Pe

EN

Christopher Ricks has held a permanent post at Boston University since 1986. He was formerly a Fellow of Worcester College, Oxford, and later a professor first at Bristol and then King Edward VII Professor of English at Cambridge University, where he was a Fellow of Christ's College. He is a Fellow of the British Academy and of the American Academy of Arts and Sciences.

His publications include *Milton's Grand Style* (1963), *Tennyson* (1972), *Keats and Embarrassment* (1974), *The Force of Poetry* (1984), *T. S. Eliot and Prejudice* (1988) and *Beckett's Dying Words* (1993). He has edited a collection of critical essays on A. E. Housman (1968), *The Poems of Tennyson* (1969, rev. 1987), *The New Oxford Book of Victorian Verse* (1987), Milton's *Paradise Lost* (Penguin Classics 1989) and *A. E. Housman: Collected Poems and Selected Prose* (Penguin Classics 1989). He was co-editor of *The State of the Language* (1980, and a new collection 1990). He is the general editor of the annotated Penguin English Poets and has also edited Volume 2 in the Penguin History of Literature series, *English Poetry and Prose: 1540–1674*.

*Titles published or forthcoming in this series:*

# ENGLISH DRAMA TO 1710

EDITED BY

## CHRISTOPHER RICKS

**VOLUME 3 OF THE**
*Penguin History of Literature*

**PENGUIN BOOKS**

**PENGUIN BOOKS**

Published by the Penguin Group
Penguin Books Ltd, 27 Wrights Lane, London W8 5TZ, England
Penguin Books USA Inc., 375 Hudson Street, New York, New York 10014, USA
Penguin Books Australia Ltd, Ringwood, Victoria, Australia
Penguin Books Canada Ltd, 10 Alcorn Avenue, Toronto, Ontario, Canada M4V 3B2
Penguin Books (NZ) Ltd, 182–190 Wairau Road, Auckland 10, New Zealand

Penguin Books Ltd, Registered Offices: Harmondsworth, Middlesex, England

First published by Sphere Books 1971
Revised edition 1987
Published in Penguin Books 1993
1 3 5 7 9 10 8 6 4 2

Printed in England by Clays Ltd, St Ives plc

# CONTENTS

# INTRODUCTION

Literature is the texts. Literary history is the contexts. The essays commissioned to form Volume 3 of the *Sphere History of Literature* are intended to give a modern reader a sense of the many contexts within which literature – in this case, drama – exists. Without an understanding of context it is too easy to misunderstand or misjudge a work of the past. *Context*, rather than *background*, because the word context is likely to remind us that we cannot so easily hive off the pure work of art itself from the circumstances and expectations within which it was created and which may often be truly said to form part of its meaning.

There is no rule which will tell in advance which of the various possible contexts is going to prove the most illuminating for any particular writer or work. The contributors to this volume have been free to select their own emphases. But the volume necessarily begins with a full account, by Glynne Wickham, of that essential context which distinguishes drama from other forms of literature, and which even calls in question to what extent drama should be thought of as a form of literature: the context of stage and staging, of 'Play, Player, Public and Place', from the beginnings of English drama through to the Jacobean playhouse. From this account of the stage and drama (which has been fully revised by Professor Wickham for this edition), there follows naturally Brian Morris's substantial survey of the whole of Elizabethan and Jacobean drama – a map which is not only striking in itself, but which provides a context for the major dramatists who figure later in the volume. The first of such major dramatists is Christopher Marlowe; here Gāmini Salgādo sees the essential context as that furnished by the writer's life and times.

Shakespeare stands as the core of the volume, just as he is the core not only of dramatic achievement in English but of all literary achievement. Richard Proudfoot charts Shakespeare's career and development, setting down lucidly and compactly the essential known facts. Further essays then treat the plays chronologically and generically: Philip Brockbank on the histories, John Wilders on the comedies, Anne Barton on the tragedies, and Stephen Wall on the later plays. Each has been moved by the particular nature of the dramatic achievement with which he is dealing to give priority to a different approach. That Stephen Wall, for example, should make much more use of recent literary criticism of Shakespeare's late plays than does Mrs Barton of recent criticism of Shakespeare's tragedies is not a fact about the contributors, but a fact about the nature of the late plays and about the nature of recent criticism. Two new essays, specially commissioned for this second edition, deal with matters newly of great moment: John Kerrigan elucidates the strong current debate on Shakespeare's texts and on their having been revised by Shakespeare; and Cedric Watts attends to the controversial new interpretations of Shakespeare's plays politically considered, some Marxist, some feminist, all dissenting from traditional praises, or emphases.

From Shakespeare to his greatest dramatic contemporary, the first great man of letters in English: Ben Jonson. Ian Donaldson's essay establishes that the central problem for a modern audience or reader is that created by the highly specific, highly topical nature of Jonson's work; the essay then succeeds in showing not just that Jonson ought still to be accessible, but that, properly approached, he is so. One kind of inaccessibility is that created by literary and dramatic conventions; it is the context of conventions, with the further relationship to symbols and imagery, which the essay by the present editor explores, and within which it attempts to urge critical discriminations and to clarify critical disagreements.

Neither poem nor play, the masque has long been a baffling form, both in terms of literary history (when and why was it born? when and why did it die?) and in terms of literary criticism (what exactly did it set itself to do?). The form is here elucidated and assessed by the foremost recent scholar of the masque, Stephen Orgel. After a brief account by Glynne Wickham of stage and staging in the Restoration theatre, the volume ends with a comprehensive counterpart to Brian Morris's earlier survey: an account of drama from the Restoration till 1710, by John Barnard. Here Restoration comedy can be seen both as the descendant of Jacobean drama and as the ancestor or brother of Augustan literature.

One of the obvious advantages of a multiplicity of vantage-points is that more aspects of any particular work or author can be seen. So Jonson is revealed both by bringing his whole dramatic *oeuvre* to bear, and by bringing to bear the traditions and rivals which gave life to his career – and then by the further realization of how important were Jonson's masques. Another advantage of the multiplicity is that important critical disagreements are neither shirked nor factitiously ('stimulatingly') invented. The present editor thinks much less highly of Webster than does Mr Morris – and this is not just a matter of frames of mind, but of frames of argument. The *Sphere History* is not committed to any single doctrine, though it prefers some doctrines to others because there is more to be said for them. It is committed to the belief that one of the critic-historian's duties may simply be to be informative, and that a literary history should therefore not be too afraid of deploying a good many out-of-the-way matters of fact if in any particular case such facts will help to make past literature accessible to a modern reader. Mr Orgel's essay on the masque is, for this reason, more manifestly factual than Mr Wilders's on Shakespearean comedy – and this itself tells us something about the difference between the masque and Shakespearean comedy. But a successful literary history will not *inform* its readers only in the sense of telling them things, but also in the sense 'to inspire or imbue somebody with feelings, principles, qualities'.

At the end is a table of dates which will help to integrate one essay with another by presenting an outline of the main historical and literary-historical developments. Following the final essay there is a bibliography which lists the major editions and critical works. Editions from which quotations are made have been asterisked; except where otherwise noted, all quotations from Shakespeare are from the New (Cambridge) Shakespeare, edited by John Dover Wilson and others. When there is no standard edition, quotations are from the original editions unmodernized. But modern practice has been followed in differentiating i/j, u/v and than/then, and with regard to the printing of words in italics and in capitals.

C R

# 1

# THE BEGINNINGS OF ENGLISH DRAMA: STAGE AND DRAMA TILL 1660

*Glynne Wickham*

## (i)

## PLAY, PLAYER, PUBLIC AND PLACE

### I *Game and Play*

Drama is only a literary art by extension, not by nature. Its origins lie on the release of human energy, physical or spiritual, and its earliest manifestations are to be found (in Britain as elsewhere) in religious and secular festivities. However obscure these origins may be and however slender the evidence of the earliest forms of play and theatre that survive to us, the truth of this is made plain in the actual words, whether Latin, French, German or Anglo-Saxon, that were employed to describe dramatic entertainments of any kind. The most important of these is the Latin word *ludus* and its Anglo-Saxon equivalent *pleg*. Both can be translated as 'recreation' in the broadest sense or, in a narrower sense, as 'game' or 'play'. In both languages it was usual to particularize the exact nature of the recreational activity in question by adding a descriptive prefix or suffix; thus *ludus gladiatorum* or *hastiludus*, gladiatoral games or spear-play in Latin or, in Anglo-Saxon, *swerd-pleg* or *plegman*, sword-play or athlete (lit: games-man). The French word *jeu* and the German word *spiel* were used in a similar way.

Of the two words in current English use, 'game' and 'play', game is initially the more important in this context: for this word can still easily be stretched in two directions, first *via* sports like rugger, boxing or fencing towards war and, secondly, *via* dance and song towards the art of courtship and the make-believe actions of opera, ballet and stage-plays. This ambiguity latent within the word 'game' (most noticeable perhaps in the nursery or in Kindergarten) was always present in the words *ludus* and *pleg* and should thus guide us to a truer understanding of the earliest forms of drama in Britain than any approach made exclusively through surviving texts of scripted plays. In any case scripts are the product of a relatively sophisticated society, an oral tradition of transmission from one generation to the next being more usual among primitive or illiterate peoples: instances of this may still be encountered in respect of the Mummers' Play performed annually on Boxing Day in the village of Marshfield near Bristol or the Hobby Horse Play at Padstow in Cornwall.

Given this ambiguity in the meaning of the words 'game' and 'play', there are at least some common factors in the sense of them whichever way we stretch them. Chief among these is the idea of activity, of doing, of a release of energy in which both body and feelings are engaged. Scarcely less important to the sense of the words are the ideas of order and pretence; for the order or structure of the game controls its nature and provides the boundary between the make-believe action and the reality for which it is in some sense a substitute or preparation. For example, tournaments were often violent affairs and could result in the death of a combatant; but they were organized invariably as battle-schools for training in the arts of war and were never regarded as a form of war itself. Similarly, where the death of the hero at the hands of the villain and his subsequent revival by the doctor is an obligatory scene in the Mummers' Play, both the death and the resurrection of the champion are feigned, not real.

Games therefore of all sorts entail as their prime requirements doers or actors and a locality appropriate to the activity in question – a game- or play-place. Although an audience is by no means essential, spectators nevertheless quickly discover that a vicarious excitement or amusement stems from watching games or play of any sort and in this way become participants at one or two removes. As direct supporters of a particular faction they are closely involved; as neutral observers their involvement is restricted and they are likely to become critics. Either way, however, the addition of an audience for any form of game or play brings with it both the need to accommodate these *voyeurs* and the possibility of exacting some kind of charge for the privilege of viewing the activity in question: and once the principle of an admission charge has been conceded, the hierarchies of social rank, literacy and personal income which are present in any given community will reflect themselves in the style and construction of the auditorium, and this, in its turn, will open up to the performers the possibility of translating an occasional, unremunerated (and thus amateur) pastime into a regular and remunerative (and thus professional) activity.

This concept of game, complete with performers, spectators, play-place and auditorium could of course be extended to include entertainments provided at one extreme exclusively by animals and at the other exclusively by puppets instead of human actors or athletes. The *ludi circenses* of Roman times thus had its English equivalents in bear-baiting, bull-baiting and cock-fighting as late as the seventeenth century, while a pantomimic tradition of puppetry survived both the social upheavals of war and revolution and the political taboos of censorship and suppression that constantly imperilled the live theatre.

## II *Players*

Of the words used in Roman times to describe the participants in a *ludus*, *lusores* was the most usual although *histriones* and *mimes* were also used quite frequently. Both *histrio* and *mimus* however were relatively sophisticated terms when employed in a specifically theatrical context: *histrio* was confined to actors in the sense of stage-players while *mimus* was even more closely restricted to comic actors or farcical comedians. *Lusor(es)*, by contrast, retained the ambiguity implicit in the word *ludus* and could thus be as appropriately applied to gladiators or wrestlers as to singers, dancers or actors of stage-plays. This Latin word thus corresponds in its usage to both the Anglo-Saxon *plegman* and the French *joueur*, all three words being applied loosely to embrace every sort of performer from the aristocratic knight in the jousting arena and the clerical performer in the music-drama of Church ritual on the one hand to the keeper of a troupe of acrobatic monkeys or the owner of a one-man band on the other. Great confusion was destined to flow from this loose terminology.

With the advent of new languages in civilized society in medieval Europe new words came into existence to differentiate one type of performer from another and to take note of the most readily distinguishable forms of sophisticated entertainment. It was in Provence that the rival traditions of the Teutonic and Celtic North merged with those of the Latin South in the eleventh and twelfth centuries, and it was there that the *scôp* and the gleeman with his sagas of the north-western regions merged with the reciter of epic and romance poetry from the south to become the *trouvère*, the troubadour or singer of the *chanson de geste*, who was destined to become the leader of the medieval minstrel troupe. Under his name, and relying for security on the strength of his reputation, were assembled bizarre assortments of entertainers that included musicians, jugglers, dancers and mimes known collectively as *jongleurs*. In Chaucer's England they were called 'tregetoures' or minstrels, and came to form a normal part of any noble household having the status of servants with special privileges (including that of travelling to other houses) and being identifiable by the wearing of their master's livery. In Paris they even banded into a guild and occupied a special district of the city. Thus organized and identified in medieval society, the minstrels under their leader, the troubadour, came to acquire professional status. No such claim was made either for or by the clerical and lay performers of scriptural drama or the silent mummers of town and village or the aristocratic jousters, singers and dancers who adopted emblematic disguises to enliven and decorate their private festivities. Like the disguises they adopted, their claims to be considered as *lusores* or 'players' remained strictly occasional and amateur.

The increasing stability, wealth and sense of national identity in language, dress and custom that characterized European states in the fourteenth and fifteenth centuries brought changes, however, in both the form and activities of the quasi-professional minstrel troupes. The musicians parted company from their erstwhile colleagues and formed groups of their own retaining the name of minstrels. The mimes and the troubadours also split away to form distinct groups of *lusores* or 'players' to which the old Roman terms of *histriones* and *mimes* could once again be applied with some claim to accuracy. In England the Latin titles were fused into the generic English name of 'players of interludes'. When Henry VII came to the throne in 1485 he maintained a private company of four actors led by John English, known as *lusores regis* or 'the King's players'. And since these men were specialists in the presentation of stage-plays they needed both a repertoire of scripted plays and certain minimal physical conveniences for their performances. These household servants, their scripts, their stages and the arrangements they made for their audiences, formed the nucleus out of which the professional, commercial theatre in England as we know it would slowly develop. Parasitically it drew to itself and absorbed over the next hundred and fifty years all that was serviceable and digestible within the rival amateur traditions, leaving the latter a tame and exhausted corpse that had to wait till late in the nineteenth century for resuscitation.

## III *Play-places*

The earliest formalized concept in Europe of a place for the presentation of stage-plays was the Θεάτρον of ancient Greece. This consisted of a circular edifice virtually bisected into two halves, the one containing a dancing floor and tiered seating rising from it for spectators, the other containing a raised platform and a changing room divided from the platform by a wall with doors in it. This relatively simple structure was copied by the Romans and modified in two directions: the *teatrum* was greatly elaborated with decorative ornament and scenic machinery for their *ludi scenici* (stage-plays), on the one hand, and adapted to form a circular or elliptical auditorium surrounding an open arena for their *ludi circenses* (athletic games) on the other. This new kind of structure was called *amphiteatrum* and was generally much larger than the original *teatrum*. Splendid examples of the amphitheatre survive in France at Lyons, in Yugoslavia at Pula, in Italy at Verona and in the Coliseum in Rome itself. Good examples of both styles of building may be seen in England in the theatre at Verulamium (St Albans) and the amphitheatre at Caerleon near Newport, Gwent.

Of these two types of building the amphitheatre was to prove the more influential on the subsequent history of dramatic entertainments in Britain, at least initially. For when the *Pax Romana* was challenged by invading barbarians from Scandinavia and Germany, amphitheatres proved to be readily convertible into citadels or fortified camps for the final defence of the local community. Use of these buildings first to resist invasion and, following defeat by the invaders, as quarries to provide stone for new houses quickly reduced them to the level of earlier and simpler earthwork camps. Both kinds of circular, flat spaces were then taken over by the Norse and Saxon settlers as the most obvious natural sites for their own recreational activities and became known as *pleg-stów*, i.e. 'game-place' or 'play-place'. The paucity of written records in the six hundred years between the departure of the Romans and the Norman Conquest has led to great confusion in our understanding of these 'rounds' which only systematic archaeological excavation in future years can resolve. All that can be said in the present state of our knowledge is that these flat arenas with a raised, surrounding earthwork wall survived for use in the Middle Ages for 'games' of both athletic and dramatic sorts. Some kind of connection undoubtedly exists between them and that form of Tournament known in the twelfth and thirteenth centuries as 'round tables', as it does between them and those religious stage-plays of the fourteenth and fifteenth centuries like the Cornish Cycle of Miracles or *The Castle of Perseverance*, the manuscripts of which contain ground-plans for performance in the round.[1] In the latter, the arena (as opposed to the surrounding earthwork) has become the *platea* or 'place' meaning the acting-area and thus 'the stage'.

The position is further complicated by the existence of the Anglo-Saxon word *pleg-hús* meaning game or play house. Beyond indicating that some sort of roofed building existed in addition to the open *pleg-stów*, this word tells us little. It may simply have been a name for the normal banquet-hall of a palace or large fortified house; but again the awkward fact has to be explained that it is this word, and neither *teatrum* nor *amphiteatrum*, which is employed in the sixteenth century in its senses of both 'game' and 'play' to describe auditoriums specially erected in wood or stone for public entertainments. The first sixteenth-century example of which record survives is a game-house at Great Yarmouth built in 1538 from the stone of a dissolved Priory.[2] Game-house is obviously an appropriate name for the bull- and bear-baiting arenas shown on maps of London in the middle of the century. It is also to be noted that when Philip Henslowe and Edward Alleyn came to build the Hope Theatre on Bankside in 1613 the building is described throughout the contract as 'this Game or Play house': it was to be modelled on The Swan, the interior appearance of which is known to us in De Witt's sketch of 1596, and was to be used for the baiting of animals three days a week and for stage plays on the other three.[3] No entertainments were allowed on Sundays.

When the word 'theatre' enters the English language it comes as the name for a particular playhouse, *The Theater*, built in 1576 in the dissolved Priory of Hollywell in Shoreditch by James Burbage, a carpenter-turned-actor, with financial help from John Brayne, a wealthy grocer. It was not until the seventeenth century, however, that the word 'theatre' came back into general use as an alternative to the word playhouse, both words being then applied in the original Latin and Greek senses of a building used exclusively for the

---

[1] See R. Southern, *The Medieval Theatre in the Round*, London, 1957, and Neville Denny, 'Arena Staging and Dramatic Quality in the Cornish Passion Play', *Stratford upon Avon Studies 16: Medieval Drama*, London, 1973.

[2] See G. Wickham, *Early English Stages*, London, 1959–81, ii (I), 166–7.

[3] See C. Walter Hodges, *The Globe Restored*, London, 1953, reprint 1958, pp. 165–9; and G. Wickham, *Early English Stages*, ii (I), 168–9.

*proscaenium ludus* or *ludi scenici*, i.e. for scripted stage-plays performed by professional actors.

These actors were the direct descendants of the players of interludes and thus of the *lusores* of the medieval minstrel troupes. As servants of royal and noble masters their normal 'play-house' throughout the fifteenth century and for most of the sixteenth was the rectangular banquet hall. At one end was the dais with the high-table for the master of the house and his principal guests. At the other end was the screen separating the hall from the kitchen. This screen normally contained two doors for servants to bring in food and take out used dishes without colliding into each other. Over this screen was a gallery for musicians. For interludes, the *platea*, place or acting-area was the floor space adjoining the screen: this gave the actors two doors for exit and entrance, a convenient changing room in the kitchen area and the upper level of the musicians' gallery if required. The rest of the hall was available for spectators. Large numbers of spectators packed into such relatively small spaces gave rise to a very intimate form of actor–audience relationship.

Revival of interest in the stage conventions of ancient Rome resulted in the introduction of a raised stage adjacent to the screen. This was introduced into England from Italy early in the sixteenth century by Henry VIII at Court and was swiftly copied elsewhere. When companies of actors travelled therefore in the provinces, these were the conditions they looked for: this accounts for their normal choice of the guildhall or town hall when a banquet hall was not available. And when, towards the end of the century, they moved into public game or play-houses they thus took with them a raised stage, a changing room and a screen with two doors in it dividing the two areas from each other. In this way the *pleg-stów* and *pleg-hús* came to be translated first into the English 'game' or 'play' house and ultimately into the playhouse or theatre of modern times. Thus, notwithstanding the dislocation and destruction of war and the social and political upheavals of frequent invasions with all their implications for religious and cultural institutions and even for language itself, the Latin *ludi* with all their ambiguity survived into Tudor England where, under the words play, player and playhouse, they were destined to flower again in a scripted drama eclipsing anything known in Imperial Rome.

## IV *High days and Holy-days*

So successfully have the miracles of modern science eliminated from our daily lives the sense of sharp contrasts existing in nature that great imaginative effort is required today to appreciate how striking these contrasts appeared to our forefathers. The mere turning of a knob or operation of a switch translates night into day for us or winter's cold into summer's heat. We move in a matter of hours from one continent to another and have the means to avail ourselves of professional entertainment at almost any hour of the day or night. For many who live in the concrete jungles of our cities all contact with seasonal growth and decay has been lost with the result that the environment produced by science is more 'natural' than anything in nature itself. In large areas of the Third World, however, famine remains the starkest reality of life.

When we come therefore to consider the drama of the Greeks, the Romans and of medieval Christendom we must first banish from our minds this uniformity in day-to-day life to which all western nations have become accustomed and try to regain something of that vivid awareness of contrasts that characterized *their* environments. Chief among these was a sense of death in life and life in death borne home upon them by the high rate of infant mortality, the short expectancy of life, the dangers of drought and famine, the perils of plague, of travel and of winter's cold. No less real and vivid was the contrast between work and leisure. With work geared far more closely to the demands and limitations of agriculture, the seasons and the climate than it is now, leisure and the use made of it was correspondingly rarer and more valuable. These conditions in their turn provoked a much greater respect for those forces in nature which controlled life and death on the one hand and a much keener sense of community in recreational activities on the other. In general the latter tended to reflect the former. The power of nature was constantly acknowledged in Festivals for the deities thought to preside over the fertility of crops, flocks and the human race. Other Festivals were organized to keep evil spirits at a distance. At the centre of all these Festivals was a respect for energy as a source of life and survival expressed in athletic or imitative activity. Games were thus as appropriate to funerals as to births and other new beginnings, while song and imitative dance formed as good an outlet for expression of grief as of joy or thanksgiving. In this way Festivals grew up throughout Europe associated with especially significant moments in the seasonal year – the longest and shortest days (the summer and winter solstices), spring sowing and autumn harvest. Invasion and conquest served to impose one set of Festivals upon another, new Gods for old and on some occasions to dislocate old cultural patterns in point of date or ceremonial from their origins and, with the passage of time, to add or subtract features of consequence in some instances or to occasion coalescence in others. Important Roman Festivals like the Saturnalia or the Kalends made an indelible impression on countries in North-western Europe that had come within the *Pax Romana* Christianity, when it came, added its own Feast-days, but was content in many instances simply to take over an existing Festival and to endow it with a new significance. The Lenten vigil accompanied by fasting thus came to be geared to the tail-end of winter when food of any sort was at its scarcest, while the great Feast-days of Christ's birth and resurrection were synchronized respectively with the winter solstice and the vernal equinox. Christianity added many Festivals of its own of a local character commemorating the lives of particular saints and martyrs, each of which became a holiday of some importance in the area in question: and as these holidays became established, so fairs and festivities, athletic and dramatic, attached themselves as annual fixtures in the life of the local community. St Anne at Lincoln, St Werburgh at Chester or St Thomas à Becket at Canterbury came to be venerated in this way. Thus a merger came about between the Christian year and the agricultural year, seasonal time and ritual time, folk customs of great antiquity and new festivities inspired by the innovations of Christian belief. To these were added the strictly occasional festivities provoked by weddings, birth, coronations and other such events of great importance to the survival of the local community at one end of the scale and to the nation as a whole at the other.

The contrast between the drab and frugal working conditions of everyday life and these festive occasions was immense and may fairly be compared, in architectural terms, to the visual contrast between the average dwelling house and the huge castles, priories and cathedrals which shaped the landscape for miles around. Dominating all other festivals in importance in Christian Europe were the twelve-day feast of Christmas, the two-day feast of Shrovetide immediately preceding Lent, and the celebration of Easter. After 1313 these great holidays were joined and to some extent eclipsed by a fourth in mid-summer, the Feast of Corpus Christi. All of these Festivals were marked by recreational activities which included sports, singing, dancing and, from late in the fourteenth century onwards, by carefully organized and fully scripted dramatic entertainments. In this way men of letters came to be recalled to the service of the drama.

With the Reformation all these Calendar holidays received a severe jolt. The first to go was Corpus Christi, suppressed in 1548; Sunday sports were the next to come under attack; after them, the rising tide of Puritan opinion fed its kill-joy appetite first upon the entertainments associated with Christian Festivals because they were of Roman Catholic origin and thus superstitious, and then upon all others because they were of pagan origin and thus idolatrous. These efforts met with such success that by the middle of the seventeenth century not only had all the great, traditional Festivals and fairs been suppressed but the English Sunday had arrived.

## V *Roman and Celto-Teutonic Preludes*

The notion, still popular in some quarters, that drama in England begins with Marlowe or, if allowance is made to include the work of monkish ignorance and superstition represented by the early religious stage, with fifteenth-century dramatizations of the Bible, derives from an equation of drama with literature. This assumes drama to be a branch of poetry, history and moral philosophy – in the case of Shakespeare, of all three – and curiously omits theology, notwithstanding the precedence accorded to that branch of learning and letters in the sixteenth and seventeenth centuries. More naturally it ignores the actor (craft, status and economy) altogether, and allows concern with theatre architecture and production to be pursued as necessary, but peripheral, adjuncts to the study of the written texts.

This approach to the study of English drama has come under heavy attack during the past fifty years from a 'new wave' of historians and critics. Their work has taught us that the drama of the Middle Ages was a much more highly organized and subtle form of art than it was ever allowed to be by either Protestant or humanist scholars of an earlier generation.[1] No less important, the

---

[1] Important works propounding the new approach include books like Willard Farnham's *The Medieval Heritage of Elizabethan Tragedy* (1936), G. R. Kernodle's *From Art to Theatre* (1944), H. C. Gardiner's *Mysteries' End* (1946), C. Walter Hodges' *The Globe Restored* (1953) and T. W. Craik's *The Tudor Interlude* (1958), or, more recently, O. B. Hardison's *Christian Rite and Christian Drama* (1965),

many revivals of these early plays in recent years in York, Chester and London and in the Drama Departments of English and American universities have reinforced most of the views in a practical manner.[1]

One of the most significant of these early revivals was that of the twelfth-century *Ludus Danielis* (*The Play of Daniel*) by the New York Pro Musica, first presented in America in 1958 and, shortly afterwards, in Europe: it has since been recorded in stereo (Brunswick, 5XA, 4001) being sung throughout and thus more nearly resembling early opera than our ideas of a stage-play.

The prologue to this remarkable music-drama tells us that it was prepared by clerical scholars from Beauvais. The manuscript now resides in the British Museum. Although the story is taken from the Bible and concerns the Prophet Daniel, his relations with Nebuchadnezzar King of Babylon and Darius King of Persia, and his familiar confinement in the lions' den, use of the word *Ludus* tells us quite clearly that the treatment to be accorded to the story is that of a game or play: it is not an *Ordo*, or liturgical rite. Written (c.1100) in Latin interspersed with passages in vernacular French and scored for fifteen solo voices, chorus and elaborate instrumental accompaniment, this highly organized and beautiful work of art stands at the gateway between two worlds. After seeing, or even hearing it, there is little left to surprise us in the subsequent development of this sort of drama. At the same time, use of the word *Ludus* to describe it throws us back into an earlier theatrical world of which the physical remains of those *teatra* or *amphiteatra* which archaeologists have brought to light continue to remind us.

Tenuous therefore as the connection between the formal drama of Roman Britain and the English vernacular drama of the Middle Ages probably was, we are put on our guard against assuming that the Celto-Teutonic cultures which intervened either banished or lost sight of all forms of dramatic art: the *pleg, plegman* and *plegstów* of Anglo-Saxon Britain stand between. Indeed, buildings and folk

---

V. A. Kolve's *The Play Called Corpus Christi* (1966), Emily Prosser's *Revenge Tragedy* (1968), *Stratford-Upon-Avon Studies 16: Medieval Drama*, ed. Neville Denny (1973), Richard Axton's *European Drama of the Early Middle Ages* (1974), Stanley J. Kahrl's *Traditions of Medieval Drama* (1974) and William Tydeman's *The Theatre in the Middle Ages* (1978).

[1] The first Cycle to be revived in its entirety was that at York in 1951; the Wakefield Cycle was presented at the Mermaid Theatre in London in 1961. Since then virtually all surviving texts of English medieval plays have been revived, enabling all who have seen them to acquire a new and lively appreciation of them as plays in performance.

custom inform us to the contrary: so do both the new ideas given to society by the gleeman and the *scóp* and the continued study of the old culture in the monastic schools of Ireland, Iona, Jarrow, Lindisfarne, Tours and St Gall, where Irish and English scholars studied the Latin authors and, by passing on the ideas associated with it from one generation to the next, enabled the nun Hrostwitha to write plays in Latin after the manner of Terence. Whether or not her plays were ever performed is unimportant: what matters is that the Latin tradition survived, albeit in fragments, and only awaited more stable and sophisticated conditions for *ludus* to unite with *pleg, lusores* with *plegmen, amphiteatrum* with *plegstów* into the play, player and playhouse of Tudor England. The key to this fusion lies in the new languages flowing out of Provence in the twelfth century. The new drama, when it came, was thus still discernibly Latin in its forms but transformed in its content by Celtic and Teutonic ideas and Christian manners. If therefore we ignore these preludes to our national drama, of one thing we may be sure: we shall misunderstand its forms and misinterpret its content.

# ENGLISH DRAMA OF THE MIDDLE AGES

## I *The Drama of Christ the King*

On one point all historians of medieval drama are agreed: the drama of the Roman Catholic Church in England began in the ceremony adopted in the tenth century to introduce Mass on Easter morning. This ceremony was called the Introit and formed part of what was known as the Proper (as opposed to the Ordinary) within the Mass. The Ordinary was that portion of the service which remained constant every time Mass was sung throughout the year: the Proper was that portion which was particular to each major Festival. The Introit proper to Easter Day was a text from the Latin Bible describing the visit of the three Maries to Christ's tomb and their meeting with the angel before the empty sepulchre. It was sung antiphonally – that is to say by two voices or groups of voices, the one responding to the initiative taken by the other. The text in question happens to take the form of a question and an answer:

CANTOR: Whom seek ye at the sepulchre, O followers of Christ?
RESPONSOR: Jesus of Nazareth who was crucified, O heavenly creature.
CANTOR: He is risen.

Given the dialogue form of this Introit, it is of course quite easy for a congregation to make a mental equation between the deacons and cantors of the antiphon and the angel and the Maries whose words before Christ's tomb now form the subject of the antiphon before the altar: and once the singers too have made this equation – one voice for the angel and three for the Maries – they may be said to be impersonating the characters whose words and gestures they are re-creating and thus to be engaged in a brief commemorative drama.

Perhaps the most important single feature of this ceremony is the naturalness of its evolution. Like mosaic, fresco, and every form of musical addition to the Church's liturgies between the eighth and tenth centuries, it was initially no more than an ornamental elaboration, the purpose of which was to mark the nature and the importance of this particular Festival, Easter Sunday. Easter was of course the most important Festival of the entire Church year and thus the occasion that cried out above all others for decorative elaboration commensurate with Christian joy and thanksgiving for the miracle of Christ's resurrection. In this sense it was quite natural to carry the elaboration of ceremonial beyond painting and beyond music into the commemoration of this historical event by annual re-enactment of it. It was in this way that the drama of Christ the King who died to conquer Death came into existence.

A scarcely less important event in Christian history was Christ's birth. It is hardly surprising therefore that the Introit for Christmas Day – 'Whom seek ye in the cradle?' – should have been accorded similar treatment shortly afterwards. Though we may recognize in commemorative re-enactments of historical events involving impersonation the beginnings of drama, it is important to realize that Churchmen of the tenth century regarded them strictly as liturgical ceremonies proper to the Feasts in question and not as plays or *ludi*. The earliest records that we have of them describe each as an *Ordo* or *Officium* and not as a *ludus*: moreover it is precisely on this account that none of these ceremonies could coalesce with each other to form a group or sequence of plays, since it would have been entirely inappropriate to celebrate events other than those proper to the particular Feast. Christmas Day, for example, was Christmas Day, and it was meaningless to perform liturgical rituals particular to the Annunciation or to Epiphany within the liturgical context of Christmas Day itself. It should also be noted that translation from Latin into the vernacular could in no way affect this principle.

In England the earliest information we have of this liturgical music drama comes from the diocese of Winchester. In a book of liturgical canticles known as *The Winchester Troper* we have our first text of the Easter Introit, and in another book, the *Regularis Concordia* of St Ethelwold, we have this Bishop's manual of instructions for the proper administration of this and other Church ceremonies.[1] A later and more elaborate version of the Easter Office survives from Dublin in which Peter and John join the three Maries at the tomb.

The strictly liturgical nature of these early mimetic ceremonies is made quite explicit in St Ethelwold's regulations for the proper conduct of the Easter Introit.

While the third lesson is being chanted, let four brethren vest themselves. Let one of these, vested in an alb, enter as though to take part in the service, and let him approach the sepulchre without attracting attention and sit there quietly with a palm in his hand. While the third response is

[1] Printed by J. M. Manly, *Specimens of the Pre-Shakespearean Drama*, Boston, 1897, 2 vols, i, xix–xxi.

chanted, let the remaining three follow, and let them all, vested in copes, bearing in their hands thuribles with incense, and stepping delicately as those who seek something, approach the sepulchre. These things are done in imitation of the angel sitting in the monument, and the women with spices coming to anoint the body of Jesus. When therefore he who sits there beholds the three approach him like folk lost and seeking something, let him begin in a dulcet voice of medium pitch to sing *'Quem quaeritis . . . ?'* And when he has sung it to the end, let the three reply in unison *'Ihesu Nazarenum'*. So he, *'Non est hic, surrexit sicut praedixerat. Ite, nuntiate quia surrexit a mortuis'*. At the word of bidding let those three turn to the choir and say *'Alleluia! resurrexit Dominus!'* This said, let the one, still sitting there and as if recalling them, say the anthem *'Venite et videte locum'*. And saying this, let him rise, and lift the veil, and show them the place bare of the cross [i.e. the altar cross placed in the sepulchre below the altar on Good Friday] but only the clothes laid there in which the cross was wrapped. And when they have seen this, let them set down the thuribles which they bare in that same sepulchre, and take the cloth and hold it up in the face of the clergy, and as if to demonstrate that the Lord has risen and is no longer wrapped therein, let them sing the anthem *'Surrexit Dominus de sepulchro'*, and lay the cloth upon the altar. When the anthem is done, let the prior, sharing in their gladness at the triumph of our king, in that having vanquished death, He rose again, begin the hymn *'Te Deum laudamus'*. And this begun all the bells shall chime out together.[1]

The importance of these instructions can scarcely be exaggerated: not only do they inform us that the Easter Introit was conceived of as an Office and not as a play, but they give us a vivid picture of the style of acting, and the means adopted to identify character and locality in this 'Imitation of the angel sitting in the monument, and the women with spices coming to annoint the body of Jesus'. It was clearly intended that the congregation should be confronted with a double image. The Maries are men, not women. They wear copes, not fashionable female attire or historical 'period' dress. The dialogue is in Latin not English and is punctuated with anthems and hymns. The climax is the *Te Deum*, the most famous and familiar of Christian hymns of praise and thanksgiving, in which actors and audience participate together. Thus the event of Christ's resurrection is commemorated by re-enactment in the most artificial and formal manner imaginable: yet what is patently a highly ornate ritual from one standpoint is just as patently a dramatic representation of a turning point in Christian history when viewed from another. The dichotomy of this double image within the Easter Office and others modelled upon it is carried over into more self-consciously

[1] E. K. Chambers, *The Medieval Stage*, Oxford, 1903, 2 vols, ii, 14–15.

dramatic representations, religious and secular, in the Middle Ages, but with a difference: the latter are not and cannot be described as an *ordo* or 'Office' for they have become *ludus*, or 'play', in its sense of mimetic illustration.

It should be noted that the dramatic Offices not only develop within the strict limits imposed by each Calendar Feast itself, but continue to be presented on the appropriate feast days notwithstanding the development of far more sophisticated religious *ludi* like *The Play of Daniel* or the Corpus Christi Cycles. Indeed this drama of Christ the King was never superseded by vernacular or secularized dramatic treatments of scripture, nor did the latter develop out of the former any more than 'Morality Plays' developed out of the Cycles. These are myths grounded in Darwinian evolutionary hypotheses erroneously applied to the history of drama where the need to postulate progress from small beginnings to bigger (and thus better) things takes precedence over religious, artistic and social logic all of which, individually and collectively, argue a different course of development. This story occupies the next two sections of this chapter.

## II *The Drama of Christ Crucified*

One of the most striking features of those dramatic representations of scriptural events within the liturgical Offices of the Christian Church is the absence of any attempt to re-enact the crucifixion itself. To our minds this is undoubtedly the most dramatic, indeed tragic, single event associated with Christianity; yet dramatic treatment of it was avoided until late in the thirteenth century in some countries and until early in the fourteenth century in others. Why?

Two answers present themselves, one artistic and the other doctrinal: the two are interrelated. Liturgically, Good Friday was the nadir of the Christian year, a day of unparalleled sorrow and the climax towards which the forty days of fasting and penance that constituted the period of Lent starting on Ash Wednesday inexorably led. Anything less appropriate than artistic expressions of joy and thanksgiving within this period cannot be imagined. Paintings and sculptures were screened from view. Music there was, but of a kind designed to accord with the words of penitential hymns and psalms. The Last Supper was commemorated liturgically on Maundy Thursday, and the altar cross was taken down on Good Friday, wrapped in a cloth, and placed in the open space below the altar as an emblem of Christ's crucifixion and burial; all the lights in the Church were extinguished. Out of this darkness and contrition blazed the light of the re-lit candles of Easter Day; pictures and sculptures again delighted the eye, and anthems of praise and joy echoed round the churches. The triumph of Christ the King over sin and death was thus fitly symbolized artistically by the exploitation of that contrast, aural and visual, between the rejoicing of Easter morning itself and the gloom of the long penitential vigil that had preceded it. Involvement of the congregation was made complete in the choice of this moment for the admission of converts to Christian baptism and for the readmission of those who had lapsed into sin and heresy into full communion with their fellows. There was never the same incentive therefore to translate the *Ordo Deposito Crucis* (the liturgy governing the removal of the cross from the altar) into mimetic re-enactment as there was to bring the *Ordo Elevatio Crucis* to life in the *Ordo Visitatio Sepulchri*. And without dramatization of the crucifixion, growth of dramatic ceremonial (notwithstanding subsequent translation of *Ordo* into *Ludus*) could not possibly extend to any linking of Christmas plays with Easter plays. Only after some three hundred years and in a very different climate of opinion – religious, social and artistic – was the church ready to experiment in this direction.

The starting point of this new initiative was the Reform movement within the Church's own monastic life, spearheaded by the founding of the Cistercian Order in 1098 at Cîteaux, which proceeded through the course of the twelfth century. As this new Order spread and established new houses in both Eastern and Western Europe, it attracted the attention and loyalty of both the aristocratic Orders of Knighthood and many laymen of humbler origin seeking to follow the example of Christ's own disciples as defenders of the faith and as His missionaries. This reaction against the old, introverted and contemplative forms of monasticism towards an extrovert evangelism found strong support in the rapidly expanding trading cities and led, by the start of the thirteenth century, to the founding of the Dominican and Franciscan Orders of friars preacher, and to the establishment of Europe's first universities in which they played an influential role as teachers.

These changes affected all aspects of medieval life, religious and social, creating a clamour for translation of the Bible, a growing appreciation of the human aspects of Christ's personality and, with it, an alarming number of heretical sects – not least the Cathars. It was within this context of change, dissidence and debate that the concept of creating out of *ludi* (stage plays) an instrument for the instruction of largely illiterate audiences began to emerge within the ranks of the orthodox Catholic Church which could be used to satirize the vanity and folly of pretentiousness in all walks of life, and the accompanying dangers of the many temptations to stray from the tenets of the Christian faith into those of Satan and Anti-Christ.

Where religious *ludi* were concerned the doctrine of Transubstantiation, instituted by the Papacy in 1215, had given to the Eucharist a new importance – the status of a miracle on a par with those of virgin birth and resurrection from the dead. Yet the liturgical Calendar, developed over the centuries, was not equipped to deal adequately with this new concept; and while some ecclesiastics were preoccupied with this problem others were no less deeply engaged with the problem of how to fortify a converted but spiritually lazy Europe in its faith. The radical reappraisal of basic thought patterns and customs which accompanied these changes brought with it, amongst other things, a new drama centred on the Eucharist, emphasizing the humanity rather than the divinity of Christ's ministry and avowedly didactic in intention rather than ritualistic and ornamental. In consequence it was conceived from the outset as a *Ludus*, in the vernacular languages of the individual nations of Christendom and not in universal Latin, spoken not chanted. A corresponding change in architecture and the fine arts gave rise to the replacement of what we term Romanesque by the Gothic style.

The catalyst behind this great leap forward was the promulgation of the Feast of Corpus Christi by Pope Urban IV in 1269 and its institution by Pope Clement V in 1313. Pope Urban, in his Bull announcing the new Feast, speaking of the Eucharist says:

For on the day of the Supper of our Lord [i.e. the eve of Good Friday] – the day on which Christ himself instituted this sacrament – the entire Church, fully occupied as she is with the reconciliation of penitents, the ritual administration of the holy oil, the filling of the commandment concerning the washing of feet, and other matters, does not have adequate time for the celebration of this greatest sacrament.[1]

Since the mood is wrong and the time is inadequate on Maundy Thursday, Pope Urban goes on to prescribe another Thursday, the first after Trinity Sunday, when the Church is less preoccupied, for the proper celebration of the redemptive power of the Eucharist

[1] V. A. Kolve, *The Play Called Corpus Christi*, Stanford, 1966, p 44.

itself. The purpose of this new Festival is thus not to be the commemoration of historical event but to give thanks for man's salvation. We are thus taken out of ritual time into universal time: for the Eucharist has no significance in this context of man's salvation without taking account of the Fall of Adam on the one hand and of Christ's Harrowing of Hell and Doomsday on the other when man himself is to be judged. Here then, in the purpose and nature of the new Feast we have the dramatic structure of the plays which were to be so closely associated with it as to carry its name. No question of translation or coalescence arises. The plays are possessed of what we call cyclic form from their inception – a doctrinal pattern of Fall, Redemption and Judgement which parallels the Aristotelian dramatic pattern of sharply defined beginning, middle and end bequeathed by the Greeks to the Romans. From the outset therefore the Crucifixion and the Harrowing of Hell formed the climax or 'middle' of this new vernacular and didactic drama of Corpus Christi in which Old Testament history was seen as a prefigurement of that of the New Testament. Christ replaces Adam, Mary replaces Eve and the cross on Calvary replaces the Tree of Knowledge in the Garden of Eden; and since, in the context of medieval time, the past is reflected in the present and the future, the proper dramatic environment for the depiction of these events is fourteenth-century Britain.[1] Thus Pontius Pilate becomes Sir Pilate, J.P., Annas and Caiaphas become Bishops, the shepherds of Bethlehem shepherds of the Cotswolds or the Pennines; Herod swears by Mahomet, and Noah becomes a shipwright of the Tyne or the Humber or the Dee.

The scarcity of evidence surviving from the fourteenth century makes it difficult to say in what precise way and at what precise date the Cycles came into being as part of the normal Corpus Christi festivities. We know that the Feast was generally observed in England by 1318, that apart from an obligation to carry the Host out of the principal church in any district and to process with it round the town or village, local bishops were allowed to determine what form the celebration of the Feast should take; we know that the trade guilds marched in the procession accompanying the Host in their proper liveries and carrying banners displaying emblems of their crafts, that the Black Death decimated the population between

<hr />

[1] For examples and fuller discussion see Emily Prosser, *Drama and Religion in the English Mystery Plays*, Stanford, 1961; Sandra Sticca (ed.), *The Medieval Drama*, New York, 1972; G. Wickham, *Early English Stages*, iii, London, 1981; and William Tydeman, *English Medieval Theatre, 1400–1500*, London, 1986.

1345 and 1360 giving the English language an ascendancy over both Latin and French thereafter, and that plays directly associated with the Feast are noted in civic records at Beverley and York around 1377–8 and at London during the reign of Henry IV. The few texts we still possess mostly date from the fifteenth century; but all five surviving manuscripts of the Chester Cycle are copies dating from 1591 and after. Although the Feast of Corpus Christi fell near mid-summer (as good a time as any for performance of plays in the open air) in some instances these Cycles were shifted to coincide with other established summer Festivals, like the Chester plays to the three-day Feast of Whitsun or those at Lincoln to the day of the Patron Saint, St Anne.

Despite these many uncertainties, most of the important features of the Corpus Christi plays and their performance in their fully cyclic form are not in any serious doubt. We know that they were regarded by all concerned as *ludi* (that is, as plays and not as Offices), that the Church encouraged the laity to participate actively in the new Festival for the doctrinal reasons already discussed and that this participation included a large measure of responsibility for organizing and financing production of Corpus Christi plays. Sufficient texts survive to indicate that the selection of source-material for inclusion in the Cycles was carefully ordered by highly educated clerics and not left to chance or to the whims of tradesmen. We know from Church and guild account books that costumes and scenic devices for identifying place (including stage machinery) were elaborate and expensive, that guilds vied with one another competitively for the privilege of possessing a pageant-wagon and that care was taken to store these costly capital assets for use on future occasions. We know that it was a routine practice to rewrite old plays, to add new ones and withdraw others as local conditions suggested. It is to this practice that we owe the inclusion of the work of 'the Wakefield Master' within the Towneley Cycle and the suppression before the Reformation of plays devoted to the life of the Virgin within the Chester and York Cycles.

Close reading of the texts, moreover, reveals a growing, *but controlled*, intrusion of dramatic devices – literary, musical and histrionic – drawn from a co-existing and competitive secular tradition. This tradition had developed during the thirteenth and fourteenth centuries in part from the popular sports, and mimetic games of earlier times, and in part from the more sophisticated satirical and romantic entertainments devised by university students, known as 'golliards', who travelled from one town or castle to another supplementing a precarious livelihood by placing their poetic and musical talents at the service of any aristocratic or bourgeois patron who chose to employ them (see section IV, pp. 24–9 below). In this way all religious drama, devised primarily to instruct, became more widely enjoyable with the enrichment of characterization, the variety and flexibility of its verse-forms and its overt theatricality.

The Reformation, coming as it did in England as a violent and controversial disturbance of established traditions, swiftly translated the religious stage into a major political issue involving Parliamentary legislation. This will be discussed in the next section of this Chapter and in the second section of Part (iii). It is a testimony however to the strength of the tradition and its hold upon the people that it was still sufficiently active half a century after Henry VIII's break with Rome to require forcible suppression by the government of Elizabeth I in Whitehall. The last recorded performance of a complete Cycle was in Coventry in 1581 when Shakespeare was already seventeen. The drama of Christ crucified therefore, with its stories of the Fall of Lucifer, of Adam and of Cain, its vivid characterizations of Herod, Pilate, Judas and Mary Magdalen, its homely treatment of shepherds, the Noah family and common soldiers, its unflinchingly realistic portrayal of Mary's pregnancy, of the Massacre of the Innocents and of the Crucifixion itself, combined to imprint a wide range of dramatic images upon people's minds throughout the social hierarchy and throughout the country which became points of reference in their own right for dramatists and audiences alike long after the Cycles themselves had been banned from English stages.

## III *The Drama of Crime and Punishment*

If the doctrine of Transubstantiation, with the subsequent emphasis placed upon the redemptive power of the Eucharist, was a major factor in the genesis of the English vernacular Cycles of Miracle Plays, the preaching of the mendicant friars with its emphasis upon Judgement Day was at least as important to the birth of a third kind of religious *ludus*, the Morality Play. Like the Cycles, the Moralities were deliberately didactic, but aimed not so much at instructing the populace in the salient points of Christian history as at bringing home to each individual the application of his faith to his own daily life and conduct; and if the source of the texts of the Cycles was the *lectio*, or readings from the Latin Bible, the source of the texts of the

Moralities was the single vernacular item within the liturgy, the sermon.

Preaching was developed as an oratorical art with wide popular appeal during the fourteenth century, especially by the Franciscan and Dominican friars with their message that Christ was not for Churches-and-Sundays only but for every man, every day and everywhere, and that the reward for crime was punishment throughout eternity. With Christ's example before him man could hope to combat and defeat the devils of Hell dancing attendance upon the spectral figure of Death and so attain to personal salvation. Man's soul thus came to be depicted as the prime objective of both the forces of good and the forces of evil in the world who were engaged in a kind of everlasting tournament with the ultimate salvation or damnation of man's soul as the prize. The forces lined up on either side were presented by the preachers to their congregations as 'vices' and 'virtues'. Chief among the former were the seven deadly sins; and, ranged against them, were the four daughters of God – Truth, Justice, Temperance and Mercy – and the three Cardinal Virtues – Faith, Hope and Charity. By emulating these virtues man could acquire protection against Sloth, Pride, Covetousness, Anger, Envy, Greed and Lechery, the principal agents sent to ensnare him in this world and capture his soul in the next world. Described again and again in the most vivid language by the preachers, these abstractions came to acquire equally vivid characterization within lengthy verbal debates and physical combat in realistic human situations; and these word-pictures were constantly reinforced by painters with their grim pictures of the *Danse Macabre*. It was thus a relatively simple step to transfer this concept of man himself, together with virtues and vices, from the rhetorical environment of the sermon to the dramatic environment of the *ludus* or 'interlude'. In both contexts, sermon and play, the great advantage enjoyed by the preachers (and subsequently by the dramatists) was their power to transcend the limitations of literacy and to communicate with those listeners and spectators who could neither read nor write.

The earliest of these Morality Plays surviving to us is *The Castle of Perseverance* (c.1405), the dramatic structure of which is borrowed directly from a popular form of Tournament, the Pas d'Armes. It was designed for performance in the open air and assumes a highly sophisticated form of staging within a circular *pleg-stów* or 'round'. A much shorter Morality Play is the famous *Everyman* (c.1495) which is much less demanding in its staging requirements and can easily be presented indoors in any hall or church: so too can the earlier *Mankind* and the later *Hick Scorner*, both of which are highly comic.[1] All three of these plays are by unnamed authors.

It has frequently been said that the Morality Play is an extension or offshoot, rather late in time, of the vernacular cycles: yet the evidence of chronology itself, of religious content and of artistic form all argue to the contrary. It is the differences – not the similarities – between the Cycles and the Moralities which are striking. Almost the only resemblance of any consequence between the two sorts of play is the basic, Christian ritual pattern of fall from grace followed by a reversal admitting the regaining of lost grace. That said, the precedence given to historical narrative in the Cycles is reserved for theme or argument in the Moralities; the respective *dramatis personae* differ accordingly. Perhaps most important of all – at least where subsequent development is concerned – Morality Plays were not attached directly to any single or particular Festival and could be performed as appropriately by professional players as by amateurs whether priests or tradesmen. Unlike the early liturgical playlets rooted in particular Offices, or the vernacular Cycles harnessed just as firmly to the Feast of Corpus Christi, Morality Plays needed no other justification than a holiday, an audience and a suitable auditorium for their performance: one company, therefore, possessed of a play that had met with success, could repeat it several times within a single year. The shorter and more compact the play, the easier it was for the actors to travel with it from one district to another and thus to acquire new audiences. Moreover the structure and content of these plays was such as to permit an extension of the original ethical debate about personal conduct to debates about the social and political conduct of governments: nor was it difficult to graft to this root-stock ideas taken from a culture as alien and as secular as the literature of classical mythology and even Roman Comedy.

An exceptionally interesting play in this context is Henry Medwall's *Fulgens and Lucres* (1497); for not only does it contain a parody of a Tournament, a dumb-show and a lengthy moral debate, but it sets out by satiric means to compare the newly emerging

---

[1] See Robert Potter, *The English Morality Play*, London, 1975, and Sumiko Miyajima, *The Theatre of Man*, Clevedon, Avon, 1977; also E. T. Schell and J. D. Shuckter (eds), *English Morality Plays and Moral Interludes*, London, 1969; G. Wickham, *English Moral Interludes*, London, 1976, 2nd edn., 1985; Peter Happé, *Tudor Interludes*, ed. for Penguin English Library, London, 1972; and A. C. Cawley, *Everyman*, Manchester, 1961.

social values of England under Henry VII with those of Republican Rome.[1] Granted this kind of treatment, both the lengthy Morality Play and the shorter Moral Interlude could readily be adapted a generation later to serve the cause of Reformation polemic. The initiative for this departure appears to have been taken in Germany in the early 1530s, but it was swiftly copied in England at the instigation of Lord Chancellor Cromwell and Archbishop Cranmer. The technique was simply to equate the Pope, Cardinals, monks and friars with Lucifer and the Deadly Sins on the one hand, and Henry VIII and the pioneers of the reformed religion with the heavenly virtues on the other and to substitute Commonwealth or Widow England for the Everyman or Mankind figure of the earlier plays. John Bale in England and Sir David Lyndsay in Scotland led the way with this type of play and in doing so brought the whole religious stage into the centre of the political arena; for the offence given by these performances to devout Catholics led to breaches of the peace and rioting on a scale that demanded police action in the first instance, censorship in the second and, following the Catholic reaction under Queen Mary, the total suppression of all overtly religious plays during the reign of Elizabeth I.

## IV *The Drama of Social Recreation*

The insistence characterizing most histories of the theatre that drama is primarily a branch of literature has resulted, where medieval drama is concerned, in a disproportionate emphasis being placed upon discussion of the religious stage (because texts exist, albeit in Latin, from the tenth century onwards) at the expense of secular dramatic activity (for which English texts only begin to become available for study in the fourteenth century). The effect of this approach has been to distort the picture of drama and its development in England in at least three ways.

First, it has deflected attention away from the concept of *ludus, pleg,* 'game' and 'play' which, in fact, dominated the development of drama in Christian society from the tenth to the seventeenth century, towards a classical and theoretical concept of dramatic genre (tragedy, comedy, tragi-comedy, etc.) which, in fact, only came to be accepted as a factor of serious consequence in the

---

[1] For editions of *Fulgens and Lucres* see F. S. Boas and A. W. Reed for the Tudor and Stuart Library, Oxford, 1926, and G. Wickham, *English Moral Interludes*, London, 1976; 2nd edn., 1985, pp 37–107.

sixteenth century. (See Part (iii) section V, pp. 46–53 below.) Secondly, it has deflected attention away from the creative contribution of the actor or entertainer to the development of dramatic forms and given an unwarranted precedence to the dramatic poet whose status in the theatre in England was in fact strictly subservient (as a 'maker of Interludes' or 'play-maker') to that of the leading actors and impresarios who controlled the companies and their repertoires until Ben Jonson chose to challenge this situation during the reign of James I. Thirdly, it has occasioned an almost total neglect of those traditions of stagecraft that were formulated in the context of Mummings, Disguisings, Masques and other dramatic entertainments that developed from a nucleus of song and dance in a strictly secular environment from the twelfth century onwards.

In a brief discussion such as this it is only possible to single out the salient points from within a complex and controversial subject for attention here. Reference has already been made to the festivals of the agricultural year (pp. 8–10 above) as opposed to those of the Christian Calendar, and especially to the dead season of midwinter. If this period of climatically enforced leisure is to be transformed from one of unmitigated boredom into one of relative pleasure, the recreations adopted must respect the nature of the season. It is for this reason that the hall of the palace or castle in Saxon and Norman England was at least a potential rival to churches as a suitable locality in which to present dramatic entertainments. In an atmosphere where sensory perceptiveness is heightened by music and by alcohol, the elementary rituals of courtship provide an incentive for dramatic decoration at least as powerful as the incentive provided by the rituals of worship in religious environments. Thus, if praise and thanksgiving in song within Christian worship provided the effective nucleus of a religious drama in England, the stimulation of dancing as the most intimate confrontation of men and women within the normal routines of social intercourse provided the effective nucleus of a secular drama.

To this nucleus was grafted the heterogeneous entertainments provided by the minstrel troupes discussed in Chapter 1 (pp. 3–4); and in the course of time the two strains came to mingle with each other until a point was reached when the dancing became formally organized within a literary context, and decorated with special costumes, scenic devices, songs and a text appropriate to the chosen theme.

An important external element in this process was the ancient custom of Mumming. The name 'mummers' was adopted by or given to social inferiors and dependants who at goodwill seasons of the year came to their overlords disguised in exotic manner to exchange gifts and good wishes. 'To keep mum' is a phrase, still in current English use, meaning 'to be silent', more particularly, 'not to betray a secret'; and there is little cause to doubt that the mummers were so called because they conducted their surprise visits in total silence. We possess a detailed description of a visit of this sort made by the citizens of London to King Richard II in 1377, when Christmas was spent at Kennington. On this occasion the mummers had assumed the disguise of Popes, Cardinals and African Princes. They rode to the palace carrying their gifts with them, played a game called 'mumchance' with loaded dice with the young king, thus ensuring that he would win the gift as a prize; they danced among themselves, the courtiers dancing on the other side of the room, and then left as silently as they had come.

Early in the fifteenth century, this custom was forbidden not only in London but also in the Provinces. Here is an example from London, dated 1418:

The Mayor and Aldermen of London chargen on the Kynges behalf, and this Cite, that no manner persons, of what astate, degre, or condicioun that evere he be, duryng this holy tyme of Cristemas be so hardy in eny wyse to walk by nyght in any manere mommyng, pleyes, enterludes, or any other disgisynges with eny feynyd berdis, peynted visers, diffourmyd or colourid visages in eny wyse . . .

The reason for this action is clear enough: disguise, in troubled times, could be used by the unscrupulous to conceal the identity of thieves and murderers.[1] A custom like this, however, sanctified by centuries of use, does not die easily. In this instance mumming did not die: it simply changed its nature. From being a visitation of genuine strangers it became a visitation from friends pretending to be strangers. This new 'game' brought with it a rudimentary text in the form of a spoken, explanatory Prologue.

Several of these 'prefaces' written by the Dominican poet, John Lydgate, survive to us. All of them are important historical documents since one of them at least – *The Mumming at Hertford* – trembles on the brink of dramatic dialogue: three disguised figures speak in turn, all in *oratio recta*, and a judgement is called for from the audience. Others of them call not only for disguise of the

---

[1] Shakespeare makes use of a threat of this sort to the life of Henry Bolingbroke in *Richard II*.

persons involved, but for use of substantial scenic properties.[1] This brings us at once into the same theatrical context as the *entremets* of the French and Burgundian Courts and the activities of the joculators and 'tregetoures' of Chaucer's *Canterbury Tales*. The Lydgate texts come from the period 1427–35, the *entremets* and Chaucer's *Canterbury Tales* from the last decades of the fourteenth century.[2]

Three factors of general consequence to the development of the theatre in this period may be taken in conjunction: the established nature of the minstrel troupes in aristocratic households, the birth in Provence of vernacular Romance literature, and the advent of religious *ludi* in vernacular languages in the principal cities of France, England and the Low Countries. It is only to be expected that they should have interacted upon each other.

Where indoor entertainment is concerned, the minstrel troupes (who were now sufficiently well organized to claim and be granted Guild status) could only view the fast-growing Corpus Christi and Morality Plays with covetous eyes; moreover, since the *trouvères* among them possessed a fund of new narrative material which could just as easily be subjected to dramatic treatment as the Bible and sermons, they were well situated to provide an alternative *ludus* centred upon their own already familiar and popular *gestes*, or recitations chanted in the Homeric manner, concerning the Siege of Troy, the Conquest of Jerusalem or the exploits of King Richard the Lionheart. What was there to prevent stirring and romantic stories of this kind being given three-dimensional vitality in the banquet hall in the same manner as the re-enactments of scriptural history that were attracting large audiences to the market place and the *pleg-stów*? Only, it seems, a change of grouping within the minstrel troupe itself – a direct association between the *trouvères* and the mimes within the troupe on the one hand, coupled with a breaking down of the metrical romances into dialogue form on the other, the latter change being a logical sequel to the former. In France this process was already well advanced by the late fourteenth century. Remarkable entertainments were provided in

---

[1] All these texts are printed by H. N. MacCracken, *The Minor Poems of John Lydgate* (ed. for EETS, Oxford 1911–34, 2 vols), ii, 668–701. See also G. Wickham, *English Moral Interludes*, edn cit., pp 204–13.

[2] For fuller discussion of these entertainments and others like them see E. Welsford, *The Court Masque*, Cambridge, 1927; G. Wickham, *Early English Stages*, i, 179–228; and Richard Axton, *European Drama of the Early Middle Ages*, London, 1974.

Paris in 1378 and 1389 representing respectively the Conquest of Jerusalem and the Siege of Troy. The scenic properties required for the latter as described by Froissart included a castle for Troy and a ship and a pavilion for the Greeks. All these items moved on wheels concealed from public view.

In England Chaucer described similar scenic devices in his 'Franklyn's Tale' (lines 1136–51) attributing their invention and operation to 'subtile tregetoures . . . with-inne an halle large'. By 1418 the word 'enterlude' is in use and by 1425, Lydgate is writing texts which assume the presence of mimes and of scenic equipment even if dialogue is still avoided. Interestingly enough Lydgate uses the word Disguising almost as a synonym for Mumming to describe his entertainments. It would thus seem that we are here at the parting of the ways between two rival forms of *ludus* – the Disguising (which in the next century was to translate itself again into the Masque) preserving choreographic compliment as its *raison d'être*, and the Interlude which preserved the characteristic features of song and dance as embellishments while concentrating upon enacted narrative in dialogue form. And just as Lydgate could use scriptural or mythological or farcical themes for his Mummings-cum-Disguisings, so the 'players of enterludes' of the late fifteenth century could and did take the subject matter of their plays from the Bible and from sermons as alternatives to their own romances and the ribald fables of their entourage. The fact that many clerics were closely concerned with minstrelsy on their own account only encouraged this cross-fertilization of dramatic initiatives. John Lydgate at one end of the fifteenth century is a case in point and so at the other end is the author of *Fulgens and Lucres*, Henry Medwall, who at the time of its composition was chaplain to Cardinal Morton. A similar traffic in the opposite direction was encouraged by the aristocratic patronage under which this secular dramatic tradition was fostered and developed; for the nobility were themselves as much concerned with *ludi* in their athletic context – notably in all forms of warlike sport (described collectively as Tournaments) – as in *ludi* of the mimetic kind. Thus the conventions of Heraldry in the identification of person and place came to be placed at the disposal of the *lusores* and *interludentes* as an alternative to those formulated within the theatre of worship. Livery, blazons and head-dresses are all examples of this sort of contribution to stage costume, while the various forms of physical combat ranging from hand-to-hand jousting to the team-games of the 'Round Tables' provided models ideally suited to alliance with verbal debate in the development of dramatic structure. And since, at Court, the evening revels frequently came to be regarded as epilogues to the Tournaments of daylight hours when Mars' champions received their prizes from Venus' votaries, the same personalities and the same costumes and scenic devices that had decorated the *ludi circenses* served double duty in the *ludi scenici* of the Revels.

This linking of the sports of the field with those of the hall (*plegstów* with *pleg-hús*) was most in evidence both in England and on the Continent in the case of the Disguising and, subsequently, the Masque. The word Masque is derived from the Italian *maschera*; but the only structural difference between the two forms of entertainment lies in the nature of the final dance. In Disguisings the participants and the spectators, as in the earlier Mummings, remained aloof and danced apart; the Italian habit of letting the disguised performers seek partners from among their audience in the final dance was introduced into England by Henry VIII in 1512 and was regarded at the time as a scandalous innovation and no less daring in its own time than mini-skirts or 'punk' hair-styles in recent times. If, as popular tradition asserts, Henry VIII first met Ann Boleyn when indulging in this new fashion, the English secular theatre has much to answer for in the consequences of this encounter.

## V *Amateurs and Professionals*

No change was of greater consequence to the development of English drama between the tenth and the seventeenth centuries than that from occasional performances by amateur players to regular playing by professional actors. This process may be said to have begun within the minstrel troupes late in the fourteenth century, to have accelerated with the advent of small companies of *lusores, histriones* and *interludentes* in the fifteenth century and again as the impact of the Reformation on the religious stage came to be felt in the sixteenth century and to have been completed with James I's actions to regulate players, playing and playhouses in the first decade of the seventeenth century.

In the early Middle Ages playing was restricted to, and thus regulated by, the annual religious and agricultural festivals on the one hand and by the rare occasions requiring special celebration like weddings and coronations. In these circumstances *ludi* of any kind were necessarily amateur in character. In other words it was normal for every individual to earn his living in the first place within a routine occupation, trade or profession and, according to talent, to volunteer his services as an entertainer as occasion demanded. The Church, while more than ready to smile on this state of affairs, even where its own priests were concerned, was stoutly opposed to any attempts to translate a service that could be described as 'honest recreation' into a regular form of life. This attitude was directed with as much energy and force against participants in the more warlike forms of 'game' like Tournaments as at entertainers of the mimetic variety: the most probable reason for this was the reminder which both forms of *ludi* provided of Roman *spectacula* in which early Christians had been ridiculed or martyred to entertain the populace in the theatres and amphitheatres of the Empire. By the fourteenth century however many young men of noble family were devoting their time and fortunes almost exclusively to travelling Europe in quest of chivalric adventure, taking large numbers of heralds and entertainers in their wake; and the minstrel who was prepared to travel, like the knight his master, had much better expectations of finding new audiences for a limited repertoire of entertainments than the minstrel who stayed at home. Their patrons moreover found it much less expensive to maintain a troupe who paid for a large proportion of their upkeep from their own earnings, and thus encouraged them to travel. In this way the more adventurous and talented troupes began to acquire a measure at least of that freedom which comes with a professional status and economy.

Nothing however which these relatively small groups of nomadic players could offer to audiences could compare with the epic dramas sponsored by the Church and frequently organized and financed by the local population in the mid-summer months. The Corpus Christi Cycles, the Saint Plays, the Paternoster Plays, Creed Plays and lengthy Moralities were of their very nature spectacular community offerings and thus remained amateur ventures in the best sense of that word. Yet the more firmly established these *ludi* became as Calendar fixtures and in general popularity, the harder it became for the Church to advance any effective opposition to the growing professionalism of the minstrel troupes. By the start of the sixteenth century therefore both Church and State had come to accept (if only by general consent) *ludi* of all descriptions as a usual part of national life and to include within this tolerance the co-existence of amateur and professional players. Gradual and real however as was this change of attitude, it did not protect the aspiring professional against sporadic outbursts of hostility grounded in envy for a way of life that seemed to offer both an escape from the normal burden of Adam's yoke and a means of jumping over the strict barriers of class on which an hierarchical and still largely feudal society was based. Regarded in many quarters as a parasite upon his hard-working fellows and as living by means of fraudulent pretence instead of by honest toil, the professional player was an object of frequent verbal attack long before the Reformation. His best defence against these attacks lay in the growing support which he was coming to receive from royal and academic patrons.

Henry VII maintained a company of four actors led by John English whose number was extended to eight by Henry VIII and to twelve by Elizabeth I. Academic interest developed around the need for a new and varied repertoire of texts without which the swiftly multiplying groups of actors could not hope to retain their professional status for long. The Reformation only served to encourage this tendency, since the suppression of the monasteries brought with it a severe curtailment of clerical playmakers which could most easily be made good by recourse to the services of choïrmasters, schoolmasters and university graduates whose profession lay in letters. Few of these men had any basis as yet on which to prepare scripts other than direct commission; and the evidence of the texts which men like Heywood, John Redford or the Rastels supplied indicates clearly enough that they were ready to respect the requirements of the companies very closely. This expresses itself in a corpus of short, compact plays known as Interludes written for small groups of players accustomed to doubling roles and respecting in general the stage conventions developed and employed in the earlier amateur *ludi* of Church Festivals and banquet revels.

Stage costume and scenic devices were still simple and regarded essentially as aids to swift identification of character and place.[1] Both were accordingly conceived of in emblematic rather than in realistic or photographic terms. The greatest advantage which this convention offered to the actors and their playmakers was control over time and distance in story-telling. By regarding the *platea*, 'place', floorspace or acting-area as neutral ground, it could be made to possess an endless variety of localized identities in part through dialogue of the actors and in part through their own mimetic actions in relation to the *loca*, *aedes*, 'mansions' or scenic emblems placed on the edge of the *platea*. The mimetic actions

[1] See T. W. Craik, *The Tudor Interlude*, Leicester, 1958; also G. Wickham, *Early English Stages*, iii, 83–123.

associated with a particular scenic emblem at once endowed the acting area with that identity in a general way which could then be particularized by the dialogue. It thus became possible to present stage action in places geographically as far apart as Bethlehem and Egypt or Galilee and Rome within the course of a play, and to travel between them in a matter of minutes if the story-line required it. These principles applied no matter what form of stage and auditorium was used: it was only necessary to determine the nature of the *platea* – 'round', fixed stage in market-square, pageant-float or hall-floor – and then set out on or around it the scenic emblems required in the play to be performed.[1]

Responsibility for making these emblems lay with the appropriate craftsmen – joiners, metalworkers, clocksmiths and painters. These men, together with the providers of costumes, were paid for their materials and labour, and the costs were met by the actors. In the case of the Corpus Christi plays funds were raised by a tax known as 'pageant-silver' or 'pageant-pence'. Companies using 'rounds' could control entry and make a charge for admission. Professional *lusores* gave performances in halls for fixed rewards from the owners and took recourse to the collecting-box when playing to public as opposed to privately invited audiences.

*Ludi* of all kinds, amateur and professional, were advertised in advance by Proclamation, the 'crying of the Banns' (that is, spoken plot-synopsis), dress parades and a rudimentary form of poster. Rehearsal periods could be long and discpline strict, bad performances or presentation being penalized with fines. All these conditions varied considerably from place to place with local topography and government playing a large part in determining what plays were presented, by what groups, at what seasons of the year and how they were performed. Despite these variants however between actual theatrical practice in, say, London and Chester, Chester and York, or all of them and Lincoln, the general picture that emerges in late medieval and early Tudor England is one of an energetic, disciplined and skilfully organized drama widely practised, deeply rooted in public affection, and triumphantly transcending the formidable barriers of class and literacy that governed society itself.

[1] For examples see G. Wickham, *Early English Stages*, i, 149–76, and Alan H. Nelson, *The Medieval English Stage*, Chicago, 1974.

## REFORMATION AND RENAISSANCE

### I *Academic Drama: Schools, Universities and Inns of Court*

A feature distinguishing the theatre of sixteenth-century England from that of both the fifteenth-century past and the seventeenth-century future was the active interest displayed in it by men of letters in every kind of academic environment. The stimuli behind this interest were in part educational and in part literary: both had their *fons et origo* in the study of classical Latin and Greek in Italian City-States, notably Venice, Florence, Ferrara, Urbino and Rome itself in the latter half of the fifteenth century. Latin, it must be remembered, was still a living language, and an ability to speak it as well as write it was still an accomplishment which no one seeking office in Church or State could do without. No such utilitarian purpose informed the study of Greek. Yet the flood of Greek and Hellenistic manuscripts that came into Western Europe at this time, due in part to the acquisitiveness of Italian merchant princes and in part to the fall of Constantinople to the Turks in 1456, provided Greek language and literature with a new importance of its own. For not only was Greek the precursor of Latin, but it was also the language in which the New Testament had first been written.

Interest in both languages advanced rapidly in England under Henry VII, championed by Erasmus, Sir Thomas More, William Grocyn, John Colet and other notable scholars. Under their influence the Universities and leading schools began to take a special interest in surviving examples of Greek and Latin oratory, notably plays: thus, while Erasmus at Cambridge was translating two of Euripides' plays, attempts were being made in choir-schools like St Paul's to revive plays by Plautus for performance in the classroom and for transfer to Court.[1] This in its turn stimulated interest in the practical theatrical conditions under which such plays were originally staged. A result of these amateur experiments was that professional actors were persuaded to introduce a raised stage into their banquet-hall playhouses. These first-fruits of the Italian Renaissance developed rapidly in England under Henry VIII until his attempts to obtain a divorce from Katherine of Aragon brought everything associated with the Papacy, Rome and the Latin

[1] See T. H. Vail Motter, *The School Drama in England*, London, 1929; and F. S. Boas, *University Drama in the Tudor Age*, Oxford, 1914.

language into question. The frost which blighted humanist studies in consequence (in England as in Germany and the Low Countries) was destined to be of singular importance to plays, players and playhouses for the next fifty years, giving to all three a flavour altogether different from that governing development of the drama in Italy itself, or in France and Spain.

In the first place, that form of Protestantism which ensued from Henry VIII's break with Rome automatically brought the whole religious stage into the political arena: this is a subject that will be discussed in the next section. Secondly it endowed any public display of enthusiasm for Latin studies with overtones of sedition and advanced the cause of Greek studies proportionately; this state of affairs was of course reversed under the Marian reaction, only to be reversed again under Elizabeth I. Elizabeth, as Queen, made no secret of the fact that she could both write and speak Greek. Such conditions as these precluded the establishment of academies like those which grew up in several Italian cities devoted to the study of Roman drama and theatre. The result was a strange dichotomy in English theatrical development: a marked reversion on the one hand to traditional, and thus Gothic, methods of playwriting and production, and a continuing interest on the other (pursued by isolated individuals in schools and universities) in classical drama, Latin and Greek. The latter, however dangerous for the individuals concerned (many faced exile for their pains) and dependent though it was on amateur patronage, sufficed to bring to life on the stage not only plays by Plautus, Terence, Aristophanes, Euripides and Seneca but translations and free adaptations in English.[1] These performances proceeded against a background, nevertheless, of growing controversy, with the Humanists advancing the precedent of classical antiquity in support and with the neo-Platonists in alliance with extreme Protestant opinion denouncing not only these plays but the theatre itself as a fraudulent and corrupting influence in society. This argument reached its climax in the University of Oxford in the 1590s with the respective factions championed by William Gager and John Rainolds.

It was within this controversial environment that Robert Greene, John Lyly, Christopher Marlowe, George Peele, John Marston, George Chapman and Ben Jonson (known collectively with some others as the University Wits) reached their maturity and, together with Shakespeare, started to provide the principal acting companies

---

[1] See L. B. Campbell, *Scenes and Machines on the English Stage During the Renaissance*, Cambridge, 1923; reprint 1961.

of their day with plays for performance at Court, in 'private' theatres, and in public game- or play-houses, and in provincial halls. When therefore they started to write they already had a richly varied repertoire of examples upon which to model their own efforts. When, moreover, they came to accept commissions from the professional companies they could be reasonably sure of receiving fairly firm directives as to what to write about and how to set about it; and they could be just as certain that with copyright passing into the actors' hands upon delivery of the script, they would have no redress if the actors chose to cut, edit or otherwise amend their texts as rehearsal and performance suggested. It is hardly surprising therefore that some of them should have preferred to write for companies of boys who, being still under the control of their masters, could be better relied upon to respect the text; yet when comparison is made between these plays and those handled by the adult companies in the sixteenth century it is noticeable that very few of the former have been thought capable of revival by later generations.

Of the schoolmasters, choirmasters and university dons who led the way in experimenting with classical plays, William Cornish, John Rightwise, John Rastell, John Heywood, Nicholas Udall, John Redford, Ralph Radcliffe, Nicholas Grimald, Roger Ascham, Sir John Dee, William Hunis and Richard Edwards all made notable contributions to the development of English drama before Elizabeth I's accession in 1558.[1] Rastell, Heywood and Redford brought a new freedom both in subject matter and treatment to the moral interlude, while Nicholas Udall (headmaster successively of Eton and Westminster) with his neo-Plautine farce *Ralph Roister Doister* (c.1552) gave the English theatre a play that married originality and native wit to Latin stylistic precedent as effectively as Machiavelli had done in Florence forty years earlier with his *Mandragola*. Grimald at Oxford by casting Biblical drama in a Latin form, Dee at Cambridge with the staging of Aristophanes' *Pax*, and Ascham (tutor to the Princess Elizabeth) with his translation of Sophocles, provide other examples from the 1540s of pioneer efforts which widened theatrical horizons in as many directions as the rapidly developing censorship was blacking them out in others.

A similar service was rendered by the Inns of Court – which might fairly be described as a University devoted to studies of the law, situated in London – in the latter half of the century. Both

[1] See Alfred Harbage, *Annals of English Drama, 975–1700*, rev. S. Schoenbaum, London, 1964.

Latin and Greek continued to be regarded there as subjects of vocational importance and, as a recreation, an interest in classical tragedy developed in this environment akin to the interest in classical comedy which had grown up in the schools. *Gorboduc* by T. Norton and T. Sackville (1561), George Gascoigne's *Jocasta* (1566) and *The Misfortunes of Arthur* by T. Hughes (1588) were among the tragedies in the Senecan manner which these young men presented for their own and their friends' edification and entertainment. Masques were no less popular. It is difficult to attribute any precise measure of responsibility for the actual development of English drama to the Inns of Court; but, situated as they were between the Court and the public playhouses, and responsible as they were for presenting comedies, histories, tragedies and masques which attracted the attention of both the Queen and Shakespeare, they undoubtedly assisted in bringing about that fusion of academic and popular traditions of play construction which gave Elizabethan and Jacobean drama its unique character and vitality.

## II *Stage Censorship: Biblical Drama in Transition*

Censorship in the English theatre began as a simple police operation to control unruly behaviour in the auditorium but progressed rapidly from these relatively innocent beginnings to incorporate first the 'prompt-copies' of plays to be acted, then the manuscripts of plays prepared for the printer, and finally the suppression of all plays devoted to religious subject matter. This process extended over a period of sixty years between 1530 and 1590. The start of it may be recognized in the deletion from the Banns of the Chester Cycle of Miracle Plays in 1531 by the Town Clerk of all references to the Pope's promises of pardon and threats of cursing in relation to audience behaviour at performances of the Cycle.[1] It is virtually complete after 1589 when a Licensing Commission to exercise control over plays, players and playhouses was set up in London by the Government of Elizabeth I consisting of the Archbishop of Canterbury, the Lord Mayor of London and the Lord Chamberlain or their Deputies. The Deputy for the Lord Chamberlain was the Master of the Revels who, in effect, came to exercise an autocratic control over the theatre at the expense of both his colleagues and superiors.[2]

[1] See H. C. Gardiner, *Mysteries' End*, New Haven, 1946; reprint 1967.
[2] See V. C. Gildersleeve, *Government Regulation of Elizabethan Drama*, New York, 1900; reprint 1965.

Trouble began in earnest with the commissioning and performance of moral interludes devoted to Reformation polemic. Inspired by the German example of *Pammachius* which the author, Thomas Kirchmeyer, had dedicated to Archbishop Cranmer, Thomas Cromwell (Wolsey's successor as Lord Chancellor) commissioned John Bale, Bishop of Ossary to write plays attacking the Pope, monks, friars and all articles of Roman Catholic faith which Protestant opinion considered to be idolatrous or superstitious. His quasi-historical Morality Play *Kyng Johan* survives to prove how successfully he carried out his orders. This kind of play being offensive to Catholic opinion in the auditorium provoked riots. By 1543 the situation had deteriorated to the point where Henry VIII felt it necessary to introduce an Act of Parliament forbidding makers of interludes and anyone concerned with the performance of plays from attempting to interpret scripture 'and matters of doctrine now in question' on the stage. This Act was repealed by Protector Somerset on behalf of the young Edward VI in 1549. With the accession of the Catholic Mary I the process was simply put into reverse with Protestants penalized for presenting anti-Catholic plays and Catholics encouraged to copy Protestant example by pillorying the Reformers in stage-plays. The anonymous *Respublica* (1553 and now attributed to Nicholas Udall) provides the only example of this type of Roman Catholic polemical play to have survived in England. The Feast of Corpus Christi, suppressed in 1548, was revived in 1553 and with it the Cycles of plays associated with the Feast. London saw the last performance of its plays in 1557, for, with the accession of the Protestant Elizabeth I the tables were reversed again, but this time more effectively since the Government in Whitehall was beginning to discover how to enforce its own orders.

In 1572 the Privy Council decided to introduce an Act of Parliament restricting and controlling professional acting companies, to instigate an enquiry into the working of the Revels Office and to take steps through its Ecclesiastical Commissions to stamp out all remaining Miracle and Morality Plays. These decisions were occasioned in part by the pressure put upon the Government by the extreme opinions of loyal and influential Protestants recently returned from exile on the continent, but more especially by the threats to the security of Church and State implicit in the Northern Rebellion of 1569 and the excommunication of the Queen in 1570.[1]

[1] See G. Wickham, *Early English Stages*, ii (I), Chapters 1–4.

The impact of these disciplinary actions was felt immediately throughout the entire fabric of the English theatre and served to make this decade a watershed in the history of its fortunes. Between 1574 and 1581 the surviving annual performances of the great Cycles in the midlands and the north of England were suppressed, an action which struck a savage blow at the continuance of drama as a legitimate recreation for amateurs. During the same period the Revels Office was translated into the official government instrument for the censorship of plays and for the control of professional actors and playing places. One such company, the Earl of Leicester's, was given a Royal Patent in 1574 to perform regularly on weekdays in London; another Royal Patent established Edmund Tilney in 1581 as Master of the Revels with an explicit statement of his duties as the agent of the Lord Chamberlain in charge of the theatre. Leicester's Company, led by James Burbage (who was a carpenter by trade and an actor by vocation), at once took advantage of this changed situation and, with financial assistance from a wealthy grocer, John Brayne, built a playhouse in 1576 in the ruins of the dissolved Priory of Holywell in Shoreditch, and called it the Theater. In this same year Richard Farrant acquired and converted part of the refectory in the dissolved Blackfriars Priory near St Paul's Cathedral into a playhouse for performances of plays written for the children of the Chapels Royal and given there before privately invited audiences. This action was followed a year later by the building of another playhouse in the same neighbourhood called the Curtain. These developments, taken collectively, swung the delicate balance that had hitherto existed between professional and amateur dramatic activity irreversibly towards professionalism, and at the same time offered to young university graduates with great literary ambitions and very little money the chance to provide the professional companies with play-scripts for modest financial rewards.

This situation was allowed to develop with little interference until the 1590s when further restrictive actions were taken by the Government following the Martin Marprelate Conspiracy of 1589 and the performance of a play called *The Isle of Dogs* by Ben Jonson and Thomas Nashe at the Swan Theatre in 1597. The action taken was twofold. Marlowe's *Doctor Faustus* (1588–9), Peele's *The Love of King David and Fair Bethsabe* and Greene's *Friar Bacon and Friar Bungay* of about the same time bring to an end, even on the professional stage, the long line of overtly religious plays in England; and a revision in 1598 of the Act of Parliament of 1572 governing the maintenance of acting companies restricted this privilege to the nobility alone. James I on his accession in 1603 withdrew this privilege, permitting acting companies to pursue their profession as household servants of the Royal Family or not at all; he also tightened up the censorship on play texts in respect of oaths. The results of this action may be judged by a comparison of the Quarto and Folio texts of *Othello* published respectively before and after this final turn of the screw. Only after the closing of the theatres with the advent of the Civil War in 1642 was any attempt made to return to the old territory of Biblical drama – and then for largely personal reasons and with little intention of actual stage performance – by John Milton in *Samson Agonistes*, the one tragic drama in English that can stand comparison in form and quality with the tragedies of his near contemporary in France, Jean Racine.[1]

## III *Common Players and Their Playhouses*

The story of how the wide variety of play-places that had served the needs of medieval and early Tudor actors came to be translated into the formalized playhouse or theatre that we know today is inextricably linked with the fortunes of the professional or 'common' player. As we have seen, government action against the religious stage in the 1570s struck a savage blow against the continuance of amateur acting and, in doing so, provided the companies of professional players with an opportunity they were quick to seize.

The extension of the number of actors in a company from eight to twelve which became usual in the early years of Elizabeth's reign made it possible for both the players and their playmakers to extend the scope of their entertainments from the relatively narrow confines of the early Interludes to include historical and romantic subject matter and thus to attempt longer and more complex plays. A comparison of Thomas Preston's *Cambises* (1561) or the anonymous *Clyomen and Clamydes* (1570) with any of John Heywood's Interludes will swiftly reveal the difference, more especially since the text of *Cambises* is complete with the actual distribution of the roles among the players.[2] These advantages accruing to the larger company however brought with them a

---

[1] See Murray Roston, *Biblical Drama in England from the Middle Ages to the Present Day*, London, 1968, Chapter IV.

[2] Printed by J. M. Manly, *Specimens of the Pre-Shakespearean Drama*.

corresponding need to increase its income in rewards and admission charges, a need which in its turn obliged the company to give urgent attention to the size and security of tenure of stages and auditoriums.

Long experience of banquet-halls made any large, 'open' or public room of general assembly like a refectory or town hall attractive; no less interesting in their possibilities were the amphitheatres or 'game-houses' used for the baiting of bulls and bears. The yards and back gardens of inns offered yet another alternative, but one which grew steadily less attractive as City Fathers stepped up the penalties attaching to performances of plays in any place where liquor was readly obtainable, on account of the ensuing brawls and riots. As between halls and game-houses, the former offered the better performing conditions while the latter accommodated far more people and brought in a better commercial return from each performance.[1]

The knowledge that we have about the first playhouses built in London – the Theater, the Curtain, the Rose and the Swan – meagre though it is – at least suffices to suggest that a compromise was reached by which the advantages of both were combined and in which certain features derived from experience of inns (like the provision of refreshments) were incorporated. Nevertheless no compromise is ever regarded as entirely satisfactory, and any *regular* user of such a building will always struggle to modify it in the directions most relevant to his own interests. Elizabethan and Jacobean acting companies were no exception. All the information that we have about the building of the first and second Globes, the first and second Fortunes, the Red Bull and the Hope and about the structural modifications made to the Boar's Head Inn, the Blackfriars, the Phoenix, the Cockpit-in-Court, and other buildings used for the staging of plays between 1598 and 1640, indicates that the actors and managers took every opportunity that came their way to improve both the physical conditions on and behind the stage and the commercial profitability of the auditorium.[2] And in the last analysis it was their original banquet-hall homes that the actors yearned for and reverted to when the opportunity came to construct private playhouses in London. If the price they had to pay for this was a substantial cut in the number of spectators that could be accommodated, the sacrifice was amply recompensed by the pro-

[1] See G. Wickham, *Early English Stages*, ii (I), Chapter 5.
[2] See C. Walter Hodges, *The Globe Restored*, London 1953, 2nd edn, 1968; also Herbert Berry, *The Boar's Head Playhouse*, London, 1986.

tection from the hazards of climate and weather which fully-roofed and heated buildings afforded them and by the higher admission prices which this degree of protection and comfort in the auditorium allowed them to charge. Yet higher prices inevitably eliminate those patrons who can no longer afford to pay them; and this change, just as inevitably, alters the balance of interests and tastes within the auditorium. These changes in the private theatres of Jacobean and Caroline London resulted in sophisticated tastes of a primarily academic and literary kind coming to take precedence over the more popular and specifically mimetic elements of traditional English dramaturgy. No one could claim that this was disastrous so long as the actors continued to use their public, gamehouse-style of theatres as well and to tour in the provinces. (See section V, pp. 46–53 below.)

Neither of these conditions, however, was destined to last for very long. In the provinces the audiences which had supported the amateur religious stage of their own creation, switched their patronage to the professional companies when their own, home-made drama was suppressed, and in sufficient numbers to allow some companies to earn their living exclusively from provincial tours. The absenteeism which these performances on weekdays as opposed to holidays encouraged turned employers against these visiting actors who contributed nothing to the welfare of the local community but fed off it like parasites. This was an attitude that could readily be exploited by Puritan opinion eager to win allies for its own campaign to ban plays and players altogether. And wherever these two factions combined, the acting companies began to find that they were at first paid by the Mayor and Aldermen to agree to refrain from playing in that town and then banned from coming near the town on pain of fines and imprisonment. This habit spread steadily in Caroline England until those towns and cities that would still accept visiting companies were in a small minority. With the closing of the London theatres by Act of Parliament in 1642, provincial touring by professional companies came to a final end.

After the Restoration of the Monarchy in 1660 it was not resumed (at least not officially), and the public which returned to the new theatres in the capital represented the coterie audiences of the pre-war private theatres much more nearly than the popular audiences which had given Marlowe, Shakespeare and Jonson their support in the capacious wooden-Os of the common playhouses. For all their love of violent action and racy bawdry and their lack of interest in the niceties of unities of time and place, these audiences had been representative of the English nation as a whole and provided a forum for serious discussion of every aspect of the nation's life and welfare. Their defection or banishment from the theatre after 1660 was destined to impoverish English drama for centuries to come.

Underlying this attack on the theatre was a large element of envy. In a society like that of Jacobean and Caroline England, where people were growing impatient with the static nature of a strict, feudal hierarchy that made little allowance for natural ability, the theatre offered one of the few paths to wealth and reputation open to the peasant or the artisan. Edward Alleyn, the leader first of the Lord Admiral's Company and then of Prince Henry's, acquired a fortune sufficient to found and endow the College of God's Gift at Dulwich, while Shakespeare was able to buy New Place with its large garden in his home-town of Stratford-upon-Avon. Such fortunes were regarded by many worthy citizens as immoral since they seemed to have been amassed with relatively little effort and out of the pockets of the poor and needy: in fact they were the product of hard work, a high degree of discipline, loyalty and self-help within each company and a willingness to take risks. An outbreak of plague could close all London theatres for months on end and a fire could just as easily destroy a playhouse, a wardrobe full of costumes and a library of prompt-copies of play-scripts: nor did any insurance schemes exist to protect the players against the resulting financial losses. Only their own savings and gifts from their own patrons could redeem such disasters. Yet it was this very relationship with aristocratic and powerful patrons which fanned the flames of jealousy against the actors: for when they found themselves in a tight spot they could claim the protection of their masters' liveries (and after 1603 of Royal Patents) and thus claim to be immune from the penalities of the common-law. When the country divided itself in Civil War it is significant that only one actor, Elliard Swanston, is known to have taken the Parliament's side.[1] Not for nothing, therefore, did Sir William D'Avenant observe that 'they who would have no King would have no play': nor has the belief that the live theatre is the play-thing of the rich and leisured few altogether disappeared from society today.

---

[1] On the London theatres during the Civil War and Commonwealth see L. Hotson, *The Commonwealth and Restoration Stage*, Cambridge, Mass., 1928.

## IV  *Stages, Costumes and Settings*

The emblematic approach to the identification of character and locality on the stage devised within the theatres of worship and social recreation during the Middle Ages was one which proved to be resilient enough to outlast the Tudor censorship and to survive on the English professional stage until the Civil War. The dramatist Thomas Dekker, in discussing the theatre of his day, uses the phrases 'speaking pictures' and 'dumb poesie'; by 'speaking pictures' he meant the actors' dialogue reinforced by their gestures and expressions, and by 'dumb poesie' he meant the information conveyed visually to audiences by the use of the stage itself, of costume and of scenic units.

Medieval playmakers and actors never conceived of the theatre as anything but artifice, pretence, make-believe – a play or a game. In not making any attempt to simulate actuality in a photographic sense, they were content to present themselves (and expected their audiences to accept) a double image where stage-action was concerned. The actor was at once both himself *and* the character he portrayed; the *platea* was at once both the floor of the church *and* that of the cattle-manger at Bethlehem, or the floor of the banquet hall *and* that of Fulgens's house or the lawn of Lucres's garden. The fictional aspect of any theatrical performance was thus frankly acknowledged from the outset, and many advantages flowed from it. In the first place it permitted the actors to provide their audiences with essential directives rather than replicas and, in the second, it allowed audiences the freedom to fill out the details with their imaginations rather than restricting them to a single and particular example which might be meaningful to one spectator but not to others. This concept could be applied as easily to a character like Justice or Caiphas or Mercury as to localities like gardens, temples or houses. Equipped with a sword and balances and a red dress the lady so attired *represented* Justice; a couple of trees in tubs and a bench *represented* a garden. These conventions could be multiplied *ad infinitum*; and, so long as they were both codified and respected, everyone could understand them whether he was literate or not. As Shakespeare observed in *Coriolanus*: 'The eyes of the ignorant are more learned than their ears.'

The process of codification was carried out slowly over the centuries in part by the Church in the iconography of mosaic, fresco, stained-glass, statuary and vestments reinforced verbally in sermons, and in part by the nobility in the figurations of heraldic blazon, tapestry and book-illumination reinforced verbally by sagas and *chansons de gestes*. In this way whole galleries of figures – Muses, Liberal Arts, Virtues, Vices, the Worthies, Biblical heroes and villains, characters of myth and legend – came to be readily identifiable to the eye simply by the garments that they wore and the properties which they carried. A haloed figure carrying keys, no matter what his face or stature, was automatically St Peter; a figure in a helmet surmounted by a crown and with a blazon of the fleur-de-lys (even with his vizor down) was automatically the King of France. By the same token a scenic 'hill' could represent the Mount of Olives, Olympus or Parnassus: the characters, their costumes and their actions in association with the hill sufficed to provide the appropriate label.[1]

Colour could also be pressed into service as an additional aid. Livery is a case in point. There is the traditional blue gown for the Virgin Mary; there is red hair for Judas Iscariot.[2] Where scenic units were concerned, a brown and a green hill in conjunction could be used to represent Spain and England (as happened in 1501 in an entertainment welcoming Katherine of Aragon) or, as on another occasion and in another context, to represent a decayed and a flourishing Commonwealth.[3]

These conventions gave actors and playmakers the liberty to cover great distances in space and time within the action of a play, and reduced theories and rules governing unity of time and place on the stage to tiresome irrelevancies. To suppose therefore that medieval, Tudor and Jacobean stages were devoid of spectacle is a dangerous delusion. Even the mechanicals of *A Midsummer Night's Dream* equip themselves with scenic emblems when presenting their play of 'Pyramus and Thisbe' at Duke Theseus' Court. Journeys between one locality and another were represented, as often as not, by 'a passage across the stage' very much as they are today in the Chinese and Japanese classical theatre.

How then, we may ask, did the actors cope with plays which were so rhetorical in style and so formal in presentation? The answer is to be found in two phrases in the Latin rubrics (stage-directions) of the earliest liturgical plays: *quasi* and *quomodum*, 'as if' and 'in the manner of'. These requirements relate to postures and are approximations. There is not the least suggestion that any attempt

---

[1] See R. Withington, *English Pageantry*, Cambridge, Mass., 1918–20, 2 vols, and G. Wickham, *Early English Stages*, iii, 63–170.

[2] See T. W. Craik, *The Tudor Interlude*.

[3] G. Wickham, *Early English Stages*, i, Chapters 6 and 7, and ii (I) Chapter 6.

should be made to copy behaviour in any detail: only the gist or essence of a character, his style of utterance and manner of behaviour, is called for. A tyrant, like Herod, was expected to rage vocally and rampage visually, just as the three priests representing the three Maries visiting Christ's sepulchre were expected to 'step delicately' and to appear 'as if seeking for something'. The art of acting of course did not stand still. Rather did it advance and keep pace with the playmaker's art. When, in the Elizabethan theatre, Shakespeare both laughed at the crudeness of Bottom the Weaver's approach to acting and instructed the players at Elsinore through Hamlet's lips to 'hold the mirror up to nature' he was not talking about the behaviourist school of acting that suits television serials like *Coronation Street* or *Dallas* today. He was simply telling actors who called themselves professionals that they must acquire an appropriate technique to match in their posture, gesture and vocal delivery the modulations of mood and atmosphere provided by their playmakers. There must be no crude leaping from one primary emotion to another, no absurd exaggeration of a particular passion, no mumbling or 'ad-libbing' to blur or dislocate the sense for the viewer and listener. It is the sort of advice that would at once be appreciated by an opera singer today: for to *sing* a text is quite as artificial or formal as anything that was required of Elizabethan actors, yet the artificiality of this convention only becomes tiresome and absurd in the auditorium when the singer himself is not in control of his voice or person. Were we, with the aid of some time-machine, to be transported back into the auditorium of the Globe, the Blackfriars or the Cockpit-in-Court and find ourselves watching a performance of *The Spanish Tragedy*, *The Alchemist* or *The Duchess of Malfi* what we saw and heard would undoubtedly appear as strange to us as the spectacle of a Japanese Nōh play in performance; but the resemblance would extend to include that harmony between all the component elements which is so distinctive a feature of that Eastern, emblematic art.

It was only when Inigo Jones, Master Surveyor of the Works first to Prince Henry and then to Charles I, came into collision with Ben Jonson on the order of precedence to be accorded to their respective contributions to Court Masques that this harmony was seriously challenged. The outcome of this struggle resolved itself in Jones's favour; so, when the London theatre re-opened after the Civil War with Jones's collaborator, Sir William D'Avenant, and Jones's pupil, John Webb, as its leaders, its character was changed. The old emblematic stage went into eclipse and a new stage, with pictorial realism as its main concern, came into being.[1]

## V Dramatic Genre

### (a) 1300–1500

When the Shakespeare First Folio was published in 1623 its editors decided to present his plays to readers as Comedies, Histories and Tragedies. There are two features which may surprise today's readers about this: the first is the lack of correspondence with the dramatic theory of classical antiquity which had prescribed Tragedy, Comedy and Satyr Play as the normal genres appropriate to dramatic ·literature; the second (as with hindsight we can see now) is that the History, or Chronicle, Play was a genre of English invention which was as distinct as it was short-lived.

In seeking an explanation we must retrace our steps in time behind the Reformation to the religious plays of the Middle Ages that were the foster-children of the Roman Catholic Church – Miracle Cycles, Moralities and Saint Plays. None of these categories of plays owed anything to the dramatic theory of classical antiquity: rather were all such plays governed in their structure by the religious doctrine which they existed to expound and illuminate.

Preaching in the vernacular languages of medieval Europe, when authorized by the Papal Curia early in the thirteenth century, was closely restricted to those priests and friars trained and licensed to comment upon Scripture: only so could the propagation of heretical doctrine be avoided or, failing that, controlled. Thus, as the writing and performance of religious plays in vernacular languages came to be regarded during the fourteenth century as a logical extension of an evangelistic missionary crusade to laymen, so the preaching of Repentance as the gateway to Salvation served to impose upon the texts of these plays a doctrinal pattern of Fall from Grace, Redemption through Repentance and Atonement, followed by a final return to Grace: in short, a dramatic form that was neither wholly tragic, nor wholly comic, but invariably tragi-comic (see Part (ii), pp. 19–21 above). In England there was therefore no incentive to regard what Sir Philip Sidney was much later to describe as 'mongrel tragi-comedy' as anything but the normal dramatic form until Henry VII started to encourage his Court to take an active interest

[1] See Richard Southern, *Changeable Scenery*, London, 1952, Chapters 1–8; also Chapter 8, pp 375–9 below.

in the classical revival proceeding in Italy during the closing decades of the fifteenth century.

Moreover, since the subject matter of all stage-plays sponsored by the Church was derived either directly from the Bible and the legendary lives of Apostles, Saints and Martyrs, or from allegorized expositions and commentaries upon them, English religious plays of the fourteenth and fifteenth centuries, unlike those of classical antiquity, admitted of no artifical, or unnatural, distinctions and divisions between persons of varying social status in a play. If both God the Father and Christ himself could walk the stage, so could shepherds rub shoulders with kings at the manger in Bethlehem, or priests with merchants, prostitutes and beggars in the temple at Jerusalem. Nor could serious exposition of faith and doctrine on the one hand preclude within stage dialogue naive, humorous and often bawdy expressions of disbelief, even blasphemy, on the other: both belonged to the wicked mortal world that Christ had died to save. This was a theatrical world in which the critical niceties of Aristotelian dramatic theory had no place at all. Storyline, assisted by the rhetorical skills of the actors, with its power to awake faith and to stir emotion where largely illiterate audiences were concerned, was allowed to assume an importance in Miracle Plays and Saint Plays overriding all other considerations: for these were re-enactments of historical events in time-present, and to be regarded by their audiences as of abiding significance for the whole community time-without-end.

By contrast, the most potent images behind the playwright's pen when writing a Morality Play which existed to teach wilful Mankind how to recognize the Devil, his assistants and his methods, and how to distinguish between the path of Virtue that would lead him to Salvation from that of Vice leading to Damnation, were the 'Dance of Death' and the spectacle of Tournaments. The former depicted Death as a skeleton, equipped with hour-glass and scythe, behind whom followed Kings, Queens, merchants, lawyers, priests and peasants: the latter glamorized physical combat between noblemen, and dramatized war-games into epic and romantic spectacles for presentation before ladies. Morality Plays, as has already been remarked, were *not* histories but arguments: they were shorter and more frequently addressed to literate than to popular audiences: they were also less tightly attached to Calendar Feasts in their subject matter, and thus less closely tied to any single, particular occasion for their performance (see Part (ii), p. 23 above). All these factors made them attractive to actors as plays suitable for touring, provided always that the playmaker had taken care so to order the appearance of characters and their dialogue as to make the doubling or trebling of roles a possibility: and it is in this type of play that we find the small companies of quasi-professional 'players of Inter-ludes' appearing during the latter half of the fifteenth century (see Part (ii), section V, pp. 29–32). In such plays, as in Miracle and Saint Plays, a time span from cradle to grave and the need to depict on stage an after-life in Heaven and Hell, made any concept of unity of time or place ridiculous. Yet here again doctrine prescribed a happy issue out of affliction, and thus tragi-comic form, no matter which of the Seven Deadly Sins was assigned by Lucifer to ensnare the protagonist's soul.[1]

While the monopoly enjoyed by the Church over education throughout the Middle Ages ensured that most plays would be devised and presented as vehicles for doctrinal instruction skilfully disguised as entertainment – honest recreation for Calendar holidays – it is important to recognize that following the founding of Europe's earliest universities, and in the wake of the rapid rise of a bourgeois merchant class in major cities and trading ports during the thirteenth century, drama more closely in touch with the secular concerns of daily life and farcical in character began to be written and performed, especially in northern France and Flanders.[2] Only four specifically English examples of such texts have survived the ravages of time, but between them they span the period 1300–1500. The earliest is *The Interlude of the Student and the Girl* (c.1300), but only its first scene survives. The second is a play about profiteering among leatherworkers which was to have been publicly presented in Exeter in August, 1352, but performance of which was banned by the Bishop lest riots should ensue: no text or title survives. The third is John Lydgate's *Mumming at Hertford*, a courtly en-tertainment presented to Henry VI at Christmas, c.1425, which takes the form of a debate about mastery in the home between six rugged tradesmen and their shrewish wives. The fourth is Henry Medwall's *Fulgens and Lucres* I and II, commissioned for performance at a banquet held in Lambeth Palace at Christmas, 1497, at which the Flemish Ambassadors were present.[3]

---

[1] See G. Wickham, *Early English Stages*, iii, Chapter 8.
[2] See Richard Axton, *European Drama of the Early Middle Ages*, Chapter 7.
[3] For texts of these plays see G. Wickham, *English Moral Interludes*, London, 1976; 2nd edn, 1985.

### (b) *1500–1642*

The spread of interest in the art and literature of classical antiquity that becomes noticeable at the Courts of Henry VII and Henry VIII and in the English schools and universities during the early decades of the sixteenth century aroused poets and playmakers to a dawning awareness of Roman and Greek dramatic theory and practice. This becomes evident both in the records of revivals of plays by Plautus and Terence and in the texts of farces written by John Heywood (see Part (iii), pp. 33–6). Most of the early Tudor Interludes, however, whether written for choirboys, schoolboys, under-graduates or the rapidly growing number of professional 'players of interludes', preserved a strongly didactic moral content within a tragi-comic form. This conservatism was strongly reinforced through the middle decades of the century by the conflicting doctrinal pressures of the Reformation. This not only resulted in the transforming of many plays into vehicles of Protestant pro-paganda but forced Tudor governments to try to control the stage through legislation, police action and censorship (see Part (iii), pp. 36–9 above). These efforts grew steadily more severe and effective as the century proceeded; and as they did so, the relatively non-controversial alternative subject matter of Roman and Greek plays, and of Italian and French romances and farces, became more attractive to playmakers and actors since the risks of fines, impris-onment and even harsher penalties could thus be greatly reduced. Attempts therefore to copy these foreign alternatives, or to adapt them to fit an English environment, served also to familiarize playmakers with classical precedent respecting dramatic genre.

It is difficult for us to appreciate just how hard it must have been for all aspiring poets in the early years of the reign of Elizabeth I to come to terms with the radical differences of approach to every aspect of play-construction which these departures from popularly accepted norms represented. A chorus; five-act structure; no mixing of persons of high and low degree; no sub-plots; no clowning in tragedy; no stage deaths; unity of action, time and place. Given challenges as far-reaching as this, it is scarcely sur-prising that actors who depended upon a paying public for their livelihood and were acutely aware of Calvinist antipathy to all things Roman, should have questioned whether their audiences were ready to accept such radical departures from familiar Gothic types of stage-play in exchange for theoretical precepts of Italian (and thus Roman Catholic) origin.

The Elizabethan theatre was an actors' theatre: a theatre in which the adult companies commissioned their plays from such poets and journalists of the day as were prepared to do their bidding in a professional sense. The exceptions were the schoolboys and university students: they had little option but to do what they were told by their masters, and could thus be relied upon to rehearse and perform avant-garde scripts on an experimental rather than a commercial basis. The conflict that began to develop in Elizabethan London after 1576 between these two sectional attitudes to dramatic genre is nowhere better illustrated than by Sir Philip Sidney's scathing remarks in his *Apology for Poetry* (written c.1583; printed 1598) about the style of play presented by adult companies in their playhouses, and by Shakespeare's no less ascerbic comments in *Hamlet* on the pretentiousness of both the boy companies and those who wrote and directed their plays in the so-called 'Private playhouses'.

This was a conflict that could only be resolved slowly and one, moreover, which could only find its final resolution in the splitting of audiences, which in medieval and Tudor England still represented the whole community, into sections that corresponded with the swiftly developing class divisions and capitalist outlooks that had come into being under Elizabethan and Jacobean absolutist governments between 1585 and 1625.

The dominant figures among playwrights through those years were William Shakespeare, a traditional actor-sharer-dramatic poet working consistently for a single company of players, and Ben Jonson, a freelance poet, grammarian, theoretician and writer of plays and masques. In 1616 Shakespeare died having failed to publish more than half of his own plays; in that same year Jonson edited and published all his own poems, masques and plays under the grandiloquent title, *Works*. These differences are striking enough in themselves; but their implications proved to be even more significant to the future of the theatre in England. Jonson's aim was to persuade the public to accept plays deliberately designed to conform with classical theoretical principles, and thereby to transform the status of the playmaker from a despised collaborator and hack writer into that of a gentleman of letters. By the time of his death in 1637 he had realized this ambition. With the privilege of acting in London restricted to those companies employed in the service of the royal family, and with all serious dramatists acknowledging the need to publish their plays in anticipation of a critical response from their readers, drama was coming to be viewed as a branch of literature (as acceptable in the privacy of a library as in the public forum of a playhouse) and as a pastime reserved for the leisured rich instead of as the common heritage of rich and poor alike. The price structure of admission charges to the private and the public playhouses shortly before the outbreak of the Civil War provides an accurate reflection of this change in social attitudes to theatregoing. Its forms had accordingly been largely regularized to conform with those which had been postulated by such Italian theorists and critics as Scaliger and Castelvetro in the 1560s, and which the newly formed *Academie Française* in Paris was in the process of imposing upon the theatre in France.

In these terms of reference, directly derived from learned commentaries on Aristotle's *Poetics* and Horace's *Art of Poetry*, plays came to be regarded as existing to present arguments instead of to tell exciting but instructional stories. The word 'tragedy' implied a serious argument and assumed a cast-list confined to men and women in positions of authority within society who communicated with each other in lofty forms of verse appropriate to their rank. The word 'comedy' embraced witty arguments conducted largely in prose among men and women of lower rank – merchants, lawyers, doctors, academics, artisans and peasants – reflecting in an exaggerated and satirical style the manners of the time in such conventional meeting places as city streets, domestic environments or country inns. 'Tragi-comedy', it was argued, should be confined to fantasy – mythology, pastoral Arcadias and Utopias – where lyric poetry, song, dance and spectacle developed within Court Masques could all be deployed to depict ideals which mortals should aspire to imitate.

These were the new dogmas bequeathed by Ben Jonson, James Shirley, Richard Broome and other Caroline dramatists to their successors in the Restoration era; yet they themselves, being still controlled to a large extent by the innate conservatism of the actors and audiences for whom they wrote, never conformed wholly to their own doctrines; still less was this so in the case of such major figures among their contemporaries as Philip Massinger, Thomas Heywood, Thomas Middleton, John Fletcher or John Ford. Reasons for this are not hard to supply.

In the first place Shakespeare's ghost was no more amenable to quiet burial than Banquo's. While his plays continued to be revived and memories of their outstanding popularity survived, it proved impossible for other playwrights to refrain from some measure of imitation. Just as popular with Jacobean and Caroline audiences was that melodramatic and sensational form of tragic drama centred on personal revenge single-mindedly pursued which had been introduced by Thomas Kyd in the 1580s and of which his own *The Spanish Tragedy*, Shakespeare's *Hamlet* and Tourneur's *The Revenger's Tragedy* are now generally regarded as the outstanding examples. Added weight was given to this style of play in the Jacobean era by growing Calvinist concern with the total depravity of all human nature and endeavour, an idea substantially developed in the theatre by Middleton in *The Changeling*, Webster in *The Duchess of Malfi* and *The White Devil* and by Ford in *'Tis Pity She's a Whore*. Nor were English dramatists themselves willing lightly to forgo the advantages to be gained from the continued use of sub-plots as mirrors in which to reflect the principal themes of the main plot, and thus to enrich the texture of the whole play. This reluctance was further reinforced, following the signing of a Peace Treaty with Spain in 1604, by a growing interest in Spanish plays of intrigue and strong emotion arising out of love in conflict with honour, a genre introduced to the English theatre by John Fletcher in *The Maid's Tragedy*.

The major casualty of Jacobean and Caroline rationalist approaches to dramatic genre was the History Play which, like revenge tragedy, had arisen as a patriotic response to threats of foreign invasion from Scotland and Spain, organized from the Vatican during the 1580s. Episodic in structure, jingoistic in content and limited in the number of title-roles worthy of dramatization, this genre petered out after the peaceful accession of James I in 1603 without another Civil War and with all threats of foreign invasion following defeat of the Gunpowder Plot in 1605 virtually removed. Shakespeare prolonged its life-span briefly with excursions into Scottish, Roman and legendary history and, finally, in *Henry VIII* (1612) with John Fletcher as a collaborator; but a genre that no longer conformed with the changed climate of public opinion, and which could not be easily accommodated to fit within the new dramaturgical requirements demanded by the intelligentsia, had few friends left either at Court or in the public playhouses. Instead, fashion directed that attention be focussed on extravagantly ostentatious and exotic fantasy as expressed and displayed in Masques at Court, and on the uneasy and often hypocritical postures of the money-grubbing social climbers whose rise to power in the busy seaport and city of London provided playwrights with ever widening permutations of intrigue and deceit as subject matter for satirical comedy.

Once it is realized that in both of these innovative directions it was Ben Jonson who had pointed the way forward, it becomes easier to understand why it should have been Jonson, not Shakespeare, who was given a State funeral in Westminster Abbey as England's first poet laureate; why John Milton, notwithstanding his republican sympathies, should have chosen to write a Masque, *Comus* (1634) and a thoroughgoing neo-classical tragedy, *Samson Agonistes* (1671), complete with Chorus; and why the way should by then have been open for the introduction of opera to the English theatre by Sir William D'Avenant, John Dryden, John Webb and Henry Purcell following the Restoration of the Monarchy and the re-opening of theatres in London in 1660.

# 2

# ELIZABETHAN AND JACOBEAN DRAMA

## Brian Morris

> Will not a filthy play, with the blast of a trumpet, sooner call
> thither a thousand, than an hour's tolling of a bell bring to the
> sermon a hundred?
>
> John Stockwood, *A Sermon Preached at Pawles Cross*, 1578

From the opening of the first public theatres in 1576 to
their suppression in 1642, at the beginning of the Civil War, the
Puritans in England waged perpetual war upon the stage. In
sermons, in pamphlets, and in Parliament they fulminated against
this new and virulent occasion of sin. Philip Stubbes, in 1583,
blasted contemporary plays in these words:

Do they not maintain bawdry, insinuate foolery, and renew the re-
membrance of heathen idolatry? Do they not induce whoredom and un-
cleanness? Nay, are they not rather plain devourers of maidenly virginity
and chastity? For proof whereof but mark the flocking and running to
Theaters and Curtains, daily and hourly, night and day, time and tide, to
see plays and interludes, where such wanton gestures, such bawdy
speeches, such laughing and fleering, such kissing and bussing, such
clipping and culling, such winking and glancing of wanton eyes, and the like
is used, as is wonderful to behold ... And these be the fruits of plays and
interludes, for the most part.[1]

The Puritan fear arises from a sensitive instinct. The stage was
the golden calf, the actor an errant Aaron, who by imitating a sinful
action induced that sin in his beholders. Drama was literally a
diversion, a broad and easy byway tempting man from the straight
and narrow path. The key word in the passage quoted from Stubbes
is 'idolatry'. He realized that the attention which the plays commanded is not unlike the involvement of worship; the ritual participation
of actor and audience sets up a relationship between them and the

---

[1] Philip Stubbes, *The Anatomie of Abuses*, 1583, quoted in John Dover Wilson, *Life in
Shakespeare's England*, Cambridge, 1911, p 178.

experience represented by the play which has close affinities with the spiritual communion at the heart of religion. And there are lighter correspondences: the climactic structure, the compression or symbolization of everyday experience, the heightened language, the dressing up, all indicate the profound analogy between religious and dramatic expression. Stubbes' cry is against the wilful perversion of what he obscurely recognized as one of mankind's deepest instincts to the service of what he believed to be sin. In the theatre 'you will learn to contemn God and all His laws, to care neither for Heaven nor Hell, and to commit all kinds of sin and mischief'.

This intensely felt dichotomy between the Church and the playhouse, between the world of the spirit and the world of the flesh, is close to the heart of English Puritanism in the sixteenth and seventeenth centuries. The inclusive, medieval sense of the wholeness of all creation had been sharply and effectively challenged by the theology emanating from Wittenberg and Geneva, which stressed the fallen nature of Man, the unredeemed quality of created Nature, and the deadly sinfulness of sin. Until the Renaissance, drama had been dominated, and so controlled, by the Church. It served religious, ecclesiastical purposes, disseminating the incidents of the faith and making them colourful and memorable. The Mystery Cycles, despite the frequent moments of realistic human interest, were celebratory and didactic in intention, and the later Morality Plays are even more clearly concerned with presenting an audience with incitements to virtue and dissuasives from sin. When directives of this kind inform a play the true dramatic impulse operates only sporadically, and *The Castle of Perseverance* (c. 1405),[1] Skelton's *Magnificence* (1515), *Lusty Juventus* (1550), and others like them subserve a general ethical purpose which inhibits the necessary liberty of drama. Only one play of this kind, *The Summoning of Everyman* (1495), escapes all censure, and this is perhaps because of the universality of its theme. Death comes to summon Everyman, who asks various friends to accompany him on his journey. Fellowship, Kindred, Cousin and Goods refuse or desert him. Knowledge and Good Deeds go with him, though only Good Deeds get as far as Paradise. Although these abstract characters possess an unusual degree of vitality and dramatic life, it is the structural metaphor of life as a pilgrimage towards death

[1] The dating of all plays follows Alfred Harbage, *Annals of English Drama, 975–1700*, revised by S. Schoenbaum, London, 1964, except where otherwise stated, and refers to the year when the play was most probably first presented.

which gives *Everyman* a compelling unity, and raises it above the level of the routine religious dramas of the period. Elsewhere the things we now find to admire are peripheral, not central features. In the Second Shepherds' Play, of the Wakefield Cycle, it is the comedy of the lamb in the cradle which we remember, not the visit to the Christ-child. Comedy, the sharply realized moment when the occasional absurdity of the human condition is seen as itself alone, with its own, self-sufficient validity, is one of the most powerful solvents in the breakdown of the monolithic medieval drama which, for all its moments of insight, was essentially an extension of the hermeneutic principle (that of scriptural interpretation) in Christianity.

Between them, Luther and Calvin destroyed the idea of the Church as the one supranational body, to which all men equally owed allegiance, and to which all states, all princes were alike subordinate. Luther's work was largely negative, rooting out the abuses which stemmed from the power of the Papacy, cleansing, purging, and reforming the Body of Christ on earth. Calvin, by the theocracy he physically established at Geneva, as well as by the vast, ordered system of theology, ethics and ecclesiastical organization set forth in the *Institutes*, offered, for the first time in Christian history, a viable alternative to Catholicism and the Papacy. Yet both reformers are alike in the importance they give to the individual, human situation. The effect of this movement of thought upon the drama is startling. Until about 1560 the majority of plays of which records have survived were Biblical Histories, Moral Interludes, Anti-Catholic Interludes, Miracle Plays, Mystery Cycles, pageants and masques: all plays rooted in religion and illustrative of the great creative and redemptive scheme. After 1560 there appear more and more plays whose interests are secular. Classical mythology becomes the centre of interest in many, plays on English and foreign history are common in the 1590s, and the 'kinds' – comedy, history, tragedy – assert themselves on a purely secular basis. Plays tend to be less about virtues than about people.

The reasons for this shift of interest and emphasis are inextricably complex. F.P. Wilson points out that in the period from 1590 to the closing of the theatres in 1642 there was a steady development in the organization, wealth, and importance of the acting companies.[1] Puritan opposition to the theatre was made less damaging by the patronage of the Court, and both public and

[1] In F. P. Wilson, *Elizabethan and Jacobean*, Oxford, 1945, p 86.

private playhouses flourished. The various influences of Seneca, Machiavelli, Terence, Plautus, Plutarch, Castiglione, Montaigne, have often been assessed, but it has perhaps not been sufficiently emphasized that the one thing these various 'sources' share is their concern with the secular as opposed to the religious world. Religion does not supply relevant answers to the new questions that playwrights were asking, nor does the simple dramatization of myth, parable, or moral problem provide a sufficiently satisfying pattern for contemporary human life. In a rising, mercantile, politically conscious, comparatively affluent society there was a need for new visions of the good life, new paradises, new golden worlds, and even new hells. It is this newly awakened interest in the unoccupied territories of the world of thought which, in the next half-century, will bring forth Burton's *Anatomy of Melancholy*, Harvey's *Circulation of the Blood*, Hobbes' *Leviathan*, Browne's *Pseudodoxia Epidemica* and *Religio Medici*, and will see the flourishing of Gresham College and the beginnings of the Royal Society.[1] And giving local life and an enduring image to these new directions of thought will be plays like Marlowe's *Doctor Faustus*, Jonson's *Volpone*, Marston's *The Malcontent*, Chapman's *Bussy D'Ambois*, and Ford's *The Broken Heart*. If one were to seek one over-arching image to characterize the drama of the period 1580–1640 it would be the deserted altar. While Bacon in *The Advancement of Learning* (Book I, i. 3) differentiated sharply the spheres of religious and scientific thought, the dramatists, it seems, extended the hitherto religious questions – about the meaning of life, the finality of death, and the permissive limits of human happiness and joy – across the whole area of man's experience, breaking down the scholastic demarcations between the sacred and the secular, insisting upon a newly apprehended integrity of human life. Perhaps the essential quality of Elizabethan and Jacobean drama, the quality which distinguishes it from all that has gone before, is this retreat from religion, the flight from faith.

The plot of one of the earliest plays of the period begins as follows: a ruthless and mighty conqueror, one of the greatest soldiers the world has known, subdues yet another kingdom, and in doing so, takes prisoner a young and beautiful woman. The effect of her presence as his campaigns proceed is to tempt him to abandon his career of conquest and subjugation, and give up War for a life of Love. The obvious implication is that this is the first part of Marlowe's *Tamburlaine*. And so it is. But it is an equally accurate

[1] See Christopher Hill, *Intellectual Origins of the English Revolution*, Oxford, 1965, especially pp 14–84.

description of the opening of *Alexander and Campaspe* (1584) by John Lyly (1554?–1606). This play takes an ancient myth, from Pliny's *Natural History*, and dramatizes it more or less faithfully. Alexander the Great falls in love with his beautiful prisoner, Campaspe, a woman of mean parentage who lived in Thebes. As evidence of his nobility and his love he gives her her freedom, so long as she stays near him, and in spite of the warnings of his general, Hephaestion, he engages the painter Apelles to paint her portrait. Apelles falls in love with Campaspe, and she with him. Having finished the portrait, Apelles damages it to secure fresh sittings, and when he finally presents it to the king his strange behaviour betrays the fact that he is in love with Campaspe. Alexander, in his magnanimity, resigns her to him, and returns to the warlike life he had been neglecting. This is interspersed with dialogue between Alexander and a group of philosophers, including Plato and Aristotle, and especially Diogenes, whose independence, wit, and cynicism make him a major character in the play. There is also a group of young pages, as there is in nearly all Lyly's plays. Whereas Marlowe makes the female captive a dangerous and ultimately fatal intrusion into the purity of a dedicated warrior's life, Lyly makes the same theme the subject for a debate on the nature of Magnanimity – the apogee of the Aristotelian virtues. The subject is announced, and the tone set, in the opening words of the play:

CLITUS: Parmenio I cannot tel whether I should more commend in Alexanders victories, courage, or curtesie, in the one being a resolution without feare, in the other a liberality above custome: Thebes is rased, the people not racked, towers throwne down, bodies not thrust aside, a conquest without conflict, and a cruell warre in a milde peace.

The poise and balance of the prose, and the self-conscious nobility of the controlled sentiments, enact the virtue of Magnanimity itself, regardless of which side of the debate is being urged. The whole play is an investigation into 'the nature of true kingliness', and the inquiry is conducted with such civilized elegance that the issues are crystal clear. The interest in the Courtier as a model of human perfection is far older than Castiglione's *Il Cortegiano*, but the Renaissance interest in courtliness is one example of the flight from faith into fashion.

A second quality of Lyly's art which demands attention is what Fulke Greville describes as 'that hypocritical figure *Ironia*, wherein men commonly (to keep above their works) seem to make toys of the utmost they can do'.[1] To keep the strident emulation of court life

[1] *Life of Sir Philip Sidney* (ed. Nowell Smith, Oxford, 1907), p 154; cited by G. K. Hunter, *John Lyly: The Humanist as Courtier*, London, 1962, p 130.

within bounds it was important to devise a code of manners by which the courtier could display his virtue by concealing it. Assertiveness was no virtue in Elizabeth's court, where the proper attitude was a proud humility, which always promised more than it ever needed to perform. This courtly deference, almost diffidence, is an essential tone in Lyly's plays, and especially so in what is perhaps his greatest artistic achievement, *Endimion* (1588). The plot, which traces the love of Endimion for Cynthia, the attempted revenge of his former love, Tellus, and the intrigues of their various confidantes and servants, is full and complicated in itself. But above its narrative level is a second level of political allegory. All critics are agreed that Cynthia represents Queen Elizabeth, and Endimion is the Earl of Leicester. And while the plot has several covert references to the arbitrary quality of Elizabeth's judgements (when, for example, Cynthia sentences Semele to a year's silence for speaking out of turn) it does shadow forth the relationship between the Queen and Leicester with remarkable fidelity. At the end, Endimion can declare his devotion to Cynthia in terms of complete humility, and so gloss the Leicester affair with an acceptable courtly irony:

Such a difference hath the Gods sette between our states, that all must be dutie, loyaltie, and reverence; nothing (without it vouchsafe your highnes) be termed love. (V. iii. 168–70)

To call this subservience, or flattery, would be totally to mistake Lyly's tone. It is Irony, one of the most vital elements in Lyly's art.

The same qualities of courtly elegance and allegoric depth appear in most of the other plays. *Sapho and Phao* (1584) debates the issue between Love and Chastity, under a stylized classical narrative in which Venus, to prick the pride of Queen Sapho, makes her fall in love with the ferryman Phao, to whom Venus has given extraordinary beauty. The praise of Sapho throughout the play is clearly intended for Queen Elizabeth, and the conversation between the courtiers, who form the background to the action, establishes the level of brittle, valued sophistication. *Midas* (1589) similarly retells the Ovidian story, in order to present to Elizabeth's court the perils of the time – it was written soon after the Armada. These four plays form a group in which, as Professor G.K. Hunter has pointed out, the debate form and the allegoric level determine the structure. Three other plays, overlapping in time but representing a later stage of Lyly's dramatic thinking, are set in more or less 'pastoral' backgrounds and develop in an episodic or even 'fugal' way: they are *Gallathea* (1585), *Love's Metamorphosis* (1590), and *The Woman in the Moone* (1593). Gallathea and Phillida, disguised as boys, fall in love with each other, and, at Cupid's instigation, are amorously pursued by three of Diana's nymphs under the same misapprehension. The 'dance of disguises' is not resolved until Venus decides to change one of the girls into a boy, so that the right true end of love may be obtained. Just as disguising is the mainspring of *Gallathea*, so the magical changing of shape is the main motif of *Love's Metamorphosis* (1590). Fidelia, a nymph of Ceres, has been transformed into a tree, and she is accidentally killed by the farmer Erisichthon. Famine strikes him, and he sells his daugher, Protea, to a merchant. She escapes when Neptune changes her into a fisherman, and she later assumes the form of Ulysses. Elsewhere in the play three of Ceres' nymphs are transformed into a rock, a rose, and a bird, and are not permitted to recover until they accept the lovers chosen for them. This 'anatomy' of love virtually dispenses with plot in order to enhance the setting in a timeless, featureless, pastoral world, where only the delicacy of emotion and response has power to determine action. *The Woman in the Moone* (1593), probably Lyly's last play, is episodic in a different way. It deals with the creation of Woman, made by nature as a comrade for the shepherds of Utopia, and invested with the qualities of the gods who rule the planets. These gods, displeased, determine to subject her in turn to their influence. Under Saturn she becomes intransigent, under Mars aggressive, and so on. She is finally assigned a place in the Moon, and charged to 'make the moone inconstant like thy selfe'. The vision informing the structure in these three plays is that of a pastoral perfection; nature, cleansed and winnowed by Lyly's courtly art, becomes a paradise of dainty devices, which makes its oblique judgement of the real world, though the irony it asserts is preservative rather than aggressive.

*Mother Bombie* (1589) stands apart from Lyly's other plays in every way. It has no direct source, though the general model is obviously Terence. The skilfully articulated plot concerns the mysterious fortune-teller, Mother Bombie, who prognosticates the true and romantic issue of all the conflict presented to her by a group of old men and young lovers busily engaged in arranging marriages. The issues and the characters are all resolutely human; there is no pastoral paradise in this play, and the setting is urban. It is a witty and effervescent play, but strangely unlike anything else Lyly wrote.

Irony and courtly elegance are essentially secular, worldly qualities, and it is significant that an examination of Lyly's sources reveals no indebtedness to any religious tradition, but a profound interest in classical literature – particularly Ovid, and especially the Ovid of the *Metamorphoses*. Nearly all Lyly's plays were first acted by the Boys' companies, and the stern words of an unknown Puritan in 1569 'Plays will never be supprest while Her Majesty's unfledged minions flaunt it in silks and satins'[1] probably had a counterpart in the 1580s and 1590s.

At the opposite pole from the jewelled, studied elegance of Lyly stands Thomas Kyd's *The Spanish Tragedy* (c.1587), an early and most influential example of a play on the theme of revenge. 'Revenge' said Bacon, 'is a kind of wild justice', and it is the nature of Justice in the Universe that is the play's central concern. Hieronimo, when his son has been murdered, asks the question:

> O world, no world, but mass of public wrongs,
> Confus'd and fill'd with murder and misdeeds;
> O sacred heavens! If this unhallow'd deed,
> If this inhuman and barbarous attempt,
> If this incomparable murder thus
> Of mine, but now no more my son,
> Shall unreveal'd and unrevenged pass,
> How should we term your dealings to be just?
>
> (III. ii. 3–10)

The tone of the play is Senecan, its construction episodic, but the questions it poses take us back to Greek tragedy. Hieronimo's question is also the prayer of Clytemnestra in Aeschylus' *Agamemnon*, lines 349–50; in Gilbert Murray's translation:

> May good but conquer in the last incline
> Of the balance! Of all prayers that prayer is mine.

The medieval faith in a moral universe, harmonious in all its parts, has shrunk to a plea for some vestigial sign of an ultimate justice. *The Spanish Tragedy* marks the beginning of a movement in English drama because it questions and explores so many hitherto inviolate assumptions. Its revenge theme allowed the investigation of the social issue of personal honour, the political questions of tyranny and rebellion, and the spiritual problem of the relative places of human and divine vengeance. The spiritual pessimism which pervades the play is strangely accompanied by a sense of the glory inherent in the natural man. Yet however far Kyd's sphere of

[1] See E. K. Chambers, *The Elizabethan Stage*, Oxford, 1923, ii, 34.

thought is from Lyly's, they share a language, and, almost, a style. When Horatio's mutilated body is found Hieronimo says:

> Here lay my hope, and here my hope hath end:
> Here lay my heart, and here my heart was slain:
> Here lay my treasure, here my treasure lost:
> Here lay my bliss, and here my bliss bereft:
> But hope, heart, treasure, joy and bliss,
> All fled, fail'd, died, yea, all decay'd with this.
>
> (IV. iv. 90–5)

They are lines which, *mutatis mutandis*, Lyly might have written.

Courtly comedy could not for long maintain the plane of excellence which Lyly had achieved. There was a demand for comedy of a different sort from the public playhouses, a need sensed and met by one of the shrewdest writers of the age, Robert Greene (1560?–1592). He was one of the first who set out to entertain, professionally, the widest possible public. After the success of Lyly's *Euphues*, Greene began writing romantic novels, in the early 1580s, and his best work is found in his later prose journalism – the 'coney-catching' pamphlets, and the autobiographical pieces, especially *Greene's Groatsworth of Wit*. His plays belong to the years about 1587–91, and the three early ones have found few defenders and fewer producers. *Alphonsus King of Aragon* (1587) was probably written to rival Marlowe's *Tamburlaine*, and shows how Greene could pick up the rant but not the grandeur of his model. The play was a failure when it first appeared on the stage, and Greene gave up the idea of writing a sequel. As Kenneth Muir says of it, 'The main theme . . . is interrupted in the third and fourth acts by a series of scenes concerning Amurack, scenes which contrive to be both boring and incredible'. *Orlando Furioso* (1591) has survived in a Quarto edition of 1594 and the Alleyn MS of Orlando's part, at Dulwich College. The differences between the two versions show that it would be unfair to judge Greene by the extant text of the play, but it suggests neither profundity nor wit when, in Act V, the mad Orlando is woken by a fiddler playing 'any odd toy', breaks his fiddle on his head and is rewarded with the line 'Lor, sir, you'll break my living'. *A Looking Glass for London and England* (1590), in which the prophets Oseas and Jonas preach repentance to Rasni, King of Nineveh, against a background of the multifarious life and sin of London, rises to moments of a certain bleak dignity, as Greene sometimes does in his prose pamphlets when contemplating the nature of mortality. Oseas cries:

> Looke, London, look; with inward eies behold
> What lessons the events do here unfold.
> Sinne growne to pride to misery is thrall;
> The warning bell is rung, beware to fall.
>
> (IV. v.)

The long shadow of the plague lies over such passages, and in these moments Greene is like the greatest of Elizabethan journalists, Thomas Nashe. The two remaining plays, *Friar Bacon and Friar Bungay* (1589) and *James IV* (1590), are superior in every way. *Friar Bacon* presents the 13th century philosopher Roger Bacon as a wonder-working magician who finally burned his books and died in an odour of sanctity. Parallel with this is the Edward-Margaret-Lacy plot, in which Lacy is employed to woo Margaret on Edward's behalf, and falls in love with her himself. The play has been claimed as the first successful romantic comedy, but more significantly it is the earliest of the 'double-plot' plays. Scenes showing the strength of Bacon's magic alternate with scenes displaying the 'patient Griselda' constancy of Margaret's love. As William Empson says, 'The process is simply that of dramatizing a literary metaphor – "the power of beauty is like the power of magic", both are individualist, dangerous, and outside the social order'.[1] This permits a more trenchant exploration of the comic world than the simplicity of previous comic plots had allowed, and it may partly account for the critical willingness to see in Margaret 'the first realistic heroine in Elizabethan drama', and the forebear of Rosalind, Viola and Imogen. She is not so fecund. Daniel Seltzer points out that her 'apparent liveliness owes as much to the theatrical situations which surround her as to a fully articulated character of her own'; the line in which *Friar Bacon* stands is not that of the Romantic Comedy of Peele, Shakespeare, and Dekker, but that of the more strenuously intellectual 'double-plot' plays, like *Troilus and Cressida* and Middleton and Rowley's *The Changeling*.

Several of these elements (though not the double plot) persist in what is probably Greene's last play, *James IV*. There is a triangular love-situation between the King, Dorothea, and Ida; Dorothea is herself another version of the 'patient Griselda' theme; there is the same mixture of history and fantasy, but the multiplicity of experience is increased. In the opening scene Bohan, a cynical Scot, offers to demonstrate to Oberon, King of Fairies, why he hates the world, by showing him a play about Scotland in the year 1520, when

[1] W. Empson, *Some Versions of Pastoral*, London, 1935; Penguin edn, 1966, p 33.

it was misruled 'much like our court of Scotland this day'. At once we are in two worlds, and they comment on each other. Similarities have often been urged between *James IV* and *A Midsummer Night's Dream*, but perhaps the more enlightening comparison would be with *Cymbeline*. Both plays use a historical background as a guarantee and sanction for the magical and fantastic. Both plays blur the boundary between the imagined and the real, and achieve in the end the same, basically 'friendly' effect. All Greene's plays resolve in the celebration of natural order, with the coming together of the lovers or the lost in a reconciled and peaceful society. But his journeys are into the realm of magic, of illusion and delusion, of human constancy and spiritual drift. The only feature his plays share with orthodox religious life is a fascination with repentance, and repentance is an elementary, raw religious state.

Typical of this stage of the rejection of religion by the dramatists is the rich, delicate way in which George Peele (1558?–1597?) explores the surface of things. He is not interested in the profound questions of man's estate. The key to his work lies in the fact that he was, like his father, a designer of pageants. His two London pageants, *The Pageant before Woolstone Dixie* (1585) and *Descensus Astraeae* (1591) are based on classical figures and motifs, and mark a new development in pageant technique, which had hitherto been a matter of arranging a series of folk-lore heroes in some rough order. As a dramatist Peele is always alert to the possibilities of spectacle. The coronation scene in *Edward I* (1591) requires 24 people on stage at once, and the triumphal entry of King Edward in the opening scene is certainly cleverly staged: first trumpets, then 'maimed Souldiers', then 'the Ancient borne in a Chaire', then Gloucester and Mortimer 'and others as many as may be', and then the King and Queen, followed by Edmund, Jone, Leicester, Sailors and Soldiers. To place the King in the middle doubles the apparent length of the procession, doubles the grandeur. Spectacle, and a certain journalistic appropriateness, seems the only dramatic justification for *The Battle of Alcazar* (1589), but in what is probably Peele's earliest play, *The Arraignment of Paris* (1581), his original contribution to the development of romantic comedy is vividly marked. It was written for, and performed in front of, the Queen at court, by one of the Boys' companies. The plot dramatizes the story presaging the fall of Troy in which the shepherd Paris, accompanied by his nymph Oenone, is required to award the golden apple to Juno, Venus, or Pallas. He chooses Venus, who carries him off leaving Oenone forlorn. Juno and Venus arraign him for partiality before the gods, the case is referred to Diana, and she evades the issue by presenting the apple to the nymph Eliza – the Queen herself. The pastoral world, which foreshadows the fifth act of *As You Like It*, is rich and various: the arcadianism of the classical story is complicated by a tart, country commentary involving Colin, Hobbinol, Diggon, and Thenot; their dialogue is in fourteeners, while the Greek gods discourse in couplets; the tone is heightened by music and songs (including the famous 'Cupid's curse'), and finally Peele does what Lyly is too discriminatingly courtly to do – he breaks out of the mythological and dramatic framework to award the play's apple to the Queen in the audience. The consolations of pastoral are similarly active in *The Old Wives' Tale* (1590), a romantic medley stretched over a slight plot which begins with two brothers ranging the country searching for their lost sister, and involves us with a wicked magician, Sacrapant, a braggart, Huarebango, enchanted lovers, a churchwarden, sexton, harvestmen who sing, Jack's ghost, and two heads which rise magically out of the Well of Life. They are all set in a winter's tale told by Madge, the wife of Clunch the smith. Yet the rustic and the literary elements blend strangely well; there is a control of the elements of myth, a lyricism, above all an inclusive pastoral vision which unifies what would otherwise be a farrago of unlikely events.[1] *Edward I*, on the other hand, is resolutely patriotic:

> Illustrious England, auncient seat of kings,
> Whose chivalrie hath roiallizd thy fame:
> That sounding bravely through terrestial vaile,
> Proclaiming conquests, spoiles, and victories,
> Rings glorious Ecchoes through the farthest worlde . . .
>
> (I. i. 11–15)

All the 'pageant' qualities are richly honoured throughout the play. But Peele's real achievement is the creation of Friar Hugh ap David, called Friar Tuck, a worldly, quarrelsome, lecherous, patriotic religious, whose prose marks him as a brilliant intruder into this world of organized spectacles. As he throws his dice he grumbles:

Did ever man play with such uncircumcised handes, sice ace [i.e. six and one at dice] to eleven and lose the chaunce.

---

[1] This atmosphere has recently attracted artistic interest. See *Sacrapant, the Sorcerer* (a children's drama with music based on *The Old Wives' Tale*), words by Paul Morgan, music by Peter Aston, Novello, 1968.

He comments shrewdly on the preoccupation with sin and glory which the 'nobler' characters exhibit.

Peele's greatest achievement is undoubtedly *The Love of King David and Fair Bethsabe* (1587), which unites the rich pagan pastoralism of the *Arraignment* with the renaissance patriotism and self-awareness in *Edward I*, against a finely apprehended Old Testament background. The result is anything but religious drama. The poetry makes marvellous, proleptic, allusive use of the biblical:

> Now comes my lover tripping like the roe,
> And brings my longings tangled in her hair ...
>
> (I. 92–3)

but the dramaturgical development shows Peele less interested in the sin of David than in Absalom's revolt. The proud and beautiful rebel, with whose hair 'the wanton winds Delight to play, and love to make it curl', nurtured and favoured by Nature until at last he is trapped, hanging between earth and heaven by his hair, is a new and vitally significant figure in the drama. The language fails when called upon to render the aching simplicity of David's Old Testament cry 'O my son Absolom, my son, my son Absolom! would God I had died for thee, O Absolom, my son, my son!', but it achieves rich intensity when it fuses Hebraic and Greek myth in the celebration of love:

> ... Bethsabe, the daughter of the Highest,
> Whose beauty builds the towers of Israel,
> She that in chains of pearl and unicorn
> Leads at her train the ancient golden world,
> The world that Adam held in paradise ...
>
> (XV. 20–4)

It is as if the biblical tone is no longer powerful enough to stand without support.

The humanist exploration moves significantly forward in the work of the first commanding genius to emerge in the period: Christopher Marlowe (1564–93). Indeed the whole development of humanism in drama can be outlined in the sequence of his four tragedies from *Tamburlaine* to *Edward II*. The spectacular statements of the 'Baines' document, and the contemporary reputation of his 'atheist lecture' have presented a picture of Marlowe as the blasphemous rebel against all authority in heaven and earth, daring God out of heaven in the sure confidence that he was never there. But Marlowe is no simple iconoclast; indeed, in the deepest sense he is not revolutionary at all. He works his way steadily towards a tragic vision which stands on certain quite central human values.

The two parts of *Tamburlaine the Great* (1587, 1588) are a rebel's progress. The first part is packed with allusions to the usurpers of classical legend: Phaethon, Olympians, Titans, Giants, Hercules defying the gods. The special quality of Tamburlaine is his orphic skill, his eloquence of persuasions, his 'winning words'. Theridimas declares:

> Not Hermes Prolocutor to the Gods,
> Could use perswasions more patheticall.
>
> (I. 405–6)

This godlike use of language, the mastery of hyperbole, informs the physical structure of the play. Frequently Tamburlaine's words, his 'vaunts substantial', become visual stage facts. He boasts to Bajazeth that it is his habit 'to march upon the slaughtered foe' and some 200 lines later he ascends his throne by treading on Bajazeth's neck. This enforces the division between the fully apprehended earthly felicity ('the sweet fruition of an earthly crown') and a hostile heaven. In Part II, when worldly conquest is almost complete, he threatens to 'march against the powers of heaven', and 'signifie the slaughter of the Gods', but the play's final discovery is that the 'aspiring' mind becomes the presumptuous mind – Tamburlaine's last image is of himself as Phaethon – and that man cut off from God is both glorious and ultimately impoverished.

The same paradox energizes the Morality structure of *Doctor Faustus* (1592, or possibly, 1588–9). In the opening speech the Chorus tells how

> His waxen wings did mount above his reach,
> And melting heavens conspirde his overthrow.

When Faustus says 'Divinitie, adieu' (line 76) it is he who turns from God, not God from him. Grace and mercy are continually available to him through the play; as M. M. Mahood has said 'the obstacles to Faustus's salvation are raised only by him.'[1] Marlowe understood Christian orthodoxy well enough. When Mephistophilis says:

[1] *Poetry and Humanism*, London, 1950, p 74.

> Why this is hel, nor am I out of it:
> Thinkst thou that I who saw the face of God,
> And tasted the eternal joyes of heaven,
> Am not tormented with ten thousand hels,
> In being depriv'd of everlasting blisse?

> (lines 312–16)

he speaks in the central tradition of theology, and the flames, devils, and magic of the play are obviously irrelevant to its central concern, and 'frivolous'.[1] The powerful presence of classical image and allusion in the play's poetry enforces the point that Faustus's 'despair' is stoical and pagan, rather than Christian. Although Faustus learns to feel hell invading his soul, he has no corresponding apprehension of heaven. His God is always far away, transcendent rather than immanent, and the abiding impression is of distance and distaste, and judgement given. In Marlowe's two other great plays heaven and hell hardly feature.

The world of *The Jew of Malta* (1589) is sharply materialistic, and the position of man in it has shrunk from conquering king or mighty magician to plundering merchant. Barabas's opening line asserts the controlling values:

> So that of thus much that returne was made ...

and Machiavelli, as Prologue, has already dismissed heaven from earth:

> I count Religion but a childish Toy,
> And hold there is no sinne but Ignorance.

The characters, be they Christians, Jews, or Turks, are not evaluated in moral terms; they are either clever or stupid. The stupid are the weak, and the weak go to the wall. Yet the spiritual world is not totally banished. As G. K. Hunter has shown, its symbols survive and offer a coherent religious judgement on the action. The cauldron, for example, into which Barabas falls is like the cauldron which represented hell in medieval art, and it is clearly true that Barabas's fall 'has moral meaning as well as stage excitement'. Yet the iconological judgements are of the simplest kind – the wicked shall not always flourish – and the complex vision of

---

[1] See W. Moelwyn Merchant, 'Marlowe the Orthodox', in *Christopher Marlowe* (New Mermaid Critical Commentaries), ed. B. Morris, London, 1968, pp 179–92.

the world as charged with spiritual grandeur and significance is not to be found in *The Jew of Malta*.

Still less are there spiritual resonances in *Edward II* (1592). At the beginning Gaveston, the 'minion', displays something of the qualities of the aspiring rebel. To Warwick he is an 'Ignoble vassaile that like Phaeton/Aspir'st unto the guidance of the sunne' (lines 311–12), but before the middle of the play he is dead, and all interest is focused upon Edward. The human, historical framework binds the play closely, no other play of Marlowe's is so controlled by the pressure of events: the classical mythology which has added a cultural dimension and judgement to *Tamburlaine* and *Faustus* appears here only in masques and pageants; Edward's desire is not 'the thirst of raigne', nor a longing for 'a world of profit and delight,/Of power, of honor, of omnipotence', but only for peace

> So I may have some nooke or corner left,
> To frolike with my deerest Gaveston.
>
> (lines 367–8)

Edward's death (as apt as Barabas's) comes when he has already rejected life as flat and unprofitable:

> But what are kings, when regiment is gone,
> But perfect shadowes in a sun-shine day?
>
> (lines 2012–13)

and it marks the end of a progress from the self-confidence of Tamburlaine, who can challenge the heavens, to Edward's weak, puzzled, self-questioning, as if the heavens held no meaning for him. We cannot tell whether Edward 'died a Christian', and somehow, by this time, it scarcely matters.

Perhaps the most telling example of the retreat of the Christian assertion in Elizabethan drama comes in Thomas Nashe's *Summer's Last Will and Testament* (1592). It was produced for Archbishop Whitgift's household at Croydon, and expressed the ending of a summer in which the plague had been endemic in the City. The 'pageant' is presented by a Chorus figure, fancifully assigned to the Ghost of Will Summers, Henry VIII's court fool. He 'presents' his officers, Ver, Harvest, Bacchus, and large trains of followers who dance and sing in the traditional 'festive' ways. But in Summer's song about his approaching death the words 'I am sick, I must die' have a grim, local urgency because of the plague. And the liturgical refrain 'Lord, have mercy on us' is, in this context, an acutely human cry for deliverance. The firm asseverations of faith which can carry *Everyman* triumphantly over the narrow stream of death have dwindled to a stoic refusal of sensation:

> Adieu, farewell earth's blisse,
> This world uncertaine is,
> Fond are lifes lustful joys,
> Death proves them all but toyes,
> None from his darts can flye;
> I am sick, I must die;
> Lord, have mercy on us.
>
> (lines 1574–80)

This is a far cry from the Easter faith; its allegiances are with Seneca, or with William Dunbar's 'Timor mortis conturbat me' in his 'Lament for the Markaris'.

Puritan attacks on the stage and the actors continued unabated through the reigns of James I and Charles I, though the growing importance and influence of the theatre brought about changes in the strategy of the campaign. Dramatic language was controlled by law when the statute of James I (1605–6 cap. 21) forbade the profane use of the name of God on the stage. The effect of bad language on the actors themselves is mentioned in Thomas Gainsford's *The Rich Cabinet Furnished with Varietie of Descriptions* (1616), when he says:

I speak not of execrable oathes, artificiall lyes, discoveries of cousenage, scurrulus words, obscene discourses, corrupt courtings, licentious motions, lascivious actions, and lewde jestures: for all these are incident to other men, but here is the difference: in these they come by imperfection, in them by profession.[1]

But the central Puritan assumptions about the theatre remained unsullied. In *A Shorte Treatise against Stage-Playes* (1625) the 'Humble Supplication Tendered to . . . Parliament' begins with the words

> Whereas Stage-playes are repugnant to the written
> Word and Will of Almightie God . . .

and the Puritan attitude is justly summed up in the work of William Prynne, whose *Histriomastix: Or, The Players Scourge and Actors Tragedy* appeared late in 1632, and became the most famous

---

[1] Reprinted in W. C. Hazlitt, *The English Drama and Stage 1543–1664*, printed for the Roxburghe Library, London, 1869.

document in the case. In the view of one of his recent biographers, 'Prynne here may be regarded as the embodiment of militant Puritanism, engaged in remorseless combat with the new forces in England',[1] yet it should be remembered that *Histriomastix* was only one of many books written against the theatre. From Prynne's citations it is clear that at least forty others had appeared during the late sixteenth and early seventeenth centuries. He regarded the playhouses as evil on all counts: his strictures range from the moral to the economic, and apply equally to all kinds of theatre. Although Prynne had attended only four plays in the whole of his life he had obviously read very widely, and his lack of first-hand experience is compensated by his breadth of knowledge. It was after the publication of *Histriomastix* that Prynne was arraigned before the Star Chamber on a charge of libel against the state, king and people, and his punishment was more violent than his prose. William Haller says of the situation in 1632:

Much that appears to us innocent and joyous made a stench in Prynne's nostrils; much that the Puritans condemned would have made a stench in any decent nose.[2]

This is true, but the truth was seen by Puritan pamphleteers in remarkably simple terms. Ben Jonson (1572–1637) was more delicately discriminating, though his plays are just as much moral judgements of a corrupt, acquisitive society as are Prynne's pamphlets. Even his earliest plays are complex acts of judgement; as Harry Levin says:

The comedy of humours was not arrived at as a descriptive formulation for purely critical purposes; it was seized upon as a polemical weapon to answer the Puritan attacks on the stage.[3]

*Cynthia's Revels* (1601) is a comparatively inoffensive satire on the generous excesses of Queen Elizabeth's court, from no particular, assured moral standpoint. It is not as if Jonson had Castiglione's *Courtier* at the back of his mind when he wrote. The standards are clearer, and more instantly recognizable in *The Poetaster* (1601), where contemporary dramatists are attacked, and measured against the poets of Augustan Rome. The play was part of the so-called

[1] Ethyn Williams Kirby, *William Prynne: A Study in Puritanism*, Cambridge, Mass., 1931; p 20.

[2] W. Haller, *The Rise of Puritanism*, New York, 1938, p 221.

[3] Harry Levin, Introduction to *Selected Works of Ben Jonson*, 1938; reprinted in *Ben Jonson: a Collection of Critical Essays*, ed. J. A. Barish, Englewood Cliffs, 1963, p 41.

'War of the Theatres', but Jonson's Ovid, Virgil, and Horace assert those specifically Roman virtues, and those Augustan standards of art, of which he says so much in the *Discoveries*. *The Poetaster* is Jonson's examination of his own values as a poet, and if they appear essentially Horatian it is well to remember that Jonson was one of the earliest translators of the *Ars Poetica*. He makes his allegiances clear.

*Every Man In His Humour* (1598, revised 1612) is a strangely uneven play, because Jonson's purpose is clearly to show, in an entertaining way, that poetry, as opposed to poetasting, was a valuable, serious activity; yet there is nothing within the plot of the play to enforce the point, and little in the language to demonstrate it. More prophetic of Jonson's later mode is the activity of Justice Clement in Act V, when he dispenses a rough and merry justice all round, and challenges Knowell to an extempore poetry competition. Poetry itself is not proof against Jonson's resolutely sceptical ending. In *Epicoene, or The Silent Woman* (1609) Jonson shows an old man with an obsessive dislike of noise tricked by his nephew into marrying a virago, who is eventually revealed as a boy in disguise. It is a cruel play; L. A. Beaurline describes it as 'a tissue of afflictions visited upon hermaphroditical monsters', and suggests that Jonson may have been taunting the Puritans with his boy dressed up as a woman (see *Deuteronomy*, xxii. 5). The atmosphere of perversion and freakishness is certainly the kind of thing which would have offended Prynne, and it is a quality the play shares with Jonson's later comedy, *Bartholomew Fair* (1614). The fair, with its stallholders, cut-purses, and bawds, is visited by the simpleton Bartholomew Cokes, who is robbed of his possessions one after another, while his servant Wasp, and the Puritan Zeal-of-the-land Busy end up in the stocks. Mr Justice Overdo, who should resolve the conflicts, is himself humiliated, and all that survives is the sprawling, brawling fair and the puppet show. When Busy accuses the puppet Dionysus of 'abomination' because 'the Male, among you, putteth on the apparell of the Female, and the Female of the Male', the puppet replies:

It is your old stale argument against the Players, but it will not hold against the Puppets; for we have neither Male nor Female amongst us. And that thou may'st see, if thou wilt, like a malicious purblinde zeale as thou art!
                                                                   (*takes up his garment*)

The sexless puppet is Jonson's rejoinder to the Puritan case, and he celebrates in *Bartholomew Fair* a world which is instinct with energy, and in which even Ursula the pig-woman has a recognized and honoured place. The criticism is levelled against anyone who would cramp the rich variety of life.

Jonson's two tragedies are on Roman themes. *Sejanus* (1603) is concerned with problems of government and ambition, and it is not unreasonable to assume that Jonson was asserting the parallels between ancient Rome and Jacobean England. The Emperor Tiberius is presented as an unbearable tyrant, and Sejanus as a ruthless plotter for power. Jonson is sharply conscious of the politics of mob rule, as Shakespeare is in *Coriolanus*, and his sense of the perils attending democracy is clear from the last Act, in which the populace dismember the dead body of their hero. Young and old alike

> Losing all grief in joy of his sad fall,
> Runne quite transported with their crueltie!
>
> (V. 816–17)

They 'deale small pieces of the flesh for favours', and Jonson's verdict on the unnatural riot is gravely judicial:

> What cannot oft be done, is now ore-done.

It is a dark view of humanity, whose ferocity is even more apparent in *Catiline* (1611). Jonson gives full weight to the horror: the sacramental dedication of the conspirators, the plot to burn Rome, Sulla's ghost, and the death of the hero, all expressed in a sombre blank verse of unrelieved weight, show the cheerless side of Jonson's classicism, reminding us that he could compass the tones of Juvenal and Cicero as well as sound the Horatian note.

The two masterpieces are undoubtedly *Volpone* (1606), and *The Alchemist* (1610). Both plays are about gold, but the symbol is developed in different ways. In *Volpone* gold is first of all the object of worship:

> Good morning to the. day; and, next, my gold:
> Open the shrine, that I may see my saint.
>
> (I. i. 1–2)

The blasphemous possibilities of magnificence radiate through the play, at tension with the realization that gold is no more than metal, 'filthy lucre' for which men scheme, and grasp, and bite. The animality of man in search of gold is made brutally clear in the naming of characters, but the 'labelling', the 'typecasting', is also Jonson's challenge to his audience. The play offers to debate the justice of calling one man Corbaccio, another Corvino, an advocate Voltore, and a servant Mosca. The 'comic justice' of the last Act is deliberately two-edged: villains are condemned and sentenced by villains as great as they. Volpone is no more rotten than the state of Venice, the city's moral standards are precisely his. The play ends with a horrifying sense of moral chaos, all coherence gone, and the words of Juvenal, whose presence haunts the play, come to mind: 'quis custodiet ipsos custodes'. The Alchemist is a play about Greed, about the *cupiditas* which motivates everyone and of which gold is the central but not the only symbol. Subtle, the alchemist, in alliance with Dol Common and Face, persuades all comers that he has discovered the philosopher's stone, and Jonson arranges a series of seekers after gold and motivates them variously. Dapper and Drugger are simply seeking quick profit, but Sir Epicure Mammon represents a more inclusive greed:

> I will have all my beds, blowne up: not stuft:
> Downe is too hard. And then, mine oval roome,
> Fill'd with such pictures, as Tiberius tooke
> From Elephantis: and dull Aretine
> But coldly imitated

> (II. ii. 41–5)

The quality of his hyperbole goes a long way towards creating a kind of 'golden' world, but his 'Great Solomon's Ophir' is a paradise of sensuality, set against the 'real' world of Blackfriars, Pie Corner, and the artillery-yard. The key image of the play is the figure of transmutation, the change of base into precious; yet because the search is for the alchemist's gold all the characters are chasing an *ignis fatuus*. In *Volpone* the gold is real enough, but in *The Alchemist* it is always a visionary hope. As Subtle says of Mammon:

> If his dreamè last, hee'll turne the age, to gold.

> (I. iv. 29)

The dream is never completely broken in the play. When the fifth Act provides verdicts on the action Jonson's judge is no official representative of law and order, but Lovewit, the 'jovy boy', who punishes no one, and divides the spoils equally with Face, the most intelligent of the rogues. The only real sufferers are the Puritans, Tribulation Wholesome and Ananias, who are left wholly disconsolate, to report their defeat 'to the Brethren'.

Jonson's later plays, *The Devil is an Ass* (1616), *The Staple of News* (1626), *The New Inn* (1629) and *The Magnetic Lady* (1632), were described by Dryden as his 'dotages', and they have never been successful on the stage, but it has recently been pointed out by L. S. Champion that they are constructed in accordance with precisely that comic theory which generated the great comedies, and they certainly offer the same uncompromising moral judgements on the 'acquisitive society'. In all his dramatic works – and it should not be forgotten that some of his greatest achievements are in his masques – Jonson's vision is of a Truth which is universal and beautiful, and which only Art can exemplify, and his judgements are uncompromisingly moral.

The dramatic career of John Marston (1575?–1634) is brief and spectacular. All his plays were written in the decade 1598–1608, in which he also collaborated with Jonson and Chapman, and at the end of which, in 1609, he was ordained and disappears from the literary scene to become a parish priest for the rest of his life. His ordination may be significant, for it seems as if the Church provided a stability and moral certainty for which Marston searched vainly in his plays. His first published work was non-dramatic: *Metamorphosis of Pygmalion's Image and Certain Satires* appeared in 1598, and it was followed in the same year by *The Scourge of Villainy*. Some of the satires in *The Scourge* are interpreted as attacks on Jonson, or on Gabriel Harvey, but the general tone is savage, obscure, Juvenalian, and these earliest publications show Marston obsessed by eroticism and violence. Marston's dramatic work is linked with the rise of one company, Paul's Boys, and between 1599 and 1601 he wrote or revised for them *Jack Drum's Entertainment*, revised *Histriomastix*, and wrote *Antonio and Mellida*, the first part of which was produced in 1600, and the second, *Antonio's Revenge*, in 1600–1. In 1601 again for Paul's Boys, he wrote *What You Will*. These plays have been included by Brian Gibbons among the Jacobean 'City Comedies', and the phrase points to useful connections which can be made between the work of Marston, Jonson, Dekker, and Middleton. Yet none can equal Marston in savagery. At the end of *Antonio's Revenge* there is a great ceremonial banquet scene. Antonio, revenging the murder of his father by the tyrant Piero, glories in the tortures Piero suffers, and the whole scene is reminiscent in tone of the climax of Seneca's *Thyestes*. Or in *What You Will*, Marston gives to Albano some moving words on the theme of inconstancy:

> the soul of man is rotten
> Even to the core; no sound affection.
> Our love is hollow-vaulted, stands on proppes
> Of circumstance, profit or ambitious hopes.
> The other tissue Gowne or Chaine of pearle
> Makes my coy minx to nussell twixt the breastes
> Of her lull'd husband, together Carkanet
> Deflowres that Ladies bed

(III. i)

This is grating and serious, but its effect is shattered because Albano suffers from a speech impediment, and his cry of passion dissolves in a farcical stutter. Albano subsequently becomes incoherent, incomprehensible, and mad; the audience's response is continually put out of joint. *The Fawn* (1604) is a subtler play. The name of the central figure, Faunus, suggests not only 'sycophant' (the play's alternative title is *Parasitaster*) but 'satyr', the classical giver of oracles, the woodland figure of Renaissance pastoral. The play's insistence upon truth, upon free speech, may mirror the danger in which Marston himself stood as a satirist in the early years of the seventeenth century. Hercules, speaking against flattery, says:

> Most spotless kingdom,
> And men, O happy born under good stars,
> Where what is honest you may freely think,
> Speak what you think, and write what you do speak,
> Not bound to servile soothings.

(I. ii)

Yet, at the other extreme, the play contains the foul-mouthed Zuccone, a causelessly jealous man, through whom Marston channels his relentless invective against women:

O heaven, that God made for a man no other means of procreation and maintaining the world peopled but by women! O, that we could increase like roses by being slipp'd one from another, or like flies procreate with blowing, or any other way than by a woman. . . .

(IV. i)

Sexual disillusion is even more powerful in *The Dutch Courtesan* (1605), where Frevill can cry:

> That things of beauty created for sweet use,
> Soft comfort, and as the very music of life,
> Custom should make so unutterably hellish!
> O heaven,
> What difference is in women and their life!

(V. i)

As Theodore Spencer pointed out, 'Of all the Elizabethan poets who plundered Montaigne none plundered so much as Marston', and the theme of *The Dutch Courtesan* is very like Montaigne's essay 'Upon some verses of Virgil': man's physical desires and passions must be seen clearly, recognized for what they are, and controlled and directed by reason. The play forces us to witness a lengthy process of purification, in which the rotten world is thoroughly anatomized. The anatomy of evil is what stays in the mind from Marston's last completed tragedy, *Sophonisba* (1605). She was the daughter of Hasdrubal, a Carthaginian general, but her story pales before the exploits of the lustful Syphax and the witch Erichtho, who likes nothing more than to find a corpse and 'gnaw the pale and o'ergrown nails from his dry hand'. Yet the necrophiliac horrors should not blind us to one quality in the play which appears in Marston's art for the first time. As Una Ellis-Fermor has pointed out[1] there is, in the death speech of Sophonisba, a tone of sweet stillness which anticipates the most characteristic utterance of John Ford:

> O thou for whom I drinke
> So deepe of greefe, that he must onely thinke,
> Not dare to speake, that would express my woe.

(V. ii)

His most famous play, however, is undoubtedly *The Malcontent* (1604), though it is also in many ways the most puzzling. Malevole snarls openly from his first words:

> Yaugh, God o'man, what dost thou there? Duke's Ganymede, Juno's jealous of thy long stockings. Shadow of a woman, what wouldst, weasel?

And in his first soliloquy he stresses his prerogative:

> Well, this disguise doth yet afford me that
> Which kings do seldom hear, or great men use—
> Free speech.

(I. iv)

[1] *The Jacobean Drama*, London, 1961, p 96.

Yet perhaps the most characteristic scene is that (II. iv) in which, while the Duke and his attendants prepare to kill Ferneze in the Duchess's room, the court bawd, Maquerelle, passes over the stage in conversation with two ladies on the subject of age, cosmetics, and the decay of beauty. The talk of possets, dyeing of hair, and surphling of breasts descants grotesquely on the matter of life and death. Marston is justly celebrated for the quality of his disgust, and in many ways the moral attitudes which underlie his art are Puritan, akin to those of men like Richard Rogers, who, in his Seven Treatises (1603), offers

to help the frailtie of Gods children . . . by setting before their eies as in a glasse, the infinite, secret, and deceitfull corruptions of the heart: from whence . . . sore and dangerous evils doe arise.[1]

Marston, as a dramatist, is far more acutely aware of the sin than of the grace, of the fall than of the redemption.

In the new genre which has been called 'comical satyre' Jonson and Marston take a sceptical view of human affairs. But other, more generous, kinds of comedy continued to flourish. In the period after 1600, as the surviving plays become more numerous, and the playwrights themselves more prolific and more inclined to collaborate, it is only possible to select for comment those plays which are the most important or the most characteristic in an author's output. Thomas Dekker (1572?–1632) is a good example of the new professionalism. He is generally acknowledged to have had a hand in at least seventeen plays, and to have collaborated with half a dozen of his contemporaries over a period of some thirty years. His earliest surviving play is Old Fortunatus (1599), in which Fortune offers the beggar Fortunatus a choice of gifts, and when he picks Riches, gives him a purse from which he may at any time take ten pieces of gold. The tone is set in Act I when Fortunatus says 'If I die tomorrow, I'll be merry today: if next day, I'll be merry tomorrow', and the play is frequently interrupted by music and song giving an effect of high yet wholesome entertainment, unrelated to the mundane or the moral world. The two parts of The Honest Whore belong to 1604–5, though the second part was not published until 1630. The best things about it are the scenes in Bedlam and Bridewell, but the whole play is gripped by an impeccable moralism, which frequently adopts an overt pulpit stance:

---

[1] Quoted in Haller, The Rise of Puritanism, p 117.

> Patience, my Lord: why, 'tis the soule of peace;
> Of all the vertues, 'tis neer'st kin to Heaven,
> It makes men looke like gods.
>
> (Part I. V. ii)

Dekker's firm commitment to the 'citizen morality' has its rewards as well as its perils, as L. C. Knights has shrewdly shown.[1] His dominant tone is cheerfully optimistic:

> England shall ne're be poore, if England strive
> Rather by vertue, than by wealth to thrive.
>
> (*Old Fortunatus*, V. ii)

The honest workman is the backbone of the country. It is only in one play, *The Shoemakers' Holiday* (1599), that Dekker succeeds in establishing an acceptable framework for this vision. Clearly the success of the play is largely due to the way it appealed to the citizen's pride in his trade; it comfortably 'reinforced a prevalent social attitude' (L. C. Knights, p. 199). Simon Eyre's progress from shoemaker to Sheriff to Lord Mayor was every apprentice's dream. But the real achievement of Dekker's art is to embody the bustling tradesman's energy in an appropriately rich, comic language:

Where be these boyes, these girles, these drabbes, these scoundrels, they wallow in the fat brewisse of my bounty, and licke up the crums of my table, yet wil not rise to see my walkes cleansed: come out you powder-beefe-queanes, what Nan, what Madge-Mumble-crust, come out you fatte Midriffe-swag-belly-whores, and sweepe me these kennels, that the noysome stench offende not the nose of my neighbours.

> (II. iii)

The vitality of this cheerful abuse, shielding as it does an idealized version of the relation of master and servant which belonged to the middle ages rather than the tougher Tudor economy, seems to unite the appeals of realism and nostalgia; add to this the romantic story of Rose and Lacy, and a King who moves familiarly among his subjects, and little is lacking that comedy could provide.

Like Dekker, Thomas Heywood (1575?–1641) had a hand in many plays – in two hundred and twenty if his own account is to be believed – and published many poems and pamphlets as well. What is probably his first play, *The Four Prentices of London* (1592–c. 1600), provides a clue to all the others. The prentices, Godfrey of Bouillon and his brothers, are 'all high born, Yet of the city-trades

---

[1] 'Dekker, Heywood, and Citizen Morality', in *Drama and Society in the Age of Jonson*, London, 1937.

they have no scorn'. They conquer Jerusalem yet never lose the common touch, or a strong sense of citizen virtues. Heywood turned his hand to every type of play, from romantic adventure to the pageants for the Lord Mayor's show. But everything he touches becomes domesticated. The two part play, *Edward IV* (1599) begins as a chronicle play of sorts, but other concerns rapidly dominate the action. The interlude of the Tanner of Tamworth, and the romantic story of the rise of Jane Shore, show where Heywood's interest and ability lie. The second part starts as a confused account of the king's wars in France, but rapidly becomes the story of Jane Shore's fall: the dramatist's attitude is simple, the morality obvious, the presentation of Jane Shore herself frankly sentimental. But, as John Addington Symonds pointed out in his introduction to the Mermaid volume (1888), the play 'is chiefly remarkable for the way in which Heywood sustains the character of Master Shore, who is the very mirror of sound English middle-class Christianity'. The dramatic study of a virtuous man is a central feature in *The Fair Maid of the West* (two parts, 1610 and 1631), where Master Spencer has to flee the country after killing a man while protecting Besse Bridges, 'the flower of Plymouth', from assault. Besse takes over the Windmill tavern at Fowey, and in her conduct of it displays all the qualities of female independence, domestic orderliness, and respectable thrift, which characterize Heywood's simple, colourful, moral world. The two best-known plays, *The English Traveller* (1625) and *A Woman Killed with Kindness* (1603), are similar in many ways. T. S. Eliot considered that *The English Traveller* contained Heywood's best plot: 'for the refinement of agony of the virtuous lover who has controlled his passion and then discovers that his lady has deceived both her husband, who is his friend, and himself, is really more poignant than the torment of the betrayed husband Frankford'. Yet the low key in which the suffering of Frankford and Anne is played out, the steadiness and stillness with which the pathetic scene is observed, makes *A Woman Killed with Kindness* the masterpiece of Heywood's work. One of his most recent biographers points out that apart from Dekker 'none of the other dramatists had displayed so much interest in religion and edification as Heywood; he seems to us now like a man destined for the Church whom the accidents of the time rushed into dramatic journalism'[1], and it is surprising to recall that in 1612 Heywood published *An Apology for Actors*, in defence of the stage. As Sir Edmund Chambers said, 'however

---

[1] A. M. Clark, *Thomas Heywood*, New York and Oxford, 1931, p 192.

much the Puritans and humanists might disagree, they were at one in referring their judgement of the drama to purely ethical standards of value'[1], and Heywood's pamphlet meets the Puritan case on its own ground, pointing out the countless instances in which the theatre has been an incitement to virtue rather than vice. There was no form of drama 'from which an infinite use cannot be gathered'. Yet it remains true that in Heywood's plays and pamphlets religion is primarily a matter of living a good life, and the spiritual exploration is that of an observant, but minor, artist.

Comedy, in this early Jacobean period, is strongly divided into the satiric or the domestic. The satiric comedy, of Jonson and Marston in particular, is an act of judgement upon a society which is corrupt, but also, paradoxically, energetic, witty, and strangely self-perpetuating; the domestic comedies of Dekker and Heywood, on the other hand, celebrate a central 'goodness' in humanity, stimulating and cherishing the social virtues of man seen as *zoon politikon*, a political animal. The comedies of Thomas Middleton (1580?–1627) will fit neither pattern. To T. S. Eliot he is 'a great comic writer', to L. C. Knights 'Middleton's comedies are comedies of intrigue . . . and they yield little more than the pleasure of a well-contrived marionette show', and there is every shade of critical opinion in between. The efficiency and objectivity with which Middleton's comedies are plotted, and his habit of creating powerful dramatic scenes out of stereotyped characters, lend a sense of finality to his comic judgements which sometimes rings false. This is truer of the early comedies, *The Phoenix*, *The Family of Love*, *A Mad World*, *my Masters*, *Michaelmas Term*, and *Your Five Gallants*, all of which were written before 1606, and it is noticeable that in these early plays there are virtuous characters, who must be seen to triumph, and villains who must be seen to fall. In the later, and greater, comedies this is not so. *A Trick to Catch the Old One* (1605) begins the process; the plot is complex, organized, ironic, and there is not a single 'good' character in the play. Witgood is a spendthrift, Pecunius Lucre a miserly merchant, Walkadine Hoard a usurer, and the wealthy widow around whom they all flock is a whore. The resolution of this giddily active plot avoids all question of moral turpitude. All are cheaters, all are cheated; the dramatist condemns no one. The plot has simply obeyed the logic of its own design. Middleton's so-called 'realism' is an elusive quality. It lies not so much in conformity to observable social fact as in the

[1] *The Elizabethan Stage*, i, 259–60.

concrete nature of every character's imaginings. Hoard, dreaming of a wife, says:

she's rich, she's young, she's fair, she's wise; when I wake, I think of her lands – that revives me; when I go to bed, I dream of her beauty – and that's enough for me; she's worth four hundred a year in her very smock, if a man knew how to use it.

(IV. iv. 6–9)

*A Chaste Maid in Cheapside* (1611), generally considered Middleton's finest comedy is concerned with the love between Joyce Yellowhammer, a goldsmith's daughter, and an impoverished gentleman, Touchwood Junior. But the intrigue matters more than the passion, and the play really belongs to the profligates and swindlers like Sir Walter Whorehound, Lady Kix, and the Allwit family. Allwit readily allows his wife to be Sir Walter's mistress so long as Sir Walter pays all the bills, and, indeed, he glories in the situation:

I thank him, has maintain'd my house this ten years . . .

(I. ii. 15)

It is typical of Middleton's vision that this distorted moral attitude is presented with a comic gusto which almost redeems it. Almost, but not quite. The whole play treads a razor edge between involvement and disgust, and the society it portrays is ultimately self-devouring.

Distorted lives chronicled unflinchingly – the phrase might serve as a paradigm for Middleton's two greatest plays, the tragedies *Women Beware Women* (1621) and *The Changeling* (with William Rowley, 1622). In *Women Beware Women* the widow, Livia, seduces her own niece into an adulterous affair with her uncle, and helps the Duke of Florence to seduce the happily married Bianca from her respectable husband, Leantio. As Bianca's vanity swells, her moral standards collapse, and the various intrigues are resolved in a final masque where hideously apt punishments are dispensed: Livia, for example, is suffocated with the incense offered to the marriage-goddess. The irony is trenchant and grim: the scene in Act II in which Livia and Bianca's mother play chess while the Duke seduces Bianca just above them allows a hideous play of allusion to develop as comment upon the 'mating'. Yet the morality is starkly orthodox: 'sin will pluck on sin', or in the words which end Act II:

> Sin tastes at the first draught like wormwood-water,
> But drunk again, 'tis nectar ever after.

This might also serve as a text for *The Changeling*, in which Beatrice-Joanna employs De Flores, whom she loathes, to murder her husband-to-be. De Flores blackmails her into becoming his mistress, and when she marries Alsemero, whom she really loves, she is forced into complicated trickery with De Flores to keep the truth from him. De Flores has become 'a wondrous necessary man', but their guilt is eventually revealed, and they take their own lives. The key word is 'blood', in its multiple senses: high birth, will, sensual desire, even life itself. At her death Beatrice-Joanna says to her father:

> Oh come not near me, sir, I shall defile you:
> I am that of your blood was taken from you
> For your better health; look no more upon't,
> But cast it to the ground regardlessly:
> Let the common sewer take it from distinction.
>
> (V. iii. 149–53)

Middleton understands the nature of his heroine. Here, at least, Eliot's phrase is accurate; he is writing 'without fear, without sentiment, without prejudice'. The question of the relationship between plot and sub-plot in *The Changeling* has provoked sharp differences of opinion, but it has recently come to be thought – see, for example, William Empson on 'Double Plots' in *Some Versions of Pastoral* – that the connections are close and deliberate: one kind of frenzy illuminates the other.

Many features of *The Changeling* are reminiscent of the tragedies of John Webster (1580?–1625?): the violence of the ending, the wit and delight of the villain, the brooding atmosphere of fatality, the slow disintegration of a character. The plot of *The Changeling* is very like that of *The White Devil* (1612), for in both a young woman brings about the murder of those who stand in her way. Both plays are centrally concerned with 'blood'; Vittoria Corombona's dying words might easily belong to Beatrice-Joanna:

> O my greatest sin lay in my blood.
> Now my blood pays for't.
>
> (V. vi. 240–1)

But Middleton's dramatic language is not Webster's. Una Ellis-Fermor describes the 'pitiless abstemiousness' of Middleton's verse, and its stark, relentless quality is responsible for many of the greatest effects in his plays. Webster, by comparison, looks almost baroque; his lines are laden with imagery, and the rich, evocative language achieves at times an almost overwhelming power. His earliest work was done for Philip Henslowe – a series of collaborations with Dekker, Middleton and others,[1] and it was with Dekker that he worked on *Westward Ho!* and *Northward Ho!* in 1604–5. *Appius and Virginia*, if Webster wrote it, can probably be assigned to 1608, or a little later, and G. E. Bentley dates *The Devil's Law-Case*, which is almost certainly Webster's, as 1610.[2] Of the two great tragedies *The White Devil* was written between 1609 and 1612 (F. L. Lucas favours the later date), and *The Duchess of Malfi* can be fairly accurately dated as either 1613 or 1614. All Webster's great work was written before 1616, and after that date we have only a Lord Mayor's show, *Monuments of Honour*, and a few collaborative plays, in which he worked with Dekker, Ford, Middleton, and Rowley.

Webster's two great tragedies are profoundly disturbing. Both plots are retellings of comparatively recent historical events, both are set in Italy, and both centre on the court and its life. *The White Devil* is centrally concerned with Vittoria, the 'White Devil', and the theme of the conflict between appearance and reality, especially within the context of a corrupt and corrupting court. The 'restless' quality of the dramaturgy is due in part to Webster's ever-sceptical intelligence, which ranges commandingly over the play's development, and never allows any one moral attitude to achieve a dominance. No set of values is ever the right one, no pose is ever invincible. The justice of 'courtly reward and punishment' is ironic and fortuitous, and other moral categories are equally undermined and imperilled. After Vittoria's trial scene (III. ii) an audience's response is complex: she is justly condemned, but by wicked judges; she stands alone, deserted, yet blazing with defiance; she is proud, shrewd, and guilty, with a marvellously human command of language:

> VITTORIA:
> Instruct me some good horse-leech to speak treason,
> For since you cannot take my life for deeds,
> Take it for words, – O woman's poor revenge
> Which dwells but in the tongue, – I will not weep,
> No I do scorn to call up one poor tear

---

[1] See G. E. Bentley, *The Jacobean and Caroline Stage*, 7 vols, Oxford, 1956, v, pp 1240 ff.

[2] R. W. Dent finds in the play two borrowings from Burghley's *Certaine Precepts* (1617), and dates it c. 1617 (*John Webster's Borrowing*, Berkeley and Los Angeles, 1960, p 59).

> To fawn on your injustice, – hear me hence,
> Unto this house of – what's your mitigating title?

MONTICELSO:
Of convertites.

(III. ii. 281–8)

Una Ellis-Fermor speaks of Webster's 'profound originality', and suggests that his plots are only a superficial logic of events:

> The true plot of his play is not the events which proceed upon the surface, and are flung off, as it were, as a casual expression, but the progress of the minds of the central figures towards deeper and deeper self-knowledge, the approach to the impenetrable mystery of fate perceived in the moments of intensest suffering and action, which are also the moments of clearest insight. (*The Jacobean Drama*, p. 176.)

Man is never taller than when he is on the rack. Yet Webster deliberately creates difficult theatrical situations in order to surmount them, winning some of his profoundest insights out of technical triumphs. The trial of Vittoria, for example, is prefaced by a burlesque of court proceedings involving a comic loquacious lawyer. And the death scene of Flamineo is immediately preceded by the 'mock-death' in which he invites Vittoria and Zanche to fire pistols at him, and shams a long and 'poetic' demise, which Webster then has to better with the real thing. Yet at this 'second' death Flamineo says:

> I do not look
> Who went before, nor who shall follow me;
> No, at myself I will begin and end:
> While we look up to heaven we confound
> Knowledge with knowledge, O I am in a mist.

(V. vi. 256–60)

This is the climax of the play's exploration of religion. Intensive as this exploration is, it is on an absurdly narrow front. There are some obvious parallels, like Cornelia's remark to Brachiano 'Be thy act Judas-like – betray in kissing' (I. ii. 298), and a few attempts to shock:

> Come dear Lodovico.
> You have ta'en the sacrament to prosecute
> Th'intended murder. . . .

(IV. iii. 71–3)

but apart from these the religious interest is solely in death and damnation. Religion is an insurance, a preservative. Flamineo asks Brachiano's ghost:

> In what place art thou? in yon starry gallery
> Or in the cursed dungeon? No? not speak?
> Pray, sir, resolve me, what religion's best
> For a man to die in? ...
>
> (V. iv. 127–30)

Vittoria, aware of her soul, lacks even an elementary understanding of its peril:

> My soul, like to a ship in a black storm
> Is driven I know not whither.
>
> (V. vi. 248–9)

This is her penultimate utterance, and with it, puzzled as it is, her mind comes to rest in what is for her the central discovery and moral:

> O happy they that never saw the court,
> Nor ever knew great man but by report.
>
> VITTORIA *dies*

The smell of corruption ceases at the grave, and in this play there is less concern with heavenly than with courtly judgement.

This is not true of *The Duchess of Malfi*. Again the centre of interest is a heroine, but a heroine treated as if she were virtually a Christian martyr. Webster is careful to stress her chastity. Antonia's praise of her in Act I is carefully placed and clearly phrased:

> ... in that look,
> There speaketh so divine a continence
> As cuts off all lascivious, and vain hope.
>
> (I. i. 198–200)

The evil which surrounds her does not proceed from her, it is projected upon her. Ferdinand, accusing her of lust and wanton desires, simply reveals his own; the cardinal, crying that the duchess makes religion her riding hood, is a warrior-priest with a private whore and a bad conscience. The depth of the duchess's religious insight is clear in Act III, when she is about to be separated from her husband, and sees that 'whom the Lord loveth he chasteneth':

> Must I, like to a slave-born Russian,
> Account it praise to suffer tyranny?
> And yet, O Heaven, thy heavy hand is in't.
> I have seen my little boy oft scourge his top
> And compar'd myself to't: naught made me e'er
> Go right but heaven's scourge-stick
>
> (III. v. 76–81)

This is orthodox Christian dogma on persecution, but realized vividly and with difficulty. One of the duchess's last thoughts, before her death, is the hope that her daughter will be brought up to pray, and she meets her death kneeling, a position indicating to an audience the proper Christian humility. Even Bosola, the prober and examiner of all moral pretension in the play, is moved to see her death in her own terms. As he looks at her dying body he says:

> Return, fair soul, from darkness, and lead mine
> Out of this sensible hell.
>
> (IV. ii. 342–3)

Webster, however much he may be possessed by death, is centrally concerned in this play with Christian endurance and fortitude, with life lived as a preparation for death, and the contemplation of death as a stimulus to further and higher living.

The irony which operates so powerfully (through Flamineo and Bosola especially) in Webster's moral world is made structural in *The Devil's Law-Case*. Here again he presents a strong, articulate heroine, capable of standing against convention, but, apart from the marvellous reversals and recognitions of the trial scene, the most memorable dramatic moment is when an avenger, by stabbing his sick, dying enemy, releases the poison from his festering wound and saves his life. It is this almost equal balance between heroic assertion and reductive irony that gives poise to Webster's art, and it also serves to indicate his position in the line of development from the astringent vision of Jonson and Marston to the relative flaccidity of the Caroline dramatists. In the preface to *The White Devil* he lists the contemporary dramatists he admires, and there may be signficance in the way he calls the roll:

... I have ever truly cherish'd my good opinion of other men's worthy labours, especially of that full and height'ned style of Master Chapman, the labour'd and understanding works of Master Jonson. . . .

Shakespeare comes well down the list, praised along with Master Dekker and Master Heywood for his 'right happy and copious industry'.

The qualities of George Chapman (1559?–1634) which Webster seizes upon are obvious enough in Chapman's tragedies, or in his translations of Homer, which Webster may have known, but the 'height'ned' nature of Chapman's art is not a matter confined to his language. His ideas of human personality, his concepts of heroic life, his occultism, his commanding moral precepts, all merit this description, and suggest an austere, remote, eccentric and learned figure: an impression which is in no way at variance with the known facts. Chapman seems not to have thought of himself primarily as a dramatist: his great work, 'the work that I was born to do' was the translation of Homer. His first poem *The Shadow of Night* (1594), and his *De Guiana* (1596), connect him with the circle around Sir Walter Ralegh, and with Christopher Marlowe, whose *Hero and Leander* Chapman completed in 1598. He wrote other poems, and his earliest plays, written for the Admiral's men, probably belong to the period 1595–99. He collaborated with Jonson and Marston in *Eastward Ho!* (1605), and was imprisoned with Jonson for its satire on the Scots. Seven of the comedies written by Chapman alone survive (or eight if, with T. M. Parrott, we include *Sir Giles Goosecap*), as well as six tragedies. Some of these thirteen plays are in every anthology of the drama of the period, others are totally forgotten. The best-known is certainly the tragedy of *Bussy D'Ambois* (1604, revised 1610?), based on recent French history, in which Bussy, a man of high independence, arrogance and courage comes to the court of Henry III of France. His soliloquy, with which the play opens, sets immediately the tone of effortless moral superiority which characterizes the heroes of Chapman's tragedies:

> Fortune, not Reason, rules the state of things,
> Reward goes backwards, Honour on his head;
> Who is not poor, is monstrous; only Need
> Gives form and worth to every human seed.
> As cedars beaten with continual storms,
> So great men flourish. . . .
>
> (I. i. 1–6)

The world is uncertain, human life is perilous, and 'We must to Virtue for her guide resort'. The moral pattern seems clear, the standards orthodox and simple. The subsequent career of Bussy then becomes a gradual and ultimately fatal movement away from his announced ideas of rectitude. Yet, as Peter Ure points out, this is not the only, or even the dominant, structure. Bussy exemplifies the working-out of the theme of 'greatness' in the human spirit, honour and the pursuit of glory are matters indissolubly linked with the nature of individual personality, and Bussy is a 'self-made' man in that he creates himself in his own image. At his death Bussy has achieved the degree of self-knowledge which enables him to recognize the gulf between his potential and his performance, but the discovery is made in vast natural and cosmic images, which work against the limiting quality of the judgement:

> O frail condition of strength, valour, virtue,
> In me (like warning fire upon the top
> Of some steep beacon, on a steeper hill)
> Made to express it: like a falling star
> Silently glanc'd, that like a thunderbolt
> Look'd to have stuck and shook the firmament.
>
> (V. iv. 141–6)

The sense is of the complete centrality of the human position. There is no moral and spiritual authority beyond Bussy, to whom appeal can be made. In the later tragedies this 'double vision' does not occur. In *The Conspiracy and Tragedy of Charles Duke of Byron* (1608) Chapman creates a hero so simply confident of his own greatness that he can be swayed and governed by lesser men. The real authority lies in the King, against whom he rebels, and who destroys him. It is a study of a different kind of integrity. Just as the Friar's ghost can say at the death of Bussy 'Farewell, brave relics of a complete man' and convince an audience of the rightness of that phrase, so Byron can generalize about his own nature with a confidence that has neither arrogance nor humility:

> . . . men in themselves entire
> March safe with naked feet on coals of fire:
> I build not outward, nor depend on props.
>
> (III. ii. 227–9)

The difference between *Bussy* and *Byron* is a matter of moral balance; whereas Bussy stands ambivalently at the centre of his play, Byron is eccentric, and it is Henry, the stable ruler, who is the still point of that turning world. In *The Revenge of Bussy D'Ambois* (1610) Chapman is less concerned to work out the vengeance than to develop the character of Clermont, who stands as one of his 'exemplars of calm', a man of inward peace and certainty, whose Senecan principles and fortitude provide him with a peace which passes all understanding. His revenge accomplished, and learning of the assassination of his patron, Guise, Clermont refuses to live longer amid 'all the horrors of the vicious time' and kills himself.

His death is his own, almost an artistic comment on the inviolate quality of his greatness:

> . . . th' end being proof and crown
> To all the skill and worth we truly own.
>
> (V. v. 166–7)

In *Caesar and Pompey* (1605, Parrott? 1612) we have Chapman's only attempt to write a play about the historic characters closest to the Stoic vision which informs so much of his writing. It fails not because it lacks grandeur of utterance, but because the concept of heroic integrity, exemplified elsewhere in a single, commanding character, is here split up between the figures of Pompey, Caesar, and Cato. The single figure of Chabot, the just judge, dominates *The Tragedy of Chabot, Admiral of France* (1622, Parrott 1612–13), and the action is controlled and organized to make a satisfying play, but the final impression is of a case history rather than a tragedy; the dramatist's mind is so concerned with the details of the pure analysis that the language loses the fecundity of allusion that characterized *Bussy D'Ambois*. Chapman's searching imagination is evident not only in the philosophical preoccupations of his tragedies, but in the quasi-religious explorations as well. In *Bussy D'Ambois* the hero calls upon supernatural help, not from the Church, but from Behemoth and the Prince of Darkness. Behind this occultism lies the Hermetic philosophy, and in particular Giordano Bruno, with whose work Chapman must have been familiar.[1]

Chapman's seven comedies are seldom thought of as anything more than journey-work, but in some of them the preoccupations of the tragedies are worked out in different terms. *The Blind Beggar of Alexandria* (1596) is a crude, fast-moving comedy of mistaken identity. *An Humourous Day's Mirth* (1597) is an intrigue between scarcely distinguishable court characters, relieved only by a quite keenly observed satire on the Puritan wife, Florilla. *All Fools* (1604, Parrott 1599), set in Florence, touches on more serious comic issues in its whirligig of folly. In Act V, Rinaldo begins his soliloquy:

> Fortune, the great commandress of the world,
> Hath divers ways to advance her followers.
>
> (V. i.)

---

[1] See Frances Yates, *Giordano Bruno and the Hermetic Tradition*, London, 1964, especially Chapters xi–xiii, and *Bussy D'Ambois*, ed. Maurice Evans (New Mermaid Series), London, 1965, pp xx–xxvi.

This theme has certain connections with Chapman's tragic vision, and if we pass over *May-Day* (1602), which is light-hearted romance, the serious issues are taken up in *The Gentleman Usher* (1602), where in the character of Strozza Chapman probes more deeply than his comedy requires into the nature of suffering and the possibilities of mystical healing. *Monsieur D'Olive* (1604) is Chapman's most important comedy, though probably his worst-constructed play. It concerns the comic rise and fall of that 'mongrel of a gull and a villain', Monsieur D'Olive, who produces, among other things, a brilliant anti-Puritan encomium on the smoking of tobacco, in Act III. This is set in the context of a 'romantic' comedy, in which Count St. Anne keeps the body of his dead wife, sitting in her chair, because he cannot be reconciled with mortality. Act III opens with a long discussion between Vandome and St Anne, which is a close translation from Petrarch's *Liber Secretum*, on the subject of the sweetness of death and contempt of life. This strange play ends with some unashamed borrowing from Shakespeare's *Twelfth Night*, and in many ways it is a hotch-potch of theatrical situations. Yet beneath the surface action lies a continuous and serious concern with the conflict between retirement and assertion: the idea of retirement, as Chapman presents it, stems not from Horace, but from Cicero's *Tusculan Disputations*, through general Stoic ideas of love and death, to Petrarch's recondite fusion of pagan with Christian. D'Olive's preparations for his 'embassy' form an image of heroic assertion as serious, in its comic way, as Bussy's tragic assertion. *Monsieur D'Olive* is a mysterious play. Its range, its violent contrasts of tone, its occasional profundity, make the more successful comedy *The Widow's Tears* (1605) seem thin by comparison. But in his comedies as well as his tragedies Chapman can be seen as perhaps the most spiritual, though the least religious, of the Jacobean dramatists.

The distance between the medieval morality and Jacobean theatre is nowhere greater than in *The Revenger's Tragedy* (1606). This play and *The Atheist's Tragedy* (1609) have been attributed to Cyril Tourneur (1575?–1626), though the attributions have been disputed. *The Revenger's Tragedy*, set in Italy, deals with the revenge of Vindice for the murder of his mistress by the lascivious duke, and for the attempted seduction of his sister, Castiza, by the duke's son, Lussurioso. Vindice is both the revenger and the Presenter of the play, and this double role permits him to temper horror with black humour and lurid verbal wit, until the tone of 'tragic burlesque' pervades the whole play. The language rides on great waves of imagery and accords well with the violence of the stage image in the scene where Vindice addresses the skull of his dead mistress:

> Does the silk-worm expend her yellow labours
> For thee? for thee does she undo herself?
> Are lordships sold to maintain ladyships
> For the poor benefit of a bewitching minute?
>
> (III. v. 72–75)

Apart from the violence of its tone and language the play can be seen as the confluence of two traditions. L. G. Salingar has shown that

Tourneur is writing in the contemporary Revenge convention; but behind the Revenge plays is another dramatic influence, working in harmony with Tourneur's narrowly traditionalist outlook, that of the Moralities. *The Revenger's Tragedy* is a logical development from the medieval drama.[1]

In the Moralities the characters are personified abstractions, organized about a doctrinal scheme concerned with man's progress to salvation and the obstacles along the way. In *The Revenger's Tragedy* the complete absence of any positive moral standards, any norm of human behaviour, any impulse towards altruism, to say nothing of Love, suggest not so much the Morality vision of man as redeemable, as a fascination with the possibilities of utter decadence, unrelieved sin. Vindice's last words, as he leaves the stage under guard, make it impossible to see valid moral judgements in the play's denouement:

> ... We have enough, i' faith;
> We're well, our mother turn'd, our sister true;
> We die after a nest of dukes. Adieu.
>
> (V. iii. 123–5)

*The Atheist's Tragedy* seems, in some ways, to be a reworking of the same themes in a more controlled and muted way. It provides a new twist to the Revenge theme, in that the hero, denying himself revenge because of his religious scruples, receives a satisfying worldly reward. But the central concern of the play is the conscious theorizing of D'Amville, the 'atheist', even in the heat of action, as if the dramatist is seeking to undergird what might seem motiveless malignity with materialist, philosophical principles. The result is clear, but not dramatically satisfying.

---

[1] *'The Revenger's Tragedy* and the Morality Tradition', *Scrutiny*, vi, 1938, pp. 402–24; reprinted in *Elizabethan Drama*, ed. R. J. Kaufmann, New York, 1961.

The vision of a world in which evil is regnant and rampant informs comparatively few plays of the period. Far more common are the comedies which aim to divert, amuse and entertain, without raising in any acute or painful way the larger issues. The fifty-two plays which have been assigned to Francis Beaumont (1584–1616) and John Fletcher (1579–1625) come largely within this category. The collaboration between the two is generally thought to have begun in or about 1607, and it probably ended about 1613 when Beaumont married Ursula Isley, and moved out of London. Beaumont died in 1616, but Fletcher lived on in London and wrote a great many plays, sometimes alone, and sometimes in collaboration. He died, probably of the plague, in 1625.

The first play now generally considered to have been written by Beaumont alone is *The Knight of the Burning Pestle* (1607). It is a direct parody of Thomas Heywood's *Four Prentices of London*, in which a grocer and his wife, in the audience, insist that their apprentice Ralph, shall have a part in the play on stage. The whole point is the riotous, good-humoured mockery of citizen values and popular tastes in entertainment. In the Induction the Grocer asks the speaker of the Prologue:

Why could you not be contented with 'The Legend of Whittington', or 'The Life and Death of Sir Thomas Gresham, with The Building of the Royal Exchange', or 'The Story of Queen Eleanor, with the rearing of London Bridge upon Woolsacks'?

Civic pride and commercial standards were powerful enough to invite this gentle satire, and resilient enough to absorb it. Fletcher alone wrote *The Faithful Shepherdess* (1608), reminiscent of Sidney's *Arcadia* and the golden world of Lyly and Peele. Its finest moment is the night scene in the forest where shepherds and shepherdesses assemble, and Amarillis, by dipping in a magic well, assumes the form of Amoret. The pure pastoral play did not prove popular[1], and in the Address to the Reader in the first edition of *The Faithful Shepherdess* Fletcher describes the new form of tragi-comedy, which was to be the one real contribution made by the collaborators to the development of the drama:

A tragie-comedie is not so called in respect of mirth and killing, but in respect it wants deaths, which is inough to make it no tragedie, yet brings some neere it, which is inough to make it no comedie: which must be a representation of familiar people, with such kinde of trouble as no life be

[1] See W. W. Greg, *Pastoral Poetry and Pastoral Drama*, Oxford, 1906.

questiond, so that a God is as lawfull in this as in a tragedie, and meane people as in a comedie.

The 'creation of this middle mood', which was developed from Guarini and the controversy which followed the publication of *Il Pastor Fido*, is well illustrated by one of Beaumont and Fletcher's most successful plays, *Philaster* (1609). The plot indicates the mood. The King of Calabria has usurped the throne of Sicily. Philaster, the true heir, loves the usurper's daughter Arethusa, though her father plans to marry her to Pharamond, Prince of Spain. Philaster places his page, Bellario, in Arethusa's service, and Arethusa tells her father of an affair between Pharamond and Megra, a court lady. Megra accuses Arethusa of misconduct with Bellario, and Philaster, believing this, dismisses Bellario and leaves Arethusa. Bellario is eventually revealed as the daughter of a Sicilian lord, who has assumed the disguise to follow Philaster, and all ends happily. Intrigue, perils narrowly averted, romantic love, misconduct, marriage, simple passions and uncomplicated people – these are the ingredients of *Philaster* and most of the other plays in the canon. There is no sense of tragic oppression or of the trenchant exploration of Jonsonian comedy. The terrible gulf between appearance and reality, which so preoccupies Tourneur or Marston, is here reduced to a gap, bridgeable with a commonplace. Dion says:

Every man in this age, has not a soul of Crystal for all men to read their actions through: men's hearts and faces are so far asunder, that they hold no intelligence.

(I. i)

Philaster's jealousy is expressed in easy hyperboles:

> O that I had a sea
> Within my breast, to quench the fire I feel!

(III. i)

His wish, in Act IV, to leave the courts of princes and live in rustic solitude, is typical of the play's simple moods:

> Oh, that I had been nourished in these woods
> With milk of goats and acorns, and not known
> The right of crowns, nor the dissembling trains
> Of women's looks.

The achievement lies really in the creation of a fairy-tale world, delightful enough to hold an audience's interest. *The Two Noble*

*Kinsmen* (1613), in which Shakespeare may have had a hand, is built to the same formula, following fairly closely the Chaucerian story of Palamon and Arcite, and playing the courtly game to the rules of knightly chivalry. But many of the plays have darker tones. In *Philaster* the usurper would have killed Philaster if he could have summoned the courage; in *A Wife for a Month* (1624), the tyrant of Naples tries to seduce Evanthe, and plans an ingenious revenge when he fails; in *A King and No King* (1611) the plot is built upon the possibility of incest. In some ways, *A King and No King* provides a key to the later drama of the period. Although the contemplation of incest is a central concern in the play, there is no insight. It is a matter of superficial horror, almost of titillation. Arbaces thrills at the discovery:

> Why should there be such musick in a voice,
> And sin for me to hear it? All the world
> May take delight in this, and 'tis damnation
> For me to do so.

(III. i)

The theme of 'incest averted' has appeared before: it is part of the horror in *The Revenger's Tragedy* and *The Atheist's Tragedy*, and it occurs in comedy as early as Lyly's *Mother Bombie*. Among the Jacobean plays we find it in Middleton's *Women Beware Women*, Philip Massinger's *The Unnatural Combat* and Richard Brome's *The Lovesick Court*. But only Ford, in *'Tis Pity She's a Whore*, and Beaumont and Fletcher in this play make it the central issue of the plot. And Ford is the only writer to take it seriously. The presence of these forbidden subjects in the tragi-comedies of Beaumont and Fletcher gives substance to the charge that their art reflects a general slackening of moral rigour in the age. The flight into fairy-tale is also a flight from the harsh claims of religious faith.

John Ford (1586–1640?) is often taken to represent the decadence of the Jacobean period. He is accused of 'brooding over the swamp', and dallying with interdicted subjects. But two things need to be made clear about Ford's plays: the best are seriously concerned with deep moral issues, contemplated steadily, and his verse is a marvellously flexible vehicle, capable of achieving effects of stillness and sobriety in the face of terror which no other Jacobean dramatist can match. He began writing for the theatre in 1621, collaborating with Dekker and others in at least five plays before 1625. After that date he seems to have worked alone. *The Lover's Melancholy* (1628) is a conventional romantic play, and it would be barely distinguishable from the tragi-comedies of Beaumont and Fletcher were it not for the delicacy and tact with which Ford handles difficult emotional situations. The play is an exploration of Burtonian love-melancholy, and at one point Thamasta, the sister of Amethus, falls in love with Parthenophil, who is really a girl, Eroclea, in male disguise. The scene in which Eroclea has to make her sex known is a masterpiece of sensitive organization. Thamasta's apology

> I have trespass'd, and I have been faulty;
> Let not too rude a censure doom me guilty,
> Or judge my error wilful without pardon ...

> (IV. i)

and the embarrassed yet dignified reconciliation of the two women is typical of Ford's control of reticence. In *Love's Sacrifice* (1632) the illicit love of Fernando and Bianca stops short of technical adultery, and the strain of this 'situation of honour', wire-drawn through the play, provides further possibilities for the poetic examination of constraints and restraints upon heroic passion. But the pattern of *Love's Sacrifice* is tragic, and counterpointing the theme of 'passion controlled' is a growing theatrical tension which culminates in the appearance of Fernando in a winding-sheet of Bianca's tomb, and his wild, rhetorical attack on the Duke:

> Com'st thou, Caraffa,
> To practise yet a rape upon the dead?
> Inhuman tyrant!

The play ends with an image of the need for repentance and the reassertion of reason, but the enduring spectacle of the tomb-scene enforces its own comment on the official judgement. Ford's three great plays were written in a comparatively short space of years. *The Broken Heart* (1629) is set in Sparta, and concerns the love of Orgilus for Penthea, who has been forced by her brother Ithocles to marry the aged and jealous Bassanes. Penthea goes mad and dies, while Ithocles falls in love with Calantha, the king's daughter, and she with him. Orgilus avenges Penthea by entrapping Ithocles and killing him, and Calantha, at a feast, hears of the deaths of her father, Penthea, and Ithocles. Orgilus is sentenced to death, and Calantha dies, of a broken heart. Una Ellis-Fermor describes the play as celebrating 'the immutable virtues: courage, continence, and chivalry' (*The Jacobean Drama*, p. 246), and its protracted contemplation of various forms and pressures of human suffering issues in a rare delicacy of emotion and response. Again there is a scene (III. v) in which two women enact the courtesies of social discourse with a superbly articulated concern for each other's feelings. But beneath the observed etiquette lie more powerful controls. Orgilus, watching the madness of Penthea, the death of Ithocles with its Spartan fortitude, and the ritual slaying of Orgilus, all point to an undergirding Stoic fatalism and decorum, which dictates the way to face death. Calantha, in the final scene, having disposed of her kingdom calmly and rationally, explains as she dies that her outward decorum masks an unbearable grief: 'They are the silent griefs which cut the heart-strings' (V. iii). The words are a direct translation of Seneca's 'Curae leves loquuntur, ingentes stupent'.

'Tis Pity She's a Whore (1623) is an obsessive play. Its main plot and sub-plots are concerned with disasters in marriage, and the concern focuses on the incestuous relationship between Giovanni and his sister Annabella. The seriousness with which Ford anatomizes this sensational passion is guaranteed by the scene (I. ii) in which the lovers confess their love, and, because no wedding service is possible for them, invent their own little ritual, and exchange vows:

> On my knees,
> Brother, even by our mother's dust, I charge you,
> Do not betray me to your mirth or hate,
> Love me, or kill me, brother.

This egregious relationship has no precedents, the lovers must live by the standards they forge for themselves. Only in this play does Ford allow a real presence to a moral world other than the one being explored. In 'Tis Pity we are given the citizens of Parma, with their corrupt, mercantile values, we see the moral ineptitude of Poggio and Bergetto, and we have constant reference to the scheme of Christian values and sanctions in the activity of the Friar. Ford's moral discovery is that the forbidden love may be doomed, but it is none the less real, beautiful, and ennobling. The spiritual possibilities of incestuous love are seriously set against the spiritual claims of the Christian faith.

There is nothing of this magnitude in Perkin Warbeck (1633), in which Ford takes up, in a new key, the much earlier fashion for plays on English history. He found the story in Bacon's History of the Reign of King Henry the Seventh (1622) and in Gainsford's True and Wonderful History of Perkin Warbeck (1618) and although for the most part Ford follows his sources fairly closely, there is one crucial difference. The sources state that before his death Perkin confessed that he was not the Duke of York, but Ford leaves us with a character who seems to believe that he is what he has claimed to be. The play becomes a study in delusion, and its central concern is with the integrity of human personality, and the effect of an assumed role upon the consciousness of the role-player. The later plays, *The Fancies Chaste and Noble* (1635) and *The Lady's Trial* (1638), are best forgotten, and Ford's importance lies in the unique voice which speaks unmistakably from the three great plays, and in the seriousness and candour with which he can create a moral world to challenge the received commonplaces of religious thought.

T. S. Eliot, in his essay on Philip Massinger (1583–1640), both evaluates the dramatist's work, and places him in a significant position as belonging not to Jacobean drama but to a later period:

. . . . with the end of Chapman, Middleton, Webster, Tourneur, Donne we end a period when the intellect was immediately at the tips of the senses. Sensation became word and word was sensation. The next period is the period of Milton (though still with a Marvell in it); and this period is initiated by Massinger.

Eliot's judgement is made primarily on the evidence of Massinger's verse and his attitude towards dramatic language, but the point is equally enforceable if we examine the dramaturgy of the plays. Of the thirty-seven plays attributed to him only nineteen remain, and in one or two of these he had a collaborator. Among his tragedies *The Roman Actor* (1626) is perhaps the best known, and it is said to have been the dramatist's own favourite. It is based on the life of Domitian, as told by Suetonius, but it is loosely constructed, and breaks off in the middle to include a long and irrelevant digression about the dignity of the stage. As in many of Massinger's tragedies there are strong echoes of the work of other, and greater, writers. In Act II, Paris, the Roman Actor, says:

> I once observed,
> In a tragedy of ours, in which a murder
> Was acted to the life, a guilty hearer,
> Forced by the terror of a wounded conscience,
> To make discovery of that which torture
> Could not wring from him.

The parasitic quality in Massinger's art seems never to improve upon the host. *The Duke of Milan* (1621) is fast-moving, and crammed with action, but it has no moral depth. Francisco, at his end, says defiantly:

> . . . I glory
> To be the thing I was born, I AM Francisco.

One has only to compare this statement, and this moment, with Webster's 'I am Duchess of Malfi still', or Seneca's 'Medea super est', to sense that one is in the presence of the second-rate. In *The Maid of Honour* (1621) and *Believe As You List* (1631) the passive fortitude of the principal sufferers shows that Massinger's scheme of values is basically stoic, and his ideas of endurance and fortitude in adversity are conservative and rudimentary. Massinger's real achievement lies in two comedies: *A New Way to Pay Old Debts* (1621) and *The City Madam* (1632). The earlier play has certain real affinities with Jonsonian comedy, and its social satire has an occasional basis. It deals with the discomfiture of Sir Giles Overreach, a character modelled on the notorious extortioner Sir Giles Mompesson, who was imprisoned for his financial activities. The rapacious Overreach, having obtained possession of the property of his spendthrift nephew Wellborn, treats him with unconcealed disdain, and the plot develops through Wellborn's schemes, aided by the rich widow Lady Allworth, to repossess his land and dupe his uncle. The central device of the plot is borrowed from Middleton's *A Trick to Catch the Old One*, but the development is quite different. The character of Overreach is a great comic creation, deriving from Marlowe's Barabas, Jonson's Volpone and his Epicure Mammon, and, as L. C. Knights points out, he is set in a context which displays Massinger's sure grasp of the actual:

MARRALL:

> What course take you,
> With your good patience, to hedge in the manor
> Of your neighbour, master Frugal? as 'tis said
> He will nor sell, nor borrow, nor exchange;
> And his land, lying in the midst of your many lordships,
> Is a foul blemish.

It is a chaffering society, where men are bought and sold as easily as land. The morality of *The City Madam* is more explicit. The play concerns the wife and daughters of the rich merchant Sir John Frugal, who have become extravagant, and driven away their erstwhile suitors. Sir John pretends to retire to a monastery, and hands over his property to his brother Luke, a ruined prodigal. Luke acts very harshly to the women, and to Sir John's creditors, and his hypocrisy is exposed when Sir John returns home. The comedy plays about the twin themes of hypocrisy and social pretension, and the play's judgements are often made in overtly religious terms:

> The devil – why start you at his name? If you
> Desire to wallow in wealth and worldly honours,
> You must make haste to be familiar with him.

(V. i)

Yet the effect is not of a coherent pattern in a moral universe. The ethics are somehow too glib, too thin. Eliot, in the essay already quoted, sums up Massinger's art, and with it a great deal of the dramatic output of the end of the period:

What may be considered corrupt or decadent in the morals of Massinger is not an alteration or diminution in morals; it is simply the disappearance of all the personal and real emotions which this morality supported and into which it introduced a kind of order. As soon as the emotions disappear the morality which ordered it appears hideous. Puritanism itself became repulsive only when it appeared as the survival of a restraint after the feelings which it restrained had gone.

The insight applies, broadly speaking, to James Shirley and to Richard Brome as much as it does to Massinger. What took the place of personal and real emotions in the 1630s was the cult of Platonic Love, fostered and cherished at the court of Queen Henrietta Maria. The cult fostered a number of plays, the best known of them being Sir John Suckling's *Aglaura* (1637).[1] Elizabethan and Jacobean drama, which began with the plain man's pathway to heaven, ends with a flight up the Platonic ladder into fantasy. But it is probably true to say that in its movement away from the orthodox dramatic explication of religious dogma the drama of the period opened new possibilities for asserting the sacredness of man, and for making the kind of religious statements typified by Blake's cryptic apothegm 'Everything that lives is holy'.

Such insights are not easy to bear, and it comes as no surprise to learn that when the Puritan party came to power, and closed the theatres by the *First Ordinance of the Long Parliament against Stageplays and Interludes*, 2 September 1642, the language in which they did so is sharply reminiscent of John Stockwood and Philip Stubbes:

[1] See J. B. Fletcher, 'Précieuses at the Court of Charles I' *The Journal of Comparative Literature*, i, 1903, pp 120–53.

Whereas the distressed estate of Ireland, steeped in her own blood, and the distracted estate of England, threatened with a cloud of blood by a civil war, call for all possible means to appease and avert the wrath of God appearing in these judgements: amongst which fasting and prayer, having been often tried to be very effectual, have been lately and are still enjoined . . . while these sad causes and set-times of humiliation do continue, public stage-plays shall cease and be forborne. . . .[1]

When, after the Restoration, plays reappeared in the theatres the fashion was for libertine frivolity. The dramatic impulse abandoned the stage and made its two most powerful appearances elsewhere: in *The Pilgrim's Progress* and in *Paradise Lost*.

[1] Reprinted in W. C. Hazlitt, *The English Drama and Stage 1543–1664*.

# 3

## CHRISTOPHER MARLOWE

### Gāmini Salgādo

#### I

Merling, Merlin, Marlin, Marley, Morley, Marlowe – the man who died by a stab wound from his own hand in a tavern brawl at Deptford Green on the night of 30 May 1593 was known during his lifetime by all these names. In his one surviving signature he signs himself 'Marley'. His name first appears as 'Christopher, the sonne of John Marlow' in the baptismal register of St George's Church, Canterbury on 26 February 1564 – two months to the day before the baptism at Stratford-upon-Avon of William Shakespeare. In the records of Corpus Christi College, Cambridge, where he was a student for six years, he is listed as 'Merling'; and the Middlesex jury which held the inquest on his death identifies him as 'Christopher Morley'.

The John Marlow who was Christopher's father was a prosperous shoemaker from a family whose connections with Canterbury go back at least one hundred and fifty years before the dramatist was born. John married Catherine Arthur, possibly the daughter of a Canterbury vicar. The year Christopher was born his father became a freeman of the city, having served less than the usual period of apprenticeship. Christopher was one of nine children, two of whom died in infancy – a circumstance which was by no means unusual at the time.

Sixteenth-century Canterbury had changed little from the medieval Cathedral town of Chaucer's day, though the Reformation had put an end to the practice of making pilgrimage to the shrine of St Thomas à Becket. The town was on the main Dover –London road and offered a convenient resting place for travellers to the capital and the port, as well as for soldiers to and from the European wars. Like many large towns, its activities included bull-baiting and public executions – by 1576 there were three gibbets in the town, and men were also hanged from the city walls.

City records show that during the reign of Henry VIII religious and political rebels in Canterbury were tortured by being boiled. Thus the atmosphere of cruelty, intrigue and violent death which is an immediately striking aspect of Marlowe's plays needs no special explanation in terms of the dramatist's personality – it was part of the air he breathed as a child.

But only part of it. Coming as he did from a comfortable 'middle class' background, Marlowe's early life was inevitably cushioned against many of the dangers and hardships of Elizabethan life. As a freeman of the city, his father could not be tried by any but a Canterbury jury, or imprisoned anywhere but in Canterbury. In his mother's will, the bequests include gold and silver rings, silver spoons and christening linen as well as sums of money.

In January 1579, Christopher Marlowe entered the King's School, Canterbury. He was within a few weeks of his fifteenth birthday, which was fortunate, as the School Statutes barred any boy over fifteen from admission. As a King's scholar he received an allowance of £1 each quarter from the funds of the Cathedral, in whose account book he appears as 'Christopher Marley'. Though it was laid down that the pupils of the school were to be confined to 'fifty poor boys, both destitute of the help of friends, and endowed with minds apt for learning, who shall be sustained out of the funds of the Church', this was a statute more breached than observed. Marlowe was typical of the majority of the school's pupils in being the son of a prosperous citizen.

Like most Tudor educational institutions, the King's School laid greatest emphasis on the teaching of Latin. The object was to impart a reasonable knowledge of Latin grammar and proficiency in speaking and writing the language. Among the methods used to achieve this end was the acting of plays in Latin. These school plays form part of the earliest secular drama in England.

The school day was, by modern standards, long and arduous. Lessons began and ended with psalms and ran from six in the morning till five in the afternoon. Marlowe stayed at the school till the Michaelmas term of 1580 when, at the age of sixteen, he went up to Corpus Christi College, Cambridge.

Marlowe's education at Cambridge was paid for by one of the scholarships endowed by Archbishop Parker of Canterbury, who was also Master of Corpus Christi, one of the oldest of the Cambridge Colleges. In the main, the Parker scholarships were granted on the understanding that holders should eventually take holy orders. Marlowe (or 'Merling') first appears on the college books, however, not as a student of theology but of dialectics.

He remained at Cambridge for six years, though his attendance during this period was erratic. His reading at the University brought him into contact not only with the Latin classics, but also with contemporary Italian and French literature and, even more importantly, with the writings of the sixteenth-century Florentine diplomat and political philosopher, Nicolo Machiavelli. Only a year before Marlowe went up to Corpus Christi, the Cambridge scholar Gabriel Harvey had written to the poet Edmund Spenser about his Cambridge contemporaries:

And I warrant you some good fellows amongst us begin now to be pretty well acquainted with a certain parlous book called, as I remember me, Il Principe di Nicolo Machiavelli, and I can peradventure name you an odd crew or two that are as cunning in his Discorsi, in his Historia Fiorentina, and in his Dialogues della Arte della Guerra too . . .[1]

Machiavelli introduced a new realism into European political thinking, being a keen analyst of the actualities of statecraft and the real, as opposed to the professed motives that guided those who sought or retained political power. When, in his play *The Jew of Malta*, Marlowe has the Prologue spoken by Machiavelli in person, he not only puts into his mouth nearly all the commonplaces associated with Machiavelli in the popular mind, but creates a character, the intriguer whose whole existence is based on never revealing his real character or motives to anyone but the audience, whose descendants are legion in the drama of the next few decades, and who include Shakespeare's Richard III, Edmund and Iago. The Machiavellian world of double dealing and realpolitik also provides the characters and atmosphere of Marlowe's *The Massacre at Paris*.

But Marlowe's acquaintance with the world of political intrigue was by no means merely academic and theoretical. During at least three of his six years at Cambridge he was absent from the University for several weeks at a time, and it seems reasonably certain that at least some of these absences were on secret state business – in other words, as a member of the vast anti-Catholic espionage system operated by Mr Secretary Walsingham. One of the places most closely watched was the English Catholic seminary at Rheims where missionary priests were given a training which often involved subversive religious and political activity in England. (The distinction between these two spheres, never very clear until modern

---

[1] *The Works of Gabriel Harvey*, ed. A. B. Grosart, London, 1884–5, i, 137–8.

times, was virtually obliterated, as far as English Catholics were concerned, by Pope Pius V's excommunication of Queen Elizabeth in 1570.) Among those who spied for Walsingham at the Rheims seminary were the dramatist and pamphleteer Anthony Munday and Richard Baines, possibly the same man who informed against Marlowe in 1593. A few months before he was due to receive his M.A. degree the rumour spread that Marlowe himself had decided to join the Catholic seminary at Rheims as a novice-priest. The university authorities took this and other rumours about Marlowe seriously enough to refuse him permission to take his degree, but were evidently uninformed about the real nature and scope of Marlowe's activities. At any rate a Privy Council resolution dated 29 June 1587 fairly brusquely directed that the degree be granted, while at the same time giving sóme indication of Marlowe's true profession:

Whereas it was reported that Christopher Morley was determined to have gone beyond the seas to Rheims and there to remain their Lordships thought good to certify that he had no such intent, but that in all his actions he had behaved himself orderly and discreetly whereby he had done Her Majesty good service, and deserved to be rewarded for his faithful dealing. Their Lordships request that the rumour thereof should be allayed by all possible means, and that he should be furthered in the degree he was to take this next commencement: Because it was not Her Majesty's pleasure that anyone employed as he had been in matters touching the benefit of his country should be defamed by those that are ignorant of the affairs he went about.[1]

'The affairs he went about' and the people with whom he went about them (such as Robert Poley, one of the men with him in the last few hours of his life), were the counterparts in real life of the characters and action Marlowe portrayed in *The Jew of Malta* and *The Massacre at Paris*. (Richard Baines had even made the suggestion that the entire Jesuit seminary at Rheims could be eliminated by poisoning the well, which is Barabas's bright idea in *The Jew of Malta*.) The University authorities naturally did as they were told and Marlowe took his M.A. in July 1587. But his dramatic career had already begun. *Tamburlaine the Great*, his first play, had been staged in London and had been so overwhelmingly successful that it had been speedily followed by a sequel.

The exact nature of Marlowe's espionage activities will, in the nature of the case, probably remain obscure. They certainly involved

[1] C. F. Tucker Brooke, *Life of Marlowe*, London, 1930, p 32.

him closely in the state affairs of France, Spain and probably the Low Countries. These were the feverish years before the Great Armada and Elizabeth's Government was more than usually interested in the activities abroad of English Catholics, one of whose main centres was the seminary at Rheims. It is difficult to imagine that Marlowe's work for Walsingham did not bring him into contact with the Catholics abroad, at Rheims and elsewhere. (*The Massacre at Paris* contains an explicit reference to 'a sort of English priests' who 'hatch forth treason 'gainst their natural Queen'.) And if he did have such contact, the hazy knowledge of it in the outside world would be quite sufficient to give rise to the rumour that he himself was a Catholic, or on the point of becoming one. We have Baines' word for it that Marlowe said 'That if there be any God or good religion, then it is in the papists, because the service of God is performed with more ceremonies, as elevation of the Mass, organs, singing men, shaven crowns etc'. But in its context this passage seems to indicate only the dramatist's regard for ritual and pageantry rather than any real religious sympathy for Catholicism.

Marlowe's career as a spy accounts, in part, for his comparatively small literary output (he wrote seven plays, an unfinished narrative poem, some translations and a handful of lyrics). At the same time it provides the dark and violent world of plays such as the *Jew of Malta* and more specifically the detailed knowledge of recent French political history revealed in *The Massacre at Paris*. It seems that the roots of Marlowe's attachment to the life of a secret service agent were social and economic as well as temperamental. The hostility towards Catholic Spain and the consequent suspicion of English Catholics and their activities abroad has already been mentioned as a feature of the social climate. This attitude must be seen against the background, not of England as a first class world power, which she was not to be until the beginning of the eighteenth century, but as a small island nervously aware of the hostility of an immensely rich Catholic superstate just across the ocean. Next we have to remember that the professional dramatist (and indeed, the professional secular writer) was only just beginning to emerge in Marlowe's day. The old secure system of literary patronage was breaking down and the impersonal relations between writer and public which we take for granted today were a long way in the future. Despite the fact that the first London theatre had been established a full decade before Marlowe began to write for the stage, and was quickly followed by several others, the economic position of the young men who came down from the universities and began to write plays was by no means secure. This can be clearly seen when we consider that most of them had to turn out plays at a rate which would be regarded today as consistent only with hackwork, but also from the fact that many of them had to resort to other activities than playwriting to earn a living – Robert Greene to 'coney catching' (confidence tricks), Thomas Nashe to pamphleteering and so on. Finally we have a certain amount of evidence which suggests that Marlowe was by nature drawn to a life of intrigue and violence. The dramatist Thomas Kyd, with whom Marlowe shared a room for some time, spoke of his 'rashness in attempting sudden privy injuries to men,' while Marlowe's continued association with such sinister figures as Robert Poley is also significant. In this part of his life Marlowe is nothing if not typical of his time and place.

Marlowe's spying activities must have taken him through much of northern and western Europe, though it is impossible to be certain just where and when. In October 1587, a letter to Lord Burghley written from Utrecht refers to a certain 'Morley' as a messenger though this may have been the musician Thomas Morley who was in the Low Countries at this time. In 1592 one 'Marlin' figures as a courier between the Government and the British Ambassador in Paris, Sir Henry Unton. But the next time we come across Christopher Marlowe unmistakably is in September 1589 when he was arrested, during a sword fight within the City precincts, together with Thomas Watson who today survives only in anthologies, but was the most celebrated Latin poet of his day and ranked by his contemporaries as the equal of Philip Sidney and Edmund Spenser. Marlowe was remanded (along with Watson) in Newgate prison and the prison register accords him the rank of 'yeoman' living in the prosperous suburban district of Newton Folgate. The grim conditions of Newgate prison have been vividly recorded in a contemporary pamphlet, *The Black Dog of Newgate* by Luke Hutton. They may be guessed at from the fact that more prisoners died of gaol fever than were executed. Marlowe, who was discharged with an admonition to keep the peace in December 1589, undoubtedly recalled his own experiences when he came to write the brief but unforgettable prison scenes in *Edward II*.

In addition to his familiarity with intrigue abroad and violence at home, Marlowe appears also to have been connected with a group of radical thinking young men of his day who gathered round the enigmatic figure of Sir Walter Ralegh. This group sometimes called The School of Night, which included Ralegh's half-brother Carew, the astronomer John Dee, the mathematician Thomas Harriot and several others, was associated in the popular imagination with atheism, necromancy and other sinister goings on. When Ralegh lost the Queen's favour in 1592 by marrying one of her Maids of Honour, he retired from the court to Sherborne Abbey in Dorset (a gift from the Queen in happier days) and the house soon acquired a reputation as a centre of freethought, blasphemy and worse. Marlowe's direct connection with Ralegh cannot be established with certainty, though the latter did write a reply to Marlowe's 'Passionate Shepherd' and according to an informer's report, Marlowe's friend Richard Chomley said that 'Marlowe told him that he had read the atheist lecture to Sir Walter Ralegh and others'. What is probable is that Marlowe's fascination with the movement of the planets and heavenly light and infernal darkness derives in some part from the activities and interests of men like Harriot, while John Dee's contemporary reputation seems to have been one of the sources of inspiration for the figure of Doctor Faustus.

Marlowe's fascination (if such it was) with Ralegh hardly needs any special explanation, for Ralegh fascinated most of his contemporaries. Courtier, poet, patron, explorer, polemicist, historian – Ralegh not only embodied the many-sidedness of his age, but in his failure to achieve real fulfilment in any of his activities and interests was typical of the 'aspiring mind' of his generation. In comprehensiveness of imagination and scepticism of intellect, as well as in the manner of his death Ralegh resembled not only the heroes of Marlovian drama but their creator.

It is probable that at Ralegh's London house in the Strand, where he played host to such men as the Italian humanist Giordano Bruno and John Florio, the translator of Montaigne, Marlowe came into personal contact with members of 'The School of Night'. He was certainly associated in the public mind with this group and one of its members, the poet and dramatist George Chapman, wrote a continuation of *Hero and Leander*, a narrative poem which Marlowe left unfinished at his death.

What with his mysterious dealings with suspected traitors abroad and his open association with known unbelievers at home, it was not at all surprising that within a few years Marlowe had acquired a reputation as an intriguer, a blasphemer and a libertine. Everything we know or can infer about his personality suggests that it was not a reputation which he took the least trouble to live down; indeed, it is likely that he gloried in it, though this was a dangerous thing to do, as subsequent events proved.

In 1593, five years after the defeat of The Great Armada, fears of a Catholic invasion (possibly based on the Isle of Man) were still prevalent and Elizabeth's Government very sensitive to the slightest suspicion of a Catholic plot against the Queen. Feeling against foreigners was very strong within the city and the tension was hardly lessened by a violent outbreak of plague which spread across London.

In May the dramatist Thomas Kyd was arrested, apparently on suspicion of having had a hand in the vituperative libels against foreigners which, appearing on city walls, were a principal cause of unrest among London apprentices and others. Though nothing was found to connect Kyd with these activities, the authorities did find papers which they described as 'vile and heretical conceits denying the deity of Jesus Christ'. Kyd was interrogated and his examination included the customary torture, under which he declared that the papers in question had belonged to Marlowe and dated from a time some two years earlier when they had shared a room; many people, he added, would swear that Marlowe was an atheist. In letters written later, Kyd went into some detail about his fellow-dramatist's blasphemous and heretical opinions.

Kyd's evidence led to a warrant being issued against Marlowe, which the latter duly answered. He was ordered to attend on the Privy Council. He seems to have been treated by the Council much better than Kyd (as a University graduate Marlowe was entitled to the rank of gentleman). The Council now instructed Marlowe to be available while they made further inquiries as to his activities and opinions. The principal upshot of these inquiries was a report by the informer Richard Baines, headed *A Note containing the opinion of one Christopher Marly concerning his damnable judgment of religion and scorn of God's Word*. This 'note' (which, together with Kyd's letters referred to above and some references in Greene's *Groatsworth of Wit* forms the chief source for our knowledge of Marlowe's religious views) is undated. But by the time the Queen received her copy of it Marlowe had already been dead two days.

Thanks to Mr Leslie Hotson's discovery, some forty years ago, of the proceedings of the inquest on Marlowe's death, it is now possible to reconstruct almost hour by hour the events which took place at the widow Eleanor Bull's tavern in Deptford Green on 30 May 1593. (This has not however prevented Mr Calvin Hoffman from claiming, in his book *The Man Who Was Shakespeare*, that Marlowe did not die that evening at all, but escaped and lived on to write plays under the pseudonym of – guess who?)

Besides Marlowe himself, there were three other people who met on the morning of 30 May at Mistress Bull's house. All four men were associates of Thomas Walsingham, and three of them were secret service agents. There was the sinister Robert Poley already mentioned, and Nicholas Skeres, who had worked with Poley before. The fourth man was Ingram Frizer who earlier that year had been Skere's partner in defrauding a young gentleman to the benefit, among others, of Thomas Walsingham whose business agent Frizer then was. A contemporary account tells us that it was Frizer who invited Marlowe to Deptford.

After an early dinner the four men walked about in the garden and went in for supper at about six in the evening. The meal over, Marlowe rested on a bed while the others sat playing backgammon. A dispute then arose about the bill and Marlowe suddenly sprang up, drew Frizer's dagger from his belt and began beating him on the head with it. Frizer struggled to retrieve his weapon and drove the point of the dagger into Marlowe's skull just over the right eye. Death was apparently instantaneous.

Nearly 300 years after his death, a memorial was erected at Canterbury though even then it was felt that there should not be one in Westminster Abbey on account of 'his acknowledged life and expressions'. At St Nicholas' Church, Deptford, a brass plate put up in 1919 refers 'To the Immortal Memory of Christopher Marlowe, M.A., The Founder of Grandiloquent Blank Verse'.

Christopher Marlowe died before he was thirty. His writing career lasted just over five years. During that time, in addition to producing an outstanding, though uncompleted, narrative poem and a vigorous translation of Lucan's *Pharsalia* (and a less satisfactory version of Ovid's *Amores*), Marlowe virtually single-handedly changed the nature and scope of the English drama. Of his contemporaries, only Shakespeare clearly surpasses him in achievement. And as an influence, it could be claimed that he is more important than Shakespeare, not least for his influence on Shakespeare himself.

II

None of Marlowe's poems or translations was published during his lifetime and it is not easy to determine the order of their composition. Only one lyric poem by Marlowe survives. (The 'Description of Seas, Waters, Rivers, &c.', from *England's Parnassus*,

1660 – though it continues to be reprinted as if it were the work of Marlowe – has been conclusively proved by Mr John Crow to be the work of Gervase Markham.) Marlowe's only short poem, 'The Passionate Shepherd to his Love' is one of the best-known pastoral poems in the language and exists in many versions other than the original one which appeared in another popular anthology of the time, *England's Helicon*. It is an elegant and cheerful rendering of the age-old pastoral theme of the shepherd inviting his sweetheart to share his life. The apparent naivety of the verse is deceptive, pastoral being one of the most sophisticated of literary forms and the product of highly developed urban cultures. Not only the landscape but the costume is elegant and highly mannered, far removed from true pastoral simplicity (if such a thing exists):

> A gowne made of the finest wooll,
> Which from our pretty Lambes we pull,
> Fayre lined slippers for the cold,
> With buckles of the purest gold.

> (lines 13–16)

Marlowe's poem provoked many imitations and rejoinders, and Marlowe himself makes a sardonic reference to it in Ithamore's speech to Bellamira in *The Jew of Malta* (Act IV, lines 1804–16). Sir Walter Ralegh's ironic reply is almost as well known as Marlowe's own poem.

The late sixteenth and early seventeenth century was, among other things, a period of great translations, chief among which were North's *Plutarch*, the King James Bible and Chapman's Homer (the last of which inspired Keats's famous sonnet). Marlowe was typical of his time in trying his hand at translations from the Latin. His version of Ovid's *Amores*, entitled *All Ovid's Elegies*, appeared about two years after his death, and the existence of at least six early editions shows how popular it was. It was originally printed in Middleburgh in Holland and had the distinction of being publicly burnt in 1599 by order of the ecclesiastical censors, though this may have been due to Sir John Davies' bawdy epigrams which were bound in with Marlowe's translations.

It is possible that this is the earliest of Marlowe's work that has survived. It is almost certainly the work of the young Cambridge undergraduate, shaky in his grasp of the original and often less than successful in his effort to render it into decent English. These lines from the ninth elegy give a fair idea of the staple of Marlowe's verse, even to the tottering rhythm of the last line:

> Sooth Lovers watch till sleepe the hus-band charmes,
> Who slumbering, they rise up in swelling armes.
> The keepers hands and corps-dugard to passe
> The souldiours, and poore lovers worke ere was.
> Doubtfull is warre and love, the vanquisht rise
> And who thou never think'st should fall downe lies.
>
> (lines 25–30)

But, as in everything he wrote, the dazzling energy of Marlowe's imagination occasionally bursts through the mists of obscurity and misunderstanding. *All Ovid's Elegies* may not in itself be a great translation, but there is enough in it to remind us not only that it belongs to an age of great translations, but also that it is the work of a great and original poet.

In 1599 Thomas Thorpe, the man who ten years later printed Shakespeare's sonnets, published Marlowe's translation of the first book of Lucan's *Pharsalia*. (Thorpe also published a complete translation of the *Pharsalia* by Sir Arthur Gorges in 1614.) The original is a Latin historical epic in ten books dealing with the civil war between Caesar and Pompey. Marlowe's rendering of the first book, though still full of mistranslations, often has a martial clangour which anticipates the 'mighty line' of *Tamburlaine*, as well as the latter's fascination with exotic place-names:

> Titan himselfe throand in the midst of heaven,
> His burning chariot plung'd in sable cloudes,
> And whelm'd the world in darkness, making men
> Dispaire of day, as did Thiestes towne,
> (Mycenoe) Phoebus flying through the East:
> Fierce Mulciber unbarred Aetna's gate,
> Which flamed not on high; but headlong pitcht
> Her burning head on bending Hespery.
>
> (lines 538–45)

But Marlowe's finest achievement outside the drama is the long narrative poem *Hero and Leander*, left uncompleted at his death and continued, although in a very different mode, by his friend George Chapman. The legend of Hero and Leander came to Marlowe from a fifth century poem, probably in a late sixteenth-century Latin translation; Ovid too uses the fable in his *Heroides*, though Marlowe's handling of it is almost wholly original. The story tells how Leander, a young man of Abydos, falls in love with Hero of Sestos whom he meets in the temple of Venus during the festival of Adonis. She invites him to visit her at night in her tower by the sea.

Leander spends the night with Hero and returns to Abydos, but tormented by his separation from her, swims the Hellespont to Sestos. On the way he is carried down to the sea bed by Neptune, who mistakes him for Jupiter's page, Ganymede. Leander escapes, returns to Sestos and makes love to Hero; the lovers wake to another dawn. Within the main narrative is inserted an exemplary tale above Jove, Mercury and Cupid to explain the poverty of scholars and the Fates' hostility towards true lovers.

In the spring of 1593, the London theatres were closed owing to an outbreak of the plague. It may have been then that Marlowe, who was staying at Thomas Walsingham's house in Kent, began work on this poem (which the publisher dedicated to Walsingham). If this is the case, it is his last work, and in many ways *Hero and Leander* shows a maturity of technique absent from Marlowe's other non-dramatic works. In exuberance of imagination and in the freedom of its handling of the verse form Marlowe's poem rivals and often surpasses Shakespeare's narrative poem *Venus and Adonis*, written about the same time.

When Chapman came to write his continuation of *Hero and Leander*, he did not fail to draw the pious moral – that the tragic death of the protagonists was a judgement from above on their illicit passion. No such moral scruples trouble the gaiety of Marlowe's presentation of the young lovers. The description of Hero with which the poem opens recalls Renaissance painting at those moments when it combines the celebration of the flesh with elegance and intricacy of decorative detail – say the work of Botticelli:

> She ware no gloves, for neither sunne nor wind
> Would burne or parch her hands, but to her mind,
> Or warme or coole them, for they tooke delite
> To play upon those hands, they were so white.
> Buskins of shels all silvered used she,
> And brancht with blushing corall to the knee;
> Where sparrowes pearcht, of hollow pearle and gold,
> Such as the world would woonder to behold:
> Those with sweet water oft her handmaid fils,
> Which as shee went would cherupe through the bils.
>
> (lines 27–36)

And if the description of Hero, for all its brilliant colouring, lacks a certain warmth, the portrait of Leander is alive with breathing human passion:

> His bodie was as straight as Circes wand,
> Jove might have sipt out Nectar from his hand.
> Even as delicious meat is to the tast,
> So was his necke, in touching, and surpast
> The white of Pelops shoulder. I could tell ye,
> How smoôth his brest was, and how white his bellie,
> And whose immortall fingars did imprint
> That heavenly path, with many a curious dint,
> That runs along his backe, . . .

>> (lines 61–9)

But the poem is not a mere series of set pieces, however brilliant. Incomplete though it is, it has an organic unity possessed by few of Marlowe's other works. *Hero and Leander* may be a head without a body, but it is a head which lives and breathes. The first meeting of the lovers marvellously combines delicacy and humour; and Leander's arguments against virginity – a fairly common theme of the time – are handled with a lightness and skill which suggest some of Shakespeare's sonnets or the love poems of Donne:

> This idoll which you terme Virginitie,
> Is neither essence subject to the eie,
> No, nor to any one exterior sence,
> Nor hath it any place of residence,
> Nor is't of earth or mold celestiall,
> Or capable of any forme at all.
> Of that which hath no being doe not boast,
> Things that are not at all are never lost.

>> (lines 269–76)

The burlesque of scholastic argument is controlled by the playful tenderness of tone appropriate to the speaker and his dramatic situation.

Throughout the poem Marlowe retains his characteristic blend of intensity and detachment, a Keatsian warmth together with a gently mocking wit which often puts one in mind of such a poem as Andrew Marvell's 'To His Coy Mistress'. If he had written nothing else, Marlowe would still be remembered as the author of *Hero and Leander*.

The world of classical legend was one to which writers of the Renaissance returned time and again, and Marlowe's attachment to it is shown once more in *Dido, Queen of Carthage*, possibly his earliest play, though he may have revised it at a later date before production. When Shakespeare's Hamlet discusses contemporary plays with the First Player, Marlowe's *Dido* seems to be in his mind, for though not popular ('caviare to the general') he says it was 'an excellent play, well digested in the scenes, set down with as much modesty as cunning'.

Marlowe found the simple plot in Virgil's *Aeneid* and Ovid's *Metamorphoses*. Aeneas, escaping from the sack of Troy, is wrecked on the Libyan coast where Dido, the Carthaginian queen falls in love with him, although she is already pledged to Iarbas, one of her noblemen. In a vision Mercury tells Aeneas that his destiny is to found Rome and he must therefore leave Dido. After one unsuccessful attempt he does this, whereupon Dido kills herself for sorrow, followed by her sister Anna and Iarbas.

Parts of the play are almost word-for-word renderings of passages from the first, second and fourth books of Virgil's epic but elsewhere Marlowe adapts his source material with the greatest freedom, which is one of the reasons for thinking that the play as we have it is the work of different periods of Marlowe's career. The title page of the only extant early edition (1594) tells us that *Dido* was acted by the Children of the Chapel and names Thomas Nashe as co-author of the play. It is very difficult indeed to see what part, if any, Nashe had in the composition of *Dido*. It bears no resemblance to the only dramatic work definitely known to be by Nashe, *Summer's Last Will and Testament*. Though collaboration between playwrights was very much the rule in Marlowe's day, Marlowe himself seems to have been an exception in this respect. Perhaps the partnership in this case dated from Marlowe's Cambridge days, when Nashe was his contemporary.

What is indisputable is that *Dido, Queen of Carthage* bears the unmistakable signature of Marlowe both in its language and its stage technique. Though unique among Marlowe's plays in being the only one with a central love interest, it has many links with the other plays and shows in cruder form the restlessness of spirit, the exuberance of imagination and that capacity to evoke horror by pushing the grotesque almost, but not quite, to the point of caricature, which T. S. Eliot singled out as Marlowe's peculiar strength:

> Then from the navell to the throat at once,
> He ript old Priam: at whose latter gaspe
> Joves marble statue gan to bend the brow,
> As lothing Pirrhus for this wicked act:
> Yet he undaunted tooke his fathers flagge,
> And dipt it in the old Kings chill cold bloud,
> And then in triumph ran into the streetes,
> Through which he could not passe for slaughtred men: ...
>
> (lines 550–7)

Single lines break loose from their context and haunt the memory—

> We saw Cassandra sprauling in the streetes
>
> (line 569)

> At last the souldiers puld her by the heeles,
> And swong her howling in the emptie ayre
>
> (lines 542–3)

> ... heele make me immortall with a kisse.
>
> (line 1329)

(A line that found its definitive and unforgettable context when Marlowe adapted it for Faustus' words to the phantom Helen of Troy.) Occasionally, there is an odd anticipation of Shakespeare, as in:

> See what strange artes necessitie findes out.

*Dido* is too static and too predictable in its development to be a successful drama, but occasionally we hear in it the voice of a great dramatist, confident in his capacity.

Marlowe wrote four great tragedies: *The Massacre at Paris* is not one of them. As it stands it is undoubtedly his worst play. The text, as given in the only (undated) early edition that survives, is so short and often so garbled that it is almost certainly based on an actor's memory or a theatrical abridgement. But it is not difficult to account for the contemporary popularity of the play (the great Elizabethan actor Edward Alleyn had one of his outstanding successes in the principal role of the Guise in it) for its rabid and unvarying anti-Catholicism was a faithful reflection of popular sentiment at the time.

The play, sometimes called *The Guise*, covers a period of some seventeen years, from the notorious massacre of the Huguenots on St Bartholomew's Eve 1572, to the death of Henri III in 1589, probably just a year or two before Marlowe wrote the play. The action opens with the murder of Admiral Coligny in his bed which is a prelude to the massacre of the Protestants, which in turn is followed by a series of individual killings culminating in the death of the Guise followed by that of the new king. The only variations from the unending sequence of stabbings, stranglings and poisonings are a grotesque scene where a cutpurse has his ears chopped off for trying to steal gold buttons from a wedding guest,

and a hackneyed and irrelevant sub-plot dealing with the adultery of
the Guise's wife.

The anti-Catholic bias of *The Massacre of Paris* seems to have
been strong enough to overcome the customary ban on the presentation of political and religious topics on the Elizabethan stage.
But for all the bitter strife between Protestants and Catholics which
forms the staple of his play, Marlowe appears to be singularly
uninterested in the rights and wrongs of the religious debate. The
Huguenots (twice referred to as Puritans) are portrayed as pathetic
victims without much courage or dignity, and the dying king's
concluding injunction to the English agent to

> Salute the Queene of England in my name,
> And tell her Henry dyes her faithfull freend.
>
> (lines 1256–7)

sounds more like an obligatory flourish than a deeply felt patriotic
utterance. The only real interest in the play lies in the character of
the Guise, who is presented as a thoroughgoing Machiavellian,
using religion, kinship, personal loyalty and anything else that
comes to hand in the service of a relentless and single-minded
self-seeking. In his great opening soliloquy (the longest in any of
Marlowe's plays) we recognize the authentic accent of the
Marlovian would-be superman:

> Oft have I leveld, and at last have learnd,
> That perill is the cheefest way to happines,
> And resolution honors fairest aime.
> What glory is there in a common good,
> That hanges for every peasant to atchive?
> That like I best that flyes beyond my reach.
> Set me to scale the high Peramides,
> And thereon set the Diadem of Fraunce,
> Ile either rend it with my nayles to naught,
> Or mount the top with my aspiring winges,
> Although my downfall be the deepest hell.
>
> (lines 94–104)

'That like I best that flyes beyond my reach' – it could be the
motto of Tamburlaine, the first Marlovian hero, who took the stage
by storm and became a theatrical legend even within the brief span
of his creator's lifetime. There is an appropriate irony in the fact
that the two parts of *Tamburlaine the Great*, stamped as they are in
every line with Marlowe's characteristic genius, are the only works
by Marlowe for which documentary evidence of his authorship is

lacking. No author's name appears on the title page of any of the three early editions.

From the very first lines of the Prologue it is clear that the young dramatist knows exactly what he wants to do:

> From jygging vaines of riming mother wits,
> And such conceits as clownage keepes in pay,
> Weele lead you to the stately tent of War,
> Where you shall heare the Scythian Tamburlaine
> Threatening the world with high astounding tearms
> And scourging kingdoms with his conquering sword.

The first two lines glance disparagingly at the buffoonery and the jogtrot verse typical of the early years of Elizabethan drama. But taken together these opening lines serve to define the action of Marlowe's own play: it is precisely a progress from the 'jigging veins' of the ineffectual Mycetes to the stately verse of Tamburlaine's utterance. In finding a new kind of hero Marlowe also finds the speech that gives him life; or rather, he discovers the character through the language.

Marlowe had five principal sources for his play. These were George Whetstone's *The English Mirror* (1586); a life of Tamburlaine published in Florence in 1553; Lonicerus's *History of the Turks*; the famous atlas by Abraham Ortelius (*Theatrum Orbis Terrarum*); and Paul Ive's *Practice of Fortification*, from which Marlowe took most of the details of military strategy. The real life original of his hero was Timur the Lame who ruled in Samarcand in the late fourteenth century, and whose vast empire was looked on with awe and admiration by the monarchs of Europe.

But the historical figure was little more than a point of departure for the dramatist's soaring imagination. Marlowe saw in Tamburlaine the very image of Renaissance man, entranced by the variety of the world he lived in and boundlessly confident in his ability to bend it to his will. It is no accident that the hero begins life as a humble shepherd. Drama (other than comedy) had hitherto dealt with the exploits of kings and nobles: here we have the saga of the self-made man, triumphing through no advantages of birth or inheritance, but entirely through qualities of character. (We meet a similar figure in Doctor Faustus.) Tamburlaine's attitude and career are a continuous challenge to the traditional scheme of things, where a man's life was determined by the station to which he was born, and the cardinal virtue, in religion as in politics, was humble obedience. The 'world' which Tamburlaine threatens with 'high astounding terms' is nothing less than the socio-religious order which was the medieval heritage of the Elizabethan age:

> I am a Lord, for so my deeds shall proove,
> And yet a shepheard by my Parentage: . . .
>
> (lines 230–1)

At every point Tamburlaine challenges the ethic of 'the fall of princes' as expounded in such popular treatises as *The Mirror for Magistrates* (a new edition of which appeared in 1587, the year *Tamburlaine* was first performed). Marlowe is simply not interested in enforcing the old moral that pride goeth before a fall; this is especially true if we remember that the two parts of the play were not conceived together; and that the first part concluded not with Tamburlaine punished for his pride but rather when he 'takes truce with all the world' at the height of his triumph.

Tamburlaine's physical conquests are of course an emblem of the spiritual discoveries, the 'thirst for the infinite' of Renaissance man. The language in which Tamburlaine speaks of himself leaves us in no doubt that his territorial expansion is not merely the result of squalid political ambition:

> For Fates and Oracles [of] heaven have sworne,
> To roialise the deedes of Tamburlaine:
> And make them blest that share in his attemptes.
> And doubt you not, but if you favour me,
> And let my Fortunes and my valour sway
> To some direction in your martiall deeds,
> The world will strive with hostes of men at armes
> To swarm unto the Ensigne I support.
> The host of Xerxes, which by fame is said
> To drinke the mightie Parthian Araris,
> Was but a handful to that we will have.
> Our quivering Lances shaking in the aire,
> And bullets like Joves dreadful Thunderbolts,
> Enrolde in flames and fiery smoldering mistes,
> Shall threat the Gods more than Cyclopian warres,
> And with our Sun-bright armour as we march,
> Weel chase the Stars from heaven, and dim their eies
> That stand and muse at our admyred armes.
>
> (lines 605–22)

Throughout the play Tamburlaine is identified with the sun and likens himself repeatedly to the gods. But his blasphemy goes unpunished and he climbs from victory to victory, while his enemies are shown to be pathetic, self-divided weaklings. The deeply traditional image of the wheel of Fortune with whose fickle movement men rise and fall is given a new ironic twist by Tamburlaine:

> I hold the Fates bound fast in yron chaines,
> And with my hand turne Fortunes wheel about....
>
> (lines 369–70)

He is Fortune, controlling his own destiny and those of others; and insofar as the play shows every character's fate dependent on Tamburlaine's will or whim while he himself is not subject to control, it confirms Tamburlaine's view of himself.

Marlowe is clearly fascinated by the energy, the resolve and the visionary imagination of his hero. Tamburlaine's capacity to give utterance to his ambition becomes, in the words of the play, the guarantee that the ambition is achieved. To put it in another way, Tamburlaine's eloquence is the dramatic equivalent of his military prowess; the 'high astounding terms' and the 'conquering sword' are exactly interchangeable. It is significant that the weakling Mycetes, at the very beginning of the play, finds himself 'insufficient to express' his feelings about his country because 'it requires a great and thundering speech' – the speech, in other words, of a Tamburlaine. The Marlovian hero is distinguished by his eloquence, or magniloquence, as we might expect in a theatre where the spoken word was the most powerful resource of stage-craft; the weaklings are always at a loss for words.

No doubt Marlowe's original audience, as soon as they heard Tamburlaine's arrogant utterances and saw his acts of cruelty (such as the sack of Damascus and the slaughter of the virgins), would have sat back in their seats and waited for a proper retribution to overtake him for his *hubris* in rejecting his appointed place in society and setting himself up as a rival to the gods. An audience accustomed to moralizing tracts of the *Mirror for Magistrates* variety could hardly be expected to react otherwise. But the great dramatist, though he may take his audience's stock responses into account, does not necessarily satisfy them. (Shakespeare, in his History plays, shows his awareness of the idea of the Great Chain of Being, but he is not shackled by it.) One of the reasons for the immense popularity of *Tamburlaine the Great* may well have been precisely the fact that it did *not* satisfy the audience's expectations; instead, it deflected them in a new and surprising direction. But to put it this way is also slightly misleading. For the Elizabethan age was, more than most, an age of transition. Counterpoised in the

Elizabethan mind with the medieval sanctions against 'over-reaching' was the Renaissance admiration for the 'aspiring mind'. And it is in the tension between these two that *Tamburlaine the Great* lives, moves and has its being.

If the first part of *Tamburlaine the Great* is a celebration of Renaissance individualism, the second is something like a lament for its limitations. Since he had already exhausted most of his source material in Part I, Marlowe was compelled to elaborate on Tamburlaine's further conquests in the sequel. But Part II is not simply the massacre as before. There is a dramatic development, as we see the hero become more and more drunk with power, seeing himself now not merely as 'the scourge of God' but as the rival and even the superior of the gods. Tamburlaine's growing madness, the death of his beloved wife Zenocrate and finally his own death are the shadows cast by the bright sun of Tamburlaine's imperial conquest. It is not weakness of character nor any twist of Fate that brings about Tamburlaine's downfall, if such it is. It is the very nature of man, and of human existence. Tamburlaine is a finite creature with a longing for infinity. The frustration of his *ultimate* aspiration – divinity – is implicit in the aspiration itself. It has been well said by M. M. Mahood that *Tamburlaine* is the only drama in which the death of the hero constitutes the tragedy. And the hero himself expresses this in his final piercing moment of tragic awareness:

> For Tamburlaine, the Scourge of God must die.

Like Tamburlaine, Marlowe's next hero Doctor Faustus is a man of humble birth who, when the Chorus first introduces him to us at the beginning of the play, has already established himself in the world of learning through his native abilities. This opening chorus is a cunningly contrived piece of stagecraft for it not only gives us, in a nutshell, 'the form of Faustus' fortunes good or bad' (with a brief backward glance at *Tamburlaine*) but, with that freedom of movement through space and time which was second nature to the Elizabethan dramatist, concludes by zooming down on Faustus, at this moment, with the fateful choice still before him – 'And this the man who in his study sits'. This shuffling together of past, present and future gives some sense of the inevitability of Faustus' progress to damnation while preserving inviolate the hero's capacity to choose.

In some ways *The Tragicall History of The Life and Death of Doctor Faustus* is a more deeply traditional play than *Tamburlaine*.

Marlowe's immediate source was probably an English translation of the contemporary German *Faustbuch*, but the story itself was part of European mythology. It tells how Faustus, thirsting for supreme power, sold his soul to the devil in exchange for twenty-four years of absolute dominion on earth. Built into the very bones of the story is the element of the cautionary tale, with Faustus as the horrible example of what happens when creatures rebel against their lot and aspire to the condition of the Creator. The Chorus stresses this aspect of the fable, and behind the immediate allusion to Icarus looms the distant shadow of the first rebel, Satan himself:

> Till swolne with cunning, of a selfe conceit,
> His waxen wings did mount above his reach,
> And melting heavens conspirde his overthrow.
>
> (lines 20–2)

The Good and Evil Angels who embody the struggle with Faustus' soul come straight out of medieval Morality drama and the concluding warning of the Chorus, after Faustus has met his awesome fate, is undeviatingly orthodox:

> Faustus is gone, regard his hellish fall,
> Whose fiendful fortune may exhort the wise,
> Onely to wonder at unlawful things,
> Whose deepenesse doth intise such forward wits,
> To practice more than heavenly power permits.
>
> (lines 1481–5)

But, as with *Tamburlaine*, the play invites us to regard its hero from more than one point of view. The Chorus was for Marlowe a convenient means for directing the audience's interests, but it no more represents the total tragic experience of *Doctor Faustus* than, say, Edgar's tidy moralizings represent the final judgement of *King Lear*. It is not irrelevant to remember that Marlowe himself was probably the friend of men such as John Dee, whose life's aim was 'to practise more than heavenly power permits' (at least insofar as heavenly power was incarnated in the ecclesiastical authorities), but we do not need to go outside the world of the play to be powerfully aware of the dramatist's imaginative sympathy with his protagonist. In *Tamburlaine* the hero's territorial conquests are a metaphor for the scope of his imagination, and his military and political ascendancy the outward sign of his soaring spirit. With *Doctor Faustus* we are dealing with the thing itself. The story deals directly with Faustus' spiritual ambition and its consequences. In his very first speech he surveys and rejects contemptuously the whole body of traditional learning – logic, medicine, law, theology. The Biblical reference 'The reward of sin is death' underlines the nature of the offence Faustus is about to commit, but it is difficult not to hear in his subsequent lines something more than the dramatist's creative sympathy for any of his characters:

> O what a world of profit and delight,
> Of power, of honor, of omnipotence
> Is promised to the studious Artizan?
> All things that move betweene the quiet poles
> Shal be at my commaund . . .

> (lines 81–5)

When Faustus, in this opening speech, rejects theology he takes the first fateful step towards damnation, but it is in no spirit of vindictive moralizing that Marlowe follows his hero's descent into hell. Though the outcome is certain, the tension is maintained by a series of choices throughout the action by means of which Faustus confirms himself in sin and finally puts himself beyond the reach of divine mercy. After his first rejection of God's teaching, there is his refusal to heed the Good Angel, the signing of the blood bond with Lucifer, his refusal, (or inability, perhaps, at this stage) to follow the Old Man's exhortation to repent, and his effort to forget his desperate spiritual predicament in the gratification of physical desire. Though the fable deals with aspiration and damnation at the literal level, the dramatist still has to find adequate embodiment of this conflict in word and gesture. Marlowe's verse rises magnificently to every dramatic occasion, from the opening self-assurance of Faustus rejecting all human learning, through the desolate eloquence of Mephistophilis—

> Why this is hel, nor am I out of it:
> Thinkst thou that I who saw the face of God,
> And tasted the eternal joyes of heaven,
> Am not tormented with ten thousand hels,
> In being depriv'd of everlasting blisse?

> (lines 312–16)

—to the final desperate writhings of Faustus' tormented soul:

> The starres moove stil, time runs, the clocke will strike,
> The divel wil come, and Faustus must be damnd.
> O Ile leape up to my God: who pulles me downe?
> See see where Christs blood streames in the firmament.
> One drop would save my soule, halfe a drop, ah my Christ.
> Yet wil I call on him: oh spare me Lucifer!

> (lines 1429–35)

The imagery is resonant with memories of all the great rebels of myth and religion, the Titans, Phaeton, Icarus, up to Lucifer himself, so that the hero's progress becomes in some sense the progress of the European consciousness. And though Marlowe's language carries the greatest charge of meaning and implication, the action and spectacle have retained undiminished their capacity to hold an audience enthralled. Already in *Tamburlaine* Marlowe had shown his ability to make telling use of the theatre's non-verbal resources. Tamburlaine's triumphal entry in a chariot drawn by four deposed Asian kings and the scene where the captured monarch Bajazeth is brought on in a cage against whose bars he dashes out his brains were two of the most famous 'set-pieces' in Elizabethan drama. Perhaps for us today their bravura tends to spill over into comedy. But the same cannot be said of the great moments of *Doctor Faustus* – Faustus holding his hand over a flame because the blood in which he has to sign the bond has congealed, the pageant of the Seven Deadly Sins (no less effective for being profoundly traditional), above all, the great scene where Faustus confronts his paramour, the incarnation for all Europe of a world ill lost, Helen of Troy, and utters the most poignantly ironic line in all Elizabethan drama:

'Sweet Helen, make me immortal with a kiss'

— in scenes such as this the visual presentation matches superbly the incandescent blank verse which is Marlowe's legacy to the English stage.

Though not as popular as *Tamburlaine* in Marlowe's own day, *Doctor Faustus* is the play by which its author is best known today, and it has a strong claim to be considered his best in spite of a comic sub-plot which is not completely woven into the main action. The text has come down to us in two quite different forms, the earlier, and probably more authentic of which, is found in the Quarto editions from 1604 to 1611. The Quartos from 1616 to 1631 print a version which is half as large again (though some of the original matter has been omitted or recast), but it is generally believed that most of the new material is not in fact by Marlowe at all. For the most part, it consists of crude incidents taken from the Faustbook and is probably the work of a well-known Elizabethan hack called Samuel Rowley. There is also a Quarto of 1633, containing many comic scenes adopted from Marlowe's next play *The Jew of Malta*, but this has no textual authority whatever.

To pass from *Tamburlaine* and *Doctor Faustus* to *The Jew of Malta* is like leaving the open air or a spacious palace to enter a prison cell. For his setting Marlowe abandons the freedom of Renaissance Europe and the wide plains of Asia for a tight little island in a land-locked sea. And for his hero, instead of a warrior who sweeps all before him in his triumphal progress, or a thinker whose dreams are boundless, he chooses a devious and calculating Jew, a friendless outsider in a hostile community.

Nor is this restriction of scope limited to character and setting. In both the earlier tragedies the actions and utterances of the hero evoke a world of absolute values, even if only to reject it. When Tamburlaine boasts:

> I hold the Fates bound fast in yron chaines,
> And with my hand turne Fortunes wheel about, . . .
>
> (lines 369–70)

he recalls, however scornfully, the forces in human life which set a limit to human aspiration and achievement, forces later to be embodied in the death of Zenocrate. In the same way Faustus' words—

> Thinkst thou that Faustus is so fond, to imagine,
> That after this life there is any paine?
> Tush, these are trifles and meere olde wives tales.
>
> (lines 565–7)

gain their dramatic force from the incompleteness of Faustus' commitment to them. But the mean and narrow world of *The Jew of Malta* is the only reality with which the play deals directly or by implication. It is a world whose manifesto is spoken by Machiavelli appearing as Prologue:

> And let them know that I am Machevill,
> And weigh not men, and therefore not mens words:
> Admir'd I am of those that hate me most.
> . . . . . . . . . . . . . . . . . . . . . . . . . . . . . . . . . . . . . . . . . . . . . . .
> I count Religion but a childish Toy,
> And hold there is no sinne but Ignorance.
> . . . . . . . . . . . . . . . . . . . . . . . . . . . . . . . . . . . . . . . . . . . . . . .
> Might first made Kings, and Lawes were then most sure
> When like the Dracos they were writ in blood.
>
> (lines 7–21)

There is a world of difference between Faustus' professed disbelief in an afterlife and Machiavelli's cynical definition of religion. For all his defiance, the former teeters between faith and doubt and the play in some sense proves his words wrong. The action and motivation of *The Jew of Malta* on the other hand confirm at every point that we are in a society where force and fraud are the ruling principles and lip-service to religion a handy instrument of policy.

Barabas the Jew is undoubtedly the villain of the piece, but, while Marlowe amply satisfied the audience's desire to see the Jew as scapegoat, the entire play turns on the fact that Jew, Christian and Turk without exception act in the same ruthlessly egotistic way in their pursuit of wealth and power, whatever their pious avowals. On the evidence of the play Barabas has the 'right' on his side when he declares:

> Thus loving neither, will I live with both,
> Making a profit of my policie;
> And he from whom my most advantage comes,
> Shall be my friend.
> This is the life we Jewes are us'd to lead;
> And reason too, for Christians doe the like.

> (lines 2213–18)

It is impossible not to feel the savage irony which, unknown to the speaker, comes through the words of the Christian Governor as he piously admonishes the Jew, having just confiscated all his possessions—

> Excesse of wealth is cause of covetousnesse:
> And covetousnesse, o 'tis a monstrous sinne.

> (lines 356–7)

There is something deeper than the desire to pander to the popular taste for anti-clerical satire in the scene where the two friars, fooled by Barabas's protestations that he wishes to turn Christian, try to get their hands on his fortune. In the end Barabas is left, literally, to stew in his own juice, but only because he is not Machiavellian enough: he makes the fatal error of trusting a Christian.

*The Jew of Malta* cannot be called a tragedy in any but the crudest sense, the sense in which we may call any play a tragedy in which the chief character dies. Barabas dies, but utterly without tragic illumination, and nowhere else does the play offer even the faintest glimmer of such illumination. The staple of its plot is the sheerest melodrama – poisoned porridge, poisoned flowers, stranglings, boilings in oil and the like follow one another in bloodthirsty succession. There is an undeniable comic relish in the way Marlowe depicts this world, a relish which black comedy and sick jokes may make more accessible to the modern audience:

> As for my self, I walke abroad a nights
> And kill sicke people groaning under walls:
> Sometimes I goe about and poyson wells;
> And now and then, to cherish Christian theeves,
> I am content to lose some of my Crownes;
> That I may, walking in my Gallery,
> See 'em goe pinion'd along by my doore.
>
> (lines 939–45)

Barabas never attains the near-tragic stature of Shylock any more than the play itself ever emerges from its worm's eye view of human motivation. With neither tragic insight nor comic liberation, the laughter it provokes is thoughtful and disturbing and its peculiar quality is aptly summarized in T. S. Eliot's phrase 'savage farce'.

In spite of its title, Marlowe's *Edward II* is not a 'history play', certainly not in the sense in which the phrase is applied to Shakespeare's plays dealing with kings of England. Like Shakespeare, Marlowe found his raw material in Holinshed's *Chronicles* and the *Annals* of John Stow, but there is little similarity in the use which the two dramatists made of their sources. Marlowe has little of the concern for the suffering land which runs through Shakespearean history plays, and nothing at all of the Shakespearean sense of historical change. He covers a period of over twenty years (1307–30) but we have little sense of what happens to England during this time. The dramatist's centre of interest is the relationship between the weak and frivolous Edward and his favourite, Gaveston. It has been suggested that in the figure of Gaveston Marlowe came closest to drawing a self-portrait, and certainly the dramatic character has the personal charm, the panache and the touch of cruelty which we tend to think of as the leading traits of his character, in addition to being a partner in a homosexual relationship. (According to Baines, Marlowe held that 'all they that love not tobacco and boys were fools'.) Unfortunately for the unity of the play, Gaveston disappears from it about halfway through, put to death by the nobles whom he has offended. Though Edward immediately takes new favourites, these have neither the attractiveness nor the force of personality of Gaveston, and the dramatic impact of the Gaveston – Edward relationship is gone. The lack is partly compensated for by the emergence of Mortimer as a fully fledged Machiavellian (though Marlowe has to do a certain amount of violence to his earlier portrayal of Mortimer to achieve this). The latter part of the play is largely taken up by the combined efforts of Mortimer and Queen Isabella to oust Edward from power, efforts which eventually succeed in forcing the king to abdicate in favour of his son. Mortimer tries various means of getting rid of the king and when everything else fails hires Lightborn, a specialist in ingenious means of murder. Lightborn is discovered and Mortimer put to death by the young king who also sends his mother to the tower.

Though it bears all the marks of Marlowe's impatient genius, *Edward II* is in some ways his most ambitious play. To begin with, he shows a certain amount of skill in choosing and ordering character and events from the fairly substantial material provided by his sources. Sometimes the very swiftness of the 'cutting' carries its own penalty, as for instance when we suddenly hear, towards the end of the play, of '*old* Edward', when we still think of him (as the play has made us do) as a pleasure-loving young man. But most of the time the plot, in spite of being 'broken backed' after Gaveston's exit, moves rapidly enough.

Then again, the dialogue of the play spans the entire Marlovian range, from the youthful lyricism of *Dido* (here finely tuned to the immediate dramatic occasion, as in Gaveston's account of the diversions he has planned for the king, lines 50–71) through the horror-comedy of *The Jew of Malta* to the austere splendour of *Doctor Faustus*, as in Mortimer's last words, with their anticipation of *Hamlet*:

> Farewell faire Queene, weepe not for Mortimer,
> That scornes the world, and as a traveller,
> Goes to discover countries yet unknowne.
>
> (lines 2632–4)

There is even, for Marlowe, a new kind of dialogue, a dialogue that gets its power not from splendidly extravagant statement but rather from a bare and chilling matter-of-factness applied to a grim situation (see for instance, the exchange between Lightborn, Matrevis and Gurney, lines 2476–85).

But the most distinctive thing about *Edward II* is that it is not a 'one character' play, as *Tamburlaine, Doctor Faustus* and *The Jew of Malta* tend to be. Apart from the king himself we have Gaveston and Mortimer as characters in their own right. And among the minor figures, Lightborn, the professional killer, has a deadly and totally convincing dramatic presence. (He is not found in Marlowe's sources; it is not fanciful to assume that the dramatist modelled him on some real-life acquaintance encountered in the course of his secret service activities.)

*Edward II* attempts, within the limits imposed by its historical sources, to discover the alternatives in human action to the self-seeking hedonism of a Gaveston and the Machiavellian cynicism of a Mortimer. The world-ranging conquests of a Tamburlaine have shrunk here to the pathetic dimensions of an imprisoned king standing in the filth of sewers in a dungeon below the earth. The play has little to offer in positive terms, other than the Stoic defiance of death expressed in the last words of Mortimer. This attempt to invest the acceptance of death with an autonomous significance, as a reaction against the emptiness of a life drained of value, is one that will be made repeatedly in drama in the two or three decades following Marlowe's death. We see it, for instance, in the two great tragedies of John Webster, *The White Devil* and *The Duchess of Malfi*, and in the plays of John Ford. In this, as in so much else, Marlowe first sounded the note that was to be taken up by later dramatists. But Marlowe's claim to greatness does not rest merely on his influence on others, nor on his own brilliant promise, but on a solid and varied achievement to which a fellow poet, Michael Drayton, paid a splendid tribute in his poem 'To Henry Reynolds, Of Poets and Poesy':

> ... Marlowe, bathed in the Thespian springs,
> Had in him those brave translunary things
> That your first poets had; his raptures were
> All fire and air, which made his verses clear,
> For that fine madness still he did retain
> Which rightly should possess a poet's brain.

# 4

# SHAKESPEARE

## (i)

## HIS CAREER AND DEVELOPMENT

### Richard Proudfoot

Although they afford no intimate picture of his personality, the historical facts about William Shakespeare have an essential place in any attempt to construct a context in which his works may be understood, because they anchor the works to the circumstances in which they were written and can serve as a corrective to the wilder flights of fancy to which writers about him have been peculiarly prone. What is known relates to the public events of his career, which were matters of record, but the picture that emerges of his career in his chosen occupation of actor-playwright confirms the view of Shakespeare as a practical and efficient man, using his outstanding poetic ability to ensure the continuing success of his company in pleasing a wide and discriminating audience for some twenty years with a succession of plays that achieved their originality within existing traditions and at the same time extended the range and intensity of English poetic drama to a point unequalled before or since.

The facts about Shakespeare include information about the early publication of his works. This is important not only as a major source for the chronology of his plays but because his manuscripts have not survived, so that early printed texts are the only basis for our knowledge of what he wrote. Less than half of the plays were printed in his lifetime and he was not actively concerned with the printing of any of them. Plays were the property of the companies who acted them and formed a valuable part of the companies' capital: they would not sell them to publishers without good reason. Play publication became more widespread during Shakespeare's career than it had been earlier and was especially frequent after the longest periods of closure of the theatres because of the plague, when companies unable to act in London could be persuaded to raise cash by selling some of their plays. Unfortunately, not all plays that were published were sold by the companies who owned them and some two dozen plays, at least seven of Shakespeare's among them, were printed in texts of doubtful origin and of varying degrees of inaccuracy and incompleteness. Many of these texts show signs of having been altered for acting by reduced casts, perhaps by touring groups in the provinces, and some seem further to have been compiled from memory by actors who had played minor roles in performances of the authentic versions and whose reconstructions are muddled by frequent lapses of memory and eked out with remembered phrases from other plays.

Apart from these memorial texts, the Quartos of Shakespeare's plays generally contain accurate and authentic texts well printed by the standards of the time and they remain the chief authority for the text of ten plays. Plays did not enjoy a high status as literature and printers devoted little care to formal matters in printing them. The accurate verse-lining, full stage-directions and consistent speech prefixes familiar in modern editions are not always to be found in the early editions, while other formal features, especially act and scene divisions and notes of location, were mostly introduced by eighteenth-century editors and are often positively misleading because they assume a mode of staging which came into existence long after Shakespeare was dead. Stage space was not localized by scenery in his theatres and the division of plays into five acts, separated by intervals, only became a regular practice in the private theatres of the 1620s.

The exact place and date of William Shakespeare's birth remain uncertain. He was christened on 26 April 1564 in the Church of the Holy Trinity at Stratford-upon-Avon. He was the first son and eldest surviving child of John and Mary Shakespeare: two older daughters had died in infancy. Three sons, Gilbert, Richard and Edmund, reached manhood, but died before William; his sister Joan survived him, another sister, Anne, having died in childhood. Edmund, born in 1580, was the only member of the family to follow William into the theatre: he died in London in 1607.

Both of Shakespeare's grandfathers were farmers in the environs of Stratford. His father left the farm, married the landlord's daughter, Mary Arden, and set up in the town as a glover and worker in white leather, trading also in wool and corn. John Shakespeare probably settled in Stratford shortly before its incorporation as a royal borough in 1553. He held a succession of civic offices and was elected bailiff, or mayor, for 1568–9. His early prosperity was on the wane by 1576 and ten years later he forfeited his rank as an alderman for persistent failure to attend council meetings. When a list of recusants in Stratford was compiled in 1582, his name was on it, but the reason for his absences from church was given as fear of arrest for his debts and the suggestion that he remained a Roman Catholic is hardly consistent with his civic record. John Shakespeare lived until 1601 and Mary until 1608. The grant of a coat of arms made to John in 1596 was warranted by his having held the office of bailiff: his application was presumably financed by William, whose successful career was well launched by the mid-1590s.

Little is known of William's life before 1592, by which date he was already established in London as an actor and playwright. As the plays show their author's acquaintance with the standard Latin school texts of the day we can assume that he received the free grammar school education available to him in Stratford. In 1709, Shakespeare's first biographer, Nicholas Rowe, recorded the tradition that he was taken from school early and apprenticed to a trade; certainly no record has been found of his further education at either university or at the Inns of Court. Although the Stratford grammar school had well-qualified masters and paid them well, only one Stratford boy of Shakespeare's generation is known to have proceeded to Oxford; another, Richard Field, was apprenticed to a London printer and later printed Shakespeare's *Venus and Adonis* and *Lucrece*.

Unlike many of his fellow dramatists, Shakespeare never lost touch with his birthplace: this fact lends support to the assumption that he remained in Stratford until his move to London. He married Anne Hathaway, a local farmer's daughter, in 1582. She was his senior by eight years and their first child, Susanna, was christened six months after the wedding, but no further factual basis exists for the popular myth that the marriage was an unhappy one, and the scanty records relating to Shakespeare's family life are equally consistent with the view that his marriage was happy and stable. Twin children, Hamnet and Judith, were born in 1585, but Hamnet died in 1596. Shakespeare purchased New Place, one of the two largest stone houses in Stratford, in 1597 and it remained his Stratford home until his death. His early years may have been spent in the house in Henley Street now commemorated as his birthplace.

From 1585 to 1591 no record of Shakespeare has been found. A strong tradition that he was 'in his younger yeares a Schoolmaster in the Countrey'[1] is at least consistent with his close knowledge of classical Latin texts such as Ovid's *Metamorphoses* and the comedies of Plautus and Terence which were in general use in the schools, and with the fact that his earliest plays show his most conscious and elaborate use of this knowledge. The late seventeenth-century tradition that his move to London, leaving his family behind, was occasioned by his arrest for poaching cannot be entirely discounted although it is inaccurate in detail and accords uneasily with such facts and dates as have been established. Although the precise date and occasion of his move to London is unknown, Shakespeare was probably there no later than 1590 and possibly as early as 1587. He may have gone with the specific intention of working in the theatre: he had had ample opportunity to see performances in Stratford by several London companies, whose visits are recorded from 1568, the year in which his father was bailiff. He could have joined a company on tour if a vacancy occurred, as it must have done, for instance, when William Knell of the Queen's men was killed in a fight at Thame, Oxfordshire, in 1587.

Shakespeare's name is not found in extant records relating to any theatrical company before 1595, when, in company with Richard Burbage and William Kempe, he received payment for court performances by the Chamberlain's men during the Christmas festivities of 1594. From 1590 to 1594 the story of the leading companies of players is confused and suggests that their organization was unstable. Lord Strange's men flourished from 1587 to 1594 and their patron was Earl of Derby from September 1593 until his death in April 1594. They performed a play called 'Harey the vi' in 1592, which may have been *1 Henry VI*. The Earl of Pembroke's men were active in 1592–3: they performed *3 Henry VI* and *Titus Andronicus*. *Titus* was also performed by Derby's (Strange's) men and by the Earl of Sussex's men, who acted in London in 1593–4. Whether or not Shakespeare acted with any of these companies and for which of them he may have written his earliest plays is unknown, but as a playwright his name is linked, however tenuously, with these groups rather than with the other leading companies of the day, the Queen's men and the Lord Admiral's men. He apparently brought his earliest plays with him to the newly founded Lord Chamberlain's men in 1594. Richard Burbage, whose fame is associated with leading tragic roles in

[1] E. K. Chambers, *William Shakespeare*, Oxford, 1930, ii, 254. Cited hereafter as Chambers.

Shakespeare's plays, was the youngest son of James Burbage, proprietor of the Theatre; he had earlier acted with the Admiral's men. William Kempe, the company's leading comedian until 1599, had acted with Strange's men.

Shakespeare seems to have achieved his success as a dramatist quickly. There is no clear evidence for dating any of his plays earlier than 1590–1. By 1592 he was known as the author of *Henry VI*. The publication of his narrative poems, *Venus and Adonis* in 1593 and *Lucrece* in 1594, extended his fame, especially in literary circles and in the universities, and he was soon known to have written a set of love-sonnets, although these were not published until 1609. The dedicatory epistles to *Venus and Adonis* and *Lucrece* show Shakespeare first seeking and then enjoying the patronage of the third Earl of Southampton. His other patrons were the patrons of his company, the first and second Lords Hunsdon, King James I and the Herberts, Earls of Pembroke and Montgomery, to whom his colleagues dedicated his works in 1623. Stories of his intimacy with the nobility are unsupported, and as late as 1613 he was content to receive forty-four shillings for devising an impresa or motto for the Earl of Rutland to bear on his shield at a tourney at court. Further plays which he probably wrote before the forming of the Chamberlain's men are *The Comedy of Errors*, *The Taming of the Shrew*, *The Two Gentlemen of Verona* and *Richard III*. *The Comedy of Errors* was acted at Gray's Inn in December 1594; the play called *The Taming of a Shrew*, acted by Pembroke's men and published in 1594, is probably derived from Shakespeare's play. The early dating of the other two plays is based on the internal evidence of style and structure as well as on the assumption that *Richard III*, which is a sequel to *3 Henry VI*, was written soon after it. *Titus Andronicus* was published in 1594, but no other of the earliest plays was printed in complete and accurate form until 1623. The text of *Richard III* published in 1597, although remarkably complete, is probably a memorial reconstruction of the play.

The theory that Shakespeare began his career as a reviser, or even plagiarist, of other men's plays has little to recommend it. It is based on the ambiguous attack on him in Robert Greene's *A Groatsworth of Wit*, 1592, which deserves attention as the first certain allusion to Shakespeare as actor and dramatist. Greene warns his fellow graduate playwrights against the ingratitude of the actors, 'those Puppets . . . that spake from our mouths', in failing to relieve his misery during his final illness: he sees especial danger in the recent successes of an actor-dramatist, an upstart Crow, beautified with our feathers, that with his *Tygers hart wrapt in a Players hyde*, supposes he is as well able to bombast out a blanke verse as the best of you: and being an absolute *Johannes fac totum*, is in his owne conceit the onely Shake-scene in a countrey. (Chambers, ii, 188)

'Our feathers' are most likely the plays in which Shakespeare the actor was earning a living, but the phrase has been taken as a charge of plagiarism against Shakespeare the poet. Henry Chettle, who had published Greene's attack after its author's death, came to regret that he had let the offending passage stand and later made formal apology for it:

I am as sory as if the originall fault had beene my fault, because my selfe have seene his demeanor no lesse civill than he exelent in the qualitie he professes: Besides, divers of worship have reported his uprightnes of dealing, which argues his honesty, and his facetious grace in writting, that approoves his Art. (Chambers, ii, 189)

Greene parodies a line from *3 Henry VI* (1.4.137), 'O tiger's heart wrapp'd in a woman's hide', and his alleged charge of plagiarism seemed, at one time, to account for the relationship between *2* and *3 Henry VI* and two plays printed in 1594 and 1595 as *The First Part of the Contention betwixt the Two Famous Houses of York and Lancaster* and *The True Tragedy of Richard Duke of York*. It is now generally accepted that these plays are not originals reworked by Shakespeare, but memorial versions of his *2* and *3 Henry VI*. No evidence exists for a charge of plagiarism because no play survives which is certainly an original later revamped by Shakespeare. When he did find his material in earlier plays, his transmutation of it was complete: his borrowings were never inert or mechanical but rather discoveries of new significance or shapeliness in old materials as he fused them with each other to make his plays.

Shakespeare has been proposed as author or part-author of several plays of doubtful authorship, some dating from the earliest years of his career. *The Reign of King Edward III*, printed in 1596 but written about 1591–2, contains striking verbal parallels with Shakespeare's work including the line 'Lillies that fester smel far worse than weeds',[1] which also concludes Sonnet 94. *The Tragedy of Locrine*, a play in the Senecan manner of the 1580s, was printed in 1595 as 'Newly set foorth, overseene and corrected, By *W. S.*'. No conclusive case has been made for Shakespeare's hand in these two plays, although he clearly knew *Edward III* well and echoes it in

---

[1] II. i. 451; in *The Shakespeare Apocrypha*, ed. C. F. Tucker Brooke, Oxford, 1908.

*Henry V* and *Measure for Measure*. A third play, *Sir Thomas More*, survives in manuscript: the manuscript was written by Antony Munday and was later revised, piecemeal, by several other writers. One revision, filling three pages, has been attributed to Shakespeare with a high degree of probability, on evidence ranging from style and political ideas to handwriting and orthography. The scene shows the quelling of the 'ill May-day' riots by More as sheriff of London. It was probably written before 1594 and is the only extant literary manuscript believed to be in Shakespeare's hand.

Shakespeare joined the Chamberlain's men as an actor and certainly continued to act until 1604 if not until his retirement from London. His name is high in the lists of actors in his own plays and in Jonson's *Every Man in his Humour* and *Sejanus*. He was known for his 'kingly parts', but the traditions which assign to him the roles of the Ghost in *Hamlet* and Adam in *As You Like It* are too late to be relied on. From 1594 he wrote all his plays for performance by himself and his partners. He was fortunate in his company, as they were in him. The organization continued stable throughout his career and provided him with a necessary condition for the writing of plays which often entailed an amount of preliminary reading for which he would hardly have found time in a less prosperous company. *King Lear*, *Antony and Cleopatra* and *The Winter's Tale* also presuppose an acting company of great strength and virtuosity as well as a dramatist of genius. Occasional setbacks, such as the death of their first patron, the first Lord Hunsdon, in 1596 or the closure of London theatres because of the plague, especially in 1603–4 and for lengthy periods between 1607 and 1610, were not enough to disrupt the company. Throughout Shakespeare's career his company played at Court more frequently than any other and his plays figure largely in the few records which name the plays performed there.

Comedies and English histories remained Shakespeare's main concern in the later 1590s. He seems to have written steadily at the rate of two plays a year for his new company. *Love's Labour's Lost* and *Romeo and Juliet* were among his first plays for them, followed by *A Midsummer Night's Dream* and *Richard II*, which was published in 1597. *Romeo and Juliet* was also published in 1597, in a short memorial text which was superseded by a good one in 1599. The 1598 edition of *Love's Labour's Lost* may also have been designed to replace an earlier memorial text, now lost, and was the first edition of any play to be printed with Shakespeare's name on its title-page. A young clergyman, Francis Meres, included a comprehensive and enthusiastic survey of the present state of English literature in his *Palladis Tamia* (1598). He testified to Shakespeare's high reputation for comedy and tragedy and listed twelve of his plays, providing us with good evidence for dating *King John*, *The Merchant of Venice*, *Henry IV* and *Love's Labour's Won* before the middle of 1598. Two editions of *1 Henry IV* were published in 1598. *Love's Labour's Won* is not extant under that title, but the discovery of a list of books in stock made by an Exeter book-seller in 1603 indicates that such a play was then in print. If it is to be identified with any play in the Shakespeare canon, *All's Well that Ends Well* may be the likeliest candidate, though not in its present form.

Despite its popularity in the 1590s, English history was not the safest of subjects for a dramatist. Queen Elizabeth was disposed to see allusions to herself in literary handlings of the deposition of Richard II. Shakespeare's play of *Richard II* was revived on 7 February 1601, at the instance of the supporters of the Earl of Essex, whose attempt at rebellion took place the following day. Shakespeare and his company were able to plead ignorance of any politically subversive intention and did not lose royal favour. The scene of Richard's abdication (4.1.154–318) first appeared in print in the fourth edition of the play in 1608, the first reprint after the Queen's death.

The character in *Henry IV* and *The Merry Wives of Windsor* whom we know as Sir John Falstaff was originally called Sir John Oldcastle. Oldcastle was a prominent Lollard, martyred in the reign of Henry V. His wife's descendants, the Brookes, Lords Cobham, took exception to Shakespeare's use of the name Oldcastle and induced him to change it. The Admiral's men commissioned a play of *Sir John Oldcastle* in 1599, with the dual aim of cashing in on Shakespeare's success and of presenting the true history of Oldcastle. Part 1 of this play, which was written by Michael Drayton, Antony Munday and others, was fraudulently attributed to Shakespeare in 1619.

The lease of the ground on which James Burbage had built the Theatre, the principal playhouse of the Chamberlain's men, expired in 1597. Burbage's plan was that the Chamberlain's men should move from Shoreditch into the City, to occupy a new indoor theatre in the old Blackfriars monastery. He duly bought and equipped the Parliament Chamber at the Blackfriars, but a petition by local householders led to the prohibition of its use as a public theatre. The Chamberlain's men apparently used the smaller Shoreditch theatre, the Curtain, from 1597 to 1599. The period at the Curtain probably saw the first productions of *Much Ado about Nothing, Henry V* and perhaps also of *As You Like It*. About 1595, Francis Langley had opened a new and splendid playhouse in Southwark, the Swan. The possibility that Shakespeare's company may briefly have used this theatre at some date before February 1597 is raised by the linking of Shakespeare's name with that of Langley as parties against whom William Wayte petitioned for sureties of the peace late in 1596.

James Burbage died in February 1597, leaving his sons Cuthbert and Richard two unusable playhouses. In December 1598 they took the law into their own hands and demolished the Theatre, moving its timbers to Southwark, where they were used as materials for the building of their new playhouse, the Globe. Ownership of the Globe was held by a syndicate composed of the Burbages, who owned a half share, and five leading actors, including Shakespeare, between whom the other half share was equally divided. The syndicate continued, with occasional variation in the number of sharers, until the disbanding of the company in 1642. In return for their initial investment in the building the actor-sharers were entitled to share in the half of the gallery receipts which had long been accepted as the due of the owner of a playhouse. When the company regained possession of the Blackfriars theatre in 1608, shares in the ownership were similarly distributed. Shakespeare was assessed for taxes in the parish of St Helen's, Bishopsgate, in October 1596, but he had moved to Southwark before October 1599 and finally paid his taxes there in 1601.

The Chamberlain's men began playing at the Globe in the late summer or autumn of 1599. It was there that Thomas Platter of Basle saw them perform *Julius Caesar* on 21 September, 'with at least fifteen characters very well acted'.[1] *Hamlet* and *Twelfth Night* were among the first of Shakespeare's plays for the Globe: *The Merry Wives, Troilus and Cressida* and *All's Well that Ends Well* were also written during the last years of Queen Elizabeth. *Hamlet* had been acted at Oxford and Cambridge as well as London before the publication of a very poor memorial text in 1603.

It is not certain that Shakespeare ever wrote a play for a particular occasion, but the appearance of Falstaff in *The Merry Wives* and not, as the epilogue to 2 *Henry IV* had promised, in *Henry V*, may be explained by the tradition, first recorded in 1702, that the Queen requested a play showing Sir John in love. When *Troilus and*

*Cressida* was published in 1609, its publishers made two incompatible claims in successive states of the first sheet: first, that the play had been acted at the Globe; second, that it had never been acted in public. Their first claim is the more likely, but the hypothesis that the play was specially written for performance at one of the Inns of Court has found many supporters among scholars who find its static opening and scenes of formal debate untypical of Shakespeare.

The publication in 1600 of good texts of 2 *Henry IV*, *Much Ado*, *A Midsummer Night's Dream* and *The Merchant of Venice* seems to have been authorized by the company and may reflect some financial difficulty after the great expense of building the Globe and in face of competition from the revived Boys' company to which the Burbages had leased the Blackfriars theatre. Attempts to prevent the publication of a corrupt text of *Henry V* in the same year were unsuccessful, and it was followed, in 1602 and 1603, by equally bad texts of *The Merry Wives* and *Hamlet*. Five sonnets by Shakespeare, three of them from *Love's Labour's Lost*, were printed in *The Passionate Pilgrim* 'By W. Shakespeare', published by William Jaggard in 1599. Shakespeare's annoyance at the fraudulent attribution to him of the other poems in the book is mentioned by Thomas Heywood in his complaint against Jaggard for including some of his poems in a later edition. Shakespeare was among the poets who contributed verses on the theme of the phoenix and the turtle, emblems of love and constancy, to Robert Chester's *Love's Martyr*, 1601. One further non-dramatic poem usually accepted as his is *The Lover's Complaint*, which was printed with the sonnets in 1609.

The death of Queen Elizabeth in March 1603 and the accession of James I led to the extension of royal patronage to all the London companies of players. The Chamberlain's men became the King's men, Queen Anne became patron both of Worcester's men and of the Boys' company at the Blackfriars, and Prince Henry of the Admiral's men.

During the Christmas festivities of 1604–5, the King's men gave court performances of *Measure for Measure* and *Othello*, and, in December 1606, of *King Lear*: none of these plays was much more than a year old at the time of its court performance. So far the chronology of Shakespeare's plays, though uncertain in detail, is often supported by such good evidence as dates of publication or records of performance. External evidence for dating his later plays is less frequent, and the order of composition commonly accepted depends largely on the internal evidence of style and versification, occasionally supported by clear topical references, although these are always rare in Shakespeare's work. *Macbeth*, which certainly alludes to the accession of King James and probably also to the Gunpowder Plot, may be dated 1606. References in *Macbeth* to Caesar and Antony suggest that he was at work at about the same time on *Antony and Cleopatra*, which was registered for publication in 1608, although not printed then. As the subjects of *Coriolanus* and *Timon of Athens*, like that of *Antony and Cleopatra*, are drawn from North's translation of Plutarch's *Lives*, they are reasonably assigned to the years 1607–8, although the dating of *Timon* remains problematic.

The last of Shakespeare's plays to be printed in his lifetime with the authority of his company was *Hamlet*, in the good second edition of 1604–5. Unauthorized publication continued, however, with *King Lear*, 1608, in an unrevised and badly printed text, and *Troilus and Cressida*, 1609, in a good text of doubtful origin. Three other King's men's plays were published with attributions to Shakespeare, *The London Prodigal* in 1605, *A Yorkshire Tragedy* in 1608 and *Pericles* in 1609, but only *Pericles* is his, even in part. It had been performed by 1608 and marks a new direction in Shakespeare's work, a return from the historical tragedy of the Roman plays to the haphazard conventions of medieval romance and the naive stagecraft which had attracted Sidney's scorn in the popular plays of the 1570s. The text of *Pericles* is uneven in style and it is possible that the play is reported, or Shakespeare's revision of another man's work, or a play written in collaboration. Evidence of Shakespeare's style is clearest in the last three acts.

*Cymbeline* and *The Winter's Tale* were acted at the Globe in 1611, and *The Winter's Tale* and *The Tempest* at court in the same year. *The Tempest* was written in 1611, the other two plays slightly earlier. Records exist of court performances of a play called *Cardenio* in 1612–13; no such play is extant but in 1653 a manuscript of 'The History of Cardennio, by Mr Fletcher and Shakespeare' was registered for publication by Humphrey Moseley, the stationer who had published the first collected edition of Beaumont and Fletcher's plays in 1647. The name of Shakespeare is again linked with that of his young colleague, John Fletcher, who was to succeed him as principal playwright for the King's men, on the title-page of *The Two Noble Kinsmen*, a play written and performed at the Blackfriars in 1613, but not printed until 1634. These facts have prompted the suggestion that Shakespeare's *Henry VIII* may also be the product of collaboration with Fletcher: internal evidence of style and versification supports the suggestion although the inclusion of the play in the Shakespeare Folio of 1623 may argue against it. *Henry VIII* was apparently the play acted at the Globe on 29 June 1613, perhaps for the first time. During the performance wadding from the cannon used for sound effects ignited the thatch on the roof and the Globe quickly burnt down. It was rebuilt, with a tiled roof, and re-opened the following year.

The tradition that Shakespeare retired from London to Stratford in his later years is supported by his description of himself as 'of Stratford upon Avon' when he gave evidence in the case of Stephen Belott versus Christopher Mountjoy in May 1612. The likely date of his retirement was 1610–11. His renewed dramatic activity in 1612–13 might suggest that he had some difficulty in settling down to country life, and records exist of his visits to London on several occasions after 1611, the latest being in 1614. In the course of his career, Shakespeare had invested large sums in property in and about Stratford, both in New Place and in land and a lease of the Stratford tithes, which he bought in 1602 and 1605 respectively, but his last important purchase was in London. In May 1613 he bought a house in the Blackfriars, near the theatre, for £140: this was apparently the first house that he owned in London. His residence in Southwark had ended before 1604, when, as the law-suit of 1612 indicates, he was lodging north of the river with Christopher Mountjoy, a French Huguenot tile-maker, in St Olave's parish, Cripplegate. He was at this time a near neighbour of his colleagues John Hemming and Henry Condell.

In Stratford, Susanna Shakespeare had married John Hall, a doctor of some repute, in June 1607. The Halls occupied New Place after Shakespeare's death, leaving it, in their turn, to their daughter Elizabeth. Elizabeth was twice married, first to Thomas Nash, and after his death to John Bernard. She died at Abington as Lady Bernard in 1670, Shakespeare's last surviving direct descendant. Judith Shakespeare married Thomas Quiney, son of her father's friend Richard Quiney, in February 1616, and survived their three sons to die in 1662. The house in Henley Street commemorated since 1769 as Shakespeare's birthplace was occupied by descendants of his sister, Joan Hart, until 1806.

Shakespeare's will was drafted in January 1616, but Judith's marriage necessitated alterations in it which were made in March and which entailed the rewriting of the first of its three pages: no other feature of it is exceptional. His smaller legacies included 26/8d each to his colleagues John Hemming, Richard Burbage and Henry

Condell to buy memorial rings. He died on 23 April and was buried in the chancel of the Church of the Holy Trinity on 25 April. John Ward, vicar of Stratford in the 1660s, records the story of his death current there at that date:

Shakespeare, Drayton, and Ben Jhonson, had a merry meeting, and itt seems drank too hard, for Shakespear died of a feavour there contracted ...

(Chambers, ii, 250)

The monument in the Stratford church, by Gheerart Janssen, was erected before 1623. It has suffered from restoration and repainting, but it remains, along with Martin Droeshout's engraving for the First Folio, the only visual representation of Shakespeare with any claim to authenticity. Anne Shakespeare continued to live at New Place with the Halls until her death in 1623.

Hemming and Condell did Shakespeare the outstanding service of seeing his plays published. The first collected edition of English plays was Ben Jonson's Folio of 1616. An unauthorized attempt by Thomas Pavier to publish a collected edition of Shakespeare in 1619 was foiled by the intervention of the Lord Chamberlain with the Stationers' Company. Whether activated by Pavier's attempt or carrying out a plan decided on before Shakespeare's death, his colleagues reached an agreement with Pavier's printer, William Jaggard, for an authorized collection. The book, now known as the First Folio, was published in November or December 1623. It contains thirty-six plays, of which seventeen had not previously been printed and a further six had only appeared in memorial texts: these were *The Merry Wives, The Taming of the Shrew, Henry V*, 2 and 3 *Henry VI* and *Richard III*. The remaining thirteen plays had already been published in good texts, most recently *Othello*, in 1622, but the Folio versions of five of them differed materially from those of the earlier Quartos: these were 2 *Henry IV, Troilus and Cressida, Hamlet, King Lear* and *Othello*. The greatest problems facing editors of Shakespeare are in these five plays and in *Richard III*, where choices have to be made between the many variant readings of two versions of each play whose relation to each other is still not completely certain. *Titus Andronicus* and *Richard II* each include a lengthy passage in the Folio which is not found in the Quartos and the remaining six reprinted plays contain occasional minor variations from the Quartos. The Folio omits *Pericles, Sir Thomas More, The Two Noble Kinsmen, Love's Labour's Won* and *Cardenio*, of which the first three are Shakespeare's only in part and the other two cannot certainly be identified. *Timon of Athens* may be an unfinished or collaborative play: the decision to print it was only made when printing was already far advanced.

In an epistle 'To the great variety of Readers', Hemming and Condell claimed that

> ... where (before) you were abus'd with diverse stolne, and surreptitious copies, maimed, and deformed by the frauds and stealthes of injurious impostors, that expos'd them: even those, are now offer'd to your view cur'd, and perfect of their limbes; and all the rest, absolute in their numbers, as he conceived them.
>
> (Chambers, ii, 230)

In substance this claim was justified: the manuscripts from which at least twenty-two of the plays were printed probably included some of Shakespeare's autographs as well as scribal copies carefully made from his papers, of which some were specially made for the printing of the Folio. Where plays in the Folio were printed from Quartos, the copies used were annotated, and corrected, sometimes very extensively, from the company's manuscript prompt-books of the plays. Where the only Quartos provided corrupt texts, those were replaced by good ones.

Many editions of Shakespeare still print his plays in the order adopted in the First Folio, adding *Pericles* at the end. The Folio's rough classification into comedies, histories and tragedies relates only to the subject matter of the plays, although even by these standards its classification of *Cymbeline* as a tragedy seems anomalous. *Troilus and Cressida* appears out of sequence, between the histories and tragedies, for mechanical reasons connected with copyright: it was at first intended to include it among the tragedies. The Folio classification is sanctioned by custom and provides a reminder that discussion of the plays in terms of genre is of limited value. To attempt a chronological arrangement would imply greater certainty about the order of composition than has yet been achieved.

It is nevertheless possible to consider the development of Shakespeare's art in terms of groups of plays chronologically arranged. His plays fall into four fairly coherent groups, related to the fortunes of his company and the progress of his career. The groups necessarily overlap, and his development, though constant, was not linear. The first group comprises the plays written before 1594: already Shakespeare shows his outstanding ability to impart structural and thematic unity to a wide range of material. His language still shows the pervasive influence of school rhetoric, but its relentlessly patterned cleverness goes hand in hand with a pervasive use of metaphor, much of it drawn from everyday life. Many features of the transitional plays, *Romeo and Juliet* and *Love's Labour's Lost*, link them with this group as well as with the second, which consists of the plays for the Chamberlain's men before the opening of the Globe, up to *Henry V*. Expansiveness characterizes the work of this period, which shows a growing self-consciousness about language and stagecraft and a rapidly increasing ability to particularize character made possible by the use of a freer verse movement and, in the later plays, of much prose. Structural experiment leads away from the busy plotting of the earliest plays towards a looser pattern of action whose centre is either a character as in *Richard II*, or a set of ideas, as in *King John* or *2 Henry IV*. The third group, containing the major work of Shakespeare's maturity, begins with *Julius Caesar* and extends to *Coriolanus* and *Timon*, covering the years when the Globe was the company's only theatre. Generalization about Shakespeare's major works is not profitable. What the Globe plays most clearly share is a complexity of poetic organization and a technical command which enables Shakespeare to express the whole range of human passion with a directness and conviction that remains a main reason for the continuing appeal of his work to audiences in a theatre. The basis of his plays is still a narrative, their centre often a single character, but their significance resides more and more in their simultaneous realization of the complex particularity of experience, often conveyed through metaphor, and of a wider order and pattern behind that complexity. The plays after *Pericles* may be associated with the recovery of the Blackfriars theatre, although they were also performed at the Globe. Shakespeare's latest plays retire from the passionate involvement of the tragedies to a cooler, more distant view of their romantic plots. Their 'sophisticated artlessness' expresses itself in an ever-increasing virtuosity with language together with a decreasing concern for verisimilitude in plotting and for individuality in characterization. Within an extended time span the plays include, in diminution, tragic and comic phases of experience and stress the cyclic nature of human existence. They are plays for an escapist audience by a philosophical poet, content to please, but unable to refrain from reflecting on the significance of the stories he is making into plays.

In the 1590s, Shakespeare's rate of composition was about two plays a year, but after the move to the Globe it slowed down to about one play a year. The Globe plays show signs of increasing care in their composition and the company may well have complied with a desire on the part of their leading dramatist to devote more time to each new play than he could afford to in earlier years. His reputation for fluency of composition has been taken too seriously: Ben Jonson stressed his painstaking artistry in the memorial verses he supplied for the Folio.

> . . . that he,
> Who casts to write a living line, must sweat,
>     (such as thine are) and strike the second heat
> Upon the Muses anvile: turne the same,
>     (And himselfe with it) that he thinks to frame;
> Or for the lawrell, he may gaine a scorne,
>     For a good Poet's made, as well as borne.
> And such wert thou.

(Chambers, ii, 209)

The claim that 'hee never blotted out line' (Chambers, ii, 210) can hardly apply to the major plays of his maturity, although the style of the latest plays does show an increasing freedom with syntax and vocabulary, sometimes leading to obscurity, which may be partly the reflection of a growing impatience of second thoughts.

The sense of unity and development in Shakespeare's work reflects the profound difference between his response to the task of writing plays for the public theatres of London and that of many, if not most, of his contemporaries, (one might instance Thomas Dekker or John Fletcher), whose plays succeed each other without revealing any substantial increment of experience, either of life or of art. In his simultaneous concern with the ends and the technique of his art, Shakespeare generally gives an impression of total involvement in his writing that has made it possible for critics and biographers to read his works as a commentary on his intellectual and emotional life. Such attempts are based on questionable assumptions about the relation between life and art and tend to make too easy associations between a philosophy of life attributed to Shakespeare himself and the views expressed by his characters: they ignore the impersonality of the dramatist, whose voice is that of all his characters, and they fail to recognize the extent to which Shakespeare's own supremacy results from his inclusiveness of sympathy and his power to give forceful and sympathetic utterance to diametrically opposite positions within a single play. In this respect Shakespeare is supremely the 'camelion Poet' of Keats's phrase, exhibiting the poetical character that has as much delight in conceiving an Iago as an Imogen and that does no harm from its relish of the dark side of things any more than from its taste for the bright one; because they both end in speculation.[1]

There may be some crudity but there is no naivety in the technique even of the earliest plays and his later work shows Shakespeare's constantly growing self-consciousness about the language and structure of drama. 'More matter with *more* art' would serve as a brief comment on his development, and among the greatest achievements of that art was concealment of itself: the plotting of *A Midsummer Night's Dream* is more elaborate and involves a synthesis of many more various elements than that of *The Comedy of Errors* but it impresses us as by far the simpler play of the two. Shakespeare was not, like Jonson, a critic or a writer of manifestoes, and the imputation, first voiced by Jonson, that he lacked art, has naturally recommended itself to generations of readers who have found in his works an immediately sympathetic humanity lacking in Jonson's own plays. Recent study of Shakespeare has tended increasingly to vindicate his artistry, demonstrating his fine discrimination in selecting and ordering material from his sources, analysing his ever-increasing subtlety and economy in the use of language and showing that the poetic structure of his major plays is so closely unified by the concentration of his imaginative grasp on his subject that hardly a speech can be found whose language and imagery do not relate it to the larger patterns of the whole play. The same intensive study is in danger of lending Shakespeare an academic aura foreign to the nature of his plays and of suggesting, or at least implying, that so consummate an artist could only have written for a highly educated and sophisticated audience. The story of his career indicates that he wrote throughout it for the wide and mixed audience of the public theatres of Elizabethan and Jacobean London.

[1] *The Letters of John Keats*, ed. M. Buxton Forman, 4th edn, London, 1952, p 227.

# SHAKESPEARE: HIS HISTORIES, ENGLISH AND ROMAN

## Philip Brockbank

There was tact and good sense in the decision of the Folio editors to group together as 'Histories' the ten plays about English kings from John to Henry the Eighth; it encourages us to read the plays together, and it eludes problems of definition and description that might have troubled Polonius ('tragical-comical-historical-pastoral') as they have troubled his heirs. By admitting the 'Roman Histories' alongside the English ones we risk too intrusive a preoccupation with the significance of the term 'history', with questions both comprehensive and particular. If we assume that history consists in the recognition of events and the mastery of facts, we may find it relevant to ask why Holinshed tells us that 'six counterfeit husbandmen' were used by the English to release prisoners at Cornhill while in the play (*I Henry VI*, Act 3 Scene 2) the trick is played by the French at Rouen, or why Shakespeare does not recognize that Cleopatra collaborated with Octavius and offered to assassinate Antony. If we believe history to be immediately expressive of the political situation of its makers, we may more confidently ask about the analogues between (say) the stage Henry V and the contemporary Earl of Essex. Responding, however, to the great diversity of interpretations of history current in Shakespeare's time, we may find the appropriate critical freedom and challenges. We do well to remember that Machiavelli believed that history would yield its patterns to systematic study, that Jean Bodin saw history as an instrument of political propaganda, and that Grynaeus thought it the key to the moral purposes of God.[1] But while these and other available concepts may offer creative approaches to Shaespeare's art as a history playwright, they are not its boundaries. Through the immense variety of achievements that link *Henry VI* with *Antony and Cleopatra* it is possible to trace Shakespeare's developing understanding of the way in which human consciousness both shapes and is shaped by the apparently impersonal and ineluctable movement of events. But however the later plays

[1] See L. B. Campbell, *Shakespeare's 'Histories': Mirrors of Elizabethan Policy*, San Marino, 1947.

may surpass the early ones in this or any other Shakespearean sequence, they do not displace them; each play makes its distinctive discoveries and its own contribution to Shakespeare's sense of the past.

The emergence of the history play was itself an historical event over which, it might be claimed, Shakespeare presided. A passage in Nashe's *Pierce Penniless* (1592) has been taken to indicate that a flourishing genre of 'chronicle plays' anticipated Shakespeare's first essays in history. But if we survey the two dozen surviving plays that Nashe might have had in mind when he rejoiced to see 'our forefather's valiant acts, that have lien long buried in rusty brass and worm-eaten books . . . raised from the grave of oblivion', we can find none that compare with Shakespeare's *Henry VI* in their patient attention to chronicle interpretation, in detail and in grand design. That Nashe was writing with Shakespeare in mind seems the more likely when his allusion to plays borrowed out of chronicles is set alongside his tribute to a play about the Earl of Talbot in the next paragraph of *Pierce Penniless*.[1]

How would it have joyed brave *Talbot* (the terror of the French) to thinke that after he had lyne two hundred yeares in his Tombe, hee should triumphe againe on the stage, and have his bones newe embalmed with the teares of ten thousand spectators at least, (at severall times) who, in the Tragedian that represents his person, imagine they behold him fresh bleeding.

It looks like a clear recognition of the epic and memorial quality of the scenes of Talbot's death in *I Henry VI*.

From the debris of textual and circumstantial evidence, however, we cannot now be certain of the dates and the sequence of the early plays of the Wars of the Roses; their authorship has been questioned, and attempts have been made to establish their dependence on other plays, both extant and hypothetical. In 1594 an anonymous quarto was published under the title, 'The first part of the Contention betwixt the two famous Houses of Yorke and Lancaster'; and it was followed in 1595 by an octavo, 'The true Tragedie of Richard Duke of Yorke, and the death of good King Henrie the Sixt'. These were once thought to be the sources of *Parts 2* and *3* of *Henry VI*, but they are now generally acknowledged to be 'bad' texts memorially or otherwise reconstructed from versions of the Folio plays. Henslowe's diaries record fourteen

[1] E. K. Chambers, *William Shakespeare*, Oxford, 1930, ii, 188.

successful performances of 'Harey the vj' between 3 March and 20 June 1592, with the mark 'ne' against the first entry, suggesting that it was new. We do not know if the entry refers to any one or to all three parts of *Henry VI* (consecutively performed), but that *Part 3* was known in 1592 is indicated by Robert Greene's use of a line from it shortly before his death on September 9, when he brought his notorious charge against Shakespeare:[1]

for there is an upstart Crow, beautified with our feathers, that with his *Tygers hart wrapt in a Players hyde*, supposes he is as well able to bombast out a blanke verse as the best of you . . . being . . . in his owne conceite the onely Shake-scene in a countrie.

Since the theatres were closed on 23 June, the evidence could suggest that the three parts were produced within three or four months. Some have found this hard to believe and have therefore argued that their authorship was divided and that the first part was written as an after-thought in 1592 when the other plays had been staged in the previous season. The writing of the plays, however, may have been leisured while their performance was hasty, with all three composed long before they were offered to Henslowe, at the very outset of Shakespeare's career in the theatre. Greene's jealousy might be accounted for by postulating that he was the author of a lost play on Henry V, perhaps the one that has reached us anonymously in the 'bad' text of *The Famous Victories of Henry V*.

That the *Henry VI* plays were carefully planned in advance is firmly indicated by the division of the source material between them.[2] *Part 1* draws most fully on the first forty pages of the reign in the 1587 edition of Holinshed, *Part 2* on the next twenty and *Part 3* on the remaining fifty. There is evidence too that Shakespeare glanced elsewhere in Holinshed and that he consulted other chronicles (notably Hall and Fabyan) as well as Foxe's *Book of Martyrs*. Much systematic study went to the making of the plays. The phases of the chronicle coincide with the dominant themes of the three parts, and each calls for its own mode of presentation: the loss of France, the martyrdom of the Duke of Gloucester, and the final catastrophe climaxed by Richard's slaughter of Henry.

---

[1] E. K. Chambers, *William Shakespeare*, ii, 188.

[2] For a fuller account of the sources see Geoffrey Bullough, *Narrative and Dramatic Sources of Shakespeare*, Vol. III, London, 1960, and J. P. Brockbank, 'The Frame of Disorder – "Henry VI"' *Early Shakespeare*, ed. J. R. Brown and B. Harris, London, 1961. Throughout this Chapter most source quotations can be readily located in the relevant volume of Bullough.

The theme of *Part I* required primarily a pageant of banners and devices, expressing in spectacle the changing fortunes of the war with France and the 'civil broils' at home. The stage-directions alone display the direction and even the structure of the history, from the funeral of Henry V, past the triumph of Joan in sword-fight over the French nobles, the brawl between blue coats and tawny coats outside the Tower, the boy with a linstock sniping Salisbury at Orleans (as the upper stage serves for town walls), to the plucking of the roses in the Temple garden, the death of Talbot, the impeachment of Joan, and the precarious ceremonies of fealty in the last act. The demands upon Shakespeare's art are of a limited and limiting kind. The poetry moves within the boundaries of the chronicle's understanding, often assimilating its phrases and metaphors. Holinshed, for example, says of the quarrel between Gloucester and Winchester that it was 'a great division . . . which of a sparkle was like to have grown to a great flame', and Shakespeare's Duke of Exeter is made to speak for him:

> This late dissension grown betwixt the peers
> Burns under feigned ashes of forged love
> And will at last break out into a flame.
>
> (3. 1. 189–94)

Shakespeare recasts the intricate battle material, clarifies and simplifies the quarrels of the nobility, ritualizes and intensifies the significant tensions of the reign, in order to be true not to the events only, but to their chronicle interpretation. The fictitious scene at Rouen (Act 3, Scene 2) which begins by attributing an English disguise trick to the French, ends with preparation for Bedford's exequies, and conveys very fittingly two of Holinshed's judgements upon the course of the history: the French won by subtlety, deceit and witchcraft what they could not hope to win by force, and after the death of Bedford 'the bright sunne in France toward Englishmen, began to be cloudie, and dailie to darken'.

The play reaches its crisis when Talbot dies because York ('louted by a traitor villain') and Somerset ('sulking at the unheedful, desperate, wild adventure') fail to reach Bordeaux in time. The arms of the dead father become 'young John Talbot's grave' and the play pauses, as before a monument, while Sir William Lucy ('attended: a French Herald preceding') intones the many titles of honour due to him under the old dispensation ('Worthy Saint Michael and the Golden Fleece'). Joan's jeer, 'Him that thou magnifi'st with all these titles/Stinking and flyblown lies here at our feet', measures the distance both between the English past and the English present, and between the vanities of chivalry and the grim truths of human mortality; and it returns us to the hygiene of battle. In other respects too, the play rawly but poignantly creates and destroys heroic dreams. The war with France is on both sides both brave and futile; Joan is fashioned both to honour the French claim for her (particularly in her plea to Burgundy in Act 3 Scene 3) and to justify the English charges against her. The harshness of the interpretation has given offence but it is true to the double force of the chronicle, which assimilates two rival accounts, and it creates a disconcerting theatrical figure. Similarly, the dynastic clash of York and Lancaster is at once fatuous, and a poised, stylized realization of rival vanities of power. The Temple garden scene (Act 2 Scene 4) is a fiction, but an historically appropriate one that conveys very precisely the commitment to emblems and heraldic devices which characterized the war and its memorials:

> And, by my soul, this pale and angry rose,
> As cognizance of my blood-drinking hate,
> Will I for ever and my faction wear,
> Until it wither with me to my grave
> Or flourish to the height of my degree.

> > (2. 4. 107–11)

Fear of civil war and anxiety about rights of dynastic succession were dominant in political and historical plays of the period, from *Patient Grissell* and *Gorboduc* in the 1560s to *Macbeth* and *Perkin Warbeck* in the reign of King James or later, but the plays of *Henry VI* do more to master the chronicled past in the service of contemporary political understanding than any that came before or after.

*Part 2* of the play owes to the chronicle its elementary but often poignant discovery that the virtues of the king are not the kingly virtues. 'In hym reigned shamefastnesse', wrote Hall, 'modestie, integritie, and pacience to bee marveiled at, takying and sufferyng all losses, chaunces, displeasures, and suche worldely tormentes, in good parte, and with a pacient manner, as though they had chaunced by his awne fault or negligent oversight.' The queen, however, has the rival and, as events prove, incompatible qualities: 'a woman of a great witte, and yet of no greater witte, than of haute stomacke, desirous of glory, and covetous of honor, and of reason, pollicye, counsaill, and other giftes and talentes of nature belongyng to a man, full and flowyng.' The rival values of king and queen are the equivalent in human character to the tension felt throughout the chronicle between competing historical visions, sacrificial and Machiavellian. From one point of view Henry embodies an authentic innocence, and a truth that cannot be outraged without catastrophic consequences for the realm – an atonement by blood sacrifice. But from another he culpably lacks the skill and ruthlessness proper to a ruler – a Machiavellian truth that the chroniclers did not need to learn from Machiavelli, particularly as Tito Livio, one of Machiavelli's mentors, was court-historian to Henry V.

Henry's most poignant witness to the more vulnerable virtues, however, is focused not upon himself but upon the figure of Gloucester:

> And as the butcher takes away the calf
> And binds the wretch and beats it when it strays,
> Bearing it to the bloody slaughter-house,
> Even so remorseless have they borne him hence.
>
> (3. 1. 210–13)

Gloucester's impotence, unlike Henry's, owes nothing to moral weakness; it is owed rather to the destruction of the stabilities of government by malignant faction:

> Ah, gracious lord, these days are dangerous:
> Virtue is choked with foul ambition,
> And charity chased hence by rancour's hand.
>
> (3. 1. 142–4)

The point is made out of Holinshed ('Justice and equitie clearelie exiled') but with a theatrical precision to be fully realized in the next scene when Gloucester is literally as well as figuratively 'choked'. The analogue between the plots of politicians and the plots of the playmaker is precipitating its ironies even in this early work:

> I know their complot is to have my life,
> And if my death might make this island happy,
> And prove the period of their tyranny,
> I would expend it with all willingness:
> But mine is made the prologue to their play;
> For thousands more, that yet suspect no peril,
> Will not conclude their potted tragedy.
>
> (3. 1. 147–54)

But as in the history, so in the play, some plots are more manifest than others, and Shakespeare expresses the covert opportunism of

Richard of York by allowing him in the theatre the prerogative of confidential soliloquy; where Hall says that although York was in Ireland 'yet his breath puffed, and his wynde blew dayly, in many partes of the Realme', the York of the play tells the audience that from Ireland he will stir up a storm 'shall blow ten thousand souls to heaven or hell'. Thus the theatre convention serves the history with great immediacy and the audience becomes party to the enterprise and malice of the Machiavellian politician; it is a technique that Shakespeare with intricate variations deploys through *Richard III* to *Othello*.

The unity of the play owes much to Shakespeare's recognition that York used the Cade rebellion to exploit the chaos that opens upon Gloucester's slaughter; the 'spleenful mutiny' of the commons is carried over into the Blackheath and Smithfield of the last acts, with interludes for the deaths of Winchester (by phantasmagoric guilt and terror) and of Suffolk (by malignant popular justice). The pattern of violence, however, is not determined by the class conflict between the 'infinite numbers' of the market place and the soldiery of Sir Humphrey Stafford. It happens that the virulent ambition and hostility to law that characterized the barons of the third act, equally characterize the workmen of the fourth. Borrowing material from the chronicle account of the Tyler rebellion, Shakespeare makes Cade's followers kill the lawyers, pull down the Inns of Court, and bear upon a pole the head of the Lord Chief Justice. The chronicles, however, and the anonymous play *Jack Straw* allow vulgar rebellion to fade in the bright light of kingly magnanimity, while Shakespeare's Clifford diverts it to his own cause, with a charismatic memory of Henry V, and a hint that the meanest will become 'earls and dukes' when they renew the war with France. The effect is to win sympathy for Cade:

The name of Henry the Fifth hales them to an hundred mischiefs and makes them leave me desolate.

(4. 8. 56–8)

and his defeat is an effect of plebeian treachery before his death at the hands of the 'esquire of Kent' is made symbol for the momentary restoration of a patrician order.

The second part ends on the battlefield of St Albans, dominated by the nihilistic vision of the young Clifford:

Shame and confusion! all is on the rout;
Fear frames disorder, and disorder wounds
Where it should guard . . .

(5. 2. 32–4)

The internecine terror is such that soldiers kill their fellows as readily as their enemies, and out of the ugly chronicle fact the poetry makes a frightening apocalypse:

> O, let the vile world end,
> And the premised flames of the Last Day
> Knit earth and heaven together!
> Now let the general trumpet blow his blast,
> Particularities and petty sounds
> To cease!
>
> (5. 2. 40–5)

In *Part 3* of the play Clifford's devotion to atrocity and to cataclysm is confronted by the gay histrionic malevolence of Richard of Gloucester; but it may be said that the second is generated by the first, and that it is the more evil because the fitter to survive. In a scene (Act 1 Scene 4) carefully fashioned from the chronicle material Shakespeare makes of the Battle of Wakefield a ritual destruction of all humane values. Kingship, knighthood, womanliness and fatherhood are ceremoniously desecrated in a stage recreation of what was in historical fact a cruel theatrical fantasy, with a mock coronation ('as the Jewes did unto Christ') that might have been imitated from a miracle play, and a bloody handkerchief that might have been borrowed from English Seneca:

> This cloth thou dip'dst in blood of my sweet boy,
> And I with tears do wash the blood away.
>
> (1. 4. 157–8)

The purging of the Wakefield barbarities is a dual process of pain inflicted and pain suffered. The messenger's tale of Rutland's end and York's clarifies the murderous, recriminatory and witty resolution of Richard (2. 2. 79–88) which finds its fullest expression in the celebrated soliloquy closing Act 3 Scene 2. Shakespeare attributes to Richard both the actor's and the politician's command of human nature, and with a further development of the soliloquy convention he allows him full sovereignty of the theatre.

The sovereignty of the land, however, is farcically divided throughout the third and fourth acts of the play. The impotence and isolation of Henry, lyrically voiced in the nostalgic pastoral soliloquy at Towton (2. 5. 1–54) where it had set the mess of the war in an ampler natural and human perspective, now becomes a theme for irony and comic spectacle. Warwick for a while is stage-manager to the comedy in which King Edward as well as King Henry is made to play a passive role (especially in Act 4 Scene 3, where Warwick snatches the king 'in his gown, sitting in a chair' and takes off his crown). Authority is, to use Holinshed's word, 'imbecilled'; made impotent and ridiculous by the oscillations of power.

In its last phase, however, *Part 3* finds new resources of authority in Henry's despised virtues (pity, mildness, mercy and love) and the king-slaying becomes the play's most significant act – morally, historically and theatrically. From one point of view it is Shakespeare's first essay in the direction of *Macbeth*; kingship owes its sanctity to the vulnerable and innocent qualities that sustain it (Duncan bore 'his faculties so meek' and was 'clear in his great office'), and outrage upon those qualities returns the realm to that bloody 'olden time, Ere humane statute purg'd the gentle weal'. Moved by this tragic insight, accepting the sacrificial rather than the Machiavellian interpretation of the course of events, Shakespeare virtually ignores what Hall had styled 'the prosperous reign of Edward IV'. Richard emerges as the Machiavel ordained for slaughter, his wit and political skill purging the commonweal by the shedding of blood.

It is probable that *Richard III* was written late in 1592 or in 1593 and first performed in 1594. In historical substance and in theatre technique there is a vital continuity with the earlier plays, but there is too an access of energy and liberated understanding as Shakespeare, freed from the obligation to order the sprawl of forty years of chronicled incident, gives decisive dramatic form to the events of 1477 to 1485. Much of the shaping of the historical myth had indeed already been accomplished in the chronicle account through the contributions of Polydore Vergil and Thomas More. Here, for example, is Hall's comment on the appearance of Richard before the people at Baynard's Castle, where by collusion with Buckingham he affects to refuse and then accept the crown:

But the people departed talkynge of the matter, every man as his fantasye gave him, but much they marveiled at this maner of dealing, that the matter was on both parties made so strange as though never the one part had communed with the other part thereof before, when they wiste that there was no manne so dull that heard them, but he perceyved well enough that all the matter was made betwene them. ... And so they saied, these matters be kynges games, as it were staige playes, and for the most part plaied upon scaffoldes, in which poore menne bee but lookers on, and they that wise be, will medle no farther, for they that steppe up with them when they cannot play their parts, they disorder the plaie and do their selves no good.

The incident itself is mounted by Shakespeare almost as a play within a play (Act 3 Scene 7) and the temper of the first three acts makes politics a king's game best played by accomplished actors.

Richard is bred out of the history for the service of the theatre, a master actor and a master plotter, and the executor of three kinds of law – comic, tragic and historical: comic, because he is a knave among gulls, seducing by wit and murdering by intrigue; tragic, because he both undergoes and inflicts upon others an ordeal of guilt and expiation; historical, because he is the agent of the ruthless chronicle providence whose choric voice is the play's Queen Margaret. For the greater part of the first three acts the comic mode prevails, with Richard allowed the buoyancy and moral force that stage tradition gave to the Vice, the Devil and such figures as Ambidexter and Dissimulation. Those who suffer do so within the boundaries of Senecal tragedy – Elizabeth plays a 'scene of rude impatience . . . to make an act of tragic violence', and Margaret is witness of 'a dire induction' to a 'frantic play' and 'direful pageant'. The courtship of Queen Anne is dramatic proof that the devilish comic rhetoric is more potent in human exchanges than the Senecal tragic. Richard for a while is master of events and all his earlier victims deserve to die in expurgation of the crimes inherited from the past.

The play's *peripetaeia*, its tragic reversal, occurs when Richard, mounting the throne, decides to kill the princes – his first authentically innocent victims. The change in his soliloquies registers his forfeiture of prerogative, for they are no longer confident and confidential but tense, inward and self-consuming. The play-acting falters and fails; in an early scene with Hastings (Act 3 Scene 4) Richard pretended to lose his temper; now in face of a recalcitrant Buckingham (Act 4 Scene 2), and later before the messengers (Act 4 Scene 4), he loses it indeed. Self-control and control of events are yielded at the same moment to the laws of expiation and nemesis that the play imitates from the history, and when Richard summons his last resources of vitality and wit in his wooing of Queen Elizabeth for her daughter (Act 4 Scene 4), neither the character Richard nor the playwright Shakespeare can convince us that another success of that sort is probable or possible. All that is left for the Richard of the last scenes is a nihilistic commitment to force, in an attempt to destroy by violence the moral and historical laws that announce themselves in a nightmare (as Polydore Vergil had reported) and fulfil themselves on the field of Bosworth.

There are in the chronicle two large causal processes that might fairly be called 'extra-personal': the Old Testament law of retribution, and the Tudor dynastic myth proclaiming the 'Union of the two noble families of Lancaster and York'. Both are celebrated in the play and both exposed to severe criticism. In order to display the contingencies of the history, to show how the punitive murders were carried out, Shakespeare made the immediate plot the expression of Richard's witty human will, but to reveal the larger chronicle law of retribution he made the comprehensive plot a projection of Margaret's will. Thus the devil makes Richard his factor and God makes Margaret his prophet, and the devil in the play becomes the servant of God; but it is God as the chronicle enlists him. Because Margaret's prophecies come true they have the authority of Providence behind them, but because they are also curses they express a tawdry human spleen which taints the moral order of the history:

> Did York's dread curse prevail so much with heaven
> That Henry's death, my lovely Edward's death,
> Their kingdom's loss, my woeful banishment,
> Should all but answer for that peevish brat?
>
> (1. 3. 191–4)

The play's answer to this and to her next question, 'Can curses pierce the clouds and enter heaven?' must be 'yes'.

In the scene of Clarence's death Shakespeare exposes the chronicle retribution to another criticism, for Clarence is made the spokesman of a Christian providence far more human than that which the history offers:

CLARENCE:    If God will be avengéd for the deed,
             O, know you yet he doth it publicly.
             Take not the quarrel from his powerful arm;
             He needs no indirect or lawless course
             To cut off those that have offended him.

I MURDERER:  Who made thee then a bloody minister,
             When gallant-springing brave Plantagenet,
             That princely novice, was struck dead by thee?
                                        (1. 4. 215–22)

Throughout the scene biblical texts are adroitly, comically manipulated, as Clarence fights with his wits to save himself, but he is at the same time the voice of an outraged moral sense and he moves the second murderer towards sparing him. Yet to spare Clarence would be to foil at once the course of the chronicle's justice and the antic guile of Richard.

The ironies that play upon the chronicle theology recoil too upon its movement towards dynastic union. An early Latin tragedy, Thomas Legge's *Ricardus Tertius* had in 1579 made Richmond's victory occasion for a dynastic compliment to Elizabeth on 'the happy uniting of both houses of whom the Queenes majesty came', and the closing speech of Shakespeare's play is in the same tradition from Hall's celebrated title:

The Union of the Two noble and illustre families of Lancaster and York, being long in continual dissension for the crown of this noble realm, with all the acts done in both the times of the princes, both of the one lineage and of the other, beginning at the time of King Henry the Fourth, the first author of this division, and so successively proceeding to the reign of the high and prudent prince King Henry the Eighth, the indubitable flower and very heir of the said lineages.

Over the range of histories from *Richard II* to *Richard III* the resolution of dynastic conflict is a distinct and sometimes eloquent theme: through the prophecy of Carlisle in *Richard II*, the guilty, sickly perplexities of Henry IV, the respite won by the valour and magnanimity of Henry V, the culpable weakness of Henry VI, the emergence of the scapegoat Richard of Gloucester, to the magical triumph of Henry Tudor. But in each phase contending truths are inhibiting or destroying the myth: the self-regarding impotence of Richard II, the Machiavellian skills of Prince Hal and John of Lancaster, the moral force of the martyred Henry·VI, and the savage ironies of *Richard III*.

Thomas More broke off his history at the point where Richard takes the throne, at his zenith on Fortune's wheel, but he left it ripe for development into sacrificial tragedy. Richard carried on humped shoulders all the sins of the realm and his killer promised to have the stature of a redeemer, a St George, a dragon-slayer. Some thirty years later Hall was to describe Richmond as 'more like an angelical creature than a terrestial personage' but More, writing under the crowned Richmond, Henry VII, had reason to regard him as a very terrestial personage indeed. Shakespeare eludes the embarrassment by leaving the reign of Henry VII untouched, and his Richmond at the end is able to address an Elizabethan audience ready enough to rejoice that 'Civil wounds are stopped' and 'peace lives again', but that audience would have no delusions about the rival lineages; they knew them for what they were.

It has long been believed that *King John* was written after the first Roses tetralogy and largely adapted from the anonymous play, *The Troublesome Raigne of King John*, which was published in 1591. The belief has made it possible to explain with facility both the comparative maturity of some passages of its verse and the apparent clumsiness of its construction. It has also been claimed, however, by arguments hard either to admit or wholly to set aside, that the 1591 play was derived from Shakespeare's and that *King John* therefore belongs to the late 1580s.[1] The data are intricate and intractable, consisting in part of minute interrelationships between the texts and in part of allusions to recent and contemporary events, in particular to the ordeal and death of Mary Stuart and its attendant political turbulence. The surviving facts, however, allow us only to suppose that the extant text of *The Troublesome Raigne*, with its many fragmentary recollections of other plays, is a reconstructed or pirated version of an earlier play whose relationship with *King John* must remain obscure. Literary criticism and history can only attempt to indicate the distinctive contribution that Shakespeare appears to have made to the theatre's understanding of the historical and political experience of John's reign.

It appears from Bishop John Leslie's *A defence of the honour of Marie Quene of Scotlande* (1569, reprinted 1571 and 1584) that the analogue between Queen Mary and Prince Arthur had been used by both Protestant and Catholic parties and it may plausibly be claimed of either play that the relationship between John and Hubert resembled that between Elizabeth and her Secretary of State William Davidson, who was made scapegoat for Mary's death. The political hazards of the theme must have been considerable – a circumstance perhaps reflected in the anonymity and muddled two-part state of *The Troublesome Raigne*, and in the delay in printing *King John* for the first time in the 1623 Folio. *The Troublesome Raigne*, however, like Bishop Bale's old play *King Johan*, is an unequivocal Protestant tract: John is more commemorated for his stand against the Pope's legate than censored for his part in Arthur's death, and the England of the play is an anti-papal fortress with the Bastard Fawconbridge as its most resolute voice. Shakespeare's play flourishes by more complex laws of growth, its structure allegorically expressing the death of English innocence. The effects of pathos built up about the boy prince whose name had for Tudor audiences an almost magical significance, make him in small way the heir to the qualities of mercy, peace and love prefigured in Henry VI. Arthur jumps to his death with the words:

> O me! my uncle's spirit is in these stones.
> Heaven take my soul, and England keep my bones!
>
> (4. 3. 9–10)

[1] See E. A. J. Honigmann, ed. *King John* (Arden Shakespeare), London, 1954.

The destruction of Arthur's fragile innocent body becomes for the Bastard a metaphor expressing the political and moral plight of the state:

> How easy dost thou take all England up
> From forth this morsel of dead royalty,
> The life, the right and truth of all this realm
> Is fled to heaven; and England now is left
> To tug and scamble, and to part by th'teeth
> The unowed interest of proud-swelling state.
>
> (4. 3. 142–7)

The Bastard recognizes that the England to which he now owes his allegiance is the internecine and 'proud-swelling' state. There is from this point no question of his forgiving a repentant John; the motives of patriotism become wholesomely Machiavellian, for while the Bastard cannot redeem the fled innocence, he can with his sword and his rhetoric salvage something from the moral mess:

> I am amazed, methinks, and lose my way
> Among the thorns and dangers of this world . . .
>
> (4. 3. 140–1)
>
> Now, for the bare-picked bone of majesty,
> Doth dogged war bristle his angry crest,
> And snarleth in the gentle eyes of peace:
> Now powers from home and discontents at home
> Meet in one line; and vast confusion waits,
> As doth a raven on a sick-fall'n beast,
> The imminent decay of wrested pomp.
>
> (4. 3. 148–54)

The Bastard's vision dominates this phase of the play. He outfights the French and outscolds them in the 'brabblings' of battle, in the great violent game of war, for violence is in his catechism a purer moral force·than politic compromise and 'commodity'. The nobles who desert to France fail to recognize that the moral corruption of England is ubiquitous, and the treachery which they indulge from the highest motives is retorted against them by the French from the lowest.

In the first part of the play personal heroism can look like virtue in the frame of unprincipled, cowardly makeshift, but the unhistorical conjunction of the death of Arthur (1203) with the baron's rebellion (1216) and John's yielding of the crown (1213) precipitates in both plays instabilities of value and allegiance that cannot be kept under control. The tensions are evaded in *The*

*Troublesome Raigne* by displays of facile chauvinism ('The English Archers have their quivers full') but in *King John* values and allegiances grow strained and ambiguous: Arthur is betrayed by the French, killed by the English; Europe is ruled by the expedient treacheries of both court and Church; the nobles who fight for right and truth are manifest traitors while the patriot Bastard serves a corrupt sovereign. Unlike the author of *The Troublesome Raigne*, who makes much of the pillaging of the monasteries, Shakespeare gives the monks no motive for poisoning John. It is enough that he is literally and metaphorically burned out:

> I am a scribbled form drawn with a pen
> Upon a parchment, and against this fire
> Do I shrink up.

> (5. 7. 32–4)

The King of both the history and the theatre was too passive a figure, too little the master of events, to serve as a tragic hero. The final note of the play is resonant bravado in a pageant manner well becoming to the decade of the Armada.

Shakespeare's return to the history play may have been prompted by the publication of Samuel Daniel's *Civil Wars* in 1595, since this is counted among the minor sources of *Richard II*. But the theatre offered other stimuli too; among the several English-history plays of the early 1590s were the anonymous *Woodstock*, Marlowe's *Edward II* and the anonymous *Edward III*.

*Woodstock*, owing a little to 2 *Henry VI*, vindicated the democratic English virtues of plain living and good husbandry, and King Richard's offences appear to be against the respect that he properly owes to Parliament. *Edward II* exhibits a king both vicious and victimized, disreputable in his cult of minions yet dying a martyr. Shakespeare's *Richard II* tactfully takes his bearings from *Woodstock* when Gaunt makes Woodstock's death the opening memory of his melancholy colloquy at Plashy, and in handling the misgovernment theme he contrives to keep his distance from Marlowe. It is moreover distinguished from the earlier plays by its greater historicity – not for its attentiveness to fact (which is rivalled by *Woodstock*), nor for its capacity to dramatize the chronicler's moral voice (*Edward II* does that very precisely), but for the pressure of the past on the play's present. In *Woodstock* and *Edward II* we are left with the impression that the mess of the realm is the full responsibility of those who made it; but in *Richard II* we are made to recognize that much has gone before and much has still to come.

Shakespeare's sense of the impersonal movement of events, acquired through the arduous schooling of the Roses plays, is now refined and related much more precisely to the intimate sensibility of their kingly agent. It is a feat of style; for although the style of *Richard II* resembles that of *Romeo and Juliet* and is attributable to an early phase of Shakespeare's mature development, it is used upon the historical material to historical purpose. Shakespeare's plays of fifteenth-century English history are about the paradoxes of power: power ought to be the ceremonious exercise of high moral authority, but the historical facts do not admit it. In *Richard II* the ceremony that makes 'high majesty look like itself' fails as a vehicle of government but proves a source of solace to the abdicating king; it is politically sterile but personally efficacious.

It has been claimed that in his preparation for *Richard II* Shakespeare specifically read Holinshed, Hall, Froissart, two versions of a French MS chronicle *La Traison et Mort de Richard Deux*, Créton's *Histoire*, *Woodstock* and Daniel's *Civil Wars*.[1] Apart from reservations about the accessibility of the manuscript material, there is no reason why Shakespeare's interest in the reign should not have taken him to all these sources; the play nevertheless would have been substantially the same had he read nothing outside Holinshed. More significant than the diversity of the chronicle material is its richness in accounts of tournament and pageantry, making it ripe for a pageant mode of theatre. It is probable that the play was enacted in front of that traditional pageant property, the tournament façade – a castle wall, decorated with banners and heraldic devices. In the first phase the façade is background for a throne, for a display of the rituals of government and tournament justice, and for the death of Gaunt (a death-bed memorial to England's chivalrous past under Edward III). As the play advances the importance of the façade diminishes, the splendours and symmetries of public show give place to more intimate episodes of power exercised, mourned or abdicated. The readiest way to recognize the consonance between the movement of events and the changing significance of theatrical ceremony is to compare the three scenes in which appeals are heard before authority – the first of the play, the first of Act 4 (when Fitzwater and Aumerle appear before Bolingbroke) and the third of Act 5 (when Aumerle and the Duchess plead for pardon).

In the first scene authority in the person of Richard presides from

[1] See Peter Ure, ed. *Richard II* (Arden Shakespeare), London, 1956.

the throne in full decorum, with each participant observing with precision the rules of speech and gesture designed for the occasion; the conventions of tournament are themselves the principal source of theatrical art. The language exploits the movement and metaphor of tournament ('giving reins and spurs to my free speech'), and it is no use probing beneath the bright armour of the style for the circumspect souls of Bolingbroke and Mowbray, for they are contestants in the verbal lists; we judge their skills more readily than their causes, in their territories of honour rather than of law.

For the appeal scene which virtually opens Bolingbroke's reign (Act 4 Scene 1) Shakespeare contrives a conspicuous decline in rhetorical address. Bolingbroke does not affect to compete; where Richard had declared his judicial role in nine lines beginning 'Mowbray, impartial are our eyes and ears' (1. 1. 115), Bolingbroke prevails with 'Call forth Bagot,/Now Bagot, freely speak thy mind.' The appellants persist in the old modes of speech, but without the old mastery. Shakespeare relaxes his control of ceremonious hyperbole to make the squabble uglier and its energies more dangerous, and to make Bolingbroke's laconic interventions the more decisive. The play no longer invites us to enjoy tournament rhetoric for its own sake, but rather to keep our ears tuned for the idiom that makes Bolingbroke 'thrive in this new world'; his brevities cut like sword-thrusts through the embroidery of the dialogue. The spectacle endorses the effects of the language. In the first scene Richard *presided* from the throne, but in Act 4 Scene 1 Bolingbroke *dominates* the stage platform; it is only when all the essential business has been done that he moves 'in God's name' to 'ascend the regal throne'. Power has been exercised but ceremony slighted. This is the context of word and spectacle that makes Carlisle's protest (Act 4 Scene 1) so impressive, for it is precisely a protest against the exercise of power without the ritual authority to endorse it, without the sanctity of annointment. But 'the figure of God's majesty' of Carlisle's account has become a cypher. When Richard is called in, it is in response to Bolingbroke's laconic purpose and not to Carlisle's eloquence: 'So we shall proceed without suspicion.'

The third appeal, Aumerle's in Act 5 Scene 3, is often cut from performances; but here authority has become peremptory and all ceremony turned to farce. A private rumination upon Prince Hal is interrupted by Aumerle 'amazed' and refusing to talk until the door is locked. With York shouting to be let in, the effect of the king trying to keep his temper in the face of crazy relatives is inescapable.

A momentary recovery of the old ceremonious hyperbole, as Bolingbroke responds to York's gestures of allegiance – 'Thou sheer, immaculate and silver fountain' – yields to new absurdities with the clamorous entry of the Duchess.

While the appeal scenes are not the key to the play, they do demonstrate the continuing, almost unseen, gravitation of power and allegiance to Bolingbroke, as the ceremonious rhetoric associated with government at the start of the play is exhausted. The gravitation of power is significantly impersonal. Bolingbroke enlists the populace and returns from Ireland not for England but for Lancaster. There are no battles, riots or street scenes, but the sense of a false order dissolving grows with the discovery that Richard's authority is merely a show, a pageant, like the stage-setting and like the language. But as the ceremonious spectacle and language cease to order the course of events, Shakespeare diverts them to another purpose, and through the figures of Gaunt, the Duchess of Gloucester, Richard, York and the Queen, and even the gardeners, makes them the vehicle of nostalgic emotional consolation. Gaunt redeems himself from the incapacities of guilt, age, and disease by acting out the role of dying prophet, the Duchess by acting out her mourning ('Desolate, desolate, will I hence and die'), York by performing the part of perfect subject to each king in his turn. Richard redeems himself, in his own eyes and before his audience, by his fulfilment of the kingly roles that circumstance requires him to play.

He is first the king in office, the megaphone voice of authority, the president of the lists. Off the throne he plays the impulsive reckless sophisticate ('Pray God we may make haste and come too late'), bungling the Irish affair, grabbing money and jeering at Gaunt; this is the man of 'wicked and naughty demeanour' described by the chronicles, and might be taken for the 'natural' Richard were it not for its manifest affectation. When he returns from Ireland the petulance is shed, and through the superb self-dramatizations of the third and fourth acts he plays the part of abdicating king. His language entertains the great medieval themes – the wheel of fortune, *contemptus mundi*, the dance of death and the sanctity of sovereignty, but when it has served its turn as aesthetic and imaginative consolation to the man Richard, there is nothing more it can do. It cannot salvage his political power nor stop him from sharing the vulnerabilities of other men. His public self-dramatization reaches its climax where he compares himself with Christ:

> Did they not sometime cry 'all hail' to me?
> So Judas did to Christ

(5. 1. 169–70)

The passage prompted one critic to call *Richard II* 'Shakespeare's miracle play',[1] but the miracle play is not Shakespeare's precisely, it is Richard's. Shakespeare perhaps got the idea from an observation of Holinshed's on the King's responsiveness to flattery. Bushie, he says, 'invented unused termes, and such strange names as were rather agreeable to the divine majestie of God, than to any earthly potentate'. Yet the miracle-play pose is moving both because the King speaks from his office and because the claims for sanctity are consciously ironic, made in the process of discovering his own poignant weakness. The last scenes at Pomfret require Richard (like Gaunt) to make a good end, one rich in mockery of personal vanity and impotence but still with its consolatory virtuosity – 'But for the concord of my state and time/Had not an ear to hear my true time broke'. His death purges from the commonwealth those ceremonies of authority that in his reign were dislocated from efficient government, and it is attended by a kind of self-knowledge; it is therefore a tragedy, and was aptly so described by Francis Meres in *Palladis Tamia*. Since there is reason to believe that it was performed under the patronage of the Essex faction, and that the omission of the deposition scene (4. 1. 154–318) from some of the Quartos was owed to threat of prosecution, the play was clearly (like *King John*) open to interpretation as an exercise in contemporary politics. But it remains distinctively a history, marking one phase in a continuing movement of events, and not allowing the death of the King to exhaust our interest in his realm; life ends and life goes on.

Historically speaking, *Henry IV Part 1 and 2* and *Henry V* are manifestations of that 'going on'. But each play nevertheless makes its own use of the language of the theatre and composes its own particular and self-contained experience. The topical relationships of *Henry IV Part I* with Lord Cobham (who objected to Shakespeare's use of the family name of 'Oldcastle' for Falstaff in the first performance) and with *The Merry Wives of Windsor* (written perhaps at the Queen's order for the Garter feast of April 1597), should not obscure the significance of the large historical design. The source material is so aportioned between the plays that Shakespeare must early have decided to make three plays out of the

---

[1] J. Dover Wilson develops this point in his New Cambridge edition of *Richard II*, Cambridge, 1939.

two reigns. But the ordering of chronicle material is not, in these plays, a dominant concern.

The chronicle incidents of *Part 1*, from the battles of Nesbit and Homildon to the battle of Shrewsbury, are assimilated with effacing economy; the fictions (like the Prince's rescue of his father and his slaying of Hotspur) collaborating with the facts to yield dramatized historical truths about the key human relationships. In the sequence of Shakespeare's histories, *Henry V* makes fresh discoveries about the complex interplay of political life and private; and it does so largely by exploiting the tradition of the moral interludes. At the prompting of the original version of the *Famous Victories of Henry V* (of which a bad text was published in 1594) Shakespeare makes the conversion of Hal both a political and moral event, in setting both courtly and popular. While *Part 1* owes its independent unity to the displacement of Hotspur by the Prince in the course of an heroic, sentimental and malevolent rebellion, it owes its continuity with *Part 2* to the Prince's cultivation of, and detachment from, Falstaff. The two aspects of the play engage in turn the audience's heroic sense of community (serving the country and its sovereign, making common cause against the pagans or the French), and its unheroic (meeting at the tavern, sharing a quotidian love of life); England stretches immensely between Windsor and Eastcheap.

Once again Shakespeare exploits theatrical traditions and conventions that can be made to express historical truths. All that relates the history play to public pageantry, the King's men at Shrewsbury 'glittering in golden coats like images' and Hotspur sounding 'the lofty instruments of war', is foiled by all that confesses the bond between the theatre and the inn-yard (the 'harlotry players' among the pint pots). Prince Hal's command of both modes is the central fact of the play as politics, as morality and as entertainment.

In comparison with the ascendant Bolingbroke of *Richard II*, King Henry speaks a remote and feudal dialect:

> And majesty might never yet endure
> The moody frontier of a servant brow.
>
> (1. 3. 18–19)

The characteristic tone and metaphor answer to the King's anxiety that the Prince should keep his distance from the populace:

> Had I so lavish of my presence been,
> So common-hackneyed in the eyes of man.
> So stale and cheap to vulgar company,
> Opinion, that did help me to the crown,
> Had still kept loyal to the possession.

> (3. 2. 39–43)

Neither this account of Bolingbroke's detachment nor the qualifications that follow are obviously true to the earlier play where it is he and not Richard who 'courted the common people' and 'wooed poor craftsmen with the craft of smiles'. But the nature of the bargain with the streets has subtly but decisively changed and Shakespeare has become much more interested in it. King Henry's counsel here is severely criticized by its placing in the dramatic design: for his withdrawal from the flux of common life is increasingly associated with insomnia, guilt, sickness and sterility, and with some of those enervating nostalgias that once disabled Richard, Gaunt and York, and the ironies multiply when we reflect that Henry, in a scene already burlesqued in anticipation (2. 4. 370–471) is only pleading for the rejection of Falstaff, but from reasons not moral but political.

Over the span of the four plays from *Richard II* to *Henry V* the ironies and qualifications grow richer, for the Prince who rejected Falstaff becomes the King most intimately 'enfeoff'd to popularity'. The popularity of Bolingbroke, however, had been tactically secured by the exercise of the actor's arts; for he had transiently recognized the populace as a source of political and military power. The popularity of Henry V is expressed through the camp scenes where the anonymous king recognizes in the ordinary soldiery a common humanity, and because he shares the humanity of the people he wins their allegiance. In the last play of the sequence (which from this point of view keeps a certain coherence) we are offered a most glowing optimism about the relationships between the high and the low, the courtly and the common, the heroic and the ordinary, which is not anticipated in the plays of *Henry IV*.

In between there has happened the rejection of Falstaff. What is its significance? Dominating the arguments that seek to derive Falstaff from Shakespeare's father, from Florio, Greene, Chettle, Peele, and William Brooke the tenth Lord Cobham, are those which associate him accidentally with Sir John Oldcastle (the name borrowed from the *Famous Victories*), historically with Sir John Fastolf (stripped of the Garter in 1 *Henry VI*, Act 4, Scene 1), and theatrically with the figure of Riot in the morality plays and the *miles gloriosus* in Roman comedy. Of these the analogue with Riot is most often canvassed and most fully documented. It is nevertheless a treacherous one, likely to encourage misinterpretation of Shakespeare's enlistment of morality drama and therefore to mistake the profounder insights of the play, and in a measure to falsify literary history. For Shakespeare's use of morality play does not coincide with Prince Hal's. When the Prince in Act 2 Scene 4 improvises his tavern play with Falstaff ('Thou art violently carried away from grace, there is a devil haunts thee in the likeness of an old fat man') his understanding of his own situation is urbane and absolute. Unlike, for example, Juventus in *Lusty Juventus*, he cannot forsake Riot in a spirit of genuine indignation and shame; the forsaking is from the start a part of Hal's design.

The celebrated soliloquy closing the play's second scene is not, as many have claimed, an instance of conventional reassurance to tell the audience they need not fear for the Prince's ultimate integrity. The soliloquy convention is adroitly refined and exploited in order to win for Hal the right measure of detachment both from the audience and from the stage companions. Its opening words ('I know you all') are addressed to the departed figures of Falstaff and Poins, and its closing ones have the effect of definitive inner resolution:

> I'll so offend to make offence a skill,
> Redeeming time when men think least I will.

Prince Hal gives himself therefore a politic, tactical reason for cherishing the morality plot to renounce Falstaff, and by so contriving Shakespeare sets himself an exacting challenge. When the reformation is finally accomplished at the end of *Part 2* it can be felt as a total moral and political vindication of Hal's tactics, 'glittering' not only in the eyes of its stage witness but in the eyes of its theatre audience too; for behind it is not only the insight and determination attending his companionship with Poins, but also those that move him on the death of his father:

> with his spirits sadly I survive,
> To mock the expectation of the world.
>
> (5. 2. 125–6)

His 'tide of blood' which had 'proudly flowed in vanity' ebbs 'back to the sea' to 'flow henceforth in formal majesty'. Behind the politic conversion, we are almost persuaded, is an authentic redirection of energy and purpose.

Much of the play, however, cannot be contained by this account; for it allows too much authority to the Prince's casting of Falstaff as Riot, and Falstaff is more comprehensively human than that casting will allow. Literary history might invite comparison not with the early Interludes, but with the sprawling hybrid play (morality-heroic-pastoral-fantasy) *A Looking Glass for London*, written by Lodge and Greene in about 1590. In it a figure whose name, Adam, seems to signify the unrepentantly human Old Adam in our nature, proves intractable to the reforming constraints of the law. His grumblings to the prophet Jonah are a pre-echo of Falstaff:

> I would you had never come from Jewry to this country.
> You have made me look like a lean rib of roast beef,
> Or like the picture of Lent painted upon a red herring cob.

and when commanded to fast he would 'rather suffer a short hanging than a long fasting'. When hauled off to gaol for carrying beef and beer in his slops he sees himself as a public martyr, 'I am for you. Come, let's away, and yet let me be put in the chronicles'. Without Adam or his equivalent, the play seems to claim, no history of public life is complete. Wenches, scurrilous patter and enterprising thievery are part of the total life of London and England; they are the vicious excesses of vitality.

The transition, announced by Rumour in *Part 2*, from the 'royal field of Shrewsbury' to the 'worm-eaten hold of ragged stone' (Warkworth Castle) where Northumberland 'lies crafty-sick', aptly characterizes the shift of stress between the plays. The death of Hotspur ('whose spirit lent a fire/Even to the dullest peasant in his camp') provokes from Northumberland a 'strained passion' that anticipates the cataclysmic passages of the tragedies:

> Let Order die!
> And let this world no longer be a stage
> To feed contention in a ling'ring act;
> But let one spirit of the first-born Cain
> Reign in all bosoms, that, each heart being set
> On bloody courses, the rude scene may end,
> And darkness be the burier of the dead.
>
> (1. 1. 154–60)

Falstaff's opening line ('Sirrah, you giant, what says the doctor to my water?') comically testifies to the dominion of sickness that, from one point of view, rules the play. Falstaff outfaces it; the King is subdued by it. The nihilistic ardours of youth that precipitate the slaughters of Shrewsbury and make an heroic play of *Part 1* are displaced by the quieter ordeals of living and ageing in the flesh. The morality-play is complicated by admitting alongside Hal's still active intention 'to make offence a skill', Falstaff's to 'turn diseases to commodity'. The dismissal and arrest of Falstaff, poised between absurdity and pathos, moral rigour and political virtuosity, is complicated in its clear but intricate effects by the confidence and authority it confers upon the lean and sterile figure of Prince John. It is he who announces the coming redirection of English energies ('We bear our civil swords and native fire/As far as France'), and it was clearly Shakespeare's intention, confirmed in the Epilogue, that the play which followed should be of the heroic kind.

*Henry V* was probably written in the season 1598–9 and produced in the summer of 1599 when hopes (soon to be disappointed) of Essex's victorious return from Ireland were running high (Act 5, Prologue 30–3). The play's 'Muse of fire' recovers for the service of the English community the heroic impulses and war music that had threatened to destroy it in *Henry IV*. But the community has changed and so has the heroism. The failure of the play to entertain us with Falstaff in France has led some to suppose that Shakespeare was forced by circumstance to break the promise that ended *Henry IV* – objections from the Master of Revels, perhaps, or the actor Kempe leaving the company. But the presence of Falstaff would not consort either with the critical temper of the soldiery at Agincourt or with the nostalgic recollection of English community with which the King rallies them before the battle:

> He that shall live this day, and see old age,
> Will yearly on the virgil feast his neighbours,
> And say, 'To-morrow is Saint Crispian.'

(4. 3. 44–6)

By way of Talbot, Hotspur, and Prince Hal at Shrewsbury Shakespeare has humanized, almost domesticated, the heroic idiom. The intimate, familiar fellowship that characterize the battle rhetoric of the play ('Once more unto the breach, dear friends') is generated from Shakespeare's rendering of the salient chronicle facts and takes its starting points from a few details of reported speech. But its generous realization in the camp scenes is pre-eminently Shakespeare's. Holinshed tells of the King going about to view the warders and hanging two delinquents as a warning, while Tacitus (*Annals* II. iii.) tells of Germanicus in disguise listening to his troops on the eve of battle; in Shakespeare's version the King is challenged, figuratively and literally, by the common soldier William:

I am afeard there are few die well, that die in a battle: for how can they charitably dispose of anything, when blood is their argument? Now, if these men do not die well, it will be a black matter for the king, that led them to it; who to disobey were against all portion of subjection.

(4. 1. 140–45)

The sources of Henry's popularity are clearly displayed; his arguments are imperfectly convincing, but he meets William on a point of honour and treats him generously when he proves his mettle. And there is just enough responsive reflection in the King's arguments and soliloquy to keep the battle rhetoric in perspective.

Dr Johnson grieved that Shakespeare in the love scenes gave the King the character of military grossness and unskilfulness that he had formerly ridiculed in Percy. It is true that the role of plain soldier-lover is more continuous with Hotspur's than with Hal's, and it may well have been established as a stage expectation from the original version of the *Famous Victories*. But within the play it coheres well enough; and in the sequence it can appear that his conversion is not only the calculated effect it was meant to be, but also the subduing of political and personal values to the discipline and fellowship of war.

'In the quick forge and working house of thought' the Chorus of Act 5 finds a Roman simile for an English scene; the citizens of London

> Like to the senators of th'antique Rome,
> With the plebeians swarming at their heels,
> Go forth and fetch their conquering Caesar in.

Contemporary allusions suggest that *Julius Caesar* was first produced in 1599, probably some months after *Henry V*, in the newly opened Globe theatre. Shakespeare's transition from English to Roman history looks natural enough in retrospect; the *Mirror for Magistrates* (1587) has Caesar appear among the '*Britayne* Princes' with admonitory '*Romayne* facts', and Senecal plays from France and Italy, cultivated and imitated in English court and university circles, had made the death of Caesar a theme for sophisticated political and ethical thinking in Latin or Latinate recitative. Yet, unlike *Titus Andronicus*, *Julius Caesar* owes little to the academic drama that it does not transform into popular theatre. From his experience in the English history play Shakespeare has learned to meet the Roman past halfway – has acquired a fuller sense of the relationship between perennial human dispositions and historically changing political systems and circumstances. Through the next decade, many of Shakespeare's most searching discoveries in these areas were made out of Plutarch's *Lives of Noble Grecians and Romanes*, familiar to Shakespeare in North's translation of 1579.

Whether or not he was acquainted with Pescetti's *Il Cesare* (1594) or with *Caesar's Revenge*, an English Senecal play performed at Oxford in the 1590s Shakespeare recognized the consonance between the Senecal style of play and the material he found in Plutarch. Feverous dreams, atrocities, 'unlucky signs', ruptures in the natural order and vengeful apparitions are in Plutarch matters of reported fact. They relate to experiences that Shakespeare assimilates into the play through the consciousness of the conspirators – Casca at the start of Act 1 Scene 3, and Brutus, sleepless in a waking nightmare:

> Between the acting of a dreadful thing
> And the first motion all the interim is
> Like a phantasma or a hideous dream:
> The Genius and the mortal instruments
> Are then in council, and the state of man
> Like to a little kingdom suffers then
> The nature of an insurrection.

> (2. 1. 63–9)

The intimacy of the scene in which this soliloquy is set owes its temper ('But when night came that he was in his owne house, then he was cleane chaunged') to Plutarch, but not its detail (the coming and going of the boy Lucius). Shakespeare actualizes, familiarizes, the insomnia of Brutus and at the same time confers upon it a comprehensive political and moral significance. What is a local insight in *Julius Caesar*, however, will become a structural principle in *Macbeth*, where the phantasmagoric imagination both prompts the destruction of the kingdom and state of man, and recoils upon the destroyer.

The large structure of *Julius Caesar* is less Senecal than historical and political. When Antony, however, kneels by the dead Caesar, he recognizes that his personal desolation and the blight upon the land can find redress in a Senecal outcome:

> And Caesar's spirit ranging for revenge,
> With Até by his side come hot from hell,
> Shall in these confines with a monarch's voice
> Cry 'Havoc,' and let slip the dogs of war;
> That this foul deed shall smell above the earth
> With carrion men, groaning for burial.

> (3. 1. 271–6)

Yet, from an historical point of view, the movement of events is not determined by Até 'hot from hell' but by the sequence (almost repeated from *2 Henry VI*) of plot and assassination, factitional rhetoric, street murder and civil war. Under the spell of these impersonal processes the conspirators, their victim and their enemies do what they can to shape public events out of private weaknesses, griefs and fears. The commanding figure of Caesar, in public and in private, is both a political fabrication and an achievement of histrionic art and will; the 'ragtag people' clap and hiss him 'as they use to do the players in the theatre'. And by analogous political and theatrical art, Antony moves the mob to a confusion of purposeful and arbitrary atrocities. Unlike *2 Henry VI*, however, the play has a tragic as well as a political shape; the sense that one faction has provisionally triumphed in the continuing life of Rome is muted by the sense that with the death of Brutus a poignant personal experience, of profound historical significance, is complete. Yet the rival nobilities of the Stoic Brutus and the Epicurean Cassius, the impulse of the one to honour the great movements of the moral order and of the other to work out each situation according to its own laws, seem aptly expressed in the reported misunderstandings that destroy them at Philippi. Even the tragic catastrophe has its historical truth.

It was apparently six years before Shakespeare returned to Plutarch and to the life of Marcus Antonius to write *Antony and Cleopatra* (1606–7). Shakespeare did not make it a sequel to *Julius Caesar* but conspicuously neglected an opportunity to make it so; for Plutarch reports that Antony first fell in love with Cleopatra when he called her to answer charges of assisting Cassius in the civil war. The play promptly and amply takes up the antinomies of love and empire that are so large a part of Plutarch's theme; the 'unreyned lust of con-cupiscence', as North phrases it, 'the pestilent plague and mischiefe of Cleopatraes love', that 'put out of Antonius heade, all honest and commendable thoughtes'. Shakespeare handles the ten-year chronicle from 40 B.C. to 30 B.C. deftly and representatively; the forty lines opening Act 3, for example, both convey the essential facts about the Parthian campaign and insinuate Plutarch's general point that Antony's military reputation owed much to his lieutenants. But the play is not to be measured by its fidelity to fact, nor yet by its treatment of Plutarch's moral and political wisdom. Its effects are owed to the analogues generated in the play between the lovers' imaginations and the poet's, and to a poetry that seeks to transfigure and transcend the public qualities of an Egyptian queen and a Roman commander.

Cleopatra's most spacious claims for Antony are made in the face of the cool solicitude of Dolabella:

> His legs bestrid the ocean. His reared arm
> Crested the world. His voice was propertied
> As all the tuned spheres, and that to friends.

(5. 2. 82–4)

and her climactic question:

> Think you there was, or might be, such a man
> As this I dreamed of?

does not stay for Dolabella's answer ('Gentle madam, no.') but approaches a final acclamation of the truth of the imagination:

> Nature wants stuff
> To vie strange forms with fancy; yet t'imagine
> An Antony, were nature's piece 'gainst fancy,
> Condemning shadows quite.

(5. 2. 97–100)

In the fiction of the play Cleopatra's vision is made from her experience and love of Antony; but Shakespeare's ability to define it is owed to his reading of the history with the poet's eye. Hence the analogue between lover and poet – they are both transfigurers of historical truth. This is a source of mystery and of satisfaction.

Seen in relation to the histories, *Antony and Cleopatra* is remarkable for its assimilation of 'nature' into 'fancy'. Where, for example, Plutarch makes of Antony's prodigality a Roman grumble (he 'easily gave away great seignories, realmes, and mighty nations unto some private men'), Shakespeare refashions it into Cleopatra's hyperboles:

> in his livery
> Walked crowns and crownets. Realms and islands were
> As plates dropped from his pocket.

(5. 2. 90–2)

Plutarch's data are extensively, but never inertly, transposed into poetry. Shakespeare is at once recovering the insights of *A Midsummer Night's Dream* ('The lunatic, the lover, and the poet/Are of imagination all compact') and recognizing imaginative capacities that seem, as a matter of historical truth, to have been attributes of Antony and Cleopatra. Antony, we are told, spent his time 'sometimes in warres, and otherwhile in the studie of eloquence', and 'he used a manner of phrase in his speeche, called Asiatik, which carried the best grace and estimation of that time, and was much like to his manners and life'. Cleopatra, answeringly, had a tongue that 'was an instrument of musicke to divers sports and pastimes'. And the history yields much staged incident – the 'marvellous sweete harmonie' that presages Antony's defeat, the attempt to raise the dying Antony into Cleopatra's tomb, and the circumstance of the aspic brought in a basket of figs to Cleopatra 'araied in her royall robes' on a bed of gold. More searchingly, Shakespeare could have found in Plutarch occasion for the play's attention to dissolution, both in the Roman sense (Antony is 'dissolute') and in a more comprehensive sense that takes the beginnings of life from 'the dungy earth' and 'Nilus slime' and sees its end prefigured in the clouds of the evening sky ('even with a thought/The rack dislimns and makes it indistinct/As water is in water'.) Plutarch's understanding of the past is fully active in the play, but it confronts an understanding that the nineteenth century Romantics were to find congenial – vindicating the synthetical and magical power of the imagination.

If we can trust an allusion to 'the coal of fire upon the ice' and can suppose the corn dearth a topical theme, *Coriolanus* was written early in 1608, perhaps a year after *Antony and Cleopatra*. The legend of Coriolanus had been shaped by Plutarch into a minutely circumstantial history, and Shakespeare treats it with the respect due to recorded fact (he did not so treat the material of *Lear*, *Macbeth* and *Cymbeline* in Holinshed). Since there existed no Senecal tradition for plays on Coriolanus (there were many on Caesar and on Antony and Cleopatra) Shakespeare's choice of theme was an adventurous one.[1] There is no need, however, to suppose that Shakespeare was moved to emulate Ben Jonson's Roman plays *Catiline* and *Sejanus*, for there is a clear continuity of interest in the politics of the Roman state between *Coriolanus* and *Julius Caesar*. Once again the history is made to yield the tragedy. As Plutarch presents it, the personal crisis of events coincides with the political crisis, and more momentously, so it does in the play.

'He did it to please his mother', says one of the citizens, 'and to be partly proud, which he is, even to the altitude of his virtue' (1. 1. 37–9). Thus Shakespeare attributes a common understanding of the play to a common voice. But the citizen is answered by another, 'What he cannot help in his nature you account a vice in him'. Pride, in a rich and authentic sense that returns us to the Greek

[1] See Terence Spencer, 'Shakespeare and the Elizabethan Romans', *Shakespeare Survey 10*, Cambridge, 1957.

concept of *hubris*, is the essence of Coriolanus; it is his vice and his virtue. Shakespeare so designs the play, however, that the personal quality is a specifically Roman one.

When Coriolanus scolds the patricians for letting power slip from them to the tribunes he charges them with betraying the state:

> Your dishonour
> Mangles true judgement, and bereaves the state
> Of that integrity which should become't;
> Not having the power to do the good it would,
> For th'ill which doth control't.
>
> (3. 1. 157–61)

The play is consistently probing 'the integrity which should become the state', beginning with the celebrated belly fable (1. 1. 89–154) by which Menenius subdues his Roman audience (and perhaps his Elizabethan one) to silence. The parable makes such an impression that the play's imagery can recall it at a touch: the country, it is said much later, will be 'cankered' and war poured like a purgative 'into the bowels of ungrateful Rome'. At a first response it may be taken to express the ubiquitous concept of the state as a system of mutual responsibilities. But in its setting the fable is a trick; the food is not being distributed, and the populace, not the patricians, have to make do with 'bran'. Menenius in Plutarch is the congenial elder statesman whose tale is part of an oration delivered at the request of the Senate; it leads to the appointment of tribunes. In the play Menenius betrays his private convictions by announcing Coriolanus's entry with:

> Rome and her rats are at the point of battle;
> The one side must have bale.

The 'limbs' of Rome are become 'rats'. Rome for Menenius is the patricians; but, more significantly, it is a ruthless military machine:

> you may as well
> Strike at the heaven with your staves as lift them
> Against the Roman state, whose course will on
> The way it takes; cracking ten thousand curbs
> Of more strong links asunder than can ever
> Appear in your impediment.
>
> (1. 1. 65–71)

The body politic and the body of Coriolanus will be represented in the same language – the destructive, neutrally advancing 'thing' that yields to no human obstacle.

The Rome of Coriolanus is dedicated to a single idea of virtue. 'In those dayes,' says Plutarch, 'valliantness was honoured in Rome above all other vertues: which they called *Virtus*, by the name of vertue selfe, as including in that generall name, all other speciall vertues besides. So that *Virtus* in the Latin was as muche as valliantness'. The play not only catches this idea in passing:

> It is held
> That valour is the chiefest virtue and
> Most dignifies the haver.
>
> (2. 2. 81–3)

it exhausts its possibilities. In the remorseless logic of Coriolanus valour is the whole of virtue, and those who do not exhibit it deserve neither to govern nor to live:

> Being pressed to th'war,
> Even when the navel of the state was touched,
> They would not thread the gates; this kind of service
> Did not deserve corn gratis.
>
> (3. 1. 122–5)

Coriolanus is 'too absolute'. But his integrity is not merely personal; it is related to that of the state. Menenius would 'find physic for the violent fit of the times'; he would keep the state going on the best conditions he can find for his caste. Coriolanus requires that a military ideal of virtue should be absolutely satisfied; he is more Roman than the conditions of Rome will allow.

The impersonal conflicts are intimately manifest in the relationships that Marcius has with his mother. Volumnia is distinctively a Roman educator, a weight of precepts. 'You were used to load me', says Marcius, 'With precepts that would make invincible/The heart that conned them' (4. 1. 9–11). But her character in the play shifts from a commitment to dedicated violence to a commitment to tactics. It is Coriolanus's virtue, his tragic integrity, that unlike the 'vile politician' Bolingbroke he cannot 'dissemble with his nature'.

The prudential judgements of Plutarch upon the uncompromising brashness of Coriolanus are fully represented by the Roman patricians and by Tullus Aufidius (4. 7. 35–53), but they are not unequivocally endorsed by the central experience of the play. This has to do with the persistence of Coriolanus in his Roman virtue to the extremest point of his humanity. The rigour and weight of the play's poetic dialect characteristically excludes all the qualities of pity and love that find their silent symbol in the figure of Virgilia:

> His sword, death's stamp,
> Where it did mark, it took; from face to foot
> He was a thing of blood, whose every motion
> Was timed with dying cries.
>
> (2. 2. 105–8)

He is deified for his inhumanity:

> He is their god; he leads them like a thing
> Made by some other deity than Nature,
> That shapes man better.
>
> (4. 9. 91–3)

A god that kills men as butchers kill flies.

Plutarch's imagination, before Shakespeare's, had recognized the significance for Rome of the confrontation between the kneeling Volumnia and her son. The human bonds finally prevail, and valour no longer looks like the chiefest virtue. Coriolanus weeps ('it is no little thing to make/Mine eyes to sweat compassion'), and a phase in the history of Roman values seems to come to an end.

The great Roman plays out of Plutarch (including *Timon of Athens* in so far as it concerns Alcibiades) find personal and tragic stresses at the centre of public events. The same claim cannot be made about *Henry VIII*, a play which, in view of its high incidence of personal catastrophe and suffering, is remarkably free from stress. In it the tensions and fundamental conflicts related to historical events are not clarified and heightened but evaded and diminished, or (by a more favourable account) they are transposed into threnody. The song, 'Orpheus with his lute', sung at the request of Queen Katherine, is significantly about playing that quietens pain:

> In sweet music is such art,
> Killing care and grief of heart
> Fall asleep, or hearing die.
>
> (3. 1. 12–14)

The innocent and guilty alike accept their falls and their deaths with exquisite patience. Wolsey's political frustration is translated into a mutability lament and his conversion is made a natural attribute of his humiliation:

> Vain pomp and glory of this world, I hate ye:
> I feel my heart new opened.
>
> (3. 2. 365–6)

And the Queen's farewell to both friends and tormentors is serenely accepting of the sleep of death, the atrocity of the event quite set aside:

> Remember me
> In all humility unto his highness;
> Say his long trouble now is passing
> Out of this world. Tell him in death I blessed him,
> For so I will.
>
> (4. 2. 160–4)

The tenor of the verse and action have disposed many to accept arguments first advanced in the nineteenth century and supported by word-counts, that John Fletcher worked with Shakespeare and was responsible for rather more than half of the play (including all the passages quoted above).[1] Certainly, read with Fletcher in mind, the play declares its affinities with the sentimental fashions of the Blackfriars theatre. But there is also the manifest, if not wholly reassuring, contemporaneity with Shakespeare's last plays, even if the processes by which acceptance and forgiveness encompass distress are less readily reconciled with hard historical facts than with the material of romance, legend and exotic travel.

Nevertheless, the historical veracity of the play is hard won, with an attention to detail much more in Shakespeare's mode than in Fletcher's, and with a consistency of effect that owes much to the manner and matter of Holinshed. For the chroniclers of Tudor England were not free, and probably were not disposed, to dramatize the conflicts of Henry's reign. The characteristic moral claim of the chronicle may be found in the marginal note, 'The cardinall ascribeth his fall to the just judgement of God' (compare 3. 2. 455–9). But the characteristic interest that the chronicler takes in the reign is better glimpsed in the source material for the Cardinal's entertainments: 'On a time the king came suddenlie thither in a maske with a dozen maskers all in garments like sheepheards'. The small cannon that announced the King's arrival in fact were those which, imitated in the play, evidently set fire to the Globe in 1613. The extravagance of the play as a grand costumed spectacle is in its own way very true to the chronicle

---

[1] See R. A Foakes, ed. *Henry VIII* (Arden Shakespeare), London, 1957.

ceremony, with the trumpets and the bright banners keeping the senses alive in the theatre while distancing and subduing political and moral judgements. It is an effect consonant with, if less profound than, analogous ones in the late plays; where, for example, *Cymbeline* is self-confessedly theatrical, *Henry VIII* is a representation 'full of state and woe' of 'Such noble scenes as draw the eye to flow'; it is an historical pageant.

There is also, however, a significant relationship between *Henry VIII* and two other history plays which are without comparable pageant effects. *Sir Thomas More*, to which Shakespeare probably contributed several fine passages, perhaps in or about 1600, resolves tensions with similarly effacing ease. And John Ford's *Perkin Warbeck* (registered 1634), the last in the historical mode, uses Warbeck's urbanity (owed to Bacon's history) with answering qualities in the other characters, to diffuse all violence into high politeness. It seems that an ameliorating, conciliatory spirit was for these decades mediating the English past to English audiences; the history play, as the Epilogue to *Henry VIII* puts it, is in 'The merciful construction of good women'. But it matters that this last of Shakespeare's histories, like the first, was still looking for its effects in the chronicle record: the version of *Henry VIII* that burned down the Globe theatre had as its subtitle, *All is True*.

# SHAKESPEARE: HIS COMEDIES

## John Wilders

At no time during his professional life did Shakespeare devote himself exclusively to the writing of comedy. Although most of the great tragedies were composed during the single period 1604–8, the comedies appeared intermittently during the whole course of his career. The first, *The Comedy of Errors*, was written probably in about 1592 after the four early histories. The other early comedies, *The Taming of the Shrew*, *Two Gentlemen of Verona*, *Love's Labour's Lost* and *A Midsummer Night's Dream*, belong to the years 1593–6 as do also *Romeo and Juliet* and *Richard II*. The 'mature' comedies, *The Merchant of Venice*, *Much Ado about Nothing*, *As You Like It* and *Twelfth Night*, were composed between 1596 and 1600, the years in which Shakespeare was writing the two parts of *Henry IV*, *Julius Caesar* and *Hamlet*. *The Merry Wives of Windsor*, *All's Well that Ends Well* and *Measure for Measure* were probably written between *Hamlet* (1600) and *Othello* (1604), and the last plays, *Pericles*, *Cymbeline*, *The Winter's Tale* and *The Tempest*, came between *Timon* (1607) and *Henry VIII* (1612). It is customary for critics to regard these four later plays as a separate and distinct group but they were in fact written within the structural form of comedy and three of them were included among the comedies in the First Folio edition of Shakespeare's plays.

The comedies were therefore not the expression of a particular state of mind, a sort of optimism or cheerfulness which possessed him during a distinct part of his life. Nor did he put forward any particular set of ideas or principles exclusively in these plays, for his views about personal relationships and political conduct, insofar as we can infer from his work what these were, appear indiscriminately in the comedies and tragedies alike. The reflections in *As You Like It*, for example, on the ingratitude of man anticipate those made by King Lear in the storm, and Lear's observations on the nature of justice are similar to those made by Angelo in *Measure for Measure*. It seems likely, therefore, that, when he returned from tragedy to comedy, Shakespeare did not feel he was primarily expressing a different mood or ethical view, but attempting a different kind of play with a different kind of form: *Titus Andronicus*, a tragedy in the manner of Seneca, came right after *The Comedy of Errors*, closely modelled on Plautus and *Othello* followed *Measure for Measure*. We may therefore be better able to understand individual comedies if we can first discover what, for Shakespeare, was the nature of the form in general.

He was not, of course, a literary theorist and has left us with little or no idea of his views on the subject, nor do the theories of his contemporaries have much relevance to his work. The few Elizabethans who wrote about comedy believed that it fulfilled in its own particular way what they thought to be the purpose of all literature, the moral improvement of man. The epic achieved this wholesome purpose by recounting the deeds of great heroes for our emulation, tragedy exhibited the fall of kings and princes, teaching – in the words of Sir Philip Sidney's *Defence of Poesie* – 'the uncertaintie of this world, and uppon how weak foundations guilden roofes are builded', but comedy was distinguished by its portrayal of base and foolish characters in such a way as to make them appear ridiculous and thereby discourage the spectator from indulging in such follies himself. 'Comedy' wrote Sidney, 'is an imitation of the common errors of our life which [the poet] represented in the most ridiculous and scornfull sort that may be; so as it is impossible that any beholder can be content to be such a one'. And since, for literary purposes, people of high rank were seldom, if ever, ridiculous, its characters were drawn from the lower orders of society or what George Puttenham described as 'unthrifty youthes, young damsels, old nurses, bawds, brokers, ruffians and parasites'.[1] It was, in short, a kind of dramatic satire. Such definitions, however, do not fit the comedies of Shakespeare, few of whose characters are made to look ridiculous, even though some, like Bottom or Malvolio, may be satirized from time to time and are not drawn exclusively from low life, even though they include Dogberry and Autolycus as well as Orsino and Leontes. These theories do, incidentally, describe the comedies of Ben Jonson who apparently realized that he and Shakespeare were writing different kinds of play and thought that his own were the more correct.

The most relevant theories of comedy are those of modern critics like Susanne Langer and Northrop Frye who have argued that the kind of comedy Shakespeare wrote is distinguished by its structure.[2]

---

[1] *Art of English Poesy*, ed. G. Willcock and A. Walker, Cambridge, 1936, p 32.

[2] Susanne Langer, *Feeling and Form*, London, 1953; Northrop Frye, *A Natural Perspective: the Development of Shakespearean Comedy and Romance*, New York, 1965.

Whereas the action of tragedy is concentrated on a single, isolated individual who finds himself in opposition to his society, like Romeo, or the universe, like Lear, comic action involves a group of people like the courtiers in *Love's Labour's Lost* or the pairs of lovers in *As You Like It*. Both forms take as their starting-point some kind of challenge which presents itself like a blow of fate or sudden turn of fortune's wheel. Hamlet is confronted by the news of his father's murder and his consequent obligation to take vengeance, Macbeth is presented with the chance to murder Duncan and seize the throne, Viola and Sebastian are cast ashore in an unknown land, and nearly everyone in *As You Like It* is forced to flee to the Forest of Arden. But whereas the tragic hero is incapable of rising to the challenge and either tries to avoid it, like Hamlet, or takes a course of action which is fatal to himself, like Macbeth, the comic character meets it with confidence and verve, turning it ultimately to his own advantage. As a consequence of their apparent misfortune Viola finds Orsino, Sebastian marries Olivia, Rosalind courts Orlando and the banished Duke discovers that the uses of adversity are sweet. The conventional end of tragedy is the death of the hero but the conventional end of comedy is a double or triple wedding:

> Jack shall have Jill;
> Nought shall go ill;
> The man shall have his mare again,
> And all shall be well.

Shakespeare's tragic figures die childless but his comic figures look forward to marriage not simply as a source of happiness but as a means of producing children in defiance of an adverse fortune which initially threatened them with extinction.

The initial calamity which pushes the action of Shakespeare's comedies into motion generally arrives without explanation or motive like a sudden tempest. Aegean in *The Comedy of Errors* describes in his opening monologue how his whole family has been split up by a storm at sea, an episode which Shakespeare used again in *Pericles* which he adapted from the same story. Viola makes her first appearance recovering from a shipwreck and the first scene of *The Tempest* consists of a storm which casts Prospero's enemies on the same island to which he and Miranda were carried twelve years earlier. The plots of other comedies start not with an impersonal event in nature but with a hostile act by one of the characters who assumes a role, such as that of judge or ruler, which is itself impersonal. Such is the act by which the Duke reluctantly condemns Aegean to death as an alien, or the edict by which Theseus seeks to force the marriage of Hermia to Lysander, or the command which imposes on Angelo the authority of Duke. Even when the characters are challenged by the private enmity of an individual, a Shylock or a Don John, it is given little or no explanation; the villain of Shakespearean comedy seems to be possessed by an impersonal, external force which he can neither account for nor resist. Shylock, it is true, offers several reasons for his loathing of Antonio: he hates him 'because he is a Christian' and because 'he lends out money gratis' but neither motive sufficiently accounts for the viciousness of the Jew's conduct and, indeed, in the trial scene Shylock mockingly refuses to explain himself. 'It is my humour' he says. This same 'motiveless malignity' appears in Oliver's hatred of Orlando – 'my soul (yet I know not why) hates nothing more than he' – and in Don John's hostility to the world in general which is so baldly stated that Shakespeare seems to be deliberately challenging the audience's belief: 'It must not be denied but I am a plain-dealing villain'. The motivation of such people is, of course, not Shakespeare's concern in the comedies which is rather to display the reaction which such villainy provokes in his heroes and heroines. But even when he examines this kind of personality at more leisure, as he does with Iago, he provides him with so many conflicting motives that they appear like rationalizations which leave the ultimate cause a mystery. It seems that, for Shakespeare, no explanation was possible. Though Edmund is motivated by his bastardy, Goneril and Regan like Iago and Don John are apparently born wicked, a phenomenon which perplexed King Lear and which we simply have to accept as an undeniable fact of human nature and a necessary premise for the plays. It is something which they share with the 'winter and rough weather' of creation in general.

The characters of Shakespeare's comedies meet this challenge with energy and imagination. The heroines particularly spend little time bewailing, like Hamlet or Lear, the injustice of their predicament but instinctively begin to control it. Viola has only a brief word of regret and even that is mixed with reassurance:

> And what should I do in Illyria?
> My brother he is in Elysium.
> Perchance he is not drowned.
>
> (1. 2. 3–5)

Within moments she is asserting her will to survive:

> I'll serve this duke,
> Thou shalt present me as an eunuch to him:
>            ... for I can sing,
> And speak to him in many sorts of music,
> That will allow me very worth his service.
> What else may hap to time I will commit.
>
> (1. 2. 54–9)

Like Rosalind, Portia, and Helena in *All's Well*, Viola is quick-witted, spirited and practical. These characters assume their new roles with enthusiasm and seem to delight in adversity. Shakespeare does not develop and expose their characters in such depth as the great tragic heroes but this is partly because their resources are not stretched and are entirely adequate to overcome their difficulties. It is the liveliness of his heroines which supplies the buoyancy and exuberance of these plays.

The various disguises and subterfuges which the heroines adopt are initially a means of survival but in the course of the action they overcome the motiveless, impersonal attacks of fate in a peculiarly personal way. They turn fate into providence and fall in love. It is the process of falling in love which occupies much of the action of the middle comedies, especially *As You Like It* which, after the initial catastrophes in the first act, is devoted to a series of courtships and debates on the nature of love:

> Good shepherd, tell this youth what 'tis to love ...
> It is to be all made of fantasy,
> All made of passion, and all made of wishes,
> All adoration, duty and observance,
> All humbleness, all patience, and impatience,
> All purity, all trial, all obedience.
>
> (5. 2. 79–94)

But although Silvius is here describing his own love for Phoebe and Orlando's love for Rosalind, it is of a different kind from that of the other characters, notably Touchstone who, reluctantly deprived of the pleasures of the court, consoles himself with the doubtful charms of Audrey, frankly confessing that he is drawn to her simply by the need for sexual satisfaction:

As the ox hath his bow, sir, the horse his curb, and the falcon her bells, so man hath his desires; and as pigeons bill, so wedlock would be nibbling.

(3. 3. 75–7)

He admits to this physical appetite grudgingly as a need which must be satisfied but which debases him in the process: 'we that are true lovers run into strange capers'. Rosalind, too, stands apart from the pastoral lovers in her awareness that love is ridiculous as well as ennobling, and in her dual role of boy and girl she can both mock Orlando's idealism while secretly enjoying the delight of being in love with him. She can privately confess to Celia 'how many fathom deep' she is in love and yet assure her suitor that though 'men have died from time to time, and worms have eaten them' it was not for love. Hence the action is distributed between three contrasting pairs of lovers, each couple displaying a different kind of love which is a reflection or distortion of the feelings of the others. When they are finally joined by a fourth pair (Oliver and Celia) and assemble for the marriage-rite they exemplify a whole range of human affection and become almost allegorical figures in a tableau like those displayed in court masques and public triumphs. At this point, with the entry of Hymen, a further, more religious idea is introduced which suggests that through their mutual love these people transcend themselves:

> Then is there mirth in heaven,
> When earthly things made even
> Atone together

(5. 4. 105–7)

This structural arrangement by which several similar actions are conducted in parallel had earlier been used by Shakespeare in *A Midsummer Night's Dream* where the mature, heroic love of Theseus and Hippolyta is contrasted with the delusions of the young couples and the infatuation of Titania and in *Love's Labour's Lost* where the courtiers' aspirations to learning are placed against the pedantry of Sir Nathaniel and Holofernes, the fashionable affectation of Don Armado and Costard's astonished discovery of the power of words. In later plays the interrelationships between characters become much more complicated. *The Tempest*, for example, contains a curious assortment of people – an exiled Duke, a drunken butler, an airy spirit, a savage and deformed slave – who are linked in an intricate pattern the effect of which is not simply that of a series of reflecting or distorting mirrors as in *As You Like It* but a crystal, one facet of which is geometrically related to the others in a multitude of ways.

*As You Like It* is typical of nearly all the middle comedies in that the principal characters overcome and transcend adversity by means of their capacity for affection. To begin with the most personal human loyalties are violated: the rightful Duke has been deposed by his brother, Oliver plots the murder of his brother Orlando, Rosalind and Celia are separated from their parents and the central episode of the first act is a wrestling match in which the professional tries to kill his untrained opponent. During the course of the play these links are reconstructed as a result of experience: Orlando learns to forgive his brother as a result of seeing him in danger and acquires a love which can survive the taunts of Ganymede. By a comparable process Helena wins the respect of Bertram, Claudio develops a more lasting love for Hero and Beatrice and Benedick, while apparently ridiculing each other, are in fact drawn more closely together. In general, then, the comedies present a group of contrasting characters who are brought through adverse circumstances to a closer and more lasting relationship with one another. Parents find their lost children, husbands are restored to their wives, brothers and sisters, masters and servants meet again, dukes are restored to their lost dukedoms and all are united in an ideal condition of order and happiness.

Although similarities can be seen in the plays of some of Shakespeare's predecessors such as Greene and Lyly, this kind of comedy is something essentially new in English drama. Various attempts have been made to discover its origins. It has been pointed out that the structure of Shakespeare's comedies resembles that of pagan religious rituals which often consisted of the dramatic enactment of the process of death and rebirth or 'the casting out of death', to which F. M. Cornford traced the source of early Greek comedy.[1] Certainly relics of this pattern survive in the comedies, notably those in which a character undergoes apparent death and resurrection like Hero in *Much Ado*, Thaisa in *Pericles* and Hermione in *The Winter's Tale* or in which there is a very positive progress towards marriage and procreation as in *A Midsummer Night's Dream*, *As You Like It* and *The Winter's Tale*. The question remains, however, of how such ritual performances reached the Elizabethan stage and the changes they underwent in the process. C. L. Barber has suggested a source closer to Shakespeare's own times in popular festivities such as the May Games, the Lord of Misrule (in which servants changed roles with their masters as in *The Taming of the Shrew* and *Twelfth Night*) and the mummers' play of Saint George which were themselves descended from ancient ritual. But although such primitive elements certainly survive in Shakespeare and contribute to the form and spirit of his comedies,

[1] See Janet Spens, *An Essay on Shakespeare's Relation to Tradition*, Oxford, 1916; F. M. Cornford, *The Origin of Attic Comedy*, London, 1914.

they are not the only elements which make them unique or have given them the power to last. We must also recognize more sophisticated, literary features such as dramatic irony, the subtle placing of one character against another, word-play and the verbal exuberance which Shakespeare enjoys in common with other Elizabethans such as Sidney, Spenser and Ben Jonson. The comedies grow out of a combination of many different elements and it is evidence of Shakespeare's genius that he brought them together, it would seem, instinctively. There is no doubt that he also drew on non-dramatic literature, especially the popular prose romances which, with their sudden and unexpected events, their preoccupation with romantic love, their fondness for remote, exotic settings and supernatural happenings provided the immediate source for several of his plots. Shakespeare also took from the romances the element of fantasy or make-believe which is not entirely missing even from such a sombre comedy as *Measure for Measure*. When Rosalind and Celia set out into exile, Portia puts on her lawyer's gown or Angelo plays the role of Duke, no matter how seriously they may regard their situation themselves, the audience is to some extent aware that it is fictional: apparently real people find themselves in imaginary situations. Where Shakespeare chiefly improves on these sources, however, is by making his characters in convincing depth and detail. The characters in the romances may, like Shakespeare's, be preoccupied with love but they seldom express much more than conventional, token feelings whereas Shakespeare has the power to make them live.

Modern criticism has made us more aware of the general nature of Shakespearean comedy. It has not, perhaps, sufficiently emphasized the extraordinary variety of effect which he achieved within the same dramatic form. Although *A Midsummer Night's Dream*, *Measure for Measure* and *The Tempest* may share many structural features in common each is so distinctive in its effect as to be unique; we can sympathize with the critic who declared that there was no such thing as Shakespearean comedy but merely a collection of independent plays. For though it is helpful to try and generalize about their form – it gives us some notion of the kind of thing we are dealing with – the effect of each play, especially in the theatre, is in fact quite different from the rest. Each has its own particular 'atmosphere' which a theatrical director will try to embody in stage designs, costumes and the way he instructs his actors to move. And if he is a careful director he will be guided by the strong sense of place with which Shakespeare took pains to provide him. The earliest comedies contain little or no sense of environment and it was only when he began to write *Love's Labour's Lost* that Shakespeare began to place his figures in a landscape. It is true that this play has practically no physical setting: we learn little about the geography of Navarre beyond its castle and its park, but there is a recognizable social setting with which we gradually become acquainted. This society is small, self-contained and domestic: the king seems to have no army and spends no time actually ruling. It is also a representative society with its young monarch and attendant lords, their Spanish tutor, the local parson and schoolmaster, the constable, the farmhand and the dairymaid. Though some of its members are naive they are seldom stupid – even Dull has a primitive wisdom – and, for all their battles of words, they are frequently lost in admiration of one another's wit. 'Sir,' says the parson to the schoolmaster, 'I praise the Lord for you, and so may my parishioners, for their sons are well tutored by you, and their daughters profit very greatly under you: you are a good member of the commonwealth' (4. 2. 77–80). It is also a very gentle, safe society in which people play at life rather than actually living and the young men write love-verses instead of making love. Two of the major episodes, the masque of Russians and the pageant of the nine worthies, consist of actual play-acting. The arrival of Marcade bringing news of death is therefore not unexpected but his entrance destroys a community which, though sheltered, self-absorbed and parochial, has not been without style and intelligence.

With his next comedy, *A Midsummer Night's Dream*, Shakespeare made an astonishing advance in the art of creating dramatic place and, from then onwards, Illyria, Vienna, Bohemia and the Forest of Arden are as firmly present as their inhabitants. The wood near Athens is profusely described not simply in such formal pieces as Oberon's 'I know a bank where the wild thyme grows' or 'You spotted snakes with double tongue' but in scores of incidental images and allusions:

> Sleep thou, and I will wind thee in my arms ...
> So doth the woodbine the sweet honeysuckle
> Gently entwist: the female ivy so
> Enrings the barky fingers of the elm.
>
> (4. 1. 39–43)

The moonlit, magical world of the forest also gains its power by contrast with the daylight world of law and ceremony at the court and this dramatic placing of one location against another becomes as regular a feature of the comedies as the placing of one kind of character against another which we have already noticed. The descriptive writing is, however, excessive, as though Shakespeare was carried away by the discovery of what he could do and, although the verse is probably more beautiful than that of any other play, it is an obvious beauty which exceeds its dramatic purpose and is not sufficiently integrated into the dramatic situation. Many of the descriptive passages seem like recitations and are too easily detachable from their context. The scene-setting of *The Merchant of Venice* is much more discreet and controlled. Shakespeare by now has discovered how to make his characters describe their environment while apparently talking about something else. Salerio in the opening scene appears to be discussing Antonio's unaccountable melancholy but one reason why Shakespeare allows Antonio to be baffled by his malady is in order to give Salerio a reason for describing Venice and its ships:

> Your mind is tossing on the ocean,
> There, where your argosies with portly sail—
> Like signiors and rich burghers on the flood,
> Or as it were the pageants of the sea—
> Do overpeer the petty traffickers,
> That curtsy to them, do them reverence,
> As they fly by them with their woven wings.
>
> (1. 1. 8–14)

He goes on to say that, were he a wealthy ship-owner like Antonio he would worry about

> dangerous rocks
> Which, touching but my gentle vessel's side
> Would scatter all her spices on the stream,
> Enrobe the roaring waters with my silks,
> And, in a word, but even now worth this,
> And now worth nothing.
>
> (1. 1. 31–6)

Within forty lines Shakespeare has told us something about Antonio's character, occupation and social position and at the same time has created an image of the wealthy, proud, exotic and precarious life of Venice. He has also prepared us for the catastrophe which will drop Antonio into Shylock's grasp. In due course the tough Venetian world with its financial bargaining and commercial wealth is placed in opposition to the generous opulence of Belmont with its inherited wealth and its music. This contrast is established not merely for theatrical effect but as a means of strengthening other dramatic contrasts within the play, for the confrontation between Shylock and Portia is also a clash between two opposing sets of values and these are in part the product of the two environments in which they have grown: the setting has become an integral part of the play.

*The Merchant of Venice* also displays an advance in the subtlety with which Shakespeare controlled the moral conflicts in the comedies. Among the many traditions on which he drew in the evolution of his own characteristic kind of comedy was the allegorical tradition of the morality plays. We have already noticed the allegorical effect of the conclusion of *As You Like It* but this element is already present in a comparatively crude form in *The Two Gentlemen of Verona* where Proteus is torn between his love for Julia, his love for Silvia and his loyalty to Valentine and, later, Valentine is forced to make a choice between the demands of his love for Silvia and his friendship for Proteus. The fact that both men have to choose between two conflicting principles as well as between two personal claims adds to the weightiness of their predicaments. In *The Merchant of Venice* the moral tensions are less simple and less easily resolved. Portia's eloquent plea for mercy in the trial scene appears to have been placed in a simple antithesis to Shylock's earlier demand for justice and both seem to be carrying into the public, judicial sphere attitudes they have previously shown in private. The motivation of the characters is not, however, simple nor are their moral functions in the play. Portia's eulogy of mercy is not disinterested: it is one of several tactics she resorts to in order to rescue her husband's friend and when she is no longer pleading Antonio's defence but sits in judgement over Shylock she conveniently ignores her own homily. Though love may be allied with friendship in the framework of the play and identified with mercy, it is also related to self-interest, and we may notice that Bassanio was attracted as much by Portia's money as her good looks. The characters are no longer cast in the simple roles of a morality play but reveal an uncertainty and complexity of motivation which is more true to life. Shylock may be motivated by a financial prudence which is inferior to the generosity of Antonio but he is also driven by personal malice towards Antonio, a malice which the merchant has himself aroused by his inhuman treatment of Shylock. Antonio is therefore partially to blame for his own predicament.

To say that the comedies are preoccupied with love is once again to neglect their uniqueness and the variety of forms which love is shown to take. It includes the romantic excitement of Rosalind, the generosity of Portia, the maternal care of the Countess for Helena and the lust of Angelo for Isabella. *Measure for Measure* also moves towards the discovery of a love which is not the private attraction of one individual to another but a compassion for corrupt human nature similar to that discovered by Lear in the play Shakespeare wrote a year later. It is the comedy in which moral conflict is conducted at its most intricate and intense and can be called a comedy only by virtue of its structural design. Many critics have set it apart, together with *Troilus and Cressida* and *All's Well*, as a different kind of play, a 'problem play'. But to the extent that they exhibit characters under the stress of moral conflict, most of the comedies are problem plays and *Measure for Measure* differs from the others only in the degree to which its moral tensions are sustained.

Like the characters in the other comedies, Angelo, Claudio and Isabella find themselves in sudden and baffling predicaments. Angelo is landed with the job of restoring order to a society which has grown corrupt, Claudio, a betrothed man anticipating marriage, finds himself a prisoner awaiting death, and Isabella, a novice pledged to chastity, is given the chance to save Claudio by sacrificing her maidenhead. What distinguishes these people, however, from the heroines of previous comedies is their inability to solve their dilemmas, partly because their problems are almost insurmountable and partly because they lack the qualities needed to overcome them. Claudio, though consoled for a while by the Duke's stoicism, quickly falls back into terror and panic at the prospect of death:

> Ay, but to die, and go we know not where,
> To lie in cold obstruction, and to rot,
> This sensible warm motion – to become
> A kneaded clod; and the delighted spirit
> To bathe in fiery floods, or to reside
> In thrilling region of thick-ribbed ice,
> To be imprisoned in the viewless winds
> And blown with restless violence round about
> The pendent world . . . or to be worse than worst
> Of those that lawless and incertain thoughts
> Imagine howling – 'tis too horrible.
>
> (3. 1. 117–27)

If Claudio recoils from this challenge through lack of resolution, Angelo fails in his by exercising too much. On being given full scope 'to enforce and qualify the laws' as he thinks fit, he chooses to enforce them with inhuman rigour, commanding all the brothels in the town to be demolished and condemning Claudio to death for adultery. To have allowed the law to remain idle would certainly have been wrong but so is the ruthless course which Angelo adopts. He is high-handed, taking no account of particular circumstances and in one case unjust since Claudio is at least betrothed to the woman he has made pregnant. Morality apart, he is also unrealistic: as Pompey pertinently asks 'Does your worship mean to geld and splay all the youth of the city?' and it is only when Angelo detects the sexual appetite within himself that he begins to have doubts about his conduct and to question his own authority. With the arrival of Isabella to plead for Claudio he is faced with a further dilemma. He can give way to her entreaties, pardon Claudio and be guilty of partiality or he can ignore her, execute Claudio and be inhumane. In fact he devises a third, even less defensible course and offers to free Claudio if Isabella will satisfy his mounting lust for her. And when later he reveals that, even if Isabella does give way to him, he will still execute Claudio, he forfeits all moral claim to wield authority, as he realizes himself. None of the problems which confront him can be solved easily but by being both over-scrupulous and corrupt Angelo falls into two opposing kinds of error at the same time. He is stringent in public but secretly lustful and is unable to adopt a middle course which would combine justice with compassion. Such compassion, Shakespeare suggests, can grow only from an understanding of human nature and this depends on having knowledge of oneself:

> He, who the sword of heaven will bear,
> Should be as holy as severe:
> Pattern in himself to know,
> Grace to stand, an virtue go:
> More nor less to others paying,
> Than by self-offences weighing.

(3. 2. 253–8)

When, under the stress of circumstances for which he is largely responsible, Angelo does begin to understand himself, the discovery comes almost too late to save either Claudio or himself.

Isabella's predicament is just as urgent and intractable. She can either abide by her religious vow of chastity and thereby let her brother die or, as she believes, save Claudio at the expense of the virginity she is pledged to preserve. Neither course can be entirely right and either is potentially disastrous. Her immediate, spontaneous decision, 'Then Isabel live chaste, and brother die; More than our brother is our chastity', is hardly consistent with the Christian ideals of love and sacrifice to which she aspires. In the two most exciting scenes of the play Angelo and Isabella challenge each other's ability to feel compassion and rigorously test each other's character in the place where it is most vulnerable. Under the strain of this experience they reveal themselves with an intensity and depth comparable to that of Shakespeare's tragic heroes and the clash of their personalities is made the more forceful by the fact that its outcome will affect another man's life and will mark a victory for one of several opposing principles. One reason why the scenes between them are dramatically so successful is because they raise such questions as the rights of sacred over secular law, the demands of abstract principle against human sympathy, the claims by which imperfect men may sit in judgement over their fellows and the possibility of right action in a situation where nothing is incorrupt.

Having brought his characters to an impasse in which they are compelled to act but any action must apparently be calamitous, Shakespeare then allows the Duke to intervene and impose a happy solution to their difficulties which, in the event, seems facile and contrived, a hasty attempt by Shakespeare to dispose of the problems he has raised by manufacturing rather than evolving a conclusion. It may be thought that the artistic flaws of the last act are caused by an incompatibility between the comic form of the play and its ethical content and that some problems are too serious for comedy to deal with. But there seems no reason why so flexible a form should not be capable of encompassing any issue, however serious. This lack of coherence is more probably caused by Shakespeare's failure to accommodate the comic action to characters who are simply too convincing. The plot of the last scenes is not in itself less credible than those of the previous comedies but Shakespeare has produced two characters of such depth that, for the first time, they are too lifelike for the actions he makes them undergo. Shakespeare almost certainly knew what he was doing and he seems, at this stage of his career, to be trying to discover how much weight the structure of comedy could bear without collapsing altogether. Although his experiment failed on this occasion it succeeded in the last comedies, the romances, where the denouement is extended over a much longer period and can therefore be made more acceptable. *The Tempest* in fact consists of

# SHAKESPEARE: HIS TRAGEDIES

## Anne Barton

In 1598, Francis Meres singled out six 'tragedies' by William Shakespeare for special praise. They were: *Richard II*, *Richard III*, *Henry IV*, *King John*, *Titus Andronicus* and *Romeo and Juliet*. He also listed six comedies, asserting that 'Shakespeare among the English is the most excellent in both kinds for the stage'. Meres's reluctance to make use of the new and somewhat dubious term *history* is understandable, considering that he was out to celebrate Elizabethan literature by way of comparisons with the ancient world. *Comedy* and *tragedy* were the two categories sanctioned by Aristotle and exemplified by Plautus and Seneca. *History* was only precariously respectable as a dramatic classification, while such experimental compounds as 'tragical-historical' (although by no means the purely private lunacy of Polonius) were more doubtful still. Simple conservatism cannot, however, have been entirely responsible for Meres's failure to distinguish between Shakespeare's tragedies and his history plays. Subsequent critics, while most of them have admitted *history* as a category, have not found it easy to determine where the borderline between these two dramatic forms ought to lie. Despite (or perhaps because of) the immense elaboration of tragic theory over the last three centuries, the growing conviction that this is the most special and exclusive of dramatic genres, it seems impossible to reach any general agreement as to how many of the thirty-seven plays in the Shakespeare canon ought to be read, and discussed, as tragedies.

Hemming and Condell were Shakespeare's friends and colleagues as well as being his first editors. They may have sought his advice on the plan of the First Folio. In any case, they divided his plays into Comedies, Histories and Tragedies in a fashion suggesting reasonable certainty as to the form and limits of the first group, a willingness to impose definition upon the second for the sake of convenience, and unabashed confusion with respect to the third. Disparate though they may be in date and character, the fourteen plays assembled as Comedies in the First Folio form a distinct and basically homogeneous group. Every one of them moves purposefully through five acts towards a resolution in marriage. The History section, by contrast, seems frankly arbitrary. Here, Hemming and Condell have assembled, in chronological order according to reign, a mixed lot of ten plays dealing with actual, as opposed to legendary, English kings. Two of these plays, *Richard II* and *Richard III*, had already been described quite explicitly in Quarto editions as tragedies. Several of the others are ambiguous in form. Obviously, the First Folio designated its Histories less as the result of any considered, aesthetic judgment than because Shakespeare's editors wished to present a dramatic sequence, a panorama of English history beginning with the troubles of King John and ending with those of Henry VIII.

Tragedy, as a result, became the most inchoate of the three sections. Hemming and Condell simply gathered together in this final group everything left over after they had established the other two. Of the twelve plays involved, *Cymbeline* now seems the most unlikely as a tragedy, so much so that scholars have occasionally tried to suggest that it was placed here only because the copy arrived in the printing house too late for inclusion in either of the preceding sections. There is no evidence to support such a theory. The plot of *Cymbeline*, although it comes close to destroying the pre-existing union of Imogen and Posthumus, does not work towards the accomplishment of any marriage. In this respect, it is unlike *The Winter's Tale, The Tempest*, and all the other First Folio comedies. Cymbeline himself, even by the generous standards of Elizabethan historiography, was only an imaginary British king, and so debarred from ante-dating John in the History section. The play probably joined the Tragedies simply because there was nowhere else for it to go. It is far from being the only uncertain member of the group. If *Richard II* is to be called a history, so must three out of the four Roman plays classified in the First Folio as tragedies. *Julius Caesar, Antony and Cleopatra* and *Coriolanus* not only maintain a similar balance between public and private worlds, between politics and the individual, they quite obviously develop certain of the conflicts and preoccupations of *Richard II* in a classical setting. *Romeo and Juliet, Hamlet* and *Othello* are unquestionably tragedies. *Titus Andronicus* can be excluded only on the dubious grounds that you happen to dislike it. *Macbeth* on the other hand, is a tragical-historical hybrid and so, in a different sense, are *Troilus and Cressida* and *Timon of Athens*. It is very difficult indeed to determine what formal definition binds all eleven of these plays together, and associates them logically with a twelfth: a play now generally regarded as

Shakespeare's supreme tragic achievement, which was originally published, however, in 1608 as 'M. William Shakespeare: His True Chronicle Historie of the life and death of King Lear'.

Unlike Chapman and Ben Jonson, Philip Sidney or Thomas Kyd, Shakespeare does not seem to have thought of tragedy as a particular kind of dramatic structure, or even a definable artistic form. This, surely, is one reason for the uneasiness of the First Folio classification. He tended to be evasive about the word *tragedy* itself, as he was not about *comedy*, its companion. When Berowne, in the final moments of *Love's Labour's Lost*, comments ruefully:

> Our wooing doth not end like an old play:
> Jack hath not Jill: these ladies' courtesy
> Might well have made our sport a comedy,
>
> (5. 2. 870–2)

his meaning is precise: marriage, although expected as an ultimate resolution, has had to be postponed beyond the limits of the fifth act. Shakespeare's infrequent uses of *tragedy* and *tragic* are all, by contrast, extremely vague. Certainly, Lodovico's 'Look on the tragic loading of this bed', at the end of *Othello* (5. 2. 365), has nothing like the specific force of Berowne's observation. Here, Shakespeare is employing the term in exactly that casual sense which modern literary critics like to deplore as a distortion fostered by the popular press. Lodovico's 'tragic' is little more than a way of describing calamity: events that are unusual, distressing, and associated with death. This rather cloudy, essentially emotional use of the word is entirely characteristic of Shakespeare. In fact, on those rare occasions when he does allow *tragedy* or *tragic* to assume the kind of structural meaning that it has in the work of Ben Jonson, he does so in order to mock it. This is what happens with the various attempts to describe the Pyramus and Thisbe interlude in *A Midsummer Night's Dream*, as it does with the pedantries of Polonius. Hamlet's Mouse-trap, 'The Murther of Gonzago', may seem from what we see and hear of it to qualify unequivocally as tragedy. Kyd, in his *Spanish Tragedy* a few years before, had introduced a somewhat similar inset play with a virtual disquisition on the art of tragic drama. Shakespeare, by contrast, insists in all the talk about 'The Murther of Gonzago' that it is a 'play', and nothing more. On the one occasion when it is called a tragedy, by the Prologue, the comment produces from Hamlet himself a howl of scorn (3. 2. 150).

Of the nineteen instances of *tragic* or *tragedy* listed in Bartlett's Concordance to Shakespeare's plays, no fewer than twelve come from the Henry VI plays, *Richard III* and *Titus Andronicus*: all of them early works marked by a certain, consciously literary, straining after grandiose effects. Characters tend to use these words when the action becomes especially dire, or portentous, and they are at least as likely to be thinking of something read – a 'tragic tale' (*Titus Andronicus*, 4. 1. 48) – as they are of the stage. Such usage is basically medieval. Chaucer's 'Monk's Tale', Lydgate's *Fall of Princes* and its Elizabethan successor *The Mirror for Magistrates*, had all treated tragedy as a cautionary form: a warning to great men against placing any faith in secular place and power. The three parts of *Henry VI* and *Richard III*, for all the brilliance of their construction as plays, nevertheless are associated with the older, non-dramatic tradition. They too chronicle the downward swings of Fortune's wheel. Their characters lament, in a choric fashion, the insubstantiality of ambition and its achievements, involving 'tragedy' as a synonym for disaster in a sense that Lydgate or Chaucer's monk would have understood. The didacticism of these plays is, however, imperfect. Although the idea that it is folly to trust the world comes over in them clearly enough, the pattern of retributive justice which they expose seems brutal and mechanistic. If God's Providence is reponsible for the individual fates of the knights and bishops, the pawns, kings and queens involved in this enormous game of chess – and all four plays are orthodox in suggesting that it is – then His power is undeniable. But there is no compensating sense of Heaven as a place in which human beings can place their hope, no viable alternative to the treacheries of a world which may be insecure and appalling but is also, as far as Shakespeare is concerned, the only reality. This non-committal attitude towards Providence divides the four early tragical-histories, seen as a whole, from that simpler, medieval attitude towards tragedy which individual characters occasionally invoke.

From the Henry VI plays and *Richard III*, one line of Shakespeare's characteristically amorphous and ill-defined tragic development leads on through *King John, Richard II*, the two parts of *Henry IV* and *Henry V*. Here, the emphasis shifts, fastening upon the crown itself as the source of tragic experience. To be a king and no king in the manner of John, the usurper on Arthur's rightful throne, is bad enough. The position of Richard II, no longer a king after Bolingbroke's rise to power, but not quite a private individual either, is even worse. There is a sense in which Meres was right when he classified both these plays, and *Henry IV*, as tragedies. All four of them, and *Henry V*, explore a particular kind of identity crisis in tragic terms. All emerge from that complicated view of kingship which, as Ernst Kantorowicz has shown, in *The King's Two Bodies*, Elizabethans inherited from medieval political theology. According to the doctrine of the king's two bodies, the sovereign is a being cut off from the world of private individuals by the fact that he alone possesses twin natures: a body natural, as the theorists described it, which is mystically united at the moment of coronation with a body politic. Once assumed, this dual identity is irrevocably his for life. In practice, however, it is excruciatingly difficult to maintain. With the spectres of death and deposition hovering always at his side, the king must try to support within finite time the kind of incarnation which only Christ could encompass successfully, within eternity. Enforced abdication can only reduce him, as Richard II declares, to 'nothing' (4. 1. 201), to a desperate groping after identity somewhere between the sundered halves of his former self. Shakespeare was not the only Elizabethan dramatist who recognized that tragedy of a peculiarly powerful kind can be extracted from the anomalous situation of the king deposed. Marlowe, and others, had seen this too. Where he does seem to have been unique was in his understanding that the opposite transformation, the one undergone by Bolingbroke and after him by Prince Hal, from man into king, is invariably tragic too.

When Hal declares at the end of *2 Henry IV* that the crown 'hath fed upon the body of my father' (4. 5. 159), he is not referring only to its physical ravages. The crown does indeed 'eat the bearer up' (4. 5. 164) in an even more sinister sense. The king preys off the man, reducing him to a cipher, depriving him of his personality. It has already reduced the voluble and passionate Harry Hereford of the early part of *Richard II* to the 'silent king' (*Richard II*, 4. 1. 290) of the deposition scene. In fact, Richard's own progress towards tormented individuality has been crossed and balanced by Bolingbroke's retreat into the anonymity consequent upon his acceptance of a double nature. In the two Henry IV plays, the king stands alone: a masked figure, stripped of personal relationships. The position of his son, the man born to be king, is similar. Neither with Falstaff nor with Poins is Hal free to behave purely as a private person. He lives under the shadow of the crown which will one day be his, and this means that a ghostly other self accompanies him everywhere he goes, at Gadshill as at Shrewsbury, in the Boar's Head Tavern as well as the court. Like the deposed Richard, he is a sort of half-king who wears away an uncomfortable interim playing parts, waiting for the moment when he must vanish completely into his permanent, predestined role as Henry V. His eventual success in that role is purchased at a heavy price. Fluellen's cautious inquiry after Bardolph's execution – 'If your majesty know the man' (*Henry V*, 3. 6. 98–9) – can only be answered, or evaded, with a judicial sentence reminding us that Hal has now surrendered not only his individuality but even his personal memory of time past to the requirements of a corporate identity: 'We would have all such offenders so cut off' (3. 6. 104–5). Henry's most uncomfortable moments in the play, embarrassments less spectacular but, in a sense, more disturbing than the military situation at Agincourt, are those in which an essentially personal response is exacted of him: when he confronts the treachery of his friend Scroop, or with William and Bates before the battle, or in the wooing of Katherine. Hampered as he is by the possession of twin natures, Henry cannot deal easily or straightforwardly with dialogue which engages him, primarily, as an individual. In this limitation there is tragedy.

Most of Shakespeare's Elizabethan tragedy seems to have sprung from a meditation on history: more specifically, from his awareness of the discrepancy between great political roles and the human beings who enact them. *Julius Caesar*, despite its Roman setting, nevertheless constitutes an extension and development of the plays about kingship. There were, however, certain other directions taken by Shakespeare's tragic writing in the period before the death of Elizabeth in 1603. One of them produced the two revenge plays, *Titus Andronicus* and *Hamlet*. Another links *Romeo and Juliet* with *Othello*, both of them plays about the ill-fated love of private individuals. *Troilus and Cressida* is close to *Hamlet* in date, and shares some of its characteristics, but it exists subbornly in a category of its own. Half history, half revenge play, sounding at times like a corrupt echo of *Romeo and Juliet*, it was variously described in Shakespeare's lifetime as a comedy, as a history and as a tragedy. Modern critics have, on the whole, succeeded in proving only that its genre will shift obligingly according to the manner in which the play is read.

Revenge, as a dramatic theme, is almost as old as tragedy itself. The *Agamemnon* and the *Choephori* of Aeschylus are, after all, revenge plays. As early as 1567, at least one Elizabethan dramatist had made a clumsy attempt to unite the classical story of Orestes' revenge for Agamemnon with a morality play structure. In John Pickering's *Horestes*, the hero wavers between the blandishments of his bad angel, the Vice Revenge, and the enlightened counsels of

Nature personified. Under the evil influence of the former, Horestes at last kills Clytemnestra and her lover, and so pacifies his father's spirit. This deed accomplished, he repents of it and, surprisingly, is welcomed back into a society which actually forms itself around him, as king. All the blame falls upon Revenge himself, who is ritually exiled. This use of Revenge as scapegoat, absolving the avenger himself from moral responsibility for his actions, allowed Pickering to express almost diagrammatically the characteristic Elizabethan conflict of attitudes towards the man of blood. The audience was invited to sympathize with the hero while dissociating itself from Revenge. Tactically, this is cunning, but it prevented Pickering from exploiting the tragic potential of the form. Kyd, in *The Spanish Tragedy* a few years later, pushed his figure of Revenge outside the play proper. The protagonist, as a result, bears the full burden of his decision to kill. Hieronymo's position isolates him from society with no possibility of return; it forces upon him a strange, detached view of the world, an anguished questioning of heavenly justice, and of the workings of his own heart, which points in the direction of Shakespeare's *Hamlet*. Kyd's play is immensely more assured, and also more dramatic, than Pickering's. Nevertheless, it preserves in a subtler form the same, curious, ethical contradiction. In the frame of *The Spanish Tragedy*, a kind of Senecan circle drawn around the action itself, the two spectator-characters Don Andrea and Revenge not only condone Hieronymo's vengeance, they send him at the end to live in perpetual bliss in a pagan Elysium. This essentially literary supernatural accounts, however, for only half the theology of the tragedy. Kyd also expected his audience to judge and, ultimately, to damn Hieronymo according to Christian law. Revenge may be praised in the frame; in the play, it is condemned, and no mediation between these conflicting verdicts is proposed.

   *Titus Andronicus* also operates in that ambiguous space between the official Elizabethan castigation of private revenges, and an unofficial sympathy, and practice. Like *The Spanish Tragedy*, it is stylized, rhetorical and eminently theatrical: a limited, but totally achieved, work of art. Unlike Kyd's play, it maintains a consistent attitude towards the revenge hero. *Titus Andronicus* has no frame. Revenge personified does appear in the action, but only as a bit of make-believe, one of Tamora's ill-considered devices. This mythical, half-barbaric Roman world announces itself from the beginning as an artificial construct. A society which calmly accepts human sacrifice, leaving the chief proponent of this practice to ascend the throne at the end, with the approval of the virtuous, is a society carefully distanced – like that of Marlowe's *Tamburlaine* – from Elizabethan moral realities. Although Titus himself, in the fourth act, wraps petitions for justice from the gods around the shafts of arrows, and looses them into the sky, the supernatural in this play resembles a slab of marble suspended over the heads of the characters. Inert, neutral and cold, it serves to keep them in their place without itself issuing either prohibitions or commands. Basically, the tragedy narrows down to one issue: how will Titus, beaten to earth, excluded from the court, deprived of his sons, maddened and maimed, contrive nonetheless to avenge his children? At the end, with most of the cast (including Titus himself) dead by violence, our principal reaction is gratification at the solution of a problem, at symmetry achieved. We can see exactly how, against terrible odds, Titus has achieved his purpose. Questions which go beyond the facts of the case itself are simply brushed aside as irrelevant to this intense, frightening, but wholly arbitrary view of human life.

If *Titus* seems unusual in the restriction of its vision, the amount which has been omitted from a world picture which buys sharpness of focus at the expense of range and verisimilitude, *Hamlet* of course astonishes for the opposite reason. The length of the play suggests that it was never, not even in Shakespeare's time, performed uncut. Other plays by Shakespeare are long; no other violates so strikingly the limits of audience attention, or asks for so much from its leading actor. Like *Titus*, like *The Spanish Tragedy* and that lost source play, the so-called *Ur-Hamlet*, which was probably the work of Kyd, Shakespeare's *Hamlet* is a tragedy of revenge. It concentrates, like them, upon a single, essentially sympathetic hero and it confronts precisely the same structural problem: how to linger out his vengeance for the necessary five acts. Kyd's Hieronymo (and probably his Hamlet), Shakespeare's Titus and Hamlet all require proof of the villain's identity before they can act. They are temporarily deflected from their purpose, not only by difficulties of strategy, but by a madness partly assumed and partly real. All make use of some kind of dramatic show to further their intention and all accomplish, in the end, a vengeance which, whatever the original provocation, has by this time become more than a little suspect.

As a tragic predicament, revenge has several inherent advantages. Intrigue and spectacle, madness and violence, are not the only elements native to the genre. The isolation naturally imposed upon the revenger not only encourages introspection, it destroys normal human relationships in a fundamentally tragic way. A detached, satirist's view of the society against which they war almost forces itself upon these characters. Their situation generates a corrosive doubt, reaching out to attack religious, moral and legal institutions. Kyd, Marlowe in *The Jew of Malta*, and the young Shakespeare of *Titus*, had all recognized and explored these inbuilt opportunities, at least to some extent. It was only with *Hamlet*, however, that a dramatist seized upon the form to trigger off an enquiry into the whole basis of human existence. Debate over man's right to encroach upon the prerogative of Heaven by undertaking himself what was properly God's act of retributive justice had been and, in the Jacobean period, would continue to be a feature of revenge tragedy. Even in the pagan never-never land of *Titus*, the orthodox position is stated by Titus's brother Marcus (4. 1. 129–30). *Timon of Athens* was to express the prohibition even more clearly:

> He's truly valiant that can wisely suffer
> The worst that man can breathe,
> And make his wrongs his outsides,
> To wear them like his raiment, carelessly,
> And ne'er prefer his injuries to his heart,
> To bring it into danger.
> If wrongs be evils and enforce us kill,
> What folly 'tis to hazard life for ill! ...
> You cannot make gross sins look clear:
> To revenge is no valour, but to bear.
>
> (3. 5. 31–40)

Only *Hamlet* side-steps the ethic of revenge entirely. It is one of several great silences at the heart of this play. Deliberately, Shakespeare has shifted attention away from an expected centre, from the problem of whether the prince *ought* to kill Claudius – or even whether in practical terms he *can* – to the far more complicated and subjective issue of whether or not he ultimately *will*. It is not the peculiar status of acts of private vengeance that is under review here, but the validity of all and any human action.

Although other dramatists (Marston, Webster and Tourneur especially) later used *Hamlet* as a spring-board for their own exploration of the revenge form, none of them dared to attempt a focus so wide. The range of the play and, above all, of the role of Hamlet himself, is so great that any performance must necessarily be a matter of selection, of emphases more or less arbitrarily imposed. The impossibility of presenting *Hamlet* whole and uncut is not entirely a feature of its great length. It is also bound up with its inclusiveness, with the fact that Shakespeare seems to have been determined to subject a bewildering number of people, ideas, values, kinds of relationship, emotions and social forms to the distorted but strangely clear scrutiny of a revenger so complicated himself that no attempt to describe, or act, him can be more than partial. Even more than most plays of Shakespeare, *Hamlet* is a warning against the fallacy that any critical interpretation or stage production can be definitive, or even complete.

When Hamlet cautioned Rosencrantz and Guildenstern, after the play scene, against the attempt to 'pluck out the heart of my mystery . . . sound me from my lowest note to the top of my compass' (3. 2. 368–70), he also provided a useful counsel for literary critics. The play as a whole is built upon contradition, upon the promulgation of confusion. Shakespeare gives every indication of having constructed an imaginary Denmark intended to baffle, to resist explanation as stubbornly as those mysterious facts of human existence which it illuminates without rationalizing. A distrust of what might be described as a 'play-shaped' view of the world of the falseness of clearly defined moral, theological or formal patterns imposed upon reality in the interests of art is, I think, characteristic of him throughout his dramatic career. It was to become particularly strong in his Jacobean plays. This antipathy may account, in part, for Shakespeare's apparent suspicion of *tragedy* as a term, and also for the variety and restlessness of his own formal development.

Certainly, the eschatology of *Hamlet* defies explication. The ghost of a murdered king appears from an almost embarrassingly specific Catholic Purgatory, a place of 'sulph'rous and tormenting flames' (1. 5. 3.) to which it has been confined 'till the four crimes done in my days of nature/Are burnt and purged away' (1. 5. 12–13). This spirit urges upon its beloved only son a revenge for which, by immutable Christian law, that son must be damned perpetually – sent not to Purgatory, but to the far greater torments of Hell. Neither Hamlet, the sensible Horatio nor the ghost itself ever remark upon this illogicality. Hamlet's worry is only about the truth of the ghost's accusation. If Claudius is guilty, and the Mouse-trap proves that he is, he must be killed. Not for an instant does Hamlet doubt the justice of such a course, let alone the propriety of a repentant soul spending its time in Purgatory meditating a murder. A similar inconsistency adds complications to what is already, on psychological grounds, a most ambiguous scene in Act 3. Hamlet declines to kill the king at prayers because he fears that Claudius' soul will ascend to Heaven. This, at least, is the reason he gives. He will wait to find his enemy

> drunk asleep, or in his rage,
> Or in th'incestuous pleasure of his bed,
> At game, a-swearing, or about some act
> That has no relish of salvation in't,
> Then trip him that his heels may kick at heaven,
> And that his soul may be as damned and black
> As hell whereto it goes.
>
> (3. 3. 89–95)

Here, the odd fact that Hamlet never considers that his own soul would be damned irrecoverably by the requirements of such a theology, is cunningly mingled with doubts as to whether he really means what he is saying in this speech, or whether it is a feeble excuse for postponing an explicably distasteful task.

In *Hamlet*, Shakespeare affirms a Christian supernatural in one moment to deny it in the next. The hereafter involves Purgatory, hell fire, and flights of angels. It is also silence, an eternal sleep that has nothing to do with punishment or reward. The prince talks about death as 'the undiscovered country, from whose bourn/No traveller returns' (3. 1. 79–80) out of an anguish of mind created by the return of just such a traveller. A special Providence guides the fall of the sparrow, or at least Hamlet asserts that it does just before the fatal game with the foils in Act 5. He seems to die, however, in the agnostic spirit which, a moment later, prompts Horatio's account of the catastrophe as 'accidental judgements, casual slaughters' (5. 2. 380). These conflicting views follow one another so closely in the action, and they are treated by the dramatist with such a non-committal equality, that it becomes impossible to characterize the supernatural in the play. Although we stumble from time to time over the partially submerged rocks of old beliefs, their presence only makes the obscurity of the total picture more poignant. In effect, Shakespeare has created his own, infinitely more complex version of the divided worlds of *Horestes* and *The Spanish Tragedy*. Hamlet's questions, instead of being halted artificially as Hieronymo's were by a tidy, Senecan supernatural visible to us in the audience although not to the hero, grope their way into a darkness without form or limit. Like Pickering, Shakespeare placed his spirit of Revenge inside the play itself, as a character who addresses the protagonist directly. Having done so, he proceeded disconcertingly to associate the ghost with a Christian hereafter, and refused to judge its ethic of blood vengeance. *Hamlet* never explains the nature of that silence towards which the hero moves gradually, away from us, and into which he finally vanishes.

This is one reason why the tragedy has a terror, and also a relevance to the world as we know it, lacking in Pickering and Kyd.

More perhaps than any other Shakespearean tragedy, *Hamlet* is a play obsessed with words themselves. It displaces the accustomed centre of earlier revenge drama by subordinating plot for its own sake to a new concern with the mysterious gap between thought and action, between the verbal formulation of intent and its concrete realization. The prince himself is the most articulate of Shakespeare's tragic heroes, but he combines verbal fluency with a curious paralysis of the will. When Claudius asks Laertes in Act 4 what he would do 'to show yourself your father's son in deed/More than in words' (4. 7. 124–5), Laertes replies instantly that, to be avenged, he would be happy to cut Hamlet's throat 'i'th'church'. A demonstration that 'in deed more than words' he is his father's son is conspicuously what the Hamlet of 'O, what a rogue and peasant slave am I' and 'How all occasions do inform against me' has not managed. We may respect him for this failing. Certainly, the sharply contrasted readiness of Laertes to act without thinking is unlovely. The fact remains that Hamlet is a man suffering from a peculiar malaise. In his mind, speech and event, language and its realization have become separate and disjunct. He can initiate action only when he has no time to subject it, first, to words: when he stabs impulsively through the arras and kills Polonius, when he sends Rosencrantz and Guildenstern to death *before* 'I could make a prologue to my brains' (5. 2. 30), boards the pirate ship in the heat of the moment or finally, without premeditation, kills the king. The Norwegian captain tells Hamlet in the fourth scene of Act 4 that Fortinbras is hazarding twenty thousand ducats and an army of two thousand men to gain 'a little patch of ground/That hath in it no profit but the name' (4. 4. 18–19). Fortinbras here, as in other respects, is Hamlet's diametric opposite. He has converted a mere word, a name, into a pretext for action. Hamlet, on the other hand, allows a tangible situation, the fact of a father's murder, to dissolve into words alone.

*Troilus and Cressida* was probably a play designed not for the public theatre, but for the more specialized audience of the Inns of Court. Its subject matter, the last stages of the Greek siege of Troy, with the death of Hector, was inherently tragic. Its characters in both camps were archetypal heroes. The play which Shakespeare produced, however, is tragic only according to its own highly special rules. It is not heroic at all, although at a number of points it tempts the theatre audience into believing that it is about to become so.

Caroline Spurgeon once pointed out that *Troilus and Cressida* and *Hamlet* are linked by a distinctive pattern of disease imagery. Ideas of physical sickness, of slow corruption in the flesh, characterize them both. They are also alike in their attitude towards language as disjoined from action. Like *Hamlet*, with its formal address by Claudius to his court in the second scene of Act 1, *Troilus* places close to the beginning a scene of set speeches, of formal, rhetoric display. The Greek leaders, Agamemnon, Nestor, Ulysses, debate the reasons for their lack of success in the siege of Troy. This debate is intensely intellectual, full of intricate verbal manoeuvre. It is something of a shock to find at the end of it that Ulysses's noble speech on order (1. 3. 75–137), the most famous passage in the play, has as its practical issue the petty – and also quite ineffective – plan to force Achilles out of his tent and into his armour by making him jealous of the blockish Ajax. All that Ulysses will manage to do through his subtle insults and persuasions is to make Ajax even more intolerable than he was originally, while leaving the great Achilles inactive. It is only blind chance, the accidental death of Patroclus in battle, which finally rouses Achilles and sends him out to ensure the Greek victory through a revenge so cowardly and disgusting that it undermines what little stature the play has hitherto allowed him.

Among the Greeks, there is a singular lack of connection between verbal formulation and the action that results. The Trojans are no better. In the council scene of Act 2, Hector seems for a while the one sane man in a brood of romantic hotheads. His arguments for returning Helen to her country, for ending the war, are unanswerable. It is transparently true that, as he says, 'she is not worth what she doth cost/The keeping' (2. 2. 51–2). Against Hector's beautifully rational arguments, Paris looks like a blind egotist, and Troilus like a besotted fool. Linguistically, Hector towers over the other Trojans, even as Ulysses had dominated the Greeks. When it comes, however, to the point of embodying his own words in action, he moves, bewilderingly, in the opposite direction:

> Hector's opinion
> Is this, in way of truth. Yet, ne'ertheless,
> My sprightly brethren, I propend to you
> In resolution to keep Helen still;
> For 'tis a cause that hath no mean dependence
> Upon our joint and several dignities.
>
> (2. 2. 188–93)

He had already, before urging peace in the Trojan council scene, despatched his personal challenge to the Greeks. The same kind of baffling discrepancy is visible too in the love plot, where words in the form of solemn vows and promises are contradicted so immediately by Cressida's actions when she arrives among the Greeks that it becomes hard for an audience, as well as for Troilus himself, to believe that she could ever have spoken them.

Obviously, the problem in *Troilus and Cressida* is not quite the same as the one explored in *Hamlet*. This is, after all, in its subject matter, its structure, and its general savagery of tone, a very different play. In *Hamlet*, the central character had seemed unable to move from the words of which he was so consummate a master to action of any deliberate kind. In *Troilus*, where no character can really be described as central, it is more a matter of continual non sequiturs. Greeks and Trojans alike tend to give their intentions the most elaborate linguistic embodiment and then, for no reason that they can articulate, act in a totally contradictory fashion. Nonetheless, both of these plays written just at the beginning of the seventeenth century, and certainly Shakespeare's most complex and impressive ventures up to that point, extract tragedy from a special kind of hiatus between the formulation of action, and the action itself.

To move back in time from *Troilus and Cressida* and *Hamlet*, both of them plays that stand at the entrance to the Jacobean period, to the intensely Elizabethan tragedy of *Romeo and Juliet* is to enter a simpler world. This is not to denigrate *Romeo and Juliet*. Like almost all the early work of Shakespeare, it is perfectly realized within its own, self-appointed limits. And what it lacks in terms of range and intellectual complexity, it makes up for in the singleness and force of its emotional impact. Most unusually for Shakespeare, *Romeo and Juliet* is provided with a prologue, in sonnet form, in which the situation of the tragedy to follow is outlined, and its ending revealed. It is surprising, particularly if you compare this prologue with the contorted and riddling introduction which later launched *Troilus and Cressida*, how fully and straightforwardly *Romeo and Juliet* is, in fact, summed up by these fourteen prefatory lines. Mercutio and the Nurse could not be predicted from them. Otherwise, most of the play is there in miniature, set out for us clearly. There are even certain phrases – 'A pair of star-crossed lovers', or 'The fearful passage of their death-marked love' – which seem to epitomize the nature and quality of this tragedy.

Shakespearean drama does not usually lend itself to formulas so concise.

This is a play which uses antithesis as a structural principle. Love and hate, light and darkness, revelry and the tomb, youth and age, life and death are the grand, abstract poles between which it plays. Total commitment, hasty avowals, a passion which momentarily transforms the landscape like a lightning flash, may be doubted by the cynical (like Mercutio) or feared by the timorous (like the Friar). They are still the law, and the ultimate values, in the tragedy. Against them stands a cruel, destructive Fate. There is no human villain in *Romeo and Juliet*. Paris, the husband forced upon Juliet by her parents, is as much a victim of circumstance as she. Even Tybalt, for all the destruction he initiates, is churlish rather than diabolical, an unwitting instrument of the stars. All the characters in this tragedy, but the lovers most, are Fortune's fools. Up to the very last moments, there is still a tantalizing possibility that everything will yet be well: that Juliet will wake before Romeo drinks the poison, that Friar Laurence will arrive in time to explain the misunderstanding. The element of chance, of fractional mistimings, is so strong in the play that critics have often wanted to deny its full tragic stature. This, surely, is to make the service greater than the god, to subject *tragedy* to the kind of niggling and exclusive definition that Shakespeare himself mocked. The universe of *Romeo and Juliet* is one in which, by some inexorable law, every quality, every emotion, almost every object confronts its total opposite. This principle governs the language of the play, as well as its larger, structural patterns. Not only does Shakespeare abruptly juxtapose weddings with funerals, day with night, bawdy comedy with an ecstasy of romantic love, he does so in verse which veers between the rambling colloquialism of the Nurse and a formality so extreme that Romeo and Juliet can converse with one another in perfect sonnet form. Stark and unmediated contrast is also characteristic of the imagery throughout. So, when Romeo first sees his lady at the Capulets' ball, she seems to him to 'hang upon the cheek of night/ As a rich jewel in an Ethiop's ear' (1. 5. 45–6), to be 'a snowy dove trooping with crows' (1. 5. 48). Brilliance and obscurity, black and white, heat and cold: the tragedy lies in the fact that a malign destiny sooner or later awards the victory to the dark or negative side of such pairings. On their way to extinction, however, the doomed qualities of passion, love and youth shine out with all the more integrity and splendour for the darkness against which they are set.

Although there is a prince in Verona, a ruler determined to put an end to the senseless quarrel between the two houses of Montague and Capulet, *Romeo and Juliet* is very much a tragedy of private persons. There are no great political issues dependent upon the fate of the central characters here, as there are in the tragical-histories, and also in *Titus Andronicus, Troilus and Cressida* and *Hamlet.* Not until *Antony and Cleopatra* did Shakespeare treat love as an issue affecting the state. Both *Romeo and Juliet* and *Othello* are, in a way, domestic tragedies. It is true that *Othello* takes place against the background of a threatened Turkish attack upon Cyprus, and that Othello himself is a valued servant of the Venetian state. He is, in fact, one of the Renaissance tribe of *condottieri*: men whose profession was war, who sold their services in answer to the military needs of various Italian principalities. Some of them, like the Sforzas and the Coleoni, eventually became princes in their own right. In *Othello*, however, the Turkish threat is little more than an excuse to move the action from Venice to Cyprus. The Turkish fleet is destroyed before it can reach Cyprus, not by Othello, but by Fate in the guise of a sea-storm. This same Fate also has something – although by no means everything – to do with the subsequent destruction of Othello himself.

Francis Bacon remarked that the evil for which a man is himself partly responsible is more agonizing, that 'it strikes more deadly inward' than calamities imposed purely from without. This is one of several reasons why *Othello* is so much more painful to read, or experience in the theatre, than *Romeo and Juliet.* No one, as far as I know, has ever stood up in the audience and tried to tell Romeo not to take the poison, because Juliet is really alive. Desperate attempts to enlighten Othello, to interfere with the progress of the plot are, however, a constant feature of the theatrical history of the later tragedy. *Othello* is close to being unendurable by reason of its subject matter, a sexual jealousy which is humiliating and degrading as Macbeth's ambition or Lear's lack of judgement are not, and also because the destruction at the end is so utterly irredeemable and complete. A state temporarily shattered by war and usurpation can be pieced together again by a Fortinbras, a Malcolm or an Edgar. Something can be rescued out of the carnage. The statues of the lovers in pure gold which the sorrowing Montagues and Capulets offer each other at the end of *Romeo and Juliet* are pathetic 'sacrifices of our enmity' (5. 3. 304), a poor exchange for the warm reality now extinguished in the Capulets' vault. All the same, these metal images not only symbolize peace between the two families, they perpetuate the memory and the values of a love betrayed by Fortune, but unshakeably true to itself. At the end of *Othello*, issues of state are non-existent, and so are family connections. Even Brabantio is dead. There is nothing, not even an agreed-upon memory of good, that can be rescued whole from this catastrophe. No gilded monuments will celebrate the star-crossed loves of Desdemona and the noble Moor. Instead, we are asked to accept the fact that a relationship in which, for a while, all the very considerable positives of this play world were embodied has been annihilated from within. Almost, Iago has won.

His victory is of a curious kind. The bewildering number of reasons which Iago advances at various points in the play for hating Othello and Cassio, and proceeding against their peace, has tended to find critical explanation within recent years less in terms of Coleridge's famous formula, 'the motive-hunting of a motiveless malignancy', than in attempts to trace Iago's ancestry back to the Vice of medieval morality drama: that cynical, scheming, but oddly attractive agent of the Devil whose business on earth was, precisely, to enlarge his master's kingdom. Certainly, the mysterious plurality of Iago's motives does tend to make him a generalized embodiment of evil in a way that other Shakespearean villains are not. At the end, Othello sees him for an instant as the Devil himself (5. 2. 288–9). Iago remains an individual, however, more than a type. The atrocities he commits, and the various self-justifications he advances, have a psychological and not simply a literary origin. Here, as with the changed character he imposed in *Hamlet* upon the revenge form initiated by men like Kyd and Pickering, Shakespeare has subtly altered an expected focus. Iago may preserve some of the lineaments of the old Vice, may even at times address the audience with something of his engaging jocularity. His attitudes are those of a far subtler and more modern hell.

Iago claims at one point to hate Cassio, not because Cassio was promoted over his head, nor because he suspects him with Emilia, but because 'he hath a daily beauty in his life/That makes me ugly' (5. 1. 19–20). This most intangible and, apparently, oddest of Iago's excuses is probably the most important. Iago has constructed his whole personality and way of life upon the conviction that man is an animal just like all the rest: selfish, greedy and cruel. There is no such thing as a woman both chaste and beautiful, the 'she that was ever fair and never proud' of his mocking couplets in the first scene of Act 2. Characters like Cassio, Othello and Desdemona are an affront to him because he cannot help but recognize in them values outside this brutal, reductivist philosophy. If they truly are what they seem to be, Iago stands condemned as poor and ugly. Sometimes, he tries to pretend that they are, in fact, shams: hypocrites to be unmasked. So, he can say of Desdemona, in soliloquy where there is no one to delude but himself: 'that Cassio loves her, I do well believe't', and add hopefully to this palpable fiction: 'that she loves him, 'tis apt and of great credit' (2. 1. 280–1). More usually, he finds himself up against the plain fact that Othello's much-praised nobility is genuine, that the courtesy and gentleness of Michael Cassio are real, that Desdemona is true as well as fair. These people are only human. They have faults, in the form of romantic self-magnification, a weak head for wine, or a certain girlish refusal to grow up. At the same time, the three of them represent a serious attack upon Iago's philosophy. This is why it is not enough for him to get Cassio cashiered from his lieutenancy: he must be killed. Desdemona's virtue must be turned 'into pitch' (2. 3. 353), Othello dragged down to speak Iago's language of 'goats and monkeys' (4. 1. 264) instead of his own. It is Iago's self-appointed task in the play to destroy in fact those values which he could only snipe at linguistically before, in that scene where they received their most complete celebration – the triumphant arrival of Desdemona, and then Othello, after the storm, in Cyprus.

> It gives me wònder great as my content
> To see you here before me. O my soul's joy!
> If after every tempest come such calms,
> May the winds blow till they have wakened death.
> And let the labouring bark climb hills of seas
> Olympus-high and duck again as low
> As hell's from heaven! If it were now to die,
> 'Twere now to be most happy; for I fear
> My soul hath her content so absolute
> That not another comfort like to this
> Succeeds in unknown fate.
>
> (2. 1. 180–90)

There was for a time a critical fashion, now happily superseded, which turned upon Othello himself a suspicious and carping eye not unlike Iago's. Heroic virtues, of the kind embodied by the Moor, are of course out of favour. The very word 'noble' tends to seem a little embarrassing now, although it was a concept Shakespeare was perfectly willing both to examine and to entertain. The fact is that this tragedy demands our admiration of the Othello of the first half, and of the final scene. It also exacts belief in the value of his and

Desdemona's love. If this newly formed relationship is perilous, insecure and only half understood on either side, it is in just these respects a demonstration of the risks love freely takes. Like *Romeo and Juliet, Othello* is built upon antithesis, with the difference that the contrasts here are all to be found in the union of the lovers themselves, not in the world which surrounds them. Romeo and his lady had been remarkably alike: both young, equally innocent, products of the same society and social class, neither one leading or dominating the other. The marriage of Othello and Desdemona is of a very different kind. Youth and mature age, white skin and black, innocence and experience, an intensely feminine nature weighed against a masculine extreme, the old civilization of Venice set against a barbaric world of deserts, caverns and burning suns: these are some of the antimonies which this marriage, briefly, reconciles. The *otherness* of the beloved, a source of attraction, but also something which must be understood and subtly adjusted so that it forms half of a whole, is here made as radical as possible. Quite apart from the individual worth of Othello and Desdemona as human beings, their union is precious because it stands as a living example of the harmonizing and creative power of love.

In his own, distorted way, Iago has recognized this achievement: 'O, you are well tuned now! But I'll set down/The pegs that make this music' (2. 1. 197–198). Cunningly, he plays upon Othello's quite natural sense of Desdemona as a creature still mysterious and unknown. As Iago goes on talking and insinuating, the architecture of this love begins to disintegrate, leaving the disparate elements of which it was composed scattered on the ground in confusion. Age and youth, the negro and the white woman, the Venetian and the Moor again confront each other as opposites, when handled by a man whose purpose it is to ignore and discredit the alchemy of love. Of course, Othello should not have listened to any of this. Of course, he should have kept faith. It is always easy to give detached and omniscient advice from outside a love relationship – or a play. Like most people who have given themselves totally to someone who is still a comparative stranger (and it is surely right to remember at this point the Shakespeare of the *Sonnets*) Othello is insecure. So is Desdemona, or she would not have lied, as she does in the fourth scene of Act 3, about the loss of the handkerchief. The insecurity of these two is understandably increased by the very nature of their marriage: by the chasm of time, space, and experience which it so miraculously bridges.

At the end, Othello's clear understanding of exactly what it is that he has done, of the treasure he has thrown away forever, is one of the most unbearable things in Shakespeare. Without hesitation, he shoulders responsibility for his actions, turning away wearily from Iago, sentencing and then executing himself as a common ruffian, a malignant infidel summarily, and justly, despatched in the street (5. 2. 353–8). No critical censure of Othello can be greater than that he turns upon himself. In fact, it goes too far. The very splendour of this love now broken was always bound up with its peril, as a union of extremes. Iago was no common antagonist, and yet he is only partly responsible for his own plot. The universe, hideously, was on his side. Had Desdemona not dropped the handkerchief just when she did, had Bianca not happened by in the first scene of Act 4 to confront Othello with a seeming proof of his wife's adultery, the ending of this play might have been quite different. The malignity of Fate here is like that in *Romeo and Juliet*. The situation over which it broods is, however, complex and disturbing in ways that serve to remind one that *Othello* follows *Hamlet* in the Shakespeare chronology, and precedes *King Lear*.

The precise date of *Othello* is uncertain, but it is probably the first of Shakespeare's Jacobean tragedies. Speculation as to what kind of psychological distress it was that impelled Shakespeare after 1603 into the writing of an unbroken series of tragedies, halted only by *Pericles* in 1608, is now unpopular. Tragedy was, of course, the Jacobean dramatic form *par excellence*, or at least it was for the first twelve years of James's reign. The English history play, so popular in the late sixteenth century, died with Elizabeth, or else went underground to issue in such disguised forms as *Macbeth* or John Ford's *Perkin Warbeck*. Jacobean comedy does, of course, exist. The great Jonson comedies fall mostly within this period, and he was far from being the only practitioner of the form. Nevertheless, the bias of the time, for a complex of reasons – historical, social and intellectual – was towards tragedy. This much admitted, the fact remains that Shakespeare cannot have been responding only to the taste of his Jacobean audience when he turned away so completely from comedy. *Twelfth Night, All's Well That Ends Well* and *Measure for Measure*, the three comedies he wrote at the end of the Elizabethan period, display an increasing uneasiness with their own form, a sense of dissatisfaction concentrated just where *As You Like It* or *Much Ado About Nothing* had been most secure: in the final scenes. It is at least likely that, having created over the years between *Two Gentlemen of Verona* and *Twelfth Night* a magnificent comic form, Shakespeare began to distrust its very perfection: to feel that the symmetries it imposed upon life were false and unreal. Shakespearean tragedy had always been more heterogeneous than his comedy, resistant to patterning. This may have been, at least in part, why he devoted himself to it now. In any case, he produced after *Othello* a series of five tragedies, *King Lear*, *Macbeth*, *Timon of Athens*, *Coriolanus* and *Antony and Cleopatra* which are essentially unrelated to each other, or to anything Shakespeare had written before: five planets spinning independently in space.

*King Lear* opens with what is recognizably a kind of tableau. The King, his daughters and his court present an image of order that is at once political, social and emotional. This order is no sooner stated, through the formal grouping of characters on the stage, than it begins to undo itself. Deliberately, Shakespeare robbed the love-trial in the opening scene of even that modicum of realism and psychological plausibility which it had possessed in his source play, the old, anonymous *King Leir*. The dramatic short-hand here has a purpose that goes beyond mere structural economy. For Shakespeare's original audience, this starkly presented division of the kingdom must have urged memories of old, political moralities like *Gorboduc*. A rash splitting of the succession, the ruler's abandonment of himself to the deadly sins of wrath and pride: this is just where Gorboduc himself, Rex Humanitas or Magnyfycence in those earlier, didactic plays had taken the wrong turning. Kent's lines rebuking Lear make this similarity explicit:

> Think'st thou that duty shall have dread to speak
> When power to flattery bows? To plainness honour's bound
> When majesty stoops to folly.
>
> (1. 1. 146–8)

This progression of familiar, morality play abstractions (Duty, Power, Flattery, Plainness, Majesty and Folly) invites an audience to see the whole episode in the sure and rigid terms of some Tudor interlude. Traditional absolutes seem to lie just beneath the surface, waiting to emerge. They are reinforced, apparently, by the unusually schematic way that characters are ranged on the side of good or evil. There is even a sense in which Lear himself is a man defined by his situation, is Old Age personified more than he is an individual like Hamlet or Othello. Around the old king, everyone but Albany is committed unequivocally to virtue or wickedness in a fashion familiar from morality drama, but unaccustomed in Shakespearean tragedy.

Christian absolutes are not the only ones invoked by this first scene. By stripping away the marriage intrigue of the old *Leir*, and preserving the silence about the motivations of Cordelia and her father, Shakespeare moved the love-trial closer to its archetypes in legend and myth. The testing of the daughters, Lear's violence, the wickedness of Goneril and Regan and the goodness of Cordelia associate themselves as a result with a nursery-tale world of clear-cut, arbitrary black and white. In fairy stories, daughters normally come in threes. When they do, it is virtually axiomatic that the elder two will be dreadful, while the youngest will turn out to be Cinderella, Beauty or (in Greek mythology) Psyche, the bride of Eros. Lear's three daughters belong to this pattern. Unlike the author of the old *Leir* play, however, Shakespeare insisted upon running the whole gamut of fairy-tale in his first scene. Prince Charming, in the person of the French king, makes his appearance immediately after the rejection of Cordelia, not midway through the play, as he had in the source. And he sees at once that 'she is herself a dowry'.

> Fairest Cordelia, that art most rich being poor;
> Most choice, forsaken; and most loved, despised;
> Thee and thy virtues here I seize upon.
>
> (1. 1. 249–51)

The persecuted youngest daughter, rescued in the nick of time, has made the best match of the three. She can now ride off with her prince on a white horse, leaving the wicked elder sisters to gnash their teeth with impotent rage. This is the place where fairy-tales end. It also happens to be the place where the tragedy of *King Lear* really begins. Our sense of outrage when Cordelia finally returns from France, where she ought to be living happily ever after, in order to be hanged in a prison cell before the eyes of the father she has failed to save, springs from Shakespeare's deliberate violation of material whose intrinsic nature he has made quite plain. It is as though we were asked to accept a version of 'Cinderella' in which the heroine, after her splendid marriage, went back to her old home on a generous errand only to be strangled by her sisters and cast out to die. This is not the way the story is supposed to conclude.

*King Lear* uses fairy-tale material in order to arouse certain emotional expectations which it then proceeds to frustrate. The result is to make the catastrophe particularly monstrous, shocking at an almost unconscious level rooted in our childhood memories. Shakespeare's additional suggestion of morality play absolutes makes this situation even more painful. Most of the moralities had, in their own terms, ended happily. Usually, they restored the erring hero to felicity, either on earth or else in Heaven. Even when they did not, all these plays stressed the justice of God, a divine ordering of the world in which nothing was random, haphazard, or at the mercy of blind chance. Everyman might be terribly harrassed by the rival efforts of good and bad angels to possess his soul, but at least it was obvious that Someone cared. This supernatural surveillance was ultimately comforting. Man could commit himself, in entire faith, to the hands of a just and articulate God. He knew that to disobey certain Christian laws was to run a grave risk of damnation; to respect them was to ensure eventual reward. These are certainties notably absent from *King Lear*, and their omission is not dictated simply by the pagan setting of the play. Where *Gorboduc*, where even the old *Leir* had assumed a Christian universe in despite of historical accuracy, Shakespeare opens the door upon chaos.

Characters in this tragedy are continually assigning qualities to Heaven, asking it questions, accusing it, or demanding rational and just behaviour. Gloucester and Edmund, Edgar, Albany, Kent and Lear himself all offer different views of the supernatural at different moments. Edmund's outlook is perhaps the most consistent. From the beginning, he worships a Nature conceived of in Iago-like terms as brutal, amoral law, a goddess of self-interest. Only in the final scene does this attitude seem to falter. Edgar and Albany, by contrast, are conservatives. They would like to believe in a stern but righteous supernatural which punishes human wrong-doing. Both of them find that such faith becomes increasingly difficult to maintain. Albany's 'this shows you are above,/You justicers, that these our nether crimes/So speedily can venge' (4. 2. 78–80) is an expression of relief after some doubt. The evil Cornwall has been slain by his own servant. In context, however, Albany's piety is instantly undercut by the messenger's next revelation: that Cornwall's death was, inexplicably, delayed just long enough for him to be able to put out Gloucester's other eye. Even so, Edgar, although he clings tenaciously throughout to the Old Testament idea that 'the gods are just, and of our pleasant vices/Make instruments to plague us' (5. 3. 169–70), is forced in Act 4 to impersonate a divine justice which appears to have broken down, when he stage-manages his blind father's mock suicide and restoration. For the defeat and capture of Lear and Cordelia in battle, he has no explanation to offer, only a difficult counsel of stoical acceptance.

Of the others, Kent characteristically alludes to Fortune or the stars as remote, mechanical arbiters of destiny. Only once does he try to assign a moral consciousness to Heaven, in the blessing he invokes upon Gloucester, who has risked Cornwall's displeasure by bringing Lear and his party to shelter out of the storm: 'The gods reward your kindness!' (3. 6. 5). This reward turns out to be blindness: ultimately, death. As for Gloucester and Lear himself, the two characters who suffer most excruciatingly in the tragedy, they seem to run the gamut of possible attitudes towards the divine. Gloucester appears first as an absurdly superstitious old man, mumbling darkly about planetary disorders. After his blinding, he regards the heavens in a series of contradictory ways. At one moment, he can beseech the 'kind' gods to protect the son he now realizes he has wronged (3. 7. 91); in the next, he formulates the most savage view of divine irresponsibility in the play; 'As flies to wanton boys, are we to th'gods—/They kill us for their sport' (4. 1. 36–7). In the latter part of the tragedy, his statements become markedly more orthodox. They are conditioned, however, by the fact that Edgar, as we realize but Gloucester does not, has undertaken the role of Providence in his father's life. Nor does Gloucester live, mercifully, to face the horror of the final scene. Lear himself oscillates between a belief that the storm is an agent of divine justice, seeking out concealed criminals – or even that the gods, being old themselves, must naturally incline to take his part – to the far more alarming, but equally possible, view that Jove the high-thunderer is in league with Goneril and Regan and has stirred their hearts against him. He hopes to learn from his philosopher, the Bedlam beggar, 'what is the cause of thunder' (3. 4. 155). He does not find out, and neither do we. If thunder is indeed the voice of the gods in this play, its message is equivocal: an undistinguishable blur of sound that will not resolve itself into meaning, let alone into judgements or sanctions.

In the long last scene of Act 5, all the main characters of the tragedy, except the Fool and Gloucester, come together. Here if anywhere one would expect some hint as to what it was the thunder said and meant. For a while, such an answer does seem possible. The evil of the two wicked sisters destroys itself. Edgar overcomes Edmund in the combat, and the latter repents. Albany ranges himself firmly on the side of good, and sums up the fates of Edmund, Goneril and Regan as 'this judgement of the heavens' (5. 3. 230). Something, however, has been forgotten, and it is something which entirely alters the nature of this ending. The eighteenth century was quite right to feel that the death of Cordelia was an outrage to its faith. It appears to be the product of blind chance, miscalculation, entirely gratuitous and without purpose. It may even be worse than this.

> Upon such sacrifices, my Cordelia,
> The gods themselves throw incense. Have I caught thee?
> He that parts us shall bring a brand from heaven
> And fire us hence like foxes.
>
> (5. 3. 20–3)

This is what Lear says early in the scene, as he and Cordelia are led off to prison. They *are* parted, and it is the reverse of comforting to believe that the agency at work is that of Heaven. Edmund, after all, has decided to destroy his own plot, to do some good, 'despite of mine own nature' (5. 3. 242). He will save Lear and Cordelia from death. Confidently, he stretches out his hand to arrest the progress of that monstrous machine which he has guided through five acts. But nothing happens. The machine grinds on, regardless of the changed intentions of the man who thought he controlled it. What its own nature is, its ultimate purpose (if it has one), we cannot know. All we can see is that Edmund's initial claim to self-sufficiency, to complete freedom from the will or influence of any non-human power (1. 2. 121–36), was false: as false as Albany's pious optimism, 'the gods defend her', uttered a fraction of a second before the entrance of Lear, howling like an animal, with Cordelia dead in his arms.

When Gloucester, in Act 4, gave his purse away to the Bedlam beggar, he made the curious suggestion that Heaven itself might learn to imitate such principles of charity and economic fairness. 'So distribution should undo excess,/And each man have enough' (4. 1. 69–70). One may well think that if the gods have to learn morality from man, then the kingdom of Heaven totters. This, all the same, is my feeling about this tragedy. The world of *King Lear* is not a world of total nihilism and despair, but only because there are people in it who create values essentially human, values which are assailed from all sides, disregarded by the divine powers, but whose worth we are made to understand. Although the fate which overtakes them is much the same, it is still better to be Cordelia than Goneril and Regan, to be Kent rather than Oswald, Gloucester than Edmund. The Fool's loyalty is not so foolish after all. That the good characters of *King Lear* should manage to endure what they have to endure without betraying their own nature, that they should possess so great a capacity for intelligent suffering is, in the end, a reassurance. It tells us almost nothing about the gods, but a good deal about man. We in the audience will 'never see so much, nor live so long' as Edgar and Albany, the survivors who conduct this tragedy to its broken, deliberately truncated resolution (5. 3. 326). Yet to read *Lear*, or experience it on the stage, is a kind of ordeal too. Keats recognized this when he described the process, in one of his sonnets, as a Dantesque pilgrimage through a dark wood, a dangerous, uncertain, but creative journey. Whatever Aristotle meant, in the *Poetics*, by that enigmatic term *catharsis*, it would seem possible to gain a clearer sense of it now from *King Lear* than from any other tragedy. It has something to do, perhaps, with the creation of a supreme dramatic order out of the worst that men can face.

In *Richard III*, a tragedy written early in his dramatic career, Shakespeare had traced the fortunes of an evil man, monstrous even in his physical shape, on the road to a crown which ought never to have been his. Witty, cynical and energetic, half-endearing to a theatre audience safely distanced from his machinations, Richard is through most of his play a magnificent stage presence but not quite a realistic character. Only on the night before Bosworth, when he has bad dreams, does the pronoun 'I' acquire a complexity on his lips which abruptly transforms him from a bogey-man into a frightened, perplexed human being, uncertain about the nature of the universe and also about his own self.

> What do I fear? Myself? There's none else by.
> Richard loves Richard; that is, I am I.
> Is there a murderer here? No – yes, I am.
> Then fly. What, from myself? Great reason why—
> Lest I revenge. What, myself upon myself!
> Alack, I love myself. Wherefore? For any good
> That I myself have done unto myself?
> O no! Alas, I rather hate myself
> For hateful deeds committed by myself!
> I am a villain; yet I lie, I am not.

> (5. 3. 182–91)

The fragmented 'I' of this contorted, disjunct soliloquy, the meditation of a mind turning for the first time to introspection, is diametrically opposed to the one in Richard's initial self-presentation at the beginning of the tragedy: 'Now is the winter of our discontent'. There, fourteen lines of extremely powerful verse had all borne down upon a pivotal and monolithic 'I', placed midway in the speech, which both syntactically and psychologically had received their impact without a tremor. Richard began his play assured and hardened in evil, without self-questioning or doubt. He ends it as a desperate, uncertain but also far more human figure, trying to impose some form upon a dismembered personality. This progress is the reverse of the one later traced by Macbeth.

Like *Richard III*, *Macbeth* is a tragical history. It represents, however, a radical readjustment of Shakespeare's Elizabethan form. In general, it was the task of the tragical history to explore the relationship between a public and a private world, the state and the individual. Usually, these plays moved towards a conclusion in which the voice of tragedy, expressing the fate of a Richard II, or III, a Hotspur, a Henry IV or a Brutus, was allowed to rise above and momentarily to dominate the ground-bass of historical process. There were obvious emotional as well as formal advantages to be gained from this slight tilting of the balance towards tragedy at the end. *Macbeth* forgoes them. This is a play which begins with the most intense individual focus, a searching light directed into the dark places of the protagonist's mind, and ends with generality. It starts out as a tragedy, and finishes as a history play. Macbeth himself is not even accorded the honour of an on-stage death, as Richard III was, let alone any encomium of the kind that Mark Antony speaks over the body of his enemy Brutus, in which some of the good qualities which this man once possessed might be re-membered. The brave soldier, the man of imagination and valour who earned golden opinions from his peers, is forgotten as though he had never been. Macbeth makes his last entrance as an object, a head ignominiously rammed on to a pole. It is only the last in a series of diminutions, the gradual reduction of a complex and tormented human being painfully aware of the nature and significance of his own actions, first to an hysteric, next to a psychopathic killer, then to an automaton mechanically propelled and finally, at Dunsinane, to a cornered animal distinguished only for the savagery of its last defence.

There is something curiously modern about Shakespeare's de-liberate evasion here of the traditional tragic pattern, his relentless shrinking of the protagonist in just that part of the play where Faustus or Hamlet, Hieronymo, Vittoria or Othello interest us most. The tragedy of *Macbeth* in so far as it is the story of a remarkable and ill-fated human being discovering a malign uni-verse and the unsuspected depths of his own soul, is effectively over at just the halfway point where Richard III's had, at least tentatively,

begun. Significantly, Macbeth himself speaks the epitaph that would
seem appropriate to a tragic fifth act early in the play, in the moment
that Duncan's murder is revealed:

> Had I but died an hour before this chance,
> I had liv'd a blessed time; for, from this instant,
> There's nothing serious in mortality:
> All is but toys: renown and grace is dead,
> The wine of life is drawn, and the mere lees
> Is left this vault to brag of.
>
> (2. 3. 90–5)

The lines are of course hypocritical, a cunning pretence of sorrow
for Duncan. Macbeth does not guess that he is really predicting his
own future of barbarity and inconsequence, that dreary journey
through blood in which he will first blunt and then lose his individuality. From this point in the play, the true tragic protagonist
becomes Scotland itself, an impersonal entity whose sufferings are
made manifest through the misfortunes of Banquo, Malcolm and
Donalbain, Ross, Siward, Macduff and his family, but not in those
of the butcher who has become Scotland's king.

In *King Lear*, the supernatural either kept silence or else spoke in
the ambiguous form of thunder. It takes more articulate forms in
*Macbeth*, without becoming much more comprehensible. The
witches are both frightening and disturbingly comic. They have
knowledge of the future, or part of it. Their will is evil, and they are
tempters who half compel the violence they foresee. At the same
time, there is a certain grotesque and ugly humour about their
activities and their spells, a petty malice, a determined particularity
of swine-killing and lust for chestnuts that associates them with old
wives' tales. They seem more like chance abnormalities, 'bubbles'
of the earth as Banquo calls them (1. 3. 79), than great cosmic
forces. Their relationship, if any, to those angry portents of earth-
quake, storm and unnatural behaviour in the animal kingdom which
herald Duncan's death is left unclear. More certain is the sense that
Macbeth himself, at the beginning of the play, has unconsciously
summoned them, that they come to meet him on the heath in
response to certain subterranean movements of his mind. It is their
task to give objective expression to his buried desire for the crown.
This done, they vanish, leaving him to live with a possibility which
has acquired a new, dangerous half-existence because it has been
spoken, tangibly fixed in words. Macbeth seems to kill Duncan less
out of specific ambition for the throne, less because of his wife's

goading and aspersions cast upon his masculinity, than because he has become fascinated by the bare idea of the act. He is like a man afflicted with an uncontrollable, nervous fear of heights who has been led up to the top of a tower: unless he is judiciously restrained by a companion, the overwhelming suggestion which the place breeds of a plunge into space will torment him until he buys his peace, irrationally, by yielding to it. In Macbeth's case, there is no one by his side to hold him back. And, although part of him undeniably dies with Duncan, the man he kills, there is still a kind of shadow Macbeth who lives on, running faster and faster along the road to which he has committed himself, in a pathetic effort not to lose the ground so dearly purchased.

The text of this tragedy is problematic. The play is not only suspiciously short by seventeenth-century standards, it seems oddly curtailed in certain areas (notably in the sketchy treatment of Lady Macbeth between the murder and her sleep-walking scene) to the point of suggesting loss, or drastic cutting. Even if some original material is lacking, however, the shift of interest from Macbeth himself to his multiple victims in the second half cannot be the result only of a playhouse or printing accident. The systematic deadening and coarsening of Macbeth's responses, that loss of feeling which leaves him with nothing to say about his wife's death except 'she should have died hereafter' (5. 4. 17), must always have been part of the play. Like *King Lear*, although its terms are very different, *Macbeth* seems deliberately to violate even that evasive and ill-defined sense of a Shakespearean tragic form accumulated in his Elizabethan period. At the end of *Lear*, the restoration of order in the state had been so pale and faltering as to approach the derisory. *Macbeth*, by contrast, reinstates the norm fully while jettisoning an individual, tragic exploration which had seemed initially to be the main business of the play. There is a sense in which Macbeth's steady forfeiture of awareness, his inexorable debasement, is not only a demonstration of the destructiveness of evil, but something more untidy and dispiriting than tragedy itself. Just exactly why the Shakespeare of *Richard II*, *Romeo and Juliet*, *Hamlet*, *Othello* and *King Lear* should have chosen at this point to avoid a tragic close, allowing his hero to degenerate ingloriously in what becomes, effectively, the background of the play, we cannot know. It seems to me, however, that distrust of what one might call a 'tragedy-shaped' view of the world, of those false symmetries which art imposes upon life, may well have begun to cloud this Shakespearean form too, even as it had clouded the later comedies. In any case,

Shakespeare's last three tragic dramas, *Timon of Athens, Coriolanus* and *Antony and Cleopatra*, are plays so determinedly perverse in their construction, and particularly in the way they end, that critics have persistently been forced to invent excuses for them, or even special dramatic categories.

Like *King Lear, Timon of Athens* deals with that most painful, and most oddly personal, of Shakespearean subjects: ingratitude. The date of the play and its exact place in the late chronology are uncertain, and so is the nature of the text. Many scholars have argued that this is not really a finished work, but only the first draft of a play. Shakespeare's editors Heminges and Condell, declined to include the botched text of *Pericles* in the First Folio; they included *Timon*, however, without explanation or excuse. On the whole, it would seem best to follow their example here. Although the play is undeniably strange, and may be incomplete, it is nevertheless powerful as it stands in the theatre. Its peculiarities, moreover, are of a kind which associate it with the other late tragedies.

*Timon of Athens* goes even farther than *King Lear* in the reduction of characters to types. M. C. Bradbrook has claimed that Timon himself is a role rather than a character, and this was certainly the effect produced by Paul Scofield, playing the part at Stratford-upon-Avon in 1965. Significantly, the characters surrounding Timon are designated for the most part by their occupation or social class, rather than by individual names: the poet, the painter, the jeweller, the steward, the senators, the servants. We are a long way from *Hamlet* or *Othello*, plays in which even the most minor characters had been endowed with distinct personalities. *Timon*, by contrast, seems to employ a morality play rigidity of characterization, to remember works like the anonymous *Contention Between Liberality and Prodigality*, which was performed at court in 1601. *Liberality and Prodigality* stands as a late example of a whole class of Tudor plays concerned to counsel the citizens of a new, capitalist age that while it might be better, figuratively, to lay up treasure in Heaven rather than on earth, a reasonable amount of attention to one's secular financial policy was not incompatible with godliness, let alone with good sense and certain Christian virtues. It treated Money personified as a wholly neutral character, the passive victim first of Prodigality and then of the miser Tenacity, and suffering equally from the mismanagement of both regimes. At the end, Money freely decided to serve Liberality, a judicious master who expended him in the service of faithful but unlucky courtiers, disabled soldiers, and poor but honest servants of the queen.

In *Timon of Athens*, Shakespeare seems to have endowed his central character with the features of *both* Liberality and Prodigality in the older play, mingling them to the point where judgement (the chief purpose of the Interlude) becomes virtually impossible. When he redeems a friend from debtor's prison, when he bestows a marriage portion upon his servant, Timon is following traditional patterns of magnanimity. His extravagances of food and drink, on the other hand, the lavish gifts presented without regard for the need or merit of the recipient, all suggest waste: the sin of prodigality. Yet, in the play, the same attitude governs and unites all these actions. Timon is both admirable, an example of goodness and bounty as it should be in some pre-lapsarian world, and a fool, a man wilfully blind to the truth which surrounds him. In the first half of the play, he behaves persistently as though all men were noble and generous, like himself. His optimism is mocked by Apemantus, the cynic who believes that humanity is universally depraved. Neither point of view is really reasonable. Unfortunately, the only other voice of importance in the play, that of Alcibiades, disregards moral issues entirely. For the soldier, men can be termed good or bad according to how they behave to him personally, but he neither expects much nor tries to move from individual instance to principle. Basically, Alcibiades believes in himself, and in the effectiveness of brute force. His is not an attitude which mediates between the extremes of Timon and Apemantus, nor are we encouraged to see it as central.

*Timon of Athens* is as eccentric in its dramatic construction as it is with respect to character and patterns of moral judgement. The play falls into oddly rigid and abstract halves. In the first, the world crowds to Timon's table to receive his benefactions and good things. In the second, it is still coming to him, in the forest, for a reward of curses and stones. Ingratitude does not effect a gradual change in Timon's personality, as it had in Lear's. He simply shifts at the end of Act 3 from one position to its opposite: from an excess of love to one of hate. Shakespeare makes no attempt to render this alteration psychologically credible, or to delineate its stages. It happens abruptly, but irreversibly. As for Timon's death, it is positively anti-tragic in its nature. When he has exhausted his fund of curses, Timon also comes to the end of his reason for living. Mysteriously, almost casually, in some unspecified moment of off-stage time, the protagonist of this play ceases to exist. In a theatre devoted to the rhetoric of death, to a concentration upon the final clairvoyances of the hero, this perfunctory disappearance violates tragic decorum even more strikingly than Macbeth's insignificant end. In *Timon*, moreover, it is impossible to take seriously that restoration of order in the state which here, as in *Macbeth*, occupies the last section of the play.

The concluding scene of *Timon of Athens* reads, to me, like parody. The senators, pleading for mercy from their conqueror, produce an outrageous series of lies and equivocations, crowned by the statement that the men chiefly responsible for the injustices of the past have all died of shame and broken hearts at discovering that they were, after all, *insufficiently* Machiavellian (5. 4. 26–9). Alcibiades may be, like Fortinbras or Malcolm, the new ruler who weaves together the threads of ordinary life after tragedy has exhausted itself, who establishes political coherence. It is hard to see him, with his unlovely train of harlots and greedy soldiers, as representing any very enlightened government. Most of what he says indicates that things will go on in Athens much as they have before, except that different masters will now settle comfortably into those 'great chairs of ease' (5. 4. 10–11) which Alcibiades shows no signs of wanting to overturn. The old places will simply be occupied, under the new dispensation, by himself and followers.

The resolution offered by this final scene is made still more uneasy by the fact that, although there has been no formal, tragic catastrophe, Alcibiades tries to behave as though there had. Lament and ceremonious farewell seem very hollow when their object contributes neither a physical body over which to mourn, nor even a memory at all relevant to these events. Timon, before his death, cared neither for Athens nor for Alcibiades. Only through a monstrous distortion of facts can his spirit be made to preside over this ending. Alcibiades is dishonest when he attempts to associate Timon with his own victory, or claims that 'rich conceit/Taught thee to make vast Neptune weep for aye/On thy low grave, on faults forgiven' (5. 4. 77–9). Detached, formless and utterly impersonal, the sea which washes now over Timon's corpse has, of course, no feelings of this kind. It is indifferent to anything human – which is just why the later Timon found it attractive. Alcibiades is falsifying truth, grotesquely, in the interests of a shapely, but obviously contrived tragic finale. The whole of his final speech is ostentatiously literary and, like the productions of those two shabby hypocrites the poet and the painter, earlier in the play, it is essentially a lie: a prettifying of reality in the dubious service of art.

*Coriolanus* is, in its own way, equally extreme in its denial of tragic patterning. Here, Shakespeare has chosen to do something which only the twentieth century, perhaps, can fully understand: he has placed in the centre of his play a man whose consciousness is extremely limited. Coriolanus possesses certain special excellences, but is fundamentally imperceptive, even stupid, as no protagonist in Shakespeare's tragedies had been before. We are never tempted to see the world through his eyes, because Shakespeare makes it abundantly clear from the start that this perspective (like that of the tribunes who oppose him) is brutal and meagre. Titus, Richard II, Romeo, Brutus, Hamlet, Othello, Lear and the early Macbeth had all been tortured by the very clarity and also the subtlety of their understanding, by their often horrified comprehension of the meaning and consequences of their own actions, and feelings. Coriolanus, by contrast, spends most of the play in a mist. He is really happy only when he can give himself wholly and unthinkingly to action, to the implacable rise and fall of a sword arm 'timed with dying cries' (2. 3. 108). Only once does this horizon expand. When he takes Volumnia, silently, by the hand in the third scene of Act 5, when he sees the heavens open and hears the ironical laughter of the gods at the tragi-comedy of human life, Coriolanus for an instant grasps his situation completely. If the revelation is blinding, a lightning flash that momentarily transforms the landscape, it is also disturbingly impermanent. The play does not end here. Instead, we are forced to watch Coriolanus lose touch with his own, tragic self-knowledge, unable to build upon or even remember the truth of that crisis outside the gates of Rome. In Corioli, he responds automatically to the cunning taunts of Aufidius, even as he had much earlier to the insults of the tribunes. Mechanically, he repeats an old pattern of behaviour, as though the third scene of Act 5 had taught him nothing. This time, he is killed, ignominiously torn apart by an infuriated crowd. Powerful though it is, this ending is again anti-tragic. It reminds us that life has a disconcerting way of continuing beyond the point that art would regard as climactic, that the moment of truth, even if recognized as such, seldom prevails for long over habit, over the disposition ingrained in a man. The Coriolanus who dies is the Coriolanus of Act 1, not the character briefly enlightened by pain who marched his army away from Rome midway in Act 5, because he had been forced to recognize the inescapability of human relationship.

*Antony and Cleopatra* may have preceded *Coriolanus* in time, at least marginally. It seems proper, however, to consider it last because the dislocation of tragic form here (and no one has ever suggested that this play is unfinished, or textually corrupt) is so radical as to suggest a trespass upon the territory of the final romances. Once again, it is the ending which suggests most strongly an impatience with the false symmetries of tragic art. Deliberately, Shakespeare divided the catastrophe in half, allowing Antony to die in Act 4, postponing Cleopatra's end, amid a welter of ambiguity, until Act 5. The play itself is so generous in its construction, so sublimely indifferent to ideas of dramatic economy or concentration, as to tax the resources of any theatre. As the action swings between Egypt and Rome, from palaces to galleys to the distant plains of Parthia, a feeling of perpetual movement through space is created which does not seem the servant of plot so much as plot itself. With the exception of Cleopatra, the magnet which attracts others while remaining immobile itself, almost all the characters are travellers. Antony, Octavius, Pompey, each with his retinue, seem to journey constantly from place to place. Caesar's sister Octavia is encountered first in Rome, makes her way to Athens, and limps back to Rome. Even Cleopatra's soothsayer, for no very clear reason, turns up at one point in Italy. This is a world of continual flux, in which the ceaseless coming and going of messengers seems to typify the restlessness that informs the whole.

Attitudes and personalities, too, are perplexingly in motion. When Cleopatra learns, in Act 2, that Antony has unexpectedly betrayed her by contracting a marriage with Octavia, she reaches out desperately for a verdict on this man who has so abruptly deserted her. The attempt fails.

> Let him for ever go! let him not – Charmian—
> Though he be painted one way like a Gorgon,
> The other way's a Mars.
>
> (2. 5. 115–17)

This Janus-faced Antony derives from Elizabethan 'perspectives': paintings devised and overlaid so that they altered their character, often their subject matter, according to where the viewer stood. There simply are two, contradictory Antonys: a Gorgon and a splendid Mars. They exist simultaneously, and there is no way of reconciling them or even of subordinating one aspect to the other. Cleopatra has no choice but to accept both, and wait.

A stance rather like hers is recommended by the play generally to its audience, and not solely with respect to Antony. The idea of the perspective picture, a single entity revealing two or more incompatible natures, is fundamental to this tragedy. Is Antony the triple pillar of the world, a great and magnanimous soldier who is also the master of kinds of experience unknown to the frigid Octavius, or is he merely an ageing sensualist, a strumpet's fool? How is one to separate wisdom from folly in the conflict between Rome and Egypt, value from emptiness in the love of Antony and his exasperating queen? Not even Enobarbus, that shrewd and realistic commentator, can tell the difference between Cleopatra's glorious variety and her propensity to lies. They are the same characteristic, and yet not the same. Nor, alas, can he distinguish Antony's extravagance, his culpable waste, from Antony's bounty – that godlike generosity of spirit which finally breaks Enobarbus's heart. Decision in matters of this kind seems important, and yet Shakespeare renders it impossible, for us as well as for the characters of the play. With Romeo and Juliet before, with Othello and Desdemona, even Macbeth and Lady Macbeth, evaluation of the relationship and of the two individuals concerned, had been urged, was in fact essential. With Cleopatra and Antony, it cannot be managed. They are as elusive and contradictory as people known in real life, and as difficult to assess or explain.

Where earlier tragedies had admitted the theatre audience into the secret places of their protagonists' minds, either through soliloquy or through a frank unburdening of conscience encountered far more often on the stage than in reality, *Antony and Cleopatra* offers a distant, exterior view. Our place of vantage is essentially that of Charmian or Enobarbus: people sufficiently close to their superiors to witness informal, frequently undignified behaviour, without participating in motive and reflections like a confidante in Racine. It is true, of course, that more of the picture – in range, not depth – is available to us as spectators than to these attendant characters. They cannot move, as we can, from Rome to Egypt and back again in an instant, nor are they present in all the scenes. Our own perspective on the affairs of Antony and his mistress is wider than theirs, but this very breadth makes judgement more instead of less difficult. Here, as he was to do in the final romances, Shakespeare undercuts and baffles the customary superiority of the theatre audience.

Cleopatra and Antony are like Desdemona and Othello in that they confront the *otherness* of the beloved in ways that are made deliberately extreme. They do not fully understand, let alone fully trust, one another. The audience shares this incomprehension now, as it had not in *Othello*. What was really in Antony's mind when he agreed to marry Octavia? How firm was Cleopatra's resolve to follow her lord's fortunes in life and death: is she betraying Caesar – or Antony – in the ambiguous scenes with Thidias and Seleucus? This play seems more like life itself, magnified but still unruly and only partially comprehensible, than it is like formal tragedy. What logic there is at work is that of love itself, and its pattern is characteristically circular. In the *Sonnets*, it was impossible to determine whether the young man was really an angel or a devil, innocent or horribly guilty. *Antony and Cleopatra* extends this desperately honest way of thinking about the relativity, the imperfect knowledge, of even the closest human relationships still further. It is a play about the multiple aspects of personality, situation, and of truth itself. But by the end, this bewildering, sometimes disheartening abundance has been converted into a subject for celebration, even for joy.

Cleopatra and Antony die, but they leave behind them a sense of the richness of the world, of its inexhaustible resource, unexpected in a tragic finale. Cleopatra's death in particular seems more like a triumph than a defeat. It is a hard-won victory, achieved only after she has overcome an enemy potentially more dangerous than Caesar himself, in the person of that ribald, determinedly comic countryman who brings her both annihilation, hidden in his basket of figs, and an assault upon her dignity more savage than anything Shakespeare's earlier tragic characters had had to endure at such a juncture. Cleopatra survives this attack. Patiently, she listens and responds to the clown's slanders and rambling inconsequence. She can be amused by his doubtful account ('the worm's an odd worm' 5. 2. 256–7) of the asp which is shortly to kill her. By the end of the episode, when the countryman has at last been persuaded to depart, she has earned the right to say: 'Give me my robe, put on my crown, I have/ Immortal longing in me', and she does so immediately (5. 2. 279– 80). The change of tone is startling, and was meant to be.

Although the word itself is never mentioned, Cleopatra dies ostentatiously as a *tragedy* queen. She assumes a costume and a role, gathers the minor players around her, ransacks the treasuries of rhetoric, and confronts Caesar and the soldiers, when they break in upon the scene, with a contrived and formal tableau of death which they understand as such (5. 2. 330). In a sense, this is her answer to that other, monstrous theatrical possibility which had presented itself to her just before the entrance of the clown:

> The quick comedians
> Extemporally will stage us and present
> Our Alexandrian revels; Antony
> Shall be brought drunken forth, and I shall see
> Some squeaking Cleopatra boy my greatness
> I' th' posture of a whore.
>
> (5. 2. 215–20)

A genuine horror informs Cleopatra's imagining of the debasement of her relationship with Antony through the agency of comedy. This future, satirical performance in Rome can only be an impoverishment, a cheapening of the story. Bravely, she combats it with a counter-illusion, an illusion which proceeds to walk through the fire of comedy, as represented by the countryman, and emerges from the ordeal not only unharmed, but *true*.

Endings in fiction tend to be limiting and artificial. Frank Kermode has claimed, in *The Sense of an Ending*, that the most satisfactory conclusions are those which 'frankly transfigure the events in which they were immanent'. The ending of *Antony and Cleopatra* does this in very special terms. Here at last, the bewildering multiplicity, the ceaseless shifting of the perspective picture is simplified and stilled. Cleopatra's death alters our feelings, in retrospect, about those preceding acts which it crowns. There is a curious sense, too, in which Shakespeare seems to have overcome, by very special means, what looks like his growing distrust of 'tragedy-shaped' views of human life. The play here is so constructed that it can accommodate tragedy without disruption, without even a feeling of finality. Antony's vision of a hereafter 'where souls do couch on flowers' (4. 14. 51) and where he will be companioned forever by his queen is not only elaborated by Cleopatra herself in the last scene: she manages to suggest that for Antony and herself the end of the play is really a beginning, that Caesar is defeated, not victorious, and death itself a sensuous abundance of life. Shakespeare not only admits, he goes out of his way to emphasize the fact that Cleopatra dies as a character in a tragedy. He confronts an old problem directly and, in the same moment that he does so, conducts it to a resolution. In the ending of *Antony and Cleopatra*, the worlds beyond tragedy of the final romances are prefigured: the deliberately 'playlike' finale of *Cymbeline*, the awakening of the statue in *The Winter's Tale*, Prospero's Art. In none of these plays will it be possible to distinguish the patterns of reality from those of fiction.

## (v)

## SHAKESPEARE: HIS LATER PLAYS

### Stephen Wall

The plays that Shakespeare wrote towards the end of his theatrical career have never been so highly valued as they are today. It would now be widely agreed that *The Winter's Tale* and *The Tempest* provide a noble conclusion to Shakespeare's development, and involve a profound resolution of themes apparent throughout his work. Such attitudes have little in common with the estimates of earlier periods. In 1667 audiences were so little awed by *The Tempest* that they were prepared to enjoy Dryden's and D'Avenant's adaptation of it in which Miranda is given a sister with whom she can exchange girlish confidences, and in which Caliban is paired off with a female creature as grotesque as he is. Not even the later addition of some fine music by Purcell can make up for the vulgarization of Shakespeare's text caused by the Restoration insistence on spectacle and sexual innuendo. In the middle of the eighteenth century Johnson allowed that *The Winter's Tale* was 'with all its absurdities, very entertaining', but his patience was severely strained by *Cymbeline*:

To remark the folly of the fiction, the absurdity of the conduct, the confusion of the names and manners of different times, and the impossibility of the events in any system of life, were to waste criticism upon unresisting imbecility, upon faults too evident for detection, and too gross for aggravation.

Garrick's 1756 version of *The Winter's Tale*, titled *Florizel and Perdita*, cheerfully abandoned most of Shakespeare's three earlier Acts, and substituted scenes of his own. He was congratulated by Warburton for 'giving an elegant form to a monstrous composition'.

Coleridge's analyses of *The Tempest* form an important part of his defence of Shakespeare's powers of judgement against Augustan censure. He treats it as a romantic drama which 'addresses itself entirely to the imaginative faculty'. Like Lamb, Coleridge seems to have felt the actual performance of Shakespeare's plays as distracting and intrusive:

... although the illusion may be assisted by the effect on the senses of the complicated scenery and decorations of modern times yet this sort of assistance is dangerous.

In a theatre 'the spiritual vision is apt to languish'. Coleridge anticipates the nineteenth-century tendency (maintained in a more sophisticated form by some modern critics) to think of Shakespeare as a literary rather than as a theatrical artist. His remarks about Miranda also look forward to the Victorian encomiastic sentimentalization of the women in the last plays:

Of Miranda we may say, that she possesses in herself all the ideal beauties that could be imagined by the greatest poet of any age or country.

Edward Dowden's influential *Shakespere – His Mind and Art* (1878) presents the last plays as the product of a self-mastery that is 'powerful, luminous, and calm'; they imply a 'period of large, serene wisdom', a 'clear and solemn vision'. Although his terms are now old-fashioned, Dowden's view of a philosophic Shakespeare at the end of his pilgrimage is not in essentials very different from many modern accounts. Yet even Dowden conceded that at this time Shakespeare's concentration sometimes lapsed – a point eagerly seized on by Lytton Strachey in his iconoclastic essay 'Shakespeare's Final Period' (1906), which is reprinted in *Books and Characters*. Strachey attacks the eminently Victorian assumptions underlying Dowden's view, and offers as an alternative a Shakespeare bored with everything except poetical dreams and technical effects. He also points to some harsher aspects of the late plays not properly visible in the sunset glow with which Dowden suffused his subject.

Modern critics have not often been as dismissive as Strachey, but although they mostly agree to attach great importance to the last plays, their methods of approach to them are far from being compatible. In a helpful review of twentieth-century criticism in *Shakespeare Survey* (1958), Philip Edwards summarizes various attempts to explain why *Pericles, Cymbeline, The Winter's Tale* and *The Tempest* should be grouped together, and in what ways they developed from Shakespeare's earlier work. Some have seen the new features of the romances (as these four plays are commonly called) as a response to changing theatrical tastes and a wish to exploit the scenic possibilities of the indoor Blackfriars theatre which Shakespeare's company acquired in 1608. Others have considered them in relation to Elizabethan Romance in general and to

Sir Philip Sidney's *Arcadia* in particular, and as examples of pastoral tragi-comedy. Others again see them as symbolic dramas, parables of reconciliation, and myths of immortality.

The esteem in which the last plays are held is often based on the theory that, despite their stylistic innovations, they constitute an 'answer' to the great tragedies. In *Shakespeare's Last Plays* (1938) E. M. W. Tillyard asserts their structural continuity wth the earlier works:

... one of Shakespeare's main concerns in his last plays, whether deliberately taken up or fortuitously drifted into, was to develop the final phase of the tragic pattern ...

The 'tragic pattern' referred to is the destruction of prosperity followed in its turn by re-creation; the old order dies, but a new one emerges. Even in the tragedies, Tillyard maintains, this development is hinted at; in the last plays it is fully worked out. In his 1929 essay 'Myth and Miracle' (now reprinted in *The Crown of Life*) G. Wilson Knight has also asserted that 'Tragedy is never the last word'. His view of *The Tempest* – not in itself revolutionary – as a record of Shakespeare's spiritual progress and a statement of his final vision was supported by his discovery of 'the predominating symbols' of 'loss in tempest and revival to the sounds of music'. In *The Shakespearian Tempest* (1932) Wilson Knight argues that the opposition between tempests and music was 'the only principle of unity in Shakespeare', and the terminal position of *The Tempest* itself obviously has a special significance in such a scheme. Though often eccentric, Wilson Knight's work has powerfully encouraged those who posit correspondences and connections – whether of image, symbol or 'theme' – between the last plays and their predecessors. Attitudes to the last plays are, in fact, often conditioned by the critic's views of earlier work. Those, for instance, who feel with L. C. Knights that 'for what takes place in *King Lear* we can find no other word than renewal', naturally find the concern of the romances with regeneration a logical sequence.

Such views of the last plays generally assume or attempt to demonstrate their essential unity, for, as Philip Edwards points out, 'only if they are interlocking is the critic justified in creating an "overall" pattern, made up of elements taken from each play'. However, what might be called 'separatist' interpretations of the romances, which study each play individually and without regard for its immediate neighbours, can have the effect of disintegrating the alleged unity of the last plays. Moreover, the presence of common themes in, for example, *Pericles* and *The Winter's Tale*, should not be taken to imply that the two plays are necessarily of comparable dramatic quality.

Those who call in the romances to redress the balance of the tragedies are obliged to find ways of accommodating *Antony and Cleopatra* and *Coriolanus* which, according to established chronology, come between them. These late Roman plays are sometimes regarded as forming a self-contained group (deriving from a common source in North's translation of Plutarch), and sometimes seen as concluding Shakespeare's tragic period. Several recent critics, however, have considered them as transitional works leading to the last plays. Since *Pericles* may well have been written in the same year as *Coriolanus* (1608), it is worth enquiring what features of the two Roman tragedies anticipate the plays that shortly followed them.

That *Antony and Cleopatra* is a play which shows a quite exceptional degree of energy and power – even by Shakespeare's standards – is not disputed, but there has been less agreement about the nature of the impression that it so forcefully makes. One critical tradition, running from Dowden to L. C. Knights, maintains that although Shakespeare allows both protagonists the full benefit of his vitality, he withholds from them his ultimate approval. Others postulate different kinds of reservation. John F. Danby has argued that, having in *King Lear* exhausted the long debate about 'Nature', Shakespeare turns to a pagan world without the transcendent reality that, in his view, Cordelia symbolizes. 'Shakespeare seems deliberately to adopt self-chosen limits'. Ernest Schanzer takes *Antony and Cleopatra* as the culminating example of Shakespeare's evasive technique of 'dramatic coquetry', in which the audience's affections for a character are alternately enlisted and repelled.

But although accounts of the moral attitudes behind *Antony and Cleopatra* remain conflicting, there has been an increasing appreciation of the play's technical virtuosity. Earlier scholars often felt that its construction – with its constantly shifting and often short scenes – was inept and careless; it was not until Granville-Barker in his *Preface* to the play demonstrated the brilliance of Shakespeare's exploitation of such Elizabethan conventions as the unlocalized stage that its theatrical qualities began to be understood. And it has become increasingly clear that *Antony and Cleopatra* is not an isolated *tour de force*: the remarkable qualities of its dramatic style develop the theatrical resourcefulness that Shakespeare seems to have relied on heavily in the romances.

In *Antony and Cleopatra* Shakespeare's effects reach a new level of audacity, as Coleridge sensed: 'Feliciter Audax is the motto for its style comparatively with his other works'. Of course, Shakespeare's daring was always apparent; such obvious *coups de théâtre* as the Porter's entrance after the murder of Duncan or the imagined fall of Gloucester over Dover cliff come immediately to mind. Nevertheless, *Antony and Cleopatra* and the plays that followed it are linked by a new adventurousness, almost a new restlessness, of theatrical expression. These effects do not generally seem restless or gratuitous because they rely on an extraordinarily secure estimate – developed by long experience and continual experiment – of the capacities of his stage and the responses of his audience. Moreover, Shakespeare's language had by now developed an irresistible range and authority.

Shakespeare's handling of the deaths of Antony and Cleopatra reflects this remarkable coolness of authorial nerve. Antony, after falling ineffectually on his sword in Act 4 Scene 14, finally expires at Cleopatra's monument a hundred lines later; Cleopatra applies the asp to her breast sixty lines before the end of Act 5. (Bradley called the extra Act devoted to her 'a unique compliment'.) In order to bring off this double catastrophe Shakespeare takes some theatrical risks that only a dramatist very confident of his powers would have considered.

Antony's resolve to die (thinking that Cleopatra is already dead) is expressed in the erotic terms that pervade this work:

> . . . but I will be
> A bridegroom in my death, and run into't
> As to a lover's bed.
>
> (4. 14. 99–101)

As on other heroic occasions in the play, Antony's present bungling makes a pathetic contrast with his remembered exploits as a younger man. The next scene, however, is deliberately spectacular. Cleopatra and her maids are 'aloft', that is, on the upper stage or balcony. When Antony is borne in, Cleopatra moves straight from the simple enquiry 'How now! Is he dead?', to the astonishing invocation:

> O sun,
> Burn the great sphere thou mov'st in! darkling stand
> The varying shore o'th'world.
>
> (4. 15. 9–11)

At this stage of his career Shakespeare can rely on his ability to raise the tension and the temperature of a scene by a sudden swerve into rhetoric of this quality, which calls for immense projection by the actor and which can produce an almost physical reaction in an auditor.

Cleopatra then appeals to her women and her 'good friends' (Antony's bearers) to help draw Antony up from below to her level on the upper stage. She encourages and accompanies their efforts with these extraordinary comments:

> Here's sport indeed! How heavy weighs my lord!
> Our strength is all gone into heaviness;
> That makes the weight.

> (4. 15. 32–34)

The pun on heaviness (which also means sorrow) would seem disastrous: it insists on the audience's awareness of the mechanical problem of raising the perhaps substantial actor playing Antony fifteen feet or so from the main stage to the balcony. Various theories as to how this was done have been offered, but however the manoeuvre was executed, the audience was bound to have part of its mind on the difficulties it involved. Shakespeare makes them part of Cleopatra's consciousness too. Her grim, even grotesque joke accommodates the stunt into the emotional life of the play, and reassures the audience that the dramatist is in full control of the scene.

When Antony finally dies, the verse Cleopatra is speaking immediately registers the moment of his passing by another sudden escalation of style whose soaring long-breathed line communicates an unanalysable excitement:

> Noblest of men, woo't die?
> Hast thou no care of me? shall I abide
> In this dull world, which in thy absence is
> No better than a sty? O, see, my women ...

(Antony dies)

> The crown o'th'earth doth melt. My lord!
> O, withered is the garland of the war,
> The soldier's pole is fall'n: young boys and girls
> Are level now with men: the odds is gone,
> And there is nothing left remarkable
> Beneath the visiting moon.

> (4. 5. 59–68)

Shakespeare's command of rhetoric is so obviously equal to any occasion that it is surprising that, when he comes to present Cleopatra's own death, his use of it is comparatively restrained. He handles it with a theatrical self-consciousness that becomes an essential part of his method in his later work. The sequence in Act 5 Scene 2 leading to Cleopatra's end is prefaced by a startling reference to the conditions with which Shakespeare had to reckon. Cleopatra fears that if taken to Rome as a captive

> I shall see
> Some squeaking Cleopatra boy my greatness
> I' th' posture of a whore.
>
> (5. 2. 217–19)

This, however, is not so much an apology for the limitations that must become apparent when any boy actor is asked to impersonate Cleopatra as an invitation to the audience to waive objection by acknowledging that they have grounds for one.

Cleopatra prepares for her death as if she were giving an authoritative performance to out-face the Roman burlesque:

> Show me, my women, like a queen: go fetch
> My best attires. I am again for Cydnus,
> To meet Mark Antony.
>
> (5. 2. 226–8)

She mordantly concedes, however, that this will be her last appearance; she gives Charmian 'leave/To play till doomsday', and after Cleopatra's death Charmian adds

> Your crown's awry,
> I'll mend it, and then play—
>
> (5. 2. 317–18)

In both cases the sense of 'play' hovers between the ideas of childish recreation and theatrical illusion. Cleopatra and her maids play at dressing up, they pretend (perhaps this gained an odd plausibility when the actors were children themselves); but the play itself is, of course, a pretence. Shakespeare enhances the dramatic climax by reminding the audience of its essential theatricality.

Cleopatra's volatile performance in her last scene recalls the variousness of her character; her 'I have nothing/Of woman in me . . . I am marble-constant' is disingenuous. Her jealous fear that Iras will get to Antony first; her vulgar desire to hear Antony insult Caesar; her erotic apprehension that 'The stroke of death is as a lover's pinch/Which hurts, and is desired' (as Hazlitt said, 'she tastes a luxury in death'); her tolerance of the coarse, sexual innuendo of the Clown's chatter: these and other aspects of her nature are reflected in the line-to-line transitions of style.

Cleopatra's death is so affirmatively accomplished that it has often been felt to be triumphant rather than tragic. It is as if, having exhausted every sensation life has to offer (she is, after all, 'wrinkled deep in time'), she is eager to embrace the final experience. Her attitude to death really is what Antony had hoped this would be: she runs 'into't/As to a Lover's bed'. The serenity of the play's close, the wonder it evokes, and the paradoxical sense that it is a triumph of life, have led some to see it as looking forward to the glowing and beneficent conclusions of the romances. And Cleopatra's powers as a presenter of spectacle, as Robert Ornstein has attractively suggested, anticipate Paulina's in *The Winter's Tale*, and Prospero's.

The assurance with which Shakespeare seized on the theatrical possibilities of Plutarch's narrative is accompanied by a certain loss of intimacy in the audience's relationship with Antony and Cleopatra; the dramatist seems more detached from them than from their predecessors, Hamlet, Macbeth, or Timon. In all the later plays (although *Cymbeline* is perhaps a special case), the decline of soliloquy is marked. But the absence of confidential tone is off-set by a new candour; both Antony and Cleopatra are subjected to a remarkable degree of exposure. Antony is shown drunk and out of temper; Cleopatra hales an innocent messenger up and down with a violence that makes Antony's description of her as a 'right gypsy' seem modest understatement. Her vulgarity, coarseness and ferocity make the maintenance of any kind of decorum impossible, but the dramatist's ability to accommodate such varied moods is an essential preparation for the flexibility of style in *The Winter's Tale*. In both plays we feel that we are being shown the whole truth.

Although *Coriolanus* is deeply concerned with politics, it remains uncertain what Shakespeare's own position was, if any. Right, left and centre have been able to claim the play speaks for them. However, the patrician Coriolanus himself is clearly the hero, and the abrasiveness and immaturity of his character and code are likely to inhibit a popular audience's sympathy. The methods Shakespeare uses to deflect this resistance are characteristic of his later dramatic technique.

L. C. Knights's suggestion that 'our sense of Coriolanus is created largely by poetic means' does less than justice to the play's theatrical life. The images and rhythms of the verse are effective because they are at one with the actions of the character on the stage. Coriolanus's first entrance (when he is still Caius Marcius) crackles with aggressive energy:

> What's the matter, you dissentious rogues
> That, rubbing the poor itch of your opinion,
> Make yourselves scabs?
>
> (1. 1. 163–5)

His language is constantly urged forward by the kind of violence needed to push aside strong obstruction:

> He that depends
> Upon your favours swims with fins of lead
> And hews down oaks with rushes.
>
> (1. 1. 178–80)

In general his speech is astonishingly kinetic; its velocity (leading at times almost to incoherence) is a late development of the impetuous idiom Shakespeare gave to Hotspur, in the first part of *Henry IV*.

Johnson wondered whether in *Coriolanus* 'there is too much bustle in the first act, and too little in the last'. It is precisely the bustle – the battle against the Volsces which runs from Scene 4 to Scene 9 of Act 1 – which establishes Coriolanus's dynamic utterance as the verbal correlative of his martial force. The full, staged impact of these battle scenes is needed early on because they provide the visible guarantees which support the play's poetic currency. When, in his eulogy of Coriolanus, Cominius says

> As weeds before
> A vessel under sail, so men obeyed,
> And fell below his stem. His sword, death's stamp,
> Where it did mark, it took; from face to foot
> He was a thing of blood, whose every motion
> Was timed with dying cries. Alone he ent'red
> The mortal gate of th'city, which he painted
> With shunless destiny; aidless came off,
> And with a sudden re-enforcement struck
> Corioli like a planet.
>
> (2. 2. 103–12)

If this was a mere report it would seem hyperbole, but the audience knows it is true because they have seen it happen. War is Coriolanus's element, and we must see him in his element to understand his nature. Shakespeare risked putting his battle scenes at the beginning of his play because the tragedy of Coriolanus is the tragedy of an initially irresistible force gradually immobilized. The famous stage-direction of Act 5 Scene 3 – 'Holds her by the hand, silent' – marks the point at which he finally loses momentum. The stage picture of a still Coriolanus statically enduring his mother's long appeal is made powerful by its absolute contrast with the furious dynamism of word and act which Coriolanus at first exhibited. Coriolanus himself draws attention to the 'unnatural scene'; he is like 'a dull actor' who has forgot his part.

Coriolanus is not a noble and sympathetic figure whom we are sorry to see die; rather, we watch his fate with the awe that comes from seeing the suppression and self-destruction of unequalled energies. This effect is not achieved by 'poetic means' merely, but by the integration of structure, verse, character, image, scene, and action to the point at which they become aspects of each other. And this is what happens in the greatest moments of the last plays too.

It would be misleading to claim that such moments occur in *Pericles* or *Cymbeline* as it would be to think those plays comparable to *The Winter's Tale* or *The Tempest* because they can be shown, in summary, to be concerned with similar themes. *Pericles* was not included in the First Folio, and although some critics (notably Wilson Knight in *The Crown of Life*) have argued strongly in favour of the play's integrity, most editors now agree that what we have is Shakespeare's reworking of a play by someone else. He seems to have revised the first two Acts lightly and to have rewritten the last three substantially. Perhaps, as Coleridge surmised, Shakespeare started this work in a desultory manner, but became more deeply involved in his material as he proceeded. The play's construction is uncharacteristically episodic; the first Act can be – and in performance has been – detached from the rest without much sense of loss. On the other hand, a number of scenes in *Pericles* are irresistibly Shakespearean. The words spoken by Pericles when his wife has apparently died in childbirth during a storm at sea are hardly equalled in *The Tempest* itself, whose marine imagery is so strikingly anticipated:

> A terrible childbed hast thou had, my dear;
> No light, no fire: th'unfriendly elements
> Forgot thee utterly; nor have I time
> To give thee hallowed to thy grave, but straight
> Must cast thee, scarcely coffined, in the ooze;
> Where, for a monument upon thy bones,
> And e'er-remaining lamps, the belching whale
> And humming water must o'erwhelm thy corpse,
> Lying with simple shells.
>
> (3. 1. 56–64)

*Pericles* contains some of the principal motifs of the last plays. Pericles himself may be a passive figure compared with Leontes or Prospero, but like the former he loses wife and child to have them miraculously restored, and like the latter he is carried away from his kingdom by tempest. The double reconciliation is strategically much less well handled than in *The Winter's Tale*, but the scene in which Pericles is restored by Marina's music deploys the basic symbolism which Shakespeare brought to or found in the play with great power:

> O Helicanus, strike me, honoured sir;
> Give me a gash, put me to present pain;
> Lest this great sea of joys rushing upon me
> O'erbear the shores of my mortality,
> And drown me with their sweetness. O, come hither,
> Thou that beget'st him that did thee beget;
> Thou that wast born at sea, buried at Tharsus,
> And found at sea again!
>
> (5. 1. 194–201)

Here the authentic note of rapture – so vital to the effective presentation of the last plays' family reunions – is all the more remarkable for the instability of the surrounding verse in the text as we have it.

Other features of *Pericles* which look forward to its successors include an evil foster-mother (compare the wicked step-mother in *Cymbeline*); the strewing of flowers by Marina (she is imitated by Arviragus in *Cymbeline* and Perdita in *The Winter's Tale*); the appearance and intervention of supernatural beings (see the vision in *Cymbeline*, the oracle in *The Winter's Tale*, and the spirits' masque in *The Tempest*); and a new stress on the virtue of chastity (if the term is applied not only to Marina's disastrous effect on the brothel's business in *Pericles*, but also to Imogen's 'pudency so rosy', and to Florizel's and Ferdinand's insistence that their desires run not before their honour).

*Pericles*, however, is nearer unsophisticated forms of romance than the other late plays. Its primitive structure reflects the fortuitous nature of its action. Pericles's misfortunes, unlike those of Leontes or Prospero, are not set in motion by sin or neglect of duty, and so his final felicity is not the result of expiation but merely the reward of endurance. It has been suggested that Pericles is intended as an example of the patient man in adversity, but even if this were so, the briefest reminiscence of, for example, the 'Ripeness is all' passage in *King Lear* will show how thinly the virtue is here demonstrated. Pericles, in fact, has little character in the sense of recognizable quiddity; he is without idiosyncracy.

Although the construction and execution of *Cymbeline* need no apology, it remains a matter of debate whether Shakespeare is aiming at much more than an entertainment in a new style which *Pericles* may have suggested, and which the new conditions of the Blackfriars theatre probably encouraged. *Pericles* seems to have been popular, and there was also a successful revival of an absurd old romance called *Mucedorus* (which features a 'wild man' with some affinities with Caliban, and also employs a pursuing bear, as in *The Winter's Tale*). The songs, dances, and masques of the last plays are appropriate to the Blackfriars traditions and resources and may have been specially to the taste of its more polite audience, but Shakespeare's company continued to use their old theatre, the Globe. The chronology of events in the theatre at this time is hard to establish in detail, but whatever their order, and whatever Shakespeare's degree of responsibility for them, there is clear evidence of the development of the kind of taste that *Cymbeline* seems designed to gratify.

Part of the critical confusion which surrounds the interpretation of *Cymbeline* is due to the continuing uncertainty about the responses which this new style envisaged. Cymbeline has many of the traditional materials of romance as they had come down from Greek models and from native tradition: its events are tragically arbitrary and often incredible but lead finally to a happy conclusion; lost royal children are wonderfully found; wandering, vicissitude and apparent death end in restoration and reunion. Two incidents in *Cymbeline* closely resemble one of the best-known Greek romances, Heliodorus's *Aethiopica*. But Shakespeare has presented this kind of material in a historical context – Cymbeline's refusal to pay tribute to Rome and its consequences are recorded in Holinshed – and associated it with the wager-plot involving Imogen, Iachimo and Posthumus, which is taken from Boccaccio's *Decameron*. This latter intrigue (virtually complete after the first two Acts) is of the kind found in some of Shakespeare's previous comedies, but its co-existence with the Romano-British situation has led some to class the play as a history, concerned with national destiny. There is the further possibility that the play was intended to allow topical application: the final peace-making gesture, for instance, being meant as an applausive reference to James I's diplomacy.

Whatever the effect of inherited motifs and ulterior motives on the design of *Cymbeline*, Shakespeare's resourcefulness was fully tested by the problem of co-ordinating his heterogeneous materials and providing an integrated conclusion. Older commentators tended to dismiss the long last scene of *Cymbeline* as a cynical display of opportunism and a weary lapse of judgement. Granville-Barker did much to rehabilitate the scene, and his favourable verdict on its stagecraft has been echoed by Bertram Evans who, in *Shakespeare's Comedies*, has studied the dramatist's technique of exploiting the differences of knowledge among the characters themselves and between the characters and the audience. Evans goes so far as to say that

From the point of view of the creation, maintenance, and exploitation of discrepant awareness – considered both quantitively and artistically – *Cymbeline* is Shakespeare's greatest achievement.

The test of performance is important here. Act 5 Scene 5 of *Cymbeline* resembles other final sequences in Shakespeare (such as the last scene of *Measure for Measure*) in that it looks hopeless on the page, and has been proved to work successfully in the theatre. It is significant that Granville-Barker's commendatory *Preface* is written from the point of view of a stage director of the play, and he is alert to such theatrical factors as the relative positions of the actors, and their demeanour when not speaking. The subtly varied tempo of the verse reflects the supple control of the dramatist over material that does not have the advantage of the profound implications of the comparable occasion in *The Winter's Tale*. The modulations of style – from Cymbeline's terse questions in lines 108–18, to the ornate defensiveness of Iachimo's elaborate confession in lines 153–209, to Posthumus's electrifying 'Hang there like fruit, my soul,/Till the tree die' (lines 263–4), to Belarius's elevated benediction on the two royal princes (lines 347–52) – indicate great sensitivity to the voicing and pacing of the scene. Cymbeline's incredulity and surprise may seem artless, but it is acceptable because his almost complete impercipience flatters an audience in possession of all the material facts, and anxious to feel the relief of seeing every tangle untied.

Such a virtuoso piece of manipulation is a suitable climax for a play that often seems preoccupied with its own processes. A further result of this self-consciousness is that the characters sometimes give the impression of being caught between different kinds of theatrical possibility – an inherent danger in tragi-comedy.

Imogen, Posthumus, and Iachimo are intermittently something more than the mere agents necessary for the romantic plot. They require, fitfully, what the editor of the new Arden edition of the play calls a 'destructive reality'. The nineteenth century cult of Imogen (subscribed to by both Tennyson and Swinburne) may have been the result of too biographical an approach to the plays, but it was not without foundation. Imogen's impassioned speech beside the corpse of Cloten (4. 2. 291–332) ought to have a comic effect because it rests on the absurd mistake of supposing Cloten's body to be Posthumus's, but we have come to have too much respect for Imogen's intensity and individuality to feel happy about laughing at her.

By the time Shakespeare came to write *The Winter's Tale*, probably early in 1611, he was in full control of his new effects and combined them with his customary resources with complete security; its technical assurance is comparable with *Antony and Cleopatra*'s. Shakespeare seems to have approached his subject without any formal pre-conceptions as to its treatment. He keeps closely to his source, Greene's popular prose romance *Pandosto*, when it suits him, but remains free to alter its story completely (Shakespeare's conclusion is quite different from Greene's). *The Winter's Tale*'s structure shows a large control which allows much local spontaneity. The bi-partite nature of the plot – Leontes's jealousy which apparently causes the death of Hermione, followed sixteen years later by the love of Florizel and Perdita and the reconciliation of parents through children – is reflected in the clear division of the play into two halves (to some extent parallel in layout) by the speech of Time, the chorus (Act 4, Scene 1). But the play is actually conducted in three main styles: an intense, tragic manner in the first three Acts; a festive, pastoral episode in Act 4; and finally what, for want of a more satisfactory term, has often been called symbolic drama. *The Winter's Tale* shows Shakespeare's art at its most flexible, and the extraordinary impression of hospitable inclusiveness that it gives sustains the impression of self-sufficiency already noted in the late Roman plays.

The equal stress given in *The Winter's Tale* to successive generations under the pressure of time has understandably encouraged generalizing comment. When we are shown, in effect, the whole course of a man's life (as we are with Leontes), its pattern can be established and assessed, and the play has been much discussed in terms of such processes as sin, expiation, and reconciliation, or age and winter yielding to youth and spring. And it does indeed approach the condition of myth: Hermione's resurrection can dramatize for us the human longing that is also expressed by the myth of Alcestis; Perdita justifiably invokes Prosperpina since she herself embodies the renewal of nature. But although the play does intimate such large significances, they are not suggested to us by intrusive commentary from the dramatist or by characters (such as Edgar in *King Lear*) whose function is partly to alert the mind to the wide implications of the action. The characters of *The Winter's Tale* exist within their situations, too deep in their own lives to have much time for gnomic reflection. Even the celebrated discussion between Polixenes and Perdita on the respective value to be given to Nature and Art (4. 4. 79–103) – concepts also vital, as Frank Kermode has shown, to the understanding of *The Tempest* – is primarily a dramatization of their respective situations, and the arguments they advance are ironically at variance wth the positions they are in. Polixenes advocates marrying 'A gentler scion to the wildest stock' in theory, but baulks at his son's proposal to put his theory into practice; Perdita argues against 'carnations and streaked gillyvors', unaware that she is herself a 'bud of nobler race'. The discussion, as a discussion, is unresolved. Perdita gets on with distributing the flowers since 'It is my father's will, I should take on me/The hostess-ship o' th' day'. It is her *acts*, as Florizel realizes, that are queens.

The text of *The Winter's Tale* is not a vehicle for abstraction. Much of it cannot plausibly be related to general notions, and when characters are subjected to reckless symbolizing interpretation they can, as Philip Edwards warns, become diminished rather than enhanced by the process. The mythic properties of *The Winter's Tale* are essentially mysterious and latent; recognition of their undoubted power should not override attention to the vitality of the play's local life. The action in it is conducted at different levels, in different tones, and with wide variations of intensity. Shakespeare ensures the response appropriate to its dramatic occasions with an effortless resource that seems to become a little negligent only at the end of Act 4.

He solves the problem of the immediate presentation of Leontes's jealousy (made necessary by the play's time-scheme) by enforcing its acceptance rather than by hurriedly accounting for its origin. Whether or not we agree with J. I. M. Stewart's suggestion (in *Character and Motive in Shakespeare*) that we find Leontes's emotion plausible because we intuitively recognize that it corresponds with our own internal experience of the irrational,

Shakespeare uses some patently theatrical methods of communicating disturbance. The obscurity of such speeches as that beginning 'Thou want'st a rough pash and the shoots that I have' (1. 2. 128) defies tidy-minded editors because its syntactical disorder *is* the incoherence that Leontes suffers from. A more drastic method of enforcement is contained in these lines:

> Go, play, boy, play: thy mother plays, and I
> Play too; but so disgraced a part, whose issue
> Will hiss me to my grave: contempt and clamour
> Will be my knell. . . . Go play, boy, play. There have been
> (Or I am much deceived) cuckolds ere now,
> And many a man there is (even at this present,
> Now, while I speak this) holds his wife by th'arm,
> That little thinks she has been sluiced in's absence,
> And his pond fished by his next neighbour. . . .
>
> (1. 2. 187–95)

The first three 'plays' are an accumulating pun: the boy's play is childish but the mother's is sexually provocative, and Leontes himself has therefore to assume the role of cuckold. His neurotic dwelling on the lurking lexical degradation of the word is defensive; the rest of the lines quoted aim at disquieting the audience. Leontes's picture of himself as an actor leads him to think of the men now in the audience who may be or who are afraid of being 'o'er head and ears a forked one'. He insists on involving them ('even at this present,/Now, while I speak this'); and he uncovers in his listeners those dormant suspicions which in him have become virulent. The violence of sound and metaphor in 'sluiced' and 'fished' and the brutal coarseness of the rest of the speech (down to line 207) maintain the pressure of Leontes's will on an audience which has now become an involuntary accessory to his delusion.

As M. M. Mahood points out in *Shakespeare's Wordplay*, Perdita picks up the double meaning of 'play': she talks of 'a bank, for love to lie and play on', and three lines later suddenly becomes aware of herself as a performer:

> Methinks I play as I have seen them do
> In Whitsun-pastorals: sure this robe of mine
> Does change my disposition.
>
> (4. 4. 133–5)

But this is only one of many elements in the long and marvellously handled sheep-shearing scene. Shakespeare has time not only for the argument between Polixenes and Perdita already noted and for her famous flower passage, but also for Florizel's fervent declarations and Perdita's frank replies, for the old shepherd's memories of his wife, for Autolycus's gulling of the country-people, for idle holiday chat, for three songs and two dances, as well as for Polixenes's discovery of himself and the turn in the plot that this precipitates. Here, if anywhere in Shakespeare, can his art properly be called 'spatial', since the necessary concerns of the play are accommodated in a dramatic environment which resembles the diffuse spread of real life. Like the drinking party in Shallow's orchard in *Henry IV Part 2*, this scene has a movement that is at once wayward and progressive, action that is both thematic and irrelevant. Its eddying ordinariness and sudden crises, its comprehensive attention to the whole stage, almost seem to anticipate the technique of Chekhov.

This long and leisurely scene ensures that when the last Act is reached Leontes's original crime has been sufficiently distanced; time is felt to have passed. The resurrection of Hermione is the final example of that insistence on its own theatricality that *The Winter's Tale* shares with Shakespeare's other late plays. It also gives romance the greatest resonance of which it is capable, since romance shows the fortunate end of untimely accidents, and death is the most serious of all accidents. Shakespeare has kept the audience in ignorance of Hermione's continued existence – an unprecedented secretiveness on his part – and only at the beginning of Act 5 does he allow Paulina to drop some preparatory hints. The action of the scene in which the supposed statue comes to life is beautifully integrated with its vocabulary. The opposition of life and death, the contrary properties of warmth and cold constantly recur in the verse:

> Chide me, dear stone. ...,
>     O, thus she stood,
> Even with such life of majesty (warm life,
> As now it coldly stands). ...
> ... does not the stone rebuke me,
> For being more stone than it?
> Standing like stone ...
>     ... the stone is mine ...
> The very life seems warm upon her lip.

>                                         (5. 3. 24–66)

The sequence ends with Paulina's command 'be stone no more', and Leontes exclaims, as he embraces his lost wife, 'O, she's warm!'

The simplicity is breath-taking, but it has been thoroughly prepared for. Nothing could be less abstract or theoretical than this resurrection; the statue that comes to life is not a rhetorical figure but a stage fact, and Shakespeare describes it in the most elementary terms possible, the language of primary sensation.

After Hermione's descent and her reunion with Leontes (which, in the hands of major actors, has proved immensely effective, as records of performance from Macready to Gielgud indicate), Paulina is quick to add

> That she is living,
> Were it but told you, should be hooted at
> Like an old tale . . .
>
> (5. 3. 115–17)

There is, as we have just seen, all the difference between telling and showing, but this is the last of several concessions to the play's unreality. Its apparently suicidal acknowledgement that what we have just seen is illusion in fact corresponds with what the audience ('in their senses' as Johnson reminds us) know to be true: the play is a fiction. But when this admission is shared between stage and audience, at such a moment of tension, it paradoxically allows the profounder meaning of what has been performed to penetrate all the more deeply.

*The Tempest* is even more insistent on its own unreality than *The Winter's Tale*, but its dazzling enigmas are achieved at a certain human cost. Prospero's magical powers may be what Leontes calls 'an art/ Lawful as eating', but they put a form of coercion on the other characters which effectively diminishes their freedom and their interest. Our relative closeness to Prospero involves a distance from those he controls. His comment, aside, on Miranda's offer to help Ferdinand with his log-bearing – 'Poor worm thou art infected' (3. 1. 31) – shows a discouraging flicker of contempt for her feelings, a remoteness from simple, direct emotions which is unlike anything in *The Winter's Tale*. The adherence of *The Tempest* to the unity of time, and Prospero's disposing power over its events mean that the play's conclusion lacks the accumulated experience that masses behind Hermione's restoration. As F. R. Leavis has pointed out,

With the absence of the time-gap goes also an absence of that depth and richness of significance given, in *The Winter's Tale*, by the concrete presence of time in its rhythmic processes, and by the association of human growth, decay and rebirth with the vital rhythms of nature at large.

('The Criticism of Shakespeare's Late Plays')

The poignancy of Leontes's words

> But yet, Paulina,
> Hermione was not so much wrinkled, nothing
> So aged as this seems
>
> (5. 3. 27–9)

is lacking in *The Tempest*, since the action of time is not followed through serially but shown only in the summary retrospect of Prospero's memory. Miranda finds it difficult to concentrate on his long relation in Act 1 Scene 2, and she represents (although she thereby effectively contains and neutralizes) the audience's resistance to what seems almost an interior monologue. The play more than once gives an impression of private self-absorption.

The exotic nature of the enchanted island and its inhabitants, though superficially attractive, tends in the long run to emphasize the remoteness of such glamour. As Frank Kermode has made clear, in his introduction to the new Arden edition, *The Tempest* is a profound study of themes that appear in other Elizabethan works of the pastoral kind, but here there is no reassuring relationship with English country life. Pastoral is a mode of the imagination, not a guide to rural economy, but the shepherds of *The Winter's Tale* have quotidian concerns that connect them with real life as their audience surely knew it. Caliban and Ariel, on the other hand, belong to the world of travellers' tales and shipwrecks where the remote Bermudas ride. As a variant of the 'salvage man' in Book VI of Spenser's *Faerie Queene*, Caliban may have been familiar, but he can never have been normal. Ariel wistfully acknowledges his detachment from human emotions:

> Your charm so strongly works 'em
> That if you now beheld them, your affections
> Would become tender. . . .
> Mine would, sir, were I human.
>
> (5. 1. 17–20)

Caliban and Ariel have always been regarded as the products of what Joseph Warton in 1753 called an 'amazing wildness of fancy', and they are obviously creations of the greatest imaginative suggestiveness. All the same, their tangental relationship with ordinary human nature, even while it fascinates, makes them a little desolate. However, the feebleness of the fooling of Stephano and Trinculo, to whom Shakespeare appears to have had nothing new to give, works to the advantage of Caliban and Ariel.

As a play of reconciliation, *The Tempest* is less rewarding than has sometimes been assumed. After Prospero's strikingly unserene words to his brother—

> For you – most wicked sir – whom to call brother
> Would even infect my mouth, I do forgive
> Thy rankest faults – all of them; and require
> My dukedom of thee, which, perforce, I know,
> Thou must restore.
>
> (5. 1. 131–5)

Antonio says nothing at all for the rest of the play except to offer one typically sneering comment on Caliban. He has no choice but to be forgiven on Prospero's terms, but he accepts them with bad grace.

It is even difficult to be sure whether Prospero's reconciliatory intentions are consistently maintained. Although he claims, in Act 5 Scene 1, that 'with my nobler reason, 'gainst my fury/Do I take part', it is hard to trace in any convincing detail the running conflict between the desire for revenge and the resolve to forgive that seems to be implied. Unlike the speeches of Leontes, Prospero's words often appear to act as a screen between the audience and what is happening in his mind. He tells Ferdinand

> Sir, I am vexed.
> Bear with my weakness, my old brain is troubled:
> Be not disturbed with my infirmity.
> . . . A turn or two I'll walk,
> To still my beating mind.
>
> (4. 1. 158–63)

Given his own powers and Ariel's assistance, it is hard to believe that Prospero can be seriously worried about Caliban's conspiracy, the ostensible cause of his 'anger so distempered'. He may perhaps be mortified by the fact that his art cannot change Caliban's nature; he remains an 'Abhorred slave,/Which any print of goodness will not take', a 'thing of darkness' that Prospero has finally to acknowledge his.

Prospero's preoccupation with the power and instability of his 'art' has, of course, tempted many to see his situation as a model of Shakespeare's own. The old assumption that when Prospero talks of drowning his book, he is signifying Shakespeare's intention to give up writing and retire to Stratford dies hard, despite the evidence of his continued association with the theatre afforded by his collaboration in *Henry VIII*, *Two Noble Kinsmen*, and perhaps the lost *Cardenio*, all later works than *The Tempest*. The temptation to read Prospero's 'Our revels now are ended' speech as the dramatist's palinode is naturally strong, but our uncertainty about what is going on in Prospero's consciousness should make us resist it.

Prospero is, after all, referring to the immediate theatrical situation. The terms used, however metaphorically extended, are specifically theatrical: 'revels', 'actors', 'pageant'. Even the 'rack' in 'Leave not a rack behind' probably quibbles on a technical term used for stage clouds in masques. Since Prospero and the lovers have themselves formed an audience watching an illusory and insubstantial performance, the sudden disappearance of that 'vision' makes their own status precarious. As Anne Righter puts it, in *Shakespeare and the Idea of the Play*:

Here, in *The Tempest*, the condition of the actor and the man who watches his performance in the theatre have become identical, and the relationship of the audience with the play made strangely disturbing. Always before in Shakespeare, the play metaphor had served as a bridge between the audience and the domain of the stage. . . . Now, the barriers have been swept away altogether. . . . As Prospero's explanation reaches its end, the audience in the theatre seems to lose its identity. Life has been engulfed by illusion.

It is appropriate to think of *The Tempest* as Shakespeare's final play because the process of withdrawal that can be deduced from his later work is there taken as far as it can go without his abandoning the theatre altogether. The audacity and autonomy of the late Roman plays and the romances, their theatrical self-consciousness and seeming independence of their creator, reaches in *The Tempest* a new degree of inscrutability.

## SHAKESPEARE AS REVISER

### John Kerrigan

If you want to study Wordsworth's revisions you can go to Dove Cottage where, surrounded by lakes and tourists and daffodils, you may pull sheaf upon manuscript sheaf from the shelves, each traced with 'turnings intricate of verse'. If your interests are Miltonic or Tennysonian, Cambridge has the papers, and, in the chequered gloom of the Wren Library, you can watch *Comus* and *In Memoriam* come to life in the authors' hands. With Shakespeare the situation is different. No manuscripts stand behind his *Collected Works*: our *Richard III*s and *Cymbeline*s are based on early printed texts, trimmed, corrected and judiciously corrupted by editors. The Shakespearean originals have been lost beyond recall – some, perhaps, consumed in the fire that destroyed the first Globe theatre in 1613, and others, certainly, marked up by the printers and then thrown away. From time to time, someone will claim that Shakespeare's papers are hidden in the roof of Anne Hathaway's cottage, or under the tombstone guarded by the poet's fierce curse in Holy Trinity Church. But such notions are more curious than scholarly, and only based on wishing. Nothing seems to survive in the dramatist's hand beyond certain pages in a play apparently not performed and a scattering of signatures on legal documents.

The play, *Sir Thomas More*, was kept from the stage by censorship. As Lord Chamberlain, responsible for vetting drama, Edmund Tilney judged the chronicle, with its racial unrest and food riots in the reign of Henry VIII, unacceptably close to Elizabethan politics. '[Le]ave o[ut] ye insur[rection] wholy', he commanded its authors, '& ye Cause ther off'. That such an omission would eviscerate the work may or may not have struck him. But Munday and Chettle, aware that their play required a scene resembling the uncensored riot in 2 *Henry VI*, seem to have turned at this point to Shakespeare.[1] What he wrote did not, perhaps, persuade Tilney, but it has wit, moral weight and metaphoric ingenuity. It is also littered with second thoughts. 'Whates a sorry parsnip to a good

---

[1] The evidence is usefully summarized in *The Riverside Shakespeare*, ed. G. Blakemore Evans *et al.* 1974, the source of line references throughout this section.

hart' asks John Lincoln, a rioter, in the manuscript. Yet he first called parsnips 'watrie'. 'The removing of the straingers . . . cannot choose but much advauntage the poor handycraftes' cries Betts, but he reached that resonant 'advauntage' by way of a deleted 'helpe'. Not for nothing are working sheets called 'foul papers'. Throughout this scene, words, phrases and even speech prefixes, though added last (Shakespeare composed the riot as a cacophany and then identified the voices), are subject to inky-fingered revision.

'Wee have scarse received from him a blot in his papers' declared Heminge and Condell in their preface to the Folio – that post-humous collection which is the only source we have for half the plays – and the comment has been used to challenge not only the authorship of Lincoln and Betts' riot but the idea that Shakespeare was a self-revising writer. The Folio editors do not stop, however, at their assertion of blotlessness. 'But', they add, 'it is not our pro-vince, who onely gather his works, and give them you, to praise him'. E. A. J. Honigmann has shown that fluency was such a modish accomplishment in the period that not to 'praise' Shakespeare for it would be tantamount to saying he couldn't write.[1] Admittedly Jonson echoed the phrase, declaring in *Discoveries* that his rival should have 'blotted' lines which, strictly construed, made no sense. Yet in the Folio, where a considered panegyric was called for, Jonson struck a balance between Art and Nature, celebrating Shakespearean ease but at the same time insisting, in what reads like a conscious correction of Heminge and Condell, on the artistry of Shakespeare as reviser. 'Yet must I not give Nature all', he writes:

> Thy Art,
> My gentle *Shakespeare*, must enjoy a part.
> For though the *Poets* matter, Nature be,
> His Art doth give the fashion. And, that he,
> Who casts to write a living line, must sweat,
> (such as thine are) and strike the second heat
> Upon the *Muses* anvile: turne the same,
> (And himselfe with it) that he thinkes to frame;
> Or for the lawrell, he may gaine a scorne,
> For a good *Poet's* made, as well as borne.
> And such wert thou.[2]

Certainly, the loose ends, confused attributions, double versions of single exchanges and other textual tangles which characterize

[1] *The Stability of Shakespeare's Text*, Lincoln, Nebraska, 1965, pp 22–8.
[2] 'To the memory of my beloved, The AUTHOR MR. WILLIAM SHAKESPEARE', 55–65.

plays printed from Shakespearean foul papers most plausibly stem from variant thoughts.[1] Not all point to the sweat of striking a second heat. Often Shakespeare changed things on the hoof, blotting as he went, and sometimes he did not trouble to stop and delete what had become rejected text. On occasion, however, he made foul-paper changes significant enough to deserve Jonson's strenuous description. Theseus' speech at *A Midsummer Night's Dream* 5. 1. 2–22, for instance, originally compared 'Lovers, and mad men'; but Shakespeare returned to it at a late stage of composition and, made self-conscious perhaps by what he had achieved, squeezed into the margins, to the confusion of the printer, a number of lines about poetry, including these famous words:

> The Poets eye, in a fine frenzy, rolling,
> Doth glance from heaven to earth, from earth to heaven.
> And as imagination bodies forth
> The formes of things unknown: the Poets penne
> Turnes them to shapes, and gives to ayery nothing,
> A local habitation, and a name.[2]

Every reader of the early plays will sense a great leap forward. We seem to find at the point of revision a born poet being made. Can it be doubted that striking a second heat here shaped and, in Jonson's image, 'turned' the poet with his 'forms of things unknown', through the labour of rewriting?

Whatever is learned from such a crux will be inseparable from the text; but since, in revision as elsewhere, Shakespeare works impersonally, that is not inappropriate. Compare a speech in *Hamlet*, where Laertes encounters Ophelia, driven mad by her father's death (4. 5. 154–64). In the second edition of the play, a Quarto (i.e. paperback made of sheets folded twice, into four) printed from foul papers, Ophelia enters and Laertes cries,

> O Rose of May,
> Deere maid, kind sister, sweet *Ophelia*,
> O heavens, ist possible a young maids wits
> Should be as mortall as a poore mans life.

[1] Roughly a third of the three dozen plays survive in this form. For a classic account see W. W. Greg, *The Shakespeare First Folio*, Oxford, 1955, especially on *Errors*, *2 Henry IV* and *Timon* (though this is now considered a collaboration with Middleton).

[2] Lineation corrected. The standard analysis remains J. Dover Wilson, ed. *A Midsummer Night's Dream*, New Cambridge Shakespeare, 1924, 'The Copy . . . 1600' Section C.

Coming upon this passage later – presumably while copying from foul to fair – Shakespeare decided that 'poore' was unhelpfully unfocused, since, meant to imply pathos ('poor chap'), it also suggested a degree of poverty at odds with Polonius' worldly status. The counsellor to kings was no 'poore man'. So, as the Folio (based on a transcript near the prompt-book) shows, he substituted 'old' for 'poore'. But as soon as Shakespeare registered his objection to the word, the objection itself worked on his imagination, and he was prompted to add to his speech lines developing the suppressed suggestion of value:

> . . . as mortall as an old man's life?
> Nature is fine in Love, and where 'tis fine,
> It sends some precious instance of it selfe
> After the thing it loves.

The shift from age to worth, which in F (Folio) and the modern editions which follow it seems a disjunction, is, for readers aware of the divergence from Q (Quarto), associative and Shakespearean. It's as though the 'poore mans life', bodied forth in re-imagining, had yielded its ambiguity in revision.

That paragraph is contentious. Almost all scholars accept the idea of rethinking within foul papers, and the majority believe that, in copying, Shakespeare made changes. A text like *Love's Labour's Lost* will thus be agreed to reflect both rewriting in draft (as with Q's two versions of Berowne's great speech on Love [4. 3. 285–362]) and tinkering between foul papers and a transcript, evidenced by F's divergence from Q.[1] Resistance sets in, however, with plays like *Hamlet* which vary at many points between 'good' Quarto and Folio. For reasons which have more to do with the history of textual bibliography than evidence from the theatre and print-shop, many still reject the message of early editions: that Shakespeare revised *Othello* and *King Lear* as surely as he did *Troilus and Cressida*, extensively and in detail, and that Laertes was not meant from the outset to call Polonius 'old'. Hence the most recent editor of *Hamlet* – Philip Edwards, in the New Cambridge series (1985) – accepts the principle of revision but reckons only the 222 and 83 lines unique to Q2 and F part of a rewrite, though evidence from the period suggests that authorial revisions are characterized by local variants while larger cuts and inserts can indicate non-authorial

[1] Stanley Wells, 'The Copy for the Folio Text of *Love's Labour's Lost*', *Review of English Studies*, ns 33, 1982, pp 137–47.

adaptation.[1] (There are doubtful passages of this kind in *Macbeth* and *Measure for Measure*,[2] and Hamlet himself adds 'a speech of some dosen lines, or sixteene lines' to *The Mouse-trap* [2. 2. 541–2].) Worse, the magisterial New Arden (1982) rejects authorial revision at every point but one (spurning, like Edwards, the c.1300 local variants), and judges the Folio lines on boy players an insert only because they conflict with the editor's early date for the tragedy.

Yet this passage, 2. 2. 337–62, belongs to a sequence of variants affecting Rosencrantz and Guildenstern. The king's faithful ministers in the prose analogues, they become in Q2 fellow students of the prince and Claudius' gullible agents. The Folio, as one would expect in rewriting, moves further from the received story. (A similar drift away from source can be found in Shakespeare's revision of Sonnet 2, and in the reworked war in *King Lear*.[3]) F Hamlet's friendship with the pair is stressed, not only in the 'ayrie of Children' insert but in added banter (bluntly starting 'Let me question more in particular:') about bad dreams and ambition (2. 2. 239–69). Then, in the bedchamber scene, F cuts Hamlet's hostile speech, 'Ther's letters seald, and my two Schoolefellowes,/Whom I will trust as I will Adders fang'd,/They bear the mandat[e] . . .' (3. 4. 202–10). This omission can hardly be accidental since, while Q2 confirms the prince's suspicions by having Rosencrantz and Guildenstern arrive after his speech in Claudius' company, F has the king enter to Gertrude alone, leaving the pair to be called for. Harold Jenkins, in his New Arden, invokes the 'Adders fang'd' to support Hamlet when, confronted by Horatio's cool reaction to the rewritten commission and their death, 'So *Guyldensterne* and *Rosencrans* goe too't', the prince replies, 'Why man, they did make love to this imployment' (5. 2. 56–7). 'Hamlet assumes them to be willing for the worst' Jenkins says, noting 3. 4. 202–7, 'and we are probably meant to assume it too and to accept the poetic justice of their end.' This feckless comment is a warning against conflation. For Hamlet's response is Folio-unique and linked to the chain of variants. Stung by Horatio's criticism, and less sure of the pair's

1   John Kerrigan, 'Revision, Adaptation, and the Fool in *King Lear*', in *The Division of the Kingdoms: Shakespeare's Two Versions of 'King Lear'*, ed. Gary Taylor and Michael Warren, 1983, pp 195–245.

2   3. 5 and 4. 1. 39–43, 125–32 in the tragedy (probably Middleton), 1. 2. 1–84 and, it has been argued, 4. 1. 1–20 in the problem play.

3   Gary Taylor, 'Some Manuscripts of Shakespeare's Sonnets', *Bulletin of the John Rylands University Library*, 68, 1985, pp 210–46; 'The War in *King Lear*', *Shakespeare Survey 33*, 1980, pp 27–34.

complicity in F than Q2, Hamlet shrugs off blame with a bawdy jest.[1]

As the exchange unfolds, the texts drift purposefully apart. Girding at Horatio's coolness, Hamlet asks in F whether it's not 'perfect conscience,/To quit' the king 'with this arme?', now that the commission gives proof of his villainy, and he anticipates what will be cut from Q2 a few lines later: Gertrude's suggestion that he apologize to Laertes before the duel (5. 2. 67–80). The Folio emphasis on pace is striking:

HOR: It must be shortly knowne to him from England . . .
HAM: It will be short,
The *interim's* mine, and a man life's no more
Than to say one:

and it so clearly anticipates those gaps in F which reduce the exchange with Osric (106–43)[2] and remove entirely the anonymous Lord who comes in 1604 to make sure Hamlet will fight Laertes (195–208) that Professor Jenkins's refusal to notice links begins to look perverse. But then, Philip Edwards cannot deeply care for a single word like 'one', though the ghost first appears on 'The bell then beating one' (1. 1. 39), and in the clash of 'fell incensed points' a man's life hangs on 'one' sword-thrust:

HAM: Come on sir.
LAER: Come my Lord.
HAM: One.
LAER: No.
HAM: Judgement.
OSRIC: A hit, a very palpable hit.[3]

'I do so much of my work by the critical, rather than the imaginative faculty' Yeats confessed, and we're inclined to think this unShakespearean. What the new work on revision has revealed, however, is a poet willing to engage with his own work critically, as reader and rethinker. That meshing of Shakespearean imagery and echo which works across scenes and situations to complicate our

---

[1] For 'goe too't' see *King Lear* 4. 6. 111–13; for 'make love', *Hamlet* 3. 4. 93–4.

[2] So the courtier is named at most points in Q2, presumably because his foppish headgear is plumed with ostrich feathers, but perhaps on account of his affected gait ('This Lapwing runnes away with the shell on his head' [185–6]) and his folly.

[3] 5. 2. 280–1. Contrast the iterative 'one's added to *Othello* at the same point in a tragic economy and in the context of 'Justice' and 'her Sword' (5. 2. 16–20). What makes for pace at Elsinore stresses protraction in the later ending.

responses, and which has seemed instinctive, now starts to look deliberate. If the reshaping of *Hamlet* from Q2 to F may be readily summed in general terms – cuts to hasten the arrival of the ghost (1. 1. 108–25, 1. 4. 17–38), a softening of sensual denunciation in the bedchamber (3. 4. 71–6, 78–81, 161–5, 167–70), a blunting of our scepticism towards Fortinbras so that he more securely refigures Old Hamlet, that other smiter of the Polacks (4. 4. 9–66) – the *details* of revision change our idea of Shakespeare. He becomes a self-considering artist, verbally conscious down to the chiasmus 'One./No', and too preoccupied with complex material to warble native wood notes wild. Moreover, the bias of his self-criticism must influence our own. For the first time, analysis can gain some purchase on the plays from inside. It is liberating, and creative of better discipline, to establish with exactness that Shakespeare thought some of his inspirations better than others, and not a few dispensable. We need not accept his judgements, but they are inextricably part of the texts they address. Certainly, in the light of recent research, the holistic tendency of criticism since Wilson Knight, and our habit of thinking the plays artifacts, verbal icons for actors, appears misguided. Shakespeare's imagination seems to have thrashed around within a story, establishing an area of textual potential, and he then reworked his material as the development of sources through drafts which were subject to second and, we may gather, third thoughts. His plays achieved completeness only in the approximation of performance, from a book which then might be revised.

A corollary of this is that certain analyses can be found, in the deepest sense, Shakespearean. When John Bayley, for instance, wrote his essay 'Time and the Trojans',[1] he will not have known that, as it now appears, Q *Troilus and Cressida* precedes F, reproducing the foul papers of a text lying behind the play as it was probably performed at the Inns of Court, while F stems from the prompt-book of a public theatre version revised from the work found in Q.[2] Even when faced with a blurred text, however, Bayley detected in it a distinctive quality of timelessness. Despite the long perspective of history through which its events are seen, he argued,

---

[1] *Essays in Criticism*, xxv, 1975, pp 55–73.

[2] Gary Taylor, '*Troilus and Cressida*: Bibliography, Performance, and Interpretation', *Shakespeare Studies*, 16, 1983, pp 99–136. For an interesting but unpersuasive attempt to revive Coghill's theory that F precedes Q see E. A. J. Honigmann, 'The Date and Revision of *Troilus and Cressida*', *Textual Criticism and Literary Interpretation*, ed. Jerome J. McGann, 1985, pp 38–54.

and despite the looming fall of Troy, its characters are allowed no
felt past or future. And so we look from foul papers to the second
prompt-book to find that Shakespeare has interpolated six extraordinary lines in Agamemnon's greeting of Hector. 'Worthy [of]
armes', he says in both texts, 'as welcome as to one,/That would be
rid of such an enemy.' Then, F alone,

> But that's no welcome; understand more cleere
> What's past, and what's to come, is strew'd with huskes
> And formelesse ruine of oblivion:
> But in this extant moment, faith and troth,
> Strain'd purely from all hollow bias drawing:
> Bids thee with most divine integritie,

—back to shared text – 'From heart of very heart, great *Hector*
welcome' (4. 5. 165–70). It is at least as easy to see why those
words are in the play as it is to see why they are in Agamemnon's
speech; and when that happens in Shakespeare it's always worth
asking, Why?

Most changes in *Troilus and Cressida* are of this kind, affecting the
dialogue rather than staging and structure. Shakespeare tautens
(e.g. Thersites' list of plagues [5. 1. 20–23]) and dilates (1. 3. 354–
6), cuts (2. 1. 29–30) and interpolates (4. 4. 144–8). Rare words
he replaces with familiar ones, while obvious terms become exotic.
Sometimes he seems merely to fidget, making 'worthy' 'Noble' and
'such like' 'so forth'; yet work on Middleton, Chapman, Jonson and
Dekker shows that meddling with indifferent substitutions is the
hallmark of a closely revising author.[1] Only once do the early texts
indicate a major adjustment. Where Q has Troilus dismiss
Pandarus before the epilogue (5. 10. 32–4), F duplicates the dismissal at the end of 5. 3. If F was printed from a copy of Q
annotated against the Globe prompt-book, it follows either that the
company book kept both options open (rather as F *Macbeth* allows
the hero to be killed on- or off-stage) or that the Folio printer
ignored the collator's deletion, if it was made, of 5. 10. 32–56. At
all events, the tangle shows Shakespeare first ending the play with
a seamy, cynical epilogue, and then deciding to finish with Troilus'
'Hope of reveng[e] shall hide our inward woe'. No more than
hollowly affirmative, the revised conclusion at least spares its audience the foul aftertaste of Pandarus' bequeathing his diseases.

More connectedly than *Hamlet*, and more searchingly than

---

[1] J. Kerrigan, 'Revision, Adaptation', pp 205–13 and nn. 45–66.

*Troilus*, the text of *Othello* has been rethought and recast.[1] Between Q and the post-1606 prompt-book-related F, Shakespeare works along fault lines in the story, ambiguating afresh points at which the audience's sympathy seems too readily assured. The dialogue is shot through with shifting emphases, rhythms and, above all, possessives and pronouns. A Roderigo 'I' becomes 'you' in Iago's alchemical presence (2. 1. 281); 'he ecchoes me./As if there were some monster in his thoughts' is echoically 'thou' and 'thy' in F (3. 3. 106–7); Desdemona's wedding sheets distressfully switch from 'our' to 'my' (4. 2. 105). Tiny examples; but the subtlest attention is paid in revision to that which holds between characters, and between characters and their senses of self. Consider Desdemona's murder, 5. 2. 80–91. In Q, she cries 'O Lord, Lord, Lord' as Othello strangles her, and the line is both the 'prayer' she was denied at line 83 and an anguished protest, couched in the language of obedience, to the Moor, her lord.[2] At once, a banging on the door begins – like the knocking on the castle gate, after Duncan's murder – and also the process of anagnorisis, with Emilia's 'My Lord, my lord, what ho, my Lord'; and the narrowed obsessive Moor for a moment thinks this Desdemona's voice, displaced. (Emilia's voice will again become her mistress', singing the added willow song at 5. 2. 246–8.) 'What voice is this?' he asks, 'not dead? Not yet quite dead?' In F, 'O Lord, Lord, Lord' is deleted and 'What voice is this?' correspondingly becomes 'What noise', which takes Emilia's cry to be other. Look at a modern edition like the Riverside, or Norman Sanders's New Cambridge (1985), and you find the Quarto line plus, ineptly, 'What noise'.

This detail is chosen as a hard case. F regularly removes references to God because an Act of Parliament, passed in 1606, forbade stage blasphemy. While the Shakespeare prompt-books did not suffer as keenly as, say, *Dr Faustus* under this dispensation, undesirable changes were still forced on the text. When discussing revision, it's important to remember that while certain variants (such as the inserted fly scene, 3. 2, in *Titus Andronicus*) were in Shakespeare's power, others were not. Censorship kept the

---

[1] Though Johnson comments shrewdly on the play's revision in a note to the F-only willow song (4. 3. 31–53, 55–7), the pioneering work is by Nevill Coghill, 'Revision after Performance' in *Shakespeare's Professional Skills*, 1964. See also E. A. J. Honigmann, 'Shakespeare's Revised Plays: *King Lear* and *Othello*', *The Library*, 6th series, 4, 1982, pp 142–73.

[2] Cf. 'Who is thy Lord?/He that is yours, sweet Lady', F 4. 2. 101, another added possessive twist.

deposition scene', *Richard II* 4. 1. 154–318, off page and stage during Elizabeth's lifetime; the Lord Chamberlain probably objected to *King Lear* 1. 4. 140–55, missing in F;[1] and 'O Lord, Lord, Lord' was expunged by law. So many distinctive variants are linked to oaths in *Othello*, however, that it looks as though Shakespeare himself purged the prompt-book. Certainly, many of the changes from Q to F – six lines unique to the former, a hundred and sixty added, about a thousand variants in common text – are not of the kind that can be readily attributed to a book-keeper, or scribe, or drunken compositor. Some stand alone, like the dozen lines given Roderigo to clarify the plot (1. 1. 121–37), but others connect thematically and by means of stage tableaux.

Thus F thrice foregrounds Brabantio's assertion that Othello seduced his daughter 'with Drugs or Minerals', 'Spels, and Medicines, bought of Mountebanks' (1. 2. 65, 72–7, 1. 3. 63). The Moor assures the Duke that he used no 'forced courses' to 'poison' Desdemona, but that when he told the story of his life she 'with a greedy eare/Devour[ed] up [his] discourse'. 'This onely', he says, 'is the witchcraft I have us'd' (1. 3. 110–70). At first blush the answer clears his name, but that image of an ear glutted with charm, glanced at several times in the scene, once by Iago, may give us pause. 'Thou knowest we worke by wit, and not by wi[t]chcraft' the Ensign later reminds Roderigo, yet the 'poison' he uses on Othello (3. 3. 325, F only) is called, in the F-dilated epileptic fit, 'medicine' (4. 1. 38–43). The 'Drugs' and 'Minerals' poured in dead King Hamlet's ear become verbal in *Othello*; but they are not the less dangerous for that. There may be no 'witchcraft' in renaissance Venice; but there remains as in *Macbeth* the corrosive 'suggestion' that lies like truth.

My claim is not that the Moor deceives, but that the inserts about magic are concerned with suasion too. There's a strong centripetal tendency in the tragedy, referring disparate material towards the temptation that precipitates Othello's downfall, and the 1. 3 argument about feeling and fabling decidedly looks forward to Acts 3 and 4. So, indeed, does its account of Turkish strategy. For in revising the Senate scene Shakespeare chose not to trim what might be thought an excrescence, but to expand. What are we to make of the Turkish to-and-fro, the feint towards Rhodes before the attack on Cyprus? 'Tis a Pageant,' a senator answers, 'To keepe

---

[1] Gary Taylor, 'Monopolies, Show Trials, Disaster, and Invasion: *King Lear* and Censorship', in Taylor and Warren, *Division*, pp 77–119; Annabel Patterson, *Censorship and Interpretation*, 1984, pp 58–73.

us in false gaze'. His analysis of what is against what merely seems (17–35) offers an example of caution beside which Othello can ultimately be judged, deluded as he is by false gazing and Iago's pageant with Cassio. And it is spun out in F:

> ... If we make thought of this,
> We must not thinke the Turke is so unskillfull,
> To leave that latest, which concernes him first,
> Neglecting an attempt of ease, and gaine
> To wake, and wage a danger profitlesse.

While the Duke and others are baffled by this manoeuvering, the sage First Senator is sceptical, explains in balanced phrases why, and immediately after the addition has his doubts confirmed by the arrival of a messenger from Cyprus. This may be the most extreme example in *Othello* of public affairs reflecting private experience, but the links are there, and Shakespeare's enlargement of the speech points towards his wishing them registered.

At all events, this takes us to the cluster of variants which must concern us most – in the temptation, fall and vengeance of the Moor. We also find there a counter-instance to the Bayley essay: criticism which contradicts the movement of authorial feeling. Dr Leavis, notoriously, saw Othello's behaviour in these scenes as imperceptive and egotistical. Rejecting Bradley's image of the Noble Moor, he emphasized the hero's responsiveness to Iago, and wrote of his succumbing 'with a promptness that couldn't be improved upon'.[1] Scholarship may have recomplicated the picture, but critics, always wary of siding with the credulous, remain closer to Leavis than they should. For we can deduce from the drift of variants that, after sailing close to the wind in Q, Shakespeare worked to protect Othello. His Folio 'promptness' not only could be 'improved upon': it had been in the Quarto. Indeed caution seems evident from the outset in F. While Q Othello calls Iago's suspicions 'horrible counsell', they constitute in F 3. 3. 93–162 'Some horrible Conceite' – less information than a fancy. Strikingly 'conceits' replaces 'coniects' a few lines later (148–9), where F Iago defensively plays up Othello's 'wisedome'. Meanwhile, 'close denotements' in Q's exploratory exchange become uncommitted 'dilations, working from the heart' (123) in Folio, much as F's 'For *Michael Cassio,*/I dare be sworne, I thinke that he is honest' pulls

---

[1] 'Diabolic Intellect and the Noble Hero: or The Sentimentalist's *Othello*', reprinted in F.R. Leavis, *The Common Pursuit*, London, 1952.

back the devil's horns more sharply than Q's 'I dare presume' (125). Towards the end of this sequence, we notice, Quarto Othello's explosive 'Zouns' (154) is replaced by a baffled but genuinely interrogative 'What dost thou meane?'

Howsoever that may be, by the end of the scene Shakespeare is unmistakably concerned to make the Moor less amenable. In both texts, Othello returns to the stage, after Desdemona's loss of the handkerchief and Iago's exchange with Emilia, enraged and hating his tempter. He wishes he had remained ignorant, bids farewell to the plumed troops, and insists on 'ocul[a]r proofe'. Erratic in Q, he immediately proclaims Iago's honesty and has to be prompted by the Ensign into thinking once more about evidence. 'I should be wise, for honestie's a foole', Iago says, 'And looses that it workes for:' half-line pause, characteristic of his methods:

> I see sir, you are eaten up with passion,
> I doe repent me that I put it to you,
> You wou'd be satisfied.
>     OTH. Would, nay, I will.

With the handkerchief to hand, and a plot ripening, Q Iago can risk encouraging the Moor to seek the proof he has already part-forgotten (3. 3. 382–3, 391–3). That does not happen in F; there Othello inherits Iago's half-line and says:

> By the world,
> I thinke my Wife be honest, and thinke she is not:
> I thinke that thou art just, and thinke thou art not:
> Ile have some proofe. My name that was as fresh
> As *Dians* Visage, is now begrim'd and blacke
> As mine owne face. If there be Cords, or Knives,
> Poison, or Fire, or suffocating streames,
> Ile not indure it. Would I were satisfied.

This may not be the most limber, intelligent blank verse, but its inflexible antitheses at least show Othello weighing in a balance the evidence he's heard against what he knows of the Ensign and Desdemona. Instructively, he echoes the First Senator's added idiom, with its 'If we make *thought* of this,/We must not *thinke*', its 'ease, and gaine' and 'wake, and wage'. And Othello demands, for himself, 'some proofe'.

In F this speech is a watershed, a parting of the ways, and when Iago offers 'some proofe' by mentioning the handkerchief – that scarlet-dabbled token lifted from revenge tragedy, strawberry-spotted like wedding-sheets, and woven perhaps with 'witchcraft'[1] – Othello's collapse is correspondingly extreme. His debasement is registered in the vindictive oath, expanded in F into a highly dramatic set-piece. As Othello and his Ensign kneel together (3. 3. 453–69), the revised Moor rants about the Propontic and the Hellespont and swears 'by yond Marble Heaven' to act against his wife. 'Do not rise yet', Iago answers, effective in both texts but painfully attractive in the Folio as an instant parodist:

> Witnesse you ever-burning Lights above,
> You Elements, that clip us round about,
> Witnesse that heere *Iago* doth give up
> The execution of his wit, hands, heart,
> To wrong'd *Othello's* Service . . .

Now this revision, like the congruent one in the second big Iago/Othello scene, extending the Moor's epileptic fit (from 4. 1. 35–7 to 43), might seem theatrically opportunistic. But the charge of crowd-pleasing can be discounted because the changes are linked to variants elsewhere in the tragedy, while both are consistent with Shakespeare's slightly more protective attitude towards the Folio Moor at this point in the action. 'Nature would not invest her selfe in such shadowing passion, without some I[n]struction', for instance, in the epileptic speech, shows F Othello even at the point of breakdown thinking through the possibility of delusion. In a hideous sense, it is his willingness to think about unthinkable evidence which precipitates his collapse. 'It is not words that shakes me thus,' he says: '(pish) Noses, Eares, and Lippes: is't possible?' The question is not asked in Q, and neither is the mesh which entangles the Moor so intricately displayed. The speech may lie at the limits of sanity, but nothing in it is redundant. 'O divell' it ends in F: both 'Oh *Desdemon!*' (F 5. 2. 281)[2] and 'If that thou bee'st a Diuell, I cannot kill thee [*Wounds Iago*, no more]' (5. 2. 287). Even the exclamation ('pish') works, as a classic instance of an Iago word

---

[1] Kyd, *The Spanish Tragedy* II. v; *3 Henry VI* 1. 4; Tourneur, *The Atheist's Tragedy* II. i; Freud, *Introductory Lectures* (1916–17), number 17, 'A lady, nearly thirty years of age . . .'; *Othello* 3. 4. 55–75, recalling Brabantio's additions. For a less portentous, or too naturalistic, interpretation, see Christopher Ricks below, pp 358–9.

[2] The 'demon' in '*Desdemon*' – a form which occurs after the jealousy (Anne Barton, '*Othello's* Fair Devils', unpublished lecture), in F – matching the 'hell' in 'Othello', is seen at least as clearly in Cinthio's source (where the Moor has no name): 'Disdemona' there means, as in the New Testament, 'unfortunate', but it also reads 'Hades/*demon*/feminine ending'.

carried into Othello's language; and it is carried from one sexually heightened Folio moment, in the exchange with Roderigo at 2. 1. 257–70, to another.[1]

And then, the combination of 'yond Marble Heaven' with Iago's kneeling and the 'ever-burning Lights above' generates, in F only, one of the most alarming ironies introduced by Shakespeare as reviser. Having developed 3. 3, that is, the poet went on to add an echoic sequence in which Desdemona kneels to the Ensign (4. 2. 150–9). 'By this light of heaven,' she says in both texts, 'I know not how I lost him.' But F goes on:

> Heere I kneele:
> If ere my will did trespasse 'gainst his Love,
> Either in discourse of thought, or actuall deed,
> Or that mine Eyes, mine Eares, or any Sence
> Delighted them [in] any other Forme,
> Or that I do not yet, and ever did,
> And ever will, (though he do shake me off
> To beggerly divorcement) Love him deerely,
> Comfort forsweare me.

Shakespeare once more associates heaven, light and kneeling with a sweeping vow – for this is Desdemona's version of the Propontic speech; and his doing so involved more than a black structural joke. If, in Desdemona's genuflection, we see evidence of the Ensign's growing power, F also protects Othello from the hasty rebuke of those who blame the outcome entirely on him. Another, outside the circle of macho camaraderie, and with less reason to trust Iago, bends the knee.

Yet the editors neglect this. Norman Sanders, most recently, concedes second thoughts but, like his New Arden precursor (1958), he uses signs of revision to underwrite eclecticism. Divergence is for him a local phenomenon and his *Othello* is 'arrived at by treating each pair of variants as a separate entity'. This procedure reduces textual criticism to a lucky dip, since the well-printed substantive prizes are all Shakespearean. Professor Sanders does not choose to hear the resonance of F 4. 2 in the F-only willow song and its aftermath – that argument between Desdemona and Emilia in which both swear 'by this heavenly light' (4. 3. 65–6). He does not pause to examine the Folio bolstering of Emilia there, against her mistress's rapt romanticism (86–103), nor trace through

---

[1] 'Pish' occurs nowhere else in Q/F, and only once in the rest of Shakespeare.

Act 5 the comic relativism which, associated with Iago's wife, tells against the Moor's stoic posturing (in, especially, the Folio-unique 5. 2. 151–4, 185–93 and 246–8 vs. 266–72 and F variants at 338 and 342). His conflating policy makes him miss Shakespeare returning upon himself, visibly busier than everywhere else except Q and F *King Lear*.

For that play, finally, lies at the heart of the matter. Indeed, Peter Blayney made it the *start* of the matter when he showed that a grubby *Lear* published in 1608 was confused because of circumstances in Nicholas Okes' print-shop.[1] Previous editors had dismissed Q as a 'bad' text, derived from the same lost original as F, yet supplementing it. The actors playing Goneril and Regan had hastily assembled and dictated the text from papers filched out of Shakespeare's closet. Or an assiduous stenographer, visiting the Globe many times, had botched together a draft of the play and sold it to the printer with verse lined as prose plus all sorts of passages, oddly, not in the prompt-book. But Blayney showed that Okes's press was not equipped to print plays, so that, quite quickly, the compositors ran out of wooden blocks to fill the margins for verse and had to set it as prose instead. And he traced, precisely, a shortage of full stops – plays use them heavily, after each prefix as well as in the text – which meant dialogue full of commas, seeming underpointed and eccentric. In short he showed that foul papers lay behind Q, with an authority distinct from F. Subsequent work has supported Blayney on stylistic as well as bibliographical grounds, and a growing consensus suggests that Q was set from papers preceding a prompt-book used for the first performance of the play in 1606, while F was printed from a copy of a reprint of the Quarto annotated against a prompt-book of the play as revised on or from a copy of the first Quarto probably put together in 1609–10. In a nutshell, Q and F approximate early and late versions of *King Lear*, both apparently authorial but separated by three or four years hard writing and by the experience of producing plays like *Coriolanus* and *Pericles*.

Massive in scale and intricate in detail, Shakespeare's reworking of *King Lear* offers the most extreme and revealing evidence of his willingness to rethink. The blots in *Sir Thomas More*, interlinings of the *Dream*, foul to fair changes in *Hamlet*, and post-prompt-book further thoughts there and in *Troilus* perhaps and certainly in *Othello*: changes of each kind apparently recur in *Lear*. Some 285

[1] A Cambridge Ph.D. leading to *The Texts of 'King Lear' and Their Origins*, 2 vols., i, *Nicholas Okes and the First Quarto*, 1982, and ii which is earnestly awaited.

lines in Q are cut from F, with a further 120 added. In common text, there are about 800 variants. And the changes affect most roles in the play. There is that sharp cutting in the second third of the tragedy which, combined with the removal of references to French involvement in the War for Britain, transforms the pace and temper of the play's drift towards catastrophe. Rapid and unsettling, F lacks the choric exchanges and static soliloquies which lend Q its amplitude.[1] There is the exaltation of Cordelia and diminution of Kent, the constraining of Edmund and refraction of the Fool.[2] Albany is strong in Q and has the play's last lines; in F, Edgar is more powerful, and he increasingly appropriates speeches from Quarto Albany until he inherits the kingdom.[3] There is hardly a character in the play not caught up in revision. No scene is free from rewriting of some sort. At half a dozen points, conflation produces nonsense. And Q's family tragedy is more complex and political in F.

For, if one had to isolate the 'most important' strand in revision, it would start from the abdication speech.[4] In Q, Shakespeare does nothing to make Lear seem sagacious. The old man sits there with his map, like Hotspur and the rebels in *1 Henry IV*, presumptuously putting asunder a kingdom which Nature has assembled from 'shady forrests, and wide skirted meades'. Peremptory and self-concerned, the king offers no reason for his abdication beyond a desire to shake the 'cares and busines' of government from his shoulders:

---

[1] G. Taylor, 'War in *King Lear*', and, for a useful caution suggesting theatrical involvement, 'The Structure of Performance: Act Intervals in the London Theatres, 1576–1642' in *Shakespeare Reshaped: 1606–1623* by John Jowett and Gary Taylor (Oxford, forthcoming).

[2] Michael Warren, 'The Diminution of Kent', and Kerrigan, 'Revision, Adaptation' in Taylor and Warren, *Division*, pp 59–73, pp 195–245, but also Taylor, 'War in *King Lear*', and R. A. Foakes, 'Textual Revision and the Fool in *King Lear*', *Trivium* xx, 1985, pp 33–47.

[3] Michael Warren, 'Quarto and Folio *King Lear* and the Interpretation of Albany and Edgar', *Shakespeare, Pattern of Excelling Nature*, eds. David Bevington and Jay L. Halio, 1978, pp 95–107; Steven Urkowitz, *Shakespeare's Revision of 'King Lear'*, 1980, Chapter 5.

[4] 1. 1. 36–54. My account of this speech overlaps with Thomas Clayton, '"Is this the promis'd end?": Revision in the Role of the King' and MacD. P. Jackson, 'Fluctuating Variation: Author, Annotator, or Actor?' in Taylor and Warren, *Division*, pp 121–41, pp 313–49, and Gary Taylor, *Moment By Moment By Shakespeare*, 1985, Chapter 5.

> Meane time we will expresse our darker purposes,
> The map there; know we have divided
> In three, our kingdome; and tis our first intent,
> To shake all cares and busines of our state,
> Confirming them on yonger years,
> The two great Princes *France* and *Burgundy*,
> Great rivals in our youngest daughters love,
> Long in our Court have made their amorous sojourne,
> And here are to be answerd, tell me my daughters,
> Which of you shall we say doth love us most,
> That we our largest bountie may extend,
> Where merit doth most challenge it,
> *Gonorill* our eldest borne, speak first?

The weight of this falls on paternal authority and filial love. Lear seems recklessly ready to sacrifice the realm for the sake of his comfort and a few words of flattery. All those fears of division and dissent fostered in the Elizabethan and Jacobean mind by tracts and homilies would have come to life when Shakespeare's projected audience heard this. Indeed, it's worth recalling what that audience consisted of. We are told by the Stationer's Register and title-page of Q that the original *Lear* was performed at court during the Christmas Revels of 1606. Since we know that certain other plays belonging to Shakespeare's company were written with King James's interests in mind – *Macbeth*, for instance, which shows the origins of the Stuart succession in Banquo and Fleance – it's natural to wonder what this tragedy might have offered the king. Significantly, at just this time James was trying to persuade Parliament to accept the unification of Scotland, England and Wales, something not finally achieved until the eighteenth century. Q is not propaganda, but its first scene does present a view of national unity which would have been recognized at the time as conforming to that of the king.

In the Folio, by contrast, Shakespeare allows certain complicating factors inherent in his material to surface.

> Meane time we shal expresse our darker purpose.
> Give me the Map there. Know, that we have divided
> In three our Kingdome: and 'tis our fast intent,
> To shake all Cares and Businesse from our Age,
> Conferring them on yonger strengths, while we
> Unburthen'd crawle toward death ...

What else was Lear to do? Critics are forever telling the king what he should not have done, and they quote *Gorboduc* to prove it. But what positive steps could the old man take to ensure the safety of

the realm? Given his lack of a male heir, was he to respect
primogeniture and leave the state in Goneril's less than ideal hands?
Or make the best of an intractable problem by ensuring that at least
part, the best part it seems, of Britain should be ruled by the kind
and honest Cordelia? If the latter, was it not wise of Lear to divide
the kingdom – or as Q reminds us at 1. 1. 4 'kingdomes' – before his
own death, given that, while alive, he could act as figurehead and
arbiter, helping consolidate the potentially unstable system of
tripartite government? You can watch the political issues surface.
Quarto 'To shake all cares and busines of our state' uses 'state' to
mean 'condition', 'of' as 'off'; F makes the line less ambiguous,
while transforming 'all cares . . . of our state' into one phrase in a
two-line parenthesis opened after 'Tell me my daughters': '(Since
now we will divest us both of Rule,/Interest of Territory, Cares of
State).' The change can scarcely be random since it rings, a few
lines later, in Kent's variant – remarked by Dr Johnson as evidence
of revision – 'Reverse thy doome', 'reserve thy state' (149). In Q,
the counseller questions Lear's judgement in the love-trial; in F he
engages with the issue of abdication.

At the same time, F Albany and Cornwall join Cordelia's suitors
– ciphers in Q but associated in revision with wealth and territory,
with 'The Vines of France' and 'Milke of Burgundie' (84).[1] The
Folio reminds us of the complex redistribution of power which
Lear's demotion must entail: to husbands and to foreign states as
well as daughters. 'Our son of *Cornwal*,/And you our no lesse loving
Sonne of *Albany*' it adds, at some risk of becoming a catalogue,

> We have this houre a constant will to publish
> Our daughters several Dowers, that future strife
> May be prevented now . . .

That last clause is, of course, crucial. Coleridge writes of
Shakespeare's 'characteristic preference for expectation over
surprise', and the Folio supports his insight, for, while 'prevented'

[1] A laden rift marked by Keats in his F facsimile. By no means a textual biblio-
grapher, and unread in Q (the play he knew was at this point virtually identical with
F), Keats nevertheless on the first page of facsimile (c. 88 lines) underscored
almost half the added text (totalling c. 9 lines) – with a stroke in the margin also
against the enriched 36–41 – but only c. 3 lines common to Q/F. Since the
markings show us, in a concrete form, Keats reading Shakespeare like
Shakespeare returning to himself, it is uncanny, and moving, to find on the
opposite page 'On sitting down to read King Lear once again' in holograph. For
some related thoughts see Randall McLeod, 'UN*Editing* Shak-speare',
*Sub-Stance*, 33/34, 1982, pp 26–55.

means 'staved off' in Jacobean English, it also implies 'brought forward'. Unanticipated in Q, tragedy is courted while striven against in F. And it takes effect complexly. That obsessive re-run of Q's filial love-trial, the mock-trial (3. 6), goes, while Lear's developing political awareness is emphasized in lines about 'the strong Lance of Justice', a rare addition to the stripped Act 4.[1] The family drama becomes as contingent as paradigmatic. Indeed, Goneril is in revision, if not exactly pleasant, less opaquely evil.[2] It's Regan, not her sister, who in F slaps down Cordelia after the love-trial. When Oswald neglects Lear, Kent trips him, and Goneril demands a reduction in the king's hundred knights (1. 4.), the confrontation is prepared by her in Q but not in F. Throughout the early text, she is impetuous. Revision increases Lear's impatience, and there's a real sense in F of Goneril's cruelty interacting with and responding to provocation. Cuts and close changes make her quarrel with Albany better tempered (4. 2); and, in the long last scene, F Goneril is attractively self-possessed. It's she, for example, who has the presence of mind to exclaim, when Albany challenges Edmund, 'An enterlude'. And where the Quarto Goneril says, somewhat obviously, to Regan's 'Sick, ô sicke', 'If not, Ile nere trust poison' (5. 3. 95–6), the revised sister darkly remarks, 'If not, Ile nere trust medicine.'

The glint of Iagesque irony here, 'poison' becoming 'Work on my medicine, worke', is lost in conflation. But the change shows us Shakespeare intently at work. Three scenes earlier, and in a happier part of the family drama, Cordelia had been reunited with the king, recuperating from madness in sleep. In Q, a Doctor arranges Lear's wakening. But in F his lines are either abolished or given to a Gentleman, while Cordelia revives the king – takes him, in Lear's vivid phrase, 'out o'th'grave' (4. 7. 24–47). Cerimon is, as it were, ousted by Marina. And a comparison with late Shakespeare seems inevitable. For the Doctor is in Q a Paulina figure, stage-managing the recovery, calling for music to rouse the king. In F, 'Please you draw nearer; louder the music there' is cut, and Cordelia's 'kisse' proves cordial:

> O my deere Father, restauration hang
> Thy medicine on my lippes, and let this kisse
> Repaire those violent harmes, that my two Sisters
> Have in thy Reverence made.

[1] 4. 6, 165–70. See, especially, Roger Warren, 'The Folio Omission of the Mock Trial: Motives and Consequences', in Taylor and Warren, Division, pp 45–57.

[2] Randall McLeod, 'Gon. No more, the text is foolish.', in Taylor and Warren, Division, pp 153–93.

'Restauratian hang/Thy *medicine*'. Having in F thrust this into prominence by making it the key to Lear's recovery, Shakespeare chose – as so often with decisive dramatic moments – to root it firmly into the play's verbal texture. 'If you have poison for me, I will drinke it', the restored king says (71). In the alteration of 'poison' to 'medicine' three scenes later, we can see the reviser pointing a subliminal contrast in the family plot.[1]

And he had good reason to bear those 'lippes' in mind. Not for nothing did Shakespeare work against the practice of his late romances in removing the music. He emphasized the restorative medicine hanging on Cordelia's lips to anticipate the tender concentration with which Lear bends over his daughter when she is 'hang'd' and he seeks to bring her out of the grave (5. 3. 258–75). The effort is vain; she cannot be restored; Cordelia, as in the love-trial, says nothing (272–5); and both deaths begin,

> my poor Foole is hang'd: no, no, no life?
> Why should a Dog, a Horse, a Rat have life,
> And thou no breath at all?

In Q Lear utters 'O, o, o, o', the groans which represent, in F *Hamlet*, a death rattle, but which are here, as in the fifth act of *Othello*, where the Moor sees what he has done to Desdemona, a terrible cry of despair. He faints, and wills himself to die; with 'Breake hart, I prethe breake.' In F those words are given to Kent, who seeks a loyal death like Enobarbus and Iras,[2] and Lear dies attending not to his own heart but to Cordelia's lips:

> Pray you, undo this Button. Thanke you Sir.
> Do you see this? Looke on her? Looke her lips,
> Looke there, looke there.

The ending has 'surprised' critics when they should have profoundly 'expected' it. Shakespeare, as Coleridge, worked hard to lend the lines meaning. He did not make them suddenly transcendent, raising the king above tragedy as Bradley and his followers argued. But neither did he pitch Lear's death into pointlessness and the theatre of the absurd. The conflated text encourages such critical extremism because it obscures, with its Quarto Doctor and music plus the Folio ending, the steady particularity of

[1] For a broader context, and the Shakespearean *pharmakon*, see John Kerrigan, ed. *'Sonnets' and 'A Lover's Complaint'*, 1986, p 422.

[2] *Antony and Cleopatra* 4. 9; 5. 2. 292–305.

Shakespeare's intent. As far back as 3. 4, we find F adding 'Come, unbutton here' to give us the measure of Q/F 'Pray you, undo this Button'. In such variants we glimpse Shakespeare as reviser intimately at work, preparing an outcome in which what tells are echoes of a known situation carrying into silence. Lear here realizes what time not being up might mean, and deixis suggests what could be said, given more words, about the love-trial and F's added 'Nothing's there' (1. 1. 88–9), and Desdemona coming back to life as Cordelia won't, and Pistol killing his prisoner on stage, and the order of dancers in *Much Ado*, and the history of editing in the eighteenth century[1] – about, in short, all the perplexed issues raised by being a character in Shakespeare's revised text.

[1] Gary Taylor, ed. *Henry V*, 1982, pp 65–6; Stanley Wells, 'Editorial Treatment of Foul-Paper Texts: *Much Ado About Nothing* as Test Case', *Review of English Studies*, ns xxxi, 1980, pp 1–16, 8–10; Steven Urkowitz, 'The Base Shall to th' Legitimate: The Growth of an Editorial Tradition', in Taylor and Warren, *Division*, pp 23–43.

# RECENT DEVELOPMENTS IN SHAKESPEAREAN STUDIES[1]

*Cedric Watts*

I

One rapid way of indicating 'recent developments' is to begin with a personal note. I've been teaching English Literature at Sussex University for over twenty years, and throughout that period one of our courses has been devoted solely to Shakespeare. Twenty years ago, that course was compulsory for all English majors; now, it is optional. There are various reasons for that change, and one reason is certainly that Shakespeare's prestige and the sense of 'great traditions' of English Literature have been vigorously questioned. Twenty years ago, prospective students of the course would be allocated arbitrarily to tutors, the assumption being that, although there would naturally be differing emphases, the approach of tutor A would not differ radically from that of tutor B. These days, a prospective entrant to the Shakespeare course first consults a lengthy document in which each of the many tutors summarizes his or her approach; the student then makes a choice. Some tutors offer course-descriptions which do not differ markedly from what they might have said twenty years ago, except that now a brief defence or explanation of their 'traditionalism' is added, often accompanied by a profession of willingness to consider alternatives; some tutors offer diverse feminist approaches; others profess an enthusiasm for structuralist or semiotic readings; others offer various decon-structionist, Marxist or socialist emphases; and in some there is marked interest in considering the political and cultural im-plications of the 'Shakespeare industry', of Shakespeare's im-portance in literary history and in educational institutions.

In short, the most conspicuous 'recent development' in Shakespearean studies is the sense that there have been numerous recent developments, some of which would repudiate scornfully the notion that they constituted merely 'an approach'. New vigour has

[1] Shakespearean quotations in this section are from *William Shakespeare: The Complete Works*, ed. Peter Alexander, London and Glasgow, 1951.

been imparted to the old orthodoxy that old orthodoxies need to be challenged, and tutors co-operate to publicize competing ways of scrutinizing the texts and their location in history. Earlier critical accounts of Shakespeare which once appeared politically 'neutral' or even progressively 'liberal' have come to appear conservative or 'élitist'; in England, as the influence of F. R. Leavis waned, that of Raymond Williams waxed. Some forms of 'close' textual reading can be regarded as 'closed' or myopic readings; what's more, analytic tools and terminologies have become available which make some of those previous 'close analyses' look rather amateurish. The critical habit of seeking 'organic unity' in the text has been largely superseded by the critical habit of seeking tension and contradiction. These days, the 'meaning' of a work may be regarded not as a lightly buried treasure awaiting the treasure-seeking interpreter but rather as a multiplicity of possibilities in constant process of generation and regeneration: a current cliché pugnaciously terms the text 'a site of struggle' in which 'meanings are contested'. There is now much more scepticism, not only regarding Shakespeare's 'insight', 'wisdom' and 'timelessness', but also regarding the very concepts of the veridical and of human autonomy. The term 'ideology' has proved exceptionally congenial. Definitions of the term vary but are usually capacious and pejorative: for example, 'Ideology is composed of those beliefs, practices and institutions which work to legitimate the social order – especially by the process of representing sectional or class interests as universal ones.'[1] The utility of such a definition is obvious: it implies a militant scepticism (fortified perhaps by Marx or Althusser); it postulates as forms of propaganda, overt or covert, matters which would once have been discussed in terms of truth or falsehood, right or wrong; and it imputes to the definer a capacity to evade the network of 'legitimation' in which the many are purportedly enmeshed. Nevertheless, although definitions of the term 'ideology' are usually problematic, its currency in many recent commentaries on Shakespeare indicates a particularly interesting development. Increasingly, Shakespearean studies have become part of the study of social inscription – of the ways in which individual people are inscribed by society with roles, beliefs, identities and allegiances.

---

[1] Jonathan Dollimore and Alan Sinfield, 'History and Ideology: The Instance of *Henry V*' in *Alternative Shakespeares*, ed. John Drakakis, London and New York, 1985, pp 210–11. Terry Eagleton remarks that '"ideology" is always a way of describing other people's interests rather than one's own'. The term may conceal the distinction between democratic and anti-democratic societies.

Shakespeare explores the process in which he is involved; and if his status as sage has diminished, the status of his works as illuminators of historical processes has variously been enhanced. The creator of Prospero and Jaques might smile, if a little wryly, to see that so much recent literary theory aspires to dissolve the conventional boundaries between fact and fiction, reality and illusion. The influences of Marx, Freud, Saussure, Althusser, Derrida, Barthes, Foucault and others have conspired to make many former certainties, facts or beliefs seem, at times, an 'insubstantial pageant', while disconcerting force has been conferred on the declaration that

> All the world's a stage,
> And all the men and women merely players . . .

## II

In literary theory, as in philosophy, the 'new' often proves to be an extension, elaboration or re-cycling of the old. The scepticism which haunts recent discussions would not have surprised Nietzsche, or Hume or Hobbes, or – looking further back – Euripides. Similarly, though Charles S. Peirce and Ferdinand de Saussure are frequently regarded as the founders of semiotics, much semiotic theory extends the project of Aristotle's *Poetics* to provide a useful analytic terminology for a given body of cultural material. One of the main problems for a critic or commentator who wishes to give a detailed semiotic or structuralist analysis of a Shakespearean text (whether on the page or in production) may now be that of choice, given the abundance and diversity of available terminologies. Keir Elam's *The Semiotics of Theatre and Drama* offers a lucid survey of the possibilities, and his fifth chapter gives an elaborate practical example: an eighteen-column scheme which depicts a 'micro-segmentation' of the first 79 lines of *Hamlet*, aiming to provide 'a more precise instrument than those traditionally adopted for the anatomy of language, action, character, interrelationships and the very construction of the fictional world in the drama'.[1] While such studies strive to make conspicuous the whole range of assumptions, codes and conventions which is brought to the text or performance, other semiotic accounts are less

[1] Keir Elam, *The Semiotics of Theatre and Drama*, London and New York, 1980, pp 184–207; I quote p 185.

technical and come closer to the traditional critical concern with the elucidation of themes and character-relationships. Here Italian commentators have been prominent: specular, semantic and rhetorical elements of *King Lear* have been discussed by Marcello Pagnini and Paolo Valesio,[1] and Alessandro Serpieri has given particular attention to *Othello*. Employing the fashionable distinction between the *énonciation* (the act of producing the utterance) and the *énoncé* (the utterance produced), Serpieri finds that:

Iago cannot identify with any situation or sign or *énoncé*, and is thus condemned to deconstruct through his own *énonciations* the *énoncés* of others, transforming them into simulacra . . . Iago is imprisoned in negation, the negation of eros . . . But Othello is likewise imprisoned, in hyperbolic affirmation. They live according to opposed modes of unreality: Iago through closure to others, bourgeois–puritan *extraneity* or isolation; Othello through the weight of a manifest or hidden *discrimination* . . . If Othello is the victim in dramatic terms, Iago, artificer of a destructive projection, is in turn victim at an epistemic level, namely of the very category of extraneity . . .[2]

F. R. Leavis once remarked that '[A. C.] Bradley's Othello is, rather, Othello's';[3] perhaps the semiotician's *Othello* is, rather, Iago's. We may speculate that another Shakespearean (or largely Shakespearean) play which cordially solicits the semiotician is *Titus Andronicus*. There the nauseating anthropophagous banquet is given such an ostentatiously allegorical heralding (Tamora introducing herself as Revenge and her sons as Rapine and Murder) that even an amateur of semiotics could readily see the banquet as a reific discourse in which vengeance manifests itself as cannibalistic: a starkly physical *énonciation* of what in later Shakespearean drama will be uttered as metaphor ('And appetite, an universal wolf . . ./Must . . . last eat up himself'); while a more sophisticated reading would detect a 'devouring' within the very sign-systems, the physically syntagmatic engorging the metaphoric: the word made flesh – and pie. Indeed, such a text might be said to foreground certain strengths and weaknesses of the semiotic project, which, at its boldest, seeks to convert pies into utterances, chalk and cheese

1 M. Pagnini, *Shakespeare e il paradigma della specularità*, Pisa, 1976; P. Valesio: '"That Glib and Oylie Art": Cordelia and the Rhetoric of Anti-rhetoric' in *Versus* xvi, 1977, pp 91–117.

2 A. Serpieri, 'Reading the Signs: Towards a Semiotics of Shakespearean Drama' in Drakakis, *Alternative Shakespeares*, pp 139, 142–3.

3 F. R. Leavis, *The Common Pursuit*, 1952, Harmondsworth, 1962, p 141.

into modes of discourse, and blood and tears into signifying systems.

'What's in a name?' To a large extent, semiotics, formalism, structuralism and poststructuralism are united by the ambition to extend the recognized territory of the artificial and reduce that of the natural: the Shakespearean text may now seem not to 'hold, as 'twere, the mirror up to nature' but rather to be the magnifying-glass of culture. Theorists strive zealously to reverse Polixenes' dictum that 'The art itself is nature'. Of course, some of the 'radical' theories prove on inspection to be conservative: as Terry Eagleton has pointed out, the extreme poststructuralism which dissolves virtually all experience into modes of discourse severed from notions of truth, probability and historical change 'is mischievously radical in respect of everyone else's opinions . . . while utterly conservative in every other way. Since it commits you to affirming nothing, it is as injurious as blank ammunition.'[1] An instance of the increasing emphasis on 'discourse' and of the attempted capture by left-wing writers of material which once seemed to support conservative ideas is provided by the changing treatment, over the years, of festive and saturnalian elements in Shakespeare's work.

Northrop Frye was undoubtedly one of the most important intermediaries between the preoccupation in the period 1890 to 1920 with myth and ritual (characterized notably by Sir James Frazer's *The Golden Bough* and Jessie L. Weston's *From Ritual to Romance*) and recent structuralist and poststructuralist discussions. In Frye's work we may see the influence of Frazerian anthropology, of Freud and Jung, and of the Chicago Formalists; but, again, the Aristotle of *Poetics* would not have been particularly surprised by the following remarks of Frye in 1948:

Many things are involved in the tragic catharsis, but one of them is a mental or imaginative form of the sacrificial ritual out of which tragedy arose. This is the ritual of the struggle, death, and rebirth of a God-Man, which is linked to the yearly triumph of spring over winter . . . The audience enters into communion with the body of the hero, becoming thereby a single body itself . . . The ritual pattern behind the catharsis of comedy is the resurrection that follows the death, the epiphany or manifestation of the risen hero.[2]

In particular, argued Frye, Shakespeare's comedies draw on the

---

[1] T. Eagleton, *Literary Theory: An Introduction*, Oxford, 1983, p 145.

[2] 'The Argument of Comedy' in *English Institute Essays 1948*, ed. D. A. Robertson, Jr., New York, 1949, p 64.

tradition of the 'green world', the tradition of fertility, festivity and saturnalia maintained by folk-lore and folk-tale: 'The green world charges the comedies with a symbolism in which the comic resolution contains a suggestion of the old ritual pattern of the victory of summer over winter'; and the Falstaff of *The Merry Wives of Windsor*, having been thrown into water, dressed up as a witch, beaten and furnished with horns, 'must have felt that . . . he had done about all that could reasonably be asked of any fertility spirit'.[1] There were numerous related studies, among them G. Wilson Knight's *The Crown of Life* (1947) and C. L. Barber's *Shakespeare's Festive Comedy* (1959), which saw the 'green world' and the festive, saturnalian elements as regenerative, a recognition of 'the rhythms of life' which enabled Shakespeare to achieve 'a poise which was possible because a traditional way of living connected different kinds of experience to each other'.[2] But, against this view of the festive as a replenishment of order, other critics emphasized its subversive possibilities. Mikhail Bakhtin, with his theory of the 'carnivalesque', suggested that one radical, incursionary mode of resistance to established authority had long been the element of saturnalia and festive misrule in society and in literature; and he relished what he took to be subversive bawdry in both Rabelais and Shakespeare, for it kept alive 'the utopian world'.[3] Perhaps the May-game was rehearsal for the carmagnole. Terry Eagleton explained:

The laughter of carnival is both plebeian derision and plebeian solidarity, an empty semiotic flow which in decomposing significance nonetheless courses with the impulse of comradeship.[4]

A related preoccupation informed Robert Weimann's *Shakespeare and the Popular Tradition in the Theater* (1978), a partly Marxist, partly semiotic, partly poststructuralist work which claimed that in Shakespearean drama we see a fruitful interplay between two symbolic areas, the 'locus' and the 'platea'. The locus accommodates the noble, the ceremonious and the 'illusionistic'; the platea accommodates the vulgar, the vernacular and the 'anti-illusionistic'. 'The tension as well as the unity between "naturalism" and "convention" . . . helped to constitute the universalizing pattern in Shakespeare.'[5]

[1] Ibid., p 69.
[2] *Shakespeare's Festive Comedy*, Cleveland and New York, 1963, p 238.
[3] *Rabelais and His World*, Cambridge, Mass., 1968.
[4] *Walter Benjamin or Towards a Revolutionary Criticism*, London 1981, p 146.
[5] *Shakespeare and the Popular Tradition in the Theater*, Baltimore and London, 1978, p 251.

Weimann's references to 'the universalizing pattern' and 'Shakespeare's universal vision of experience' might have seemed congenial to an older generation familiar with A. C. Bradley's *Shakespearean Tragedy* or with Wilson Knight's quest to derive a single grand vision from Shakespeare's work; but his interest in 'anti-illusionism' appealed to a younger generation familiar with the paradoxical Brechtian notion (which in turn derived partly from Shklovsky and Russian Formalism) that 'alienation effects' which prick the bubble of illusion encourage an audience not only to see more objectively but also to embrace Marxist conclusions. Given that Brecht's own dramatic practice had been inspired largely by the Elizabethan theatre (which he saw as 'a theatre full of A-effects'),[1] it was predictable that Brechtian possibilities would be discovered in Shakespeare's works: *Coriolanus* – which Brecht adapted – was seen to resemble *Galilei*, for 'the audience is discouraged from identification with the protagonist' and 'no single discourse is privileged', while *The Winter's Tale* was seen as a fine example of an 'interrogative text', for it appeared 'increasingly dismissive of its own pretensions to truth':

In this way it challenges the realist concept of art, and invites the spectators to reflect on fiction as a discursive practice and the ways in which discourse allows them to grasp their relation to the real relations in which they live.[2]

## III

When reduced to plot-summary, much of Shakespeare's work may seem politically conservative. In the tragedies and histories, those who conspire to topple legitimate rulers usually unleash a destructive cycle of violence and are themselves humbled or destroyed; while, in the comedies, conflicts between social law and individual aspirations are, on the whole, eventually resolved harmoniously. The institutionalized study of Shakespeare can be regarded as part of a related plot: the state's endeavour to effect social cohesion through an educational policy strongly imbued with middle-class values. Consequently, left-wing discussions of Shakespeare sometimes voice a frankly iconoclastic challenge: time once given to Shakespeare should be given to media studies or communication studies or 'rhetoric' – the analysis of overt and covert modes of

[1] B. Brecht, *The Messingkauf Dialogues*, London, 1965, p 58.
[2] Catherine Belsey, *Critical Practice*, London and New York, 1980, pp 96, 101, 102.

social persuasion.[1] One objection (itself left-wing) to such iconoclasm is, of course, that if the general tendency of Shakespeare's works were 'reactionary', 'the relentless investment of critical energy in their conservative interpretation since the Renaissance would have been ludicrously superfluous': indeed, such an investment might rather indicate their subversive power.[2]

A less iconoclastic approach is one which aims to salvage as much of Shakespeare as possible for socialism, and for this purpose there are various procedures which may be dignified by the terms 'deconstructionism' or 'cultural materialism'. One tactic is to argue that though Shakespeare may not deliver the political answers we would like, he asks the right questions: wittingly or unwittingly he indicates the devious operations of ideology. As the state strives to impose cohesion on conflicting class-interests, the text seeks to offer imaginative resolution of real social contradictions; both bespeak what they would deny. Where earlier critics perceived 'rich complexity' and 'qualified affirmations', deconstructionists perceive 'internal contradictions' and 'significant gaps' in the texts. Shakespeare has a friendly habit of anticipating his commentators: in *Troilus and Cressida* he anticipated E. M. W. Tillyard's *The Elizabethan World Picture* by providing a speech on hierarchy and degree which conveniently epitomized Tillyard's claims;[3] and in the same play he anticipated deconstructive opponents of Tillyard by depicting a vast ironic disparity between the postulated cosmic order and the manifest disorder of the action, a disorder reflected in the play's distinctively open, inconclusive ending. It remained for Jonathan Dollimore, aided by Brecht, Lukács, Althusser and Macherey, to supply the missing conclusion:

More strategically than nihilistically, *Troilus and Cressida* exploits disjunction and 'chaos' to promote critical awareness of both the mystifying language of the absolute and the social reality which it occludes. We are for example compelled by the apparent fact of chaos to think critically about the way characters repeatedly make fatalistic appeals to an extra-human reality or force: natural law, Jove, Chance, Time and so on . . .: in effect they all serve to legitimate fatalistic misrecognition.[4]

---

[1] T. Eagleton, *Literary Theory*, p 205.

[2] Kiernan Ryan, 'Towards a Socialist Criticism: Reclaiming the Canon' in *L. T. P. (Journal of Literature Teaching Politics)*, iii, 1984, p 7.

[3] Ulysses on 'degree': *Troilus and Cressida*, 1. 3. 75–137; quoted in Tillyard's *The Elizabethan World Picture*, 1943 (Harmondsworth, 1963), pp 18–19.

[4] *Radical Tragedy*, Brighton, 1984, pp 44–5.

Meanwhile Stephen Greenblatt, in *Renaissance Self-Fashioning* (1980), postulated a partial analogy between Desdemona's submission to Othello's lethal love and Shakespeare's submission to the prevailing culture; and one which, again, exposed the contradictions of ideology:

Shakespeare approaches his culture not, like Marlowe, as rebel and blasphemer, but rather as dutiful servant, content to improvise a part of his own within its orthodoxy. And if, after centuries, that improvisation has been revealed to us as embodying an almost boundless challenge to the culture's every tenet, a devastation of every source, the author of *Othello* would have understood that such a revelation scarcely matters . . . Shakespeare relentlessly *explores* the relations of power in a given culture . . . If there are intimations in Shakespeare of a release from the complex narrative orders in which everyone is inscribed, these intimations do not arise from bristling resistance or strident denunciation – the mood of a Jaques or a Timon. They arise paradoxically from a peculiarly intense *submission* whose downright violence undermines everything it was meant to shore up, the submission depicted not in Othello or Iago but in Desdemona.[1]

In the past, many literary critics regarded the Elizabethan period not only as a Golden Age of literature but also as a political Golden Age – that vital, colourful, questing time, when a nation, united under the Virgin Queen, defeated the Spanish Armada and sent forth her bold adventurers, Drake, Raleigh and the rest, to the far reaches of the globe. Wilson Knight shared this nostalgic enthusiasm; and, in *The Crown of Life*, he even derived from Shakespeare's later works and particularly from *Henry VIII* 'a myth of the national soul', the expression of Shakespeare's 'prophetic spirit' and of 'the spirit of England': future historians would see that Shakespeare had wisely prophesied the British Empire's power 'to raise savage peoples from superstition and blood-sacrifice, taboos and witchcraft and the attendant fears and slaveries, to a more enlightened existence'.[2] Recent left-wing commentators prefer to regard the Elizabethan period as a political Iron Age of revolts in Ireland and the north of England, of the Essex Rebellion, of repression in bloody and more subtle forms. Two such critics, making a deconstructionist approach to *Henry V*, argue that at 3. 3. 33–41, for example, 'the play dwells upon imagery of slaughter to a degree

[1] *Renaissance Self-Fashioning from More to Shakespeare*, Chicago and London, 1980, pp 253–4.

[2] *The Crown of Life*, 1947 (London, 1965), p 255.

which disrupts the harmonious unity towards which ideology strives'; and the conquest of France and eventual union of the kingdoms can be seen as 'a re-presentation of the attempt to conquer Ireland and [attain] the hoped-for unity of Britain . . . The play offers a displaced, imaginary resolution of one of the state's most intractable problems.' Thus 'Henry V can be read to reveal not only the strategies of power but also the anxieties informing them and their ideological representation'.[1] A similar tactic can be used for The Tempest. Here Francis Barker and Peter Hulme note the conspicuous disturbance of Prospero when recollection of Caliban, Stephano and Trinculo forces him to abandon his masque: 'Caliban's revolt proves uniquely disturbing to the smooth unfolding of Prospero's plot' and is 'symptomatic of the text's own anxiety about the threat posed to its decorum by the New World materials': 'The lengths to which the play has to go to achieve a legitimate ending may then be read as the quelling of a fundamental disquiet concerning its own functions within the projects of colonialist discourse.'[2]

It begins to look as though Shakespeare can't lose. Whereas conservative critics may praise him for the messages of patriotism, piety, unity, harmony and reconciliation which he proclaims to them, and middle-of-the-road critics may applaud his 'infinite variety', complexity and ambiguity, left-wing critics may commend him for the messages about ideological obfuscation which he smuggles. And within many recent commentaries, whether they advertize themselves as semiotic or deconstructionist or materialist, we may detect not only the reductively sceptical tones of a Thersites ('All the argument is a whore and a cuckold') but also the considerate

---

[1] Jonathan Dollimore and Alan Sinfield, 'History and Ideology: The Instance of Henry V' in Drakakis, Alternative Shakespeares, pp 226, 225. See also Philip Edwards, Threshold of a Nation, Cambridge, 1979, pp 74–86.

[2] Francis Barker and Peter Hulme, 'Nymphs and Reapers Heavily Vanish: The Discursive Con-Texts of The Tempest' in Drakakis, Alternative Shakespeares, pp 201–2, 203–4. Paul Brown, discussing Caliban's speech on the 'sounds and sweet airs' of the island (3. 2. 130–8), says: 'The play registers . . . a radical ambivalence at the heart of colonialist discourse, revealing that it is a site of struggle over meaning.' ('"This Thing of Darkness I Acknowledge Mine": The Tempest and the Discourse of Colonialism' in Political Shakespeare, Jonathan Dollimore and Alan Sinfield (eds), Manchester, 1985, p 66.) Terry Eagleton declares that 'the glaring contradiction on which [The Tempest] effectively founders' is 'the fact that this "organic" restoration of a traditional social order founded upon Nature and the body rests not only on a flagrant mystification of Nature, gratuitous magical device and oppressive patriarchalism, but is actually set in the context of the very colonialism which signals the imminent victory of the exploitative, "inorganic" mercantile bourgeoisie.' (William Shakespeare, Oxford, 1986, p 96).

ate tones of a Launce, voicing concern for the underdog: Shakespeare's successful monarchs and dukes must now face inquisitorial critics, while his Bateses, Williamses, Caliban and their fellows gain articulate champions. Shakespeare's women now find themselves amid a large scrutinizing sisterhood; Cordelia, Regan and Goneril, having submitted to the judgement of Lear, now present themselves for the judgement of feminism.

## IV

Feminist approaches to Shakespeare customarily give special attention to the female characters and search the text for further evidence that women have long been exploited by men but have displayed a capacity for resistance. The most popular and contentious question is whether Shakespeare's women subvert or confirm demeaning stereotypes.

In *Shakespeare and the Nature of Women* (1975), Juliet Dusinberre claimed that Shakespeare transcended masculine prejudice and aided the cause of women by popularizing the Protestant reformers' advocacy of the married state. Predominantly his plays prove that

Shakespeare saw men and women as equal in a world which declared them unequal. He did not divide human nature into the masculine and feminine, but observed in the individual woman or man an infinite variety of union between opposing impulses.[1]

Anne Barton, too, made in more polemical style a similar claim for Shakespeare:

No other writer challenges the aggressively limited feminist position, the intolerant and rigidly schematized view of human life .. with such power. At the same time, disconcertingly, no other writer has created as many memorable and sensitively understood women characters.[2]

Marilyn French, in *Shakespeare's Division of Experience* (1982), suggested that though Shakespeare experienced a pathological 'horror of sex', he showed that males needed to value and absorb 'inlaw feminine qualities': 'nutritiveness, compassion, mercy'.[3] Her study received little mercy from Lisa Jardine, however, whose *Still Harping on Daughters* (1983) claimed that, for all their apparent

[1] *Shakespeare and the Nature of Women*, London, 1975, p 308.
[2] 'Was Shakespeare a Chauvinist?' in *New York Review of Books*, 11 June 1981, p 20.
[3] *Shakespeare's Division of Experience*, London, 1982, p 196.

variety, Shakespearean women are based on stereotypes: in particular, the type of patient Griselda, self-sacrificingly submissive, imprints Julia, Hero, Helena, Desdemona, Marina, Imogen and Hermione. In *The Rape of Lucrece* we find that 'male lust and female suffering unite Lucrece and Hecuba in a compelling composite image of extreme guilt: the ultimate posture for the female hero. And behind that image lurks the guilt imputed by the patriarchy to the female sex for the lust they passively arouse'. At least *The Phoenix and the Turtle* provides a consolatory ending to Jardine's account. The phoenix was Queen Elizabeth's emblem; accordingly, Shakespeare's phoenix is described as female, and the turtle, therefore, as male 'in spite of his loyal, grieving submissiveness': so, for a moment, sex and gender attributes are transposed and the stereotypes at long last confused.[1]

For Catherine Belsey, particular interest resides in the 'transvestism' of comedies like *The Merchant of Venice* and *Twelfth Night*. 'Even while it reaffirms patriarchy, the tradition of female transvestism challenges it precisely by unsettling the categories which legitimate it.' In *Twelfth Night*, 2. 4, Viola as Cesario becomes a speaker who 'occupies a place which is not precisely masculine or feminine, where the notion of identity itself is disrupted'. Thus we may glimpse 'an image of a mode of being, which is not asexual, nor bisexual, but which disrupts the system of differences on which sexual stereotyping depends'.[2]

Some of the questions raised by feminist readings of Shakespeare could be summed up, then, as follows:

1. If Shakespeare complicates stereotypes, does he thereby propagate them or subvert them?
2. If he offers glimpses of non-stereotyped women, do those glimpses offer mere consolations (evasions of history) or attainable goals (historical possibilities)?
3. What kind of woman does the feminist advocate; how does that kind elude stereotyping; and in what form of society may that kind prevail?
4. If the liberation of women from submissive roles entails the liberation of men from the complementary dominative roles, does

---

[1] *Still Harping on Daughters*, Brighton, 1983, pp 193, 194.

[2] 'Disrupting Sexual Difference: Meaning and Gender in the Comedies' in Drakakis, *Alternative Shakespeares*, pp 180, 187, 190. Germaine Greer says that Shakespeare generally 'rejected the stereotype of the passive, sexless, unresponsive female and its inevitable concomitant, the misogynist conviction that all women were whores at heart. Instead he created a series of female characters who were both passionate and pure ...' (*Shakespeare*, Oxford, 1986, p 109.)

not feminism merge with masculism ('division grow together, To themselves yet either neither')?

To the traditionalist who says, 'But these new approaches demean Shakespeare by treating his texts as so much ammunition to be used in political battles', the familiar answer is: 'Shakespeare always has been political and has served political purposes; there is now simply a franker and fuller recognition of that fact and of the issues involved.' To those who complain, 'But what of the human interest, of the knowledge that his dramas can move us to laughter or tears, and induce awe at Shakespeare's powers of articulate intelligence, imagination and sensitivity?', the answer may be: 'Enough – or too much – has already been said on such matters; criticism needs to move away from the limited area of largely tautological appreciations and analyses and into the great arena of social struggle. Accordingly, we treat Shakespeare and our opponents as they deserve.' To which Hamlet might reply, 'Use every man after his desert, and who shall scape whipping? Use them after your own honour and dignity: the less they deserve, the more merit is in your bounty.'

# 5

## BEN JONSON

### Ian Donaldson

On more than one occasion during his lifetime, faced with a hostile audience or a suspicious government, Ben Jonson declared that he had little interest in what his contemporaries thought of his work, but that he awaited with confidence the more enlightened verdict of posterity. Posterity has not, on the whole, treated Jonson with quite the kindness he anticipated, and his reputation in modern times has never been what it was during his lifetime and the half-century following his death. At Jonson's death in August 1637, a crowd which included 'all or the greatest part of the nobilitie and gentry then in town' gathered at his house in Westminster ('under wch. you passe, as you goe out of the Church yard into the old palace') to accompany his body to its final place of rest in the Abbey.[1] This was a major public event: the passing of the dominant literary figure of the age. Such honours were the more remarkable when it is remembered that Jonson had been living for a good many years in relative obscurity. He had had no major success with the theatrical public since 1614. His library had been gutted with fire in 1623, and many of his manuscripts destroyed. In 1628 he had been stricken with paralysis, and was thereafter confined to a single room of his house, where he was visited regularly by a warm group of friends, but evidently forgotten by the public at large – the appearance of *The Magnetic Lady* in 1632 prompted one news-writer to note in mild surprise that it was by 'Ben Jonson (who, I thought, had been dead)'.[2] Shakespeare's death in April 1616 had been quite a different affair; he had been buried quietly in the chancel of his parish church in Stratford-upon-Avon, having earned this modest place of honour probably as much because of the fact that he had been a wealthy and respectable citizen of the

[1] *Ben Jonson*, ed. C. H. Herford and P. and E. Simpson, Oxford, 1925–52, i, pp 115, 179.

[2] Herford and Simpson, ix, 253.

town as because of his literary distinction; no contemporary writer noted the immediate fact of his death. Over fifty poems to the memory of Ben Jonson appeared in the four years following his death, most of them in the commemorative volume *Jonsonus Virbius* which was published early in 1638. Today we may feel a furtive sympathy for Jonson: bad luck to have been born a mere eight years after Shakespeare, and to have been forced to write under the vast shadow of his genius. Surprisingly enough, not many of Jonson's contemporaries seem to have felt like this, and throughout the tribute *Jonsonus Virbius* there is the recurrent implication that the shadow, if there was one, fell the other way. Jonson is England's 'rare Arch-Poet', 'our Poet first in merit, as in love', 'of English Drammatickes, the Prince', 'the most Excellent of English Poets'. G. E. Bentley has argued that Jonson's superlative reputation was maintained throughout the course of the seventeenth century; in each decade of the century except the last, when Shakespeare began at last to inch ahead, Jonson was still clearly acknowledged to be the English arch-poet, his works being generally taken as the immediate touchstone of poetic and dramatic excellence.[1]

In one sense it could be argued that Jonson has always maintained this primacy of place. No other native writer has exerted so powerful an influence on English comic writing as he has done. As a modern dramatist (John Arden) once said while speaking of the literal inimitability of Shakespeare's dramatic technique, Jonson is a writer with whom all would-be dramatists can profitably go to school, his craftsmanship is palpable, a lasting model for generations of pupils. Jonson's most obvious, but probably least important, influence was upon the work of the swarm of minor writers who were closely attached to him during his lifetime, men like Nathan Field, whose acting Jonson had so admired, or his 'servant', Richard Brome, and the other members of the so-called Tribe of Ben; and upon a dramatist such as Thomas Shadwell later in the century, who followed Jonson's manner competently, though with a faintly ridiculous spirit of devotion. More important is Jonson's influence upon what might be called the great tradition of English comic writing, where it is the richer for being more deeply absorbed in a variety of stronger individual talents. It is an influence which can be felt in the work of Wycherley, for instance, and of

[1] G. E. Bentley, *Shakespeare and Jonson: Their Reputations in the Seventeenth Century Compared*, Chicago, 1945, 2 vols. Bentley's methodology has been challenged by David L. Frost, *The School of Shakespeare: The Influence of Shakespeare on English Drama 1600–42*, Cambridge, 1968.

Congreve, whose letters contain some fine criticism of Jonson's plays, and who in his own comedies freely imitated Jonsonian characters and phrases, turns of plot and small details of stagecraft; in that of Fielding, who praised Jonson as a master of 'the Ridiculous' in the Preface to *Joseph Andrews*, and of Dickens, who so enjoyed playing Bobadil in the 1840s, and whose saturation in Jonson's comic style is often evident in his major novels (compare Troubleall in *Bartholomew Fair* with Miss Flite in *Bleak House*). In a quite different way, too, Jonson seems to have exerted some influence on the work of Joyce, who said that Jonson was one of the four writers whose work he had read *in toto*.[1]

Yet despite this continuous influence upon English writers (and not a few abroad), it is obvious that Jonson no longer enjoys the reputation with a wider public that once he did. We can date the beginning of this decline in reputation fairly precisely from the early part of the eighteenth century. It is no mere coincidence that it is from this period, too, that we date the beginnings of modern Shakespearean scholarship, and of Shakespeare's steep ascent to the position of unrivalled fame which he now has. For men such as Pope and Dr Johnson, the editing of Shakespeare's works was an important and obvious literary labour to be undertaken gladly; both men, by and large, ignored the work of Ben Jonson. (Pope conceded that *Epicoene* was the best comedy in the language, but was impatiently dismissive about Jonson's work as a whole: 'What trash are his works, taken all together!'[2]) Even David Garrick, who was personally responsible for keeping the best of Jonson's plays in regular performance until quite late in the century, pledged his own devoted allegiance elsewhere; there was no real rival for the god whom Garrick had publicly acclaimed in his Jubilee Ode of 1769:

> The lov'd, rever'd, immortal name!
> Shakespeare! Shakespeare! Shakespeare!

By the beginning of the nineteenth century, when the scholar William Gifford came to prepare his learned edition of his works, Jonson had been decisively relegated to minor status. In a series of lengthy and often querulous notes, placed like spiky trench-

---

[1] See J. B. Bamborough, 'Joyce and Jonson', *A Review of English Literature*, ii, 1961, pp 45–50; R. C. Churchill, 'Dickens, Drama, and Tradition', *Scrutiny*, x, 1942, pp 358–75; Robert Garis, *The Dickens Theatre*, Oxford, 1965.

[2] Joseph Spence, *Observations, Anecdotes, and Characters of Books and Men*, ed. James Osborn, Oxford, 1966, i, pp 184, 207.

defences at the foot of the text, Gifford conducted a lone battle
for the recognition which he thought Jonson deserved. While it is
not true to say that the Romantic critics ignored Jonson – Coleridge's brief notes and observations on the plays are often particularly acute – they did commend him in decidedly odd terms.[1] Take
Coleridge's devastating analogy:

It was not possible, that so bold and robust an Intellect as that of Ben
Jonson could be devoted to any form of intellectual Power vainly or even
with mediocrity of Product. He could not but be a Species of himself: tho'
like the Mammoth and Megatherion fitted and destined to live only during
a given Period, and then to exist a Skeleton, hard, dry, uncouth perhaps, yet
massive and not to be contemplated without that mixture of Wonder and
Admiration, or more accurately, that middle somewhat between both for
which we want a term – not quite even with the latter, but far above the
mere former.

A splendid fossil, but a fossil all the same. Hazlitt suggested, in an
equally eloquent analogy, that a taste for Jonson was like a taste for
olives. And later Swinburne, who was an admirer of Jonson's work,
delivered the cool verdict that he was 'one of the singers who could
not sing'. Hard, dry, and uncouth, bitter as olives and tone-deaf,
Jonson the mammoth limped along as well as the praise of his
friends would allow him. T. S. Eliot was speaking exactly in that
celebrated essay when he described what Jonson's reputation had
become:

The reputation of Jonson has been of the most deadly kind that can be
compelled upon the memory of a great poet. To be universally accepted; to
be damned by the praise that quenches all desire to read the book; to be
afflicted by the imputation of the virtues which excite the least pleasure;
and to be read only by historians and antiquaries – this is the most perfect
conspiracy of approval.

Since these words were written, some excellent studies of Jonson's
plays have appeared. Yet it is impossible not to feel the continued
truth of Eliot's judgement. For the common reader and playgoer, Jonson still seems to stand as the most daunting and formidable of English classics, an author one would more gladly walk
round about to avoid than walk in company with. How has this
reputation developed? And how fair is it to the real nature of Jonson's
work?

[1] See *Coleridge on the Seventeenth Century*, ed. R. F. Brinkley, Durham, N.C., 1955,
pp 647–8; *The Complete Works of William Hazlitt*, ed. P. P. Howe, London and
Toronto, 1931, vi, p 39; A. C. Swinburne, *A Study of Ben Jonson*, London, 1889, p 5.

Probably the first reason, historically speaking, for the shrinking of interest in Jonson's plays is a simple one: that with the passing of time they had become increasingly difficult to understand. The plays were probably not found difficult primarily because they were erudite, though erudite they could certainly be, as Jonson's own detailed notes to *Sejanus* amply testify. Jonson had been the pupil of the great scholar William Camden at Westminster School, and although he had probably attended neither of the universities he may have felt some pride in showing that in scholarship he could, when he pleased, keep pace with such friends as Bacon and Ralegh, Cotton and Selden. Yet it is significant that none of Jonson's contemporaries ever called him a pedant, though they called him many other things. The old bogey of Jonson's monstrous classical learning has certainly been exaggerated, and one of the most liberating tendencies in twentieth-century criticism of his work has been the insistence (to be felt, in different ways, in the writing of C. R. Baskervill, T. S. Eliot, Freda Townsend, and L. C. Knights) that Jonson is a dramatist who is essentially English and who belongs essentially to his own age; a dramatist who, even when ostensibly writing a play about ancient Rome, had his eye fixed upon the world in which he lived; a dramatist who drew freely upon (and critically surveyed) topical happenings and gossip, native traditions of drama and of folk-culture, and colloquial patterns of speech.

And yet it is in this very topicality that the difficulty of Jonson's plays probably lay. 'He was not of an age, but for all time!' was Jonson's tribute to Shakespeare. By the eighteenth century it may have been felt that for Jonson himself this epitaph should be reversed: he was not for all time, but for an age. It is a remarkable fact that at the Restoration, while Tate and Shadwell, Dryden and D'Avenant snipped and hacked at Shakespeare's plays, radically retailoring them in the name of 'improvement', Jonson's plays appear to have been acted in an unaltered form; such was the respect for Jonson's authority. The first alteration to Jonson's plays that we know of is an adaptation of *Every Man In His Humour* in 1725.[1] It is significant that after this date such adaptations are made very freely. Garrick and Colman were responsible for the most famous of these. Garrick spent three years rewriting *Every Man In His Humour* for performance in 1751, because, as he said later, 'The Language & Characters of Ben Jonson (and particularly of the

[1] R. G. Noyes, *Ben Jonson on the English Stage 1660–1776*, Cambridge, Mass, 1935, p 28.

Comedy in question) are much more difficult than those of any other writer.'[1] In 1752, when *Epicoene* was revived, the dramatic historian Thomas Davies thought likewise:

the frequent allusions to forgotten customs and characters render it impossible to be ever revived with any probability of success. To understand Jonson's comedies perfectly, we should have before us a satirical history of the age in which he lived.[2]

The difficulty of which Garrick and Davies speak is one that may still be felt by a modern reader. It might be said to arise out of Jonson's belief that comedy should deal 'in deedes, and language, such as men doe use', showing 'an Image of the times', as he put it in a well-known passage in the prologue to the revised version of *Every Man In His Humour*. This notion, deriving ultimately from Cicero, is stated again by Cordatus in *Every Man Out of His Humour*: comedy is *Imitatio vitae, Speculum consuetudinis, Imago veritatis*, an imitation of life, a mirror of manners, an image of truth. Dr Johnson (probably with a memory of *Hamlet*) used the same image when he praised Shakespeare as 'the poet that holds up to his readers a faithful mirrour of manners and of life'; yet in the very next breath he added an important qualification:

His characters are not modified by the customs of particular places, unpractised by the rest of the world; by the peculiarities of studies or professions, which can operate but upon small numbers; or by the accidents of transient fashions or temporary opinions: they are the progeny of common humanity, such as the world will always supply, and observation will always find. (*Preface to Shakespeare*, 1765)

Particular places, peculiar studies, transient fashions and temporary opinions are, on the other hand, precisely the materials out of which Ben Jonson wrought his comedies. The same passion which led him to anchor his tragedies in the verifiable 'truth' of history[3] led him also to set his comedies in a 'true' and recognizable context, in Blackfriars or Finstock, Smithfield or Old Jewry. He seems to have been vexed by the lack of such precision of context in Shakespeare's work; in one play (Jonson told Drummond scathingly) Shakespeare had gone so far as to bring in a number of men who said they had

---

[1] *The Letters of David Garrick*, ed. David M. Little and George M. Kahrl, London, 1963, i, 304.

[2] *Dramatic Miscellanies*, London, 1784, ii, 101–2.

[3] J. A. Bryant Jr., 'The Significance of Ben Jonson's First Requirement for Tragedy: "Truth of Argument"', *Studies in Philology*, xlix, 1952, pp 195–213.

suffered shipwreck upon the coast of Bohemia, though it was well known that Bohemia was not on the sea. His comedies turn continually, as Shakespeare's do not, to ridicule those who indulged in contemporary cults: alchemists, projectors, puritans, roaring boys. And he has a fondness for catching the ephemeral and highly specialized jargon which such cults produce, collecting with pleasure what Dr Johnson was to call disapprovingly 'hard terms' and 'fugitive cant'. His plays consequently present greater linguistic difficulties than do Shakespeare's (what are *skeldring* and *odling*? What is a *niaise* or a *shot-clog*, a *twire* or a *trig*?). Whole comic scenes are sometimes built upon obscure contemporary games of challenge and abuse, such as the games of crab and of dor in *Cynthia's Revels*, the game of vapours (and the subsequent 'circling') in *Bartholomew Fair*, and the 'jeering' scenes of *The Staple of News*.

Yet it is remarkable how swiftly many of these difficulties may evaporate in the theatre: modern revivals of *Epicoene* have shown Thomas Davies's gloomy prognostications about its chances of survival to be unfounded, while in revivals of *Bartholomew Fair* the game of vapours, somewhat surprisingly, has often turned out to be a comic highlight. The authorial side-note which tells us that the game of vapours '*is* non sense' (the *O.E.D.*'s first recorded use of this term) gives the essential clue to the reason for the success of this style of learned farce; quite simply, its obscurantism is its comic point. 'Pure and neat language I love, yet plain and customary', wrote Jonson in his *Discoveries*, yet in his comedies he repeatedly presents us with people who deviate from that ideal, whose language drifts rapidly into argot or officialese or terms of art, into mere noise and nonsense. There are people who make verbal mystification their trade – lawyers, preachers, and politicians, newsmongers and poetasters – and who often end up mystifying even themselves. The effect is one which Jonson exploits even in his tragedies; in the long, shifting, 'lapwing' letter from Tiberius to the Senate in the final act of *Sejanus*, for instance, through whose bland and sustained political rhetoric the hard truth is barely discernible. In the comedies the comic effect of such linguistic deviousness is normally broad and obvious, as it is in the first act of *Bartholomew Fair* when Zeal-of-the-Land Busy assembles his battery of theological justifications for eating and not eating pig. In the last scene of *Poetaster* the unfortunate Crispinus is given an emetic and is forced – if one may reverse the metaphor – to unswallow his words: *glibbery, lubricall, spurious, snotteries, oblatrant, furibund, prorumped.* Cozening and obscurantism have not become so rare in the modern world that we cannot find a comic relevance in such scenes as these.

It is hardly an exaggeration to say that some of Jonson's comedies are in fact about language and the ways in which it may be abused. In *The Alchemist*, for instance, all characters are absorbed by the uses to which language may be put, to gull, mystify, bully, and impress.[1] While Subtle and Face deploy their Latin and their alchemical jargon, the victims of their cozenage experiment with other forms of language. Kastril's ambition is to learn the cant of the angry boys. Surly arrives in disguise uttering fragments of Spanish (which Kastril takes to be French). Dapper deviates into Turkish. Sir Epicure Mammon claims to have a treatise on the philosopher's stone, penned by Adam in High Dutch, 'Which proves it was the primitive tongue'. For Ananias, 'All's heathen, but the Hebrew'; as Herford and Simpson point out in their note to this passage, Puritans in Jonson's day actually did want to enforce Hebrew as a universal language, considering that it was the language spoken by Adam in Paradise, subsequently handed down after the confusion of Babel to the Hebrew race. Yet what *The Alchemist* in fact depicts is a new Babel, a house in which different people try in different ways to reach the heaven of their private fantasies, yet are driven farther and farther from the common language which joins them to each other and to common sense. Cozening is a matter of abusing words; if a man understands no words, he is all the easier to fleece:

> His great
> Verdugo-ship has not a jot of language:
> So much the easier to be cossin'd, my Dolly.
>
> (III. iii. 70–2)

'Tickle him with thy mother-tongue', says Face to Dol; the only universal language is sex. In the 'Queen of the Fairies' scene (III. v), language has become a matter of mere nonsensical sounds: '*Ti, ti do ti, ti ti do, ti da*', mysterious enough to deceive the credulous Dapper. In Dol's 'fit of talking' in IV. v there is a significant theme beneath the gibberish; for in Dol's speech Jonson has actually paraphrased the writing of the Puritan Hugh Broughton on the subject of the universal language:

[1] For a fuller development of the argument of this paragraph, see my essay 'Language, Noise, and Nonsense: *The Alchemist*', in *Seventeenth-Century Imagery: Essays on Figurative Language From Donne to Farquhar*, ed. Earl Miner, Berkeley, Los Angeles, London, 1971, pp 69–82 (reprinted in Holdsworth: see Bibliography).

> For, as he sayes, except
> We call the Rabbines, and the heathen Greekes . . .
> To come from Salem, and from Athens,
> And teach the people of Great Britaine . . .
> To speake the tongue of Eber, and Javan . . .
> We shall know nothing—
>
> (IV. v. 12–17)

Dol's wild harangue on the ways of achieving universal linguistic understanding runs as a lunatic counterpoint to what is actually occuring, as (in the words of the stage-direction) *They speake together*. The scene parodies the Pentecostal miracle when the apostles 'began to speak with other tongues, as the Spirit gave them utterance'; instead of the 'sound from heaven, as of a rushing mighty wind' there comes, from the laboratory, '*A great crack and noise within*'. Language has deteriorated into noise; speech, which Jonson described in his *Discoveries* as 'the instrument of Society', 'the only benefit man hath to express his excellencie of mind above other creatures', has become untuned. Jonson is fond of such symbolic moments of noise and nonsense; they are to be found, for instance, at the end of the second act of *Bartholomew Fair* ('*They all speake together . . .*'), in the courtroom scene in the last act of *The Devil is an Ass*, or in the mounting climax of discordant fiddles and of hunting horns which drives Morose from the stage at the end of the third act of *Epicoene*. Though the detailing of such scenes may be erudite, their impact in the theatre is immediate, farcical, and direct.

A word ought also to be said about the other general characteristic of Jonson's comedy which we have just noticed, namely, its highly specific nature. One ought not to ignore the pleasure given by the profusion of incidental and topographical detail in Jonson's comedies, a pleasure rather like that we may feel in the novels of Defoe or of Dickens; Coleridge suggestively compared the *inclusiveness* of Jonson's work to that of Hogarth's. Tiny details accumulate in Jonson's work to form a precise and vivid picture of contemporary London. Morose in *Epicoene* devises a room with double walls and treble ceilings, whose windows are shut and caulked; there he lives by candlelight, his door padded with a thick quilt or flock-bed, its knocker removed; the street outside is 'so narrow at both ends, that it will receive no coaches, nor carts, nor any of these common noises', yet the fish-wives and orange-women, the chimney-sweepers and bear-wards and costard-mongers can still wander through the street if they please, uttering their cries, and must be bought off by formal treaty. The scene is as crowded and as exact as, say, Hogarth's 'The Enraged Musician'. *The Alchemist* gives a similar sense of the lay-out of the actual streets and lanes of Blackfriars (where the play is set, and where it was also performed), even of the way in which the houses and shops are constructed. Abel Drugger's tobacco shop, we are told, stands at a street-corner; Drugger himself produces a plan of the shop, and muses over the exact arrangement of its door and shelves. Face's speech of introduction lets us know just what the shop does and does not contain:

> This is my friend, Abel, an honest fellow,
> He lets me have good tabacco, and he do's not
> Sophisticate it, with sack-lees, or oyle,
> Nor washes it in muscadell, and graines,
> Nor buries it, in gravell, under ground,
> Wrap'd up in greasie leather, or piss'd clouts:
> But keeps it in fine lilly-pots, that open'd,
> Smell like conserve of roses, or french beanes.
> He has his maple block, his silver tongs,
> Winchester pipes, and fire of juniper
> A neate, spruce-honest-fellow, and no gold-smith.
>
> (I. iii. 22–32)

The survey is leisurely and precise; there is time to describe and deplore the methods of less scrupulous tobacconists before proceeding to the flattering notice of Drugger's maple block and his silver tongs. Jonson's power of suggesting the details of an interior scene is particularly rich. In the fifth act of *Volpone* Mosca absently reads over to himself the inventory of Volpone's belongings, tantalizing the other would-be beneficiaries who have come to learn the contents of Volpone's will: Turkey carpets and suits of bedding, cloth of gold and velvet, chests of linen, of diaper, and of damask, down-beds and bolsters, cabinets of onyx and ebony and mother-of-pearl – these are the rich stakes for which everyone in this game is competing, and Mosca enumerates them lovingly before sweeping them from the board.

Yet 'realism' hardly seems the word here. Such a term would be inadequate, first, because certain details and images have a way of recurring insistently throughout Jonson's plays until they reach a point at which they seem to take on the force of large, governing symbols – fire, gold, clothes, noise, parts of the body.[1] And sec-

---

[1] See, for example, Edward Partridge, 'The Symbolism of Clothes in Jonson's Last Plays', *Journal of English and Germanic Philology*, lvi, 1957, pp 396–409; Ray Heffner, 'Unifying Symbols in the Comedy of Ben Jonson' in *English Stage Comedy*, ed. W. K. Wimsatt, New York, 1954; and Christopher Ricks, '*Sejanus* and Dismemberment', *Modern Language Notes*, lxxvi, 1961, pp 301–8.

ondly, because such detailing is constantly subject to farcical exaggeration. Here, for instance, is how Jonson employs detail in a non-farcical way, when, in a verse-epistle, he good-humouredly invites a friend to come and sup with him:

> It is the faire acceptance, Sir, creates
>> The entertaynment perfect: not the cates.
> Yet shall you have, to rectifie your palate,
>> An olive, capers, or some better sallade
> Ushring the mutton; with a short-leg'd hen,
>> If we can get her, full of egs, and then,
> Limons, and wine for sauce: to these, a coney
>> Is not to be despair'd of, for our money;
> And, though fowle, now, be scarce, yet there are clarkes,
>> The skie not falling, thinke we may have larkes.
> Ile tell you of more, and lye, so you will come:
>> Of partrich, pheasant, wood-cock, of which some
> May yet be there; and godwit, if we can:
>> Knat, raile, and ruffe too . . .
>
> ('Inviting a Friend to Supper', lines 7–20)

*Moderation* is to be the key-note of this supper, and the invitation, too, strives to be moderate, promising no more than is within the realms of possibility ('a short-leg'd hen,/If we can get her'), yet allowing the precise appeal of each item to be savoured as it is proffered; finally (so delectable has the meal become in the imagining) the invitation passes into some gentle and playful exaggeration: 'Ile tell you of more, and lye . . .' Here, on the other hand, is Sir Epicure Mammon visualizing a banquet – in honour not of a friend, but of himself – quite uncircumscribed by the bounds of probability (no *ifs*, just *wills*); he also tells us of more, and lies, but does not tell us he lies:

> My foot-boy shall eate phesants, calvered salmons,
> Knots, godwits, lamprey's: I my selfe will have
> The beards of barbels, serv'd, in stead of sallades;
> Oild mushromes; and the swelling unctuous paps
> Of a fat pregnant sow, newly cut off,
> Drest with an exquisite, and poynant sauce;
> For which, Ile say unto my cooke, there's gold,
> Goe forth, and be a knight.
>
> (II. ii. 80–7)

The success of such a passage as this comes from the perfect arrangement of its considered and succulent details; despite the element of farcical exaggeration, the meal has been exactly

imagined, with the help of Apicius's *Roman Cookery Book* and other
learned sources; and the dishes seem close enough to reach. If,
unlike Marlowe, Jonson manages to make such hyperbolic passages
as this sound *possible*, it is largely because of his greater skill in
detailing. Compare this feast proposed by Tamburlaine:

> Then wil we triumph, banquet and carouse,
> Cookes shall have pensions to provide us cates,
> And glut us with the dainties of the world,
> *Lachrima Christi* and Calabrian wines
> Shall common Souldiers drink in quaffing boules,
> I, liquid golde when we have conquer'd him,
> Mingled with corall and with orient pearle:
> Come let us banquet and carrouse the whiles.
>
> (lines 2787–94; Part II)

Tamburlaine's idea of a meal is very unspecific; only an exceedingly
hungry person would be stirred by these vast and vague promises of
endless cates and dainties.

If Jonson's dense and highly specific kind of drama creates
occasional problems of comprehension, then, it also provides its
own unique rewards. But there is another, major, probable reason
why Jonson is not popular today, and that is because of an unease
about the way in which he seems to have conceived the characters of
his plays. One may begin with the women. At the imagining of one
kind of female character Jonson has never been surpassed: the
sturdy, mannish woman, lavish with her cosmetics and her tongue,
knowledgeable about 'those excellent receits' to keep her 'from
bearing of children', addressing her female acquaintance by their
surnames, feeling free to leave her husband whenever she pleases in
order to make her private assignations or to hold cabal with her
friends: such are Fulvia and Sempronia in *Catiline* (whose scene
together in the second act of the play was justly praised by Eliot),
Livia in *Sejanus*, Lady Would-be in *Volpone*, Lady Haughty and her
troop in *Epicoene*, Lady Eitherside and Lady Tailbush in *The Devil is
an Ass*. Congreve's Lady Wishfort and Sheridan's Lady Sneerwell
are the mild drawing-room descendants of this strapping
Amazonian company. Jonson is also successful in his portraits of
bossy and snobbish women of a rather lower social class, such as
Fallace in *Every Man Out of His Humour*, Chloe in *Poetaster*, Mistress Otter in *Epicoene*, and Gertrude in *Eastward Ho!* Yet with his
younger and more romantic women he is less happy. Julia in
*Poetaster*, for instance, remains quite unconvincing, and the meeting

between her and Ovid at the end of the fourth act of the play seems little more than a cardboard imitation of a Shakespearean love-scene. If there is no Juliet or Cleopatra in Jonson's work, neither is there a Viola or a Rosalind. When Jonson has a woman dress up in boy's clothing he still manages to keep her spirits subdued and her role minimal. In *The New Inn* the supposed boy Frank is dressed up, for a prank, as a young woman, in which garb he is wooed, and actually wedded, by Lord Beaufort; at the end of the play, to everyone's surprise and considerable relief, it turns out that Frank is indeed a woman after all, and not *any* woman but, as chance would have it, the long-lost daughter of the landlord of the New Inn, where she happens to have been working for some years. On such an occasion, after such long confinement in breeches, it might be thought that Frank would be glad to utter a word or two of happiness or relief or conceivably of explanation, yet to the end of the play Frank remains merely a dumb spectator of the further (equally astonishing) revelations that are made. Though he is very ingenious about the whole business of deception and disguise in this play, Jonson shows no apparent curiosity here about the psychology of disguise, never allowing us to enter into the mind of the woman, as Shakespeare does in *Twelfth Night* or Wycherley does in *The Plain Dealer*, and this lack of curiosity is one of the factors that makes the ending to this play seem nothing more than a triumph of a brisk and faintly fatuous kind of ingenuity. In a similar way at the end of *The Case is Altered* it is revealed that Rachel, hitherto thought to be the daughter of the miser Jacques de Prie, is in fact the daughter of the great Lord Chamont, yet once again, from the moment of the revelation until the end of the play, the young woman is allowed no word, being quietly pushed aside to make way for the play's busy resolution. Throughout the whole of the fifth act of *Volpone* Celia suffers almost total eclipse, being allowed to utter only three half-line exclamations.

There is a curious passivity about such women, almost as if Jonson had thought of them merely as blocks in a larger jig-saw pattern of events. One critic has spoken warmly of the 'pure, womanly good sense' of Grace Welborn in *Bartholomew Fair*,[1] yet nothing so positive as good sense seems to control Grace, who wanders absently through Smithfield, declaring that 'rather than be yoak'd with this Bridegroome is appointed me, I would take up any husband, almost upon any trust', and expressing herself so equally

---

[1] *The Times Literary Supplement*, 23 April 1938.

pleased with the first two suitors that come along that she can choose between them only by means of a device as rational as flipping a coin. She is like another equally restless and unfettered Jonsonian heroine, Awdrey Turf in *A Tale of a Tub*, who on the day of her wedding enjoys a number of amorous escapades with a number of rival suitors: 'Husbands, they say, grow thick; but thin are sowne./I care not who it be, so I have one.' Even one of Jonson's most sympathetic women, Mrs Fitzdottrel in *The Devil is an Ass*, shows the same readiness to make off from her husband for an affair with Wittipol; in all these cases, though Jonson has taken care to have the women's husbands and bridegrooms sufficiently ridiculous to make their impatience understandable, there is not a strong feeling of character controlling events. Celia in *Volpone* presents a similar mildly puzzling case. It has been argued by more than one critic that Celia is the embodiment of Christian virtue in the play; yet it is not at all clear (unless it be for the purpose of getting the plot going) why this sainted figure should drop her handkerchief to Volpone in the mountebank scene. In the seduction scene, even allowing for the fact that a victim of attempted rape can hardly be expected to play a very dominant role, Celia is oddly muted. 'One wou'd think she shou'd rend, and tear, and cry out for help, as she did afterwards with fury enough; but that wou'd ha' spoil'd the Song . . .' was the tart comment of one of the speakers in the anonymous *Comparison Between the Two Stages* (1702. Ed. S. B. Wells, Princeton, 1942, p. 31); and Coleridge wished that she and Bonario might have been given principal parts in the play. The full energy of Jonson's imagination has clearly gone into Volpone's lavish enticements:

> If thou hast wisdome, hear me, Celia.
> Thy bathes shall be the juyce of july-flowres,
> Spirit of roses, and of violets,
> The milke of unicornes, and panthers breath
> Gather'd in bagges, and mixt with cretan wines.
>
> (III. vii. 212–16)

Celia's reposts, on the other hand, tend to be terse and somewhat lifeless:

> Some serene blast me, or dire lightning strike
> This my offending face.
>
> (III. vii. 184–5)

The case is a little like that of Comus and the Lady. Here a familiar critical defence has it that it is always more glamorous to be seducer than victim, always easier to give free rein to the rhetoric of blandishment and persuasion than to write attractively on the side of defensive virtue. And yet there is no *a priori* reason why the case of defensive virtue should necessarily be dull. Shakespeare has made Isabella's 'Th'impression of keen whips I'd wear as rubies' a poignant and revealing moment in *Measure for Measure*, where Jonson's words for Celia, 'Rub these hands,/With what may cause an eating leprosie' etc., have little resonance, either on the page or on the stage; Celia remains to a large extent an unknown character. For an actress, the seduction scene in *Volpone* certainly presents some difficulty, unless it is assumed (as has sometimes been argued) that in one part of her mind Celia is always strongly tempted: an assumption which it is not easy to sustain from the text.

The mention of *Measure for Measure* leads us to a larger objection which might be brought against Jonson's method of characterization. In *Measure for Measure* (as so often elsewhere) Shakespeare is able to show us people confronting situations to which they have never expected to be exposed, finding, as they watch what Coleridge called 'the flux and reflux of their inmost nature', that their character is not the fixed and known thing they thought it to be; for such people, the discovery may cause panic or fear: 'O fie, fie, fie!/What dost thou, or what art thou, Angelo?' Jonson's characters, on the other hand, seldom introspect, and seldom experience change of this kind from within; the change they do experience is usually imposed upon them, with violence, from without. Garrulous characters, for instance, are forcibly silenced: Carlo Buffone in *Every Man Out of His Humour* and Lupus in *Poetaster* are finally gagged; in *Volpone* Peregrine plays a practical joke upon the talkative Sir Pol, forcing him to crawl for refuge inside the shell of a tortoise (an emblem of silence); Crispinus in *Poetaster* must vomit and then hold his peace. In the final scene of *Bartholomew Fair*, Wasp, Busy, Littlewit and Overdo are each in turn silenced, after a series of humiliations. In the last moments of the play Overdo sees his wife vomit: the action again suggests the completion of a comic catharsis. In *Epicoene*, Morose, ironically the most talkative character in the play, finally leaves the stage without a word, having been subjected to 'an excellent comoedy of affliction'. In the sub-plot of *Epicoene*, Captain Otter, speaking his mind about his wife at last, is overheard by her and beaten. In *The New Inn* a tailor's wife, Pinnacia Stuffe, is found wearing a dress which her husband has made for Lady Frampul, and the company at the inn take time off from their courtly games to see to it that Pinnacia is forcibly stripped of her clothes and sent home 'Divested to her flanell, in a cart'. This is not comedy of happy discovery so much as comedy of punishment and social revenge.

Jonson knew violence well enough in his own life; he had on two or three occasions spent time in prison (once for killing his fellow-actor Gabriel Spencer, and on other occasions for suspected sedition and libel), he had been branded on the thumb, and there had even been talk of slitting his ears and nose; the harsh ending to *Volpone* does not emerge solely from the literary imagination. If we think, as George Meredith did, that comedy is essentially a matter of civilized and agreeable exchanges of wit between social equals, then Jonson's rougher comedy is bound to appear dissatisfying; yet it is not easy to argue that our age is less taken by violence, either inside the theatre or out, than was the age of Jonson. All successful comedy, even that of Congreve (whom Meredith so prized), has been streaked with cruelty, and the persecution of Malvolio in *Twelfth Night* or of Parolles in *All's Well* is quite as fierce as anything in Jonson's comedy. The essential question is not whether comedy of violence is still acceptable, but whether the kind of characterization that tends to go with it is still acceptable. 'Mischiefes feed/Like beasts, till they be fat, and then they bleed', says the first avocatore at the end of *Volpone*. And indeed, Jonson's characters often do just that: swell outrageously until the point when they are struck down by the butcher's knife. 'Swell, swell, my joyes', says Sejanus at the opening of the fifth act; soon this hubristical hero is to be torn limb from limb. The explosions which occur in *The Alchemist* and *The Staple of News* mark similar moments at which vanity is spectacularly deflated. It is as if Jonson blew his characters up like balloons, then pricked them with a pin.

There is certainly some simplicity of conception here; although Shakespeare indeed has moments like these, he does not make them the central or the sole kind of 'change' which his plays depict: along with the deflation of Malvolio or Parolles he gives us also the subtler inner changes of Orsino and Olivia, of Helena and Bertram. And we are made particularly aware of this simplicity of characterization because it is so different from the characterization we have come to expect, since the time of Jane Austen, in the modern novel. Today we tend to accept as axiomatic the kind of arguments about character (as something fluid, subject to growth and change, imperfectly knowable) that were put forward by, say, D. H. Lawrence in 'Why the Novel Matters' or E. M. Forster in *Aspects of the Novel*. Other kinds of characterization, both in the drama and the novel, therefore tend to look primitive. Forster suggested that the kind of characters he called 'flat' derived ultimately from the Renaissance notion of humours. And put beside Shakespeare's or George Eliot's characters, Jonson's 'humour'[1] characters – whose lives seem to have gathered to a single obsessive point of interest, who are subjected to such beating and gagging and puncturing – may well seem little more than two-dimensional caricatures.

Certain of them are indeed just this – Corbaccio in *Volpone*, for instance – but Jonson has a curious way of varying depth in his plays, and of giving an added dimension to a character who looks at first quite simple. Corvino in the same play, for instance, is a wonderful compound of stupidity and calculation, of masochism and elaborate defensiveness. Jonson's jealous husbands are usually particularly complicated: Kitely in *Every Man In His Humour*, for instance, a part much loved by Garrick in the eighteenth century, is a subtle and compassionate transformation of a stock comic type (Malbecco in *The Faerie Queene*). An equally famous role of Garrick's, around which he rewrote the play, was that of Abel Drugger in *The Alchemist*, a part played in modern times by Alec Guinness. It is true that certain of Jonson's characters seem simply to come and go repeating a single, predictable sentence, as Forster declared 'flat' characters always do ('I never will desert Mr Micawber'): Troubleall wanders through Smithfield fair, constantly repeating his request for Justice Overdo's warrant. Yet something ought briefly to be said in defence of such two-dimensional creatures. In the middle of *Tom Jones* an unnamed lawyer makes a rapid appearance, declaring that he is so busy that if he could divide himself into four pieces he could still not accomplish all he has to do. Some hundreds of pages later, a lawyer, this time named as Lawyer Dowling, makes an equally rapid appearance, declaring that he is so busy that if he were to be divided into twenty pieces he could still not accomplish all he has to do. We enjoy the return of Lawyer Dowling and his multiplying anxieties partly because of the incremental joke, partly because we are grateful, in an exceedingly dense and complex work, to be given some simple means of recognizing and identifying an old friend. Dickens likewise often uses the simplest of phrases and gestures as clues through the labyrinths of his novels: a little man in the midst of a London crowd gives a swift back-handed shake of his right forefinger, and we know at once who he is. These are the legitimate tactics of writers who delight in

[1] For Jonson's own definition of the term, see *Every Man Out of His Humour*, Grex before Act I, lines 88–114; and Herford and Simpson, ix, 391–5.

marshalling large numbers of characters in their work, and in bringing them into unexpected relationships with each other. In the choruses to *The Magnetic Lady* Jonson described this as the art of weaving, of knotting, of perplexing, and of unravelling. Though a character considered in isolation may look simple and flat, the total effect is complex and dense. In *Bartholomew Fair* we have met nearly forty characters by the time Troubleall first appears; it is doubtful if a more sophisticated character could be tolerated at this point. Troubleall's real and surprising comic function is to upset the already established pattern of relationships in the play; it is a master-stroke (and one which allows for the comic resolution of the piece) to have Dame Purecraft fall for Troubleall at this late hour.

If change does not occur in the inner life of Jonson's characters, then, it occurs constantly in the relationships which they bear to one another. And the most compelling of all relationships in Jonson's plays are those in which two or sometimes three characters wrestle slowly against each other for ascendancy over others. Jonson depicts a struggle of this kind first in *Sejanus*, where the relationship between Tiberius and Sejanus is subject to constant slight shifts, gentle but ominous, and he depicts it again in *Volpone*, where the relationship between master and parasite undergoes gradual reversal. Mosca's subversiveness is at first suggested only by the lightest of touches: by the obvious enjoyment he derives, for instance, in assisting Corvino to abuse to his face the apparently slumbering and stone-deaf Volpone; and again by his gently excessive humility:

VOLPONE: Dispatch, dispatch: I long to have possession
Of my new present.
MOSCA: That, and thousands more,
I hope, to see you lord of.
VOLPONE: Thankes, kind Mosca.
MOSCA: And that, when I am lost in blended dust,
And hundred such, as I am, in succession—
VOLPONE: Nay, that were too much, Mosca.
MOSCA: You shall live,
Still, to delude these harpyies.
VOLPONE: Loving Mosca ...
(I. ii. 116–221)

*That were too much, Mosca.* And after Bonario has broken in upon Volpone's meeting with Celia, it is again the ironic inflation of Mosca's words that lets us know that Mosca, while he appears to glide into instant harmony with Volpone's most extravagant emotional registers, is in fact in perfect control of the situation, watching and waiting his chances:

VOLPONE: What shall we do?
MOSCA:                              I know not, if my heart
Could expiate the mischance, I'ld pluck it out.
Will you be pleas'd to hang me? or cut my
    throate?
And i'le requite you, sir. Let's die like Romanes,
Since wee have liv'd, like Grecians.
                             (III. viii. 11–15)

In *The Alchemist* the struggle is a three-cornered one; right from the quarrel between Face and Subtle upon which the play opens, the 'triple alliance' is only precariously maintained; the arrival of the nubile Dame Pliant brings the rivalry between the two men to a crisis, and with the homecoming of Lovewit things degenerate into a rapid scramble, each man for himself. Even in the plays in which the struggle for power is not a major theme, it is still often felt as an undercurrent, as in the rivalry between Quarlous and Winwife in *Bartholomew Fair*, or between Clerimont, Truewit, and Dauphine in *Epicoene*. 'That falls out often, madame', says Truewit to Lady Haughty, 'that he that thinkes himselfe the master-wit, is the master-foole'. At the end of the play it turns out that Truewit himself has been 'lurch'd ... of the better halfe of the garlande' through the cunning of Dauphine. This last-minute toppling of a presumed 'master-wit' is a characteristic Jonsonian touch.

There is a third major prejudice against Jonson's work, and that is that it is untheatrical. It must be confessed that Jonson himself did something to encourage this belief. He was deeply distrustful of the judgement of his audiences, and (unlike Shakespeare) seems to have attached a good deal of importance to the printing of his plays. He took a personal interest in the printing of the 1616 Folio, which he called his *Workes*, a title which his contemporaries seem to have found amusingly pretentious for a mere collection of plays. After *Catiline* was hissed off the stage in 1611, Jonson haughtily commended the printed text of the play to 'the Reader extraordinary'. He was forever bidding the stage a lofty farewell:

> And since our Daintie age,
>    Cannot indure reproofe,
> Make not thy selfe a Page,
>    To that strumpet the Stage,

> But sing high and aloofe,
> Safe from the wolves black jaw, and
> the dull Asses hoofe.
>
> ('An Ode. To himself', lines 31–6)

Another version of these lines was spoken on stage by the character of the 'Author' in the 'apologeticall Dialogue' at the end of *Poetaster*:

> Leave me. There's something come into my thought,
> That must, and shall be sung, high, and aloofe,
> Safe from the wolves black jaw, and the dull asses hoofe.

There is something in common here with the attitude Yeats expressed in 'The Circus Animals' Desertion', yet Jonson's recoil from the stage is fiercer, more deeply driven by contempt. For Jonson, as later for Pope, the theatre could sometimes stand as an emblem of the corruption of the whole age. Jonson has chosen his metaphors carefully when, in *Every Man In His Humour*, he has Kitely complain how Wellbred and his friends have brought his house into ill repute:

> He makes my house here common, as a Mart,
> A Theater, a publike receptacle
> For giddie humour, and diseased riot.
>
> (II. i. 61–3)

In 1629, after the disaster of *The New Inn*, Jonson angrily bade farewell to the stage again (it was not to be his last play):

> Come leave the lothed stage,
> And the more lothsome age . . .

To which, with some justice, Owen Felltham replied:

> Come leave this saucy way
> Of baiting those that pay
> Dear for the sight of your declining wit.

*Baiting* is exactly the word for this contemptuous treatment of one's audiences.

Yet it would be a mistake to confuse the anti-theatrical temperament with the untheatrical temperament.[1] A seventeenth-century commentator upon one of Jonson's stage disasters remarked that 'the only Laureat of our stage (having compos'd a Play of excellent worth, but not of equal applause) fell downe upon his knees, and gave thanks, that he had transcended the capacity of the vulgar.'[2]

---

[1] See Jonas A. Barish, 'Jonson and the Loathed Stage', in Blissett, Patrick, and Van Fossen (see Bibliography), pp 27–53; and the same author's *The Anti-Theatrical Prejudice*, Berkeley, Los Angeles, London, 1981.

[2] Herford and Simpson, ix, 241.

There is naivety about such an attitude, yet in Jonson's plays a great deal of the dramatic excitement is generated by the means of a sidelong, but perfectly obvious, attack upon the audience itself. The audience-baiting is an essential part of Jonson's drama. In *The Staple of News* he places on the stage a number of censorious gossips, who chatter unintelligently between the acts about the development of the play. Quite obviously, the gossips represent the actual audience that is watching the play. In *The Magnetic Lady* Jonson places on the stage another censorious representative of the audience, called Damplay, who also grumbles between the acts and is put down in no uncertain manner by a boy who is (we are told) the representative of the author himself.

If this were simply an assault trick there would be little to commend it; an author does not have a particular privilege to abuse an audience simply because they have paid money to see his play. The business of challenge and reproof is justifiable, however, where it enhances the whole dramatic suggestiveness of a piece, as it usually does in the case of Jonson's plays. Take *The Devil is an Ass*. In that play Wittipol presents Fitzdottrel with a rich cloak, in return for which Fitzdottrel agrees to allow Wittipol to converse for fifteen minutes with his wife. This cloak (Fitzdottrel argues to his wife, as he negotiates the bargain) is very necessary, for that day he has a special engagement:

> To day, I goe to the Black-fryers Play-house,
> Sit i' the view, salute all my acquaintance,
> Rise up between the Acts, let fall my cloake,
> Publish a handsome man, and a rich suite
> (As that's a special end, why we goe thither . . .)
>
> (I. vi. 31–5)

And the play he is going to see? *The Devil is an Ass*, which was indeed 'that day' in performance at Blackfriars. Later in the play it is decided to disguise a boy as a Spanish lady, and someone suggests that the best person for the job would be the actor Dick Robinson – who may have been playing the part of Wittipol in this very production (in the end Wittipol himself dresses up as the lady, 'Robinson' being otherwise engaged). In the course of the play Jonson converts such hall-of-mirrors tricks as these into a rich, major theme: for *The Devil is an Ass* is centrally concerned with the way in which men use deception and illusion, out-acting even that prince of players, the devil himself. *Bartholomew Fair*, too, is concerned with this theme. In the Induction to this play Jonson speaks ironically of the 'understanding' of his audience (who are 'understanding' only in the sense that they stand under the stage); yet the insult is not a gratuitous one: for the play gently enforces the point that 'understanding' is as necessary to life as to art if one is not to be duped by disguises and by robes of office, by the outward signs and protestations of honesty, by all that is subsumed in the term *hypocrisy* (to the Greeks a 'hypocrite' was an actor, to the Jacobeans it could also mean a Puritan). In *The Alchemist*, too, the relationship with the audience is of some importance: in the epilogue to the play Jonson wryly suggests that the last gulls may be the audience themselves, the master alchemist may finally be the dramatist himself, who is making a tidy sum of gold out of his house of illusions. Jonson's plays often present a magnetic centre (a house, a fairground) to which the curious and the gullible find themselves drawn. The theatre (Jonson often implies) is just such another magnetic centre: beware how, and why, you are drawn towards it; the illusion you see practised here is like the illusion that is practised in life.

The theatricality of Jonson's plays is in fact remarkable. Jonson had, of course, been trained as an actor, and though he was (as Aubrey said) 'never a good Actor' he was 'an excellent Instructor', and he appears to have taken an active professional interest in the way in which his plays were acted, and to have pondered with considerable care the details of his stagecraft, both large and small.[1] Jonson is often praised, in a dutiful way, for the fact that he observed the classical unities. It is highly unlikely that there was anything particularly dutiful about Jonson's adoption of the unities – the discussion between Cordatus, Asper, and Mitus at the opening of *Every Man Out of His Humour*, as well as a couple of celebrated passages in the *Discoveries*, sufficiently show his liberation from dutiful habits of thought. It is more likely that Jonson found that observation of the unities frankly heightened the excitement of his plays. The confined settings of *Volpone*, *The Alchemist*, and *Epicoene*, for instance, create a sense of claustrophobia which is an important part of the plays' total effect.[2] The permanent interior setting of *The Alchemist* is the first that we

---

[1] See W. A. Armstrong, 'Ben Jonson and Elizabethan Stagecraft', in *Jacobean Theatre*, ed. J. R. Brown and B. Harris, *Stratford-Upon-Avon Studies* 1, London, 1960, pp 43–61.

[2] E. K. Chambers, *The Elizabethan Stage*, Oxford, 1923, iii, 123; Ian Donaldson, 'Jonson's Magic Houses', *Essays and Studies* (English Association), 1986, pp 39–61.

know of on the English stage; its restrictiveness has an unsettling effect upon the characters of the play, and, in turn, upon the audience itself; the knocking that comes at intervals throughout the piece constantly threatens an intrusion of the outside world, the arrival of the forces of law and moral retribution ('Is he the Constable?' asks Kastril when Ananias arrives). The knocking reaches its climax at the end of the fourth act with the homecoming of Lovewit; after so carefully preparing our expectations for the arrival of a moral judge, Jonson now deftly defeats them: the master of the house is easy-going, indulgent to his servant's wit. Throughout the play Jonson keeps us constantly aware of the house as a house: it serves as a trap for others, but may equally serve as a trap for Dol, Subtle, and Face; precautions must be taken so that neighbours do not hear noises through the walls, and so that the gulls, when kept apart in separate rooms, do not overhear each other. At points of high excitement and anger, Jonson delicately reminds us of the physical confines of the place:

FACE:  Let us be light, though.
SUBTLE:  I, as balls, and bound
And hit our heads against the roofe for joy:
There's so much of our care now cast away.
(IV. v. 98–100)

FACE:  By this ayre, I call,
And loose the hinges. Dol.
(IV. iii. 81–2)

The conspiracy can be destroyed by a cry, by the swinging open of a door. In *Volpone* and *Epicoene* the confined setting creates many of the same effects, and seems also to take on a further symbolic importance. Jonson contrasts in these plays two basic kinds of people: those who keep warily to their houses, locking themselves, their wives, their cash away from the prying eyes of the public (Morose, Corvino, Volpone – for all their obvious differences); and those who are ludicrously 'open' and prodigal, wandering freely from home, and hardly caring where they send their cash or their wives, or how publicly they discuss the most intimate of matters (La-Foole, and the Would-bes). Few dramatists have so skilfully used the confinement of the stage as a means of highlighting the anxieties of domestic life.

The unity of time in Jonson's plays can create similar kinds of pressure and excitement. In *The Magnetic Lady* Jonson has his boy speak scornfully of dramatists who take greater liberties with their time-schemes:

So, if a Child could be borne, in a Play, and grow up to a man, i' the first
Scene, before hee went off the Stage: and then after to come forth a
Squire, and bee made a Knight: and that Knight to travell betweene the
Acts, and doe wonders i' the holy land, or else where; kill Paynims, wild
Boores, dun Cowes, and other Monsters; beget him a reputation, and
marry an Emperours Daughter for his Mistris; convert her Fathers
Countrey; and at last come home, lame, and all to be laden with miracles.
(Conclusion of Act I)

Jonson's own plays are all sharply restricted in time, and the
restriction creates its own pressures. It is only for the duration of a
single day (the day of La-Foole's quarter-feast) that Morose will be
tormented in *Epicoene* ("'Tis but a day, and I would suffer
heroically'). It is only for the duration of St Bartholomew's Day that
the accidents of *Bartholomew Fair* will last; those of *A Tale of a Tub*
are only for St Valentine's Day. It is only for a day that the
chambermaid Pru in *The New Inn* will remain queen of the sports
at the inn, and only for two hours that she has the right to force the
half-disdainful, half-willing Lady Frampul to hear the suit of Lovel.
Jonson allows us, through Lady Frampul's laments, to feel the rapid
flow of time throughout the play:

PRU:      And see, your second houre is almost ended.
LADY F:   It cannot be! O clip the wings of time,
          Good Pru, or make him stand still with a charme.
          Distill the gout into it, cramps, all diseases
          To' arrest him in the foot, and fix him here:
          O, for an engine, to keepe backe all clocks!
          Or make the Sunne forget his motion!
                                          (IV. iv. 225–31)

More than any other literary form, the drama can create in us a
particular awareness of the passage of time; hence to voice in a play
such traditional lover's laments as these is to strike a peculiar
resonance in one's audience, as Marlowe discovered when he had
Doctor Faustus, waiting for the midnight hour, repeat a line from
Ovid: *O lente, lente curite noctis equi.* Jonson is good at creating what
might be described as a comic analogue of the Faustus experience,
a race against the clock. It is there in *The Alchemist*, for instance.
The events of the play occur between nine o'clock in the morning
and three o'clock in the afternoon of the same day; Jonson's Oxford
editors draw up an hour-by-hour programme of events. Most of the
gulls arrive only to be sent away, to return later at an appointed

time; the confusion begins when they arrive at the wrong time, or when Face and Subtle make a slip in their programme, or when a new character (such as Surly in his disguise as the Spanish don) arrives unexpectedly. In the third act Mammon arrives suddenly, wanting to see Dol, who is already occupied being Queen of the Fairies to Dapper; after a hurried conference, Subtle and Face thrust a gag of ginger-bread into Dapper's mouth and push him into the privy, and there he remains until Act V, when he suddenly wanders out again, shattering the credibility of the story which Face is rapidly fabricating for his master's benefit. Jonson times such moments as these to a hair's breadth; he judges exactly at what point his audience will have *forgotten* about Dapper's existence (as, earlier, they may have forgotten about Lovewit's). Likewise in *Epicoene* Jonson allows both his characters and his audience to become so involved in the side-issue of the 'duel' between Daw and La-Foole that they forget Morose is still somewhere in the house; hence there is an added terror in Morose's sudden reappearance with a sword in each hand. At such small but expertly timed comic moments Jonson excels; here he is unsurpassed by Shakespeare himself.

Jonson's dramatic career was a long one, stretching from the last decade of Queen Elizabeth's reign to the last decade of Charles I's. He is sometimes seen as a dramatist whose creative aims and outlook remained more or less constant throughout this long period, but whose powers went into mysterious decline as he entered the middle years of life. Jonson's greatest period is conventionally and properly reckoned to run from about 1603 to about 1614, but revisionist critics have recently been looking with interest at Jonson's later work, arguing for a new and sympathetic understanding of those plays which Dryden dismissively termed his dotages.[1] Amongst the work of his final years are probably to be included the engaging rural comedy *A Tale of a Tub*, and his lovely unfinished piece *The Sad Shepherd*, with its vision of a vanished 'happy age' of English pastoral life. In mode and outlook, these plays are quite different not only from the busy city comedies, but also from plays such as *The New Inn* and *The Magnetic Lady* with which they are sometimes casually grouped; they also differ strikingly from each other. Jonson's entire dramatic corpus is in fact

[1] See the work of Larry Champion and, in particular, Anne Barton, mentioned in the Bibliography; and Michael Hattaway's introduction to the Revels edition of *The New Inn*, Manchester, 1984. J. B. Bamborough looks at Jonson's 'rusticity' in his late work: see *Jonson and Shakespeare*, ed. Donaldson (Bibliography).

more varied, and more variously interesting, than has traditionally been recognized; more deeply characterized by change, experiment, and innovation. Only a fraction of that corpus is familiar today to modern theatregoers. Many of his plays await the touch of an imaginative director. The challenge is worth meeting; for Jonson is, as he has always been, one of the two great poets of the English theatre.

# 6

# THE TRAGEDIES OF WEBSTER, TOURNEUR AND MIDDLETON: SYMBOLS, IMAGERY AND CONVENTIONS

## Christopher Ricks

George Bernard Shaw did it to annoy, but that does not mean he only did it to annoy. His heart was in his words when he deplored the cult of Elizabethan and Jacobean drama. Marlowe, for instance:

He is the true Elizabethan blank-verse beast, itching to frighten other people with the superstitious terrors and cruelties in which he does not himself believe, and wallowing in blood, violence, muscularity of expression and strenuous animal passion as only literary men do when they become thoroughly depraved by solitary work, sedentary cowardice, and starvation of the sympathetic centres.

When one thinks of the donnish insolence and perpetual thick-skinned swagger of Chapman over his unique achievements in sublime balderdash, and the opacity that prevented Webster, the Tussaud laureate, from appreciating his own stupidity – when one thinks of the whole rabble of dehumanized specialists in elementary blank verse posing as the choice and master-spirits of an age that had produced the stories of Chaucer and the old mystery plays, and was even then pregnant with *The Pilgrim's Progress*, it is hard to keep one's critical blood cold enough to discriminate in favour of any Elizabethan whatever.[1]

Shaw's diatribe was directed at the factitiousness of the drama, against the way in which it is all merely made up – crudely and unconvincingly made up. For Shaw, Webster is 'the Tussaud laureate' not just because he offers in effect a Chamber of Horrors, and not just because he actually makes use of waxworks (*The Duchess of Malfi*, Act IV Scene i), but because his creations are as lifeless and unconvincing as waxworks.

Shaw certainly fastened upon what is a crucial question about Elizabethan and Jacobean tragedy: whether it matters that the plots

[1] 1896 and 1898; *Our Theatres in the Nineties*, London, 1932, ii, p 182, iii, p 317.

are contrived, the events improbable, the characters inconsistent. A crucial question, but not one which gets as much attention as might be expected. In the greatest literature there is a marriage of those true minds, imagination and observation – imagination not being allowed to lord it over observation, nor observation over imagination. The great work of literature is as much discovery as invention. But some of the kinds of literary criticism at which we are now most adept – the tracing of symbolic patterns, of moral significances, of webs of imagery, of literary and dramatic conventions – tend admiringly to isolate invention and imagination at the expense of discovery and observation. So, ultimately, at the expense of invention and imagination themselves, since their fullest potentialities cannot be released in isolation from their complementary powers. A triumph of invention which is not simultaneously a triumph of discovery is going to be something less than the highest triumph of which invention is capable.

The greatness of Shakespeare is that we feel of *King Lear* not only 'how striking' and 'how beautiful', but also 'how true'. Certainly, we need to be aware of the innumerable ways, some very oblique, in which a play may legitimately be said to be true. But the fact that the criterion is difficult to apply (it must be flexible but not limp) does not justify our abandoning it. To ask that a play be true is not the same as asking that it be naturalistic, realistic, photographic – but it is to insist that there be a significant and valid relationship between what the play shows us and what we know to be 'the transactions of the world', between the play's words and the 'human sentiments in human language' which Dr Johnson found supremely reflected in Shakespeare.

But is it legitimate to invoke Shakespeare at all when considering the other Elizabethan and Jacobean dramatists? Obviously it may be superfluous to invoke him simply as a stick with which to beat them – but is a stick which measures different from a stick which beats? Professor M. C. Bradbrook spoke strongly about this in the Introduction to her *Themes and Conventions of Elizabethan Tragedy*:[1]

An equally necessary proviso is that the plays of Shakespeare should be, as far as possible, excluded from the mind when the lesser Elizabethans are being considered. Shakespeare can be judged by nineteenth-century standards (or any other dramatic standards, for that matter) without suffering any eclipse. He is so different from his contemporaries, particularly in the matter of characterization, that it is unfair to judge them by him.

[1] Cambridge, 1935, p 6.

Spenser and not Shakespeare was the typical Elizabethan poet, and the Spenserian standards are much safer to apply to the dramatists. To approach Shakespeare through his contemporaries is enlightening, but to approach his contemporaries through him is to set up false preconceptions. The difficulty is that everyone knows Shakespeare's plays the best of all, and a conscious effort to set them aside is not often made.

My own position is exactly the opposite. It seems to me that we cannot truly understand and estimate the other dramatists unless we bring the work of their great contemporary to bear upon them (and this is not the same as bringing him to overbear them). Professor Bradbrook believes that since Shakespeare is 'so different from his contemporaries, particularly in the matter of characterization', this must make it 'unfair to judge them by him'. But it may be that Shakespeare's superiority resides mainly in this very difference – in which case it would be impossible to come to a considered judgement of the other dramatists without considering exactly what it was that they forfeited or repudiated when they took so different a view from Shakespeare's as to the nature of characterization in drama. Anyway, *unfair* hardly seems a critical term – a comparison may indeed not be relevant, or it may not be discriminatingly applied or cogently argued for, but simply to rule out in advance certain comparisons as *unfair* is to reduce literary criticism to a girlish appeal to an unspecified sporting code.

Moreover, even those who believe in consciously setting Shakespeare aside are always bringing him in. The strategy for the Elizabethan apologist is to invite in Shakespeare whenever he seems to provide warrant for a comparable episode or device in an Elizabethan play, and then to forbid him to enter if it looks as if his work might constitute an indictment of a comparable episode. The index of *Themes and Conventions of Elizabethan Tragedy* will make it clear whether or not Professor Bradbrook succeeded in setting Shakespeare aside. But a witness called by the defence cannot then be whisked away before the prosecution has had a chance to question him. Either Shakespeare's work is relevant or it is not, and critics should not vacillate to suit their argumentative convenience.

Not that a comparison with Shakespeare will necessarily be a matter of wearily repeating 'And thus we see once more that Shakespeare is better than . . .'. Take the episode in Webster's *The White Devil* (Act I Scene ii) in which the credulous Camillo is invited by Flamineo to overhear a conversation between Flamineo and Camillo's wife Vittoria, throughout which Flamineo then ridicules Camillo to her under his breath. For the critic, it may be helpful to recall the scene in *Othello* (Act 4 Scene I) in which the credulous Othello is snared by Iago into overhearing (and misconstruing) a conversation between Iago and Cassio about Bianca. But the help furnished by the comparison is not that Shakespeare's use of the convention shows up Webster's; rather, that the episode in *Othello* is no more convincing, no less stagey, than that in *The White Devil*; the particular convention presents such difficulties, is so intractable, that even Shakespeare here fails to master it – and this is something to bear in mind when we consider Webster's scene.

In 1918, Ezra Pound included in his 'Credo' a statement about symbols:

I believe that the proper and perfect symbol is the natural object, that if a man uses 'symbols' he must so use them that their symbolic function does not obtrude; so that a sense, and the poetic quality of the passage, is not lost to those who do not understand the symbol as such, to whom, for instance, a hawk is a hawk.[1]

*Does not obtrude*: this is not the same as a rejection of the explicit or the emphatic in symbolism. A symbolic point may be explicit but not obtrusive. Goethe said 'Man sieht die Absicht und man wird verstimmt' – 'One sees the intention and is put off'. Keats knew that 'We hate poetry that has a palpable design upon us'; at what point does a legitimate design – whether symbolic or not – turn into something obtrusive? *Does not obtrude*: what this entails is 'does not owe its place in the work solely to' – that is, 'owes its place in the work to other considerations than solely the "symbolic function" which it is to perform'.

The truly symbolic effect, then, would be distinguished not by being more indubitably symbolic, but by being in a true relationship with the non-symbolic. With a truly symbolic effect, it would not be possible to answer such a question as 'Why does a reference to a yew-tree occur in this play?' with a *single* answer (such as 'Because the yew-tree symbolizes such-and-such'); there would inherently be more than one answer, and of these there would necessarily be an answer that is non-symbolic, that owes nothing to the artist's symbolic design: such an answer as 'Because King Lear is remembering what he did to Cordelia', or 'Because old men are forgetful'. It is not a derogation from symbolic effect that a symbol has reasons over and above its symbolizing for being present at all; on the contrary, it is only by having too a non-symbolic *raison d'être*

---

[1] 'A Retrospect'; *Literary Essays*, London, 1954, p 9.

that a symbol can fully achieve its symbolic *raison d'être* – can protect itself (as everything in an imaginative work rightly has to do) against the suspicion that it is merely made up.

Why is it that 'Freudian' symbols do not necessarily live as symbols in works of art? Not because such symbols are by nature inimical to or incompatible with art; there are certainly works of literature the literary value and insight of which are inseparable from such symbols. Yet we all know of works in which the presence of indubitable 'Freudian' symbols does nothing to effect literary power. Miss Marghanita Laski once studied pony-stories for girls, and showed that the stories were replete with symbols (Daddy's horse was called Sparking Plug, Mummy's was called Gaylad).[1] What sort of gulf are we crossing when we pass from such symbols to those in Middleton's *The Changeling*? Beatrice drops a glove in the presence of De Flores, whom she fascinatedly loathes; when he picks it up and offers it to her, she tears off the other glove:

BEATRICE:   Mischief on your officious forwardness!
            Who bade you stoop? They touch my hand no more:
            There, for t'other's sake I part with this.
            Take 'em and draw thine own skin off with 'em.
                            [*Exeunt Beatrice and Diaphanta*]

DE FLORES:  Here's a favour come, with a mischief! Now I know
            She had rather wear my pelt tann'd in a pair
            Of dancing pumps, than I should thrust my fingers
            Into her sockets here, I know she hates me,
            Yet cannot choose but love her . . .
                                        (I. i. 227–35)

There can be no doubt of the symbolism here.[2] Nor can there be much doubt as to the symbolism of the incident when De Flores, having killed Alonzo, wishes to bring Alonzo's ring (a 'love' token from Beatrice) to prove that he has carried out the murder, and so cuts off Alonzo's finger. To Beatrice: 'I could not get the ring without the finger' (III. iv. 28); and so into De Flores' insistence

---

[1] 'A Horse, A Horse', *Twentieth Century*, clxvi, 1959, pp 483–5.
[2] Jonson, *The Gypsies Metamorphosed*, 'And sounding the sockets/Of simper-the-cockets' (Herford and Simpson, vii, 571); and *Oxford English Dictionary* 4a. Also the episode of the glove in Shakespeare's *The Rape of Lucrece*, when a needle pricks Tarquin: 'As who should say "This glove to wanton tricks/Is not inured"'. On Middleton's word-play, see C. Ricks, 'The Moral and Poetic Structure of *The Changeling*', *Essays in Criticism*, x, 1960, pp 290–306; and 'Word-Play in *Women Beware Women*', *Review of English Studies*, ns, xii, 1961, pp 238–50.

upon his brutal reward from Beatrice. (Alibius had earlier urged Lollio to guard Alibius' young wife: 'I would wear my ring on my own finger'; and Lollio had agreed: 'You must keep it on still then; if it but lie by, one or other will be thrusting into 't', I. ii. 27–31.) Neither the episode of the glove nor that of the dead man's finger ('But our cold maids do dead men's fingers call them', *Hamlet*) is in Middleton's source; both are strongly symbolic, and both enforce a symbolic effect such as is not inert or merely imputed. Both, in other words, present 'Freudian' symbols which exist as valid artistic symbols. Yet the difference between Middleton's glove and the pony-stories is not that the former should be thought of as somehow more symbolical – rather, that the former gains its vitality of meaning from its relationship to the non-symbolic, from its relationship to the character of Beatrice and of De Flores and to their situation. Whereas in the pony-stories character and situation do not artistically exist at any level that could have vital filaments with the symbols. The point is not one about the author's intentions (who can say what intentions went to the making of the pony-stories?), but about achievement; the genuinely potent symbol is in a true relationship to non-symbolic creative effects which complement and support it.

King Lear kneels – or makes to kneel – to Cordelia ('No, sir, you must not kneel', 4.7.59), as earlier he had knelt, though then in savage mockery, to Regan:

> 'Dear daughter, I confess that I am old:
> Age is unnecessary; on my knees I beg
> That you'll vouchsafe me raiment, bed, and food!'
>
> (2. 4. 150–2)

But the two kneelings ignite precisely because each has its independent *raison d'être*, neither is thrust into the play in order that it may serve the cross-connection's turn. There is complete fidelity to character and situation when Lear tries the fierce but desperate bid (a king begging) and kneels to Regan, just as there is when he responds to Cordelia's kneeling by wishing rather to kneel to her.

Because of its visual impact, the kneeling is an essentially dramatic effect; the impact is not in words alone – indeed, it is relevant that the words of Act 4 Scene 7 do not make it clear whether Lear actually kneels to Cordelia or only rises to do so (there is a good note on this in the Cambridge Shakespeare). It is easy for a reader to underestimate such visual impact, and Professor Maynard Mack does well to urge that we attend to what an audience would find grasping its attention: the dramatic effect, for instance, of entrances and exits:

Equally unmistakable is the significance of the King's exit, in the first scene of *Lear*, with the man who like himself has put externals first. 'Come, noble Burgundy,' he says, and in a pairing that can be made profoundly moving on the stage, the two men go out together.[1]

Significant, yes – but also natural: both Burgundy and Lear have been wounded in their *amour propre*; Lear needs the support of Burgundy, and Burgundy – who had expected Cordelia to have a good dowry – must now be soothed. If the 'pairing' were not first of all natural, would we care about its being significant?

The same may be said of a striking sequence of visual effects in Middleton's *Women Beware Women*, by which Bianca repeatedly appears to our view framed or aloft. In Act I Scene iii, the returning Leantio is delighted to see his mother and his wife Bianca set to greet him:

> See, and she be not got on purpose now
> Into the window to look after me!
>
> (I. iii. 13–14)

But by the end of the scene, the mother and Bianca are perched up to look, not for Leantio, but – fatally – for the Duke who rides by. In Act II Scene ii, we see Bianca's seduction by the Duke, the pair framed above the stage while the mother and Livia play their game of chess; and soon the spoilt Bianca is insolently complaining to her husband Leantio:

> I'd have some pleasant lodging i' th' high street, sir;
> Or if 'twere near the court, sir, that were much better:
> 'Tis a sweet recreation for a gentlewoman
> To stand in a bay-window and see gallants.
>
> (III. i. 127–31)

Later, when Leantio too has been corrupted and appears in his new finery, there is a vivid telescoping of these 'window' moments, as Leantio remembers the initial elopement:

> I long to see how my despiser looks
> Now she's come here to court: these are her lodgings;
> She's simply now advanc'd: I took her out
> Of no such window, I remember, first;
> That was a great deal lower, and less carv'd.
>
> (IV. i. 42–6)

---

[1] 'The Jacobean Shakespeare', in *Jacobean Theatre*, eds J. R. Brown and B. Harris, London, 1960, p 29.

But Bianca from her carved window spurns him; the days of their elopement are indeed long past. These linked episodes or visual allusions have their dramatic effect – and they have it because each arises naturally and is not obtrusively fabricated for the benefit of a sequence.

My argument, then, is that linked significances, imagery, themes, symbols, and conventions are all secondary or subsequent to plot and character. This is not to say that they are less important than plot and character; since what is at issue is a relationship, the notion of comparative importance is unhelpful. (The hydrogen is not any more important than the oxygen in water.) My critical position rests on what I believe to be the nature of literature; the particular nature of drama reinforces it. Here, not surprisingly, disagreement becomes open. Professor Bradbrook insists that 'The essential structure of Elizabethan drama lies not in the narrative or the characters but in the words' (*Themes and Conventions*, p 5). This is to say – and explicitly or implicitly it has often enough been said – that an Elizabethan drama is a poem. But there are those of us who think that Ezra Pound made a crucial point about the nature of drama when he said that 'The medium of drama is not words but persons moving about on a stage using words'. In which case, the difference between a poem and a play is not simply a difference of genre (such as the difference between an epic and an epigram), but a difference of medium (such as the difference between a poem and a ballet). The medium of a poem is words – and on Professor Bradbrook's view, that too is the medium (furnishing 'the essential structure') of an Elizabethan drama. But if the medium of drama is 'not words but persons moving about on a stage using words', then the dramatist stands in quite a different relationship to persons from that of the poet; the dramatist then has quite a different responsibility towards persons – they are part of his very medium. For there to be any artistic success, the medium must be well used; for the dramatist, this would mean that persons-moving-about-on-a-stage-using-words must be well used. Granted, there are a great many forms which the 'well used' can take; but a particular responsibility towards persons will remain inherent in drama, a condition of its artistic success. Writing on the character of Iago, Professor William Empson has said: 'Some recent critics have objected to this sort of analysis, but I think it is clearly wrong to talk as if coherence of character is not needed in poetic drama, only coherence of metaphor and so on'.[1]

[1] W. Empson, *The Structure of Complex Words*, London, 1951, p 231.

It is for such reasons that William Hazlitt insisted that, of all the enemies of drama, abstraction is the worst. For drama:

is the most substantial and real of all things. It represents not only looks, but motion and speech. The painter gives only the former, looks without action or speech, and the mere writer only the latter, words without looks or action. Its business and its use is to express the thoughts and character in the most striking and instantaneous manner, in the manner most like reality. It conveys them in all their truth and subtlety, but in all their force and with all possible effect. It brings them into action, obtrudes them on the sight, embodies them in habits, in gestures, in dress, in circumstances, and in speech. It renders every thing overt and ostensible, and presents human nature not in its elementary principles or by general reflections, but exhibits its essential quality in all their variety of combination.[1]

Images and symbols matter only if they are convincingly embodied. Why should we believe in them? Did not the author just put them there, just make them up? (Which suspicion is a different matter from not acknowledging that he did indeed put them there and did indeed make them up.) It is not pattern which can persuade us that a symbolic effect is neither casual nor forced; that persuasion operates if the symbolic moments make vital sense in some other terms, and so do not owe their presence to the fact that the artist wished to have links for his chain. The dramatist's imagination has seen something, seen it in how people feel and behave, in plot and character. If command over symbol can be achieved only by violating character and event, then it is a Pyrrhic victory. One might apply to symbols in art what Henry James said about 'naivety in art':

He noted that the water-colours on the walls of the room she sat in had mainly the quality of being naive, and reflected that naivety in art is like a zero in a number: its importance depends on the figure it is united with.

('The Lesson of the Master')

But such a view of symbols is incompatible with the one implicit in L. G. Salingar's praise of Tourneur's *The Revenger's Tragedy* (endorsed in the Revels edition): the theme of the play, 'the disintegration of a whole social order',

is developed with the coherence, the precise articulation, of a dramatist assured that his symbols are significant for his audience as much as for himself.[2]

But what is the nature of such an assurance – existing apparently in

[1] 'On Modern Comedy', *Morning Chronicle*, 15 October 1813.
[2] '*The Revenger's Tragedy* and the Morality Tradition', *Scrutiny*, vi, 1938, pp 402–3.

advance of any individual creative effort – that a writer's symbols cannot but be 'significant for his audience as much as for himself'? However alive 'the Morality Tradition' may have been, no tradition can guarantee its symbols against non-significance. The unwanted implication of the statement is that, however badly Tourneur were actually to have written, his symbols could not but have had significance for his audience. But if this is so, we simply need another word for that genuine artistic significance which by its very nature has always to be created or re-created in every single work of art, and of which no tradition can 'assure' us. No tradition can assure us against artistic bankruptcy; the word 'tradition' itself needs to be seen as more strenuous than that. As T. S. Eliot said of tradition, 'it cannot be inherited, and if you want it you must obtain it by great labour' ('Tradition and the Individual Talent'). On another occasion, Eliot said that 'the blossoms of Beaumont and Fletcher's imagination draw no sustenance from the soil, but are cut and slightly withered flowers stuck into sand' ('Ben Jonson'). That would do perfectly as an emblem of all those symbolic significances which have been obtained, not by great labour, but by brisk snipping.

Swinburne, who outdid even Charles Lamb in his admiration for Elizabethan and Jacobean dramatists, quoted with approval from Buckingham's Restoration parodic satire, *The Rehearsal*: 'What the devil does the plot signify, except to bring in fine things?' (Not that Buckingham offered this sentiment for admiration, but let that pass.) Yet the wish to slight the plot, or to make it a mere byway to something more grand, is still strong in critics – though one cannot tell whether this is due to a general depreciation of plot and narrative as somehow insufficiently highbrow (though of great *theoretical* interest), or to a particular sense that plot had better be dispensable since otherwise quite a few dramatists are going to be found seriously wanting. Miss Ellis-Fermor said of *The White Devil*:

The true plot of his play is not the events which proceed upon the surface, and are flung off, as it were, as a casual expression, but the progress of the minds of the central figures towards deeper and deeper self-knowledge.[1]

But what if one believes that this antithesis is itself false to the nature of literature? That it rests upon a disjunction of the characters ('the minds of the central figures') from the plot ('the events') which is false to the nature of character, whether in literature or in life?

[1] *The Jacobean Drama*, London, fourth ed., 1961, p 176.

There is a critic who cannot be accused of being unfriendly towards Jacobean drama: T. S. Eliot, who discusses the nature of melodrama in his essay on 'Wilkie Collins and Dickens' (1927):

In *The Frozen Deep* Collins wrote a piece of pure melodrama. That is to say, it is nothing but melodrama. We are asked to accept an improbability, simply for the sake of seeing the thrilling situation which arises in consequence. But the frontier of drama and melodrama is vague; the difference is largely a matter of emphasis; perhaps no drama has ever been greatly and permanently successful without a large melodramatic element. What is the difference between *The Frozen Deep* and *Oedipus the King*? It is the difference between coincidence, set without shame or pretence, and fate – which emerges into character. It is not necessary, for high drama, that accident should be eliminated; you cannot formulate the proportion of accident that is permissible. But in great drama character is always felt to be – not more important than plot – but somehow integral with plot.[1]

Similarly, to quote Henry James on this matter is not to ask that all literature be Jamesian; it is to insist that James fixes upon a crucial truth when he refuses to disjoin character from plot, when he asks 'What is character but the determination of incident? What is incident but the illustration of character?' ('The Art of Fiction', 1884). According to Webster's editor, F. L. Lucas, 'The first thing, then, in appreciating an Elizabethan like Webster is to be as cavalier about his plots as he was himself'. True, if *appreciating* means 'getting fun out of'; false, if *appreciating* means that higher kind of enjoyment which is inseparable from 'estimating at its due worth'.

Certainly we should not have a rigid idea of what constitutes improbability or inconsistency – it comes as a salutary shock when Professor William Empson remarks: 'Perhaps I am a bad judge of inconsistency, because it seems to me that few writers have dared to make people as eccentric as they really are'.[2] But the crucial difference in critical position is between those who think that considerations of probability will always be relevant to a play (that we cannot but compare the transactions on the stage with 'the transactions of the world', and that a good play creates its meaning from the similarity – and the dissimilarity – between the two), and those who think that probability can be beside the point, that the events in Tourneur's *The Atheist's Tragedy* are not *im*probable but *a*-probable. The shortcoming of the belief in the a-probability of the events and characters is that it makes it impossible for a play positively to

---

[1] *Selected Essays*, London, 1932, p 429.
[2] 'Honest in *Othello*' in Empson, *The Structure of Complex Words*, p 244.

exploit improbability, and equally impossible for it to gain praise for its probability. The point of *Measure for Measure* is not that such events happen in life, that there may be a Duke to hand who will fling out a safety net – but, on the contrary, that such events do *not* happen in life. The play throws us back upon real life with a keener sense of how remote our fantasies are from the facts of our life, a keener sense of how intractable (not how tractable, as they would appear if we were to suspend our belief about probability) are the problems of justice and mercy. In *Measure for Measure*, improbability is so much to the point as to constitute the medium of Shakespeare's meaning and insight. The events are far-fetched, and if they were home-grown they would mean something quite different, just as the point of Byron's rhymes begins in the fact that they are far-fetched, that they are rhymes which do not present themselves as inevitable or natural, but as contrived and improbable.

Byron's rhymes ('intellectual'/'hen-pecked you all') are comic, even when his subject matter is tragic. Clearly comedy differs from tragedy in its relationship to probability. We can praise *Volpone* or *The Alchemist* as a *tour de force*; we could use such a word of *King Lear* only if our intention were to dispraise the play. Much of our pleasure in comedy comes directly from our sense of the artist at work; though we enter into comedy, we do not enter into it in the same way as with tragedy (which is not to say that in tragedy we ever forget that we are in a theatre); in comedy, much of our attention is directly fixed upon the dramatist as well as upon his characters. The ingenious intrigues of the rogues in Jonson's or Middleton's comedies share our attention with the ingenious intrigues of the author, and some part of our pleasure (and of the comedy's meaning) begins in the breathless feeling of a juggler at work. How *is* the dramatist going to make sense of all this? How *will* he manage to unravel these situations which he seems to have ravelled almost too well? The situations of comedy, like the language of comedy, draw attention to themselves more directly than do those of tragedy. We relish the very unlikeliness of what happens – relish it, ponder it, and take it seriously; we are delighted that what is so improbable has been brought to pass (more a matter of 'has been brought to pass' than of 'has come to pass'). The word which threatens Jacobean tragedy – 'preposterous' – is the triumphant compliment to Jonson's comedies. It is therefore not surprising that defenders of, for instance, Tourneur's *The Revenger's Tragedy* have claimed that it is 'a tragic satire', and have postulated a likeness to Jonson's comedies (Revels, pp xxiii, xliv). There is indeed some likeness; but the critical argument would have to deal scrupulously with the question of artistic responsibility towards one's own enterprise. Jonson commits himself responsibly; does *The Revenger's Tragedy* vividly marry two modes, or does it keep shelving the responsibility on which it has embarked and reaching instead for another responsibility which more suits its moment's purpose?

Middleton's tragedies, as is well known, are more concerned not to breach probability. N. W. Bawcutt compares *The Changeling* with its source, John Reynolds's *The Triumphs of God's Revenge against Murther*:

It would not be unfair to Reynolds to say that his characters are mere puppets, moved about according to the demands of a heavily didactic theme. The dramatists [Middleton and Rowley] not only alter their attributes, making Alsemero a man of honour and integrity, and De Flores a repellent and ugly villain instead of a handsome young man; they create in them all the force and vividness and human plausibility which have given the play its reputation. In Reynolds morality is a purely external force, that waits for the characters to make a mistake and then strikes them down; in *The Changeling* it works through the characters, who are morally responsible for themselves, and are forced to experience intimately the consequences of their own actions.

(Revels, p xxxii)

One of the earliest literary comments on the play, that by Leigh Hunt in 1844, fastened upon this interdependence: 'There is one character of his (De Flores in *The Changeling*) which, for effect at once tragical, probable, and poetical, surpasses anything I know of in the drama of domestic life' (Revels, p xlv). The three epithets are mutually supporting – the effect is tragical and poetical because it is also probable.

'Tragical, probable, and poetical': the same is true of the great moment when Beatrice realizes what it is that De Flores is demanding as his reward for having killed Alonzo. Her cry is comic in its confusion, but the playwright does not ask us suddenly to shift into a world of comic criteria rather than tragic ones, since her cry is also tragic in its hideous moral confusion:

> Why, 'tis impossible thou canst be so wicked,
> Or shelter such a cunning cruelty,
> To make his death the murderer of my honour!
> Thy language is so bold and vicious,
> I cannot see which way I can forgive it
> With any modesty.

(III. iv. 120–5)

Swinburne praised this as 'wonderfully real in its artless and in-
genuous sincerity'; 'that note of incredulous amazement' succeeds
in giving 'a lurid streak of tragic humour to the lifelike interest of
the scene'. Not injured innocence but injured guilt, as when
Macbeth of all people complains that since he has no sons the
sceptre will be wrenched from him by an unlineal hand.

Swinburne was right, too, in praising one of the best scenes in
Middleton's *Women Beware Women* for 'the straightforward
ingenuity and the serious delicacy by which the action is rendered
credible and the situation endurable'.[1] Too nineteenth-century a
way to approach a Jacobean play? But Nathaniel Richards, who
contributed complimentary verses when the play was first published
in 1657, praised it so:

> hell-bred malice, strife
> Acted in state, presented to the life.

On this particular virtue of *Women Beware Women*, the critics have
concurred through the centuries; Hazlitt admired it for 'a rich
marrowy vein of internal sentiment, with fine occasional insight into
human nature, and cool cutting irony of expression'.[2] Likewise
T. S. Eliot: 'There is hardly anything truer in Elizabethan drama
than Bianca's gradual self-will and self-importance in consequence
of her courtship by the Duke'.

It may be retorted that the tragedies of Middleton do indeed
respect probability, but that all this means is that he was doing a
different kind of thing from dramatists such as Webster and
Tourneur. No doubt Middleton was, but the further question
remains: was his kind of drama different and superior? Was he wise
(and not just in terms of his own temperament and concerns) in
granting to probability the respect which so many of his contemporaries denied? Professor R. A. Foakes reminds us that the
world of *The Revenger's Tragedy* 'is made to seem grotesque,
perverted, even mad, and we do not ask for naturalistic character or
behaviour' (Revels, p xli). Agreed, we do not ask for them – but is
that simply because we have no hope of getting them, just as we
have no hope of getting them in Ian Fleming? That would be very
different from agreeing that 'naturalistic character or behaviour'
stands as no virtue in a play, or stands as some merely marginal

---

[1] Introduction to the Mermaid *Thomas Middleton*, London, 1877, pp xxxvi–xxxvii,
xxviii.

[2] W. C. Hazlitt, *Lectures on the Dramatic Literature of the Age of Elizabeth*, 1820.

virtue. Certainly Tourneur effects a special kind of achievement (its closest affinities being not perhaps with drama at all, but with the satires of Juvenal), and he does so by severing the world of the play from 'the transactions of the world'; but that severance itself drastically limits the size and nature of the artistic achievement. 'The action unfolds lust upon lust, death upon death, in a way that cannot be accepted on any ordinary level of credibility'. But what are these unspecified extraordinary levels which credibility can have? Professor Foakes maintains that the play ensures 'that we do not mistake what we see for an illusion of reality. An image of reality it is and, within the limitations which are also its strength, the play has great power' (Revels, p xliii). But this flourish is never converted into literary criticism of any specificity; the precise sense in which *The Revenger's Tragedy* may legitimately be said to be 'an image of reality' remains unspecified, and we are never told in what way the incredibilities of the play create and enforce artistic meaning. The same is true of Tourneur's *The Atheist's Tragedy* – 'so full of ludicrous and impossible incident', according to the Revels edition (p lvi), and yet with the relationship of its ludicrousness and impossibility to artistic worth and human insight never demonstrated. Instead, a critical rhetoric invariably takes over, and the problem is graciously waived.

William Archer deplored a scene in Webster's *The Duchess of Malfi*:

The ingenious Ferdinand draws a curtain and shows the Duchess wax figures of Antonio and their son, apparently lying dead. She takes them for reality and makes ‹no move to approach them, replacing by rhetoric the instinctive action of a loving woman, which could not have failed to discover the fraud. In any case, indeed, its success is a monstrous improbability. It would have been infinitely easier, safer and more dramatic to have lied to her in words. This waxen lie is the device of a dramatist in search of crude physical horrors.[1]

What magnifies the improbability here is an audacity characteristic of Webster even in his absurdity: the audacity of having the Duchess, only eight lines after being shown 'this sad spectacle', actually speak of wax:

> it wastes me more
> Than were't my picture, fashion'd out of wax...
>
> (IV. i. 62–3)

[1] W. Archer, *The Old Drama and the New*, London, 1923, pp 57–8.

Is it fate or contrivance which gives the Duchess those ironical words?

This episode perturbed even F. L. Lucas, and John Russell Brown has undertaken to defend the scene (Act IV Scene i) with its stage-direction 'Here is discovered, behind a traverse, the artificial figures of Antonio and his children, appearing as if they were dead':

Lucas (2nd ed.) argued that only the elder son who rode off with Antonio should be shown: the duchess would not leave instructions for their care (IV. ii. 203–5) if she thought they were dead, and 'why should an avaricious Duke go to the cost and trouble of wax corpses for two children who were in a few minutes to be real ones?' But common sense is not a true measure for such a scene in a play (or in life); the stage-direction is probably authorial and we may suppose that Webster aimed at a maximum horror and cruelty. There may be dramatic point in the duchess reacting only to 'it' (lines 62–63) and 'that . . . trunk' (line 68) as if she saw Antonio only; and there may be more pathos if she forgets that she has seen her children dead when she remembers them before her own death.

(Revels, pp 110–11)

But what is the uncommon sense which can vindicate in this episode what common sense repudiates? There are artistically irresponsible ways of gaining 'a maximum horror and cruelty'. Mr Brown's closing sentence alludes to the Duchess's thought for her children just before she is murdered:

> I pray thee, look thou giv'st my little boy
> Some syrup for his cold, and let the girl
> Say her prayers, ere she sleep.

(IV. ii. 203–5)

There are two quite different, and quite incompatible, ways of responding to this apparent inconsistency. On the one hand, we can repudiate 'common sense', as Mr Brown seems at first to wish, and as Mr Irving Ribner insists: 'The inconsistency here, since she believes her children to be dead, has bothered critics, but Webster abandons logic for this striking emphasis upon his dying heroine as the creator and preserver of life'.[1] (The inconsistency has, of course, nothing to do with *logic*, but Mr Ribner finds the word useful for its suggestion of a rigour of a coldly sterile kind inappropriate to art.) To this point of view, the retort would be that there is something botched about a drama in which such a 'striking emphasis' can be achieved only by demanding that the audience forget the facts which it has recently been shown.

[1] *Jacobean Tragedy*, London, 1962, p 117.

Or, on the other hand, we can say that the apparent inconsistency is no inconsistency, but a psychological point about the Duchess on the brink of her death. Mr Brown does not seem eager to embrace such an explanation ('there may be more pathos . . .'), but he is prepared to flirt with it. His adoption of both of these (incompatible) positions lends him an air very common in literary critics of these plays – the air of a barrister insisting both that his client did not do it, and that his client did it in self-defence.[1] But what if we adopt the suggestion that the Duchess later forgets that her children are dead? Pathos, indeed, but at what cost? At the cost of blurring the single-minded unflinching gaze with which the Duchess meets her death: 'I am Duchess of Malfi still' (IV. ii. 142). Her clear-eyed courage is exactly what the critics have praised in her – and in Webster – in this scene. But she would not be Duchess of Malfi still, if her sense of her tragic predicament were now so shattered that she could no longer face the fact that her children – whom she had been shown dead – were dead. Given the other 'irreducible contradictions' in the plot (Revels, p lv), is it not more likely that Webster was simply – but irresponsibly – hoping that nobody would notice?

'Whole scenes are linked together, behind the dialogue, as if in a diagram': those are the terms in which Mr Brown praises the ironies and contrasts of *The Duchess of Malfi*'s structure (Revels, p xlii). But *diagram* is a disconcerting word, suggesting as it does an art which may be diagrammatic, too imperiously overriding the human contingency of plot and character. Can a diagram move us as a painting does? When Charlemont in *The Atheist's Tragedy* (III. ii. 35–6) exclaims, to the ghost who urges revenge,

> You torture me between the passion of
> My blood and the religion of my soul,

the point remains merely diagrammatic (as it does not in *Hamlet*) because Charlemont does not sufficiently exist as a person, does not sufficiently possess a soul, for there to be any substance to the cry that he is tortured.

The wicked plotters continually praise their intrigues for their ingenuity: "Twas somewhat witty carried, though we say it' (Vindice in *The Revenger's Tragedy*, V. iii. 97); 'I would have our plot be

---

[1] Mr Brown elsewhere has some excellent defences, on grounds of psychological truth, for what might at first seem contradictions or improbabilities; e.g. Revels, pp 67–8 (Ferdinand's long delay), and p 132 (Ferdinand and the 'treasure').

ingenious' (Lodovico in Webster's *The White Devil*, V. i. 75). Such plotting hopes that a similar praise may accrue to the dramatist's plot. But the plot seldom rises to what D'Amville, relishing his murder of Montferrers, knew were the essential virtues of the plotting – his words indict all that in the plot which is 'forced or done on purpose':

> Ay, mark the plot. Not any circumstance
> That stood within the reach of the design
> Of persons, dispositions, matter, time,
> Or place, but by this brain of mine was made
> An instrumental help, yet nothing from
> Th' induction to th' accomplishment seem'd forc'd
> Or done o' purpose, but by accident.
>
> (II. iv. 103–9)

When, by calamitous mistake, Bosola kills Antonio in *The Duchess of Malfi*, he accuses fate:

> Antonio!
> The man I would have sav'd 'bove mine own life!
> We are merely the stars' tennis-balls, struck and banded
> Which way please them –
>
> (V. iv. 52–5)

But it needs something more than the dramatist's *fiat* to make such an accusation telling; about the whole episode there hangs the unexalted suspicion that the characters (and the audience) are not the stars' tennis-balls but Webster's – struck and banded which way please him.

There have always been problems, too, with that other manifestation of fate: poetic justice, which is a harder notion to make effective in a play than neo-classical critics acknowledged. Pedro in *The White Devil* gloatingly anticipates Bracciano's death:

> He could not have invented his own ruin,
> Had he despair'd, with more propriety.
>
> (V. i. 66–7)

But can there not be too much propriety? The effect depends upon our feeling that Bracciano is fatally playing into the conspirators' hands, not into Webster's hands.

In *Macbeth*, Duncan expresses to Lady Macbeth his gratitude for Macbeth's swift journeying home:

> And his great love (sharp as his spur) hath holp him
> To his home before us.
>
> (1. 6. 23–4)

Thirty lines later, Macbeth bares that spur:

> I have no spur
> To prick the sides of my intent, but only
> Vaulting ambition . . .
>
> (1. 7. 25–7)

Macbeth's 'love' is indeed as 'sharp as his spur', his spur ambition – and how the word *sharp* then catches the light! Yet the power of the cross-connection is inseperable from the conviction that Shakespeare has not merely put words into the mouths of Duncan and Macbeth in order that they may repay him with a significant reverberation. Significance in any worthwhile case is a double relationship: not just between *a* and *b*, but between both *a* and *b* and all the context of the non-significant (not insignificant) which authenticates such utterances or moments at all. For what could be more natural, what could be less susceptible to the suspicion that Shakespeare is obtrusively at work laying the ground for a significance thirty lines later, than Duncan's royal courtesy to Lady Macbeth?

> Where's the thane of Cawdor?
> We coursed him at the heels, and had a purpose
> To be his purveyor: but he rides well,
> And his great love (sharp as his spur) hath holp him
> To his home before us.
>
> (1. 6. 20–4)

Duncan's compliment would not be gracious and grateful if it were forced; Duncan's words compliment Macbeth's own apparent compliment in hastening home, and they are words which are rooted in a convincing ceremoniousness and aptness. And what again could be more natural than that Macbeth should recollect his spur? He had a metal spur which could hasten him home, but now what? His unease finds a self-lacerating form of words (he rides himself to destruction). His words follow hard upon his unmetaphorical riding, and then they evolve with compelling naturalness from his terrible imagining:

> Besides, this Duncan
> Hath borne his faculties so meek, hath been
> So clear in his great office, that his virtues
> Will plead like angels, trumpet-tongued, against
> The deep damnation of his taking-off:
> And pity, like a naked new-born babe,
> Striding the blast, or, Heaven's cherubim, horsed
> Upon the sightless couriers of the air,
> Shall blow the horrid deed in every eye,
> That tears shall drown the wind. I have no spur
> To prick the sides of my intent, but only
> Vaulting ambition, which o'erleaps itself,
> And falls on th' other.
>
> (1. 7. 16–28)

So that the artistic worth of the cross-connection (from *spur* to *spur*) cannot validly be detached from considerations as to the authenticity of each of the moments that then connect. Joseph Warton put the general point excellently when he said in 1753: 'Shakespeare seems to be the only poet who possesses the power of uniting poetry with propriety of character'. Significance – whether it is that of imagery, themes, or symbols – raises itself above a diagrammatic point-making only when it is in a true relationship with all those other important ways in which literature works upon us, ways which are non-significant but which must marry with significance if either is to release its potentialities. This is why much of the ubiquitous praise of the imagery of Webster or Tourneur is not as it stands cogent:

Poison was associated especially with the Machiavellian 'politician', and therefore the fact that Brachiano is often called 'poisonous' is significant. Cornelia says he blights like a mildew (*White Devil*, I. ii. 272) and his wife hopes to

> Charm his poison, force it to obeying
> And keep him chaste from an infected straying.
>
> (II. i. 17–18)

It is therefore appropriate that he should die by poison since it was 'his art'. (Bradbrook, *Themes and Conventions*, p 191)

But it is the easiest thing in the world for a dramatist to ensure that one of his characters is often called 'poisonous': in itself, this does not create anything 'significant'. The same goes for 'It is therefore appropriate . . .': any writer can make up events which are appropriate to his characters – but everything turns on how such appropriateness is achieved, whether it is factitious and fabricated or authentic. Appropriate it certainly is that Sir Clifford Chatterley, in *Lady Chatterley's Lover*, should be paralysed; but because of the way in which this appropriateness is achieved, this becomes not the virtue of the book but the book's grave flaw. As Dr Leavis has drily said, 'Sir Clifford's paralysis, so usefully symbolic to exegetes and experts, is not altogether a felicity'.[1]

So that to praise Webster in those terms is like praising one curve of an arch: the praise will not be worth much unless the other curve (supporting and supported) is also true. Granted, Professor Bradbrook's study was a pioneering one; she was opening up many new ways of exploring imagery in Jacobean tragedy. But unfortunately it has been too easy for subsequent critics to elaborate descriptions rather than to further inquiry. It has been too easy to write as if it were inherently valuable for a play to have a comprehensive web of imagery, as if imagery were a self-validating artistry. Repeatedly our attention is drawn to a fine pattern, and then repeatedly our attention is not drawn to the question of the value of such a pattern – which is inescapably a question as to the relationship between the pattern and those other things in the work which are not pattern (such as justness of plot, accuracy of observation).

Hereward T. Price makes his case in mapping 'The Function of Imagery in Webster',[2] but the case which he makes does not – cannot, given the terms in which it is conducted, given the emphasis given to 'Function' – go much beyond establishing that Webster's plays include a great deal of linked imagery. 'The relentless repetition of the same kind of figure, the heaping up of the same words, time and again, cannot be accidental'. But what is not accidental in a work of literature is not necessarily good (indeed, it may be so little accidental, so coercively willed, as to be bad); and there are bad as well as good artistic ways of being 'relentless'. A critic who is going to get anywhere further with the subject of Webster's imagery is going to have to be engaged in an irreducibly twofold task: he cannot peel off the facts about frequency and function from the other considerations as to how the dramatist achieves such frequency and such function.

It is true that Mr Price is concerned to show the relationship

[1] *Anna Karenina and Other Essays*, London, 1967, p 238.

[2] *PMLA*, lxx, 1955, 717–39. A stronger and more vivid argument as to 'the function of imagery in the poetic drama' had been put by Alan S. Downer, 'The Life of Our Design', *Hudson Review*, ii, 1949, pp 242–60.

between the play's images and its events, between 'figure in action and figure in word': John Russell Brown acknowledges a debt to him in observing that 'Conjuring, poison, disguises and dissimulation are not only images, but recurrent episodes in the very action' of *The White Devil* (Revels, p li). But this in itself is to shift the critical question back a stage: the images are perhaps more than merely foisted images since they are corroborated by or engrained in the events of the play – but at that point we face, inevitably, the question of the events in the play, and whether Webster has not so ordered his dramatic universe that he may all too easily call up any events he pleases. Macbeth's *spur* is certainly authenticated by an event of the play, his hurried riding; but does the poisoning or the conjuring in *The White Devil* then possess an authenticity of event comparable to that of the riding in *Macbeth*? That is not a rhetorical question, and it may be that it can be answered to Webster's credit; the crucial point initially is not whether the question can be answered by an admirer of Webster, but whether it would have to be if the high praise accorded to Webster's imagery were to mean much.

R. A. Foakes has charted the imagery and the key-words of *The Revenger's Tragedy*. Yet in his summary, a single conjunction, *but*, seems to me to point firmly in the wrong direction:

The characters are, of course, more than personifications, as having feelings and intelligence, being able to plan and intrigue, so that their behaviour is not fully predictable; *but* [my italics] there is a potent relationship between the way they are conceived and the range of personifications in the dialogue.

(Revels, p xxxvi)

But insofar as the relationship between character and dialogue is indeed 'potent' in *The Revenger's Tragedy*, that will be due to the very fact which *but* tries to set aside: that the characters are 'more than personifications'. Professor Foakes's *but* implies 'and yet all the same', whereas the conjunction needed is *and so*. Character-personifications are precisely what cannot validate (or make potent) dialogue-personifications – whereas characters can. Which is why the personifications in Vindice's speeches ('Advance thee, O thou terror to fat folks . . .', I. i. 45) are much more – not equally or less – 'potent' than those in, say, Lussurioso's speeches.

Similarly, Irving Ribner's praise of the imagery in *The Atheist's Tragedy* meets some of the objections to which imagery may be liable (that it is functionless, for example), but it ignores the legitimate objection which may be invoked from the opposite flank (that it is nothing but function, for example). 'The building imagery ... is closely integrated with the play's structure and moral argument' (Revels, p lviii): agreed, but how is the integration achieved, and what does such integration amount to? What saves the integration from being merely an unstrenuous collusion? 'We are not struck by a random piling of image upon image, with a rich profusion of sensory impressions. There is, rather, a logical movement from image to image in which each succeeds the former in a proper order' (p lx). But there is an equally bad alternative to the random: the coercive. *Logical, proper*: what do such words mean in drama when they are divorced from considerations of plot and character? Should not a play more resemble exposition than imposition? Function, yes; it is good advice to anything in a play that we should urge 'Don't just stand there, do something'. But Kenneth Tynan has quoted the opposite injunction which some actors need: 'Don't just do something, stand there'. Fuss, fidget, function. Like the actors, the images (and the themes and the symbols) must not just do something, they must stand there.

Dr Johnson, pondering *Samson Agonistes*, decided that 'Milton would not have excelled in dramatic writing: he knew human nature only in the gross, and had never studied the shades of character, nor the combinations of concurring, or the perplexity of contending, passions'. Johnson is, in my view, absolutely right in making 'the shades of character' indispensable to excellence in drama. But his words may also remind us ('he knew human nature only in the gross') that there is such a thing as a generalized psychology in literature, a knowledge of how people behave which is not identical with the evocation of a fully characterized individual and his behaviour. (Johnson's *Rasselas* is itself a supreme instance of a generalized psychology.) The knowledge of 'human nature in the gross' may also work to authenticate the patterns woven by a play. In *The Changeling*, De Flores has his obsessive turns of speech; the words *act* and *deed*, which for him so indispensably compact his murderous act and the sexual act which will be his reward, recur as the essence of his character, of his need for sardonic *double-entendre* and his unsentimental lucidity as to the inescapable relationships of person to person and of act to consequence. He is rebuffed but can menacingly bide his time.

BEATRICE:    I would not hear so much offence again
             For such another deed.
DE FLORES:                      Soft, lady, soft;
             The last is not yet paid for! Oh, this act
             Has put me into spirit!

                                        (III. iv. 104–7)

That clinging sexual pun on 'spirit' is true to De Flores the individual; and it is true to a generalized psychology of the relationship
between murderous violence and lust. De Flores had been sexually
excited at the prospect of murdering Alonzo, and he is sexually
excited after he has committed the murder. So that the elaborate
patterning of words like *blood* (murder and lust), *act* and *deed* in *The
Changeling* does not ask to be valued for itself alone, but for its
relationship both to an individual psychology and to a general one.
Middleton's insight here exists in the same realm as D. H.
Lawrence's in *Kangaroo*:

He turned round to Somers, and the strangest grin in the world was on his
face, all the lines curved upwards.

'Tell you what, boy,' he said in a hoarse whisper, 'I settled *three* of 'em –
three!' There was an indescribable gloating joy in his tones, like a man
telling of the good time he has had with a strange mistress – 'Gawr, but I
was lucky. I got one of them iron bars from the windows, and I stirred the
brains of a couple of them with it, and I broke the neck of a third. Why it
was as good as a sword to defend yourself with, see –'

He reached his face towards Somers with weird, gruesome exultation,
and continued in a hoarse, secret voice:

'Cripes, there's *nothing* bucks you up sometimes like killing a man –
*nothing*. You feel a perfect *angel* after it.'

Richard felt the same torn feeling in his abdomen, and his eyes watched
the other man.

'When it comes over you, you know, there's nothing else like it. *I* never
knew, till the war. And I wouldn't believe it then, not for many a while. But
it's *there*. Cripes, it's there right enough. Having a woman's something, isn't
it? But it's a flea-bite, nothing, compared to killing your man when your
blood comes up.'

And his eyes glowed with exultant satisfaction.

'And the best of it is,' he said, 'you feel a perfect *angel* after it. You don't
feel you've done any harm. Feel as gentle as a lamb all round. I can go to
Victoria, now, and be as gentle –' He jerked his head in the direction of
Victoria's room. 'And you bet she'll like me.'

His eyes glowed with a sort of exaltation.

'Killing's natural to a man, you know,' he said. 'It is just as natural as
lying with a woman. Don't you think?'

And still Richard did not answer.

(Chapter XVI)

What matters about theatrical conventions is the same as that about all historical information: that we are liable to miss the point if we are unaware of certain things which the playwright and his audience shared and which they legitimately agreed not to re-create from scratch on every single occasion. Perhaps allusions and references. Perhaps a convention, defined by Professor Bradbrook as 'an agreement between writers and readers, whereby the artist is allowed to limit and simplify his material in order to secure greater concentration through a control of the distribution of emphasis' (*Themes and Conventions of Elizabethan Tragedy*, p 4). This ought to be straightforward enough, and so it is, provided we steer straight forward and don't get sucked towards the whirlpool Charybdis or the rock Scylla. Charybdis is the critic's danger, the danger of being too inflexibly rooted in our own century and too indifferent to the age in which the work was created. Ignorance can minister to arrogance − 'Whatever is, is right', and if the works of the past aren't what we now expect, so much the worse for them. As if one of the supreme values of past literature might not precisely be as an urgent reminder of what a past age truly knew but our age seems to have forgotten. Yet there is the opposite danger, the scholar's Scylla: the danger of being too rooted in an earlier age, too indifferent to our own age and to the possibility that in certain respects it may be our age which more truly sees what is the case. The scholar's antiquarianism and pedantry rest upon an exorbitant humility: 'Whatever was, was right' (great scholars are usually implacable conservatives); if that is how they used to write, then it's up to us to enjoy and admire it.

What the scholar and the critic have to do is demonstrate that some of the dead are not dead but alive. This is a very different thing from bringing the dead to life, a feat for which the price is too high, as Robert Graves observed:

> To bring the dead to life
> Is no great magic . . .
>
> So grant him life, but reckon
> That the grave which housed him
> May not be empty now:
> You in his spotted garments
> Shall yourself lie wrapped.

Thomas Churchyard lives! – but Professor X, who says so, lies wrapped in spotted garments.

William Archer, friend of Shaw and translator of Ibsen, steered too near Charybdis. *The Old Drama and the New* attacked Elizabethan and Jacobean drama very intelligently, but is marred by a refusal to permit any conventions at all. The aside is swept aside as incorrigibly improbable, and Archer will not grant that, if sensitively handled, it can be effectively compact – and not just as trickery. Archer, in other words, refuses to allow for 'an agreement between writers and readers'. On the other hand, many apologists steer too far from this, and seem willing to accept any use of the aside as satisfactory just because the aside is an ancient practice. Hence cross-purposes, with the critic complaining that a particular moment in a play is inane, and the scholar retorting 'What do you mean, it's inane? – it's a convention'. A. E. Housman once pointed out that some textual arguments unhelpfully couch themselves in the form 'Which weighs most, a tall man or a fat man?', in which the right considerations have got generalized into the wrong question. But the argument needs to be reconstructed so that 'It's a convention' is not offered, absurdly, as an answer to 'It's inane', but is offered as where an answer may in a particular case appropriately begin. Of the two different kinds of liberty taken with ordinary handwriting, it is short-hand, not forgery, which should epitomize the convention.

The agreement must be fair, and not rigged in order to make things easy for the writer, who can then sit back and let his audience do all the work – or, equally unsatisfactory, let it do no work. Some of the worst things in Elizabethan and Jacobean drama are the result of irresponsible agreements. When author and audience agreed – as they seem sometimes to have done – that there was no need for any motivation on occasions when women are temptingly whispered to and fall, they were being lazy. The best dramatists (and Shakespeare above all) maintained a bracing rigour in the use of conventions, and didn't relax as writers because the audience, for its part, was – like all other audiences – only too willing to relax.

In Thomas Heywood's *A Woman Killed with Kindness* (acted 1603), Mrs Frankford welcomes her husband's friend Wendoll, who turns aside and mutters about how wicked he is for being about to try her:

> [*Aside*] Give me a name, you whose infectious tongues
> Are tipp'd with gall and poison; as you would
> Think on a man that had your father slain,
> Murd'red your children, made your wives base strumpets,
> So call me, call me so! Print in my face
> The most stigmatic title of a villain,
> For hatching treason to so true a friend.
>
> (Scene VI, 81-7)

This is so unconvincingly handled that the aside shrinks, as T. S. Eliot said, from being a convention to being a subterfuge: 'It is not Heywood who assumes that asides are inaudible, it is Mrs Frankford who *pretends* not to hear Wendoll'.[1] For the fact is that Wendoll's self-reproaches don't reveal anything about his character (and so cannot be more than cumbrous signposts) for the simple reason that in the play Wendoll has no character to reveal. It is the dramatist, not the character, who speaks, surreptitiously asking us please to translate first-person speech into the third person: Wendoll will 'injure himself, wrong her, deceive Frankford's trust'. The aside here is no more than a way of simultaneously evading the responsibilities both of first-person and third-person speech, while under the necessity of urging the audience to attend to that which it might be forgiven for not noticing: the purported importance of what is happening.

The maladroit use of the aside makes the effect faintly comic:

> Speak I must –
> Injure myself, wrong her, deceive his trust –

it sounds like the incident in the Bernstein and Wilbur musical of Voltaire's *Candide*, when the Governor deliberately sends Candide to sea in a sinking boat, and then reproaches his own villainy in some Jacobean asides:

> Oh but I'm bad, oh but I'm bad,
> Playing such a very dirty trick on such a fine lad.
> I'm a low cad, I'm a low cad,
> Every time I do this sort of thing it makes me so sad,
> Ever so sad,
> Oh but I'm bad . . .

What level of artistic skill is represented by having D'Amville in *The Atheist's Tragedy* (III. iv. 32) turn aside with the words: 'I must

---

[1] 'Four Elizabethan Dramatists', 1924; *Selected Essays*, p 112.

temporize'? The implication of using the aside so blankly is that otherwise the audience could not be relied upon to realize that D'Amville *is* temporizing. But how grossly uncomprehending would not an audience have to be, to fail to take the point unassisted? And how feeble would the dramatist's command over D'Amville's idiom have to be, if unable to convey through that idiom that D'Amville is temporizing? Flamineo in *The White Devil* (III. i. 30–1) lets us know that 'I do put on this feigned garb of mirth/To gull suspicion'. But who is being gulled by such art? Would not Flamineo's 'feigned garb', within an art of any subtlety, be evident enough?

The artistic justification of an aside will be that it achieves what otherwise could not have been so satisfactorily achieved. Yet when Supervacuo in *The Revenger's Tragedy* (III. vi. 35) greets 'the yet bleeding head' of his brother, with the aside 'Ha, ha, excellent!', can it be maintained that an audience would otherwise be unaware of how Supervacuo is inwardly reacting? Is the case not rather that the dramatist makes Supervacuo say 'Ha, ha, excellent!' only so that the smile can unmistakably (not subtly) be wiped off his face a moment later when he finds the head is that of the wrong.brother? (Foiled again . . .) Too often the aside is crassly superfluous in psychological terms, and equally often it is nothing but a plot-reminder. When Lussurioso rails at

> that slave-pander,
> Piato, whom we threatened last
> With irons in perpetual prisonment,
> (IV. ii. 128–30)

it may be prudent of Tourneur thus to make Vindice remind the audience about all the disguisings (*Aside*: 'All this is I'), but it is a prudence which is artistically demeaning, betraying an uneasiness about the plot and yet placating it rather than rectifying it.

As with the character and plot, so with significance, the aside being often no more than a crude underlining of that which hardly stands in need of any further underlining.

LUSSURIOSO:    He has been cold and stiff, who knows how long?
VINDICE: [*Aside*]  Marry, that do I!

> (V. i. 72–3)

Would the irony of Vindice's sentiment be any less accessible to us if unspoken? Yet who would argue that, given the kind of characterization accorded to Vindice, any genuine point about Vindice's own character was being made in that aside? After so many mechanical asides, one cannot but feel grateful for Spurio's un-spurious grotesquerie (*Aside*: 'Old dad dead?', V. i. 115,) and even more grateful when an aside by Vindice is a genuine distillation:

LUSSURIOSO: Where be those two that did affirm to us
My lord the duke was privately rid forth?
FIRST NOBLE: O, pardon us, my lords; he gave that charge
Upon our lives, if he were miss'd at court,
To answer so. He rode not anywhere;
We left him private with that fellow here.
VINDICE: [*Aside*] Confirm'd.

(V. i. 119–25)

An aside which earns its keep; in the words of the Revels edition, 'Vindice is congratulating himself on the success of his plot to make others appear guilty of the duke's murder, and the word carries two meanings, both "True enough" (i.e., I can corroborate that) and "My innocence is confirmed"'. A cut above the usual aside in *The Revenger's Tragedy*, the one which is always yet another periphrasis for 'I gloat'.

At its worst, the effect of the aside is like sitting next to an eager point-taker who keeps nudging you in the ribs. We have heard much about how quick and sensitive was an Elizabethan or Jacobean audience to verbal effects and to wordplay, yet the dramatists' frequent wish to nail down an ironical pun with an aside would suggest a certain uneasiness. The Duchess of Malfi, preg-nant, speaks of being 'so troubled with the mother' (that is, hysteria – II. i. 117): is the pun then sharpened or is it blunted by having Bosola at once say, aside, 'I fear too much'? *Too much*, the audience may echo, anticipating the echo scene ('Shall I never see her more?' '*Never see her more*', V. iii. 42). All that such an aside does is threaten the naturalness of the dialogue. It is one thing for the Duchess to be drawn persistently to *double-entendre* (she is both fearful and happy in her fear: 'you'll say/Love mix'd with fear is sweetest', III, ii. 65–6); the combination of 'Freudian' impulse with timidity and in-genuous audacity is psychologically true, a kind of flirting:

This green fruit and my stomach are not friends –
How they swell me!

(II. i. 154–5)

But to have Bosola at once cap this with an aside ('Nay, you are too much swell'd already') is for the dramatist to set a momentary flick above any stable respect for his own creation. Such an aside cannot but suggest that the Duchess has had the words put into her mouth in order to suit Webster's immediate ironic convenience. The effect is demeaning, as all pat effects must be. The true aside will not be a pointing hand in the margin – it will be a hand that newly grasps something.

JULIA:   You will mar me with commendation,
     Put yourself to the charge of courting me
     Whereas now I woo you.
BOSOLA: [*Aside*] I have it, I will work upon this creature –
    [*To her*] Let us grow most amorously familiar . . .

            (*Duchess of Malfi*, V. ii. 181–5)

Bosola there clenches together his lust and his plot, with a pun on 'work upon' and with 'creature' both amatory and manipulable (in the sense of 'instrument'). So that the aside here acts as an advance and not just as a needless retrospection.

Within the plays of Webster and Tourneur, then, the same convention can be found abused or used. Any convention will constitute a standing temptation, and must sometimes dwindle into too palpable a convenience. It is in Middleton, and particularly in *The Changeling*, that the aside is artistically vindicated. Its two powers in Act II Scene ii have been distinguished by N. W. Bawcutt:

One is to reveal the effect and inner significance of each remark with an intimacy and fullness of detail that we might otherwise expect only from a novelist. The other is to show in varying degrees the extent to which the characters are isolated from each other, withdrawn into a private world of reverie and preoccupation.

            (Revels, p xlix)

Here the artistic validity of the aside is inseparable from the psychological and moral analysis which is the tissue of the play. Unlike wicked Wendoll in *A Woman Killed with Kindness*, De Flores has a character with which his asides can be in a relation. In Act II Scene ii of *The Changeling*, the self-contained egotisms of De Flores and of Beatrice both create the asides and are created by them; each egotism thinks only of its own wishes, and makes only as much contact with the other as will further its own plans. The convention vindicates, and is vindicated by, the psychological portrayal: Beatrice and De Flores do talk to each other without for a moment sacrificing their isolation, and because they exist as characters the aside can be a legitimate epitome of this lack of contact, this tragi-comic misunderstanding.

The artistic effectiveness of a convention (which is not the same as its 'having an effect') cannot be detached from considerations of character, and it is therefore not surprising that as Middleton's villain (asides and all) is a greater achievement than Heywood's, so Shakespeare's (asides and all) is a greater achievement than Middleton's. Iago does not permit himself many asides – that may make them all the more telling. Soliloquies, yes (because – despite what the literary historians may say about the 'frank artificiality' of both the aside and the soliloquy – soliloquies cannot but feel safer?). Shakespeare finely exploits the hinterland that lies between the aside and the soliloquy, as when Iago ends Act 5 Scene 1:

> Emilia, run you to the citadel,
> And tell my lord and lady what hath happed.
> Will you go on afore? [*aside*] This is the night
> That either makes me or fordoes me quite.

If Emilia has already left, those last words show Iago soliloquizing; if not, he has an aside. Shakespeare compresses the advantages of both, presenting Iago as at once furtive and isolated.

There is a similar skill, gaining the advantages of the aside without incurring what can be its grosser improbabilities, when Iago gloats over Othello's body after Othello's fit:

> Work on,
> My medicine, work! Thus credulous fools are caught;
> And many worthy and chaste dames even thus,
> All guiltless, meet reproach. What, ho! my lord!
> My lord, I say! Othello! ...

$$(4. 1. 44–8)$$

This has all the gloating active immediacy of an aside – Othello is before our eyes, and we see the hideous effects of Iago's 'medicine' even while he caresses his success and looks down upon his victim-patient. Two men are present, not one – to that extent, it is not a soliloquy. But because Othello is unconscious, Iago's words are in effect spoken alone: they do not seem to have as much risk as an aside, although – since Othello will come round at any moment – they have enough risk to spice Iago's pleasure. Iago gloats, but his aside is not reducible to 'I gloat'.

One of the very few moments in *Othello* when Iago indulges in a full-blooded aside is when Othello and Desdemona are safely reunited in Cyprus after the perilous crossing:

OTHELLO:    I cannot speak enough of this content:
        It stops me here; it is too much of joy.
        And this, and this, the greatest discords be
                                    *[they kiss]*
        That e'er our hearts shall make!
IAGO: [*Aside*]             O, you are well tuned now!
        But I'll set down the pegs that make this music,
        As honest as I am.
OTHELLO:                Come, let's to the castle.
        News, friends: our wars are done; the Turks
                      are drowned . . . (2. 1. 193–9)[1]

Why does this outdo Heywood and even Middleton? First, because of the moment: Iago speaks when Othello and Desdemona are rapt, embracing, and – one might say – lost to the world; and this matters not just because it lends to the aside a tinge of naturalness (how could lovers possibly have ears for anyone else at such a moment of reunion?), but also because it is apt to Iago. In the ordinary way, he does not permit himself the luxury of an aside – what then goads him into it here? The sight of Othello and Desdemona embracing. Just such a sight was likewise to cause Milton's Satan to break into a bitter aside, when he saw Adam and Eve 'Imparadis't in one anothers arms': 'Sight hateful, sight tormenting! . . .' (*Paradise Lost*, iv. 505).

The second source of Shakespeare's power here is the way in which Iago takes up the music of which Othello had spoken, though of course perverting it from romanticism to cynicism, from 'the greatest discords be' to 'I'll set down the pegs that make this music'. What this creates is not reducible to patterning (though 'the Othello music', in G. Wilson Knight's words, does indeed pattern the play), but is as importantly a matter of naturalness. Since it takes up and distorts Othello's way of speaking, the aside gathers some of the natural reciprocity, the give and take, of dialogue. Yet no audience could predict the precise terms of Iago's aside, whereas Bosola's worst asides come lumbering into sight long before they are uttered. The naturalness of the moment in *Othello*, then, concurs with the naturalness that continues (with taut but conversational relish) the musical metaphor. Shakespeare adds a further unobtrusive skill, one that subtly increases our sense of the naturalness with which he is using the convention: Iago's aside is, as it were, embedded in the middle of a line spoken by Othello, and it does not disturb the run

---

[1] The lines are given with the Quarto lineation, not the Folio lineation followed by the Cambridge Shakespeare.

of Othello's speaking.[1] It really is an aside, and not heard by the others – if you simply ignore the aside, you are left with a line of Othello's verse: 'That e'er our hearts shall make! Come let's to the castle'. Not that we need to notice, consciously, this seamless skill when the lines are spoken in the theatre – the effect will make its point (a naturalistic one) without our being aware of it. Othello takes up his words where he had broken off, and this cannot but reinforce the impression that he has not heard what Iago has purred. The aside, like any other convention, can release artistic energies, but it cannot guarantee them nor can it circumscribe them in advance.

Similar discriminations have still to be made when we move from conventions of speech to those of plot and character. Take one of the most famous, and potentially most grotesque: the substitution of one woman for another in bed without the man's realizing. It is patently a device which lends itself to sensationalism and brutality, and we ought not to follow Professor Bradbrook into receiving it with an invariable equanimity: 'Such old tricks as the substitution of one woman for another (which Shakespeare used twice) had no moral valency at all' (p 60). One can't help expecting some sort of adverse comment when one gets to the end of that sentence – but there is none, nor is there anything else said about this convention or 'trick'. Now if it were true that the convention was used completely without moral valency, this would hardly seem to argue that the art of the Elizabethan and Jacobean dramatists was a sensitive art. Are we being asked to accept that such a convention – one which totally removes moral meaning from sexual intercourse – is simply to be accepted and endorsed because such was the playwrights' practice? If the playwrights really did use this convention in such a way, then this explains, not why there are some great plays, but why most Elizabethan and Jacobean drama is crude stuff.

But the fact is that they did not always use this convention without any moral valency. For one thing, there is *The Changeling*. Beatrice has had Alonzo murdered by De Flores so that she can marry her new passion Alsemero; but blackmail by De Flores makes him her bedfellow; and so when the wedding night comes, she must lose the prize for which she played. In terror that Alsemero will

---

[1] For an interesting, though disputed, discussion of asides and line-division, see R. Flatter, *Shakespeare's Producing Hand*, New York, 1948. R. A. Foakes discusses Tourneur's way with interjected cries, à propos the text of *The Revenger's Tragedy* (Revels, p lxi); his observations have an implicit critical relevance, since Tourneur's handling of the lineation makes its point about such cries and other characters' response to them.

discover that she has lost her virginity, she bribes her willing maid Diaphanta to sleep with Alsemero. Professor Helen Gardner has compared Beatrice's empty success with that enjoyed by Macbeth:

In the centre of *Macbeth* we have the banquet, the concrete image of a hollow kingship; in the centre of *The Changeling* is the marriage that is no marriage . . . She too has given away her 'eternal jewel' and got nothing in exchange.[1]

What we have in *The Changeling* is a use of this convention for psychological and moral purposes; in effecting something important (though certainly imperfect – the comparison with *Macbeth* cannot but enforce a sense of the extent to which, in comparison, the episode in *The Changeling* invites the damaging word 'trick') by means of the convention, *The Changeling* cannot but constitute a criticism of those plays for which the convention is vacantly convenient. Not that Professor Bradbrook's wording ('which Shakespeare used twice') does justice to *Measure for Measure*, a play which carries its inquiry into the very nature of 'moral valency' to the point of an exacerbated perplexity.[2] The substitution of Mariana for Isabella in bed with Angelo does not exist independently of the innumerable moral entanglements which the play proposes and disposes. Shakespeare does nothing to remove the bed-substitution from the world of moral concern, and moreover he takes pains to mitigate its improbability:

DUKE:      Are there no other tokens
           Between you 'greed, concerning her observance?
ISABELLA:  No: none, but only a repair i' th' dark,
           And that I have possessed him my most stay
           Can be but brief: for I have made him know
           I have a servant comes with me along,
           That stays upon me; whose persuasion is,
           I come about my brother.
DUKE:              'Tis well borne up.

                                             (4. 1. 41–8)

Yes, it is well borne up; a reason exists for the brevity of her stay – and of course the unwilling Isabella would have wanted to stay only

---

[1] 'Milton's Satan and the Theme of Damnation in Elizabethan Tragedy', *English Studies* (i.e. *Essays and Studies*), 1948.

[2] For two illuminating accounts of this convention of 'The Substituted Bedmate', see the Arden *Measure for Measure*, ed. J. W. Lever, London, 1965, pp li–lv; and the Arden *All's Well*, ed. G. K. Hunter, London, 1959, pp xliv–xlv.

briefly. And there is a reason, in the character of Isabella, a novice from the nunnery, why the encounter should take place in the dark: there is nothing there that would arouse Angelo's suspicions. Whereas in *The Changeling* there is no reason why Beatrice should at no time be seen in the light by her husband; she is not obliged by her situation to act so, and therefore she may be suspected, instead, of obliging Middleton in the matter.

Or take the convention summarized by Professor Bradbrook in these words: 'A sudden repentance of the villain is on a similar level. It is never convincing, but it is never to be questioned' (p 60). Never *was* questioned, or never should be? We are not obliged to accept the original audience's terms if we judge them to entail a prostrate or enervating goodwill. But of course 'never convincing' is not true; the good dramatist did make such a repentance convincing; he did ensure that the suddenness of the repentance was a justifiable telescoping, a warranted compression of processes whose length made them unwieldy for the stage – a compression which answered to an inner truth, to the facts of human behaviour. There is admittedly an alternative, quite as warranted artistically, which would be for the dramatist to present such a repentance as *not* answering to the facts of human behaviour, with this '*not*' being exactly the point; to show things *as they are not* may indeed be a valid artistic procedure – provided that this very fact, that things in life are otherwise than as here shown, is itself the medium within which the dramatist creates and enforces meaning. Yet this alternative (which is more native to comedy than to tragedy) cannot be feasible if all such swift repentances belong always to the category of the 'never convincing', since how then could we distinguish between a botched attempt at a convincing repentance and a deliberate artistic use of the not-probable?

Does Edmund's repentance in *King Lear* belong in the category of the 'never convincing but never to be questioned'? What Edmund's repentance shows is that on the occasions when a convention is being consummately used, it is no longer necessary specifically to invoke the word 'convention', since the convention has come to coincide with experience of life. Professor Empson has written superbly of Edmund's death:

I want also to put in a word against a fine phrase by Mr Wilson Knight, about the decision of Edmund to try to save Lear and Cordelia; 'again', he says, 'the Lear universe travails and brings forth its miracle'. I think this idea would only occur to a critic who assumes that bad characters on the stage are meant to be devils. Edmund has not been shown as a bloodthirsty man, but simply as a ruthlessly ambitious one; he has no longer any reason for wanting to kill these people. (If he hoped to survive, his only chance would be to save them at once.) ... The line between good and bad characters is drawn very sharply in this play, but the first-night audience was, I should think, more ready than we are to see the merits of Edmund. So I do not think this good action surprising, but I agree that the movement of thought which leads to it is a very striking one. 'Yet Edmund was beloved' implies that this is the only thing he can look back on with any sense of peace, with any assurance that his life was not worthless; both sisters have died of their lust for him, so after all he was somebody.[1]

'Never to be questioned'? The snag about such apparent critical kindness is that it necessitates doing less than justice to a repentance like Edmund's which deserves the compliment of being questioned, since it can return so subtle and truthful an answer.

Nor should it surprise us that Shakespeare makes no use at all of this convention when he is dealing with a villain who, unlike Edmund, is obdurate in malignity: Iago. A lesser dramatist might well have given us a last-minute repentance by Iago (there are weirder things in Jacobean drama), but Shakespeare knew better: he knew that even if his audience would have been content – or happy – to be proferred a repentant Iago, he was right to have a stricter artistic conscience than audiences have. He knew that Iago's wickedness was the sort that clamps its mouth shut and is adamant:

> Demand me nothing: what you know, you know;
> From this time forth I never will speak word.
>
> (5. 2. 305–6)

Iago is not likely to speak under the tortures that are threatened him; and De Flores in *The Changeling* outwits Vermandero, who cries 'Keep life in him for further tortures', by killing himself. No repentance here; rather, a grim satisfaction at what is inalienably his:

> her honour's prize
> Was my reward; I thank life for nothing
> But that pleasure: it was so sweet to me
> That I have drunk up all, left none behind
> For any man to pledge me.
>
> (V. iii. 167–71)

Webster's Flamineo repents: ''Tis well yet there's some goodness in my death./My life was a black charnel' (*The White Devil*, V. vi.

---

[1] Empson, 'Fool in *Lear*', *The Structure of Complex Words*, p 149.

269–70). So does Bosola: 'The last part of my life/Hath done me best service' (*Duchess of Malfi*, V. v. 64–5). But the artistic worth, the human insight, of these repentances is inseparable from considerations of their convincingness; it is impossible to see that any service is done to Webster by insisting that these repentances exist in a specially protected world of the 'never convincing but never to be questioned'. Webster's admirers will value the repentances because Flamineo and Bosola finally let themselves be ruled by an integrity which has all along been struggling within them: Webster's detractors will reject the repentances as a 'high-minded' moral equivalent to sending a film villain down a lift-shaft – a moral stand deliberately delayed in order that the play can first irresponsibly enjoy all the good effects of Flamineo's and Bosola's badness. (It is after all convenient that a character should only belatedly be struck by a – far from invisible – moral point. In *The Revenger's Tragedy*, Vindice feels obliged to tell of his mother's corruption to Lussurioso lest he be forsworn; then a few minutes later, it dawns on him that he need not have done so, and he asseverates: 'I was a villain not to be forsworn' (II. ii. 37, 100). True – it was crass of you, Vindice, not to think of that at the time. But then there is method in this dramatic practice of endowing one's characters with a moral *esprit d'escalier*.) Such a critical argument is a genuine one. But to speak as if all conventions are self-authenticating ('never to be questioned') simply makes it impossible either to admire or to deplore Webster. A procedure which could in no circumstances be mishandled cannot be praised for being handled.

In *The Atheist's Tragedy*, D'Amville 'is no longer an atheist when he dies': the comment is Irving Ribner's, and he remarks that 'D'Amville plays the traditional role of the dying sinner coming too late to recognize the error of his ways, which recalls the deaths of Marlowe's Faustus and Shakespeare's Richard III and Macbeth' (Revels, pp xlvi–xlvii). But if one stops to consider the precise achievement represented by the last scene of *Doctor Faustus*, does 'the traditional role of the dying sinner' seem accurate, let alone adequate, as a description of Faustus? *Dying* is significantly not quite the word, since it suggests that Faustus is wounded or ill, whereas he is in health – there is a crucial difference between D'Amville (fatally wounded, like Middleton's Beatrice, like Shakespeare's Edmund) and Faustus, unwounded but doomed, the doom the more terrifying because there is no wound. More important, is Faustus 'a dying sinner coming too late to recognize the error of his ways'? Repentance, after all, would not be quite the word for Faustus (why else is he not saved?), and there can be no summary judgement as to just how much Faustus 'recognizes' as he waits for the expiry of his lease. Similar considerations apply to Macbeth: his last hours cannot without violation be assimilated to the last minutes of D'Amville, D'Amville exclaiming in his penitence – as Macbeth does not, could not – that 'Yond' power that struck me knew/The judgment I deserv'd, and gave it' (*Atheist's Tragedy*, V. ii. 265–6).

There is no harm in beginning a critical point by suggesting a similarity between the dying D'Amville, Faustus, Richard III and Macbeth, but there is great harm in leaving the matter there. The achievement of Marlowe and Shakespeare can be recognized only by noticing how very imperfectly Faustus and Macbeth fit such a description as 'the dying sinner'. Mr Ribner later returns to the repentance:

Even more striking is the relation of D'Amville to Shakespeare's Edmund, who espouses the same naturalistic philosophy and who undergoes the same kind of death-bed repentance when the folly of his dependence upon a reason not guided by divine grace has been revealed to him.

(Revels, p lxiv)

But except as a starting point, 'the same kind of death-bed repentance' is far too approximate to be able to deal with any subtle art; the assimilation does not, as it hopes, provide authority for D'Amville's repentance – all it does is maltreat Edmund's. It is not in itself an accusation against D'Amville's repentance that it differs significantly from Edmund's; the question is whether D'Amville's does not represent a much more perfunctory or schematic kind of art. To answer this would entail those considerations of plot and character which too immediate a recourse to the word 'convention' disguises.

De Flores kills himself; many Jacobean villains do not. Within a drama of any subtlety and artistic ambition, that some do and some do not would have to be referable to differences of character and differences of situation. But if we press such considerations we find that a good deal of Elizabethan and Jacobean drama is arbitrary, inordinately devoted to its own technical convenience – hence Professor Bradbrook's recourse to a good-humour which is to elide all such considerations:

Murder and suicide were committed on the slightest provocation. At the end of a tragedy, in particular, there was no need to discriminate the causes of slaughter. In *Selimus* the physician Abraham takes some of the poison he has administered to the king in a cup of wine, only because

> Faith: I am old as well as Bajazet
>
> And have not many months to live on earth:
> I care not much to end my life with him –
>
> (lines 1829–31) (p 31)

'No need'? O reason not the need. . . . There are many kinds of need. Doubtless there was no need for the dramatist to 'discriminate the causes of slaughter' if his need was to earn a living or to earn plaudits; but artistic needs are another matter, and they are not something from which others can generously exonerate an artist. If the deaths at the end of a tragedy are to mean anything, they cannot be indiscriminately caused. If suicide is committed 'at the slightest provocation' and it is impermissible for a critic to do more than note the fact, we then remove any possibility of responding with a justified admiration to those suicides the force and meaning of which inhere in the fact that what provoked them was not 'slightest'. Cleopatra's, for instance. Nor would there be any way of entering into the significance of the non-suicides, those characters who endure tragic provocation without choosing suicide. If all provocations to suicide are equal, and all divorced from real human considerations of behaviour, then there is nothing available to our understanding in the behaviour of those sufferers in Elizabethan and Jacobean drama who elect, some of them, to commit suicide, and, others, not to. The strange broken-hearted death of Enobarbus in *Antony and Cleopatra* is not the same as the death of De Flores in *The Changeling*, and neither much resembles Abraham swigging poison in order graciously to disembarrass the play of his presence. All these deaths may have connections with the same convention, and it is worth being aware of that – but only if we immediately press forward to the crucial differences which the very likeness cannot but raise. The only area to which one can press forward is that of plot and character.

Nor is it true that Jacobean tragedies never discriminate the causes of slaughter. The end of *The Changeling* does, and it is superior to the massacre which unties *Women Beware Women* just because it grows more convincingly out of the characters and events of the previous acts. The murderous masque which ends *Women Beware Women* is not short of thematic and symbolic links with the events of the play, but these are achieved only by violating the principles of a just concatenation which had hitherto applied.

And if *Hamlet* is superior to Kyd's *Spanish Tragedy*, among the innumerable reasons is the fact that the end of *Hamlet*, though ostensibly
similar, more truly discriminates the causes of slaughter.

Professor Leavis makes a crucial point in insisting that: 'When
Shakespeare uses the "same" convention as Beaumont and
Fletcher, Dryden and Voltaire, his use is apt to be such that only by
a feat of abstraction can the convention be said to be the same'.[1]
Again and again we find that the good play, or good episode within a
play, only ostensibly resembles those others which are said to evince
the 'same' convention. Such an *ostensibly* certainly has its critical
relevance, but because it opens up the right critical speculations,
not because it closes them down. A list can blur. Professor
Bradbrook gives many examples of a particular convention which
she defines as

a kind of double emotional response by which the spectator or reader is
allowed to indulge a feeling which does not lead anywhere, and is contradicted later on. For example, there are several reports of deaths, described in speeches of great pathos so that the full emotional implications of
such a death are felt; but afterwards the reports are disproved and the
feeling counts for nothing. In [Henry Chettle's] *Hoffman*, Lucibel and her
lover are mortally wounded and they have a final dialogue (a kind of
'positively last appearance') in which they describe their hopes of Heaven
and how they will ascend together, and so on. But Lucibel is required later
in the play, so that her 'death' turns out only to be a swoon and she
recovers. (pp 60–61).

This is all very wittily put, but one can't help wondering what
Professor Bradbrook is so cheerful about. Is this 'double emotional
response', deployed with the intentions and in the way that she
describes, to be accepted as simply one of the things that
Elizabethan and Jacobean dramatists did? No convention is self-
evidently bad or unusable, but some are harder to handle than
others; and this particular one offers itself readily to a vacant
sensationalism, a wish to enjoy the thrill of death without the
embarrassment – moral or technical – of a corpse on the stage or in
the plot. Yet consider the list, which has – in addition to *Hoffman* –
*Antonio's Revenge* (twice), *The Malcontent*, *The Atheist's Tragedy*,
*Thierry and Theodoret*, *Satiromastix*, and *The Honest Whore*. Is it a
coincidence that *The Atheist's Tragedy* – which is, apart from
Marston's *The Malcontent*, the only play in that list which still stands

[1] 'Diabolic Intellect and the Noble Hero', *The Common Pursuit*, London, 1952, p
156.

as some sort of achievement – does not precisely fit Professor Bradbrook's account of this convention? The important difference is the word *afterwards* ('afterwards the reports are disproved'), which carries with it *contradicted* ('contradicted later on'). For we know that D'Amville is plotting against the absent Charlemont, and D'Amville has given instructions to his accomplice Borachio:

> Go presently and buy a crimson scarf
> Like Charlemont's. Prepare thee a disguise
> I' th' habit of a soldier, hurt and lame,
> And then be ready at the wedding feast,
> Where thou shalt have employment in a work
> Will please thy disposition.

(I. ii. 235–40)

So we are not unprepared or credulous when, in the next Act, Borachio enters in disguise and tells of the 'death' of Charlemont. The speech does indeed have great pathos, and it certainly elicits 'a double emotional response', yet it is not a matter of a pretence by the dramatist but of a deception by his characters. The device in *The Atheist's Tragedy* is so used, then, as not to require for its defence the generalized forgiveness or averting of eyes which some other instances might be grateful for. The fictitious account of the finding of Charlemont's body constitutes the finest passage of poetry in the play (T. S. Eliot, who quotes superbly from these dramatists, picked it out as 'masterly but artificial'):

> Walking next day upon the fatal shore,
> Among the slaughter'd bodies of their men
> Which the full-stomach'd sea had cast upon
> The sands, it was m' unhappy chance to light
> Upon a face, whose favour when it liv'd
> My astonish'd mind inform'd me I had seen.
> He lay in's armour as if that had been
> His coffin, and the weeping sea, like one
> Whose milder temper doth lament the death
> Of him whom in his rage he slew, runs up
> The shore, embraces him, kisses his cheek,
> Goes back again, and forces up the sands
> To bury him, and ev'ry time it parts
> Sheds tears upon him, till at last, as if
> It could no longer endure to see the man
> Whom it had slain, yet loath to leave him, with

> A kind of unresolv'd unwilling pace,
> Winding her waves one in another, like
> A man that folds his arms or wrings his hands
> For grief, ebb'd from the body and descends,
> As if it would sink down into the earth
> And hide itself for shame of such a deed.
>
> (II. i. 73–94)

The quality of that passage is perhaps not unconnected with the fact that what we find in the reported death is significantly different from what is suggested by Professor Bradbrook's description of the device. Yet the quality, too, should lead to further critical inquiry, since there is something strange about the fact that it should be a speech of hypocrisy which most elicited the dramatist's powers. It is as if markedly the finest speech in *Macbeth* were to be Macbeth's

> Here lay Duncan,
> His silver skin laced with his golden blood....
>
> (2. 3. 111–12)

Or take the convention of the incriminating evidence which the villain exploits. There is nothing inherently inane about the convention – such things happen in life. Yet was William Archer right to find preposterous the following incident from *The Duchess of Malfi*?

We see Bosola ferreting around the Duchess's apartments at the time of her lying-in; and his suspicions are confirmed when he picks up a calculation of the child's nativity, which Antonio has casually dropped, beginning 'The Duchess was delivered of a son, 'tween the hours of twelve and one in the night, *Anno Dom.* 1504'. What should we say of a modern dramatist who should bring about the revelation of a deadly secret through the inconceivable folly of a leading character, who first composes a compromising document, and then drops it in the actual presence of a man whom he knows to be a spy! (*The Old Drama and the New*, p 54)

Archer's summary is somewhat too fierce. Yet on meeting Bosola in this scene (Act II Scene iii), Antonio has murmured 'This mole does undermine me'. 'This fellow will undo me'; so that Antonio's suspicions of Bosola are certainly part of the tissue of the scene. 'Inconceivable folly'? John Russell Brown suggests that it is the omen of blood on Antonio's handkerchief that precipitates the fatal accident: 'busied with this, he drops the copy of the horoscope' (Revels, p 56). Such a comment implies that the dropping of the horoscope does belong within a world where criteria of probability are relevant, since it offers a suggestion as to why Antonio's folly need not be 'inconceivable'. But it does not provide much to validate the incident, and many people will find that Archer's snort carries more conviction.

The familiar alternative remains to assert that given such a convention, all considerations of probability become inherently irrelevant – a convention bypasses probability. But it is as well to be aware of a crucial implication of that view. In life, there would always be one possible explanation as to how it came about that Antonio could be so fatally careless: that in some sense he wanted to drop the horoscope, wanted to be discovered. (In the same way, an explanation for the Duchess's 'inconceivable folly' in making all those puns about her pregnancy might be that she wanted – or some part of her wanted – to take the risk, found pleasure in it.) In fact, Antonio does at times behave in the play like a man who would prefer to know he was doomed, who would like to get it all over, the fear and the insecurity. Still, the point is not so much whether Antonio's behaviour in dropping the horoscope should be interpreted in such a 'Freudian' way; the point is that, if we say that with the entry of such a convention all considerations of psychology and probability vanish, it could never be possible for a dramatist to present to us a character who drops incriminating evidence because in some sense he fatally wants to. In other words, an authentic and important situation in life (even if a rare one) would be inherently incapable of being artistically rendered in such drama. In life there are straight accidents and there are 'accidents' (and often a blend of the two – what else is it to be 'accident-prone'?); in drama, it is only if we permit considerations of probability, of how people behave, to enter in some form into our response, that it will be conceivable for a dramatist ever to show us, not an accident, but an 'accident' or an accident-prone man.

My own view is that Webster's Antonio is indeed accident-prone, oppressed by the sense that he will never get away with it, half-happy to slump into the only anxiety-free state of mind available to him: death. But the crucial point is not how to interpret the instance (the dropping of the horoscope), but the general implications of a critical commitment to 'convention' which would indeed free all such incidents from any possibility of being damagingly improbable, but only at the price of making it impossible for such drama ever to create or enforce some distinctions which would be pertinent or urgent if what we were pondering were life rather than literature.

Plainly it would just as much abolish a crucial distinction if we were to treat all accidents as 'Freudian'. Some seem to be straight accidents, and then what casually happens wreaks its casualties. But considerations of probability remain to the point. Yet what of *Othello*? Doesn't the disaster depend on the handkerchief that Desdemona dropped and which Iago exploited to convince Othello of her infidelity with Cassio? So at least the neo-classical critic Thomas Rymer argued in 1693; he insisted that one of the morals of the play must be 'a warning to all good wives that they look well to their linen', and he protested:

So much ado, so much stress, so much passion and repetition about an handkerchief! Why was not this called the *Tragedy of the Handkerchief?* ... Had it been Desdemona's garter, the sagacious Moor might have smelled a rat: but the handkerchief is so remote a trifle, no booby, on this side Mauritania, could make any consequence from it.[1]

But Shakespeare's handling of the incident dissolves (not evades) such critical accusations. He evokes a moment when both Desdemona and Othello are profoundly distressed – he by his thoughts of her infidelity, she by his strangeness and illness. There is the by-play with the handkerchief as Desdemona tries to soothe his headache by binding his head with it; Othello, thinking of his cuckold's horns, mutters 'Your napkin is too little', and the handkerchief falls unnoticed to the ground – falls as it were between them, just as it is easy to let fall something when each thinks that the other has got hold of it. The immediate exit is naturally prepared for, and Shakespeare – while not repudiating the element of monstrous evil luck – sets limits to coincidence. For one thing, he has the handkerchief found, not by Iago (contrast Webster's Bosola), but by Emilia. Second, he has Emilia inform us that Iago has often urged her to steal the handkerchief from Desdemona – this too lessens the dependence on coincidence, since there is a sense that Iago's determination would somehow or other have got hold of the handkerchief; so that, although the element of grim luck is engrained in the tragedy, the disaster doesn't exactly depend on the dropping of the handkerchief. Again, it comes out that Desdemona always has the handkerchief with her, kissing it – a natural circumstance since Othello has warned her of its value, but also one that makes it not 'inconceivable' that it might sometime or other slip from her.

All these circumstances are adroitly and naturally compacted by Shakespeare; and the final touch comes when Iago has been given the handkerchief by Emilia, and decides:

[1] *A Short View of Tragedy*; excerpts are in the Signet *Othello*.

> I will in Cassio's lodging lose this napkin,
> And let him find it. Trifles light as air
> Are to the jealous confirmations strong
> As proofs of Holy Writ: this may do something.
>
> (3. 3. 323–6)

Iago – and the words wonderfully, and responsibly, protect Shakespeare – well knows that the handkerchief is only a trifle. And after all, the world is full of usable trifles; if it had not been the handkerchief, could it not have been something else coming to Iago's hand? Indeed, Rymer's bluff psychologizing seems itself to be psychologically injudicious; his suggestion that if it had been Desdemona's garter Othello would have had something to worry about, ignores the fact that from one point of view such an item as a garter would be too incriminating, might hint a frame-up. The great thing, the fatal thing, about the handkerchief is that it is a trifle.

Shakespeare's mastery is urgently relevant to the drama of Webster, Tourneur and Middleton because his art shows that the greatest effects are created when the dramatic medium is at its most taxing, its most resistant, when it is least conciliatory to the dramatist's whims. William Archer was right to give such stress to this question of the medium, as when he deplored Chapman's *Bussy d'Ambois*: 'Dramatists who could produce effects with such total disregard of nature, probability and common-sense, worked in a soft medium'.[1] The literary critic who follows the dramatists into disregarding nature, probability and common-sense is himself then working in a soft medium.

---

[1] *The Old Drama and the New*, p 46.

# 7

## THE MASQUE

### Stephen Orgel

The masque is only in a very qualified sense a chapter in the history of English drama. Its origins are to be found in Christmas mummings, in courtly dances and in spectacular entertainments, but not until the seventeenth century is the composition of court masques regularly undertaken by a professional playwright. Ben Jonson gave the masque its most characteristic form, and we might begin by observing that his selection as masque writer for the court of James I, and – initially at least – his remarkable success, had more to do with his qualities as a poet than as a playwright. Indeed, his gradual development of the form is paralleled by a growing dissatisfaction with and withdrawal from the world of drama and the public stage. Nor are Jonson's occasional rivals in the field associated on the whole with drama; and when professional playwrights like Chapman and Beaumont do undertake the composition of court masques, they produce works that are sufficiently different from stage plays to make it clear that they feel the masque to be a quite separate genre.

Understanding the nature of the genre is complicated by the fact that, for the modern reader, a masque is necessarily represented by its text. Indeed, the texts of Ben Jonson's twenty-seven court masques constitute a considerable literary achievement, and one that he recognized as such by including them in his published works. But to the contemporary spectator the text was only part of a masque, and not necessarily the most important part at that. The form was by nature a composite one, the joint creation of poet, designer, composer and choreographer; and in the seventeenth century it nearly always culminated in an hour or more of ballroom dancing in which both courtly masquers and spectators participated. This was called the *revels*, and it came to be a defining feature of the genre. This element alone indicates the extent to which masques were necessarily involved with court protocol, and serves more than anything else to set them off from the world of the public theatre: masques were games as well as shows, balls as well as ballets; what the spectator watched he ultimately became. Thus all the rules of court decorum had to be observed in masques. Courtiers might dance but not take speaking parts; dancing is the prerogative of every lady and gentleman, but playing a part belongs to the world of the common actor. Hence all the speaking roles in masques were played by professionals – and under James I, usually by The King's Men, Shakespeare's company – who naturally did not join in the revels.

It is a little misleading to speak of the masque as a *form*, since novelty was in itself a virtue in such entertainments, and therefore its norms were constantly changing. But certain requisites were present from the very beginning, and those seventeenth-century writers who, like Jonson, first strove to treat the genre as literature faced a number of special problems that were in a sense historically determined. We may briefly trace the history of the genre to see what traditions and, more important, what expectations, lay behind the Jacobean and Caroline masque.

The word in the sixteenth century implied simply an entertainment that involved the wearing of masks or disguises: the disguisers could be either courtiers or professional players. Anything from the simplest masquerade and grotesque acrobatic entertainment to the most elaborate allegorical display was a masque – the term implied nothing about form, structure or subject matter. But one element was constant, and that was its function on the simplest level as an entertainment of the court, and on the most complex level as a celebration of the court it entertained. The more elaborate the work, the more likely it was to involve allegorical or symbolic representations of its strictly occasional subjects, so that the court was diverted with idealizations of itself and hymns to its own glory, in which particular moments were translated into myth.

Although productions of this sort are recorded throughout the fifteenth century, and even earlier, it is not until the reign of Henry VIII that the term 'masque' becomes current, and that the form takes on real consistency. The king's love of dancing and disguises went hand in hand with his determination to make the English court as cultured as any on the continent. The historian Edward Halle's account of the masque for Twelfth-night, 1512 makes clear both the novelty of the performance and its provenance:

On the day of the Epiphany at night, the king with eleven other were disguised, after the manner of Italy, called a masque, a thing not seen afore in England. . . . After the banquet . . . these masquers came in . . . and desired the ladies to dance. Some were content, and some that knew the fashion of it refused, because it was not a thing commonly seen. And after they danced and commoned together, as the fashion of the masques is, they took their leave and departed, and so did the queen and all the ladies.[1]

Obviously both court balls and disguisings had been seen in England before 1512; what was new and Italianate was the wholehearted entry of the king into the spectacle, the sudden appearance of the monarch as masquer. But the most startling innovation was the introduction of the revels, the merging of masquers and spectators in a final dance. What the ladies objected to was precisely that Italianate quality that made it so attractive to the king; for ladies to dance and 'common' with disguisers carried overtones of licentiousness and breaches of decorum. But once the chief courtier has become the chief masquer, the court cannot refuse to enter into the spectacle with him.

Henry's interest in the masque remained throughout his reign energetic and lavish, and under his sponsorship the form appears to have taken on a consistency and scope that were not reached again for almost a century. Such entertainments were used to celebrate any extraordinary event, and became staples of the Christmas season: disguisings had always served to express the saturnalian aspects of Christmas, and were, of course, especially appropriate to the revelations of Epiphany. Henry's masques were regularly prepared by the Master of the Chapel Royal, who also provided the king's music. The choice can hardly have been accidental, for the king liked to think of himself as a composer and musician; and it meant that until 1523 he had at the service of his revels the great composer William Cornysshe.

No texts of Cornysshe's productions remain, but from a number of synopses and descriptions it is possible to determine what the mature Tudor masque looked like. Here is an account, taken again from Halle, of a masque of 1527, devised by Cornysshe's successor William Crane as an entertainment for the French ambassadors:

After a speech about the new concord between England and France, eight choristers entered singing at either side of the hall, bringing with them two richly dressed figures. These two then debated the relative merits of riches

[1] The passage (here modernized) is cited and discussed in the context of the Tudor masque generally in my book *The Jonsonian Masque*, Cambridge, Mass., 1965, pp 27ff.

and love. Unable to agree, each summoned three knights, who fought at barriers across a golden bar that suddenly dropped from an arch in the centre of the hall. Again the outcome was inconclusive, and the knights withdrew. 'Then,' recounts Halle, 'came in an old man with a silver beard, and he concluded that love and riches both be necessary for princes; that is to say, by love to be obeyed and served, and with riches to reward his lovers and friends; and with this conclusion the dialogue ended.' Immediately the masquing began: 'Then at the nether end, by letting down of a curtain, appeared a goodly mount' with a fortress; the mount was studded with precious stones and planted with roses and pomegranates. On it were eight lords gorgeously dressed, who descended, took partners from the audience, and danced. 'Then out of a cave issued out the Lady Mary, daughter to the king, and with her seven ladies,' who danced with the eight lords of the mount; 'and as they danced, suddenly entered six personages' in silver and black; 'their garments were long, after the fashion of Iceland,' and they wore 'visors with silver beards so that they were not known.' They too took partners from the audience and 'danced lustily about the place.' Then suddenly the king, who had secretly left the hall, entered with seven lords in Venetian dress, their faces vizarded with beards of gold. 'Then with minstrelsy these eight ... danced long with the ladies, and when they had danced their fill, then the queen plucked off the king's visor, and so did the ladies the visors of the other lords and then all were known'.[1]

Both the composite nature of the work and its highly sophisticated organization are apparent. Each of the elements is clearly defined – the dialogue, with its interlude of barriers, followed by the masque dances and revels – but the parts are also connected both symbolically and dramatically. The opening debate resolves the apparent antithesis of riches and love; at once a pageant enters displaying symbols of their reunion and bearing masquers. The dances then become a kind of ballet on the theme of the dialogue, and the final merging of richly costumed disguisers with loving courtiers completes the resolution.

Henry VIII spent enormous sums on such entertainments, in which he himself regularly took part. The masque is by its nature heavily dependent on patronage, and it did not flower again in so complex and spectacular a form until the reign of Charles I, another monarch who loved to conceive himself as the centre of an idealized fiction, and was willing to spend a fortune on doing so. The reigns of Edward VI and Mary Tudor were too troubled to support so extravagant an indulgence of the royal fancy, though Mary did

[1] *The Jonsonian Masque*, pp 29ff.

retain Nicholas Udall to provide the court with plays and masques; and Elizabeth, whose strength, like that of her grandfather, lay in a firm grasp of the realities of her situation, was content to leave the idealization of herself to her subjects. This does not mean that the court went without masques after the death of Henry VIII, but that under his three children the form became, with occasional exceptions, markedly less ambitious. In 1551, for example, 'the masks ... were of apes and bagpipes, of cats, of Greek worthies, and of "medyoxes" ("double visaged, th'one syde lyke a man, th'other lyke death")'.[1] Here the taste for both grotesquerie and pageantry is obvious. Such productions were, of course, performed by professional actors and acrobats, but they would have been followed by a general dance of courtiers, and hence the basic structure of the Tudor disguising is still visible. This sort of 'antic masque' continued to be a staple of court entertainments until the Civil War brought an end to masques of all kinds. Ben Jonson made dramatic capital of it by incorporating it into the structure of his idealized courtly visions as an introductory *antimasque*, where it served to embody the disorder or vice over which the world of the revels ultimately triumphed.

The few more ambitious productions are those of the small number of Elizabethan poets who began to regard the masque as a viable literary form. Viewed in this way, the work became a type of occasional poetry, and the central dramatic problem was to invent a fiction within which the monarch and court could properly be included, and the revels justified. As early as 1575, George Gascoigne published a wedding masque among the 'flowers' of his *Posies*; in 1578, for a visit of Queen Elizabeth to Leicester's estate at Wanstead, Sir Philip Sidney, the most admired court poet of the age, produced *The Lady of May*, a model of the literary entertainment; and a few other instances assure us of the literary potential of the form. Nevertheless, the Elizabethan masque suffered under the good sense of the queen, and had no real home at court. The most elaborate productions were provided by courtiers for the entertainment of Elizabeth on her occasional progresses, and thus the quality of continuity so evident in the Stuart masques is wholly lacking.

The situation changed radically with the accession of James I in 1603. The new king took the form seriously; he had, indeed,

[1] E. K. Chambers, *The Medieval Stage*, Oxford, 1903, i, 406.

composed a masque himself.[1] For the first time in half a century, professional writers were retained to devise the texts of the royal entertainments, and – ultimately more important – the greatest theatrical designer of the age was called upon to create a spectacular context for them. By far the most serious, prolific and successful Jacobean masque writer was Ben Jonson, who between 1605 and the king's death in 1625 produced twenty-five court masques, more than one a year. (Most prolific after Jonson was Campion, who wrote three; and under Charles I, D'Avenant, who wrote five.) His collaboration with Inigo Jones produced nothing less than a radical transformation of the English stage.

It is primarily Jonson's doing that we are able to find in the Stuart masque some measure of continuity. After 1605 the form was, in a sense, his to define, and therefore a summary of his career as masque writer is in order. His earliest productions are characterized by arcane symbolism and didacticism. The masques of *Blackness and Beauty*, and the two wedding masques *Hymenaei* and *The Haddington Masque*, rely heavily on emblematic devices and 'mute hieroglyphs', and are supported by an enormous weight of scholarship, both classical and modern, which in the printed versions Jonson anatomizes in detailed marginal glosses. The hermetic and abstruse qualities of these productions formed part of their attraction for contemporary audiences: the Renaissance spectator enjoyed being in the presence of mysteries that expressed (or concealed) the wisdom of the ancients; and for those few who comprehended the symbols and allusions, or who subsequently deciphered them with the help of Jonson's notes, there was the added pleasure of feeling confirmed as a member of an intellectual élite. The masques through 1612 were prepared not for the king but at the command and expense of Queen Anne and Prince Henry, the young Prince of Wales, for whom Jonson composed *Prince Henry's Barriers* in 1610 and *Oberon* in 1611. In part Jonson seems to have conceived the function of his masques as the education of this prince, who commissioned the learned annotations to both *The Masque of Queens* and *Oberon*. After the prince's early death in 1612 the most obviously didactic aspects of the form disappeared. Nevertheless, Jonson continued to treat the masque as basically moral and educative, leading the court towards that ideal world his poetry was creating.

---

[1] In 1588. See *Poems of James VI of Scotland*, ed. J. Craigie, Edinburgh, 1958, ii, 134–44.

But hand in hand with the didacticism of the early masques went a tremendous spectacular bias: the emblems, symbols, allegorical actions and moral confrontations demanded for their realization the full resources of Inigo Jones's theatrical ingenuity, and it was for these productions, not for plays, that Italian stage machinery and illusionistic settings were first imported and domesticated. The spectacle, indeed, produced the strongest part of the effect of a masque in performance, and contemporary commentators make it clear that this was an effect radically different from that provided by even the most elaborate private playhouses. It is a measure of the consistency of Jonson's imagination that he was able to make the spectacle integral to the structure of his masques, and to find means of expressing in the printed texts the significance and at least a little of the wonder of Jones's marvellous transformations. How different this sort of theatrical experience was from drama may be briefly illustrated by considering two spectacular moments in the masques of *Beauty* (1608) and *Queens* (1609).[1]

Here a curtain was drawn in which the night was painted, and the scene discovered, which ... I devised should be an island floating on a calm water. In the midst thereof was a seat of state, called the Throne of Beauty, erected, divided into eight squares, and distinguished by so many Ionic pilasters. In these squares the sixteen masquers were placed by couples; behind them in the centre of the throne was a tralucent pillar shining with several-colored lights that reflected on their backs. From the top of which pillar went several arches to the pilasters that sustained the roof of the throne, which was likewise adorned with lights and garlands; and between the pilasters, in front, little Cupids in flying posture, waving of wreaths and lights, bore up the cornice, over which were placed eight figures representing the elements of beauty. ... This throne, as the whole island moved forward on the water, had a circular motion of its own, imitating that which we call *motum mundi*, from the east to the west, or the right to the left side. The steps whereon the Cupids sat had a motion contrary, with analogy *ad motum planetarum*, from the west to the east; both which turned with their several lights. And with these three varied motions at once, the whole scene shot itself to the land.

(*Beauty*, lines 144–223)

It is obvious that the stage here has become a dramatic entity; that is, it is not the setting in which actions take place, but is itself the

---

[1] *Beauty* was not designed by Jones, but the production was strictly in his style. All quotations are from the Yale edition of *Ben Jonson: the Complete Masques*, ed. S. Orgel, New Haven, 1969. Line numbers in parentheses are references to the texts in this edition.

action. At the same time, the *meaning* of this moment in the masque is dependent on Jonson's account of it, which relates the eight figures to the elements of beauty, the 'three varied motions at once' to the movement of the cosmos. Since there is no way for the spectator to be aware of the identity of the figures, or of the symbolic point of the island's motions, Jonson's text is both less than the masque in production, and much more.

*The Masque of Queens* opens upon 'an ugly hell, which flaming beneath, smoked unto the top of the roof' (lines 21–22). One after another twelve witches appear, singing incantations and performing grotesque dances. They are conceived, Jonson says, as the antithesis to the moral virtues embodied in the queens of the title, who are to be danced by Queen Anne and her ladies. The witches are abstract figures, 'sustaining the persons of Ignorance, Suspicion, Credulity, etc., the opposites to good Fame' (lines 15–16), and hence the worlds of antimasque and revels are mutually exclusive. The moral victory, then, the triumph of virtue, is accomplished not through dramatic action, but through Inigo Jones's stage machine, which Jonson employs to make a symbolic statement about the world of his fiction:

In the heat of their dance on the sudden was heard a sound of loud music, as if many instruments had made one blast; with which not only the hags themselves but the hell into which they ran quite vanished, and the whole face of the scene altered, scarce suffering the memory of such a thing. But in the place of it appeared a glorious and magnificent building figuring the House of Fame, in the top of which were discovered the twelve masquers sitting upon a throne triumphal erected in form of a pyramid and circled with all store of light.

(lines 334ff.)

The structure of the masque does not simply allow for this spectacular machine, but requires it. The transition from antimasque to masque is a metamorphosis, and the theatrical machine is crucial to its achievement. Symbolically the total disappearance of the witches and their hell demonstrates that the world of evil is not real. It exists at all only in relation to the world of ideals, which are the norms of the masque's universe. So the antimasque, for all its energy, is in fact powerless, and ultimately, when the transition takes place, without status even as a concept, 'scarce suffering the memory of such a thing'.

Though the spectacular potentialities of this sort of theatre are considerable, it lacks flexibility, especially as the context for action of some dramatic complexity. Within two years, Jonson and Jones had moved beyond it to a significant redefinition of the form in *Oberon* (1611). The masque is set in fairyland; its antimasquers are satyrs, unruly but goodnatured, whose pleasures are courtly ones, dancing and drinking. These figures need not be banished by the advent of the Fairy Prince, for Silenus, the exemplar of wisdom, presides over them. Through him they are educated to the virtues of reason and decorum, and led to submit to the rule of Oberon.

Jones's designs for this masque have been preserved.[1] Jonson's direction for the opening scene (or is it his description of it?) calls for 'all wildness that could be presented' (line 22), but in fact Jones's landscape, like the figures it contains, is clearly controlled by principles of decorum, balanced and symmetrical. This was presumably painted on one or more pairs of shutters. Halfway through the masque, 'the whole scene opened, and within was discovered the frontispiece of a bright and glorious palace whose gates and walls were transparent (lines 97–8). In this second scene the stage is now framed by high rocks – the outermost panels from the first scene have not been removed – and the palace is a curious combination of rustication and elegance, a medieval fortress with a Palladian balustrade and pediment, surmounted by a very Italian dome. Here as in the action of the masque, the ideal is classic order, attained by gradual stages. With the opening of the next set of shutters, the full depth of the perspective scene finally appears:

There the whole palace opened, and the nation of fays were discovered . . . and within, afar off in perspective, the knights masquers sitting in their several sieges. At the further end of all, Oberon, in a chariot.

(lines 213–16)

The spectator now sees the inside of the palace. Unlike the illusionistic settings of the first two scenes, the third is a pavilion from the emblematic theatre of earlier masques, a Renaissance classical temple; but we see through it and beyond it down the whole length of a perspective scene. It is from the depths of this image of order, now fully realized, that Oberon's chariot comes forth, and that the masquers at last move out into the Renaissance classical world of the audience, the columned and galleried banqueting house at Whitehall.

Jones's stage here is wholly co-ordinated with Jonson's text, and indeed may be considered an aspect of it. The setting is the medium

[1] See S. Orgel and R. Strong, *Inigo Jones: the Theatre of the Stuart Court*, London, 1973.

for action; unlike the floating island in *Beauty* it has no independent existence. More than this, the world it represents, however idealized, is a version of the spectators' own world, and scenic realism has become a prerequisite of symbolic glory.

By the end of the decade Jones had devised a scenic machine that enabled him to control visual illusions to an unprecedented degree. The stage was conceived as a total picture, working inward and backward from a proscenium wall. It is worth stressing the point that no English theatre of the period offered anything like this sort of visual experience; and it was not until 1634 that an English play was presented with such a setting, at which time the effect was rightly considered revolutionary. For the student of drama, the most significant aspect of the court masque is the stage that was invented for it, which transformed not only the spectator's experience of the action of a play, but the very nature of the action that a playwright could represent. It opened the way for a theatre of marvels and illusions, but also, paradoxically, for a new kind of realism. But most important, it transformed the theatregoer's experience from a basically auditory one to a basically visual one, turning *audiences* into *spectators*, remaking the drama from an essentially rhetorical structure into a succession of scenes.

The most important developments in Jones's stage were achieved after his return from Italy in 1614, and Jonson's response to his collaborator's machines and perspectives is evident in the masques of the years immediately following. Despite their famous quarrel, the poet's awareness of the potentialities of the new theatre was clearly unambiguous; the masque became for the first time a unified form, fully co-ordinating action, settings and text. For the masque of 1615, *The Golden Age Restored*, Jones devised another series of perspectives – rocks and clouds, then Elysian bowers, then 'the scene of light'. Jonson, abandoning drama, allowed the scenic metamorphoses full rein. The masque is a set of lyric statements; the Iron Age is banished and the Golden Age restored by poetry, finally embodied in the persons of Chaucer, Gower, Lydgate and Spenser, who are summoned up for the occasion. In the next year, the two artists created *Mercury Vindicated from the Alchemists at Court*. Its antimasque is a tiny comic drama, and it opens on something we would recognize as a full dramatic stage, a detailed and realistic alchemist's workshop. Its very consistency would have been part of the masque's point for the audience at Whitehall: the alchemists are practising below stairs at court. When the transformation comes, it is from naturalism to Nature: 'the whole scene changed to a glorious bower wherein Nature was placed, with Prometheus at her feet, and the twelve masquers standing about them' (lines 172–4). For *The Vision of Delight* (1617) Jones's stage is even more flexible. The masque is again non-dramatic: it anatomizes the true nature of courtly pleasures in a series of scenes which constitute a gradual progression from the baser delights to the higher, from anti-masque to revels. The stage moves from the perspective street of Italian comedy to a cloudy dream world to a pastoral bower, from afternoon to night to morning, from winter to spring. Part of this is accomplished illusionistically, part symbolically. Jones was able to use the conventions of both emblematic and realistic theatres without feeling a sense of strain.

The masque for 1618 was *Pleasure Reconciled to Virtue*. In Jonson's moral fable, Hercules is the courtly hero; he banishes the pleasures of Comus – gluttony, drunkenness, riot – in favour of the rational delights of song and formal dancing. For this production, Jones provides a central symbol, Mount Atlas, the embodiment of wisdom, and this device commands the scene throughout the performance. According to Jonson, the peak of the mountain was 'the figure of an old man, his head and beard all hoary and frost as if his shoulders were covered with snow' (lines 1–3). A contemporary observer adds the information that it rolled its eyes and moved itself very cleverly.[1] The action begins in an ivy grove at the foot of the mountain; when Comus is banished, the grove vanishes, revealing musicians and the goddesses of Pleasure and Virtue. Presently the masquers are called forth from the lap of the mountain, which remains open during the dances and revels, after which the masquers 'returned into the scene, which closed and was a mountain again as before' (lines 318–19). Everything in the masque proceeds from the mountain or disappears into it. Always in view, it serves as both symbol and locale and provides both unity of place and unity of action.

It is worthwhile considering the implications of Jones's new stage. Perspective settings establish their particular kind of reality by depending on a set of assumptions that the English spectator was not, on the whole, used to exercising in the theatre. These assumptions are not moral ones, such as that beauty is better than blackness or that man is a microcosm, but empirical ones, involving not what we believe but how we perceive our world. Actions on such a stage begin necessarily to take on the quality of empirical data: the

[1] The whole account is reprinted in C. H. Herford, P. and E. Simpson, *Ben Jonson*, Oxford, 1925–52, x, 580–4.

abstract vices and virtues of *Queens* gradually become the exemplary figures of *Pleasure Reconciled to Virtue*; and, in part, the increasing appearance of dramatic characters in the masque, rather than symbolic figures, is an aspect of this movement. The transition obviously was neither immediate nor self-conscious, and nothing in *The Golden Age Restored* suggests that Jonson was aware of the implications of his collaborator's new stage. Theatrical historians regularly chide Jonson for failing to give detailed accounts of Jones's settings, but the very lack of commentary in the texts reflects the character of the new theatre: symbols must be explained, but facts are self-evident. This bears also on the movement of the later masques toward comedy, with its empirical assumptions and worldly realities. This is an organic movement, part of the joint development of poet and architect. It grows directly and logically out of the new stage and Jonson's response to its nature and possibilities.

While masques were making a gradual approach toward drama during the Jacobean age, the drama was finding considerable use for the masque. This subject deserves a separate study, but a few brief notes may serve to point some useful directions. Playwrights were naturally attracted to the form for its spectacular qualities, but often too for the special nature of its action and view of the world. The action of masques is not limited by chronological time or dramatic interchange; their metamorphoses could provide potent alternatives to the demands of politics or mutability; their idealized or symbolic figures could move the drama, however momentarily, away from a world of action and passion and towards the realization of another sort of possibility. Thus – to limit our consideration to only the most brilliant example – Prospero's masque in *The Tempest* has at its centre Ceres and Juno: the goddess of agriculture directs the play back to a world of civilized nature, away from Caliban's search for pig-nuts, 'young scammels', dams for fish; and the goddess of both majesty and marriage points the way to a resolution of the play's political conflicts, to the proper exercise of authority and the uniting of ancient enemies in the harmony of marriage. The agent of all this is Iris, the rainbow, pledge of God's providence after the universal flood. And the action of the masque, in what is temporally the most tightly and precisely organized of all Shakespeare's plays, moves in its brief span from 'spongy April' through spring and the fruition of summer to the entry of 'sunburnt sicklemen, of August weary', after which (as Ceres assures Miranda and Ferdinand) there will be not winter but

> Spring come to you, at the farthest,
> In the very end of harvest!
>
> (4. 1. 114–15)

So the masque's world is able to banish even winter; its natural cycle contains no death. Appropriately, it is at this point that the magician interrupts this 'vanity of mine art' to recall himself and his play from the dangerous pleasures of fantasy to the realities of the world of action. 'I had forgot that foul conspiracy/Of the beast Caliban' (4. 1. 139–40): it is precisely death, in the persons of Caliban, Stephano and Trinculo, that threatens at this very moment. Prospero's awareness of time – both the masque's time and the play's – constitutes both his art and his power, his vision of his world as an 'insubstantial pageant' on the one hand, and on the other, his total command of the action moment by moment. Nowhere else in the age is the immense and ambiguous vitality of the masque's world-view better exemplified than in *The Tempest*.

The last real court masque in England was Inigo Jones's and William D'Avenant's *Salmacida Spolia*, produced on the eve of the Civil War, in January 1640. The spoils of Salmacis are the spoils of peace; staged with unparalleled splendour, the masque presented the banishment of Discord by the wisdom of Charles I, followed by a superb vision of the riches and harmony of his reign. Doubtless it seemed ironic to a fair number of contemporary spectators. Still, Jones's and D'Avenant's sense of the moment did allow their idealizing fable to include a little of Prospero's tragic perspective, though necessarily muted and coloured for the occasion:

> If it be Kingly patience to out last
> Those stormes the peoples giddy fury raise,
> Till like fantastick windes themselves they waste,
> The wisedome of that patience is thy prayse[1]

This was the culmination of a decade of complex and brilliant masques by such poets as D'Avenant, Thomas Carew and Aurelian Townshend. The guiding spirit throughout was Jones; Jonson had fallen from favour with the death of King James in 1625. The productions were visually far more elaborate than any Jones had designed with Jonson; and their texts, conceived by more courtly imaginations, rely heavily on both French and Italian entertainments and the rich symbolism of contemporary neo-Platonic philosophy. Unlike James, his son and daughter-in-law took active

---

[1] London, 1639, fol. DIV.

roles in their masques, and consequently the form focused with a new intensity on the king and queen, and on the nature of royalty. Charles's notion of kingship was at the centre of Jones's greatest masques, and when that notion died, the masque died with it.

But the extent to which the theatre took on the qualities of the masque may be gauged from Anthony à Wood's account of a production of William Strode's play *The Floating Island*, in 1636:

It was acted on a goodly stage reaching from the upper end of the hall almost to the hearth place, and had on it three or four openings on each side thereof, and partitions between them, much resembling the desks or studies in a library, out of which the actors issued forth. The said partitions they could draw in and out at their pleasure upon a sudden, and thrust out new in their places according to the nature of the screen, whereon were represented churches, dwelling-houses, palaces, etc., which for its variety bred very great admiration. Over all was delicate painting, resembling the sky, clouds, etc. At the upper end a great fair shut[ter] of two leaves that opened and shut without any visible help. Within which was set forth the emblem of the whole play in a mysterious manner. Therein was the perfect resemblance of the billows of the sea rolling, and an artificial island with churches and houses waving up and down and floating, as also rocks, trees and hills. Many other fine pieces of work and landscapes did also appear at sundry openings thereof, and a chair was also seen to come gliding on the stage without any visible help.[1]

It is the stage as a scenic machine; a purely visual phenomenon, that commands Wood's total attention here. He recognizes this as new to the theatre; it is in fact directly adopted from the masque. The significance of this moment in the history of English drama can hardly be overestimated, for the masque machine was to become the normal dramatic stage for the next three hundred years.

[1] Reprinted in Herford and Simpson, x, 410–11.

# 8

# THE RESTORATION THEATRE

## Glynne Wickham

Following the Restoration of the monarchy in 1660 attempts were made to re-establish professional theatre in London as though there had been no break with the past, no war and no period of closure. Sir Henry Herbert, Master of the Revels under Charles I, fought vigorously and with success to recover his lost office, and the two men granted patents by Charles II to collect companies in the King's name and that of his brother, the Duke of York, were both survivors from the theatre world of pre-war days.

Thomas Killigrew, who could claim to have been born in Shakespeare's lifetime (1612), had seen several of his own tragi-comedies performed before the theatres were closed. Sir William D'Avenant was six years his senior, was Shakespeare's godson and had established himself under Charles I as playwright, librettist of masques and as manager of the Phoenix theatre. D'Avenant, moreover, could claim the friendship of Inigo Jones's protégé, John Webb, and thus a close familiarity with the scenic, musical and choreographic aspects of the Caroline theatre as well as with the conduct of its private and public playhouses.

Yet despite this semblance of continuity, the theatre of the Restoration era both lacked genuine roots in the popular theatre of the earlier period and had aspirations to move in new directions of its own.[1] In the first place a generation had grown up with no provision made for the systematic training of boys to play women's parts; nor had any boys graduated within companies during this period to play male juveniles. While therefore there were some actors from the earlier era, they were numerically insufficient to dominate the new companies or catch the imagination of their new audiences: nor were the old theatres in an adequate state of repair for the new companies to regard them as permanent bases. D'Avenant in any case was more enamoured of the spectacle associated with masques

[1] See Eleanor Boswell, *The Restoration Court Stage*, Cambridge, Mass., 1932.

than with the drama, and was determined to possess himself of a building that would accommodate it. In this desire, that section of the audience who had acquired a taste for French *Ballets de Cours* during their exile with the King was more than ready to support him. Thus Killigrew, who was the more reactionary of the two licensed impresarios, found himself forced to follow the trend set by D'Avenant both in seeking to accommodate scenic spectacle and in repairing the gaps in his company, where the playing of female roles was concerned, by admitting women to the ranks of the acting profession.

After brief sojourns in tennis courts adapted to resemble private playhouses, both managers secured permission and funds to build new theatres carrying their patrons' names. Killigrew established himself in the King's House in Drury Lane, while D'Avenant prepared to move from the Duke's House in Lincoln's Inn Fields into a new theatre in Dorset Gardens, but died before it was completed. Killigrew's enterprise was almost wrecked by a fire which destroyed the theatre, that had cost £2,400 to build, within five years of its opening in 1663. However, undismayed, he set about rebuilding it at once and secured Sir Christopher Wren as his architect. The new theatre, which cost almost twice as much to build as its predecessor, was opened in the presence of the King and Queen in 1674. Although this theatre too was destined to be destroyed by fire, documents which have recently been discovered in Bristol indicate that the Theatre Royal in King Street in that city, which was built between 1764 and 1766, was closely modelled on Wren's design: and since that theatre is still in active use by the Bristol Old Vic Company some idea can still be obtained today of what an early Restoration Playhouse looked like.

D'Avenant's theatre for the Duke's Company at Dorset Garden was also designed by Wren: costing £9,000 – a prodigious sum for those days – it was paid for by public subscription. It opened in 1671, three years after D'Avenant's death, when the management of it passed to his widow.[1] With the death of Charles II the fortunes of this playhouse, which catered for opera as well as drama, steadily declined until it was replaced early in the eighteenth century by a new theatre in Covent Garden. Such strolling players as could get a hearing in the provinces did so in booths at the annual Fairs; but nowhere outside London was there the money or the will to erect any building comparable with the Duke's Theatre or the Theatre Royal. Anyone therefore who wished to acquaint himself with opera or with plays written to be staged with changeable scenery had perforce to travel to the metropolis to see it.

[1] See L. B. Campbell, *Scenes and Machines on the English Stage*, Cambridge, 1923, Chapters 18–25.

Once inside one of the new theatres the principal difference that a playgoer familiar with the old-style Caroline playhouses would have noticed was the proscenium arch imported from the court masques with flat wings behind it on either side of the stage and a large painted cloth in the background. Painted shutters, which moved in grooves between the wing flats, allowed the backcloth to be cut off from view and a new scene to take its place. When the shutters opened again another scene could be revealed by changing the backcloth and the furniture that had been set there in the first place.

The stage itself still projected into the pit as in the private playhouses but was now flanked by two doors set in front of the proscenium arch on either side of the stage with boxes above each. In the King's Theatre those on one side were reserved for the orchestra, but at the Duke's Theatre a special music room was constructed over the centre of the proscenium arch. Songs and musical interludes punctuated the action of a play during which time the settings were changed in public view. The illumination of the scenic area behind the proscenium arch was achieved by rows of candles and oil lamps placed in brackets and coloured by the use of protective, stained glass or strips of coloured silk. The forestage and auditorium were also illuminated by candles, most of the light being provided by candelabra suspended over the forestage; the actors gained additional frontal illumination from 'footlights' installed at the front edge of the forestage.[1]

The actors of course now included actresses among their number. This made for changes in the allocation of space behind and above the scenic area of the stage so that separate dressing accommodation could be provided. Among the ladies first to establish themselves in public favour in their new métier were Mrs Barry, Mrs Coleman, Mrs Mountford and Nell Gwyn. By the close of the century they were sufficiently secure for parts to be specially written for them, a notable instance being the association between Mrs Bracegirdle and the heroines of Congreve's comedies.[2]

Of the actors who had played in London under Charles I and resumed their profession after the Restoration, Michael Mohun had served an apprenticeship as a boy-actor and had already graduated to male roles before the closing of the theatres. Charles Hart had likewise learnt his craft as a boy player of female roles.

---

[1] See Richard Southern, *Changeable Scenery*, London, 1952.
[2] See Jocelyn Powell, *Restoration Theatre Production*, London, 1984.

Both joined Killigrew in the King's Company where they trained Ned Kynaston to follow in their own steps. It may however be on this account that Killigrew's company failed to keep pace either in public esteem or financially in its later years, being too retrospective in its policies and insufficiently adventurous in its outlook. D'Avenant's company, by contrast, with women as firmly established in its ranks as provision for scenic spectacle and operatic performances was incorporated in its building, and with the young Thomas Betterton at its head, was at least equipped to move forward in such directions as the winds of court taste were likely to blow. In this context it should be noted that Betterton himself married one of the new actresses, Mary Sanderson, thus initiating that long line of married couples in leading roles which has so endeared itself to English taste as to persuade many dramatists from Dryden and Congreve onwards to cater specifically for it. Yet Betterton was not so *avant garde* in his attitude as to ignore what past experience could teach him, for it is recorded that he learnt how to handle the part of Shakespeare's King Henry VIII from D'Avenant who was himself taught by the actor, John Lowin, who in his turn had been produced in the part by Shakespeare himself. Betterton's Hamlet had a similarly distinguished lineage. Nevertheless, we must not read too much into this, in view of the liberties that we know both D'Avenant and Betterton to have taken in adapting Shakespeare's plays to suit the tastes of Restoration audiences. The texts of their version of *The Tempest* and *Macbeth* for instance themselves stand as an awful warning; and with such examples from such sources as authority, it is scarcely surprising that audiences and actors alike for the next two centuries saw fit to give more weight to suiting their own inclinations in adapting Shakespeare's plays than to any intentions Shakespeare himself may have entertained in writing them.

The audiences that supported the new companies were drawn almost exclusively from the monied classes since admission prices started at one shilling and rose to four shillings. They were seated in the pit, the boxes which surrounded it and in the two galleries which surmounted the boxes. Given an audience thus restricted to courtiers and to wealthy merchants seeking titles or government office, the repertoires of the two theatres reflected sophisticated and fashionable taste. This centred upon French and Italian novelties together with a reflection of their own lives and manners; yet it also accorded greater scope to music in the theatre than it had enjoyed since the earliest days of liturgical drama, and produced in

Purcell's *Dido and Aeneas* an opera universally recognized as a work of genius. The ways in which dramatists set about catering for these tastes, and adapting their initial preferences for heroic sentiment and glittering wit to make room for the less imaginative tastes of the middle classes who began to return to the theatre after 'the Glorious Revolution' of 1688, are discussed in the following chapter.

# 9

# COMEDY FROM THE RESTORATION TILL 1710

## John Barnard

### I

The most puzzling feature of Restoration drama is how an audience could appreciate simultaneously the bombast of Nathaniel Lee's *Sophonisba* (1675) and the dialectical toughness of George Etherege's *Man of Mode* (1676) without suffering from intellectual schizophrenia. A further difficulty is to define the differences between writers who deal with a remarkably constant body of themes, images, and situations, and whose comedy is concerned with a narrow section of seventeenth-century society – the idle young men of a *rentier class*, pursuing love and wealth in the person of their mistress. Finally, there is the notorious red herring of the comedies' obscenity and immorality. Macaulay, taking up the cudgels wielded by Jeremy Collier in *A Short View of the Immorality and Profaneness of the English Stage* (1698), is an extreme but representative opponent of Restoration comedy when he writes of Wycherley.

... [his] indecency is protected against the critics as a skunk is protected against the hunters. It is safe, because it is too filthy to handle, and too noisome even to approach.[1]

The moralists' assault over the last two and a half centuries is ultimately extra-literary, and misunderstands both the comedies themselves and the nature of comedy. Recent criticism has gone a long way towards righting the prudery of earlier criticism, and has focussed attention on the plays as plays. The various modes developed by Etherege, William Wycherley and William Congreve have been analysed, and a closer knowledge of the intellectual and social climate has thrown into contrast the comedies' typical forms

[1] 'The Comic Dramatists of the Restoration' in *Critical and Historical Essays*, London, 1843. See also L. C. Knights, who characterized the comedy as 'trivial, gross, and dull'.

and insistent concerns. It is now possible to consider them as 'serious' drama without being defensive or apologetic.

The comedy written between 1660 and 1710 is the greatest achievement in English drama outside the Elizabethan and Jacobean period. These years are also remarkable for an out-pouring of heroic tragedies, tragi-comedies, adaptations of earlier writers, translations, operas and sentimental comedies, none of which is a major literary work, and many of which attain depths of bathos and vulgarity rarely equalled. Even Thomas Otway's *Venice Preserv'd* (1682) and Dryden's *All for Love* (acted 1677) are finally less interesting as drama than as strata laid down for the patient exploration of social and intellectual historians. It is the comedies of Etherege, Wycherley, and Congreve, and, to a lesser extent, those of Dryden, John Vanbrugh and George Farquhar, which are the vehicle of the major expression of the Restoration and post-Restoration dramatic imagination, creating 'the first modern comedies'.

The years between 1660 and 1710 are not homogeneous. Etherege's comedies certainly propose the forms of a new 'genteel comedy',[1] and so identify the problems and attitudes of an era[2] much as *Look Back in Anger*, along with *Lucky Jim*, expressed and defined the dissentience of the early Fifties. Wycherley and Dryden can be grouped with Etherege in the development of this first phase. With the Revolution of 1688, and the passing of the worldly and cynical ethos of Charles II's court, there is a significant change. Congreve's comedies written in the 1690s bear the impress of a new sensibility.

The dichotomy between the grandiloquent nonsense of heroic tragedy and the scepticism of 'genteel comedy' is more compre-hensible if both the tragedy and the later sentimental drama are seen as forms developed in a continuing, but unsuccessful, search for a proper dramatic form to embody the powerful tendency towards idealization present in aesthetic and political rhetoric throughout the Restoration and Augustan periods. This idealization is complemented and answered by the realism of the comedy of manners.

'Verisimilitude' meant either the search for a delusionist imi-tation of the surface of reality (Pepys's excessive admiration of Van

---

[1] This, the seventeenth-century term, is more precise than the later formulation, 'the comedy of manners'. See F. W. Bateson, 'Contributions to a Dictionary of Critical Terms: I. "Comedy of Manners"', *Essays in Criticism*, i, 1951, pp 89–93.

[2] Gray and Walpole make frequent reference to Congreve's plays in their letters, suggesting that in the middle of the eighteenth century Congreve was still a touchstone of 'polite' style.

Hoogstraaten's *tromp d'oeil* paintings is characteristic of the age), or, alternatively, a search for a higher reality beyond the mundane. The divorce between the actual and the mythic appears nowhere more clearly than in the metaphoric equation of seventeenth-century London with Augustan Rome. Throughout these years artists and politicians look to the grandeur that was Rome's for the metaphors and types to delineate the aspirations which it was felt should, or even did, lie behind mercenary political jobbing and behind London's urban squalor. Dryden's *Aeneid*, Addison's *Cato*, and Pope's *Homer* all attempt to realize the cultural and political ideals of their time in the dress of ancient Rome.

Restoration comedy responds to two very different forms adopted by these idealizing drives. In the first phase, Etherege and Wycherley satirize the dying aristocratic idealism, which derived from Renaissance romance and drama: at the other end, Congreve is threatened by a bourgeois sentimentality, which is based upon a Christian ethic and heavily flavoured by Puritan attitudes to marriage. Sentimental drama transposed 'heroic magnanimity' from the exotic and superhuman worlds of Aureng-Zebe and Almanzor to the everyday world of middle-class merchant families. There, 'magnanimity' appears as impossible good-heartedness, and pathos replaces 'admiration'. The unease (and hilarity) with which heroic drama is read results from the fact that tragedy has degenerated into a variety of pastoral, bearing little relationship to the increasingly mercantile society of seventeenth-century England.

Heroic tragedy, whose hey-day lasted for over a decade (1664–77), is nothing if not ambitious, flamboyant, and over-wrought. It attempted to fuse the fine-drawn intensity of Corneille's classicism with the romance of Ariosto and the human and superhuman scale of the epic. Love and valour were its subjects, and its effect 'admiration'. Characters and their motives are larger than life, and are presented in an almost operatic manner, heavily patterned and often overwhelmed by elaborate stage effects. It is, in effect, the seventeenth-century equivalent of the Hollywood 'spectacular', with the addition of elements from the musical.

The characteristic products of this genre are marked by the rigidity with which poetic justice simplifies the human condition. Dryden's adaptation of *Antony and Cleopatra* as *All for Love, or, The World Well Lost* (acted 1677) re-arranges Shakespeare to exhibit the 'excellency of the moral', namely that 'the chief Persons represented, were famous Patterns of unlawful Love; and their end accordingly was unfortunate'. Such alterations were common, the most notorious being Nahum Tate's version of *King Lear* (1681), which avoids a painful ending by restoring Lear, saving Cordelia, and supplying her with a lover in Edgar. Villains, and on occasions, heroes, may rail at the unthinking universe, but the immutable heavens mechanically settle their moral debit and credit accounts.

The major exponent of the form is, of course, Dryden (1631–1700). After his collaboration with Sir Robert Howard in *The Indian Queen* (acted 1664), which is set in Mexico and resolved by the belated discovery that Montezuma is of royal blood, he next attempted heroics with the rather more intellectual *Tyrannick Love, or, The Royal Martyr* (acted 1669), in which Maximin dies raging against the gods –

> And shoving back this earth on which I sit,
> I'll mount, and scatter all the Gods I hit.

This was followed by the extravagant two-part *The Conquest of Granada* (acted 1670, 1671). Dryden's final rhymed heroic play, *Aureng-Zebe*, was performed in 1675. Critics have been puzzled by these plays. Douglas Jefferson argues, with ingenuity, that they show Dryden developing his skills both as a debater in discursive verse, and as a satirist – the very artificiality of the mode enabled Dryden to direct an undercurrent against the pretensions of his heroes and their rhetoric. Other critics (among them, A. C. Kirsch and Bruce King) have stressed that Dryden's heroic drama is packed with material for the history of ideas, have claimed that they are successful within their own alien terms, and have pointed out that the emphasis upon domestic and private emotions in, for example, *Aureng-Zebe*, anticipates the later sentimental drama.

Thomas Otway (1652–85) shows in his brief career a marked shift towards pathos, which culminates in *The Orphan* (1680) and *Venice Preserv'd* (acted 1681) – though, as is characteristic of the period, the latter mingles its pathos with political satire and bawdy comic scenes. The eleven tragedies of Nathaniel Lee (c. 1649–92) are marked by a certain poetic ability, and an imagery which equals the violence of the action. Intended sublimity often appears as turgid rant, and the success of *The Rival Queens* (1677) must have depended heavily upon the powers of Thomas Betterton's acting.

The morbidity and disillusion which appear in the plays of Lee and Otway echo – as Anne Righter suggests – the violence and near-hysteria of Wycherley's *The Plain Dealer* (acted 1676). These later plays contrast markedly with the buoyancy of Dryden's first ventures into heroic drama, where a degree of sincerity is present in the heroics. Just as Charles II was dissolute in fact, but could still be *imagined* as Augustus, so heroic tragedy is a tribute to an unattainable *idea* of human grandeur. In this panegyrical mode, Almanzor was a possible dream.

II

The extremities of heroic tragedy result from the destruction of the intellectual bases of heroic obligation by the events of the Civil War and Interregnum. Dryden and his contemporaries knew the unreality of the ideal, for after the Revolution, presuppositions about the nature of man and society could never again be the same. Shakespeare's reliance upon a hierarchical scheme of values, governing individuals, kings, states and the universe itself, and the unquestioning Elizabethan acceptance of the inter-linking and God-given social obligations which such a world view implied, was not possible after the Civil War, whose impact Lord Clarendon described in the following terms:

All Relations were confounded by the several Sects in Religion, which discountenanced all Forms of Reverence and Respect. . . . Parents had no Manner of Authority over their Children, nor Children any Obedience or Submission to their Parents; but *every one did that which was good in his own Eyes*. This unnatural Antipathy had its first Rise from the Beginning of the Rebellion, when the Fathers and Sons engaged themselves in the contrary Parties. . . . The Relation between Masters and Servants had been long since dissolved by the Parliament, that their Army might be increased by the Prentices against their Masters' Consent. . . . In the Place of Generosity, a vile and sordid Love of Money was entertained as the truest Wisdom, and any Thing lawful that would contribute towards being rich.[1]

These are the causes of Restoration cynicism and 'gaiety'. An established social order, based on degree and obligation, had been ousted by a permissive society. Relationship and kinship had broken down under the pressure of disagreement over basic concepts of state and hierarchy, and the outcome of the Revolution itself was resolved by power. This, along with Hobbes's demonstration of the rationality of politics, meant that 'interest' displaced obligation –

[1] *The Continuation of the Life of Edward, Earl of Clarendon* printed with *The Life*, London, 1759, ii, 21–22. See the whole passage in Clarendon. My account of the drama of this period is indebted to Christopher Hill's *Puritanism and Revolution*, London, 1958, especially Chapters 6, 9 and 14.

Oathes and Obligations in the Affaires of the world are like Ribbons and Knots in dressing, that seem to ty something, but do not at all. For nothing but interest does really oblige.[1]

Living in a period of uncertainty, materialism and opportunism, with the memory of Cromwell's sequestrations behind them, and the success of the city merchants' finance capitalism everywhere evident in London, the upper classes fell back upon their conservative faith in real estate: 'Whatsoever is of Civility and good Manners, all that is of Art and Beauty, or of real and solid Wealth in the World, is the . . . child of beloved Propriety [i.e., property]. . . .' wrote Lord Clarendon.[2] In this society, the ethics behind marriage became predominantly mercenary. If the Royalists, impoverished by their exertions for Charles I, needed to repair their fallen fortunes, rising merchants struggled to marry their daughters to a good estate, since this would bring them not only wealth, but also the additional perquisites of landed property and social status. Samuel Butler is relevant and pithy:

> For Matrimony's but a bargain made
> To serve the Turns of Interest and Trade;
> Not out of Love or kindness, but designs,
> To settle Land and Tenements like Fines.[3]

Marriage contracts were not concerned with feelings but with finance. Young men suffered as much as young women in the affront to their humanity when their personal life was subjected to accountancy, but the newly married woman suffered even more heavily in law. Primogeniture, coupled with the lack of any Married Women's Property Act, meant that all her property became her husband's: for a wealthy young woman, her husband was her only and final investment.

Restoration comedy, satirizes these mercenary evaluations of human beings. The depth of Wycherley's concern with 'the intrusion of mercenary values into the sphere of personal relationships' is evident from the titles of his poems such as 'An Heroic Epistle. To the Most Honourable Match-Maker, a Bawd, call'd J.C. –; proving Free Love more Honourable, than Slavish, Mercenary Marriage'.

[1] Samuel Butler, *Characters and Passages* from *Notebooks*, London, 1908, p 292.
[2] *A Brief View of the Dangerous and Pernicious Errors in Mr Hobbes's Leviathan*, London, 1676, p 111 (quoted Hill, *Puritanism and Revolution*, p 211).
[3] 'Marriage', *Satires and Miscellaneous Poetry and Prose*, ed. R. Lamar, London, 1928, p 218.

Relationships directed by 'interest' were coupled, both in love and everyday life, with lip-service to the older notions of 'honour'. The disguise of his true intentions was essential to the man of business or pleasure. Pepys cried out, 'But good God! what an age is this, and what a world is this! that a man cannot live without playing the knave and dissimulation!' But dissimulation could be seen more light-heartedly. In *The Gentleman Dancing-Master*, Wycherley's Hippolita describes her 'masquerading Age' as a 'pleasant-well-bred-complacent-free-frolick-good-natur'd-pretty-Age'. Disguise, commonly used in their escapades by the court wits, is a crucial metaphor in the comedies of the period.

In the latter part of the seventeenth century, outward form not only differs from inward nature, but in some areas of human conduct it *ought* to differ. In social intercourse feelings and passions were expressed through the artifices of 'politeness'. Horace Walpole brings out the connection between the social forms and 'genteel comedy':

> ... affectation, politeness, fashion, art, interest, and the attentions exacted by society, restrain the sallies of passion, colour over vice, disguise crimes, and confine man to an uniformity of behaviour, that is composed to the standard of not shocking, or alarming, or offending those who profess the same rule of exterior conduct. . . . Yet under all these disguises nature lets out its symptoms. . . . Ceremonious behaviour is the substitute for pride, and equally demands return of respect. A fashionable man banters those whom in a state of nature he would affront. . . . The first instance of good breeding in a world was complimenting the fair sex with substituting the word *love* for *lust*.[1]

Aggression, pride, and lust are disguised by and expressed through the 'forms', 'proprieties', and 'decorums' of Restoration comedy.

The modernity of this comedy is its ability to recognize and successfully dramatize the division between private and public self. It also insists that the two be reconciled. The conflicts between love and honour in the tragedies of the period, and between love and 'interest' in the comedies, are debates about balancing emotional needs against the maintenance of a proper self-respect towards both one's lover and the world.

---

[1] 'Thoughts on Comedy', probably written in 1775 and 1776, but with additions made subsequently. First printed in Walpole's *Works*, 1798, ii, 313–22; reprinted in *Essays in Criticism*, xv, 1965, pp 162–70.

## III

Etherege and Wycherley dominate the beginnings of Restoration comedy. *The Comical Revenge; or, Love in a Tub*, first performed at the Duke's Theatre in Dorset Garden in March 1664, 'got the Company more Reputation and Profit than any preceding Comedy. . . .'[1] Although Etherege (c. 1635–91) does not, in this play, cut free from Elizabethan and Caroline drama, *The Comical Revenge*'s hybrid nature reveals the anti-heroic roots of early Restoration comedy. The play sets a high plot against a farcical gulling, with a mediating middle level. It is this last which is crucial. Sir Frederick Frollick, the initiator of a long line of rake-heroes, brings together the high and low worlds of the play. By rank he belongs with the gentlemen, Beaufort and Bevil, but he does not share their one-dimensional dedication to the neo-platonic concept of honour.

The serious plot has the symmetry and romance of Cavalier drama, and its pathos turns on a conflict between love and honour: Graciana is loved by both Lord Beaufort and Colonel Bruce, while the latter is loved by Aurelia, Graciana's sister. Beaufort and Bruce fight a duel for Graciana. Beaufort is victorious, but he generously spares Bruce, who in an excess of self-destructive love tries to kill himself. Colonel Bruce's 'magnanimity' wins over Graciana, and leaves her sister and Beaufort to discover their love for one another. No wonder that Graciana should burst out,

> In what a Maze, Graciana, dost thou tread!
> Which is the Path that doth to Honour lead?
> I in this Lab'rynth so resolve to move,
> That none shall judg I am misled by Love.
>
> (IV. v, 28–31)

Heroic excess is matched by comic excess. Sir Nicholas Cully is tricked at cards, forced to fight a coward's duel, and almost married off to a whore by the two tricksters, Palmer and Wheadle. This part of the play belongs firmly to Elizabethan antecedents, though the dupe has been up-dated to a Cromwellian knight. Sir Nicholas is only saved by Sir Frederick's last minute interposition, and Sir Frederick's interference in the serious duel is equally important. When Bruce's second also attempts to commit an honourable suicide, Sir Frederick prevents him – 'the Frollick's not to go round, as I take it' (IV. iv. 101–2). Sir Frederick, that is, curbs the extremes of both high and low plot. He satirizes the idealization of

[1] John Downes, *Roscius Anglicanus*, London, 1708, p 25.

love in the bodiless realm of love and honour, as well as the unchecked preying of men on one another's weaknesses which characterizes the low plot. His ability to fight honourably or to beat up his widow's quarters means that Sir Frederick is a complete man, able to recognize and so manage the pretences of both worlds. Appetite and high feelings meet in him, along with the knowledge that aggression is present even in the etherialized love matches of the romantic heroes, and takes a physical and metaphorical form in their duelling.

Consequently, the relations between Sir Frederick and his widow are those of opposing troops parleying – and the metaphors drawn from war, from hunting, or from cards, all emphasize this aspect of love, just as the animal images which describe love emphasize the inevitable presence of appetite. The equality of this contest between the sexes is as typical of Mirabell and Millamant as of Sir Frederick and his widow, although by Congreve's time the contest was much more genteel, and the comedy freed of the heroic and low-life components. Nevertheless, *The Comical Revenge* isolates that concern with realistic solutions, unimpaired by the unworldly idealization of heroic tragedy or of Madame de Scudéry's romance, which characterizes Restoration comedy.

Success brought Etherege into the circle of wits and rakes surrounding Charles II. One of the 'mob of gentlemen who wrote with ease', Etherege portrayed the age he knew. In company with Rochester, Sir Charles Sedley, and other court wits, he broke windows, beat the watch and pursued drabs with as much vigour as any of his fictional heroes. Clearly, Etherege and his heroes belong to the class of gentlemen attacked by Clement Ellis in 1660, when he reported that the word 'gentleman',

is indeed allready made to be of no better a signification than this, to Denote a Person of a Licentious and an unbridled life; for though it be as 'tis used, a word of a very uncertaine and equivocall sound . . . a Gentleman must be thought only such a man, as may without Controle doe what he lists, and sin with applause: One that esteems it base and ungentile, to Feare a God, to own a Law, or Practice a Religion; One who has studied to bring Sin so much into Fashion, and with so much unhappy Successe, that he is now accounted a Clown that is not proud to be thought a Sinner; and he is as ridiculous as an Antique, who will not, without all Scruple, proclaime himself an Atheist.[1]

---

[1] The *Gentile Sinner, or, England's Brave Gentleman: Characterized in a Letter to a Friend, Both As he is, and as he should be*, Oxford, 1660, p 11. Ellis was a Royalist divine and poet, and *The Gentile Sinner* reached its seventh edition by 1690.

The intellectual forces behind the gallants' apparent cynicism were many – neo-Epicureanism, Hobbesian rationality, Pyrrhonism, libertinism, Renaissance scepticism, all contributed, as Dale Underwood points out – but the temper of Etherege's drama is sceptical rather than cynical or atheistic. He did indeed reject conventional Christianity –

I have ever enjoy'd a liberty of Opinion in Matters of Religion; 'tis indifferent to me whether there be any other in the world who thinks as I do; this makes me have no temptation to talk of the business, but quietly following the light within me, I leave that to them, who were born with the ambition of becoming Prophets or Legislators.[1]

Etherege's 'inner light' was not the illumination of the Quakers, but a final belief in worldly 'good nature'. Late in life he wrote to a friend –

I need not tell you I am good-natured; I who have forgiven so many mistresses who have been false to me can well forgive a friend who has only been negligent. My heart was never touched for any for whom there remains not still some impression of kindness.[2]

There is more to Etherege's 'good nature' than the open-handedness of the reprobate, for it is based upon an awareness of the ways of the world and of the heart. Sir Frederick Frollick and Dorimant look not to heaven but to the men and women about them.

When Clement Ellis eulogizes the 'Christian gentleman' in the following terms –

There is a brave Heroick Vertue, which is as a second soul unto the true Gentleman, and Enspirits every part of him, with an admirable Gallantry; I mean, Christian Magnanimity and Greatnesse of Soul. This precisely heaves him up to that size that the wide world seems too strait and narrow to contain him, or afford room enough for him to expresse the activity of his Spirit. (*The Gentile Sinner*, p 133)

– he outlines the 'Heroick Virtue' and superhuman 'Magnanimity' which support Beaufort and Bevil, that is, heroic tragedy, while the rake satirizes these pretensions and brings them down to earth. Projected into the eighteenth century, this division between the worldly-wise and heavenly-good appears in the Christian magnanimity of Steele's heroes, as compared to the essential good-

---

[1] To an unnamed correspondent, 19 December 1687; *The Dramatic Works*, i, p lxi.
[2] *The Letter Book of Sir George Etherege*, ed. S. Rosenfeld, Oxford, 1928, p 206.

heartedness of Tom Jones. The gaiety and cynicism of Dorimant, the new sobriety of Mirabell, the scapegrace Tom Jones, are all variations on the same comic figure, the prodigal reformed.

Etherege's second comedy, *She Wou'd if She Cou'd*, is a considerable advance upon *The Comical Revenge*. The high and low plots of the earlier play give way to a single middle-class ethos. At the same time, the dramatist's dependence upon farcical incidents such as Dufoy's being locked in a tub, the duel and the mock duel, have begun to be replaced by a dramatic action which resides in language and dialogue. The comedy has as its centre the ways in which generations utilize the division between appearance and reality. Where the younger generation, represented by Freeman and Courtall, and Ariana and Gatty, disguise their feelings in order to satisfy their private needs, Sir Oliver and Lady Cockwood, the one pretending to a virility of which he is incapable, the other to a chastity of which she is entirely free, cannot distinguish between the real and unreal in their own natures or private life. For the gay couples, however, disguise is used, only to make way for a final openness.

*She Wou'd if She Cou'd* establishes definitively the opposition between Town and Country. (It should be noted that the gallants depend upon landed property for their income. As members of the 'Tory' land-owning class they came to London to apply the principles of the chase to the pursuit of women during the 'season'.) In part the country represents an outmoded acceptance of morality – 'if one chance but to couple himself with his Neighbours Daughter, without the help of the Parson of the Parish and leave a little testimony of his kindness behind him, there is presently such an uproar, that a poor man is fain to flee his country. . . .' (I. i. 83–7). For Sir Oliver, and Etherege's heroes, the state of nature exists paradoxically in the town, which is made for anonymity, and is therefore a place for intrigue and the gratification of appetite.

Further, the imagery of the play insistently converts the feelings of love and honour downwards metaphorically towards images of animality and mercenary contests. 'Pimps' are 'Knights of the Industry', pursuits of whores is 'business', love is on a level with backing horses, or gaming, or hawking. Unlike *The Comical Revenge*, whose plot structure is anti-heroic, *She Wou'd if She Cou'd* internalizes the anti-heroic satire through its imagery.

After the production of Etherege's second play, the London audience had to wait another eight years before his final, great comedy. *The Man of Mode: or, Sir Fopling Flutter* was first acted at the Dorset Garden Theatre in 1676. Its success was rapid, and in it Etherege achieves – in Richard Steele's words – 'the pattern of genteel comedy' (*The Spectator*, 15 May 1711). The eagerness of early audiences to identify Dorimant and Medely as portraits of Rochester, Sedley, Beau Hewitt, or Etherege himself, points to the crucial question about the play. How far does *The Man of Mode* invite the audience to identify with Dorimant? Is Dorimant – who begins the play by throwing off one mistress, Loveit, in pursuit of another, Bellinda, and concludes the play not only with the promise of the heroine and her fortune, but with the possibility of continued relations with *both* Loveit and Bellinda – condoned for his promiscuous cynicism? Is the 'gaiety' merely heartless?

Certainly, Dorimant's naturalism is used, like Sir Frederick's, to place the pretensions of others about him, but unlike the earlier play, *The Man of Mode* invites the audience to judge Dorimant. Insofar as Dorimant is attractive, it is because, as a libertine, he is an 'honest man' – he knows that his motives are based on appetite. But his attractions are dubious ones. His ability to control appearances, and the duplicity of his intrigues, are those of the Machiavellian dissembler, for Dorimant is – as Dale Underwood suggested – a comic descendant of the Elizabethan and Jacobean villain typified by Shakespeare's Edmund. Both figures might, with equal ambiguity, proclaim, 'Thou, Nature, art my goddess.' For Dorimant, sexual gratification is not an end in itself, but a means to power. It is Loveit, herself a victim of the heroic passion which is the antithesis to Dorimant's calculation, who says to Dorimant, 'You . . . have more pleasure in the ruine of a womans reputation than in the indearments of her love' (V. i. 193–4). Bellinda perceives that the aim of Dorimant's conquests is 'glory', for 'he is never well but when he triumphs, nay! glories to a Womans face in his Villanies' (V. i. 279–80). In this Dorimant acts as Hobbesian man, for *Leviathan* exactly describes his 'glory': 'Joy, arising from imagination of a man's own power and ability, is that exultation of the mind which is called *Glorying*', for the 'general inclination of all mankind [is] a perpetual and restless desire of power after power, that closeth only in death. . . .'[1]

The irony is that Dorimant, to the extent that he seeks 'glory' the comic counterpart of 'admiration' in the battles of love, is self-regarding, for he must care for his 'reputation'. He is as much a 'man of mode' as the tailor's man Sir Fopling Flutter, who has given

[1] Ed. M. Oakeshott, Oxford, 1946, pp 35, 64.

up any inner reality to the 'shadow of a man' that appears in his mirror. The comparison between Dorimant and Sir Fopling is not altogether flattering to the hero – at least Sir Fopling is not malicious, and shows consistent good nature. Both, however, are guilty in differing ways, of aggression towards others, 'the one open, bumptious, and repelled, the other covert, mannered and success- ful' (Underwood, p 85).

Dorimant's opening exchanges with the orange-woman stress that his scurrilous banter is that of a good-hearted rake, just as his indulgence of his servants argues a certain kind of liberality. As the comedy progresses, his 'glory' in power and his malice are revealed, and even his success with Harriet is qualified when she says, 'When your Love's grown strong, enough to make you bear being laugh'd at, I'll give you leave to trouble me with it' (IV. i. 181–3). In view of Dorimant's final arrangements with his cast mistresses, Harriet's may be a Pyrrhic victory, yet her strength is that she alone sees that Dorimant too is affected: 'He's agreeable and pleasant I must own, but he does so much affect being so, he displeases me' (III. iii. 24– 5). And Harriet's view of the future, despite her own 'wildness', is conventional, for as Bellair warns Dorimant, '. . . without Church security there's no taking up there' (IV. ii. 190). Here 'taking up' has, as Bliss Carnochan has pointed out, the force not only of 'taking up house' and a bawdy pun, but also the commercial meaning of 'borrowing at interest'.[1] The heavenly and commercial ties of marriage may, together, tame Dorimant's 'wildness'.

The freedom with which Dorimant and Harriet choose one another suggests how far they have moved from the older generation, which is typified by Old Bellair's half-admiring out- burst, 'Out a pise on 'em, . . . the Rogues ha' got an ill habit of preferring Beauty. . . .' Harriet demands that Dorimant give up part of his freedom to form a basis for a reciprocal relationship – and he must begin by visiting her in the country. But Dorimant is not Mirabell: that is a role for Bellair who is, significantly, pushed to one side of *The Man of Mode*. Dorimant may be duping himself, Loveit or Harriet when he says that the basis of his marriage is mercenary and will 'repair the ruines of my estate that needs it' (V. ii. 292–3). Like the play as a whole, Dorimant is in precarious balance. The order imposed by the comic structure, namely, the reformation of the prodigal through love, is a transformation not fully achieved, and it is further threatened by the audience's

---

[1] *The Man of Mode*, ed. W. B. Carnochan (Regents Restoration Drama), London, 1966, p xx.

awareness of the ambivalence of hero and heroine. The wisdom of *The Man of Mode* is comic, and lies in its exposure of necessary limits, the unalterable confusions of the human condition, and the recognition of mutually exclusive truths.

Etherege's major play is exploratory and sceptical, and is directed against all its characters. The genius of William Wycherley (1640?–1716) is of a quite different order, and his greatest plays, *The Country Wife* (1675) and *The Plain Dealer* (acted 1676), aim directly at the audience. Satire not exploration is his concern. In Wycherley, upside down though it may appear on the surface, there is a strong sense of right and wrong, of passionate moralizing. Of all the dramatists who wrote comedy between 1660 and 1710, Wycherley was, and remains, the most disconcerting for his audience. His work refuses to rest neatly within the boundaries of 'manly' satire: there is a violence, a dark energy, which threatens the decorum of Etherege and Congreve.

Wycherley's dramatic beginnings were not particularly auspicious, and his two first comedies are apprentice work. Despite its popular success, *Love in a Wood* (acted 1671) is crude. It is divided between high and low plots, though both levels, unlike Etherege's *The Comical Revenge*, are treated realistically. Marriage is the central theme – Mrs Joyner attempts to bring about matches at the farcical level, while Vincent fulfills the same role, though as a friend, in the upper reaches of the comedy. The concluding lines –

> The end of Marriage, now is liberty
> And two are bound – to set each other free

– could serve as a motto for the satire which Restoration comedy directs against the prevailing *mariage de convenance* of seventeenth-century society. Wycherley argues that the ritual and contract of marriage can, and ought to, release the private life of its participants.

*The Gentleman Dancing-Master* met with little success when it was first performed at the Dorset Garden theatre in 1672. Based on Calderón's *El Maestro de Danzar*, it has a clear-cut quality often missing in Restoration comedy. None of the romanticism, which later appears in Manly and Fidelia, impinges upon the attempts of Hippolita to win her gallant, Gerrard. In its motives the love plot is almost Shakespearean. Hippolita, kept innocent of the world, nevertheless falls in love with Gerrard, a man about town. Her first problem is how, as a woman, she can make an advance without compromising her modesty, and when she has achieved this step, how to ensure that Gerrard's feelings are genuine. But where Shakespeare, looking back to the courtly love debates of medieval and Renaissance romance, would have emphasized the heroine's dilemma, Wycherley presents her situation in more prosaic terms. Hippolita's father, a 'Canary Merchant', keeps her locked up at home partly because of his affectation of Spanish 'gravity' and 'policy' (he even calls himself 'Don Diego'), but more importantly because Hippolita has £1200 a year he cannot touch, which, Hippolita remarks, 'is the chiefest reason . . . why he keeps me up so close'. Yet, as Hippolita realizes, for her modesty and purity to have any real meaning, Don Diego must 'be oblig'd to me for my vertue' (i, 162). In 'this Masquerading Age' the fourteen-year-old Hippolita can only 'enfranchize' herself in spite of the older generation. Threatened by her father's choice of a husband for her, the Frenchified city-heir, Monsieur de Paris, she sees clearly that she must marry for love, or act the part of a prostitute within marriage. At the end of Act II she asks for the song 'I dream't [of] all night', which ends:

> The Match soon made is happy still.
>     For only Love has there to do:
> Let no one marry 'gainst her will,
>     But stand off, when her Parents woo.
>
> And only to their Suits be coy,
>     For she whom Joynter[1] can obtain.
> To let a Fop her Bed enjoy,
>     Is but a lawful Wench for gain. . . .

Hippolita's only weapon against her father's tyranny is her ability to hide behind an appearance of innocence, which is allied to her perception that both her father and Monsieur de Paris exist only through their sartorial affectation. Consequently, on the grounds that Monsieur should make a jest of his jealousy – 'you shou'd railly your Rival, and rather make a Jest of your Quarrel to him, and that I suppose is *French* too' (i, 161) – Hippolita forces him to *persuade* Gerrard, who has never met her, to attempt to ravish Hippolita from her home. Even Gerrard (who gives the play its title when he disguises himself as a dancing-master to ensure his access to his mistress's presence) is taken in by Hippolita, the apparent *ingénue* with the 'innocency of an Angel'. Only when she has tested Gerrard, by pretending to have no fortune, can they finally marry.

---

[1] 'Jointure', marriage agreement.

The true lovers discover their true selves and throw off their disguises in the course of the play.

It is not Gerrard who is the gentleman dancing-master, the mere 'tripping outside of a Gentleman', but the foppish Monsieur. The hero and heroine's true marriage is directly contrasted with Monsieur's final situation, when he is forced into 'keeping' a prostitute, Flirt, with even more onerous stipulations than those of marriage itself, complete with 'Articles and Settlements' for Flirt's 'separate Maintenance'. 'Keeping' thus becomes the extreme example of a sexual relationship based on purely commercial factors: it is an anti-marriage, just as that between Hippolita and Monsieur would have been.

There are points in *The Gentleman Dancing-Master*, a predominantly 'gay' comedy, which suggest the mature Wycherley. The satire of Don Diego and Monsieur is as unremitting as that upon 'keeping': in both cases, Wycherley demands that the audience see the point and relate it to their own situation. If this emphatic satire threatens the comedy's 'gaiety', so does the head-on comparison of the mercenary-marriage-as-keeping metaphor with the true marriage, which is so abrupt as to be almost heavy-handed. But although the moral appears overwhelmingly clear-cut at this point in the play, Flirt's epilogue undermines that simplicity – Hippolita, she points out, is an 'unnatural' character: city heiresses lack her attractions, honesty, or intelligence. As so often in Wycherley, *The Gentleman Dancing-Master* concludes with the statement that it is only a play.[1]

With *The Country Wife* (1675), Wycherley leaps into maturity. It has two major satiric targets. The first, the hypocrisy of upper-class women, who hide their rampant sexual desires behind a reputation for 'honour', is exposed through the 'satyr-satirist',[2] Horner, and contrasted with the spontaneity of the unaffected country wife, Margery Pinchwife. The second aim of the comedy is to examine the nature of marriage relationships through a comparison of four relationships, and this theme occupies the larger part of the play, so much so that Garrick's version of *The Country Wife* omits Horner altogether.

---

[1] See the discussion between Monsieur, played by Edward Nokes, and Hippolita about the relative merits of Nokes and Edward Angel (?Don Diego) at i, 186–7. *The Plain Dealer* contains a discussion of the china scene in *The Country Wife*.

[2] Behind the roughness of Horner and Manly lies the Elizabethan etymological confusion of 'satyr' (half-goat, half-man) with 'satire'. See R. A. Zimbardo, *Wycherley's Drama*, New Haven, 1965, pp 60ff.

Wycherley's discussion of marital and sexual relationships is a more mature and complex consideration of the issues raised in *The Gentleman Dancing-Master*. So Jasper Fidget puts his business before his wife – 'business must be preferr'd always before Love and Ceremony with the wise Mr Horner' (ii, 13), he says, leaving Lady Fidget in the latter's capable hands. The ageing whoremaster, Pinchwife, whose marriage suggests that he has reformed, has done so in appearance only. His jealousy of Margery, a simple country girl who wishes, to satisfy the calls of nature as expeditiously as possible, results from Pinchwife's knowledge that he has no hold over her but force. As Horner tells him, 'you only marry'd to keep a Whore to your self' (ii, 20). Finally, Alithea's engagement to the fop, Sparkish, is set against her relationship with Harcourt. Here Wycherley's romanticism significantly alters the conventional pattern, for Alithea, the rich and sophisticated heroine, wishes to marry the fop who regards her as a property to be exhibited to others. She mistakes Sparkish's lack of jealousy for nobility of feeling – ''tis Sparkish's confidence in my truth, that obliges me to be so faithful to him' (ii, 51). Because she believes that 'Love proceeds from esteem' she cannot break the engagement, despite her developing feelings towards Harcourt. Eventually, however, Sparkish is exposed, and the lovers who have discovered love and mutual respect prepare for a matrimonial happiness which is starkly contrasted to the inevitable cuckolding of Pinchwife and Sir Jasper.

The other centre of the play, Horner's pretence that an 'English-French Disaster' has deprived him of his manhood, overshadows Alithea and Harcourt. Structurally, Horner's divertissements are meant to complement the discussion of marriage. Just as Monsieur's 'keeping' is the antithesis of Hippolita's marriage in *The Gentleman Dancing-Master*, so Horner's strategy means that he attains sexual gratification but loses the possibility of the emotional satisfaction available to Alithea and Harcourt. This far, then, Horner functions as a satiric device. It is not his monomania which is attacked, but the husbands and ladies of mode who ensure that his trick works – cuckolds and adultresses make themselves.

However, Horner's one-dimensional needs confer upon him a demonic quality, and no account of *The Country Wife* which centres on Alithea and Harcourt, at the expense of Horner, can explain the peculiar force of the play as a whole, or the sense of exhilaration and growing unease with which the audience follows Horner's exploits. Wycherley puts a fantasy of male omnipotence, common to clubroom tales, on the stage, so that the exhilaration which results from the loosening of taboos, is threatened by Wycherley's relentless presentation of the reality of that fantasy. The force of the brilliant (and notorious) china scene comes from the fact that the joke goes on too long.[1]

For Dryden and his contemporaries, *The Plain Dealer* (acted 1676), rather than *The Country Wife*, was Wycherley's greatest work. It is distinguished by the urgency with which Wycherley realizes the coarsest kind of realism and simultaneously portrays an idealism bordering on romanticism. This mixture, and the perverse collocation of roles thrust upon its protagonist, Manly, threaten the success of *The Plain Dealer*. Like Horner, Manly is an 'honest man', and is used as a device to satirize society, but he is also, quite unlike Horner, a man of deeply romantic tendencies which make him an easy dupe. Is Manly a misanthrope, a psychopath, a 'satyr-satirist' who is himself infected by the vices he castigates, or is he a comic gull whose unbalanced honesty is measured by the sanity of Freeman, who complies with the world? And is the play itself a jarring mixture of satire and high tragedy, a comedy of manners, or even a romantic comedy?[2]

In fact *The Plain Dealer* is open-ended, and can include all of these possibilities. Manly is, from one aspect, a device, as he makes clear his Prologue –

> I, only, Act a Part like none of you;
> And yet, you'll say, it is a Fools Part too:
> An honest Man; who, like you, never winks
> At faults; but unlike you, speaks what he thinks. . . .

His 'honest, surly, nice humour' rejects the social pretence and hypocrisy of everyday life. The play opens:

MANLY. Tell not me (my good Lord Plausible) of your Decorums, supercilious Forms, and slavish Ceremonies; your little Tricks, which you the Spaniels of the World do daily over and over, for, and to one another; not out of love or duty, but your servile fear.

LORD PLAUSIBLE. Nay, i'faith, i'faith, you are too passionate, and I must humbly beg your pardon and leave to tell you, they are the Arts and Rules, the prudent of the World walk by.

---

[1] See F. W. Bateson's illuminating discussion in 'L. C. Knights and Restoration Comedy', *Essays in Criticism*, vii, 1957, pp 56–67.

[2] See especially Ian Donaldson's essay, '"Tables Turned": *The Plain Dealer*', *Essays in Criticism*, xvii, 1967, pp 304–21.

Manly rejects prudence and Walpole's explanation of the civilizing effect of the 'forms'. Passionate and singular, his speeches burst from him, flaying the least departure from honesty.

Despite his plain dealing Manly is unable to see what is before his eyes. Like most Restoration dupes, though for opposite reasons, he mistakes appearance for reality. Olivia, with very powerful irony, deceives Manly through the kind of pretence he rejects – 'I knew he loved his own singular moroseness so well, as to dote upon any Copy of it; wherefore I feign'd an Hatred to the World too, that he might love me in earnest . . .' (ii, 171). As a result, Manly leaves half his fortune in her trust while he is at sea, only to find on his return that Olivia has married Vernish, his 'Bosom, and onely Friend', and appropriated his money. The doubly betrayed Manly, finding Olivia attracted by his cabin-boy (in reality, Fidelia in disguise), seeks revenge through an attempted bed-trick, thus descending to the very dissimulation he despises.

Manly's emotions are violently confused. They oscillate violently, as Ian Donaldson points out, between lust and hatred:

Her Love! – a Whores, a Witches Love! – But, what, did she not kiss well, Sir? I'm sure I thought her Lips – but must not think of 'em more – but yet they are such I cou'd still kiss – grow to – and then tear off with my teeth, grind 'em into mammocks, and spit 'em into her Cuckolds face.

(ii, 160)

Even more obviously than in *The Country Wife*, physical jealousy consumes and confuses the lover. It is both ridiculous and tragic, and in consequence the play moves between tragic rant and bitter satire, between romance and vituperation.

The sub-plot, in which Manly's lieutenant, Freeman, 'complies' with the world, provides no satisfactory alternative. Although he defeats the litigious Widow Blackacre and frees her son Jeremy by utilizing the appearance – reality dichotomy, his feelings are not explored: rather, he is another satiric device, and, significantly, the relationship between Freeman and Eliza is never developed. The effect is to throw the weight of the whole play upon Manly and Fidelia.

Manly cannot fit into the London 'world', and the naked aggression of a state of nature is more attractive to Manly than the covert warring of civilized man:

I rather choose to go where honest, down-right Barbarity is profest, where men devour one another like generous hungry Lyons and Tygers, not like Crocodiles; where they think the Devil white, of our complexion, and I am already so far an Indian. . . .

(ii, 118)

Yet Manly never attains his distant idyll of honest aggression, for at the conclusion of the play he is reconciled to the 'world' by the love, and unexpected fortune, of Fidelia. This final scene is unconvincing. Manly's conversion from a blindly heroic malcontent into a man of the world is, at the very least, unlikely, and his conversion is brought about by a character who belongs not in a comedy but in pastoral. Fidelia's love for Manly is such that she disguises herself to follow Manly to war, and even puts Olivia before herself. The effect is to suggest that Manly's kind of purity is possible only outside the real world of the play, and the audience is left ambiguously poised between admiration of Manly's honesty and the realization that to act as he does is inhuman if not downright stupid.

Outside the major comic achievement of Etherege and Wycherley, this first phase also produced the vigorous but clumsy comedies of humours written by Thomas Shadwell (c. 1642–92). His most successful plays, *The Sullen Lovers* (1668), *Epsom Wells* (acted 1672), *The Squire of Alsatia* (1688) and *Bury Fair* (1689), are indebted to Molière as well as to Jonson, and they represent low life more extensively than the more middle-class dramatists. Dryden's comedies, often under-rated in the past, show independence and originality. *Marriage à la Mode* (acted 1671 or 1672) is a striking mixture of cynical and idealistic attitudes, while *The Kind Keeper or, Mr Limberham* (acted 1678) has a remarkable gusto and broadness of satire.

IV

By the end of Charles II's reign the major forms of Restoration drama had been realized, and one form, rhymed heroic tragedy, had died. Shadwell's comedy of humours, Wycherley's satire, the comedy of intrigue, and Etherege's 'genteel comedy' provided the basic patterns for comedy in the last decade of the seventeenth century. In 1690 the situation was not propitious. The only new dramatist of any note was Thomas Southerne (1660–1746), Etherege was soon to die, Wycherley had retired from the stage, and Lee and Otway were dead. Dryden's unwilling return to the stage with *Don Sebastian* (acted 1689) was marked by a singularly dispirited Preface:

Having been longer acquainted with the Stage, than any other Poet now living, and having observed how difficult it was to please; that the Humours of Comedy were almost spent, that Love and Honor (the mistaken Topicks of Tragedy) were quite worn out, that the Theatres could not support their Charges, and that the Audience forsook them. ... All these Discouragements had not only wean'd me from the Stage, but had also given me a Loathing of it. But enough of this: the Difficulties continue; they encrease, and I am still condemn'd to dig in those exhausted Mines.

It was, as Dryden perceived, the beginning of a transitional period, and in 1690 Dryden could not foresee the final flowering of Restoration comedy in William Congreve's plays, which borrow from all the modes, and fuse them into a new harmony. As Dryden recognized, however, in 1694,

> In Him all Beauties of this Age we see;
> Etherege his Courtship, Southern's Purity;
> The Satire, Wit, and Strength of Manly Wicherly.
>
> ('To Mr Congreve')

More than any other dramatist in this last phase, Congreve was able to reconcile the strengths of Restoration comedy with the new emphasis upon 'sententiousness', feeling, and melodrama.

Meanwhile, tragedy, including Congreve's own *Mourning Bride* (1697), turned more and more from public themes to private feeling. Southerne's tragi-comedies, even when like *Oroonoko* (1696) they have exotic settings, move towards pathos not admiration. The 'passionate distress' of Isobella in his *The Fatal Marriage* (1694), in which the heroine discovers she is married to two men when her first husband, presumed dead for eight years, returns, is a preparation for the innocent agitation of pure hearts which dominates sentimental drama.

Congreve's first play, *The Old Batchelour* (1693), excludes these themes, and explores instead the strengths of the traditional themes and material of Restoration comedy. It avoids the broken-backed yoking of high and low plot, and its multiplicity of actions creates the effect of 'gaiety'. Heartwell, a simplified Manly, thinks that men should be what they seem, a humour which is punished by a narrowly avoided marriage to Sylvia, a woman of the town. The usual cuckolding of the city-Puritan, Fondlewife, is achieved by Bellmour, while the doubled love affairs between Vainlove and Araminta, Bellmour and Belinda, provide the 'genteel' level. There is also a straightforward Jonsonian sub-plot in which the braggadoccio, Captain Bluffe, and the foolish Sir Joseph Wittoll, are gulled by Sharper.

*The Old Batchelour* does not fully unify these various strands. In general, it follows many other Restoration comedies in demonstrating the superiority of youthful *libertin* values over those of a self-deceiving older generation, shackled by outmoded notions of honesty (Heartwell) or limited by inability (Fondlewife). The plotting is extrinsic to the themes in the parallel love affairs of the rakes. Here the motivating principle is not intrigue, as in Etherege, but 'humour' or affectation. The 'obstacle' which faces Bellmour and Vainlove is not external, such as guardian figures or wills, but internal. It is Vainlove's own 'nicety' in love which causes Araminta to refuse an immediate marriage – as Bellmour comments, 'O my Conscience she dares not consent, for fear he shou'd recant'. (Bellmour has benefited from Vainlove's 'humour': Vainlove rouses the game only to give it over to Bellmour's enjoyment.) Similarly, the only barrier between Bellmour and his mistress is her 'affected coyness'.

Notable too is Congreve's emphasis upon the image of life as a play and upon theatrical artifice. Heartwell's despairing apostrophe on women is interrupted by Bellmour's 'Now George, What Rhyming!' (ed. Summers, i, 220). All the characters, whether of humour or affectation, are actors, and their success is dependent upon the ability with which they play their roles. Consequently, Heartwell's improbable rescue by the rakes from Silvia, which is for some critics the play's weak point, is deliberately factitious. Heartwell may earn his release in comedy, but not in life.

The imagery of *The Old Batchelour* portrays the ambivalent aspects of love. Both Belinda and Heartwell liken lovers to asses (i, 182, 174). Vainlove says that 'Love is a Deity, he must be serv'd by Prayer' (i, 185), but elsewhere love is a 'baited hook' (i, 174, 187), while 'Marriage is entering into a course of Physick' (i, 175). The characters are similarly ambivalent. If Heartwell is a fool, his desire for integrity is admirable. Vainlove's inability to enjoy the fruits of his amours undercuts his pretensions as a lover (as does his name). While the gallants remain apparently safe, *The Old Batchelour* maintains an undercurrent which puts them at risk, and their savage mockery of Heartwell which touches a 'gall'd-beast till he winch'd' (i, 221), has overtones of Wycherley's violence. The comedy closes with Heartwell's middle-aged warning about marriage – *The Old Batchelour's* libertine 'gaiety' barely holds up to the implications of its *dénouement*.

Congreve's second play, *The Double-Dealer* (acted 1693) is not a success, even though Lord and Lady Froth, Brisk, and Lord and Lady Plyant are brilliant comic creations. Actions or theme is continually subordinated to plot in *The Double-Dealer*, so that the complexities of the intrigue perplex rather than illuminate. Worse, the comedy ranges black against white. Maskwell, the villain (modelled on Terence's Syrus), deceives his victims by telling them his intentions, and is the active agent in the plot, while Mellefont remains almost wholly passive. Mellefont cannot fulfil his role as hero, which is to defeat the wiles of Lady Touchwood, a condition set by his mistress Cynthia, because the play must show 'Secret Vice' defeating itself. Well might Aaron Hill complain in *The Prompter* of 11 November 1735 that the proper punishment for Maskwell was not through comedy but by law.

*The Double-Dealer's* fundamental misapprehension of the nature of comedy resulted from Congreve's determination to obey the neo-classical critical rules. He was 'resolved to preserve the three Unities of the Drama' and to that end, he says, 'I design'd the Moral first, and to that Moral I invented the Fable . . .' (Dedication). The moral is given in the concluding lines –

> Let secret Villany from hence be warn'd;
> How e're in private, Mischiefs are conceiv'd,
> Torture and shame attend their open Birth;
> Like Vipers in the Womb, base Treach'ry lies,
> Still gnawing that, whence, first it did arise;
> No sooner born, but the Vile Parent dies.

The didacticism and histrionic elevation of tone appear only too clearly in the passionate scenes between Maskwell and Lady Touchwood, and in exchanges like the following, where the hero is tricked into seeming to be his aunt's lover:

LADY TOUCHWOOD: [*Aloud*] Never, never! I'le grow to the ground, be buried quick beneath it, e're I'll be consenting to so damn'd a Sin as Incest! unnatural Incest!
MELLEFONT: Ha!
LADY TOUCHWOOD: O cruel Man, will you not let me go? – I'le forgive all that's past. O Heaven, you will not ravish me?
MELLEFONT: Damnation!
LORD TOUCHWOOD: Monster, Dog! your Life shall answer this!
*Draws and runs at Mellefont, is held by Lady Touchwood.*
LADY TOUCHWOOD: O Heavens, my Lord! Hold, hold, for Heaven's sake.
MELLEFONT: Confusion, my Uncle! O the damn'd Sorceress.

(ii, 63)

*Love for Love* (1695) looks back in atmosphere and relative formal freedom to *The Old Batchelour*. Unlike *The Double-Dealer*, which had presented an upper-class society, physically contained within a country house, *Love for Love* is set within the middle and merchant classes. Its sources are not in neo-classical formalism, but in Elizabethan and Jacobean plays. The main plot is based on Fletcher's *Elder Brother* (1637), there are echoes of *Hamlet*, and something of the atmosphere of *A Midsummer Night's Dream*,[1] while the 'honest hoax' pattern is one used by Middleton and Massinger. As in Massinger's *A New Way to Pay Old Debts* and Middleton's *Tricks to Catch the Old One*, the prodigal has become a constant lover before the play opens. The hoax is a trick on the part of youth to gain inherited wealth from its parents' generation. However, in *Love for Love*, unlike the two earlier plays, love is more important than the legacy intrigue: indeed, interest is subordinated to love.

The comedy opens with Valentine imprisoned in his chambers by the crippling debts incurred in his attempts to win Angelica, a rich heiress. His lodgings are a symbol of inward constriction as well as outward. The action of *Love for Love* shows the progressive definition of Valentine as a disinterested lover. Its first four acts are taken up with Valentine's rejection of the earlier answers supplied by Restoration comedy for men in his dilemma. In Act I, Valentine tries out various roles – that of the wise man scorning poverty, that of the poet, that of the railer, which Scandal carefully puts to one side:

Rail? At whom? the whole World? Impotent and Vain! Who would die a Martyr to Sense in a Country where the Religion is Folly.

(ii, 101–2)

Valentine, debarred from living off anything but inherited wealth, has only two alternatives. He first asks his father's mercy, but Sir Sampson's refusal precipitates a struggle between unnatural father and prodigal (or 'natural') son. Valentine is driven to his last resort, trickery, and his feigned madness is the culmination of his attempts to free himself from his debts in order to win Angelica. Only when these attempts to combine love with interest have *failed* completely can the plot be resolved.

Finally, Valentine, convinced that Angelica really wishes to marry his father, gives up his pursuit of her:

[1] See K. M. Lynch, *The Social Mode of Restoration Comedy*, New York, 1926, pp 191–2; Norman N. Holland, *The First Modern Comedies*, Cambridge, Mass., 1959, pp 161–2; and P. and M. Mueschke, *A New View of Congreve's Way of the World*, Ann Arbor, 1958, p 71.

I never valu'd Fortune, but as it was subservient to my Pleasure; and my only Pleasure was to please this Lady: I have made many vain Attempts, and find at last that nothing but my Ruine can effect it: Which, for that Reason, I will Sign to – Give me the Paper.

(ii, 170)

Now that Valentine has committed a really 'mad' act in the terms of the traditional rake hero, for he is doing nothing less than sign away his inheritance, Angelica admits her love:

Had I the World to give you, it could not make me worthy of so generous and faithful a Passion: Here's my Hand, my Heart was always yours, and struggl'd very hard to make this utmost Tryal of your Virtue.

Angelica's affectation of pretending indifference to Valentine until he has acted 'generously', re-defines the problem traditionally set by the comedy of manners. Her dominance and her persistent refusal of the still worldly Valentine conclude in the statement that love requires love in return, and not a reconciliation between love and interest.

The regeneration theme would be less convincing in *Love for Love* if it were not presented as a necessary response on Valentine's part to the society about him. As Norman Holland has demonstrated, Angelica's name, Valentine's renouncing of the world, and the neo-Platonic imagery employed in the final stages of their courtship, place the two lovers on a supra-social level. To win Angelica, Valentine must appeal to her outside the realities of the *marriage de convenance*. At the opposite extreme are the 'natural' characters, Ben and Prue. The latter climbs up, under the instruction of Tattle, into the middle group of characters, the inhabitants of everyday society, whose humours, cuckoldings, and masked marriages belong to the normal world of the comedy of manners. Here the ability to distinguish between appearance and reality, and to arrange appearance to one's own benefit, are the only ways to success. Valentine's regeneration is subversive of the earlier drama, since it silences scepticism and reason by recourse to an ideal of true love.[1]

After the success of *Love for Love* Congreve, rather surprisingly, turned to tragedy. *The Mourning Bride* (1697) may, as Herbert Davis suggested, have been written to flatter the taste of Princess Anne.

---

[1] Aubrey Williams has argued that Congreve's comedies are worked out under the aegis of Providence, *An Approach to Congreve*, New Haven, 1979. This seems to me to ignore the emphasis upon the 'world' and society found in *The Way of the World*.

Congreve's only tragedy held the stage through the following century, for it was an excellent vehicle for the tragic talent of actresses like Mrs Barry and Mrs Bracegirdle, and later, Mrs Siddons. The play is set in Granada, where the imperious and ungovernable passion of Zara threatens the love of Almeria and Alphonso. This domestic drama takes place within the larger context of a struggle to overthrow a tyrant. Although it exhibits the familiar rhetoric of the heroic drama, Congreve's play does concern itself with its characters. Manuel, Thomas Davies remarked, is a combination of 'pompous phraseology with an outrageous vehemence of temper' yet he is 'still . . . a character'.[1]

Congreve's final comedy, *The Way of the World* (1700), is a summit of Restoration comedy. Mirabell's 'sententiousness' may indicate that sensibility has begun to qualify scepticism, and the violent scenes between Fainall and Mrs Marwood are reminiscent of those between Maskwell and Lady Touchwood, but the play reconciles these elements within a more comprehensive exploration of the 'world', that is, society, than any other of the period's major comedies.

Structurally *The Way of the World* resembles *The Double-Dealer*. It observes a less strict version of the 'rules of the stage', and Mirabell's match with Millamant is threatened by the machinations of the 'Hobbist' cynic, Fainall, and his mistress, Mrs Marwood. *The Way of the World* also has a moral firmly stated on the title-page[2] which is restated in the concluding quatrain,

> From hence let those be warn'd, who mean to wed;
> Lest mutual Falsehood stain the Bridal-Bed:
> For each Deceiver to his Cost may find,
> That Marriage Frauds too oft are paid in kind.

Unlike *The Double-Dealer*, the comedy has in Mirabell a hero who is a sufficient protagonist, and whose values are supported by the play's themes and structure.

*The Way of the World* turns on a legacy conflict.[3] Lady Wishfort, the last remaining representative of the preceding generation, holds

---

[1] *Dramatic Miscellanies*, Dublin, 1784, iii, 204.

[2] 'Audire est Operae pretium, procedere recte/ . . . Qui maechis non vultis. . . . Metuat doti deprensa' ('It is worth your while to listen you who don't want things to turn out well for adulterers . . . she who is found out fears for her dowry') Horace, *Satires*, I. ii. 37–8, 131.

[3] My discussion is indebted to the work of P. and M. Mueschke.

half the fortune of her niece, Millamant, and has power over her daughter, Mrs Fainall, a newly married widow. The aim of both sides is to control Lady Wishfort's irrevocable disposition of these fortunes. Both Fainall and Mrs Marwood are self-seekers, and, like Mirabell and Mrs Fainall, have been lovers before the play opens. Mirabell, however, has the 'generosity' to feel obligation. When he fears that his widowed mistress is pregnant, he helps her to marry Fainall, but arranges to have her property put in his trust. This legal document is only revealed at the end of the comedy by Mirabell, when Fainall's scheming has uncovered Mirabell's impropriety as well as his own adultery with Mrs Marwood. Mirabell is thus able to destroy Fainall's apparently unshakeable power over Lady Wishfort. Law, as an expression of human relationships, resolves the play, and the famous proviso scene between Mirabell and Millamant provides a metaphor which embodies this way of viewing the world.

The apparent intricacy of the plot disguises the strength and clarity of the comedy's movement. From the very beginning Fainall and Mirabell are opposed, though their ability to conduct themselves in conversation may at first obscure the differences. For both of them, as for the women, conversation is a continual exploration and analysis of feeling. Act I, set in the male domain of the chocolate house, allows Fainall to probe Mirabell's unsuccessful attempt to gain access to Millamant by pretending to court her superannuated aunt, Lady Wishfort:

FAINALL: The Discovery of your sham Addresses to her to conceal your Love to her Niece, has provok'd this Separation: Had you dissembl'd better, Things might have continu'd in the State of Nature.
MIRABELL: I did as much as Man cou'd, with any reasonable Conscience; I proceeded to the very last Act of Flattery with her, and was guilty of a Song in her Commendation . . . The Devil's in't, if an old Woman is to be flatter'd further, unless a Man shou'd endeavour downright personally to debauch her; and that my Virtue forbad me.

(iii, 16)

Mirabell is an *honnête homme* of a new style. Fainall lives, he mistakenly thinks, in a 'State of Nature' uncontrolled by any laws save those of personal gratification. Mirabell, the man of sense, avoids being attenuated to a mere sentimental nonentity in reply to Fainall because his sharp awareness of the rights and feelings of others is circumscribed by his own danger: he must suffer for his past actions, as do all the other characters in the play.

Congreve's greatest achievement in *The Way of the World* is a style and verbal alertness which places the characters by means of their own words. The coquettish Lady Wishfort, endlessly concerned about her reputation for modesty, swerves wildly between images drawn from the scurrility of servants and the unreal pastoral language she uses when speaking to Mrs Marwood in Act V. Every minor character, including the servants, has his or her particular idiom, from the affected pronunciation of Millamant's maid, Mincing, to the blustering goodwill of Sir Wilfull. Legal and gaming images are taken up throughout the play. The opening words, 'You are a fortunate Man, Mr Fainall', which are spoken by Mirabell on '*Rising from Cards*' must be put against Petulant's comment on the great last scene, '. . . what's the matter? who's Hand's out?' (iii, 75). Fainall, the practised and fortunate gambler (the man of the world in fact), fails to gain his ends because he regards the wills which leave the fortunes in Lady Wishfort's hands as mere stakes in a game of chance. He cannot allow for the 'generosity' of Mirabell and his wife, nor does he realize that legal documents ought to be contractual formulations of existing or future human relationships. Consequently, Fainall's Hobbesian individualism is destroyed by Mirabell's society built on obligation and contract. Locke, rather than innate benevolence, resolves *The Way of the World*.

Artifice, passion, and self-fulfilment are intimately linked in *The Way of the World*. Law itself is man-made, and so too the 'regularity' of the play sets up an analogy between its structure, ordered by dramatic laws, and the dénouement, whose legal provisos and instruments indicate that law is a necessary artifice, like the 'decorums' of 'polite' behaviour, and these are the basis of society. Passion must be reconciled with reason, order, and the social proprieties.

Consequently, Mirabell's 'generosity' results not in the re-establishment of a lost order, as in Shakespearean comedy, but is the hard-won foundation of a new society based specifically on the expulsion of Fainall's egocentricity, and the destruction of Lady Wishfort's power. The dance which concludes the play celebrates a contracted marriage, based on a reciprocal relationship, in a 'world' ordered by mutual obligation. Restoration comedy is resolutely secular in its conclusions.

The achievements of other writers in this last phase are more modest than Congreve's, but hardly inconsiderable. Sir John Vanbrugh (1664–1726), architect, playwright, and theatrical entrepreneur, is a difficult writer to place since of his eleven plays, only two, *The Relapse* (acted 1696) and *The Provok'd Wife* (1697), are wholly his own. The posthumous fragment, *A Journey to London*, was finished by Cibber as *The Provok'd Husband* in 1728. Otherwise his comedies consist of an adaptation of Fletcher, *The Pilgrim* (1700); *The False Friend* (1702) from the Spanish via Le Sage; one translation from Boursault, *Aesop* (1696–7); two from Dancourt, *The Country House* (acted 1703) and *The Confederacy* (1705); and three from Molière, *Squire Trelooby* (1704),[1] *The Mistake* (acted 1705), and *The Cuckold in Conceit* (1707, unpublished). How far these free and vigorous translations should be regarded as original, in view of Vanbrugh's often radical alterations of emphasis and tone, has not yet been properly explored.

Vanbrugh's two original plays and the fragmentary *A Journey to London*, have been frequently passed over as being coarse-grained. Cibber's remark that 'the Style of no Author whatsoever gave [actors'] Memory less trouble than that of Sir John Vanbrugh', has been interpreted as meaning that Vanbrugh was careless of detail and only superficially concerned with the problems which his comedies dramatize.

*The Relapse* and *The Provok'd Wife* both aim for a kind of naturalism denied by Congreve, whose structural and verbal artifice holds the audience at a distance precisely because he conceives of characters' relationships as ones which must be, in the first instance at least, perceived and expressed through a man-made code of manners. There is never any doubt about the coarseness of Vanbrugh's Sir John Brute or of Loveless's duplicity, whereas there is, at first, little sign of Fainall's corroding cynicism. Vanbrugh's realism appears in both these plays in his decision to deal with relationships within marriage, and in the pungent directness with which he points out that a coquette wishes to have the disruptive power given by promiscuity, without the allied need for sexual performance:

> ... they (against Nature) keep their Chastity, only because they find more Pleasure in doing Mischief with it, than they shou'd have in parting with it.[2]

The immediate impetus behind *The Relapse* was Cibber's *Love's Last Shift* (1696), which had reformed the debauched Loveless in the

---

[1] Written in collaboration with Congreve and William Walsh: no authoritative text was published.

[2] *A Journey to London; The Complete Works of Sir John Vanbrugh*, ed. B. Dobrée and G. Webb, London, 1927, iii, 152.

fifth act through the shining faith and virtue of his wife, Amanda. Vanbrugh's intention was to show that Cibber's improbable sentimental ending could not stand the test of reality or time. Hence Loveless is tempted by Berinthia, while Amanda's virtue is put to an extreme test through her feelings towards Worthy. Amanda's last-minute retreat from a willing rape assaults the audience by taking them to the very edge of the deed. Titillation is carried beyond the safety of theatrical voyeurism, and the point made that even virtuous married women may be severely tempted – and might actually fall.

Vanbrugh's strength is his unblushing presentation of the facts. The homosexual proclivities of Coupler in the sub-plot query the 'gaiety' of Young Fashion's pursuit of Miss Hoyden, his elder brother's wife-to-be, while the magnificent comic foolishness of Lord Foppington himself questions the wisdom of primogeniture, which leaves Foppington free to satisfy his vanity, but condemns Young Fashion to poverty and dissimulation.

*The Provok'd Wife* returns to Amanda's problem, but in a more acute form. Lady Brute is saddled with a boorish sot, who opens the comedy by railing against marriage with the stock attacks developed over the years in Restoration comedy. The effect on Lady Brute, who is a normal woman, is to make her doubt the strength of her obligations – 'he han't kept his Word – Why then I'm absolv'd from mine' (ed. Dobrée and Webb, i, 116). Although, like Amanda, Lady Brute does not carry thought into deed, her virtue, though temporarily safe, does not look as if it will long continue so. Vanbrugh's play is an energetic one, which presents the facts and implies an alternative. Replying to Jeremy Collier, he wrote:

If therefore I have shew'd ... upon the Stage, what generally the Thing call'd a Fine Gentleman is off on't, I think I have done what I shou'd do. I have laid open his Vices as well as his Virtues: 'Tis the Business of the Audience to observe where his Flaws lessen his Value; and by considering the Deformity of his Blemishes, become sensible how much a Finer Thing he wou'd be without 'em.[1]

Vanbrugh's realism, which is centred on the marriage relationship, appears in a different form in the comedy of George Farquhar (1678–1707). As William Archer put it,

Farquhar broke away altogether from the purlieus of Covent Garden, and took comedy into the highways and byways. ... Farquhar introduced us to

[1] *A Short Vindication of The Relapse and The Provok'd Wife*, 1698, in *Complete Works*, ed. Dobrée and Webb, i, 206–7.

the life of the inn, the market-place, and the manor house. He showed us the squire, the justice, the innkeeper, the highwayman, the recruiting sergeant, the charitable lady, the country belle, the chambermaid, and half a score of excellent rustic types.[1]

Archer, quite rightly, puts a positive valuation on what Pope called Farquhar's 'pert, low dialogue', for it enlarges the field of Restoration comedy to depict a society which is recognizably that of Fielding's novels. Farquhar, though he remains within the patterns of earlier comedies, can include coal-miners in his drama. *Love and a Bottle* (acted 1698) was not highly regarded when it first came out, but with *The Constant Couple* (acted 1699) Farquhar won his first success, which led to a sequel, *Sir Harry Wildair* (1707). Activity and variety are the chief attractions of *The Constant Couple*, and the energy which Sir Harry and Colonel Standard show in cudgelling dupes had early been censored by Etherege. *The Recruiting Officer* (1706) and *The Beaux' Stratagem* (1707) reflect Farquhar's own experience, and though he does not aim at social satire, he presents the reality of the early eighteenth century with robust humour and knowledge.

If Farquhar shows a possible direction comedy might have taken but for his death, Colley Cibber (1671–1757) acts as a weathervane in a period of transitional taste. Affected by Collier's attack on the immorality of the stage and by the shift in taste which Collier marked, Cibber's careers as an actor and future manager enabled him to supply what was called for. *Love's Last Shift* (1696) did not initiate sentimental comedy, but Cibber's liking in this play, and in *The Careless Husband* (acted 1704), for a sudden and unlikely reform of the prodigal in the last act, shows, more than the work of any other dramatist, the clash between old and new in these years. Yet Cibber, who was admired by Horace Walpole for his ability to catch the tone of 'society', has a sharp sense of 'la vie quotidienne'.[2]

The début of Richard Steele (1672–1729) with *The Funeral* (acted 1701) signals a decisive switch towards sentimental comedy, not completed until the production of his *The Conscious Lovers* in 1722. In these plays, as well as in *The Lying Lover* (acted 1703) and *The Tender Husband* (1705), Steele shifts the norms of comedy from scepticism to benevolence, to middle-class respectability, and to a vapid Christianity. Steele himself put down the failure of *The Lying Lover* to a piety premature for the taste of its audience.

---

[1] *George Farquhar*, London, 1906, p 24.
[2] F. W. Bateson, *English Comic Drama 1700–1750*, Oxford, 1929, p 33.

Steele's drama belongs properly to a history of eighteenth-century drama. A sense of the precariousness of Congreve's achievement is gained when *The Double-Dealer* is set in this context, for his second comedy is prophetic of the new sensibility. 'What is finer', Horace Walpole was to exclaim, 'than the serious scenes of Maskwell and Lady Touchwood. . . ?' Walpole saw clearly that the *comédie larmoyante*, or sentimental comedy, was an attempt to treat bourgeois life as intensely and tragically as tragedy treated courtly and kingly life. 'Had tragedy descended to people of subordinate stations', he writes, 'authors would have found the language too pompous'; hence they used the language of comedy 'to represent a melancholy story in private life.' If this had been called a *'tragédie bourgeoise'*, he argues, a new genre would have been created. Walpole's analysis is surely a correct description of Steele's aim in *The Conscious Lovers*. The misfortune is that the sceptical mode of comedy is fundamentally at odds with the innate benevolence of a character like Young Bevil. What Steele could not foresee was that the proper form for a true *tragédie bourgeoise* would be created, not in the drama, but in the novel – in Samuel Richardson's *Clarissa*.

# BIBLIOGRAPHY

*Editions from which quotations are made have been asterisked.

Abbreviations: RRDS = Regents Renaissance Drama Series
RP     = The Revels Plays
NM     = The New Mermaid Series

## 1. *The Beginnings of English Drama*

### Stage and Drama till 1660

Richard Axton, *European Drama of the Early Middle Ages*, London, 1974.

F. S. Boas, *University Drama in the Tudor Age*, Oxford, 1914.

Herbert Berry, *The Boar's Head Playhouse*, London, 1986.

Eleanor Boswell, *The Restoration Court Stage*, Cambridge, Mass., 1932.

L. B. Campbell, *Scenes and Machines on the English Stage during the Renaissance*, Cambridge, 1923; reprint 1961.

A. C. Cawley, *Everyman*, Manchester, 1961.

E. K. Chambers, *The Medieval Stage*, 2 vols, Oxford, 1903.

T. W. Craik, *The Tudor Interlude*, Leicester, 1958.

Neville Denny, ed., *The Medieval Drama: Stratford-Upon-Avon Studies 16*, London, 1973.

Willard Farnham, *The Medieval Heritage of Elizabethan Tragedy*, Berkeley, 1936.

H. C. Gardiner, *Mysteries' End*, New Haven, 1946; reprint 1967.

V. C. Gildersleeve, *Government Regulation of Elizabethan Drama*, New York, 1900; reprint 1965.

Peter Happé, *Tudor Interludes*, edited for Penguin English Library, London, 1972.

A. Harbage, *Annals of English Drama, 975–1700*, rev. S. Schoenbaum, London, 1964.

O. B. Hardison Jr., *Christian Rite and Christian Drama in the Middle Ages*, Baltimore, 1965.

C. Walter Hodges, *The Globe Restored*, London, 1953; 2nd edn 1958.

Leslie Hotson, *The Commonwealth and Restoration Stage*, Cambridge, Mass., 1928.

Stanley J. Kahrl, *Traditions of Medieval Drama*, London, 1974.

G. R. Kernodle, *From Art to Theatre*, Chicago, 1944.

V. A. Kolve, *The Play Called Corpus Christi*, Stanford, 1966.

John Lydgate, *Minor Poems*, ed. for EETS by H. N. MacCracken, Oxford, 2 vols, 1911–34.

J. M. Manly, *Specimens of the Pre-Shakespearean Drama*, Boston, 2 vols, 1897.

T. H. Vail Motter, *The School Drama in England*, London, 1929.

Sumiko Miyajima, *The Theatre of Man*, Clevedon, Avon, 1977.

Alan H. Nelson, *The Medieval English Stage*, Chicago, 1974.

Robert Potter, *The English Morality Play*, London, 1975.

Jocelyn Powell, *Restoration Theatre Production*, London, 1984.

Emily Prosser, *Drama and Religion in the English Mystery Plays*, Stanford, 1961.

M. Roston, *Biblical Drama in England from the Middle Ages to the Present Day*, London, 1968.

E. T. Schell and J. D. Shuckter, eds, *English Morality Plays and Moral Interludes*, London, 1969.

Richard Southern, *Changeable Scenery*, London, 1952.

—— *The Medieval Theatre in the Round*, London, 1957.

Sandra Sticca, *The Medieval Drama*, New York, 1972.

William Tydeman, *English Medieval Theatre, 1400–1500*, London, 1986.

—— *The Theatre in the Middle Ages*, Cambridge, 1978.

Enid Welsford, *The Court Masque*, Cambridge, 1927.

G. Wickham, *Early English Stages*, London, 3 vols in 4, 1959–81.

—— *English Moral Interludes*, London, 1976; 2nd edn 1985.

—— *The Medieval Theatre* London, 1974; 2nd edn 1980.

—— *Shakespeare's Dramatic Heritage*, London, 1969.

F. P. Wilson, *The English Drama 1485–1585*, ed. G. K. Hunter, Oxford, 1969.

R. Withington, *English Pageantry*, Cambridge, Mass., 2 vols, 1918–20.

## 2. Elizabethan and Jacobean Drama

### Reference

Gerald Eades Bentley, *The Jacobean and Caroline Stage*, 7 vols, Oxford, 1941–68.

E. K. Chambers, *The Elizabethan Stage*, 4 vols, Oxford, 1923.

T. W. Craik and Clifford Leech, gen. eds, *The Revels History of Drama in English:* vol. III 1576–1613, London, 1975; vol. IV 1613–1660, London, 1981.

A. Harbage, *Annals of English Drama 975–1700*, revised by S. Schoenbaum, London, 1964.

W. C. Hazlitt, *The English Drama and Stage 1543–1664*, London, 1869.

T. P. Logan and D. S. Smith, eds, *A Survey and Bibliography of Recent Studies in English Renaissance Drama*, London, 1973–8.

Glynne Wickham, *Early English Stages 1300–1660*, 3 vols, London, 1959–72.

### General

Joel B. Altman, *The Tudor Play of Mind: Rhetorical Inquiry and the Development of Elizabethan Drama*, Berkeley, 1978.

Robert Ashton, *The English Civil War*, London, 1978.

Marie Axton and Raymond Williams, eds, *English Drama: Forms and Development*, Cambridge, 1977.

J. W. Bennett, O. Cargill, and V. Hall, eds, *Studies in English Renaissance Drama*, New York, 1959.

Gerald Eades Bentley, *The Profession of Dramatist in Shakespeare's Time 1590–1642*, Princeton, N.J., 1971.

—— (ed.) *The Seventeenth Century Stage* Chicago, 1968.

M. Bluestone and N. Rabkin, eds, *Shakespeare's Contemporaries: Modern Studies in English Renaissance Drama*, Princeton, N.J., 1961.

M. C. Bradbrook, *A History of Elizabethan Drama*, 6 vols, Cambridge, 1979. Revised editions of: *Themes and Conventions of Elizabethan Tragedy; The Growth and Structure of Elizabethan Comedy; Shakespeare and Elizabethan Poetry; The Rise of the Common Player; Shakespeare The Craftsman; The Living Monument; Shakespeare and the Theatre of His Time.*

Wolfgang Clemen, *English Tragedy Before Shakespeare*, trans. T. S. Dorsch, London, 1961.

T. S. Eliot, *Selected Essays*, London, 1932; essays on Marlowe, Jonson, Webster, Tourneur, Middleton, Chapman, Heywood, Ford, Marston, and Massinger.

Una Ellis-Fermor, *The Jacobean Drama*, London, 1936.

William Empson, *Some Versions of Pastoral*, London, 1935.

David L. Frost, *The School of Shakespeare: The Influence of Shakespeare on English Drama 1600–1642*, Cambridge, 1968.

B. Gibbons, *Jacobean City Comedy*, London, 1968.

W. W. Greg, *Pastoral Poetry and Pastoral Drama*, Oxford, 1906.

A. Harbage, *Cavalier Drama*, London, 1936.

Harriett Hawkins, *Likenesses of Truth in Elizabethan and Restoration Drama*, Oxford, 1972.

—— *Poetic Freedom and Poetic Truth: Chaucer, Shakespeare, Marlowe, Milton*, Oxford, 1976.

Christopher Hill, *Intellectual Origins of the English Revolution*, Oxford, 1965.

Richard Hosley, ed., *Essays on Shakespeare and Elizabethan Drama in Honour of Hardin Craig*, London, 1963.

G. K. Hunter, *Dramatic Identities and Cultural Tradition: Studies in Shakespeare and His Contemporaries*, Liverpool, 1978.

R. J. Kaufmann, ed., *Elizabethan Drama: Modern Essays in Criticism*, New York, 1961.

A. C. Kirsch, *Jacobean Dramatic Perspectives*, Charlottesville, Va., 1972.

L. C. Knights, *Drama and Society in the Age of Jonson*, London, 1937.

J. W. Lever, *The Tragedy of State*, London, 1971.

Richard Levin, *The Multiple Plot in English Renaissance Drama*, Chicago, Ill., 1971.

—— *New Readings vs. Old Plays: Recent Trends in the Reinterpretation of English Renaissance Drama*, London, 1979.

Robert Ornstein, *The Moral Vision of Jacobean Tragedy*, Madison, Wis., 1960.

S. Gorley Putt, *The Golden Age of English Drama*, Cambridge, 1981.

Conrad Russell, ed., *The Origins of the English Civil War*, London, 1973.

S. Schoenbaum, *Shakespeare and Others*, London, 1985.

Peter Ure, *Elizabethan and Jacobean Drama*, Liverpool, 1974.

Eugene M. Waith, *The Herculean Hero in Marlowe, Chapman, Shakespeare, and Dryden*, London, 1962.

F. P. Wilson, *Elizabethan and Jacobean*, Oxford, 1945.

## Series

Among proliferating collections of essays, the following series can be recommended:

*The Elizabethan Theatre*, vols I–III, ed. David Galloway, vols IV –VIII, ed. G. R. Hibbard, Waterloo, Ontario, 1969.

*Medieval and Renaissance Drama in England*, ed. J. Leeds Barroll II *et al*, New York, 1984–.

*Renaissance Drama*, New Series, founding editor S. Schoenbaum, Evanston, 1968–.

*Stratford-Upon-Avon Studies*, vols 1–10, ed. John Russell and Bernard Harris, vols 11–, ed. Malcolm Bradbury and David Palmer, London, 1960–, especially *1 Jacobean Theatre* (1960), *3 Early Shakespeare* (1961), *9 Elizabethan Theatre* (1967), *8 Later Shakespeare* (1966).

*Studies in English Literature*. A quarterly which devotes one issue each year to this period.

## Beaumont and Fletcher

\**The Works of Francis Beaumont and John Fletcher*, eds A. Glover and A. R. Waller, 10 vols, Cambridge, 1905–12. Based on the Second Folio, 1679.

*A King and No King*, ed. Robert K. Turner Jr., RRDS, London, 1964.

\**The Knight of the Burning Pestle*, ed. M. Hattaway, NM, London, 1969.

*The Maid's Tragedy*, ed. Howard B. Norland, RRDS, London, 1968.

\**Philaster, or Love Lies A-bleeding*, ed. Andrew Gurr, RP, London, 1969.

*The Dramatic Works in the Beaumont and Fletcher Canon*, general editor Fredson Bowers, 10 vols projected, Cambridge, 1966–. On the question of attribution, see the series of articles by Cyrus Hoy, *Studies in Bibliography*, vols viii–xv.

John F. Danby, *Elizabethan and Jacobean Poets*, London, 1965.

Clifford Leech, *The John Fletcher Plays*, London, 1962.

Eugene M. Waith, *The Patterns of Tragi-Comedy in Beaumont and Fletcher*, New Haven, Conn., 1952.

## Chapman

\**The Plays*, ed. T. M. Parrott, 4 vols, London, 1910–14; reprint New York, 1961.

*The Plays of George Chapman: The Comedies. A Critical Edition*, gen. ed. Allan Holaday, assisted by Michael Kiernan, London, 1970.

*The Poems*, ed. Phyllis Brooks Bartlett, London, 1941.

*Chapman's Homer*, ed. A. Nicoll, 2 vols, London, 1957.

*All Fools*, ed. F. Manley, RRDS, London, 1968.

*Bussy D'Ambois*, ed. M. Evans, NM, London, 1965; ed. N. Brooke, RP, London, 1964; ed. Robert J. Lordi, RRDS, London, 1964.

*The Conspiracy and Tragedy of Charles, Duke of Byron*, ed. George Ray, 2 vols, Garland Publishing, 1979.

*Eastward Ho!* by G. Chapman, Ben Jonson, and John Marston, ed. R. W. Van Fossen, RP, Manchester, 1979.

*The Gentleman Usher*, ed. John Hazel Smith, RRDS, London, 1970.

*The Widow's Tears*, ed. E. M. Smeak, RRDS, London, 1967; ed. A. Yamada, RP, London, 1975.

Richard S. Ide, *Possessed With Greatness: The Heroic Tragedies of Chapman and Shakespeare*, Chapel Hill, N.C., 1980.

Millar MacLure, *George Chapman: A Critical Study*, Toronto, 1966.

Edwin Muir, 'Royal Man: Notes on the Tragedies of George Chapman', in *Essays On Literature and Society*, London, 1949.

Ennis Rees, *The Tragedies of Chapman: Renaissance Ethics in Action*, Cambridge, Mass., 1954.

Peter Ure, 'Chapman's Tragedies' in *Jacobean Theatre: Stratford-Upon-Avon Studies 1*, eds J. R. Brown and Bernard Harris, London, 1960.

### Dekker

*\*The Dramatic Works*, ed. Fredson Bowers, 4 vols, Cambridge, 1953–61.

*The Shoemakers' Holiday*, ed. D. J. Palmer, NM, London, 1975; eds R. L. Smallwood and Stanley Wells, RP, Manchester, 1979.

*The Witch of Edmonton: A Critical Edition*, ed. Etta Soiref Onat, New York, 1980.

James H. Conover, *Thomas Dekker: An Analysis of Dramatic Structure*, The Hague, 1969.

G. R. Price, *Thomas Dekker*, New York, 1969.

### Ford

*\*Works*, ed. W. Gifford, revised A. Dyce, London, 1869.

*The Selected Plays*, ed. Colin Gibson, Cambridge, 1986.

*The Broken Heart*, ed. Brian Morris, NM, London, 1965; ed. D. K. Anderson Jr., RRDS, London, 1968.

*'Tis Pity She's a Whore*, ed. N. W. Bawcutt, RRDS, London, 1966; ed. Brian Morris, NM, London, 1968; ed. Derek Roper, Methuen, London, 1975.

*Perkin Warbeck*, ed. D. K. Anderson Jr., RRDS, London, 1966; ed. Peter Ure, RP, London, 1968.

*The Lover's Melancholy*, ed. R. F. Hill, RP, Manchester, 1985.
S. B. Ewing, *Burtonian Melancholy in the Plays of John Ford*, Princeton, N.J., 1940.
Dorothy M. Farr, *John Ford and the Caroline Theatre*, London, 1979.
Ronald Huebert, *John Ford: Baroque English Dramatist*, London, 1977.
Clifford Leech, *John Ford and the Drama of his Time*, London, 1957.
Tucker Orbison, *The Tragic Vision of John Ford*, Salzburg, 1974.
M. Joan Sargeaunt, *John Ford*, Oxford, 1935 (biography).
M. Stavig, *John Ford and the Traditional Moral Order*, Wisconsin, 1968.

## Greene

*Life and Complete Works*, ed. A. B. Grosart, 15 vols, London, 1881–6. Reissued 1964. The only complete edition.
\*Plays and Poems*, ed. J. Churton ·Collins, 2 vols, Oxford, 1905. Often inaccurate.
*Friar Bacon and Friar Bungay*, ed. D. Selzer, RRDS, London, 1964; ed. J. A. Lavin, NM, London, 1969.
*James the Fourth*, ed. J. A. Lavin, NM, London, 1967; ed. Norman Sanders, RP, London, 1970.
Kenneth Muir, 'Robert Greene as Dramatist' in *Essays In Honour of Hardin Craig*, ed. R. Hosley, London, 1963.
Norman Sanders, 'The Comedy of Greene and Shakespeare', in *Early Shakespeare: Stratford-Upon-Avon Studies 3*, London, 1961.

## Heywood

*Dramatic Works*, ed. R. H. Shepherd, 6 vols, London, 1874. The only complete edition.
*Thomas Heywood*, ed. A. W. Verity, Mermaid, London, 1888. Selected plays.
*The Fair Maid of The West: Parts I and II*, ed. Robert K. Turner, Jr., RRDS, London, 1968.
*A Woman Killed With Kindness*, ed. R. W. Van Fossen, RP, London, 1961; ed. Brian W. M. Scobie, NM, London, 1985.
Frederick S. Boas, *Thomas Heywood*, London, 1950.

## *Jonson*

See also Section 5.

*Epicoene*, ed. L. A. Beaurline, RRDS, London, 1966; ed. R. V. Holdsworth, NM, London, 1979.

L. S. Champion, *Ben Jonson's 'Dotages'*, Kentucky, 1968.

## *Kyd*

*Works*, ed. Frederick S. Boas, Oxford, 1901.

*\*The Spanish Tragedy*, ed. Philip Edwards, RP, London, 1959; ed B. L. Joseph, NM, London, 1964; ed. Andrew S. Cairncross, RRDS, London, 1967; ed. J. R. Mulryne, NM, London, 1970.

Jonas A. Barish, 'The Spanish Tragedy; or, The Pleasures and Perils of Rhetoric', in *Stratford-Upon-Avon Studies 9*, London, 1966.

Philip W. Edwards, *Thomas Kyd and Early Elizabethan Tragedy*, London, 1966.

## *Lyly*

*\*Complete Works*, ed. R. W. Bond, 3 vols, Oxford, 1902. There is a new edition, ed. G. K. Hunter, in progress.

*Galathea and Midas*, ed. Anne Begor Lancashire, RRDS, London, 1970.

*Mother Bombie*, in *Four Tudor Comedies*, ed. W. Tydeman, Harmondsworth, 1984.

G. K. Hunter, *John Lyly: The Humanist as Courtier*, London, 1962.

—— *Lyly and Peele*, London, 1968.

Jocelyn Powell, 'John Lyly and the Language of Play', in *Stratford-Upon-Avon Studies 9*, London, 1966.

Peter Saccio, *The Court Comedies of John Lyly: A Study in Allegorical Dramaturgy*, Princeton, N.J., 1969.

## *Marlowe*

See also Section 3.

G. K. Hunter, 'The Theology of *The Jew of Malta*', reprinted in *Dramatic Identities and Cultural Tradition: Studies in Shakespeare and His Contemporaries*, Liverpool, 1978.

W. Moelwyn Merchant, 'Marlowe the Orthodox', in *Christopher Marlowe*, New Mermaid Critical Commentaries, ed. Brian Morris, London, 1968.

## Marston

∗*The Plays*, ed. H. Harvey Wood, 3 vols, Edinburgh, 1934–9.
∗*The Selected Plays of John Marston*, eds P. Jackson and Michael Neill, Cambridge, 1986.
*Antonio and Mellida*, ed. G. K. Hunter, RRDS, London, 1965.
*Antonio's Revenge*, ed. G. K. Hunter, RRDS, London, 1966; ed. W. R. Gair, RP, Manchester, 1978.
*The Dutch Courtesan*, ed. Martin Wine, RRDS, London, 1965.
*The Malcontent*, ed. Martin Wine, RRDS, London, 1964.; ed. Brian Harris, NM, London, 1967; ed. G. K. Hunter, London, 1975.
*Parasiter, or, The Fawn*, ed. David A. Blostein, RP, Manchester, 1978.
*What You Will*, ed. M. R. Woodhead, Nottingham Drama Texts, Nottingham, 1980.
*The Wonder of Women, or, The Tragedy of Sophonisba*, ed. William Kemp, Garland Publishing, London, 1979.
Anthony Caputi, *John Marston, Satirist*, Ithaca, N.Y., 1961.
John Scott Colley, *John Marston's Theatrical Drama*, Salzburg, 1974.
Philip J. Finkelpearl, *John Marston of the Middle Temple, An Elizabethan Dramatist in His Social Setting*, Cambridge, Mass., 1967.
R. W. Ingram, *John Marston*, Boston, 1978.

## Massinger

∗*The Plays and Poems of Philip Massinger*, ed. Philip Edwards and Colin Gibson, 5 vols, Oxford, 1976.
*The Selected Plays of Philip Massinger*, ed. Colin Gibson, Cambridge, 1978.
*A New Way To Pay Old Debts*, ed. T. W. Craik, NM, London, 1963.
*The City Madam*, ed. T. W. Craik, NM, London, 1963; ed. Cyrus Hoy, RRDS, London, 1966.
Thomas A. Dunn, *Philip Massinger, The Man and The Playwright*, London, 1957.
Douglas Howard, ed. *Philip Massinger: A Critical Reassessment*, Cambridge, 1985.

## Middleton

See also Section 6.
∗*The Selected Plays of Thomas Middleton*, ed. David L. Frost, Cambridge, 1978.
*The Changeling*, ed. N. W. Bawcutt, RP, London, 1961; ed. Patricia Thomson, NM, London, 1964.

*A Chaste Maid In Cheapside*, ed. A. Brissenden, NM, London, 1968; ed. Brian Parker, RP, London, 1969.

*A Fair Quarrel*, with William Rowley, ed. R. V. Holdsworth, NM, London, 1974; ed. George E. Price, RRDS, London, 1977.

*A Game At Chess*, ed. J. W. Harper, NM, London, 1966.

*The Roaring Girl*, with Thomas Dekker, ed. Andor Gomme, NM, London, 1976.

*Women Beware Women*, ed. Roma Gill, NM, London, 1968; ed. J. R. Mulryne, RP, London, 1975.

*A Trick to Catch the Old One*, ed. G. J. Watson, NM, London, 1968.

## Nashe

\*_The Works_, ed. R. B. McKerrow, rev. F. P. Wilson, 5 vols, Oxford, 1958.

Stephen S. Hilliard, *The Singularity of Thomas Nashe*, London, 1986.

Donald J. McGinn, *Thomas Nashe*, Boston, Mass., 1981.

Charles Nicholl, *A Cup of News: The Life of Thomas Nashe*, London, 1984.

## Peele

\*_The Life and Works of George Peele_, gen. ed. C. T. Prouty, 3 vols, London, 1952–70.

*The Old Wives Tale*, ed. Patricia Binnie, RP, Manchester, 1980.

Inga-Stina Ekeblad, 'The Love of King David and Fair Bethsabe', in *English Studies*, xxxix, 1958, 1–6.

—— 'The House of David in Renaissance Drama', in *Renaissance Drama*, 1965.

—— '"What words, what looks, what wonders?": Language and Spectacle in the Theatre of George Peele', in *The Elizabethan Theatre V*, ed. G. R. Hibbard, Ontario, 1975.

## Tourneur

See Section 6.

## Webster

See Section 6.

## 3.  Christopher Marlowe

*Editions*

*The Works and Life of Christopher Marlowe*, gen. ed. R. H. Case, 6 vols, London, 1930–3.

*The Complete Works of Christopher Marlowe* (old spelling edition), ed. Fredson Bowers, 2 vols, Cambridge, 1973.

*The Complete Poems and Translations*, ed. Stephen Orgel, Harmondsworth, 1971.

*Poems*, ed. M. MacLure, RP, London, 1968.

*Dido, Queen of Carthage* and *The Massacre at Paris*, ed. H. J. Oliver, RP, London, 1968.

*Tamburlaine The Great: Parts I and II*, ed. John D. Jump, RRDS, London, 1967; ed. J. W. Harper, NM, London, 1971; ed. J. S. Cunningham, RP, Manchester, 1981.

*The Jew of Malta*, ed. T. W. Craik, NM, London, 1967; ed. Richard W. Van Fossen, RRDS, London, 1965; ed. N. W. Bawcutt, RP, Manchester, 1978.

*Marlowe's 'Doctor Faustus', 1610–1616* (parallel texts), ed. W. W. Greg, Oxford, 1950.

*The Tragical History of the Life and Death of Doctor Faustus: a conjectural reconstruction*, ed. W. W. Greg, Oxford, 1959.

\**Doctor Faustus*, ed. John D. Jump, RP, London, 1962.

*Christopher Marlowe's 'Doctor Faustus', Text and Major Criticism*, ed. Irving Ribner, New York, 1966.

*Doctor Faustus: Text and Performance*, ed. William Tydeman, Basingstoke, 1984.

*Edward II*, ed. H. B. Charlton and R. D. Waller, London, 1933, rev. F. N. Lees, 1955; ed. W. Moelwyn Merchant, NM, London, 1967; ed. Roma Gill, London, 1967.


*Reference*

Robert J. Fehrenbach, Lea Ann Boone and Mario A. Di Cesare, eds, *A Concordance to the Plays, Poems, and Translations of Christopher Marlowe*, London, 1982. Keyed to Fredson Bowers's edition.

Millar MacLure, ed., *Marlowe: The Critical Heritage 1588–1896*, London, 1979.

## Biography and Criticism

R. W. Battenhouse, *Marlowe's 'Tamburlaine': A Study in Renaissance Moral Philosophy*, 2nd edn, Nashville, 1964.

F. S. Boas, *Marlowe and His Circle*, Oxford, 1929. On Marlowe's intellectual milieu; contains facsimiles and documents.

—— *Christopher Marlowe: A Biographical and Critical Study*, Oxford, 1940, rev. 1964.

M. C. Bradbrook, *Themes and Conventions of Elizabethan Tragedy*, Cambridge, 1935, rev. 1979.

—— *The School of Night*, London, 1936.

—— *Collected Papers Volume One: The Artist and Society in Shakespeare's England*, London, 1982.

John Russell Brown, ed., *Marlowe: Tamburlaine the Great, Edward the Second and The Jew of Malta: A Casebook*, London, 1982.

Wolfgang Clemen, *English Tragedy Before Shakespeare*, trans. T. S. Dorsch, London, 1961.

Sukanta Chaudhuri, *Infirm Glory: Shakespeare and the Renaissance Image of Man*, Oxford, 1981.

G. I. Duthie, 'The Dramatic Structure of *Tamburlaine*', in *English Studies* (i.e. *Essays and Studies*), London, 1948.

T. S. Eliot, 'Christopher Marlowe' (1918), in *Selected Essays*, London, 1932.

U. Ellis-Fermor, *Christopher Marlowe*, London, 1927.

—— *The Jacobean Drama*, London, 1936, 4th edn, 1961.

W. Farnham, ed., *Twentieth Century Interpretations of 'Doctor Faustus': a Collection of Critical Essays*, Englewood Cliffs, N.J., 1969.

H. Gardner, 'Milton's Satan and The Theme of Damnation in Elizabethan Tragedy', in *English Studies* (i.e. *Essays and Studies*), London, 1948; reprinted in R. J. Kaufmann, ed., *Elizabethan Drama*, New York, 1961.

J. L. Hotson, *The Death of Christopher Marlowe*, London, 1925.

John D. Jump, ed., *Doctor Faustus: A Casebook*, London, 1969.

Alvin Kernan, *Two Renaissance Myth Makers: Christopher Marlowe and Ben Jonson. Selected Papers from the English Institute 1975–1976*, Johns Hopkins University Press, 1977.

P. H. Kocher, *Christopher Marlowe: A Study of His Thought, Learning, and Character*, North Carolina, 1946.

Clifford Leech, 'Marlowe's Edward II', *Critical Quarterly*, i, 1959, 181–96, reprinted in Judith O'Neill, ed., *Critics On Marlowe*, London, 1969.

Clifford Leech, ed., *Marlowe: A Collection of Critical Essays* (Twentieth Century Views), Englewood Cliffs, N.J., 1964.

H. Levin, *The Overreacher*, London, 1946.

C. S. Lewis, 'Hero and Leander', in *Proceedings of the British Academy*, London, xxxviii, 1952; reprinted in Judith O'Neill, ed., *Critics On Marlowe*, London, 1969.

M. M. Mahood, *Poetry and Humanism*, London, 1950.

Christopher Ricks, '*Doctor Faustus* and Hell on Earth' in *Essays in Criticism*, xxxv, 1985.

Wilbur Sanders, *The Dramatist and The Received Idea*, Cambridge, 1968.

J. B. Steane, *Marlowe: A Critical Study*, Cambridge, 1964.

Eugene M. Waith, *The Herculean Hero In Marlowe, Chapman, Shakespeare and Dryden*, London, 1962.

Judith Weil, *Christopher Marlowe: Merlin's Prophet*, Cambridge, 1977.

## 4. Shakespeare

### Editions and Text

*Complete Works*, ed. P. Alexander, London and Glasgow, 1951.

*The Riverside Shakespeare*, ed. G. Blakemore Evans, Boston, 1974.

*The Complete Works*, ed. Alfred Harbage and others, the Pelican Shakespeare; 38 vols, 1956–7; as one vol., Baltimore and London, 1969.

*William Shakespeare: The Complete Works*, ed. Stanley Wells and Gary Taylor, Oxford, 1986.

*The Norton Facsimile: The First Folio of Shakespeare*, ed. C. Hinman, London, 1969.

*Shakespeare Plays in Quarto: A Facsimile of Copies Primarily from the Henry E. Huntington Library*, ed. Michael J. B. Allen and Kenneth Muir, Berkeley, Los Angeles, 1982.

*The New Arden Shakespeare*, ed. U. Ellis-Fermor, H. Jenkins, H. Brooks, and others, London, 1951–.

*The New Shakespeare*, ed. A. Quiller Couch, J. Dover Wilson, and others, Cambridge, 1921–66.

*Shakespeare's Lost Play 'Edmund Ironside'*, ed. Eric Sams, London, 1985. A doubtful attribution.

*The Shakespeare Apocrypha*, ed. C. F. Tucker Brooke, Oxford, 1908; reprint 1967: contains fourteen plays at some time attributed to Shakespeare.

W. W. Greg, *The Editorial Problem in Shakespeare*, Oxford, 1942.

—— *The Shakespeare First Folio*, Oxford, 1955.

E. A. J. Honigmann, *The Stability of Shakespeare's Text*, Lincoln, Nebraska, 1965.

Gary Taylor and Michael Warren, eds, *The Division of the Kingdoms: Shakespeare's Two Versions of 'King Lear'*, Oxford, 1983.

Stanley Wells, *Re-editing Shakespeare for the Modern Reader*, Washington, D.C., 1984.

### Life, Times and Career

P. Alexander, *Shakespeare's Life and Art*, London, 1939.

Marie Axton, *The Queen's Two Bodies: Drama and the Elizabethan Succession*, London, 1977.

T. W. Baldwin, *William Shakespeare's Small Latine and Lesse Greeke*, 2 vols, Urbana, Ill., 1944.

—— *Shakespeare's 'Love Labor's Won'*, Carbondale, Ill., 1957.

G. E. Bentley, *Shakespeare: A Biographical Handbook*, New Haven, Conn., 1961.

M. C. Bradbrook, *The Poet in His World*, London, 1978.

E. K. Chambers, *William Shakespeare. A Study of Facts and Problems*, 2 vols, Oxford, 1930. The standard reference book on the life of Shakespeare.

M. Eccles, *Shakespeare in Warwickshire*, Madison, 1961.

Andrew Gurr, *The Shakespearean Stage 1574–1642*, 2nd edn, Cambridge, 1980.

E. A. J. Honigmann, *Shakespeare: the 'Lost Years'*, Manchester, 1985.

J. L. Hotson, *I, William Shakespeare*, London, 1937.

H. Levin, *Shakespeare and the Revolution of the Times*, London, 1976.

Kenneth Muir and S. Schoenbaum, eds, *A New Companion to Shakespeare Studies*, Cambridge, 1971.

A. Nicoll, ed., *Shakespeare in His Own Age: Shakespeare Survey 17*, Cambridge, 1964.

C. T. Onions, ed., *Shakespeare's England*, 2 vols, Oxford, 1916.

Norman Rabkin, *Shakespeare and the Common Understanding*, London, 1967.

Wilbur Sanders, *The Dramatist and the Received Idea: Studies in the Plays of Marlowe and Shakespeare*, Cambridge, 1968.

Samuel Schoenbaum, *Shakespeare: A Documentary Life*, Oxford, 1975.

F. P. Wilson, *The Plague in Shakespeare's London*, Oxford, 1927.

*Reference*

E. A. Abbott, *A Shakespearian Grammar*, 3rd edn, London, 1870.

O. J. Campbell and E. G. Quinn, eds, *The Reader's Encyclopedia of Shakespeare*, London, 1966.

T. H. Howard-Hill ed., *Oxford Shakespeare Concordances*, Oxford, 1969–. Keyed to the text of the First Folio.

H. Kökeritz, *Shakespeare's Pronunciation*, New Haven, 1953.

C. T. Onions, *A Shakespeare Glossary*, rev. edn Oxford, 1953.

A. Schmidt, *Shakespeare-Lexicon*, 2 vols, Berlin and London, 1886.

M. Spevack, *A New and Systematic Concordance to the Works of Shakespeare*, 6 vols, Hildesheim, 1968–70.

—— *Harvard Concordance to Shakespeare*, Cambridge, Mass., 1973. (These are both keyed to *The Riverside Shakespeare*.)

*Criticism and Literary History*

S. L. Bethell, *Shakespeare and the Popular Dramatic Tradition*, London, 1944.

N. F. Blake, *Shakespeare's Language: An Introduction*, London, 1983.

G. Bullough, *Narrative and Dramatic Sources of Shakespeare*, 8 vols, London, 1957–.

Gerald W. Chapman, ed., *Essays on Shakespeare*, Princeton, N.J., 1965.

W. H. Clemen, *The Development of Shakespeare's Imagery*, London, 1951.

S. T. Coleridge, *Shakespearean Criticism*, ed. T. M. Raysor, 2 vols, London, 1930.

Patrick Cruttwell, *The Shakespearean Moment and its Place in the Poetry of the Seventeenth Century*, London, 1954.

Una Ellis-Fermor, *Shakespeare the Dramatist* (essays), ed. Kenneth Muir, London, 1961.

William Empson, *Essays on Shakespeare*, ed. David B. Pirie, Cambridge, 1986.

W. F. and E. S. Friedman, *The Shakespearian Ciphers Examined*, Cambridge, 1957.

H. N. Gibson, *The Shakespeare Claimants*, London, 1962.

H. Granville-Barker, *Prefaces to Shakespeare*, 5 series, London, 1927–48.

A. Harbage, *As They Liked It*, New York, 1947.

—— *Shakespeare and the Rival Traditions*, New York, 1952.

W. Hazlitt, *Characters of Shakespear's Plays*, London, 1817.

S. Johnson, *Johnson on Shakespeare*, ed. A. Sherbo, New Haven, 1968: vols vii and viii of the Yale Johnson.

—— *Johnson on Shakespeare*, ed. R. W. Desai, rev. edn, New Delhi, 1985. See also W. K. Wimsatt's selection, Penguin, 1969.

Emrys Jones, *Scenic Form In Shakespeare*, Oxford, 1971.

Sister Miriam Joseph C.S.C., *Shakespeare's Use of the Arts of Language*, New York, 1947.

Frank Kermode, ed., *Four Centuries of Shakespeare Criticism*, London, 1965.

Alvin B. Kernan, ed., *Modern Shakespearean Criticism*, New York, 1970.

L. C. Knights, *Some Shakespearian Themes*, London, 1959.

John H. Long, *Shakespeare's Use of Music: A Study of the Music and Its Performance in the Original Production of Seven Comedies*, Gainsville, Florida, 1955.

—— *Shakespeare's Use of Music: The Final Comedies*, Florida, 1961.

—— *Shakespeare's Use of Music: The Histories and Tragedies*, Florida, 1971.

M. M. Mahood, *Shakespeare's Wordplay*, London, 1957.

W. M. Merchant, *Shakespeare and the Artist*, London, 1959.

Kenneth Muir, *The Sources of Shakespeare's Plays*, London, 1977.

A. D. Nuttall, *A New Mimesis: Shakespeare and the Representation of Reality*, London, 1985.

G. C. D. Odell, *Shakespeare from Betterton to Irving*, New York, 1920.

A. Righter, *Shakespeare and the Idea of the Play*, London, 1962.

D. Nichol Smith, ed., *Eighteenth Century Essays on Shakespeare*, 2nd edn, Oxford, 1963.

James Smith, *Shakespearean and Other Essays*, Cambridge, 1974.

T. Spencer, *Shakespeare and the Nature of Man*, New York, 1942.

A. C. Sprague, *Shakespeare and the Actors*, Cambridge, Mass., 1948.

C. F. E. Spurgeon, *Shakespeare's Imagery*, Cambridge, 1935.

F. W. Sternfield, *Music in Shakespearean Tragedy*, Oxford, 1963.

J. I. M. Stewart, *Character and Motive in Shakespeare*, London, 1949.

Derek Traversi, *An Approach to Shakespeare*, rev. edn, New York, 1956.

Brian Vickers, ed., *Shakespeare: The Critical Heritage*, 6 vols, London, 1973–81.

Walter Whiter, *A Specimen of a Commentary on Shakespeare*, eds A. Over and M. Bell, London, 1967.

## Series

*Casebooks*, London, 1968–, which cover most of the plays.

*Shakespeare Quarterly*, New York, 1950–.

*Shakespeare Survey*, Cambridge, 1948–.

*Stratford-Upon-Avon Studies*, London, 1960–; especially *1 Jacobean Theatre, 3 Early Shakespeare, 5 Hamlet, 8 Later Shakespeare, 9 Elizabethan Theatre*, (eds J. R. Brown and Brian Harris); and also *14 Shakespearian Comedy, 20 Shakespearean Tragedy*, (eds Malcolm Bradbury and David Palmer).

*Twentieth Century Interpretations*, Englewood Cliffs, 1968–.

## Primarily on the English and Roman Histories

J. C. Bromley, *The Shakespearean Kings*, Colorado, 1971.

R. A. Brower, *Hero and Saint: Shakespeare and the Graeco-Roman Heroic Tradition*, Oxford, 1972.

David L. Frey, *The First Tetralogy: Shakespeare's Scrutiny of the Tudor Myth*, The Hague, 1976.

A. R. Humphreys, 'Shakespeare's Histories and the "Emotion of the Multitude"', Annual Shakespeare Lecture of the British Academy, 1968.

Emrys Jones, *The Origins of Shakespeare*, Oxford, 1977.

Henry A. Kelly, *Divine Providence in the England of Shakespeare's Histories*, Cambridge, Mass., 1970.

L. C. Knights, *Shakespeare: The Histories*, London, 1962.

Clifford Leech, *Shakespeare: The Chronicles*, London, 1962.

Julian Markel, *The Pillar of the World: 'Antony and Cleopatra' in Shakespeare's Development*, Ohio, 1968.

Robert Miola, *Shakespeare's Rome*, Cambridge, 1983.

R. B. Pierce, *Shakespeare's History Plays*, Ohio, 1972.

Michael Platt, *Rome and the Romans According to Shakespeare*, Salzburg, 1972.

Don M. Ricks, *Shakespeare's Emergent Form: A Study of the Structure of the Henry VI Plays*, Utah, 1968.

David Riggs, *Shakespeare's Heroical Histories: 'Henry VI' and its Literary Tradition*, Cambridge, Mass., 1971.

Peter Saccio, *Shakespeare's English Kings: History, Chronicle, and Drama*, Oxford, 1977.

T. J. B. Spencer, *Shakespeare: The Roman Plays*, London, 1962.

Stanley Wells, ed., *Shakespeare Survey 38*, 'Shakespeare and History', Cambridge, 1985. Includes a survey of books and articles 1952–83.

John Wilders, *The Lost Garden*, London, 1978.

## Primarily on the Comedies

C. L. Barber, *Shakespeare's Festive Comedy*, Princeton, N.J., 1959.

Ralph Berry, *Shakespeare's Comedies: Explorations in Form*, Princeton, N.J., 1972.

M. C. Bradbrook, *Shakespeare and Elizabethan Poetry*, London, 1951.

M. Bradbury and D. J. Palmer, eds, *Shakespearean Comedy, Stratford-Upon-Avon Studies 14*, London, 1972.

J. Russell Brown, *Shakespeare and His Comedies*, London, 1957.

J. Russell Brown, ed., *'Much Ado About Nothing' and 'As You Like It'* (Casebook Series), London, 1979.

William C. Carroll, *The Great Feast of Language in Love's Labour's Lost*, Princeton, N.J., 1976.

Lawrence Danson, *The Harmonies of 'The Merchant of Venice'*, New Haven and London, 1978.

B. Evans, *Shakespeare's Comedies*, Oxford, 1960.

R. A. Foakes, *Shakespeare. The Dark Comedies to the Last Plays*, London, 1971.

Northrop Frye, *A Natural Perspective*, New York, 1965.

Darryl J. Gless, *'Measure for Measure': The Law and the Convent*, Princeton, N.J., 1979.

G. K. Hunter, *Shakespeare: The Later Comedies*, London, 1962.

R. G. Hunter, *Shakespeare and the Comedy of Forgiveness*, New York, 1965.

Mary Lascelles, *Shakespeare's 'Measure for Measure'*, London, 1953.

Alexander Leggatt, *Shakespeare's Comedy of Love*, London, 1974.

Kenneth Muir, *Shakespeare's Comic Sequence*, Liverpool, 1979.

Kenneth Muir, ed., *Shakespeare: The Comedies. A Collection of Critical Essays*, Englewood Cliffs, 1965.

—— *Shakespeare Survey 22*, Cambridge, 1971.

D. J. Palmer, ed., *Twelfth Night* (Casebook Series), London, 1972.

John Palmer, *Comic Characters of Shakespeare*, London, 1949.

E. C. Pettet, *Shakespeare and the Romance Tradition*, London, 1949.

P. G. Phialas, *Shakespeare's Romantic Comedies*, Chapel Hill, N.C., 1966.

Antony Price, ed., *A Midsummer Night's Dream* (Casebook Series), London, 1983.

J. G. Price, *The Unfortunate Comedy: A Study of 'All's Well that Ends Well' and its Critics*, Toronto, 1968.

J. A. Roberts, *Shakespeare's English Comedy: 'The Merry Wives of Windsor' in Context*, Lincoln, Nebraska, and London, 1979.

L. G. Salingar, *Shakespeare and the Traditions of Comedy*, Cambridge, 1974.

E. Schanzer, *The Problem Plays of Shakespeare*, London, 1963.

S. C. Sen Gupta, *Shakespearean Comedy*, London, 1950.

James Smith, *Shakespearean and Other Essays*, Cambridge, 1974.

C. K. Stead, ed., *Measure for Measure* (Casebook Series), London, 1971.

Patrick Swinden, *An Introduction to Shakespeare's Comedies*, London, 1973.

E. M. W. Tillyard, *Shakespeare's Early Comedies*, London, 1965.

D. Traversi, *Shakespeare: The Early Comedies*, London , 1960.

C. Watts, *William Shakespeare: 'Measure for Measure'*, Harmondsworth, 1986.

J. Wilders, ed., *The Merchant of Venice* (Casebook Series), London, 1969.

J. Dover Wilson, *Shakespeare's Happy Comedies*, London, 1962.

David P. Young, *Something of Great Constancy: The Art of 'A Midsummer Night's Dream'*, New Haven, 1966.

## Primarily on the Tragedies

Jane Adamson, *'Othello' as Tragedy: Some Problems of Judgment and Feeling*, Cambridge, 1980.

J. Bayley, *The Characters of Love*, London, 1960.

A. C. Bradley, *Shakespearean Tragedy*, London, 1904.

—— 'Shakespeare's *Antony and Cleopatra*', in *Oxford Lectures on Poetry*, London, 1909.

—— '*Coriolanus*', *A Miscellany*, London, 1929.

N. Brooke, *King Lear*, London, 1963.

—— *Shakespeare's Early Tragedies*, London, 1968.

John F. Danby, *Shakespeare's Doctrine of Nature: a Study of 'King Lear'*, London, 1949.

Lawrence Danson, *Tragic Alphabet: Shakespeare's Drama of Language*, London, 1974.

Martin Dodsworth, *'Hamlet' Closely Observed*, London, 1985.

William Empson, *The Structure of Complex Words*, London, 1951.

Bertram Evans, *Shakespeare's Tragic Practice*, Oxford, 1979.

S. L. Goldberg, *An Essay On 'King Lear'*, Cambridge, 1974.

Michael Goldman, *Acting and Action in Shakespearean Tragedy*, Princeton, N.J., 1985.

A. Harbage, ed., *Shakespeare: The Tragedies. A Collection of Critical Essays*, Englewood Cliffs, 1964.

J. Holloway, *The Story of the Night*, London, 1961.

E. Kantorowicz, *The King's Two Bodies*, Princeton, N.J., 1957.

G. Wilson Knight, *The Wheel of Fire*, London, 1930.

—— *The Imperial Theme*, London, 1931.

C. Leech, *Shakespeare's Tragedies*, London, 1961.

Laurence Lerner, ed., *Shakespeare's Tragedies: An Anthology of Modern Criticism*, Harmondsworth, 1963.

Harry Levin, *The Question of 'Hamlet'*, Oxford, 1959.

Kenneth Muir, *Shakespeare's Tragic Sequence*, Liverpool, 1979.

Kenneth Muir and Philip Edwards, eds, *Aspects of 'Macbeth'*, Cambridge, 1977.

——*Aspects of 'Othello'* Cambridge, 1977. Essays reprinted from the *Shakespeare Survey*.

Kenneth Muir and S. Wells, eds, *Aspects of 'Hamlet'*, Cambridge, 1979.

*Shakespeare Survey 13*, Cambridge, 1960. Notable for W. Nowottny's 'Aspects of the Style of *King Lear*'.

Henry N. Paul, *The Royal Play of 'Macbeth'*, New York, 1971.

B. Spivack, *Shakespeare and the Allegory of Evil*, New York, 1958.

### Primarily on the Later Plays

W. H. Auden, 'The Sea and the Mirror' in *For the Time Being*, New York, 1944.

S. L. Bethell, *The Winter's Tale: a Study*, London, 1947.

J. F. Danby, *Elizabethan and Jacobean Poets*, London, 1965, originally published as *Poets On Fortune's Hill*.

Howard Felperin, *Shakespearian Romance*, Princeton, N.J., 1972.

R. A. Foakes, *Shakespeare: The Dark Comedies to The Last Plays*, London, 1971.

C. M. Kay and Henry E. Jacobs, eds, *Shakespeare's Romances Reconsidered*, Lincoln, Nebraska, 1978.

G. Wilson Knight, *The Crown of Life*, London, 1948.

—— *The Shakespearian Tempest*, 3rd edn, London, 1953.

F. R. Leavis, 'The Criticism of Shakespeare's Late Plays – a Caveat', *The Common Pursuit*, London, 1952.

Kenneth Muir and S. Wells, *Aspects of Shakespeare's 'Problem Plays'*, Cambridge, 1982. Essays reprinted from the *Shakespeare Survey*.

D. J. Palmer, ed., *Shakespeare's Later Comedies. An Anthology of Modern Criticism*, Harmondsworth, 1971.

E. C. Pettet, *Shakespeare and the Romance Tradition*, London, 1949.

Hallett Smith, *Shakespeare's Romances*, San Marino, 1972.

E. M. W. Tillyard, *Shakespeare's Last Plays*, London, 1938.

Derek Traversi, *Shakespeare: the Last Phase*, London, 1954.

Frances A. Yates, *Shakespeare's Last Plays, a New Approach*, London, 1975.

David P. Young, *The Heart's Forest: A Study of Shakespeare's Plays*, New Haven, 1972.

## 5. Ben Jonson

### Editions

The standard edition is *Ben Jonson*, ed. C. H. Herford and P. and E. Simpson, Oxford, 1925–52, 11 vols. G. A. Wilkes has produced a modern-spelling edition of the plays from the Herford and Simpson text, in 4 vols (Oxford 1981–2). There are well-annotated editions of individual plays in the Yale Ben Jonson series (*Every Man in His Humour, Sejanus, Volpone, Epicoene, The Alchemist, Bartholomew Fair*), in the Revels Plays series (*Volpone, The Alchemist, Bartholomew Fair, The New Inn, Eastward Ho!*), and the London Medieval and Renaissance series (*Volpone*). Other good editions are available in the New Mermaid, the Regents Renaissance Drama, the Penguin English Dramatists, and the Oxford Authors series.

### Scholarship and Criticism

J. B. Bamborough, *Ben Jonson*, London, 1970.

Jonas A. Barish, *Ben Jonson and the Language of Prose Comedy*, Cambridge, Mass., 1960.

Jonas A. Barish, ed., *Ben Jonson: A Collection of Critical Essays* (Twentieth Century Views), Englewood Cliffs, 1963.

—— *Jonson, 'Volpone': A Casebook*, London and Basingstoke, 1972.

Anne Barton, *Ben Jonson: Dramatist*, Cambridge, 1984.

C. R. Baskervill, *English Elements in Jonson's Early Comedy*, Texas, 1911.

D. Boughner, *The Devil's Disciple: Ben Jonson's Debt to Machiavelli*, New York, 1968.

W. Blissett, J. Patrick, and R. W. Van Fossen, eds, *A Celebration of Ben Jonson*, Toronto, 1973.

Larry S. Champion, *Ben Jonson's 'Dotages': A Reconsideration of the Late Plays*, Lexington, Kentucky, 1967.

Ian Donaldson, *The World Upside-Down: Comedy from Jonson to Fielding*, Oxford, 1970.

Ian Donaldson, ed., *Jonson and Shakespeare*, London and Basingstoke, 1983.

Douglas Duncan, *Ben Jonson and the Lucianic Tradition*, Cambridge, 1979.

T. S. Eliot, 'Ben Jonson' (1919), in *Selected Essays*, London, 1932.

J. J. Enck, *Jonson and the Comic Truth*, Madison, 1957.

N. Frye, *A Natural Perspective*, New York and London, 1965.

Brian Gibbons, *Jacobean City Comedy*, London, 1968.

R. V. Holdsworth, ed., *'Every Man in His Humour' and 'The Alchemist': A Casebook*, London and Basingstoke, 1978.

G. B. Jackson, *Vision and Judgement in Ben Jonson's Drama*, New Haven and London, 1968.

Ben Jonson: Quadricentennial Essays, *Studies in the Literary Imagination*, vi, 1973.

L. C. Knights, *Drama and Society in the Age of Jonson*, London, 1937.

Alexander Leggatt, *Ben Jonson: His Vision and His Art*, London and New York, 1981.

Walter D. Lehrman, Dolores J. Sarafinski, Elizabeth Savage, SSJ, *The Plays of Ben Jonson: A Reference Guide*, Boston, Mass., 1980.

R. G. Noyes, *Ben Jonson on the English Stage 1660–1776*, Cambridge, Mass., 1935.

George Parfitt, *Ben Jonson: Public Poet and Private Man*, London, 1976.

E. B. Partridge, *The Broken Compass: A Study of the Major Comedies of Ben Jonson*, London, 1958.

F. Townsend, *Apologie for Bartholomew Fayre: the Art of Jonson's Comedies*, New York, 1947.

Irving Wardle, Peter Barnes, Colin Blakeley, Terry Hands (discussion), 'Ben Jonson and the Modern Stage', *Gambit: International Theatre Review*, xxii, 1972, 5–30.

E. Wilson, 'Morose Ben Jonson', in *The Triple Thinkers*, Oxford, 1938.

Peter Womack, *Ben Jonson*, Oxford, 1986.

## 6. *The Tragedies of Webster, Tourneur, and Middleton*

### General

W. Archer, *The Old Drama and the New*, London, 1923.

F. Bowers, *Elizabethan Revenge Tragedy*, Princeton, N.J., 1940.

M. C. Bradbrook, *Themes and Conventions of Elizabethan Tragedy*, Cambridge, 1935.

Nicholas Brooke, *Horrid Laughter in Jacobean Tragedy*, London, 1979.

A. S. Downer, 'The Life of Our Design', *Hudson Review*, ii, 1949, pp 242–60; reprinted in *Perspectives on Drama*, ed. J. L. Calderwood and H. E. Toliver, New York, 1968.

T. S. Eliot, *Selected Essays*, London, 1932.

J. Henning, R. Kimbrough and R. Knowles, eds, *English Renaissance Drama*, London, 1976.

R. J. Kaufmann, ed., *Elizabethan Drama: Modern Essays in Criticism*, New York, 1961.

A. C. Kirsch, *Jacobean Dramatic Perspectives*, Charlottesville, Va., 1972.

I. Ribner, *Jacobean Tragedy: The Quest for Moral Order*, London, 1962.

### Middleton

*Works*, ed. A. H. Bullen, 8 vols, London, 1885–6.

*Thomas Middleton*, with an introduction by A. C. Swinburne, Mermaid, London, 1887.

*Selected Plays*, ed. David L. Frost, Cambridge, 1978.

*The Changeling*, ed. N. W. Bawcutt, RP, London, 1958; ed. P. Thompson, NM, London, 1964.

*Women Beware Women*, ed. Roma Gill, NM, London, 1968; ed. J. R. Mulryne, RP, London, 1975.

N. A. Brittin, *Thomas Middleton*, London, 1972.

Dorothy M. Farr, *Thomas Middleton and the Drama of Realism: A Study of Some Representative Plays*, Edinburgh, 1973.

Kenneth Friedenreich, ed., *'Accompaninge the Players': Essays Celebrating Thomas Middleton 1580–1980*, New York, 1983.

H. Gardner, 'Milton's Satan and the Theme of Damnation in Elizabethan Tragedy', *English Studies* (i.e. *Essays and Studies*), 1948; reprinted in *Elizabethan Drama*, ed. Kaufmann.

Margot Heinemann, *Puritanism and the Theatre: Thomas Middleton and Opposition Drama Under the Early Stuarts*, Cambridge, 1980.

S. Schoenbaum, *Middleton's Tragedies*, New York, 1955.

### Tourneur

*The Plays of Cyril Tourneur*, ed. George Parfitt, Cambridge, 1978.

*The Atheist's Tragedy*, ed. I. Ribner, RP, London, 1964; eds Brian Morris and Roma Gill, NM, London, 1976.

*The Revenger's Tragedy*, ed. R. A. Foakes, RP, London, 1966; ed. B. Gibbons, NM, London, 1967; ed. Lawrence J. Ross, RRDS, London, 1967.

J. A. Barish, 'The True and False Families of *The Revenger's Tragedy*', *English Renaissance Drama*, London, 1976.

R. A. Foakes, *Marston and Tourneur*, Harlow, 1978.

P. B. Murray, *A Study of Cyril Tourneur*, Pennsylvania, 1964.

A. Nicoll, '*The Revenger's Tragedy* and the Virtue of Anonymity', in *Essays on Shakespeare and Elizabethan Drama*, ed. R. Hosley, Columbia, 1963. On attribution.

J. Peter, *Complaint and Satire in Early English Literature*, Oxford, 1956.

L. G. Salingar, '*The Revenger's Tragedy* and the Morality Tradition', *Scrutiny*, vi, 1938, pp 402–24; reprinted in *Elizabethan Drama*, ed. Kaufmann (see *General* above).

S. Schoenbaum, *Internal Evidence and Elizabethan Dramatic Authorship*, London, 1966.

Samuel Schuman, *Cyril Tourneur*, Boston, 1977.

### Webster

*Complete Works*, ed. F. L. Lucas, 4 vols, London, 1927.

*The Selected Plays of John Webster*, eds Jonathan Dollimore and Alan Sinfield, Cambridge, 1983.

*The Duchess of Malfi*, ed. John Russell Brown, RP, London, 1964; ed. E. Brennan, NM, London, 1964.

*The White Devil*, ed. John Russell Brown, RP, London, 1960; ed. E. Brennan, NM, London, 1964; ed. Simon Trussler and Jacquie Russell, London, 1986.

*The Devil's Law-Case*, ed. Frances A. Shirley, RRDS, London, 1972; ed. E. Brennan, NM, London, 1975.

Ralph Berry, *The Art of John Webster*, Oxford, 1972.

T. Bogard, *The Tragic Satire of John Webster*, Berkeley, 1955.

M. C. Bradbrook, *John Webster: Citizen and Dramatist*, London, 1980.

R. W. Dent, *John Webster's Borrowing*, Berkeley and Los Angeles, 1960.

I.-S. Ekeblad, 'The "Impure Art" of John Webster', *Review of English Studies*, ns ix, 1958, pp 253–67; reprinted in Kaufmann, Rabkin, and Hunter.

R. V. Holdsworth, ed., *Webster, 'The White Devil' and 'The Duchess of Malfi': A Casebook*, London, 1975.

G. K. and S. K. Hunter, eds, *Webster: a Penguin Critical Anthology*, Harmondsworth, 1969.

Don D. Moore, ed., *Webster: The Critical Heritage*, London, 1981.

Brian Morris, ed., *John Webster: Mermaid Critical Anthologies*, London, 1970.

Jacqueline Pearson, *Tragedy and Tragi-comedy in the Plays of John Webster*, Manchester, 1980.

H. T. Price, 'The Function of Imagery in Webster', *Publications of the Modern Language Association of America*, lxx, 1955, pp 717–39; reprinted in Kaufmann and Hunter.

N. Rabkin, ed., *Twentieth Century Interpretations of 'The Duchess of Malfi'*, Englewood Cliffs, 1968.

## 7. The Masque

### Editions

Of the Jonson masques: C. H. Herford, P. and E. Simpson, *Ben Jonson*, 11 vols, Oxford, 1925–52. The standard modern edition. Volume ii contains the Introduction, volume vii the texts, volume x the notes.

*Stephen Orgel, *Ben Jonson: The Complete Masques*, New Haven, 1969; *Selected Masques*, 1970. A modernized edition with fuller critical commentary than Herford and Simpson.

Campion's masques have been modernized and edited by Walter Davis in *The Works of Thomas Campion*, New York, 1967. Aurelian Townshend's three masques are in Cedric Brown's *The Poems and Masques of Aurelian Townshend*, Reading, 1983, and Thomas Carew's great *Coelum Britannicum* is in *The Poems of Thomas Carew*, ed. Rhodes Dunlap, Oxford, 1949.

A good general selection of Stuart masques is in H. A. Evans, *English Masques*, London, 1897. It is under-annotated by modern standards, but its Introduction, despite its age, remains one of the best general essays on the history of the form in England. A less good selection, erratically edited, is in *A Book of Masques*, Cambridge, 1967.

Indispensable to the study of the English masque is the collection of Inigo Jones's complete theatrical designs, for the most part for masques at court, published and analysed in Stephen Orgel and Roy Strong, *Inigo Jones: The Theatre of the Stuart Court*, 2 vols, London and Berkeley, 1973. This also includes the texts of all the masques for which drawings have been preserved, and an extensive introduction.

### Criticism

General studies: The relevant chapters in E. K. Chambers's *Medieval Stage* and *Elizabethan Stage* are essential, and Paul Reyher's *Les Masques Anglais*, Paris, 1909, remains, despite its age, an excellent general work, as does H. A. Evans's long introductory essay to his 1897 collection of English masques (see above). The classic book-length general survey in English, Enid Welsford's *The Court Masque*, Cambridge, 1927, is unscholarly, confused and misleading; it remains, however, the most detailed attempt to consider the English masque in relation to continental models. Stephen Orgel's *The Illusion of Power*, Berkeley, 1974, analyses the masque in its political context, and his essay 'The Poetics of Spectacle', *New Literary History* 2, 1971 (reprinted in *Inigo Jones*), undertakes to establish the theoretical bases of the form. Important material on the early masque will be found in Gordon Kipling, *The Triumph of Honour*, Leiden, 1977, and Sydney Anglo, *Spectacle, Pageantry, and Early Tudor Policy*, Oxford, 1969. D. J. Gordon's seminal studies of individual masques and of the masque in general have been collected in *The Renaissance Imagination*, Berkeley, 1975. Graham Parry considers the social and political implications of the Stuart masque in *The Golden Age Restored*, London and New York, 1981. David Lindley's recent collection *The Court Masque*, Manchester, 1984, contains a number of useful essays; especially notable are David Norbrook on 'The Reformation of the Masque', and Lindley's own essay, 'Music, Masque and Meaning in *The Tempest*'. The most detailed information on production and stage history will be found in Stephen Orgel and Roy Strong, *Inigo Jones*.

On Jonson's Masques: Stephen Orgel, *The Jonsonian Masque*, Cambridge, Mass., 1965, new edn New York, 1981, though primarily a literary study of Jonson, includes an introductory historical survey. John C. Meagher, *Method and Meaning in Jonson's Masques*, Notre Dame, Ind., 1966, treats the masques in relation to the Renaissance intellectual context. The long Introduction to Stephen Orgel's edition of Jonson's masques (see above) discusses the masque in relation to the development of Inigo Jones's stage. Important studies of the political implications of Jonson's work are in Jonathan Goldberg, *James I and the Politics of Literature*, Baltimore, 1983. The occasional genetics of the Jonsonian masque are anatomized in Leah Marcus, 'Present Occasions and the Shaping of Ben Jonson's Masques', *English Literary History* xlv, 1978, and in other more specialized essays; and Joseph Loewenstein, *Responsive Readings*, New Haven, 1984, considers the Jonsonian masque's aesthetic, philosophical and cultural implications.

A detailed bibliography has been prepared by David M. Bergeron, *Twentieth-Century Criticism of English Masques, Pageants, and Entertainments: 1558–1642*, San Antonio, 1972.

## 9. Comedy from the Restoration till 1710

### History of Drama

G. E. Bentley, *The Jacobean and Caroline Stage*, 7 vols, Oxford, 1941–68.

Eleanor Boswell, *The Restoration Court Stage 1660–1702*, Cambridge, Mass., 1932.

Leslie Hotson, *The Commonwealth and Restoration Stage*, London, 1928.

Robert D. Hume, *The Development of English Drama in the Late Seventeenth Century*, Oxford, 1976.

Gerard Langbaine, *An Account of the English Dramatic Poets*, 1691, rep. The Scolar Press, Menston, Yorks, 1971, and Augustan Reprint Society, Los Angeles, 1971.

John Loftus, *The Politics of Drama in Augustan England*, Oxford, 1963.

John Loftus *et al*, eds, *The 'Revels' History of Drama in English*, vol v, 1660–1750, London, 1976.

Harold Love, *Restoration Literature: Critical Approaches*, London, 1972.

Judith Milhous, *Thomas Betterton and the Management of Lincoln's Inn Fields, 1695–1708*, Carbondale, Ill., 1979.

—— and Robert D. Hume, *Vice-Chamberlain Coke's Theatrical Papers, 1706–1715*, Carbondale, Ill., 1982.

A. Nicoll, *A History of English Drama*, vols i and ii, 4th edn, London, 1952.

Sarup Singh, *The Theory of Drama in the Restoration*, Bombay, 1963.

J. Sutherland, *English Literature of the Late Seventeenth Century*, Oxford, 1969. Unusually full on secondary writers.

H. T. Swedenberg Jr., ed., *England in the Restoration and Early Eighteenth Century*, Berkeley, 1972.

W. Van Lennep and E. L. Avery, *The London Stage 1660–1800*, Carbondale, Ill., 1960–8, parts i and ii.

J. H. Wilson, *A Preface to Restoration Drama*, Cambridge, Mass., 1965.

### Mainly on Tragedy

C. V. Deane, *Dramatic Theory and the Rhymed Heroic Play*, London, 1931.

B. Dobrée, *Restoration Tragedy*, Oxford, 1929.

B. Dobrée, ed., *Five Heroic Plays*, London, 1960.

C. Leech, 'Restoration Tragedy: A Reconsideration', *Durham University Journal*, xi, 1950, pp 106–15.

John Loftis, *The Spanish Plays of Neoclassical England*, New Haven, 1973.

A. Righter, 'Heroic Tragedy', in *Restoration Theatre: Stratford- Upon- Avon Studies 6*, eds J. R. Brown and B. Harris, London, 1965.

E. Rothstein, *Restoration Tragedy*, Madison, 1967.

J. Sutherland, ed., *Restoration Tragedies*, Oxford, 1977.

Eugene M. Waith, *The Herculean Hero in Marlowe, Chapman, Shakespeare and Dryden*, New York, 1962.

—— *Heroic Drama In England*, London, 1971.

*Mainly on Comedy*

G. S. Alleman, *Matrimonial Law and the Materials of Restoration Comedy*, Wallingford, Penn., 1941.

F. W. Bateson, *English Comic Drama, 1700–1750*, Oxford, 1929.

—— 'L. C. Knights and Restoration Comedy', in *Essays in Criticism*, vii, 1957, pp 56–7.

E. Bernbaum, *The Drama of Sensibility*, Cambridge, Mass., 1915.

Virginia Ogden Birdsall, *Wild Civility: The English Comic Spirit on the Restoration Stage*, Bloomington, Ind., 1970.

J. R. Brown and B. Harris, eds, *Restoration Theatre: Stratford-Upon- Avon Studies 6*, London, 1965.

D. Davison, ed., *Restoration Comedies*, London, 1970.

B. Dobrée, *Restoration Comedy*, Oxford, 1924.

Ian Donaldson, *The World Upside-down: Comedy from Jonson to Fielding*, Oxford, 1970.

T. H. Fujimara, *The Restoration Comedy of Wit*, Princeton, N.J., 1952.

Harriett Hawkins, *Likenesses of Truth in Elizabethan and Restoration Drama*, Oxford, 1972.

N. N. Holland, *The First Modern Comedies: The Significance of Etherege, Wycherley, and Congreve*, Cambridge, Mass., 1959.

Peter Holland, *The Ornament of Action*, Cambridge, 1981.

Robert D. Hume, *The Rakish Stage: Studies in English Drama 1660–1800*, Carbondale, Ill., 1983.

L. C. Knights, 'Restoration Comedy: The Reality and the Myth', *Scrutiny*, vi, 1937, in *Explorations*, London, 1946.

J. W. Krutch, *Comedy and Conscience After the Restoration*, New York, 1924.

Charles Lamb, 'On the Artificial Comedy of the Last Age', in *Essays of Elia*, London, 1823.

C. Leech, 'Restoration Comedy: The First Phase', *Essays in Criticism*, i, 1951, pp 165–84.

J. Loftis, *Comedy and Society From Congreve to Fielding*, Stanford, 1959.

J. Loftis, ed., *Restoration Drama: Modern Essays in Criticism*, New York, 1966.

K. M. Lynch, *The Social Mode of Restoration Comedy*, New York, 1926.

Thomas Babington Macaulay, 'The Dramatic Works of Wycherley, Congreve, Vanbrugh, and Farquhar', *Edinburgh Review*, lxxii, 1841, pp 490–528.

E. L. Mignon, *Crabbed Age and Youth: The Old Men and Women in the Restoration Comedy of Manners*, Durham, N.C., 1947.

Judith Milhous and Robert D. Hume, *Producible Interpretation: Eight English Plays, 1675–1707*, Carbondale, Ill., 1985.

E. Miner, ed., *Restoration Dramatists: A Collection of Critical Essays*, Twentieth Century Views, Englewood Cliffs, 1966.

K. Muir, *The Comedy of Manners*, London, 1970.

A. Sherbo, *English Sentimental Drama*, East Lansing, 1957.

J. H. Smith, *The Gay Couple in Restoration Comedy*, Cambridge, Mass., 1948.

Susan Staves, *Players' Scepters: Fictions of Authority in the Restoration*, Lincoln, Neb., 1979.

J. Wain, 'Restoration Comedy and its Modern Critics', *Preliminary Essays*, London, 1957.

Horace Walpole, 'Thoughts on Comedy' (published 1798); reprinted in *Essays in Criticism*, xv, 1965, pp 162–70.


## Behn

The Works of Aphra Behn, ed. M. Summers, 6 vols, 1915; reprint 1967.

The Lucky Chance, ed. F. Morgan, Royal Court Writers Series, London, 1984.

The Rover, ed. F. M. Link, RRDS, 1967.

M. Duffy, *The Passionate Shepherdess: Aphra Behn, 1640–89*, London, 1977.

See also:

The Female Wits: Women Playwrights on the London Stage, 1660–1720, ed. Fidelis Morgan, London, 1981.

## Cibber

*The Dramatic Works*, 5 vols, London, 1777; reprinted New York, 1966. As yet there is no definitive modern edition.

*\*Three Sentimental Comedies*, ed. Maureen Sullivan, New Haven, Conn., 1973.

*The Careless Husband*, ed. William W. Appleton, RRDS, London, 1967.

*An Apology for the Life of Mr Colley Cibber, Comedian*, ed. R. M. Lowe, 2 vols, London, 1889; ed. B. R. S. Fone, Ann Arbor, 1968.

B. R. S. Fone, 'Cibber's *Love's Last Shift* and Sentimental Comedy', in *Restoration and Eighteenth Century Theatre Research*, 7 May 1968.

R. N. Leonard, *Cibber*, Ashley, 1965.

Lois Potter, 'Colley Cibber: The Fop as Hero', in *Augustan Worlds: Essays in Honour of A. R. Humphreys*, eds J. C. Hilson, M. M. B. Jones and J. R. Watson, Leicester, 1978.

## Congreve

*Complete Works*, ed. M. Summers, 4 vols, London, 1923. Follows the Quarto text.

*\*Complete Plays*, ed. H. J. Davis, Chicago, 1966. Quarto text collated with 1710 *Works*.

*The Comedies*, ed. B. Dobrée, London, 1925. Follows 1710 edition which Congreve intended posterity to read.

*\*The Comedies*, ed. Anthony G. Henderson, Cambridge, 1982.

*The Comedies*, ed. Eric S. Rump, Harmondsworth, 1985.

*The Double-Dealer*, ed. J. C. Ross, NM, London, 1981.

*Love for Love*, ed. Emmett L. Avery, RRDS, London, 1967; ed. M. Kelsall, NM, London, 1969.

*The Mourning Bride*, ed. B. Dobrée, London, 1928.

*The Way of the World*, ed. Brian Gibbons, NM, London, 1971; ed. Kathleen M. Lynch, RRDS, London, 1975; ed. John Barnard, Edinburgh, 1972.

*Concerning Humour in Comedy* (1696), in *European Theories of the Drama*, ed. Barrett H. Clark, revised by Henry Popkin, New York, 1965. Also in *The Comedies*, ed. B. Dobrée.

*William Congreve: Letters and Documents*, ed. J. C. Hodges, New York, 1964.

J. C. Hodges, *William Congreve the Man*, New York, 1941. New information about the life.

Harold Love, *Congreve*, Oxford, 1974.

Patrick Lyons, ed., *Congreve, Comedies: 'The Old Batchelour', 'The Double-Dealer', 'Love for Love', 'The Way of the World': A Casebook*, London, 1982.

Brian Morris, ed., *William Congreve: a Collection of Critical Studies*, London, 1972.

P. and M. Mueschke, *A New View of Congreve's 'Way of the World'*, Ann Arbor, 1958.

Maximillian E. Novak, *Congreve*, New York, 1971.

W. Van Voris, *The Cultivated Stance: The Designs of Congreve's Plays*, Dublin, 1965.

Aubrey Williams, *An Approach to Congreve*, New Haven, 1979.


*Dryden*

*Dramatic Works*, ed. M. Summers, 6 vols, London, 1931–2.

*Works*, ed. E. N. Hooker and H. T. Swedenberg Jr., Berkeley and Los Angeles, 1956–.

*John Dryden: Four Tragedies* and *John Dryden: Four Comedies*, eds L. A. Beaurline and F. Bowers, Chicago, 1967.

*All For Love*, ed. N. J. Andrew, NM, London, 1975.

*Marriage à La Mode*, ed. Mark S. Auburn, RRDS, London, 1981.

*Essays*, ed. W. P. Ker, 2 vols, Oxford, 1900.

*Of Dramatic Poesy and Other Critical Essays*, ed. G. Watson, 2 vols, London, 1962.

Anne T. Barbeau, *The Intellectual Design of Dryden's Heroic Plays*, London, 1970.

David Hopkins, *John Dryden*, Cambridge, 1986.

Derek Hughes, *Dryden's Heroic Plays*, London, 1981.

Robert D. Hume, *Dryden's Criticism*, Ithaca, N.Y., 1970.

D. Jefferson, 'The Significance of Dryden's Heroic Plays', *Proceedings of the Leeds Philosophical and Literary Society*, v, 1940, pp 125–39. In *Restoration Drama: Modern Essays in Criticism*, ed. J. Loftis, New York, 1966.

—— '"All, all of a piece throughout": Thoughts on Dryden's Dramatic Poetry', in *Restoration Theatre: Stratford-Upon-Avon Studies 6*, eds J. R. Brown and B. Harris, London, 1965.

B. King, *Dryden's Major Plays*, Edinburgh, 1966.

B. King, ed., *Twentieth Century Interpretations of 'All for Love': A Collection of Critical Essays*, Englewood Cliffs, 1968.

A. C. Kirsch, *Dryden's Heroic Drama*, Princeton, N.J., 1965.

F. H. Moore, *The Nobler Pleasure: Dryden's Comedy in Theory and Practice*, Chapel Hill, 1963.

John M. Wallace, 'John Dryden's Plays and the Conception of an Heroic Society' in *Culture and Politics from Puritanism to the Enlightenment*, ed. P. Zagorin, London, 1980.

C. M. Ward, *The Life of John Dryden*, Chapel Hill, 1961.

## Etherege

\*Works, ed. H. F. B. Brett-Smith, 2 vols, Oxford, 1927.

*The Plays of Sir George Etherege*, ed. Michael Cordner, Cambridge, 1982.

*The Man of Mode*, ed. W. B. Carnochan, RRDS, London, 1967; ed. John Conaghan, Edinburgh, 1973; ed. John Barnard, London, 1979.

*She Would If She Could*, ed. C. M. Taylor, RRDS, London, 1973.

*The Letterbook of Sir George Etherege*, ed. S. Rosenfeld, Oxford, 1928. See also *Review of English Studies*, x, 1934, pp 177–89; viii, 1932, pp 458–9; and ns iii, 1952, pp 19–27.

D. Underwood, *Etherege and the Seventeenth-Century Comedy of Manners*, New Haven, 1957.

## Farquhar

*Complete Works*, ed. C. A. Stonehill, 2 vols, London, 1930.

*George Farquhar*, ed. W. Archer, Mermaid, London, 1906, reprinted 1949. Useful introduction.

*The Beaux' Stratagem*, ed. A. Norman Jeffares, London, 1972; ed. Michael Cordner, NM, London, 1976; ed. Charles N. Fifer, RRDS, London, 1978.

*The Recruiting Officer*, ed. A. Norman Jeffares, London, 1973; ed. John Ross, NM, London, 1977; ed. Peter Dixon, RP, Manchester, 1986.

*A Discourse Upon Comedy With Reference To The English Stage* (1702), in *European Theories of the Drama*, ed. Barrett H. Clark, revised by Henry Popkin, New York, 1965.

W. Connely, *Young George Farquhar*, London, 1949.

Eugene M. James, *Development of Farquhar as a Comic Dramatist*, The Hague, 1972.

Eric Rothstein, *Farquhar*, New York, 1967.

## Lee

*Works*, eds T. B. Stroup and A. L. Cooke, 2 vols, New Brunswick, 1954–5.

*Lucius Junius Brutus*, ed. John Loftus, RRDS, London, 1968.

*The Rival Queens*, ed. P. F. Vernon, RRDS, London, 1970.
J. M. Armistead, *Nathaniel Lee*, Boston, 1979.
R. G. Ham, *Otway and Lee*, New Haven, 1931.

## Otway

*Works*, ed. J. C. Ghosh, 2 vols, Oxford, 1932.
*The Orphan*, ed. Aline MacKenzie Taylor, RRDS, London, 1977.
*Venice Preserved*, ed. Malcolm Kelsall, RRDS, London, 1969.
R. G. Ham, *Otway and Lee*, New Haven, 1931.
A. M. Taylor, *Next to Shakespeare: Otway's 'Venice Preserv'd' and 'The Orphan'*, Durham, N.C., 1950.

## Shadwell

*Complete Works*, ed. M. Summers, 5 vols, London, 1927. Uneven but useful notes.
*The Virtuoso*, ed. Marjorie Hope Nicolson and David Stuart Rodes, RRDS, London, 1966.
A. S. Borgman, *Thomas Shadwell: His Life and Comedies*, New York, 1928.

## Steele

*The Plays of Richard Steele*, ed. S. S. Kenny, Oxford, 1971.
*The Conscious Lovers*, ed. S. S. Kenny, RRDS, London, 1968.
*The Tender Husband*, ed. C. Winton, RRDS, London, 1967.
G. A. Aitken, *The Life of Richard Steele*, London, 1889.
J. Loftis, *Steele at Drury Lane*, Stanford, 1952.
C. Winton, *Captain Steele*, Baltimore, 1964.
—— *Sir Richard Steele M.P.: the Later Career*, Baltimore, 1970.

## Vanbrugh

*Complete Works*, ed. B. Dobrée and G. Webb, 4 vols, London, 1927–7.
*The Provoked Wife*, ed. James L. Smith, NM, London, 1974; ed. Anthony Coleman, RP, Manchester, 1982.
*The Relapse*, ed. Curt A. Zimansky, RRDS, London, 1979; ed. Bernard Harris, NM, London, 1971.
Gerald M. Berkowitz, *Sir John Vanbrugh and the End of Restoration Comedy*, Amsterdam, 1981.
Madeleine Bingham, *Masks and Facades: Vanbrugh: The Man in his Setting*, London, 1974.

Bernard Harris, *Sir John Vanbrugh*, London, 1967.

A. R. Huseboe, *Sir John Vanbrugh*, Boston, 1976.

P. Mueschke and J. Fleisher, 'A Re-Valuation of Vanbrugh', *Publications of the Modern Language Association of America*, xlix, 1934, pp 848–89.

L. Whistler, *Sir John Vanbrugh: Architect and Dramatist*, London, 1938. More interesting on Vanbrugh as architect, as is his later book on Vanbrugh, 1954.

## Wycherley

*Complete Works*, ed. M. Summers, 4 vols, London, 1924. Uneven, but useful notes.

*The Complete Plays*, ed. Gerald Weales, New York, 1966.

*Plays*, ed. Arthur Friedman, Oxford, 1979.

*The Plays of William Wycherley*, ed. Peter Holland, Cambridge, 1981.

*The Country Wife*, ed. Thomas H. Fujimura, RRDS, London, 1965; ed. J. Dixon Hunt, NM, London, 1973; eds David Cook and John Swannell, London, 1975.

*The Plain Dealer*, ed. Leo Hughes, RRDS, London, 1968; ed. James L. Smith, NM, London, 1979.

W. Connely, *Brawny Wycherley*, London, 1930.

I. Donaldson, '"Tables Turned": The Plain Dealer', *Essays in Criticism*, xvii, 1967, pp 304–21.

P. Holland, *The Ornament of Action*, Cambridge, 1979.

B. Eugene McCarthy, *William Wycherley, a Biography*, Athens, Ohio, 1979.

K. M. Rogers, *William Wycherley*, New York, 1972.

J. Thompson, *Language in Wycherley's Plays: Seventeenth-Century Language Theory and Drama*, Alabama, 1984.

R. A. Zimbardo, *Wycherley's Drama: A Link in the Development of English Satire*, New Haven, 1965.

# TABLE OF DATES

## (Titles are modernized)

| | |
|---|---|
| 1495 | *Everyman* acted (?) |
| 1503 | Sir Thomas Wyatt b. (?) |
| 1509 | Accession of Henry VIII |
| 1515 | John Skelton, *Magnificence* acted |
| 1516 | Sir Thomas More, *Utopia* (Latin; English translation, 1551) |
| 1517 | Henry Howard, Earl of Surrey b. |
| 1520 | William Dunbar d. (?) |
| 1529 | Skelton d. |
| 1533 | Ariosto d. |
| | Montaigne b. |
| 1535 | More executed |
| 1536 | Erasmus d. William Tyndale burnt |
| 1539 | The Great Bible |
| 1542 | Wyatt d. |
| 1547 | Henry VIII d. Accession of Edward VI |
| | Earl of Surrey executed |
| | Cervantes b. |
| 1549 | The Book of Common Prayer, largely the work of Cranmer |
| 1552 | Sir Walter Ralegh b. Edmund Spenser b. (?) |
| | Nicholas Udall, *Ralph Roister Doister* acted (?) |
| 1553 | Edward VI d. Accession of Queen Mary |
| | Rabelais d. |
| 1554 | Richard Hooker b. John Lyly b. (?) Sir Philip Sidney b. |
| 1555 | Latimer and Ridley burnt |
| 1556 | Cranmer burnt |
| 1557 | Richard Tottel and Nicholas Grimold (ed.) *Songs and Sonnets* (*Tottel's Miscellany*, which included Wyatt and Surrey) |
| 1558 | Queen Mary d. Accession of Elizabeth I |
| | Thomas Lodge b. (?) |

1559    George Chapman b. (?)

William Baldwin (ed.), *A Mirror for Magistrates*

1560    Robert Greene b. (?)

1561    Sir Francis Bacon b.

Sir Thomas Hoby, *The Courtier* (translation of Castiglione's *Il Cortegiano*)

Thomas Norton and Thomas Sackville, *Gorboduc* acted

1564    Calvin d. Michelangelo d.

Galileo b. Christopher Marlowe b. William Shakespeare b.

1565    Arthur Golding, translation of Ovid's *Metamorphoses* I–IV

1567    Thomas Campion b. Thomas Nashe b.

1572    Thomas Dekker b. (?) John Donne b. Ben Jonson b.

1575    Thomas Heywood b. (?) John Marston b. (?) Cyril Tourneur b. (?)

Tasso, *Gerusalemme Liberata*

1576    The Theater built, the first in London

1577    Robert Burton b.

1579    John Fletcher b.

Sir Thomas North, translation of Plutarch's *Lives*; Spenser, *The Shepherd's Calendar*

1580    Thomas Middleton b. (?) John Webster b. (?)

Montaigne, *Essais* I–II

1582    Richard Hakluyt, *Diverse Voyages*

1583    Philip Massinger b.

1584    Francis Beaumont b.

1586    Sidney d.

John Ford b.

1587    Mary, Queen of Scots executed

Kyd, *The Spanish Tragedy* acted; Marlowe, *Tamburlaine* acted; Peele, *The Love of King David and Fair Bethsabe* acted

1588    The Spanish Armada defeated

Thomas Hobbes b.

Lyly, *Endimion* acted

1588–9    Marlowe, *Doctor Faustus* acted (or 1592)

1589    George Puttenham, *The Art of English Poesy*

Greene, *Friar Bacon and Friar Bungay* acted; Marlowe, *The Jew of Malta* acted

1590    Sidney (d. 1586), *The Countess of Pembroke's Arcadia*; Spenser, *The Faerie Queene* I–III

1591    Robert Herrick b.

Sidney (d. 1586), *Astrophel and Stella*

| 1592 | Greene d. |
| | Nashe, *Piers Penniless* |
| | Marlowe, *Edward II* acted |
| 1593 | Marlowe d. |
| | George Herbert b. Izaak Walton b. |
| | Shakespeare, *Venus and Adonis* |
| 1594 | Hooker, *Of the Laws of Ecclesiastical Polity* I–IV; Nashe, *The Unfortunate Traveller*; Shakespeare, *The Rape of Lucrece*, *The Comedy of Errors* acted |
| 1595 | Sidney (d. 1586), *Apology for Poetry* (*Defence of Poesie*); Spenser, *Epithalamion* |
| 1596 | Peele d. |
| | Descartes b. |
| | Spenser, *Prothalamion*, and *The Faerie Queene* IV–VI, with a revision of I–III |
| 1597 | Bacon, *Essays*; John Dowland, *First Book of Songs*; Shakespeare, *Richard II*, *Romeo and Juliet* |
| 1598 | Chapman, first part of his translation of the *Iliad*; Marlowe (d. 1593), *Hero and Leander*, completed by Chapman; Shakespeare, *Henry IV, Part I* |
| | Jonson, *Every Man In His Humour* acted |
| 1599 | Spenser d. |
| | Oliver Cromwell b. |
| | Dekker, *The Shoemakers' Holiday* acted; Shakespeare, *Julius Caesar* acted |
| 1600 | Hooker d. |
| 1601 | Nashe d. |
| | Robert Chester (ed.), *Love's Martyr*, including Shakespeare's *The Phoenix and the Turtle* |
| | Shakespeare, *Twelfth Night* acted |
| 1603 | Elizabeth I d. Accession of James I (James VI of Scotland) |
| | John Florio, translation of Montaigne's *Essays*; Shakespeare, *Hamlet* |
| | Heywood, *A Woman Killed with Kindness* acted; Jonson, *Sejanus* acted |
| 1604 | Chapman, *Bussy D'Ambois* acted; Marston, *The Malcontent* acted; Shakespeare, *Othello* acted |
| 1605 | The Gunpowder Plot |
| | Sir Thomas Browne b. |
| | Bacon, *Advancement of Learning* |

| | |
|---|---|
| 1606 | Lyly d. |
| | Corneille b. |
| | Jonson, *Volpone* acted; Shakespeare, *King Lear* acted; Tourneur, *The Revenger's Tragedy* acted |
| 1607 | Beaumont, *The Knight of the Burning Pestle* acted |
| 1608 | John Milton b. |
| | Joseph Hall, *Characters*; Shakespeare, *Antony and Cleopatra* registered for publication |
| | Jonson, *Masque of Beauty* acted; Shakespeare, *Pericles* acted |
| 1609 | Edward Hyde, Earl of Clarendon b. |
| | Shakespeare, *Sonnets* |
| | Beaumont and Fletcher, *Philaster* acted; Jonson, *Masque of Queens* acted; Tourneur, *The Atheist's Tragedy* acted |
| 1610 | Campion, *Two Books of Airs* |
| | Jonson, *The Alchemist* acted |
| 1610–11 | Shakespeare, *The Tempest*, *Cymbeline* and *The Winter's Tale* acted |
| 1611 | The Authorized Version of the Bible; Donne, *Anatomy of the World* |
| | Middleton, *A Chaste Maid in Cheapside* acted (perhaps 1613) |
| 1612 | Samuel Butler b. Richard Crashaw b. (?) |
| | Webster, *The White Devil* acted |
| 1613 | Webster, *The Duchess of Malfi* acted (?) |
| 1614 | Ralegh, *History of the World* |
| 1616 | Beaumont d. Cervantes d. Shakespeare d. |
| | Jonson, the First Folio of his *Works* |
| 1618 | Start of the Thirty Years War |
| | Ralegh executed |
| | Jonson, *Pleasure Reconciled to Virtue* acted |
| 1620 | The Pilgrim Fathers to America in the *Mayflower* |
| | Campion d. |
| | Bacon, *Instauratio Magna* |
| 1621 | La Fontaine b. Andrew Marvell b. |
| | Burton, *Anatomy of Melancholy* (subsequently much revised) |
| | Massinger, *A New Way to Pay Old Debts* acted; Middleton, *Women Beware Women* acted |
| 1622 | Molière b. Henry Vaughan b. |
| | Middleton, *The Changeling* acted |
| 1623 | Pascal b. |
| | Shakespeare, the First Folio of his *Works* |

| 1625 | James I d. Accession of Charles I |
| | Fletcher d. Webster d. (?) |
| 1626 | Bacon d. |
| 1627 | Middleton d. Tourneur d. |
| 1628 | John Bunyan b. |
| | John Earle, *Microcosmography* |
| 1629 | Ford, *The Broken Heart* acted |
| 1631 | Donne d. |
| | John Dryden b. |
| 1632 | Dekker d. |
| | John Locke b. Spinoza b. Sir Christopher Wren b. |
| | William Prynne, *Histriomastix* |
| | Ford, *'Tis Pity She's a Whore* acted; Massinger, *The City Madam* acted |
| 1633 | Herbert d. |
| | Samuel Pepys b. |
| | Donne (d. 1631), *Poems*; Herbert, *The Temple* |
| 1634 | Chapman d. Marston d. |
| | Milton, *A Mask* (*Comus*) acted |
| 1635 | Founding of the Académie Française |
| 1636 | Boileau b. |
| | Corneille, *Le Cid* |
| 1637 | Jonson d. |
| 1638 | Milton, *Lycidas* |
| 1639 | Racine b. |
| 1640 | Burton d. Ford (?) Massinger d. |
| | William Wycherley b. (?) |
| | Carew, *Poems*; Walton, *Life of Donne* |
| 1641 | Heywood d. |
| 1642 | Civil War. Closing of the theatres |
| | Galileo d. Suckling d. |
| | Isaac Newton b. Thomas Shadwell b. (?) |
| 1643 | Browne, *Religio Medici* (first authorized ed.) |
| 1644 | Milton, *Areopagitica* |
| 1645 | Milton, *Poems* |
| 1646 | Virtual end of Civil War |
| 1647 | John Wilmot, Earl of Rochester b. |
| 1648 | Second Civil War |
| 1649 | Charles I executed. Commonwealth |
| | Crashaw d. |
| | Dryden, *Upon the Death of the Lord Hastings* |
| 1650 | Descartes d. |

| | |
|---|---|
| 1651 | Hobbes, *Leviathan* |
| 1652 | Thomas Otway b. |
| 1653 | Cromwell made Protector |
| | Sir Thomas Urquhart, translation of Rabelais I–II |
| 1655 | Marvell, *The First Anniversary of the Government under O.C.* |
| 1658 | Cromwell d. |
| 1660 | Parliament recalls Charles II: The Restoration. The Royal Society established |
| | Daniel Defoe b. |
| | Dryden, *Astraea Redux* |
| 1662 | Pascal d. |
| | Butler, *Hudibras, Part I* (II, 1663; III, 1677) |
| 1664 | Matthew Prior b. Sir John Vanbrugh b. |
| 1665 | The Great Plague |
| | La Rochefoucauld, *Maximes*; Marvell, *The Character of Holland* |
| 1666 | The Fire of London |
| | Boileau, *Satires*; Molière, *Le Misanthrope* |
| 1667 | Jonathan Swift b. |
| | Dryden, *Annus Mirabilis;* Milton, *Paradise Lost*; Molière, *Tartuffe*; Racine, *Andromaque* |
| 1668 | Dryden Poet Laureate |
| | La Fontaine, *Fables* I |
| 1670 | William Congreve b. |
| | Pascal, *Pensées* |
| 1671 | Milton, *Paradise Regained* and *Samson Agonistes* |
| 1672 | Joseph Addison b. Richard Steele b. |
| 1673 | Molière d. |
| 1674 | Milton d. |
| 1675 | Dryden, *Aureng-Zebe* acted; Wycherley, *The Country Wife* acted |
| 1676 | Etherege, *The Man of Mode* acted; Wycherley, *The Plain Dealer* acted |
| 1677 | Racine, *Phèdre* |
| | Dryden, *All for Love* acted |
| 1678 | The Popish Plot |
| | Marvell d. |
| | George Farquhar b. |
| | Bunyan, *The Pilgrim's Progress* I |
| 1680 | Butler d. Rochester d. |
| | Rochester, *Poems* |

# INDEX

# READ MORE IN PENGUIN

In every corner of the world, on every subject under the sun, Penguin represents quality and variety – the very best in publishing today.

For complete information about books available from Penguin – including Puffins, Penguin Classics and Arkana – and how to order them, write to us at the appropriate address below. Please note that for copyright reasons the selection of books varies from country to country.

**In the United Kingdom**: Please write to *Dept. JC, Penguin Books Ltd, FREEPOST, West Drayton, Middlesex UB7 OBR*

If you have any difficulty in obtaining a title, please send your order with the correct money, plus ten per cent for postage and packaging, to *PO Box No. 11, West Drayton, Middlesex UB7 OBR*

**In the United States**: Please write to *Penguin USA Inc., 375 Hudson Street, New York, NY 10014*

**In Canada**: Please write to *Penguin Books Canada Ltd, 10 Alcorn Avenue, Suite 300, Toronto, Ontario M4V 3B2*

**In Australia**: Please write to *Penguin Books Australia Ltd, 487 Maroondah Highway, Ringwood, Victoria 3134*

**In New Zealand**: Please write to *Penguin Books (NZ) Ltd,182–190 Wairau Road, Private Bag, Takapuna, Auckland 9*

**In India**: Please write to *Penguin Books India Pvt Ltd, 706 Eros Apartments, 56 Nehru Place, New Delhi 110 019*

**In the Netherlands**: Please write to *Penguin Books Netherlands B.V., Keizersgracht 231 NL–1016 DV Amsterdam*

**In Germany**: Please write to *Penguin Books Deutschland GmbH, Friedrichstrasse 10–12, W–6000 Frankfurt/Main 1*

**In Spain**: Please write to *Penguin Books S. A., C. San Bernardo 117–6° E–28015 Madrid*

**In Italy**: Please write to *Penguin Italia s.r.l., Via Felice Casati 20, I–20124 Milano*

**In France**: Please write to *Penguin France S. A., 17 rue Lejeune, F–31000 Toulouse*

**In Japan**: Please write to *Penguin Books Japan, Ishikiribashi Building, 2–5–4, Suido, Tokyo 112*

**In Greece**: Please write to *Penguin Hellas Ltd, Dimocritou 3, GR–106 71 Athens*

**In South Africa**: Please write to *Longman Penguin Southern Africa (Pty) Ltd, Private Bag X08, Bertsham 2013*

# READ MORE IN PENGUIN

## THE PENGUIN HISTORY OF LITERATURE

Published in ten volumes, *The Penguin History of Literature* is a superb critical survey of English and American literature covering fourteen centuries, from the Anglo-Saxons to the present, and written by some of the most distinguished academics in their fields.

**The Middle Ages**
Edited by W. F. Bolton

**English Poetry and Prose 1540–1674**
Edited by Christopher Ricks

**English Drama to 1710**
Edited by Christopher Ricks

**Dryden to Johnson**
Edited by Roger Lonsdale

**The Romantic Period**
Edited by David B. Pirie

**The Victorians**
Edited by Arthur Pollard

**The Twentieth Century**
Edited by Martin Dodsworth

**American Literature to 1900**
Edited by Marcus Cunliffe

**American Literature since 1900**
Edited by Marcus Cunliffe

**The English Language**
Edited by W. F. Bolton and David Crystal